T0211612

Lecture Notes in Computer Science   11586

Commenced Publication in 1973
Founding and Former Series Editors:
Gerhard Goos, Juris Hartmanis, and Jan van Leeuwen

Editorial Board Members

More information about this series at http://www.springer.com/series/7409

Aaron Marcus · Wentao Wang (Eds.)

Design, User Experience, and Usability

Practice and Case Studies

8th International Conference, DUXU 2019
Held as Part of the 21st HCI International Conference, HCII 2019
Orlando, FL, USA, July 26–31, 2019
Proceedings, Part IV

 Springer

Editors
Aaron Marcus
Aaron Marcus and Associates
Berkeley, CA, USA

Wentao Wang
Zuoyebang, K12 education
Beijing, China

ISSN 0302-9743 ISSN 1611-3349 (electronic)
Lecture Notes in Computer Science
ISBN 978-3-030-23534-5 ISBN 978-3-030-23535-2 (eBook)
https://doi.org/10.1007/978-3-030-23535-2

LNCS Sublibrary: SL3 – Information Systems and Applications, incl. Internet/Web, and HCI

This Springer imprint is published by the registered company Springer Nature Switzerland AG
The registered company address is: Gewerbestrasse 11, 6330 Cham, Switzerland

Foreword

The 21st International Conference on Human-Computer Interaction, HCI International 2019, was held in Orlando, FL, USA, during July 26–31, 2019. The event incorporated the 18 thematic areas and affiliated conferences listed on the following page.

A total of 5,029 individuals from academia, research institutes, industry, and governmental agencies from 73 countries submitted contributions, and 1,274 papers and 209 posters were included in the pre-conference proceedings. These contributions address the latest research and development efforts and highlight the human aspects of design and use of computing systems. The contributions thoroughly cover the entire field of human-computer interaction, addressing major advances in knowledge and effective use of computers in a variety of application areas. The volumes constituting the full set of the pre-conference proceedings are listed in the following pages.

This year the HCI International (HCII) conference introduced the new option of "late-breaking work." This applies both for papers and posters and the corresponding volume(s) of the proceedings will be published just after the conference. Full papers will be included in the *HCII 2019 Late-Breaking Work Papers Proceedings* volume of the proceedings to be published in the Springer LNCS series, while poster extended abstracts will be included as short papers in the HCII 2019 *Late-Breaking Work Poster Extended Abstracts* volume to be published in the Springer CCIS series.

I would like to thank the program board chairs and the members of the program boards of all thematic areas and affiliated conferences for their contribution to the highest scientific quality and the overall success of the HCI International 2019 conference.

This conference would not have been possible without the continuous and unwavering support and advice of the founder, Conference General Chair Emeritus and Conference Scientific Advisor Prof. Gavriel Salvendy. For his outstanding efforts, I would like to express my appreciation to the communications chair and editor of *HCI International News,* Dr. Abbas Moallem.

July 2019   Constantine Stephanidis

HCI International 2019 Thematic Areas and Affiliated Conferences

Thematic areas:

- HCI 2019: Human-Computer Interaction
- HIMI 2019: Human Interface and the Management of Information

Affiliated conferences:

- EPCE 2019: 16th International Conference on Engineering Psychology and Cognitive Ergonomics
- UAHCI 2019: 13th International Conference on Universal Access in Human-Computer Interaction
- VAMR 2019: 11th International Conference on Virtual, Augmented and Mixed Reality
- CCD 2019: 11th International Conference on Cross-Cultural Design
- SCSM 2019: 11th International Conference on Social Computing and Social Media
- AC 2019: 13th International Conference on Augmented Cognition
- DHM 2019: 10th International Conference on Digital Human Modeling and Applications in Health, Safety, Ergonomics and Risk Management
- DUXU 2019: 8th International Conference on Design, User Experience, and Usability
- DAPI 2019: 7th International Conference on Distributed, Ambient and Pervasive Interactions
- HCIBGO 2019: 6th International Conference on HCI in Business, Government and Organizations
- LCT 2019: 6th International Conference on Learning and Collaboration Technologies
- ITAP 2019: 5th International Conference on Human Aspects of IT for the Aged Population
- HCI-CPT 2019: First International Conference on HCI for Cybersecurity, Privacy and Trust
- HCI-Games 2019: First International Conference on HCI in Games
- MobiTAS 2019: First International Conference on HCI in Mobility, Transport, and Automotive Systems
- AIS 2019: First International Conference on Adaptive Instructional Systems

Pre-conference Proceedings Volumes Full List

1. LNCS 11566, Human-Computer Interaction: Perspectives on Design (Part I), edited by Masaaki Kurosu
2. LNCS 11567, Human-Computer Interaction: Recognition and Interaction Technologies (Part II), edited by Masaaki Kurosu
3. LNCS 11568, Human-Computer Interaction: Design Practice in Contemporary Societies (Part III), edited by Masaaki Kurosu
4. LNCS 11569, Human Interface and the Management of Information: Visual Information and Knowledge Management (Part I), edited by Sakae Yamamoto and Hirohiko Mori
5. LNCS 11570, Human Interface and the Management of Information: Information in Intelligent Systems (Part II), edited by Sakae Yamamoto and Hirohiko Mori
6. LNAI 11571, Engineering Psychology and Cognitive Ergonomics, edited by Don Harris
7. LNCS 11572, Universal Access in Human-Computer Interaction: Theory, Methods and Tools (Part I), edited by Margherita Antona and Constantine Stephanidis
8. LNCS 11573, Universal Access in Human-Computer Interaction: Multimodality and Assistive Environments (Part II), edited by Margherita Antona and Constantine Stephanidis
9. LNCS 11574, Virtual, Augmented and Mixed Reality: Multimodal Interaction (Part I), edited by Jessie Y. C. Chen and Gino Fragomeni
10. LNCS 11575, Virtual, Augmented and Mixed Reality: Applications and Case Studies (Part II), edited by Jessie Y. C. Chen and Gino Fragomeni
11. LNCS 11576, Cross-Cultural Design: Methods, Tools and User Experience (Part I), edited by P. L. Patrick Rau
12. LNCS 11577, Cross-Cultural Design: Culture and Society (Part II), edited by P. L. Patrick Rau
13. LNCS 11578, Social Computing and Social Media: Design, Human Behavior and Analytics (Part I), edited by Gabriele Meiselwitz
14. LNCS 11579, Social Computing and Social Media: Communication and Social Communities (Part II), edited by Gabriele Meiselwitz
15. LNAI 11580, Augmented Cognition, edited by Dylan D. Schmorrow and Cali M. Fidopiastis
16. LNCS 11581, Digital Human Modeling and Applications in Health, Safety, Ergonomics and Risk Management: Human Body and Motion (Part I), edited by Vincent G. Duffy

34. CCIS 1033, HCI International 2019 - Posters (Part II), edited by Constantine Stephanidis
35. CCIS 1034, HCI International 2019 - Posters (Part III), edited by Constantine Stephanidis

http://2019.hci.international/proceedings

8th International Conference on Design, User Experience, and Usability (DUXU 2019)

Program Board Chair(s): **Aaron Marcus,** *USA,* **and Wentao Wang,** *P.R. China*

- Sisira Adikari, Australia
- Claire Ancient, UK
- Jan Brejcha, Czech Republic
- Silvia De los Rios, Spain
- Marc Fabri, UK
- Josh Halstead, USA
- Wei Liu, P.R. China
- Yang Meng, P.R. China

- Judith Moldenhauer, USA
- Jingyan Qin, P.R. China
- Francisco Rebelo, Portugal
- Christine Riedmann-Streitz, Germany
- Elizabeth Rosenzweig, USA
- Patricia Search, USA
- Marcelo Soares, P.R. China
- Carla G. Spinillo, Brazil

The full list with the Program Board Chairs and the members of the Program Boards of all thematic areas and affiliated conferences is available online at:

http://www.hci.international/board-members-2019.php

HCI International 2020

The 22nd International Conference on Human-Computer Interaction, HCI International 2020, will be held jointly with the affiliated conferences in Copenhagen, Denmark, at the Bella Center Copenhagen, July 19–24, 2020. It will cover a broad spectrum of themes related to HCI, including theoretical issues, methods, tools, processes, and case studies in HCI design, as well as novel interaction techniques, interfaces, and applications. The proceedings will be published by Springer. More information will be available on the conference website: http://2020.hci.international/.

General Chair
Prof. Constantine Stephanidis
University of Crete and ICS-FORTH
Heraklion, Crete, Greece
E-mail: general_chair@hcii2020.org

http://2020.hci.international/

Contents – Part IV

DUXU Practice

DUXU Case Studies

User Experience Evaluation Methods and Tools

Development and Validation of Usability Heuristics for Evaluation of Interfaces in ATMs

Cristhian Chanco[1(✉)], Arturo Moquillaza[1,2], and Freddy Paz[1]

[1] Pontificia Universidad Católica del Perú, Lima 32, Lima, Peru
{cristhian.chanco, amoquillaza, fpaz}@pucp.pe
[2] Universidad San Ignacio de Loyola, Lima 12, Lima, Peru
miguel.moquillaza@usil.pe

Abstract. ATM systems are part of the devices that have more managed approach and facilitate the use of financial services for people. However, on occasions, displayed interfaces can be frustrating to use. Usability is a principle that contemplates such situations, so it is necessary to have appropriate tools to evaluate ease of use on the products. For this reason, we present a revised version of eighteen usability heuristics proposed for ATM applications. In this paper, we describe the process that is followed from the collection of information, creation of the heuristic set, validation and refinement.

Keywords: Human-Computer Interaction · User-centered design · Usability evaluation · Usability heuristics · Automatic teller machine

1 Introduction

The banks are in a constant search for designing new ways to interact with their users [1]. Thus, thanks to technological advances, today, it is possible that clients can perform many of their transactions through channels other than the traditional bank offices [2]. The automated teller machine (ATM) is one of these new types of emerging technologies.

Nowadays, due to rapid technological advancement, ATMs acquire new features other than the provision of cash [3, 4]. However, in many cases they have severe problems that hinder its usability [5, 6]. Therefore, companies are in a constant search for tools that allow software applications to deliver a proper experience of interaction with the user [1]. However, this information is very limited when it comes to the development of ATM interfaces, compared to the large number of existing heuristics for the development of web interfaces [7].

The best-known set of heuristics to perform usability evaluations is the proposal of Nielsen [8–10], who establishes ten principles to problems of usability in software products. However, this tool does not adapt to the diversity of types of software that currently exist and in many cases elude own characteristics in certain types of applications [8, 10, 12].

© Springer Nature Switzerland AG 2019
A. Marcus and W. Wang (Eds.): HCII 2019, LNCS 11586, pp. 3–18, 2019.
https://doi.org/10.1007/978-3-030-23535-2_1

The paper presents the development and validation of a new proposal of heuristic principles for the evaluation of ATM interfaces. The new inspection tool was based in the heuristic existing proposals, the characteristic features of the ATM and the difficulties expressed by the users.

Finally, on the basis of the comments received, in reference to the quantity and quality of perceived problems when applying the heuristic evaluation (HE) and user tests, we can conclude that the proposal has obtained positive results.

2 Methodology to Develop Usability Heuristics

In order to create an appropriate set of heuristics for evaluation of interfaces usable ATM, in general, we use the proposal of the studies of Quiñones et al. [10, 12, 13]. These focused on developing heuristics of usability for emerging information technologies. This methodology involves several iterations of nine steps (see Fig. 1).

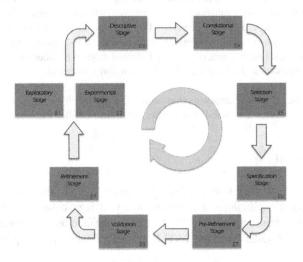

Fig. 1. Methodology for the development of heuristics.

In relation to the "Validation stage", Granollers [10] considers heuristic evaluation is an effective method to assess user interfaces by taking the recommendations based on user-centered design (UCD) principles; nevertheless, this technique need for adapting the heuristic set to the specific features of each interactive system. For this reason, this stage begins with the application of the heuristic evaluation from the set of heuristics of usability that we have created. In addition, Smith and Mayes [15] state that "usability is now recognized as a vital determining factor in the success of any new computer system"; so, we use usability test to analyze these aspects and complement the results of the evaluation of the ATM interfaces.

2.1 Exploratory Stage

In this first step, we collect the literature related to the subject of research. Specifically, in this activity is conducted a systematic review related aspect relevant and heuristics in the domains of ATM and similar contexts.

2.2 Experimental Stage

This second stage is to compile the information provided by the experts of the domain or users, because they are constantly interacting with the system. To achieve this task was carried out interviews in search of relevant characteristics and possible problems or non-conformities.

2.3 Descriptive Stage

In this third step, all the information collected in the previous stages is processed. The activity consisted in grouping and classifying the information on two relevant topics: heuristics identified in similar domains and the list of problems established.

2.4 Correlational Stage

This fourth step is to relate previously classified information, in other words, the characteristics of the application domain and the problems identified are associated with the found heuristics.

2.5 Selection Stage

In this fifth step, we maintain, adapt and/or discard each found heuristic. At this stage, we create the new set of ATM heuristics, so that the main problems previously identified can be covered.

2.6 Specification Stage

In this sixth step, is formally described the proposal of heuristic using standard template indicated by Quiñones et al. [11]. The fields used are:

- ID and name: Heuristic's identifier.
- Definition: A brief but concise definition of heuristics.
- Explanation: Detailed explanation of heuristics.
- Examples: Case of compliance and/or breach of heuristics.

2.7 Pre-refinement Stage

In this seventh step, be carried out an initial refinement through the application of Expert Judgment. The purpose of this activity is that the set of heuristics is easy to understand, and that there are no major inconveniences to evaluate them.

2.8   Validation Stage

In this eighth step, the set of proposed heuristics is validated through the implementation of User Test. For which, based on the set of rectified heuristics, we applied the heuristic evaluation to a set of ATM interfaces. This evaluation allows us to obtain a list of usability problems, whose resolution allows the elaboration of new interfaces designs. Finally, we complement the results through the use of usability tests with real users in both sets of interfaces.

2.9   Refinement Stage

Finally, a second update based on feedback obtained by the heuristic evaluation carried out in the previous stage is performed. These conditions allow the final set of heuristics to be useful and easy to understand by the domain experts (Figs. 2, 3).

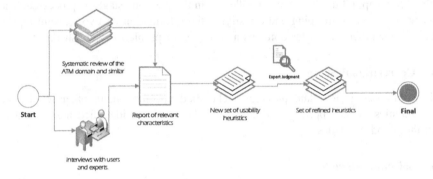

Fig. 2. Detailed list of the steps made for the development of the ATM heuristics – Part 1.

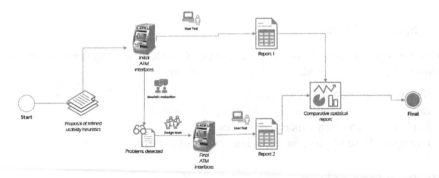

Fig. 3. Detailed list of the steps made for the development of the ATM heuristics – Part 2.

3 Case Study: Usability Heuristics for the Evaluation of the ATM Interfaces

3.1 Purpose of Study

The purpose of this study was to develop and validate a set of usability heuristics for ATM that is useful and easy to use by domain experts, and thus improve the level of usability offered by ATM interfaces.

In order to make usability tests as realistic as possible, we had the collaboration of a banking entity: the BBVA Continental Bank. BBVA provided all the necessary information, as well as collaborated in the design of the final interfaces.

We established three objectives to be developed throughout the study:

- Display a set of usability heuristics for ATM that meets the needs of users and domain-specific.
- Propose a new design of ATM interfaces that correspond to the problems detected by the application of the heuristic principles elaborated.
- Validate that the level of usability obtained with the group of final interfaces is significantly higher than that achieved by the initial interfaces.

3.2 Exploratory Stage

As mentioned, the amount of information regarding heuristics focused on the characteristics of an ATM is very scarce; therefore, the systematic review was addressed under three additional domains: Banking, touchscreen-based [16] and autoservices. In order to obtain an orderly inspection, two research questions were also proposed:

PI1: What problems and difficulties are most reported by users when using ATM interfaces?

PI2: What are the heuristic existing proposals in the domains of banking, touchscreen-based and autoservices?

The systematic review conducted in the databases SCOPUS, Springer, IEEE Xplore and ACM Digital Library obtained twelve relevant articles. In Table 1, we list the relevant articles, their authors and group them according to their topic of interest.

Table 1. Topics of the relevant articles.

Author	Topic
Curran and King [17]	ATM usability problems
Altin Gumussoy [18]	
Paz [8]	Heuristics in the domains of ATM and similar contexts
Nielsen [19]	
Lynch, Schwerha, and Johanson [20]	
Inostroza et al. [16]	
Mujinga and Eloff [21]	
Moquillaza et al. [7]	Characteristics of design on ATM interfaces
Moquillaza and Paz [22]	
Jung and Ko [6]	
Hernández, Soriano, López, and Gómez [23]	Design difficulties in older people
Chan, Wong, Lee, and Chi [24]	

3.3 Experimental Stage

We conducted an interview with nine people among users and experts in HCI and the ATM domain, trying to cover the different profiles of the clients. The interview was about thirty questions and focused on validate or expand each previously identified problem. In Table 2, we list an extract of the questions asked.

In the feedback and ideas that were obtained, it was evidenced a greater emphasis in that the flow of the transactions is very long, the client only knows which are available bills when using the ATM and that the time that shows the information on screen is very short.

Table 2. Questions asked during the interview (extract).

No.	Question
1	What do you think of the current design in ATM interfaces? Have you presented any kind of inconvenience?
2	How easy is it to distinguish the relevant information from the rest?
3	Do you think the time interval in which the on-screen information is displayed is the right one?
4	Do you usually read all the information displayed on the screen before continuing the interaction?
5	How often do products/services appear that do not correspond to the transaction you are doing? What is your opinion on these actions?

3.4 Descriptive Stage

We proceeded to analyze, group and classify all the information obtained in the previous stages. Additionally, we discard those problems and heuristics related only to hardware aspects. A total of twenty-five identified problems and thirty-three heuristic principles were obtained. In Table 3 is listed an extract of the complete set of heuristic.

Table 3. Heuristics identified in similar domains (extract).

Heuristic	Definition
PH01: Visibility and clarity of elements of the system	There are elements that are essential to the achievement of the objectives of the users within the system
PH02: Visibility of system status	This principle refers to keep informed the user about what is happening in the system
PH03: Visibility of security	The interface should keep users informed about the status of connection of the system and its level of protection
PH04: Informative commentary	Users should receive fast and informative comments about his actions
PH05: Correspondence between the system and the cultural aspects of the user	The fulfillment of cultural aspects should be verified for those users to whom the system is oriented and include characteristics in order to encompass a greater cultural diversity

3.5   Correlational Stage

Thus, we proceeded to relate the problems identified in the literature and interviews with the found heuristics. In Table 4, we can see the lack of specific heuristics that allow to address certain problems.

Table 4. Matches among identified problems and the existing heuristics (extract).

No.	Problem	Heuristic
1	Help messages should be clear, specific and used a colloquial language	Help users recognize, diagnose, and recover from errors
2	Sometimes there are no bills of certain denomination but this is only known when the client uses the ATM	–
3	There are features or texts that should be removed for not oversaturate the screens	Aesthetic and minimalist design

3.6   Selection Stage

Then, we started with the creation of the heuristics set. From Nielsen's proposal [19], the *"Help and documentation"* heuristic was eliminated because an ATM system has a time limit to complete the transaction. The implementation of a section focused on the tasks of the user is not the most appropriate in these systems because it would cause a delay in the process.

In addition, five heuristics were created in order to address specific problems that were not addressed by some principle.

3.7   Specification Stage

As a result, the first revision of the heuristic proposal has a total of nineteen heuristics that address the ATM's characteristics. Then, we formally describe each proposed heuristic:

– PHC01: Visibility of system status.

The system should always keep the user informed of the state of the system through appropriate feedback within reasonable time.

– PHC02: Visibility of transaction status.

The system should inform the users about the status, successful or wrong, of the operation performed or progress of tasks at moderate intervals.

– PHC03: Visibility and clarity of the relevant elements of the system.

The system should expose the elements of greatest importance clear and highly visible way for the user.

- PHC04: Match between system and the real world.

The system should follow the conventions of the real world, using words, phrases and concepts easy to understand that they are familiar to the user.

- PHC05: User control and freedom.

The system should be able to offer options that the user can easily undo his actions in situations unwanted or wrong [19].

- PHC06: Consistency between the elements of the system.

The system should maintain a similar design style, a well-organized structure, a consistency in the functionality of each element and ensure that it is consistent across the entire system [8].

- PHC07: Adaptation to standards.

The system should follow the established design conventions, commonly used structures, and locations of elements widely known for their continued implementation [8].

- PHC08: Error prevention.

The system should be able to prevent the occurrence of situations that cause the occurrence of errors or confusion for users [19].

- PHC09: Recognition rather than recall.

The user should not have to remember information from one part of the dialogue to another [8, 9].

- PHC10: Appropriate flexibility of features.

The system should be able to adapt to users with different levels of experience. It is important that the system allows you to customize common actions to accelerate tasks.

- PHC11: Aesthetic and minimalist design.

The system should provide content to support the achievement of the objectives or goals of the user, avoiding irrelevant, unnecessary, or complex information [25].

- PHC12: Help users recognize, diagnose, and recover from errors.

The system should be able to express the error messages in a clear language, precisely indicate the problem and suggest concrete and simple steps to recover from the inconvenience [19].

- PHC13: Proper distribution of the content display time.

The system should ensure that the display time of the information on the screen is long enough so that users do not have any difficulty in completing the task successfully. The allocated time should vary depending on the relevance of the type of content being exposed.

– PHC14: Correct and expected functionality.

The system should do what it promises the user. The features must be properly implemented and must offer what the user expects from them [8].

– PHC15: Recoverability of information against failures.

The system should be able to protect the integrity and consistency of the user's personal, private, and financial information against abrupt system failures.

– PHC16: Visibility of exchange rates.

The system should exhibit on initial screens the availability of the types of monetary denomination.

– PHC17: Customization in the design of the interface.

The system should allow users to customize aesthetically design the interface so that it adapts to your visual preferences.

– PHC18: Prevention of forgetting the bank card.

The system should ensure that, after the transaction is completed, the logic of return of bank card prevents a possible oblivion.

– PHC19: Efficiency and agility of transactions.

The system should support that the user successfully performs the desired operation in the minimum possible time. To do this, you need to minimize the steps needed to run a task, as well as the response and execution times should reach optimal levels.

3.8   Pre-refinement Stage

The refining stage began with the application of Expert Judgement to three experts on usability issues, and with extensive knowledge in the elaboration of heuristics. Table 5 lists the encountered difficulties, as well as the heuristics related to each problem.

Table 5. Problems identified by usability experts.

Problem	Heuristic
The heuristic name does not represent what is indicated in their definition and explanation fields	PHC02: Visibility of transaction status
	PHC07: Adaptation to standards
	PHC10: Appropriate flexibility of features
The heuristics are confused with features; therefore, they need a change	PHC13: Proper distribution of the content display time
	PHC16: Visibility of exchange rates
	PHC18: Prevention of forgetting the bank card
The number of heuristics is too great	All

Then, we proceeded to make the necessary modifications according to the feedback received. The following changes are presented:

(a) Change of name:

Before: PHC02 - Visibility of transaction status.
Changed to: PHC02 - Visibility of the progress and final status of the transaction.

Before: PHC07 - Adaptation to standards.
Changed to: PHC07 - Compliance with standards.

Before: PHC10 - Appropriate flexibility of features.
Changed to: PHC10 - Adaptability of the functionalities to the user profile.

(b) Complete modification of each heuristic:

Before: PHC13 - Proper distribution of the content display time.
Changed to:
PHC13 - Appropriate session time distribution to display content.
The system should ensure that the session time is long enough for users to be able to properly view the contents and successfully complete the task. The allocated time should vary depending on the relevance of the type of content being exposed.

Before: PHC16 - Visibility of exchange rates.
Changed to:
PHC16 - Early-stage visibility of interaction restrictions
The system should display in initial screens the impediments that limit the interaction of the user, avoiding unnecessary navigation that causes loss of time and discomfort in the client.

Before: PHC18 - Prevention of forgetting the bank card.
Changed to:
PHC18 – Prevention of the capture of the cash and bank card.
The system should ensure that any effort involved in the delivery, reception, return and capture of money, as well as the bank card, prevents any inconvenience that may result in the client losing his cash or card.

3.9   Validation Stage

After obtaining the set of rectified heuristics, we proceeded to perform the heuristic evaluation, which is one of the most popular inspection methods [10, 26]. In order to focus the inspection, two sets of different interfaces were evaluated, corresponding to the screens associated with the *"Bank Loan"* and *"Cash Withdrawal"* process, respectively. In both situations, the appropriate distribution of the *"Main Menu"* is examined.

For the first case, the set of ATM interfaces and the evaluation process was carried out by different groups of undergraduate students participating in the course Human-Computer Interaction (INF647) taught at the Pontificia Universidad Católica del Perú.

In addition, this proposal holds the fulfillment of several previous design methods carried out throughout the course.

The second case corresponds to a group of interfaces belonging to the BBVA Continental (see Fig. 4) for which was obtained the corresponding support of the relevant authorities. The profile of the members who formed the team assigned to this evaluation consisted of three usability experts, with extensive experience in the creation of evaluation heuristics and three novice evaluators.

Fig. 4. Set of ATM interfaces of BBVA Continental.

After applying the heuristic evaluation in both cases, the total list of identified problems was made available by the respective authorities of the BBVA Continental. Which, depending on the resources available and the technical limitations of the hardware, solved the main obstacles encountered through a process of improving the interfaces. The improvement tasks performed for the conception of the new prototype are:

- Increase the size of the letters of conditions on the display of *"Retiro Seguro"*.
- Standardize the buttons.
- Change the *"Retiro rápido"* button to *"Continuar con Retiro rápido"*.
- In the option *"Otros retiros"* place the text *"Más cuentas"* next to the scroll arrow of other bank accounts.
- In the *"Main Menu"*, perform a redistribution of the buttons.
- In advertising displays, add an informative tape *"Procesando…"*
- The final message for the *"Cash Withdrawal"* process will be divided into: *"Retira tu tarjeta"* y *"Retira tu efectivo y voucher"*.

After completing the new interface design, we proceeded to perform a cross-usability test with eight collaborators. This evaluation was carried out in a controlled laboratory environment, in which each participant was exposed to the two ATM corresponding to the interfaces to be examined. The objective of the test is to capture the level of satisfaction perceived. In the Table 6, we can see the values obtained in each prototype design.

Table 6. Average value of perceived satisfaction level.

Design prototype	Level of satisfaction perceived
Initial interface: BBVA Continental's designs	3.26
Final interface: design that solves the problems identified by the application of the heuristic evaluation	3.70

According to the information obtained, numerical experimentation was carried out to verify if there are significant differences in the perception of the level of satisfaction perceived between the new design proposal and the current prototype.

The base hypothesis was defined that the data follow a normal distribution. It was decided to perform the test of Saphiro-Wilk due to the small amount of data (n = 8). The results obtained validated the initial hypothesis.

In addition, the T-Student test is the appropriate statistical technique for the analysis of these variables because the samples are related. Table 7 shows that the T-Student test got a less than 5% significance level. Thus, we can conclude that the final design proposal is perceived with a higher level of satisfaction than the current prototype.

Table 7. T-Student test in related samples that examines the level of satisfaction.

Variable of perception	Standard deviation	gl	Significance (bilateral)
Level of satisfaction perceived	0.383	7	0.015

3.10 Refinement Stage

Finally, we proceeded to analyze the results obtained by the heuristic evaluation. In Fig. 5 shows the results of the percentage of the number of problems identified by each heuristic in both groups.

We can observe that, for the heuristics *PHC10, PHC12, PHC15, PHC16* and *PHC18* not associated them any problems. We also realized that there were problems mistakenly associated to the heuristics *"PCH03 – Visibility and clarity of the relevant elements of the system"* y *"PHC07 – Compliance with standards"*.

In order to validate the first condition, a survey was carried out to the usability experts who carried out the evaluation. The results obtained allowed to certify that difficulties were not associated with these heuristics because the interfaces inspected comply with the indicated guidelines. Similarly, the results validated the utility provided by each heuristic indicated.

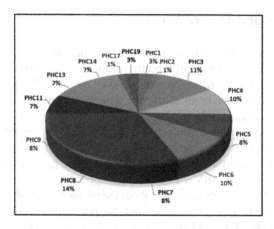

Fig. 5. Total percentage of problems identified by heuristics.

With regard to the second condition, due to the large number of erroneously associated difficulties, we opted to remove the *PHC03* heuristic and attach its information to the *PHC07* heuristic.

In summary, the Table 8 exhibits the set of heuristics final refined and validated:

Table 8. A set of refined final heuristics.

ID	Heuristic
PHC01	Visibility of system status
PHC02	Visibility of the progress and final status of the transaction
PHC03	Visibility and clarity of the relevant elements of the system
PHC04	Match between system and the real world
PHC05	User control and freedom
PHC06	Consistency between the elements of the system
PHC07	Error prevention
PHC08	Recognition rather than recall
PHC09	Adaptability of the functionalities to the user profile
PHC10	Aesthetic and minimalist design
PHC11	Help users recognize, diagnose, and recover from errors
PHC12	Appropriate session time distribution to display content
PHC13	Correct and expected functionality
PHC14	Recoverability of information against failures
PHC15	Early-stage visibility of interaction restrictions
PHC16	Customization in the design of the interface
PHC17	Prevention of the capture of the cash and bank card
PHC18	Efficiency and agility of transactions

4   Conclusions and Future Works

Usability is an aspect that increasingly takes on the different software products. Therefore, there is a need to create specific evaluation methods for each software application. The usability heuristics created by Jakob Nielsen offer acceptable but very generic results and fail to cover all aspects of specific systems.

In this study we elaborate a set of usability heuristics focused on ATM software. The results of the validation consolidated that the heuristic proposal is capable of identifying characteristic and important problems in the ATM environment. However, it is necessary to note that the results could differ in more general contexts.

Also, the perception of BBVA Continental's specialists, who collaborated in the inspection process, has been very positive about the problems identified by the heuristic evaluation and User Test. They indicate that the problems found are coherent and correspond to aspects of the ATM, as well as, they were able to identify several problems that the UX team could not find.

As a future work, we are working on enriching the process through extending the study's approach to creating heuristics that address the perception of customer security. The interaction with ATMs located in a banking agency is different from what a public environment can offer, such as a faucet.

Additionally, the study has a bias associated with the prototype of interfaces used as a basis in the validation phase. The scheme used is focused on the design aspects of BBVA Continental and the "Cash Withdrawal" and "Bank Loan" transactions. Consequently, we want to validate if we continue to obtain optimal results for case studies corresponding to the interfaces of other financial institutions and/or different banking transactions.

Finally, the large number of heuristics presented may prove to be a demotivating aspect in their use because it's difficult to apply in practice [11]. So, we are working on reducing its amount through multiple refinements.

Acknowledgments. The authors thanks to all the participants involved into the experience required to perform the presented study. This work was highly supported by the BBVA Continental, and HCI, Design, User Experience, Accessibility and Innovation Technologies (HCI-DUXAIT) Research Group of the "Pontificia Universidad Católica del Perú", in Peru.

References

1. EY: Los retos que traen las nuevas tecnologías en el sector financiero (2016)
2. ASBANC: Impacto económico del uso de los cajeros automáticos en el Perú, pp. 1–14 (2016)
3. BBC Mundo: La curiosa historia de cómo nació el cajero automático hace 50 años (2017). http://www.bbc.com/mundo/noticias-40417156. Accessed 22 Apr 2018
4. ATMIA: ATM Benchmarking Study 2016 and Industry Report (2016)
5. Muneeb, S., Naseem, M., Shahid, S.: A usability study of an assistive touch voice interface based automated teller machine (ATM). In: Proceedings of the 2015 Annual Symposium on Computing for Development, DEV 2015, pp. 114–115 (2015). https://doi.org/10.1145/2830629.2830635

6. Jung, H., Ko, Y.: ATM Design Applying the Universal Design Concept, pp. 123–137 (2017)
7. Moquillaza, A., et al.: Developing an ATM interface using user-centered design techniques. In: Marcus, A., Wang, W. (eds.) DUXU 2017. LNCS, vol. 10290, pp. 690–701. Springer, Cham (2017). https://doi.org/10.1007/978-3-319-58640-3_49
8. Paz, F.: Heurísticas de usabilidad para sitios web transaccionales. Pontif Univ Católica del Perú (2014)
9. Nielsen, J.: Usability 101: introduction to usability (2012). https://www.nngroup.com/articles/usability-101-introduction-to-usability/. Accessed 16 Apr 2018
10. Granollers, T.: Design, User Experience, and Usability: Theory and Practice. Springer, Berlin (2018)
11. Quiñones, D., Rusu, C., Rusu, V.: A methodology to develop usability/user experience heuristics. Comput. Stand. Interfaces 59, 109–129 (2018). https://doi.org/10.1016/j.csi.2018.03.002
12. Joyce, G., Lilley, M.: Towards the development of usability heuristics for native smartphone mobile applications. In: Marcus, A. (ed.) DUXU 2014. LNCS, vol. 8517, pp. 465–474. Springer, Cham (2014). https://doi.org/10.1007/978-3-319-07668-3_45
13. Quiñones, D., Rusu, C.: How to develop usability heuristics: a systematic literature review. Comput. Stand. Interfaces 53, 89–122 (2017). https://doi.org/10.1016/j.csi.2017.03.009
14. Durães Dourado, M.A., Dias Canedo, E.: Usability heuristics for mobile applications—a systematic review. In: Proceedings of the 20th International Conference on Enterprise Information Systems, vol. 2, pp. 483–494 (2018). https://doi.org/10.5220/0006781404830494
15. Ghasemifard, N., Shamsi, M., Rasouli Kenari, A.R., Ahmadi, V.: A new view at usability test methods of interfaces for human–computer interaction. Glob. J. Comput. Sci. Technol. A Hardw. Comput. 15, 17–24 (2015)
16. Inostroza, R., Rusu, C., Roncagliolo, S., Jiménez, C., Rusu, V.: Usability heuristics for touchscreen-based mobile devices. In: Proceedings of the 9th International Conference on Information Science and Technology ITNG 2012, pp. 662–667 (2012). https://doi.org/10.1109/itng.2012.134
17. Curran, K., King, D.: Investigating the human–computer interaction problems with automated teller machine navigation menus. Interact. Technol. Smart Educ. 5, 59–79 (2008). https://doi.org/10.1108/17415650810871583
18. Altin Gumussoy, C.: Usability guideline for banking software design. Comput. Hum. Behav. 62, 277–285 (2016). https://doi.org/10.1016/j.chb.2016.04.001
19. Nielsen, J.: 10 Usability heuristics for user interface design (1995). https://www.nngroup.com/articles/ten-usability-heuristics/. Accessed 17 Apr 2018
20. Lynch, K.R., Schwerha, D.J., Johanson, G.A.: Development of a weighted heuristic for website evaluation for older adults. Int. J. Hum. Comput. Interact. 29, 404–418 (2013). https://doi.org/10.1080/10447318.2012.715277
21. Mujinga, M., Eloff, M.M., Kroeze, J.: Towards a heuristic model for usable and secure online banking. In: 24th Australasian Conference on Information Systems, 4–6 December 2013, Melbourne (2013). https://doi.org/10.3127/ajis.v18i3.1094
22. Moquillaza, A., Paz, F.: Applying a user-centered design methodology to develop usable interfaces for an Automated Teller Machine. In: Proceedings of the XVIII International Conference on Human Computer Interaction – Interacción 2017, pp. 1–4 (2017). https://doi.org/10.1145/3123818.3123833
23. Hernández, J.L., Soriano, C., López, G., Gómez, L.M.: Servicios bancarios. Ahora mucho más fácil para la persona mayor. Rev. biomecánica, 40–48 (2015)

24. Chan, C.C.H., Wong, A.W.K., Lee, T.M.C., Chi, I.: Modified automatic teller machine prototype for older adults: a case study of participative approach to inclusive design. Appl. Ergon. **40**, 151–160 (2009). https://doi.org/10.1016/j.apergo.2008.02.023
25. Fierro Díaz, N.Y.: Heurísticas para evaluar la usabilidad de aplicaciones web bancarias. Pontif Univ Católica del Perú (2016)
26. Anganes, A., Pfaff, M.S., Drury, J.L., O'Toole, C.M.: The heuristic quality scale. Interact. Comput. **28**, 587–597 (2016). https://doi.org/10.1093/iwc/iwv031

Usability and Playability Heuristics for Augmented Reality Video Games in Smartphones

Alberto Chang[✉], Lourdes Montalvo, and Freddy Paz

Pontificia Universidad Católica del Perú, Lima 32, Peru
{alberto.chang1, fpaz}@pucp.pe,
montalvo.lourdes@pucp.edu.pe

Abstract. Nowadays, Augmented reality technology is being used in many applications of the industry. This technology generates new user experiences by mixing elements of the real world with virtual objects. Its use in video games is one of the most prominent, which expands the ways in which players interact with the game and its characters. This article presents a proposal of usability and playability heuristics for the evaluation of augmented reality video games on smartphones. The proposal was validated with surveys and a case study, with the help of end users and usability experts.

Keywords: Human computer interaction · Usability heuristics ·
Playability heuristics · Video games · Augmented reality

1 Introduction

The usability of a software product, which refers to the ease that a system can be learned and used, greatly influences the user experience. This aspect is a critical condition for the system, because if it is not understandable and difficult to use, users will stop using it [1].

There are different methods, techniques and tools related to the treatment of usability issues in software products. A usability evaluation method is a procedure composed of a set of well-defined activities for the collection of data related to the interaction between a user and the software product; and how these specific properties of the product contribute to achieve a certain degree of usability [2]. There are several methods for evaluating usability, which vary according to the time/benefit cost, rigor, number of users, number of evaluators and the knowledge they possess. Holzinger proposes a classification for these methods using two categories: inspection methods and test methods [3].

Among the methods of inspection is the heuristic evaluation, which, according to Nielsen [4], is "a discount engineering method that involves having usability specialists to judge whether each item evaluated follows established usability principles". Heuristics are general design rules and not specific guidelines [5].

Nielsen proposed the ten usability heuristics for the design of user interfaces [6]. Other authors designed specific heuristics for some types of software [7, 8]. In a previous study [9], from the literature some usability and playability heuristics were gathered for video games on mobile devices and others for augmented reality applications.

© Springer Nature Switzerland AG 2019
A. Marcus and W. Wang (Eds.): HCII 2019, LNCS 11586, pp. 19–29, 2019.
https://doi.org/10.1007/978-3-030-23535-2_2

The aim of this work is to formalize the development process of a proposal of usability and playability heuristics for augmented reality video games for smartphones. This article is structured as follow: In Sect. 2, we present the methodology used in this study, then in Sect. 3, we show a survey made for end users and usability experts with the purpose of validate the preliminary set of heuristics from a previous study, after that in Sect. 4, we analyze a case study of the videogame Park AR where the set of heuristics was used as an evaluation tool, and finally in Sect. 5, we present the heuristic set formally.

2   Methodology

To formalize the development of the heuristic proposal, a methodology was used. This methodology was created by Daniela Quiñones [10] to establish usability heuristics and control lists associated with usability. It has six defined and ordered stages: Exploratory Stage, Descriptive Stage, Correlational Stage, Explanatory Stage, Validation Stage and Refining Stage.

2.1   Systematic Review

In a previous work [9], a study of systematic literature mapping of the use of augmented reality in educational video games was carried out. In this systematic review, after applying the inclusion and exclusion criteria mentioned in the article, six studies were selected, which are shown in Table 1.

Table 1. Selected studies [9].

ID	Authors	Year	Title	Description
S1 [11]	Korhonen and Koivisto	2006	Playability Heuristics for Mobile Games	It proposes 29 heuristics separating them by usability, mobility and gameplay
S2 [12]	Korhonen and Koivisto	2007	Playability Heuristics for Mobile Multi-Player	It proposes 8 heuristics for multiplayer
S3 [13]	Wetzel et al.	2008	Guidelines for Designing Augmented Reality	It proposes 12 guidelines for augmented reality games on mobile devices
S4 [14]	Soomro et al.	2012	A Preliminary Study on Heuristics for Mobile Games	It proposes 10 heuristics to complement those of Korhonen (S1)
S5 [15]	Paiva and Martins	2014	A checklist to evaluate Augmented Reality Applications	It proposes 13 usability guidelines for augmented reality applications
S6 [16]	Mohd et al.	2016	Preliminary Usability and Heuristics Model for Mobile Games, in the aspect of Control Feature	It proposes 5 usability heuristics for video game controls on touch screen devices

Finally, from the six selected studies, 45 heuristics were taken as a result of a comparative analysis. In this analysis, the authors filtered the preliminary set by taking some criteria such as discarding those heuristics related to multiplayer video games or some very general guidelines about game design, and comparing those ones with similar approach. The set of heuristics as result of the previous study can be seen in Table 2.

Table 2. List of heuristics from a previous study [9].

ID	Heuristic
S1	Audio-visual representation supports the game
	Screen layout is efficient and visually pleasing
	Device UI and game UI are used for their own purposes
	Indicators are visible
	The player understands the terminology
	Navigation is consistent, logical, and minimalist
	Control keys are consistent and follow standard conventions
	Game controls are convenient and flexible
	The game gives feedback on the player's actions
	The player cannot make irreversible errors
	The player does not have to memorize things unnecessarily
	The game contains help
	The game and play sessions can be started quickly
	The game accommodates with the surroundings
	The game provides clear goals or supports player-created goals
	The player sees the progress in the game and can compare the results
	The players are rewarded and rewards are meaningful
	The player is in control
	Challenge, strategy, and pace are in balance
	The first-time experience is encouraging
	The game story supports the gameplay and is meaningful
	There are no repetitive or boring tasks
	The players can express themselves
S2	The game supports different playing styles
	The game does not stagnate
	The game is consistent
	The game uses orthogonal unit differentiation
	The player does not lose any hard-won possessions
S3	Experiences First, Technology Second
	Use Various Social Elements
	Show Reality
	Do not just convert
	Create meaningful content

(*continued*)

Table 2. (*continued*)

ID	Heuristic
S4	The player able to save the game anytime
	Game objectives are moderate (not to easy-nor to difficult)
	Player able to skip movies & images (non-playable)
	Game allow customization
	Game can handle interruptions (internal)
	Player able to pause the game anytime
S5	Visibility of the system status
	Accuracy
	Environment setup
	Satisfaction
S6	Visible control status and feedback
	Naturally mapped control

3 Surveys for End Users and Usability Experts

A survey is a method in which information about a sample of individuals is collected [17]. For this research, two surveys were carried out whose objective was to validate and evaluate the set of initial heuristics of Table 2. One survey was focused on usability experts and the other, on end users (with a player profile). Before starting the surveys, a usability heuristic was added to the initial set to make a total of 46 heuristics.

Initially, a basic design of the surveys was carried out, that is, some questions were found in both surveys. The surveys had two parts: the first was used in order to highlight the profile of the participant and the second part for the assessment of the set of heuristics. For the assessment of the heuristics, the LIKERT measurement scale was applied using three levels (Not very important, Important, Very important).

The survey for players had 58 participants who answered it voluntarily. The participants were contacted in various ways: mail, forums, social networks, etc. Some characteristics of the participants were the following: the majority were male, they were between 19 and 42 years old, most were university students (in process), some participants knew about Augmented Reality video games like Pokemon Go and Ingress and almost all the participants use to play video games a maximum of 2 h a day. With respect to the assessment of the heuristics, the average of the rating awarded by each player was extracted for each heuristic and 3 of the heuristics obtained an average score lower than 2 (Important). The heuristics with the score lower than the average in this survey can be seen in Table 3.

Table 3. Heuristics with the score lower than the average in the end user surveys.

Heuristic
The player cannot make irreversible errors)
Game objectives are moderate(not to easy-nor to difficult)
Naturally mapped control

The survey for experts had 5 participants. The participants were contacted by mail. Some characteristics of the participants were the following: the majority were female, they were between 34 and 40 years old, most with the Master's degree, all had experience performing heuristic evaluations, everyone knew the augmented reality video game Pokemon Go, and most use to play video games a maximum of 2 h a day. With respect to the assessment of the heuristics, the average of the rating awarded by each usability expert was extracted for each heuristic and 8 of the heuristics obtained an average score lower than 2 (Important). The heuristics with the score lower than the average in this survey can be seen in Table 4.

Table 4. Heuristics with the score lower than the average in the usability expert surveys.

Heuristic
The players are rewarded and rewards are meaningful
There are no repetitive or boring tasks
The players can express themselves
The game uses orthogonal unit differentiation
The player does not lose any hard-won possessions
Game objectives are moderate(not to easy-nor to difficult)
Use Various Social Elements
Naturally mapped control

The results of the surveys were compared and it could be observed that 2 of the heuristics of the set were rated with a score lower than average. The two heuristics that were eliminated from the set are shown in Table 5.

Table 5. Heuristics eliminated after the surveys.

Heuristic
Game objectives are moderate(not to easy-nor to difficult)
Naturally mapped control

Before the survey had 46 heuristics, after this, the whole was reduced to 44 due to the coincidental assessment by experts and players regarding 2 heuristics. At the end of the surveys, a new heuristic was proposed related to the way in which users interact with the controls in video games.

4   Case Study - Park AR

After the surveys, a case study was conducted in order to use the set of heuristics obtained as an evaluation tool. The videogame Park AR was selected for this case study because it fits into the profile of the type of software covered in this study.

The case study was conducted by 5 usability experts. The objective of this study was to identify aspects that are not being covered by the set of heuristics and, if the situation arises, to formulate new heuristics to add them.

The analysis was started by verifying that the problems identified were correctly associated with a heuristic. This result can be seen in Table 6.

Table 6. Results from the case study - Park AR.

Evaluator	Number of correct associations	Number of wrong associations	Identified problems
1	10	6	16
2	7	2	9
3	11	8	19
4	18	4	22
5	14	3	17
Total	60	23	83

Then, a unique list of problems was developed based on those identified by each evaluator. In total, the list contained 61 usability problems. From these problems and their associated heuristics could be described in a better way some proposed heuristics in the formal specification of these.

5 Formal Specification of the Heuristics for Augmented Reality Videogames on Smartphones

Finally, some definitions of the heuristics were corrected as a result of the usability problems identified in the case study. There were a total of 45 heuristics, which will be formally presented with the help of the template proposed by Quiñones and Rusu [10]. The resulting set was named HARVS due to its acronyms "Heuristics for Augmented Reality Videogames on Smartphones". Table 7 shows the proposed set of heuristics.

Table 7. Heuristics for Augmented Reality Video games on Smartphones (ID, name).

ID	Name
HARVS01	Audio-visual representation supports the game
HARVS02	Screen layout is efficient and visually pleasing
HARVS03	Device UI and game UI are used for their own purposes
HARVS04	Indicators are visible
HARVS05	The player understands the terminology
HARVS06	Navigation is consistent, logical, and minimalist
HARVS07	Control keys are consistent and follow standard conventions
HARVS08	Game controls are convenient and flexible

(continued)

Table 7. (*continued*)

ID	Name
HARVS09	The game gives feedback on the player's actions
HARVS10	The player cannot make irreversible errors
HARVS11	The player does not have to memorize things unnecessarily
HARVS12	The game contains help
HARVS13	Player able to skip movies & images (non-playable)
HARVS14	Game allow customization
HARVS15	Visibility of the system status
HARVS16	The game and play sessions can be started quickly
HARVS17	The game accommodates with the surroundings
HARVS18	Game can handle interruptions (internal)
HARVS19	Player able to pause the game anytime
HARVS20	The game provides clear goals or supports player created goals
HARVS21	The player sees the progress in the game and can compare the results
HARVS22	The players are rewarded and rewards are meaningful
HARVS23	The player is in control
HARVS24	Challenge, strategy, and pace are in balance
HARVS25	The first-time experience is encouraging
HARVS26	The game story supports the gameplay and is meaningful
HARVS27	There are no repetitive or boring tasks
HARVS28	The players can express themselves
HARVS29	The game supports different playing styles
HARVS30	The game does not stagnate
HARVS31	The game is consistent
HARVS32	The game uses orthogonal unit differentiation
HARVS33	The player does not lose any hard-won possessions
HARVS34	The player able to save the game anytime
HARVS35	Experiences First, Technology Second
HARVS36	Use Various Social Elements
HARVS37	Show Reality
HARVS38	Do not just convert
HARVS39	Create meaningful content
HARVS40	Accuracy
HARVS41	Environment setup
HARVS42	Satisfaction
HARVS43	Visible control status and feedback
HARVS44	If the game contains advertising, it must be in non-playable moments
HARVS45	Include a left-handed mode for player controls

Next, the descriptions of each heuristic will be placed:

- HARVS01: The music and the game are in sync.
- HARVS02: The design of the interface provides enough information to correctly understand and generate a correct interaction between the player and the game.
- HARVS03: The user interface of the game has the necessary options to not depend on the user interface of the device.
- HARVS04: The indicators referred to the game screen are correctly located and are distinguished in the user interface. In addition, they are easy to understand for the player.
- HARVS05: The player is capable to understand the context of the video game.
- HARVS06: Navigation through the application provides logical and appropriate guidance for the understanding of the game.
- HARVS07: The control keys are not repeated in the interface, perform the expected action and maintain a standard convention. These control keys must be self explanatory.
- HARVS08: The game controls are easy to recognize and use, they are also in an appropriate position on the interface and do not hinder the interaction with the game.
- HARVS09: The game reacts efficiently and quickly to the interaction of the player and the controls of the game.
- HARVS10: The player cannot fall into infinite loops where the game cannot continue.
- HARVS11: The game should provide guides on what things to do or see in the game so that the player does not have to overload his memory remembering this information.
- HARVS12: The game has an instruction manual and frequently asked questions (FAQ).
- HARVS13: You should not go through many user interfaces to start the game or the game sessions.
- HARVS14: The game is portable.
- HARVS15: The game provides clear objectives or supports the objectives created by the player providing advice or instructions to achieve them.
- HARVS16: The player has access to the results obtained in each game.
- HARVS17: Players get rewards that motivate, loyalty and can be useful in the game.
- HARVS18: The player always makes decisions based on the main objective of the game.
- HARVS19: The elements and mechanics of the game are in balance so that the game can be finalized by a player.
- HARVS20: The first experience with the video game should give a good impression of everything that the game has: story, characters, enemies, difficulty, etc.
- HARVS21: The defined story must be portrayed in the objectives of the game and the form of victory.
- HARVS22: The tasks defined by the game do not become repetitive, so each game is different from the previous one.
- HARVS23: Players can express themselves as they are.

- HARVS24: There are different ways to achieve the objectives of the game.
- HARVS25: It is not related to the performance of the device. That is, there is no way for the player to be "stuck" at some point within the application.
- HARVS26: Players should not ask themselves if the different words used in the game, situations or actions of different options mean the same thing.
- HARVS27: The game uses orthogonal differentiation of units, that is, each virtual unit has different functionalities.
- HARVS28: The player is capable to collect different possessions won during the game without fear of losing them.
- HARVS29: The player must be capable to save the game at any time and at any stage of the game, due to the limited resources of the mobile phone, the player must be able to save the game each time he wants to save it, and then the player can continue from the saved stage.
- HARVS30: The player is capable to skip non-playable content such as films or introductory images, the player must have control over whether to watch those contents or not, they should be able to avoid if the player wishes.
- HARVS31: The game should allow user customization, so users can play the game at the desired difficulty and at the desired speed. In mobile phones it is difficult to play at speed because of the inconvenience of the control keys. The control keys, sometimes, are not convenient to play easily, to react to quick decisions, that is, to respond right away.
- HARVS32: The game should be able to handle internal interruptions. These interruptions can be generated by calls, text messages, emails, etc. The game must be paused only so that the player can continue playing after the interruption, otherwise the player will feel frustrated and turn off the game.
- HARVS33: To handle external interruptions, these interruptions are those that occur in the environment of the player for example if someone speaks to the player while playing, or the player is waiting for the train and this arrives so the player needs to stop the game to be able to continue it at the exact moment in which it stopped him.
- HARVS34: First design the experience generated by the game, then decide the appropriate technology.
- HARVS35: Allow players to interact with virtual characters and other players.
- HARVS36: Do not completely convert the real environment into a virtual one, because the components of reality will be overshadowed.
- HARVS37: Not only convert existing video games to augmented reality. After a few times of playing it, the initial emotion disappears, since the game only tries to be visually more attractive than the originals, but does not include really genuine game mechanics.
- HARVS38: The 3D content in the game should add something interesting to the game.
- HARVS39: Evaluate how the system is viewed by the user. Users should receive feedback on what is happening in the system. The augmented reality applications use tracking systems to determine the position of the virtual content in the real scene, which must be fast and reliable, otherwise, the users will be lost when interacting with the application.
- HARVS40: How accurate is the system during interactions. The position of the virtual content in the interface is determined by the tracking system and should not vary.

- HARVS41: Augmented reality applications require special devices such as sensors and/or cameras. In addition, bookmarks may be necessary, such as reference markers. The configuration of the environment should be as simple as possible.
- HARVS42: This measures the degree to which the augmented reality application exceeds the user's expectations. Interaction is an important aspect in augmented reality applications, and the user must have positive attitudes towards the system.
- HARVS43: It keeps the user informed about what is happening when interacting with the game controls.
- HARVS44: If the game runs commercials with advertising, you must choose non-playable moments to add them.
- HARVS45: The controls must have an option for left-handed people in which the main controls are inverted for the player's comfort, this mode in spite of having a defined order can be edited by the player.

6 Conclusions and Future Works

The present work tries to cover the different aspects of usability and playability when evaluating augmented reality video games. The authors designed this set of heuristics based on a previous study, which was evaluated and tested through surveys and a case study. However, more tests and studies are needed to verify that the set covers all aspects of applications in this domain.

It was possible to determine, from the surveys carried out, that both experts and users with a profile of players accept the majority of the initial set of heuristics. However, then some heuristics were added and removed, so in a future work we must re-survey people with these profiles using the final set proposed to confirm their acceptance. Besides, we will use this results to build a numerical analysis.

With the case study it was possible to verify that the set can be employed as an evaluation tool for video games of augmented reality in smartphones. Furthermore, we discovered some mistakes in the description of some of the heuristics that caused confusion in the preliminary set.

As part of a future study, an augmented reality video game for smartphones will be designed using the heuristics proposed in this work in order to validate that the set also can be used to design applications of this type. The design of this video game will be employed to add or remove more heuristics to the whole of the present proposal.

Acknowledgments. The authors would like to thank all the participants involved in the preliminary experiments such as the surveys and the case study, especially the members of "HCI - DUXAIT" (HCI, Design, User Experience, Accessibility & Innovation Technologies). HCI - DUXAIT is a research group of the *Pontificia Universidad Católica del Perú* (PUCP).

References

1. Nielsen, J.: Usability 101: Introduction to usability (2012). https://www.nngroup.com/articles/usability-101-introduction-to-usability/
2. Fernandez, A., Insfran, E., Abrahão, S.: Usability evaluation methods for the web: a systematic mapping study. Inf. Softw. Technol. **53**(8), 789–817 (2011)
3. Holzinger, A.: Usability engineering methods for software developers. Commun. ACM **48** (1), 71–74 (2005)
4. Nielsen, J.: Usability inspection methods. In: Conference Companion on Human factors in computing systems, pp. 413–414 (1994)
5. Nielsen, J.: Designing Web Usability: The Practice of Simplicity. New Riders Publishing, Thousand Oaks (1999)
6. Nielsen, J.: 10 Usability heuristics for user interface design (1995). https://www.nngroup.com/articles/ten-usability-heuristics/
7. Inostroza, R., Rusu, C., Roncagliolo, S., Rusu, V.: Usability heuristics for touchscreen-based mobile devices: update. In: Proceedings of the 2013 Chilean Conference on Human–Computer Interaction, pp. 24–29 (2013)
8. Paz, F., Paz, F.A., Pow-Sang, J.A., Collantes, L.: Usability heuristics for transactional web sites. In: 2014 11th International Conference on Information Technology: New Generations (ITNG), pp. 627–628 (2014)
9. Chang, A., Paz, F., Arenas, J.J., Díaz, J.: Augmented reality and usability best practices: a systematic literature mapping for educational videogames. In: 2018 IEEE Sciences and Humanities International Research Conference (SHIRCON), pp. 1–5 (2018)
10. Quinones, D., Rusu, C., Roncagliolo, S., Rusu, V., Collazos, C.A.: Developing usability heuristics: a formal or informal process? IEEE Lat. Am. Trans. **14**(7), 3400–3409 (2016)
11. Korhonen, H., Koivisto, E.M.: Playability heuristics for mobile games. In: Proceedings of the 8th Conference on Human-Computer Interaction with Mobile Devices and Services, pp. 9–16 (2006)
12. Korhonen, H., Koivisto, E.M.: Playability heuristics for mobile multi-player. In: Proceedings of the 2nd International Conference on Digital Interactive Media in Entertainment and Arts, pp. 28–35 (2007)
13. Wetzel, R., McCall, R., Braun, A.K., Broll, W.: Guidelines for designing augmented reality games. In: Proceedings of the 2008 Conference on Future Play: Research, Play, Share, pp. 173–180 (2008)
14. Soomro, S., Ahmad, W.F.W., Sulaiman, S.: A preliminary study on heuristics for mobile games. In: 2012 International Conference on Computer & Information Science (ICCIS), vol. 2, pp. 1030–1035 (2012)
15. de Paiva Guimarães, M., Martins, V.F.: A checklist to evaluate augmented reality applications. In: 2014 XVI Symposium on Virtual and Augmented Reality, pp. 45–52 (2014)
16. Mohd, F., Daud, E.H.C., Mokhtar, S.A.: Preliminary usability and heuristics model for mobile games, in the aspect of control feature. In: 2016 2nd International Symposium on Agent, Multi-Agent Systems and Robotics (ISAMSR), pp. 112–116 (2016)
17. Scheuren, F.: What is a Survey?. American Statistical Association, Alexandria (2004)

The Potential of User Experience (UX) as an Approach of Evaluation in Tangible User Interfaces (TUI)

Vinicius Krüger da Costa[✉], Andréia Sias Rodrigues,
Lucas Barreiro Agostini[✉], Marcelo Bender Machado,
Natália Toralles Darley[✉], Rafael da Cunha Cardoso,
and Tatiana Aires Tavares[✉]

Pós Graduação em Ciências da Computação,
Universidade Federal de Pelotas (UFPel) e Instituto Federal Sul-rio-grandense
(IFSul), Pelotas, RS, Brazil
{viniciusdacosta,andreia.sias,lbagostini,mb.machado,ntdarley,
rc.cardoso,tatianatavares}@inf.ufpel.edu.br
http://www.ufpel.edu.br

Abstract. The objective of this paper its presents the potential of using UX as the main evaluation approach in TUI, starting from results of a Systematic Review of Literature (SRL), in which it found other studies published in the last five years that evaluate TUI applications, analyzing the methods and tools used to perform them, relating these with an experiment of evaluation at AR Sandbox application, discuss in order to contribute of the proposal of new methodologies that aim to evaluate the applications of tangible interfaces, considering their due particularity.

Keywords: Tangible User Interface · Evaluation · User Experience

1 Introduction

Human-Computer Interaction (HCI) is a multidisciplinary area that is concerned with providing design guidelines to developers who create applications to users needs and expectations. In this process, the HCI includes the **project**, the **implementation**, and **evaluation** of the interaction between users and the computer systems [40].

The evaluation is specifically performed for validation of the application from the user's point of view and, depending on the type of interface, an analysis methodology is chosen. The literature presented some approaches of evaluations that focus on **Usability** and **User Experience** [44].

Usability aims to evaluate how the communication between the user and the system is. How easy and quick it is for the user to understand the application, interact with it, evaluate the effectiveness of the User Interface (UI) in execution tasks, and how the system and the user react to an error [48]. Then

© Springer Nature Switzerland AG 2019
A. Marcus and W. Wang (Eds.): HCII 2019, LNCS 11586, pp. 30–48, 2019.
https://doi.org/10.1007/978-3-030-23535-2_3

User Experience is an approach that evaluates not only the usability of the system but the user's feelings and perceptions.

UI evaluation approaches for everyday devices, such as smartphones and computers, are based on **Graphical User Interface (GUI)**, where interaction occurs through the screen, with graphic elements manipulated by touch, or auxiliary devices such as the mouse and the keyboard [44].

The difference for the applications based on **Tangible User Interfaces (TUI)** is the presence of physical objects as elements of interaction. In a scenario of tangible interactions, there is the object and a set of movements or actions that the user can perform with this physical element that recognizes this interaction and reacts visually or about the object itself or the environment [30].

Hence, if in a TUI the physical element is the input and output device of the interface, it can be assumed that the interaction process is more intuitive and natural for the user with a real-world analogy [29].

Interacting in a TUI application is different from a GUI, it is suggested that the evaluation methods currently used regularly for common graphical interfaces may not fit fully into the evaluation of a tangible application.

The objective of this paper its presents the potential of using UX [57] as the main evaluation approach in TUI, starting from results of a Systematic Review of Literature (SRL), in which it found other studies published in the last five years that evaluate TUI applications, analyzing the methods and tools used to perform them, relating these with an experiment of evaluation at AR Sandbox application, discuss in order to contribute of the proposal of new methodologies that aim to evaluate the applications of tangible interfaces, considering their due particularity.

Next section presents a theoretical background about Tangible Interaction, Evaluation Methods and Tools; Sect. 3 presents and discuss the results of the Systematic Review of Literature (SRL) about Evaluation Methods and Tools used in TUI applications; Sect. 4 describes a practical experiment of TUI application evaluation using AR Sandbox; and Sect. 5 discusses the results and main contribution of this article which is to show the potential of the UX approach to evaluation in TUI.

2   Tangible Interaction, Evaluation Methods and Tools

The development of TUI applications is a new process and recent research is emerging that discusses a way to evaluate this type of interface. Usually, the methods that are being applied for the development of TUIs are the same methods for UI already used in daily life. Therefore, it is probably that there are specific evaluation criteria for tangible interfaces, since this is an unconventional approach to human-computer communication.

Tangible Interaction is a term suggested by Hornecker and Buur to present a comprehensive field than TUI, considering social interaction through tangible applications, thus including the issue of interaction with the environment and body gesticulation [26].

[31] brought the term Reality-Based Interaction to conceptualize new user interaction styles for user skills. This context suggests that interaction with digital information is closer to interaction with the real world.

Reality-Based Interaction has four concepts:

- **Intuitive Physics:** the user's perception of the real world;
- **Body consciousness:** the user's notion of his body and the ability to coordinate his gestures;
- **Environmental awareness:** the user's perception of the environment around him and his ability to interact with it;
- **Social understanding:** the perception that the user has with other users in the same environment, the communication between them and the ability to perform tasks together to achieve the same goal.

In the literature, there are already different approaches and evaluation tools that could measure these concepts of Reality-Based interaction in TUI applications. Several instruments are used, which can be quantitative and/or qualitative. The obtained results are grouped, with an analysis in order to discuss some conclusions about what was intended to be evaluated and/or validated at the application.

Some evaluation instruments are:

- **Interview:** the evaluator asks a user a series of questions in order to understand how his experience was when using the application; during the course of the interview other issues may also be addressed;
- **Questionnaire:** After the user makes use of the application, a questionnaire is applied with a set of questions that can be for descriptive or scaled answers between two opposing adjectives (I liked-dislike/agree-disagree);
- **Observation:** the user is monitored while using the application and can be recorded for later analysis, it is possible to capture the user's behavior and abilities;
- **Think Aloud:** the evaluator takes notes that the user expressed orally while using the application.

For each type of evaluation methodology, it is possible to use one or more evaluation instruments. The choice of evaluation instrument is an important issue to consider in planning phases of evaluation and, specifically with TUI applications, determines how the result is useful.

About the evaluation tools and methodologies for TUI applications (especially User Experience), the next section search to verify the existence, adaptations or suggestions of use that contemplate the concepts of Reality-Based Interaction.

3   Systematic Review of Literature (SRL) of TUI Applications Evaluations Methods

The SRL method was used for the delimitation of this study of the evaluation methods/tools used in TUIs. SRL is an exploratory analysis methodology, through search engines of scientific articles. Following specific protocols that allow a better understanding of state of art on what was published/researched in a certain area of knowledge.

3.1 Methodology

The systematization of this SRL used the software StArt (State of the Art through Systematic Review) as a tool[1] [19], which allows the creation, execution, selection, and extraction of data, within an information management software that can be shared by a group of researchers.

Two research questions were answered in the articles raised:

- (a) What approaches are used in TUIs evaluation?
- (b) What tools/instruments are used to measure the proposed goal in these TUIs evaluation?

The SRL protocol also demands to specify the search string generated based on a set of keywords defined from the most recurring ones found in the articles preliminary listed in the search:

("TUI" or "tangible user interface" or "tangible interface") AND ("evaluate" OR "evaluating") AND ("UX" OR "usability" OR "communicability")

This search string was applied to scientific indexers who returned the collection of articles. In this mapping the following Academic Search Engines (ASEs) were adopted:

- *ACM Digital Library*[2];
- *IEEE Xplore Digital Library*[3];
- *Science Direct*[4];
- *Springer*[5].

These ASEs were selected because they aggregate a considerable amount of work within the research area considered.

In order to restrict the amount of work retrieved in this stage of selection, for subsequent extraction of the data, some criteria were used for the exclusion/inclusion of articles.

Criteria for inclusion of articles:

- Full articles;
- Published as of 2013;
- Presents some TUI application with the evaluation process;

---

[1] Tool to support the planning and execution of systematic reviews. Available at: http://lapes.dc.ufscar.br/tools/.
[2] http://dl.acm.org.
[3] http://ieeexplore.ieee.org.
[4] http://www.sciencedirect.com.
[5] http://link.springer.com/.

Exclusion Criteria for Articles:

- Complete book, abstract, poster or short article;
- Be focused on another research area other than HCI discussion;
- This article presents TUI application but does not present the evaluation process.

3.2 Results and Discuss

The SRL was performed on the ASEs and as a result, **703 references were returned**, retrieved and stored in the StArt tool. The total set of articles resulting from this initial phase, classified according to the search engine used, is presented in Table 1.

Table 1. Distribution of articles found in each ASE

Search engine	Result	Selected
ACM Digital Library	10	4
IEEE Xplore Digital	3	0
Science Direct	230	11
Springer	455	33
IHC	5	2
Total	**703**	**50**

The first filter the group of researchers carried out a screening by analyzing: title, keywords and abstract. In order to make this selection, we used the exclusion and inclusion criteria of articles, established on SRL protocol, resulting in a subset of **86 articles**. Then, the final filtering cycle involved the three researchers with a complete reading of the articles to identify the answers to the research questions. Thus the final set listed in this SRL comprises the total of **50 articles**.

About the research questions listed above, the answers give some information to discuss:

(a) What approaches are used in TUIs evaluation?
As shown in Fig. 1, most articles use the approach focused on **usability** for evaluations. This validates the operation of the technology, as designed, evaluating its efficiency/effectiveness.

The listed articles that work with usability focused approach are: [2, 6–12, 15, 20, 21, 25, 27, 28, 32, 33, 37–39, 41, 42, 45, 46, 49–52] e [61].

User Experience was the second most commonly used approach, considering the user's perceptions and feelings regarding their relationship with a TUI application.

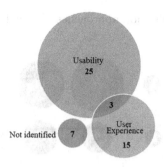

Fig. 1. Evaluation approaches used in selected articles

These are the listed articles that work with a User Experience approach: [8,13,17,18,22,24,34,37,49,54–56,58–60] e [3].

Seven articles presented tests that did not allow a categorization about the evaluation approach used, applied only functional tests of the developed technologies: [4,5,35,36,43,47,53].

Of the articles listed, three of them [8,37,49] combined the Usability and User Experience approach, using a questionnaire as the main evaluation tool.

[37] is an example of this joint approach, presents a scenario of evaluations about perceived spatial affordances of hover interaction above Tabletop Surfaces.

At the same time that efficiency-effectiveness tests are presented with quantitative performance and error rates, there is concern about sensations in the use of the application. Was applied attractiveness measurement tools and the care given with characteristics that go beyond the standard questionnaire used, such as the height and size of participants' arms, for example.

(b) What tools/instruments are used to measure the proposed goal in these TUIs evaluation?

In general, there are very different types of instruments that have been used to answer the evaluation objective within a given proposed approach.

Table 2 shows, the use of interviews (structured or semi-structured), questionnaires and the observation of the specialists were the instruments most used for TUI application evaluations returned at SRL articles.

Table 2. Evaluation instruments used in selected articles

Type of evaluation instrument	Number of articles
Interviews	10
Questionnaires	24
Observation	28
Think Aloud	5
Others	2

Figure 2 relates the evaluation approaches used with instruments that used.

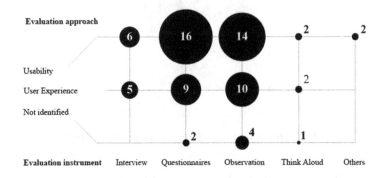

Fig. 2. Evaluation approach vs. evaluation instrument in selected articles

Interviews were usually used in a semi-structured way, with some key questions and others free, in order to evaluate how a certain group of users felt (UX) about the execution of certain tasks (Usability) in TUIs application.

[8] presents and his paper an evaluation of TUI application which goal was to improve learning conditions of children with dyslexia and attention disorder. In this scenario, a simplified questionnaire with children "liked or disliked" type, combined with interview applied to therapists, allowed a more accurate evaluation.

Focus groups were used in [28,34] and [21] as a way of generating a collaborative observational quality in association with interviews.

Although relevant, the interviews had a much lower occurrence of use in the selected articles than the use of questionnaires and observation of the process by specialists.

Several patterns of questionnaires established have emerged from articles, such as the Scale Usability System (SUS) [14], used in [15] and also in [21] combined with Focus Group.

Another recurrent questionnaire model was the AttrackDiff [23], which an instrument to measure the attractiveness of interactive products and UX. This instrument was used in [37,49] and [16].

The observation was the most referenced instrument in the final articles selected. Figure 2 gives indications that there is a relation to the use of this in a complementary way to the use of questionnaires. This is justified because questionnaires focus on user-generated perceptions, while observations are organized by specialists and mediators of the evaluation process. For example, [55] used the concepts of "gamification" for history teaching to primary school students using an augmented reality application in a TUI. In this work [55], a questionnaire was used to evaluate the interaction process with the students, and direct observation of the use was made by the specialists who recorded all the sections of the evaluation.

Based on SRL results, some observations about evaluation processes applied to TUIs:

- Most articles did not use an only single evaluation instrument or approach to evaluate TUI applications. This use of more than one approach evidences the concern of not only the efficiency of the application but also UX. At this point, the use of instruments that allow users to collaborate during the evaluation process is growing.
- There was no exact correlation between a particular TUI application evaluation approach and a specific package of instruments. According to the proposed objectives, the scenario or user profile (for example, children) defines which instruments will be used. Evaluation with children, for example, the reports of the articles indicate the difficulty of use questionnaires or more specific tools, requiring the involvement of other professionals in the evaluation process.
- None of the selected articles proposes any specific evaluation tool that considers the more general characteristics of interaction with TUIs, nor adaptations of existing tools.
- The concepts of Reality-Based Interaction, considering: intuitive physics, body consciousness, environmental awareness, and social understanding was not reflected in evaluation tools or instruments used. Observations on some points such as the height of the elements by the hands of users, arrangement and lighting of the environment, the design of the elements and use of materials more suitable for that type of interaction, although, none evaluation considered these particularities or how they can impact the interaction process.
- Another important issue is that none of the articles (even the 703 from the initial phase) proposes to discuss a specific evaluation process with tangible interactions or to review the application of several existing methods in TUI.

The next section presents a practical of UX evaluation at TUI application named AR Sandbox using some instruments listed at SRL.

4   AR Sandbox: UX Evaluation for a TUI Application

AR Sandbox is a project developed by UC Davis[6], consists of a sandbox where a topographic map is projected on top of the surface (Fig. 3). The user shapes the sand to represent reliefs as if shaping the topographic map and, raising his hand over the sandbox, the system recognizes it as a cloud and simulates the flow of water.

The project consists of a didactic and educational TUI application that offers the user a dynamic practice of representing the topographic map. Users can apply their topography knowledge to compose scenarios, simulate precipitation and observe flow, as well as can shape real-world scenarios, rather than creating

---

[6] University of California, Davis https://www.ucdavis.edu/.

Fig. 3. Users testing AR Sandbox

a model, the user can play it in the AR Sandbox by turning the relief into a moldable and interactive material.

In the work [16], this TUI application was implemented and the usability and UX evaluation were done. This section discusses the procedures and results of this evaluation, relating them to SRL conclusions.

4.1   Procedures

To evaluate the AR Sandbox application, the AttrakDiff tool was used, offering questionnaires for users, as well as generate graphs with the result obtained from the answers.

The evaluations of UX in AttrackDiff are separated by dimensions, which are: PQ, HQ-I, HQ-S, and ATT, where:

- **PQ (Pragmatic Quality):** describes the functional quality of an application and indicates the degree of success through the user's objectives achieved using it;
- **HQ-I (Hedonic Quality - Identity):** indicates the level of immediate identification of the user with the application;
- **HQ-S (Hedonic Quality - Stimulus):** indicates if the application supports the user's needs concerning originality, interest and, especially, stimulus;
- **ATT (Attractiveness):** it is the most comprehensive measure that quantifies the overall attractiveness of the application, based on the perception of quality by the user.

For evaluation, users freely experimented the application, executing some tasks such as shaping the topographic map, reproducing mountain, plateau, plain, depression, beaches, simulating rainfall and observing water flow.

After the experiment, each user evaluated the TUI application through 2 questionnaires: one form containing the Usability evaluation, and another form containing the UX. Questions and graphs of both forms were based on Attrack-Diff instrument.

80 volunteers participated in the evaluation, 74 undergraduate students, two post-graduation students, three teachers and one "other". 43 considered themselves as "Non-specialist" (computer science students or teachers), and 37 were considered "Specialist" (geology or hydric engineering students or teachers).

4.2 Results and Discuss

Figure 4 presents the UX evaluation of the AR Sandbox. The questionnaire users indicated their opinions on a semantic scale that varies from one adjective to another.

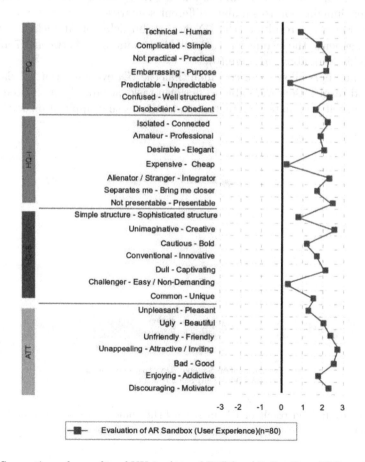

Fig. 4. Semantic scale results of UX in AttrackDiff for AR Sandbox TUI application.

The first pair "Technical - Human" received 0.7 scores, most of the users were in doubt of the meaning of Technical and Humanized adjectives for the application, therefore, they did not know to answer and they marked neutral. Other users indicated "Human" because the interaction is "more natural".

"Predictable - Unpredictable" pair received a 0.4 scores, the response range for this question was −3 to 3, but the evaluation shows that the mean of the responses tended to be "Unpredictable", indicating that users believe the AR Sandbox it is surprising.

"Expensive - Cheap" pair received 0.2 scores, users believed that the cost to implement the AR Sandbox is not cheap. They had difficulty evaluating this issue because they did not know the value of the equipment or the complexity of the computational system.

Furthermore, the "Challenger - Easy/Not Demanding" pair received a rating of 0.3 scores, which indicates that although application manipulation is simple (shaping the topographic map and simulating rain), other users were motivated to use their imagination to simulate different scenarios.

In the Fig. 5 the results of the UX evaluation fields of AttrackDiff are displayed. In general, the evaluation of the fields was uniform, between 1.7 and 1.8, and all fields were above average (0).

These numbers allow us to conclude that the UX evaluation of AR Sandbox had a good result, users were able to perform tasks accurately, interested in the application, felt stimulated, attracted, and believes that application works.

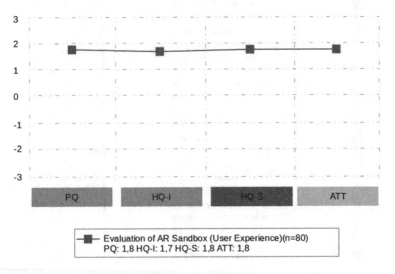

Fig. 5. The evaluation result of UX in AttrackDiff dimensions for AR Sandbox TUI application

Introducing the discussion of the UX evaluation results of the AttrackDiff questionnaire for the AR Sandbox application, many considerations are related to observations in the SRL about evaluation methods in TUI:

- Questionnaires quoted in the SRL, and the AttrackDiff that used in this evaluation with the AR Sandbox, do not consider a full observation for a TUI application. Environmental factors, physical body limits for use of this type of interface are ignored.
- Specialists comments on the use of the AR Sandbox allowed the discussion of questions that could help in the evaluation and design of the TUI application.
- Accessibility is not included in the AttrackDiff questionnaire nor in the others cited in the SRL. When applying evaluation with the AR Sandbox a wheelchair user had difficulty using the TUI application because of the height of the table. There are not topics about how accessible the application is for a person with any kind of disabilities or about the environmental factor that could interfere in the UX.
- A TUI application aims to extract the user's physical abilities for interaction in a natural way with their interface. During the tests of AR Sandbox, users proved that this characteristic is present, but do not explain or evaluate this at questionnaire. The tasks performed were simple and intuitive, requiring no further explanation for use of the interface.
- Facial expressions of satisfaction and how users interact with each other encourages collaboration in the use of the application. As for example, some groups of students simulated the dam breaking to observe the flow of water and other groups shaped the highest mountains. However, the AttrackDiff questionnaires and several other instruments cited in the SRL are answered individually and do not present questions about social engagement and collaboration about TUI application use.
- Some questions in AttrackDiff instrument were unusual, repetitive and others were not relevant for the evaluator. For example, the "Technical - Humanized" and "Cheap - Expensive" adjective pairs were questions that the users had different interpretations, causing some confusion of evaluation of the application.

5   The Potential of UX for TUI Evaluation

Academic research and commercial applications with TUI have been growing at the HCI area. Although the projects in TUI are more specific application contexts, it was noticed at SRL and in the experiment of evaluation with AR Sandbox, these evaluation methods currently used privilege interactions through GUI.

The concept of usability has become more comprehensive, but still, evaluations with this approach have as their main objective to assess the quality of software, efficiency, and effectiveness with a look to technology. Because TUIs are a relatively recent technology, most of the benchmarked evaluations focus on testing whether the "application works".

On the other hand, according to ISO 9241-110: 2010, UX is defined as: "user perceptions, feelings, and sensations that result in the use and/or use of a product, system or service" [57].

In this way, UX is a more comprehensive approach of evaluation that allows analyzing TUI applications not only by the functional characteristics of the system. UX takes into account user interaction with the entire application, evaluating user's thoughts and feelings [1].

To evaluate a product by UX, qualitative methods such as interviews, questionnaires, and written documents can be used. The data collected by observations can be verbal quotations from the user expressing their opinions, feelings, and knowledge.

This was verified with this work since the closed questionnaires do not usually provide space for dialogue between the evaluators with the users and between them.

The results from the observations are detailed descriptions of the behavior and actions of the user and the data collected in documents are summaries, citations or reports.

Quantitative methods allow the grouping of the answers of users in order to analyze what is common between the answers, and with the generalization, can extract information for comparisons, ideas and meanings of the events occurred in the evaluation.

The evaluation of UX with the application AR Sandbox used the AttrackDiff, which is one of the instruments referenced to evaluate with this approach and allows to relate that the ergonomic quality takes into consideration the usability because the user feels more comfortable when it has the control of the situation.

But, even AttrackDiff does not present basic questions that contemplate the full scope of the interaction experience with a TUI. If evaluations are made with the inadequate instruments there may be a misinterpretation of the results and design of new applications in TUI may have impacts.

Thus, the first step in proposing a specific methodology for TUIs is to understand that existing instruments are flawed. For most applications today use the GUI the evaluation tools do not extract the maximum potential when used in TUI.

Hence, it is suggested to adopt some basic considerations to enhance the use of the UX approach to TUI evaluation:

- The main element of TUI applications are physical objects as elements of interaction, the choice of how this object will be and how to evaluate its use is an important issue when developing the application, where designers should be concerned with the size, object, as this should interfere directly with the UX.
- TUIs demand the user's body gestures to shape and move objects in the interaction process and such aspects should be present in the evaluation of the application. Consider that people have different biotypes and may not have all the preserved capabilities (accessibility).

– Do not use only a single instrument to evaluate UX in TUI, but consider using them together depending on the context of a specific use of that application, user profile. For example, with children, a particular instrument will not bring results while with adults it can works.
– Social collaboration is a basic and fundamental characteristic during the use of a TUI application. It has a major impact on UX and creating ways to evaluate this during the interaction process is critical. Focus groups, thinking aloud, expert observations or methods that enable users to talk to each other and with evaluator should be incorporated.
– Consider the concepts of Reality-Based Interaction (intuitive physics, body consciousness, environmental awareness, and social understanding) during the evaluation process. If the instruments used to allow this type of information to be interpreted or if it is necessary to adapt or build a specific tool for it.

Also, from the general analysis of the articles referenced in the SRL, it is possible to generate categories of evaluation types based on the proposed objectives:

– **Comparison of user interfaces:** aims to compare the use of traditional interfaces, such as GUI, in the relation of TUI, evaluating the gains/benefits of tangible interaction. Usually, they use the same traditional evaluation tools, with criteria developed for GUI, applied in a new use with TUI, having questionnaires and usability as a focus;
– **Collaborative interaction:** TUI has as the main characteristic to privilege the process of collaborative interaction, in a certain physical space. This group of articles tries precisely to evaluate if this characteristic of the TUIs potentiates a certain UX in an application that needs more of this process of collaboration. In these cases, the use of evaluation approaches and instruments such as focus groups, observations, and UX questionnaires is preferred;
– **Education instrument:** aims to propose solutions based on tools focused on the teaching/learning process for children and young people. They are of specific contexts and presented a variation in the instruments of evaluation, precisely due to the complexity inherent in the application of structured questionnaires with children.

These categorization groups help in the understanding that the evaluations have several solution proposals and that realizing this potentiates the results. How objective is pursued in the evaluation process impacts the prescription of the UX evaluation method itself.

6   Conclusion and Future Works

Applications that make use of Tangible User Interfaces are something new and incorporate various forms of interaction, and just as common interfaces are evaluated the TUIs should also be.

The forms of interaction of the TUIs are diverse, the possibility of the user interacting with their body to manipulate the interaction element and the responding application in the same object stimulates the feeling of immersion.

This work evidenced the need to develop an appropriate methodology for TUIs. According to the results of the SRL developed in this work, inadequate methods are being applied in a generic way for TUIs, complicating the possibility to improve the applications.

Between them, even though it is not the most used, the User Experience is the closest approach to evaluating TUIs. UX shows its potential to be applied in the evaluations process for this type of interface, required customization according to TUI application to adapt to the many particularities that the interaction has to offer.

From this study, as future works, it is intended to elaborate a set of guidelines on how best to apply a UX evaluation approach in TUI applications, incorporating the issues discussed in this paper, to be validated during the test stage with users for evaluation of interface, consolidating in a methodology for TUI evaluation.

References

1. Albert, W., Tullis, T.: Measuring the User Experience: Collecting, Analyzing, and Presenting Usability Metrics. Newnes, Oxford (2013)
2. Almukadi, W., Boy, G.A.: Enhancing collaboration and facilitating children's learning using TUIs: a human-centered design approach. In: Zaphiris, P., Ioannou, A. (eds.) LCT 2016. LNCS, vol. 9753, pp. 105–114. Springer, Cham (2016). https://doi.org/10.1007/978-3-319-39483-1_10
3. Alrashed, T., et al.: An observational study of usability in collaborative tangible interfaces for complex planning systems. Procedia Manuf. **3**, 1974–1980 (2015)
4. Anastasiou, D., Maquil, V., Ras, E.: Gesture analysis in a case study with a tangible user interface for collaborative problem solving. J. Multimodal User Interfaces 8(3), 305–317 (2014)
5. Anastasiou, D., Ras, E.: Case study analysis on collaborative problem solving using a tangible interface. In: Joosten-ten Brinke, D., Laanpere, M. (eds.) TEA 2016. CCIS, vol. 653, pp. 11–22. Springer, Cham (2017). https://doi.org/10.1007/978-3-319-57744-9_2
6. Angelini, L., et al.: WheelSense: enabling tangible gestures on the steering wheel for in-car natural interaction. In: Kurosu, M. (ed.) HCI 2013. LNCS, vol. 8005, pp. 531–540. Springer, Heidelberg (2013). https://doi.org/10.1007/978-3-642-39262-7_60
7. Antonijoan, M., Miralles, D.: Tangible interface for controlling toys-to-life characters emotions. In: Proceedings of the 2016 CHI Conference Extended Abstracts on Human Factors in Computing Systems, CHI EA 2016, pp. 2387–2394. ACM, New York (2016). http://doi.acm.org/10.1145/2851581.2892330
8. Ayala, A., Guerrero, G., Mateu, J., Casades, L., Alamán, X.: Virtual touch FlyStick and PrimBox: two case studies of mixed reality for teaching geometry. In: García-Chamizo, J.M., Fortino, G., Ochoa, S.F. (eds.) UCAmI 2015. LNCS, vol. 9454, pp. 309–320. Springer, Cham (2015). https://doi.org/10.1007/978-3-319-26401-1_29

9. Besançon, L., Issartel, P., Ammi, M., Isenberg, T.: Mouse, tactile, and tangible input for 3D manipulation. In: Proceedings of the 2017 CHI Conference on Human Factors in Computing Systems, CHI 2017, pp. 4727–4740. ACM, New York (2017). http://doi.acm.org/10.1145/3025453.3025863

10. Blagojevic, R., Plimmer, B.: CapTUI: geometric drawing with tangibles on a capacitive multi-touch display. In: Kotzé, P., Marsden, G., Lindgaard, G., Wesson, J., Winckler, M. (eds.) INTERACT 2013. LNCS, vol. 8117, pp. 511–528. Springer, Heidelberg (2013). https://doi.org/10.1007/978-3-642-40483-2_37

11. Bonillo, C., Baldassarri, S., Marco, J., Cerezo, E.: Tackling developmental delays with therapeutic activities based on tangible tabletops. Univers. Access Inf. Soc. 18, 1–17 (2017)

12. Bonillo, C., Cerezo, E., Marco, J., Baldassarri, S.: Designing therapeutic activities based on tangible interaction for children with developmental delay. In: Antona, M., Stephanidis, C. (eds.) UAHCI 2016. LNCS, vol. 9739, pp. 183–192. Springer, Cham (2016). https://doi.org/10.1007/978-3-319-40238-3_18

13. Bouabid, A., Lepreux, S., Kolski, C.: Design and evaluation of distributed user interfaces between tangible tabletops. Univers. Access Inf. Soc. 1–19 (2017)

14. Brooke, J., et al.: SUS - a quick and dirty usability scale. Usability Eval. Industry 189(194), 4–7 (1996)

15. Bruun, A., Jensen, K., Kristensen, D.: Usability of single- and multi-factor authentication methods on tabletops: a comparative study. In: Sauer, S., Bogdan, C., Forbrig, P., Bernhaupt, R., Winckler, M. (eds.) HCSE 2014. LNCS, vol. 8742, pp. 299–306. Springer, Heidelberg (2014). https://doi.org/10.1007/978-3-662-44811-3_22

16. Darley, N.T., Tavares, T.A., Costa, V., Collares, G., Terra, V.: Tangible interfaces: an analysis of user experience using the AR sandbox project. In: XVI Brazilian Symposium on Human Factors in Computing Systems IHC 2017, October 2017

17. De Croon, R., Cardoso, B., Klerkx, J., Abeele, V.V., Verbert, K.: MeViTa: interactive visualizations to help older adults with their medication intake using a camera-projector system. In: Bernhaupt, R., Dalvi, G., Joshi, A., Balkrishan, D.K., O'Neill, J., Winckler, M. (eds.) INTERACT 2017. LNCS, vol. 10513, pp. 132–152. Springer, Cham (2017). https://doi.org/10.1007/978-3-319-67744-6_9

18. Duckworth, J., et al.: Resonance: an interactive tabletop artwork for co-located group rehabilitation and play. In: Antona, M., Stephanidis, C. (eds.) UAHCI 2015. LNCS, vol. 9177, pp. 420–431. Springer, Cham (2015). https://doi.org/10.1007/978-3-319-20684-4_41

19. Fabbri, S., Silva, C., Hernandes, E., Octaviano, F., Di Thommazo, A., Belgamo, A.: Improvements in the start tool to better support the systematic review process. In: Proceedings of the 20th International Conference on Evaluation and Assessment in Software Engineering, EASE 2016, pp. 21:1–21:5. ACM, New York (2016). http://doi.acm.org/10.1145/2915970.2916013

20. Garcia-Sanjuan, F., Jaen, J., Nacher, V., Catala, A.: Design and evaluation of a tangible-mediated robot for kindergarten instruction. In: Proceedings of the 12th International Conference on Advances in Computer Entertainment Technology, p. 3. ACM (2015)

21. Guerlain, C., Cortina, S., Renault, S.: Towards a collaborative geographical information system to support collective decision making for urban logistics initiative. Transp. Res. Procedia 12, 634–643 (2016)

22. Gupta, A., Padhi, A., Sorathia, K., Varma, S., Sharma, B.: MuBiks: tangible music player for visually challenged. In: Stephanidis, C., Antona, M. (eds.) UAHCI 2014. LNCS, vol. 8513, pp. 346–356. Springer, Cham (2014). https://doi.org/10.1007/978-3-319-07437-5_33

23. Hassenzahl, M., Burmester, M., Koller, F.: Attrakdiff: Ein fragebogen zur messung wahrgenommener hedonischer und pragmatischer qualität. Mensch Comput. **2003**, 187–196 (2003)

24. He, G., et al.: ARDock: a web-AR based real-time tangible edugame for molecular docking. In: El Rhalibi, A., Tian, F., Pan, Z., Liu, B. (eds.) Edutainment 2016. LNCS, vol. 9654, pp. 37–49. Springer, Cham (2016). https://doi.org/10.1007/978-3-319-40259-8_4

25. Hoe, Z.Y., Lee, I.J., Chen, C.H., Chang, K.P.: Using an augmented reality-based training system to promote spatial visualization ability for the elderly. Univers. Access Inf. Soc. **18**, 327–342 (2017)

26. Hornecker, E., Buur, J.: Getting a grip on tangible interaction: a framework on physical space and social interaction. In: Proceedings of the SIGCHI Conference on Human Factors in Computing Systems, pp. 437–446 (2006). http://doi.acm.org/10.1145/1124772.1124838

27. Hotta, M., Oka, M., Mori, H.: Liquid tangible user interface: using liquid in TUI. In: Yamamoto, S. (ed.) HCI 2014. LNCS, vol. 8521, pp. 167–176. Springer, Cham (2014). https://doi.org/10.1007/978-3-319-07731-4_17

28. Ionita, D., Wieringa, R., Bullee, J.-W., Vasenev, A.: Tangible modelling to elicit domain knowledge: an experiment and focus group. In: Johannesson, P., Lee, M.L., Liddle, S.W., Opdahl, A.L., López, Ó.P. (eds.) ER 2015. LNCS, vol. 9381, pp. 558–565. Springer, Cham (2015). https://doi.org/10.1007/978-3-319-25264-3_42

29. Ishii, H.: Tangible bits: beyond pixels. In: Proceedings of the 2nd International Conference on Tangible and Embedded Interaction, pp. xv–xxv. ACM (2008)

30. Ishii, H., Ullmer, B.: Tangible bits: towards seamless interfaces between people, bits and atoms. In: Proceedings of the ACM SIGCHI Conference on Human Factors in Computing Systems, pp. 234–241. ACM (1997)

31. Jacob, R.J., et al.: Reality-based interaction: a framework for post-wimp interfaces. In: Proceedings of the SIGCHI Conference on Human Factors in Computing Systems, pp. 201–210. ACM (2008)

32. Jadán-Guerrero, J., López, G., Guerrero, L.A.: Use of tangible interfaces to support a literacy system in children with intellectual disabilities. In: Hervás, R., Lee, S., Nugent, C., Bravo, J. (eds.) UCAmI 2014. LNCS, vol. 8867, pp. 108–115. Springer, Cham (2014). https://doi.org/10.1007/978-3-319-13102-3_20

33. Jones, C.E., Maquil, V.: Towards geospatial tangible user interfaces: an observational user study exploring geospatial interactions of the novice. In: Grueau, C., Gustavo Rocha, J. (eds.) GISTAM 2015. CCIS, vol. 582, pp. 104–123. Springer, Cham (2016). https://doi.org/10.1007/978-3-319-29589-3_7

34. Lee, T.H., Wu, F.G., Chen, H.T.: Innovation & evaluation of tangible direct manipulation digital drawing pens for children. Appl. Ergon. **60**, 207–219 (2017)

35. Leversund, A.H., Krzywinski, A., Chen, W.: Children's collaborative storytelling on a tangible multitouch tabletop. In: Streitz, N., Markopoulos, P. (eds.) DAPI 2014. LNCS, vol. 8530, pp. 142–153. Springer, Cham (2014). https://doi.org/10.1007/978-3-319-07788-8_14

36. Li, N., Willett, W., Sharlin, E., Sousa, M.C.: Visibility perception and dynamic viewsheds for topographic maps and models. In: Proceedings of the 5th Symposium on Spatial User Interaction, pp. 39–47. ACM (2017)

37. Lubos, P., Ariza, O., Bruder, G., Daiber, F., Steinicke, F., Krüger, A.: HoverSpace. In: Abascal, J., Barbosa, S., Fetter, M., Gross, T., Palanque, P., Winckler, M. (eds.) INTERACT 2015. LNCS, vol. 9298, pp. 259–277. Springer, Cham (2015). https://doi.org/10.1007/978-3-319-22698-9_17

38. Maquil, V., Leopold, U., De Sousa, L.M., Schwartz, L., Tobias, E.: Towards a framework for geospatial tangible user interfaces in collaborative urban planning. J. Geograph. Syst. **20**, 185–206 (2018)

39. Maquil, V., Tobias, E., Latour, T.: Tangible voting: a technique for interacting with group choices on a tangible tabletop. In: Abascal, J., Barbosa, S., Fetter, M., Gross, T., Palanque, P., Winckler, M. (eds.) INTERACT 2015. LNCS, vol. 9299, pp. 79–86. Springer, Cham (2015). https://doi.org/10.1007/978-3-319-22723-8_7

40. Marsh, S.: Human computer interaction: an operational definition. SIGCHI Bull. **22**(1), 16–22 (1990). https://doi.org/10.1145/101288.101291

41. Mora, S., Di Loreto, I., Divitini, M.: The interactive-token approach to board games. In: De Ruyter, B., Kameas, A., Chatzimisios, P., Mavrommati, I. (eds.) AmI 2015. LNCS, vol. 9425, pp. 138–154. Springer, Cham (2015). https://doi.org/10.1007/978-3-319-26005-1_10

42. Park, H., Moon, H.C.: Design evaluation of information appliances using augmented reality-based tangible interaction. Comput. Ind. **64**(7), 854–868 (2013)

43. Pomboza-Junez, G., Holgado-Terriza, J.A., Medina-Medina, N.: Toward the gestural interface: comparative analysis between touch user interfaces versus gesture-based user interfaces on mobile devices. Univers. Access Inf. Soc. **18**, 107–126 (2017)

44. Preece, J., Rogers, Y., Sharp, H.: Design de Interação - 3rd edn. Bookman Editora (2013)

45. Sapounidis, T., Demetriadis, S.: Tangible versus graphical user interfaces for robot programming: exploring cross-age children's preferences. Pers. Ubiquit. Comput. **17**(8), 1775–1786 (2013)

46. Seo, D.W., Lee, J.Y.: Physical query interface for tangible augmented tagging and interaction. Expert Syst. Appl. **40**(6), 2032–2042 (2013)

47. Shen, Y.T., Lu, P.W.: BlowBrush: a design of tangible painting system using blowing action. In: Streitz, N., Markopoulos, P. (eds.) DAPI 2014. LNCS, vol. 8530, pp. 184–195. Springer, Cham (2014). https://doi.org/10.1007/978-3-319-07788-8_18

48. Shneiderman, B.: Designing the User Interface: Strategies for Effective Human-Computer Interaction. Pearson Education India, Bangalore (2010)

49. Skulmowski, A., Pradel, S., Kühnert, T., Brunnett, G., Rey, G.D.: Embodied learning using a tangible user interface: the effects of haptic perception and selective pointing on a spatial learning task. Comput. Educ. **92**, 64–75 (2016)

50. Sun, H.H., Wu, F.G.: Applied motion analysis on tui design for lovers cooking together. Procedia Manuf. **3**, 6258–6265 (2015)

51. Suzuki, H., Sato, H., Hayami, H.: "Make your own planet": workshop for digital expression and physical creation. In: Shumaker, R., Lackey, S. (eds.) VAMR 2014. LNCS, vol. 8526, pp. 116–123. Springer, Cham (2014). https://doi.org/10.1007/978-3-319-07464-1_11

52. Sylla, C., Coutinho, C., Branco, P., Müller, W.: Investigating the use of digital manipulatives for storytelling in pre-school. Int. J. Child-Comput. Interact. **6**, 39–48 (2015)

53. Tada, K., Tanaka, J.: Tangible programming environment using paper cards as command objects. Procedia Manuf. **3**, 5482–5489 (2015)

54. Teh, T.T.L., Ng, K.H., Parhizkar, B.: TraceIt: an air tracing reading tool for children with dyslexia. In: Badioze Zaman, H., et al. (eds.) IVIC 2015. LNCS, vol. 9429, pp. 356–366. Springer, Cham (2015). https://doi.org/10.1007/978-3-319-25939-0_32

55. Triantafyllidou, I., Chatzitsakiroglou, A.-M., Georgiadou, S., Palaigeorgiou, G.: FingerTrips on tangible augmented 3D maps for learning history. In: Auer, M.E., Tsiatsos, T. (eds.) IMCL 2017. AISC, vol. 725, pp. 465–476. Springer, Cham (2018). https://doi.org/10.1007/978-3-319-75175-7_46

56. Van Camp, M., Van Campenhout, L., De Bruyne, G.: Rematerializing the user interface of a digitized toy through tokens: a comparative user study with children aged five to six. In: Chung, W.J., Shin, C.S. (eds.) AHFE 2017. AISC, vol. 585, pp. 16–24. Springer, Cham (2018). https://doi.org/10.1007/978-3-319-60495-4_2

57. Vermeeren, A.P., Law, E.L.C., Roto, V., Obrist, M., Hoonhout, J., Väänänen-Vainio-Mattila, K.: User experience evaluation methods: current state and development needs. In: Proceedings of the 6th Nordic Conference on Human-Computer Interaction: Extending Boundaries, pp. 521–530. ACM (2010)

58. Walther, J.U., Bærentzen, J.A., Aanæs, H.: Tangible 3D modeling of coherent and themed structures. Comput. Graph. **58**, 53–65 (2016)

59. Wang, D., He, L., Dou, K.: StoryCube: supporting children's storytelling with a tangible tool. J. Supercomput. **70**(1), 269–283 (2014)

60. Yannier, N., Koedinger, K.R., Hudson, S.E.: Tangible collaborative learning with a mixed-reality game: EarthShake. In: Lane, H.C., Yacef, K., Mostow, J., Pavlik, P. (eds.) AIED 2013. LNCS (LNAI), vol. 7926, pp. 131–140. Springer, Heidelberg (2013). https://doi.org/10.1007/978-3-642-39112-5_14

61. Zuckerman, O., Gal-Oz, A.: To TUI or not to TUI: evaluating performance and preference in tangible vs. graphical user interfaces. Int. J. Hum.-Comput. Stud. **71**(7–8), 803–820 (2013)

Which Instrument Should I Use? Supporting Decision-Making About the Evaluation of User Experience

Ticianne Darin$^{(\boxtimes)}$, Bianca Coelho$^{(\boxtimes)}$, and Bosco Borges$^{(\boxtimes)}$

Virtual University Institute, Federal University of Ceará, Humberto Monte, S/N,
Fortaleza, Brazil
`ticianne@virtual.ufc.br`, `biancasmd@alu.ufc.br`,
`boscofilho4@gmail.com`

Abstract. User Experience (UX) has been intensively investigated lately, resulting in the proposal of several evaluation instruments, methods, and techniques. However, the definition of UX and its constructs is still a work in progress, making User Experience a concept open to various interpretations. Consequently, the development of UX evaluation methods and instruments rely on very different assumptions, often making professionals and beginning researchers uncertain about choosing the right methods to evaluate user evaluation aspects. Aiming to help fill in this gap, in this work we present the results of a systematic snowballing procedure conducted to investigate the characteristics of the UX evaluation instruments that have been proposed and used by HCI community in the last years. We compiled information about 116 instruments aiming to assist researchers and practitioners in making informed choices about which instruments can support UX data collection, according to their research goals. In addition to that, the data analysis provided a glance on the directions the research on UX evaluation instruments is taking.

Keywords: User Experience (UX) · Evaluation methods · UX measurement

1 Introduction

The last years in Human Computer Interaction (HCI) literature have been characterized by an intense and rich exploration of user experience (UX) related concepts. Researchers have been investigating definitions and understanding of UX across different cultures and perspectives [1–3]; establishing concepts, frameworks and models for supporting design and development processes [4, 5]; and developing and evaluating methods, techniques, instruments and measures for evaluating UX [6–9]. Particularly, researchers have been calling attention to the relevance of and the need for a theoretical discussion around UX research and practice [10]. The theoretical roots used to develop different types of UX work are a broad work in progress, including a range of different types of theories, models and conceptual frameworks [1]. For instance, UX research has been based on psychological models and theories, formalist aesthetics and product semiotics, Gestalt theory, theories about communication, and theories inspired by the art and design fields [1]. Consequently, there are several possible understandings about

© Springer Nature Switzerland AG 2019
A. Marcus and W. Wang (Eds.): HCII 2019, LNCS 11586, pp. 49–67, 2019.
https://doi.org/10.1007/978-3-030-23535-2_4

the meaning of UX, each proposing different approaches for evaluating its qualities, which results in broadly different evaluation methods, techniques, and instruments.

Despite the established standards that define usability (ISO 9241-11:2018) and UX (ISO 9241-210), there is also a growing discussion intending to clarify the distinction between these often confused concepts [78: 104]. Because UX remains a rather vague concept, difficult to fully understand for both researchers and practitioners [11, 12], UX measurement is frequently confused with usability measurement while satisfaction, which is a component of usability [13, 14], is indistinctly treated as a UX quality - sometimes the one and only necessary to assess user experience [15]. Besides, the literature has demonstrated that several factors, including social and cultural changes, can directly interfere in the way UX is understood and hence practiced [12, 16].

The problem behind UX underdeveloped concept is the danger that user experience and its related concepts such as trust, loyalty, identity, and engagement will not be fully realized in studies of people and technology [17]. In this scenario, selecting a combination of UX evaluation methods commonly relies on individuals' experience and expertise rather than on information about the UX constructs that can be measured in empirical studies [18], and on which instruments can support UX measurement [19]. Although the literature has not yet established standard UX metrics and several philosophical arguments on UX measurement have been raised [18], evaluators should not conduct UX evaluations mostly based on their personal experience and a very restricted knowledge of the methods and instruments employed [20]. There is a huge need for UX professionals, researchers and HCI learners to make informed and conscious choices to select right instruments and methods when evaluating UX qualities [21].

Aiming to help fill in this gap, in this work we present the results of a systematic snowballing procedure [22] conducted to investigate the characteristics of the UX evaluation instruments that have been proposed and used by HCI community in the last years. Our main goal in this research is to compile a large quantity of knowledge covering a wide variety of types of UX evaluation instruments, updating the literature on UX evaluation, and to provide researchers and practitioners with a useful catalog of UX instruments. We present a compilation of 116 instruments to assist researchers and practitioners in making informed choices about which instruments can support UX data collection, according to their research goals. In addition to that, the data analysis provided a glance on how the initial list of instruments evolved, allowing us to contribute with a discussion on the directions the research on UX evaluation instruments is taking.

2 Related Work

For a long time, usability figured as the main HCI criterion on which researchers and practitioners relied for measuring the quality interactive systems interaction. According to Bargas-Avila and Hornbæk, usability focus on the efficiency and the accomplishment of tasks was one of the instigating factors for the development of user experience as a concept of quality of use that addresses hedonic qualities and emotional factors, in addition to the utility and pragmatic aspects commonly covered by usability [15].

Bevan, Nigel, and Miles presented an overview of tools developed to assess user performance, user satisfaction, cognitive workload, and analytic measures [23]. Some of the concepts they analyzed, such as perceived usability, were later understood as part of UX qualities.

Agarwal and Meyer conducted a survey to list existing instruments, motivated by the idea of identifying methods that went beyond usability, i.e., methods that more explicitly included emotions, relating directly to User Experience [24]. They identified verbal, nonverbal and physiological measurement tools and discussed that good usability metrics are often indicative of good user experience. Roto, Obrist and Vää-nänen-Vainio-Mattila categorized User experience Evaluation Methods (UXEM) for academic and industrial contexts, gathered in a special interest group session (SIG) [25]. They distinguished UX and usability methods based on pragmatic and hedonic model [26], and classified them according to their methodology.

Reviews have also been conducted to investigate UX evaluation in specific application domains and UX measurement. Ganglbauer et al. conducted an overall review about psychophysiological methods used in HCI, describing in details different psychophysiological methods, such as electroencephalography (EEG), electromyography (EMG), electrodermal activity (EDA) [27]. Nacke, Drachen and Göbel presented a classification of methods to measure Game Experience, presenting three categories of experience related to games: (1) quality of product, (2) quality of human-product interaction and (3) quality of interaction in a given social, temporal, spatial or other context. Yiing, Chee and Robert described categories for HCI qualitative methods that are used to evaluate interface of video-games, focusing in Affective User-Centered Design [28]. Aiming to guide professionals in choosing UX methods, they classified methods into user feedback and non-invasive categories. Hung and Parsons conducted a survey with emphasis on the Engagement construct, cataloging instruments self-reported instruments related to UX, engagement, communication, emotion, and other qualities, excluding later those that did not belong to the HCI field [29].

Although several important studies have been investigating different types of UX evaluation methods and instruments, Vermeeren's et al. list of UX evaluation methods was used as basis for our work, as it consists in one of the most complete and well-known compilation of methods presented in UX literature [30]. They collected data from workshops and SIGs, and also searched literature for previously categorizations of UX methods. As a result, they categorized 96 methods according to specific information, such as study type, development phase, requirements, type of approach and applications. In the present work, we chose to focus on practical and well defined evaluation instruments, instead of including UX frameworks, techniques, methods and models. Hence, we analyze the original instruments listed by Vermeeren's et al. under a different point of view, including new instruments.

3 Methodology

The present study classifies and catalogs a set of 116 UX evaluation instruments gathered from a snowball sampling [22], which consists in gathering research subjects through the identification of an initial subject which is used to provide other related subjects. Our initial subject was a subset of the papers listed by Vermeeren et al., which is a seminal and highly cited paper in the area. This subset consists in the 39 papers that describe UX tools and instruments in Vermeeren's et al. list, since it also includes methods, models and frameworks, which are out of this work scope. The 39 papers - which describe 49 UX evaluation instruments - were used as start set in the snowballing technique. As a result, we obtained a final set of 116 instruments, which include updated versions of the ones originally listed, in addition to novel instruments proposed for different domains, such as the Internet of Things, and for specific audiences, for example, children.

Figure 1 provides a schematics of the methodology followed in this research, which have three main steps: (1) Selection of Initial Set of Instruments, (2) Snowballing [22] and (3) Instruments Cataloging.

The first step of this research methodology was to select a start set of papers to use for the snowballing procedure. Having chosen Vermeeren's et al. list as our basis, we analyzed the 86 UX evaluation artifacts[1] made available by authors in their site *al-laboutux.com*. For each artifact, two researchers independently read the name, description, and intended applications. For purposes of selecting the papers to be included in the start set, we considered UX evaluation instruments as *planned and validated tools designed to systematically collect qualitative data/measure quantitative data related to UX constructs from a variety of participants, producing results based on psychometric properties in a format ready for analysis/interpretation.* The two sets selected by the researchers were later compared and consolidated, after being checked by an expert researcher, which resolved the inconsistencies. The inclusion criteria were: (a) the artifact must match the adopted definition of UX evaluation of instrument; (b) the artifact paper must be available in Portuguese, English or Spanish; and (c) the paper have to be available in a digital library. By the end of this phase, we had selected 39 papers as our start set.

Then, to execute the snowballing sampling, the 39 papers were distributed between two researchers, which applied independently a forward snowballing technique in order to find new instruments. Forward snowballing refers to identifying new papers based on those papers citing the paper being examined [5]. The citations to the paper being examined were studied using Google Scholar and, for each original paper, researchers verified how many times it had been cited by others. If the number of citations was greater than 100, they should select among them the 25 most relevant papers in addition to the 10 most recent articles, totalizing 35 new papers for each original papers with more than 100 citations. In case the original paper had less than 100 citations, the 25 most relevant papers were included. We acknowledge this procedure limited our capacity to catalog as many instruments as possible. Given our constraints, however, we adopted this procedure to make significant work more likely to be included, as well papers from authors that regularly publish in the area.

---

[1] Although the original research paper reports 96 methods, the online list at allaboutux.com, mentioned by the authors in the same paper, currently only presents 86 evaluation artifacts (among methods, frameworks, models and instruments).

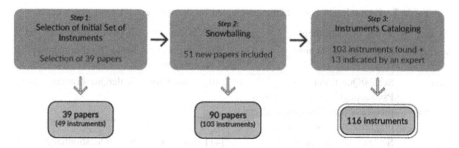

Fig. 1. Summary of methodology steps.

Given these criteria, each candidate paper citing the original paper was examined. The first screening was done based on the reading of paper title, abstract, and keywords. If this information was insufficient for a decision, the citing paper was studied in more detail and the place citing the paper already included was examined. If this was insufficient too, then the full text was studied to make a decision regarding the new paper. The goal was to identify any evidence that the citing paper proposed a new UX evaluation artifact or an update of an existing one. In this phase, from the 39 start set, 1001 citing papers were screened, 221 papers were read and analyzed, resulting in the inclusion of 51 papers. By the end of this phase, we had a set of 96 papers describing 103 UX evaluation instruments.

Finally, the instrument cataloging step consisted in the data extraction of the selected papers. In this step, 13 new papers were included after the indication of a senior researcher, helping to mitigate the limitation of our paper search process. Two researchers read the full text of 103 papers describing 116 UX evaluation instruments - as some papers described more than one instrument [e.g. 31 and 32], and cataloged them. The cataloging process consisted of extracting and tabulating the following data for each instrument: reference, publication year, instrument name, type of instrument (scales, psychophysiology, post-test pictures, two-dimensional graph area, other [21]), UX qualities (overall UX, affect, emotion, fun, enjoyment, aesthetics, hedonic, engagement, flow, motivation [15, 21]), type of approach (quantitative, qualitative or quali-quantitative), main idea, general procedure, applications, and target users.

The oldest instrument cataloged is from 1982 [33], and the newest are from 2018 [34, 35]. The complete categorization of the 116 UX evaluation instruments is available at https://bit.ly/2N7K2ly. We intend to keep periodically updating and expanding the information available.

4 Results

From the 116 UX evaluation instruments identified, 48 (41.38%) come from the start set of papers gathered from Vermeeren's et al. list, and 68 (58.62%) are instruments developed from 2011 onwards, identified using the methodology described before. The cataloged instruments reported addressing 29 different UX qualities, which can be evaluated by eight different types of instruments, as exemplified in Table 1.

Table 1. Examples of UX qualities evaluated by the different types of instruments

UX quality	Types of instrument	Ex.	UX quality	Types of instrument	Ex.
Aesthetics	Scales/Questionnaires	[39]	Human-robot trust	Scale/Questionnaire	[42]
Affect	Scales/Questionnaires; Psychophysiological; Post-test picture/object; Two-dimensional diagram/graph area; Others	[40]	Immersion	Scale/Questionnaire	[43]
Appraisal	Scales/Questionnaires	[41]	Intrinsic motivation	Scale/Questionnaire	[33]
Emotion	Post-test Picture/object; Scale/Questionnaire; Two-dimensional Diagrams/Graph area; Psychophysiology; Others	[31]	Stress	Software/equipment	[44]

Scales and questionnaires constitute 62.07% of the 116 instruments identified. The second most common type of instrument is classified as psychophysiology (10.34%), followed by two-dimensional diagrams/graph area (7.76%) and software/equipment (7.76%), and post-test picture/object (6.90%). Other types of instruments occurred less frequently, being usually developed for specific contexts, such as: diary templates [36, 37], scale combined with two-dimensional graph area [16, 38] and observational checklist [34]. These trends are suggestive of the directions research has taken in this field, and are further described in the remainder of this Section.

We classified scales and questionnaires in the same category ("scale/questionnaire"), although we acknowledge there is a conceptual difference between their definitions. Still, we grouped them together because often authors use the terms interchangeably and, in some cases, scales are developed for specific questionnaires [45]. Good questionnaires can be described as a well-defined and well-written set of questions to which an individual is asked to respond open-ended or closed-ended questions [46]. Scales are used in closed-ended questions to support an ordered response from a number of given choices, in some logical order [47].

The prevalence of self-reported UX data collection is clear in the 72 scales/questionnaires identified, which report to evaluate a range of 26 different UX qualities (Table 2). From these, seven (9.72%) evaluate general aspects of UX (i.e. the authors do not describe any specific UX quality) such as [48], seven (9.72%) evaluate specific sets of UX qualities [49], as shown in Table 3, and six (8.33%) evaluate satisfaction [50]. It is important to notice that is out of this research scope to analyze whether different terms employed by authors refer to a same UX quality.

The UX scales found target nine different types of application. Thirty seven (51.39%) are classified as "application-independent" (i.e. they are reportedly suitable to evaluate UX in three or more types of application), such as [51]. Thirteen (18.06%) aims to evaluate UX in games and virtual environments [52], eight (11.11%) are focused on online platforms [45], four (5.56%) are for mobile devices and three (4.17%) target intelligent systems, environments and objects [53].

Table 2. Examples of UX qualities evaluated by scales/questionnaires

Scales/Questionnaires			
UX quality	Examples	UX quality	Examples
Affect	[40]	Human-robot trust	[42]
Aesthetics	[39]	Immersion	[57]
Appraisal	[41]	Intrinsic motivation	[33]
Aspects of game experience	[54]	Mental effort	[44]
Cognitive absorption	[55]	Perceived usability	[58]
Cybersickness	[56]	Presence	[57]

Table 3. Examples of specific sets of UX qualities evaluated by scales/questionnaires

Scales/Questionnaires			
Set of UX qualities	Reference	Set of UX qualities	Reference
Challenge & control Fantasy Creative and constructive expressions Social experiences Body and senses	[59]	Attractiveness Perspicuity Efficiency Dependability Stimulation Novelty	[60]
Usability Trust Appearance Loyalty	[49]	Affect Efficiency Learnability Helpuness Control	[51]

The variety of UX qualities evaluated by scales and questionnaires is greater than in other types of instruments. While the 72 scales and questionnaires measure 26 different UX qualities, the remaining 44 instruments evaluate only 8 different qualities. Regarding the target users, 58 scales/questionnaires (80.56%) aim to evaluate user experience for all type of users [51], while eight (11.11%) are aimed at children [61], five (6.94%) were designed for users performing specific roles, such as journalists [48] and consumers [62], and one scale/questionnaire (1.39%) is aimed at people with disabilities [50]. Scales and questionnaire are more common than other types of instruments, nevertheless, this predominance seems to be decreasing over the last years, considering the cataloged instruments. Between 1982 and 1999, 14 out of 16 (87.50%) instruments are scales/questionnaires, while in the next 10 years (2000 to 2009) its quantity drops to 33 out of 48 (68.75%). Finally, from 2010 to 2018, it constitutes 25 out of 52 (48.08%) of the UX instruments identified (Fig. 2).

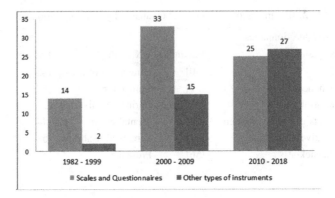

Fig. 2. Comparison between scales/questionnaires and other instruments by year.

4.1 Psychophysiological, Graphs, Software Instruments and Post-Test Pictures

The second most recurrent type of UX evaluation instrument cataloged is psychophysiological, in which user's physiological responses are recorded and measured, usually with sensors attached to the participant. The 12 psychophysiological instruments (10.34%) identified reported evaluating 4 different UX qualities: affect, emotion, generic user experience and specific sets of qualities (Table 4). Nine of the psychophysiological instruments found (75%) evaluate emotion [63]. One of them evaluates affect [64], another evaluates generic user experience [65] and the other targets a set of UX qualities: emotion and perception [66]. Most of these instruments are "application-independent" (91.67%), and one is specific to evaluate UX in audiovisual applications [65]. The most common purpose of the psychophysiological instruments found is to measure emotion in any types of applications (75%). All the 12 psychophysiological instruments aim to evaluate user experience for all types of users.

The third most common type of instrument identified is two-dimensional diagrams/graph area (7.76%). This category of type of instrument covers diagrams, charts, timelines and two-dimensional graph areas through which the users can report their experiences. We found nine instruments of this category, which evaluate three types of UX qualities. Four of these instruments (44.44%) evaluate emotion [63] and also four (44.44%) evaluates specific sets of UX qualities, such as attractiveness (appeal) of the product, ease of use and utility [67], and usability, challenge, quantity of play and general impression [19], while one (11.11%) evaluates affect [68]. In addition to application-independent instruments [63] - which were the most common target of this type of instrument (66.67%) - they target four different types of application: audiovisual [69], games and virtual environments [19] intelligent systems, environments and objects [70]. Eight of the two-dimensional diagrams/graph area instruments (88.89%) target all types of users, and one aim to evaluate UX specifically for children [19].

We also identified nine UX evaluation instruments developed as software or specific equipments. They evaluate seven different UX qualities: affect [71], aspects of

Table 4. Examples of UX qualities evaluated by psychophysiological, two-dimensional diagrams/chart area and software/equipment instruments.

Psychophysiological		Two-dimensional		Software/Equipment	
UX quality	*Examples*	*UX Quality*	*Examples*	*UX quality*	*Examples*
Affect	[64]	Emotion	[63]	Feelings	[74]
Emotion	[63]	Affect	[68]	Aspects of game experience	[72]
Generic user experience	[65]	Emotion and contextual details	[32]	Stress	[75]
Emotion and perception	[66]	Attractiveness (appeal) of the product, ease of use and utility	[67]	Behavior	[73]

game experience [72], behavior [73], emotion [35], feelings [74], stress [75] and generic user experience [76]. The most common target of software instruments are aspects of game experience (33.33%). The software/equipment group aims to evaluate games and virtual environments [77] and online platform [76], besides those that are application-independent [75]. With regard to the target users, eight (88.89%) software/equipment instruments evaluate user experience for all type of users and one (11.11%) is specific for product customers [74].

Eight of the 116 instruments are post-test pictures/objects. Among of these, three different UX qualities were revealed: emotion, evaluated by five (62.50%) instruments, affect, evaluated by two (25.00%) instruments and one (12.50%) instrument is to evaluate a specific set of UX qualities [78], which consists in: emotion, ease of use, usefulness and intention to use. Six (75.00%) of the post-test pictures/objects instruments evaluate UX holistically and two (25.00%) are for intelligent systems, environments and objects. One (12.50%) of these instruments are specifically to evaluate UX for childrens [79] and the seven others (87.50%) are suitable for all types of users.

4.2   Catalog of UX Evaluation Instruments

The set of UX evaluation instruments identified was organized as a catalog, systematizing and relating the data extracted from the papers describing each instrument. The catalog compiles 116 instruments intending to assist researchers and practitioners in making informed choices about which instruments can support UX data collection, according to their research goals. For now, the catalog is presented as a set of spreadsheets, but as this research goes on we will periodically update the information available. As future work, we are going to develop and make available an interactive version of the catalog. For each instrument, the catalog describes: reference, publication year, instrument name, main idea, general procedure, type of instrument, type of approach, UX quality, target users and applications.

Main idea and general procedure are summarized textual descriptions that provide the reader, respectively, with an overall understanding of the purpose of an instrument, and with information on how to conduct an evaluation using it. Instruments are categorized in six categories: scale/questionnaire, psychophysiological, software/equipment, two-dimensional diagrams/graph area, post-test pictures/objects and others. Each category groups two or more types of instruments (Table 5).

Table 5. Categories of types of instruments

Scales/Questionnaires			
Categories	Types of instruments included	Categories	Types of instruments included
Post-test picture/objects	Tangible manikins; shaped objects; post-test picture	Psychophysiological	Eyetracker-based; polygraphic data; multimodal sensor; psychophysiological
Two-dimensional diagram/chart area	Diagrams; charts; two-dimensional graph areas	Scale/questionnaire	Scales; questionnaires
Software/equipment	Auto text collector software; maps/geographic information; survey tool; telemetry tool; software	Others	Observational checklist; diary entry templates; combined scales and two-dimensional graphs

The type of approach can be either qualitative, quali-quantitative, or quantitative. Applications are divided in eight categories: (i) online platform, (ii) audiovisual, (iii) intelligent systems, environments and objects, (iv) games and virtual environments, (v) hardware and robotics, (vi) mobile devices, and (vii) e-learning. Besides these, there is also the application-independent category that describes instruments aiming to evaluate UX in three or more different types of applications. Each category includes two or more types of applications cited in instruments papers (Table 6). Finally, target users are categorized in four main groups: children, people with disabilities and role-specific, a category that characterize instruments developed to evaluate UX with persons performing specific functions or roles. Besides, the category "all types of users" describes instruments aiming to be used with any users.

All these aspects are presented in the catalog as filters, to help people interested in conducting UX evaluation in analyzing which instruments to choose, depending on the goals of their evaluation, the type of application, the UX qualities to be evaluated, and the target users. In addition to present the classification of each instrument, the catalog also shows the relationships between categories and instruments descriptors, as depicted in Fig. 3. The full version of the catalog can be accessed in this link https://bit.ly/2N7K2ly.

Table 6. Categories of types of applications

Category	Applications included	Category	Applications includes
Online platform	Web, shopping websites, and Social systems	Games and VE	Virtual environments; games; virtual reality
Application independent	Generic and those addressing three or more applications	Hardware and robotics	Robots; hardware
Audiovisual	360 videos; Generic audiovisual; Gameplay streaming	Mobile devices	Mobile; portable interactive devices (PIDs)
Intelligent systems, environ. and objects	Ambient intelligent environment; Internet of Things; home appliances; automated systems	E-learning applications	Educational software for children; Internet-based learning systems

Mobile Devices	Scale / Questionnaire	Generic User Experience	Attrak-Work Questionnaire; Emoji UX Questionnaire
		Success	[no name informed]
		Usability	Mobile Phone Usability Questionnaire
	Diary Template	Generic User Experience	Experience Diary
E-learning applications	Scale / Questionnaire	Usability	Pedagogically Meaninful Learning Questionnaire; [no name informed]
		Cognitive absorption	TAM
Online Platform	Scale / Questionnaire	Aesthetics	Aesthetics scale; VisAWI
		Service Experience	ServUX questionnaire
		Satisfaction	WAMMI; End-user computing satisfaction; WEBsite USability Evaluation Tool
		Usability	UFOS-V2
		Usability, Trust, Appearance and loyalty	SUPR-Q
	Software/equipment	Generic User Experience	UUX-Posts
Laboratory Experiments	Scale / Questionnaire	Intrinsic motivation	Intrinsic Motivation Scale

Fig. 3. Portion of the UX instruments catalog.

5 Discussion

The term "instrument" is traditionally associated with the measurability of UX qualities [18, 21]. Although it is far from our intention to define what characterizes a user experience instrument, in this research, UX instruments are addressed in a broader way. They are seen as evaluation artifacts designed to collect user data and to facilitate observation and/or measurement of UX qualities. In our understanding, given the nature of the user experience, qualitative and quantitative approaches have to be articulated to a thorough evaluation and deeper understanding of the UX qualities. Hence, our focus is on stimulating practical UX work by cataloging tools with diverse approaches, designed to systematically collect data related to UX constructs from a variety of participants.

In the remainder of this section we discuss some insights, trends and concerns yielded during data analysis about the use and development of UX evaluation instruments and how they incorporate UX qualities.

5.1   (Re)Use of UX Evaluation Scales/Questionnaires

Overall, our findings show a consistent picture that indicates scales and questionnaires as the most common types of UX instruments, also addressing a greater variety of UX qualities than all the other types of instruments. This indicates that the trend once identified in the early 2010s [21], that scales are commonly used with most UX qualities, remains unchanged. However, a rising trend seems to be combining traditional techniques for capturing self-reported data with UX measurement, in quali-quantitative approaches.

Some parsimony is necessary in the development and utilization of UX evaluation questionnaires, since this type of instrument can either be structured, well-tested, robust, and result in data with a high level of validity, or poorly done, resulting in data of questionable validity [46]. This type of instrument is often used not because it is the most appropriate method but because it is the easiest method [46]. A clear example of this situation is the experience report presented by Lallemand and Koenig [7] in which they report a bad experience using a UX questionnaire that was supposed to be standardized and validated. The problem they faced came from the fact that scales are often considered validated after a single validation study which leads to conclusion that the scale psychometrics properties are good and can therefore be considered as valid.

Hence, before creating new UX scales we must consider if, given the great quantity and variety of existing instruments, it is really necessary to create new ones. Wouldn't these instruments be more robust if we focused our efforts on validating, translating, expanding and improving already existing scales? It would be an effective way to improve UX instruments and make them suitable for the widest range of users possible. This is the case of MemoLine [19], an adaptation for kids arised from UX Curve [67]; AttrakWork [48], that proposes to "support the evaluation of user experience of mobile systems in the context of mobile news journalism" which is based on AttrakDiff [79]; and TangiSAM [80], a Braille adaptation of the Self Assessment Manekin [40]. In this regard, researchers have been discussing about the holistic UX questionnaires trend to follow a "one size fits all" approach [7]. In this regard, we agree with Lallemand and Koenig [7] when they state that the development of more specific methods, targeted at particular application domains is necessary. We further add that more generic evaluation instruments that already exist should be used as basis for this development.

5.2   Different Perspectives on How to Consider UX Qualities

Several instruments propose evaluating specific UX qualities such Emotion, Affect, Presence and Immersion, or even a specific set of qualities, such as Aesthetics and Emotion combined [53]. The fact that in the last years more instruments are focusing on evaluating the subjective components of user interaction is positive, because it demonstrates that researchers begun to reflect in a more deeply way about the specificities of user experience. Thus, a broad spectrum of UX qualities have been evaluated, addressing particular types of applications and users' characteristics. Some important examples of contributions designed to evaluate UX in specific and complex situations are a questionnaire developed for measuring emotions and satisfaction of Brazilian deaf users [50], and a scale developed to measure specific sets of UX qualities with preschoolers: (1) challenge and control, (2) fantasy, (3) creative and constructive expressions, (4) social experiences and (5) body and senses [61].

In a different direction, as listed in Sect. 4, some instruments have been proposed to evaluate UX without specifying which qualities are taken into account [37], following a more generalist UX evaluation approach. This can be a consequence of the lack of consensus about what User Experience means [12], since the different understandings of this concept impacts the effectiveness, development and even teaching of this discipline [81]. There are also instruments that define User Experience as a sum of qualities [e.g. 82 and 31]. Those were classified by us as instruments that measures specific sets of UX qualities. However, the set of qualities that characterize UX varies widely from one instrument to another, which is, again, a consequence of the lack of a shared UX definition.

These situations depict a scenario where the term User Experience seems to be used almost instinctively in some cases, making it hard to know what is assessed when an instrument claims evaluate UX. For instance, [83] and [67] are respectively a questionnaire and a two-dimensional graph area, both aimed at evaluating experience with a product/artifact focus, targeted at all types of users, and application-independent. However, the first one understands UX as usability, desirability, credibility, aesthetics, technical adequacy and usefulness, while the second one considers attractiveness of the product, ease of use and utility.

A similar scenario occurs for specific UX qualities, such as emotion, the most frequently evaluated UX quality, according to our results. For measuring emotion, [84] examines levels of desire, surprise, inspiration, amusement, admiration and satisfaction, while [85] measures valence, arousal and engagement, and [86] analyses anger, fear, happiness, and sadness. Although one may argue that they were constructed under the assumptions of different theoretical roots, often the reasoning behind the instruments psychometrics is not explicit. Consequently, perhaps the evaluator - specially in case of professionals - is not even aware of these differences when choosing a UX evaluation instrument or method.

However, there are some UX qualities that seem to be more established in the literature, such as affect. Most of the instruments that measure affect are based on or adapted from the PAD scale [87] and PANAS scale [88], evaluating a commonly defined set of aspects that describe affect. In this context, it is important to highlight that instruments with good psychometric properties in one culture may not have the same properties when translated for another culture, hence the relations between UX components have to be validated [89].

Although the concept of UX still needs to be better established, the commitment of researchers and practitioners in investigating definitions and improving the understanding of UX factors has been very constructive to the community. The joint efforts to develop effective evaluation methods have been resulting in a variety of instruments for diverse application domains and groups of users. Also, psychophysiological measures like [64] provide the opportunity to cross self-reported and observation measures with psychophysiological information, enriching data. This type of instrument was the second most frequently found in our cataloging, which seems to be an indication that HCI community is following the UX research agenda proposed by Law and Van Schaik [89].

6 Conclusion

This work presented an analysis and compilation of a variety of types of UX evaluation instruments and qualities, providing researchers and practitioners with a systematized catalog of UX instruments. Although this research has some limitations previously discussed, our goal is to help supporting researchers and professionals in making informed decisions about the choice of instruments for UX evaluation in their every day work. We also shared some insights and concerns about the directions research on UX evaluation has been taking, that we expect to inspire the community. Our future work include expanding the collection and analysis of UX evaluation instruments, comprise more categories of analysis, types of applications and target users, and developing an interactive version of the catalog presented in this paper.

References

1. Obrist, M., Law, E., Väänänen-Vainio-Mattila, K., Roto, V., Vermeeren, A., Kuutti, K.: UX research: what theoretical roots do we build on–if any? In: CHI'11 Extended Abstracts on Human Factors in Computing Systems, pp. 165–168. ACM (2011)
2. Law, E.L.C., Roto, V., Hassenzahl, M., Vermeeren, A.P., Kort, J.: Understanding, scoping and defining user experience: a survey approach. In: Proceedings of the SIGCHI Conference on Human Factors in Computing Systems, pp. 719–728. ACM (2009)
3. Ardito, C., Buono, P., Caivano, D., Costabile, M.F., Lanzilotti, R.: Investigating and promoting UX practice in industry: an experimental study. Int. J. Hum.-Comput. Stud. **72**, 542–551 (2014)
4. Pucillo, F., Cascini, G.: A framework for user experience, needs and affordances. Des. Stud. **35**(2), 160–179 (2014)
5. Wright, P., McCarthy, J., Meekison, L.: Making sense of experience. In: Blythe, M., Monk, A. (eds.) Funology 2, pp. 315–330. Springer, Cham (2018). https://doi.org/10.1007/978-3-319-68213-6_20
6. Obrist, M., Roto, V., Väänänen-Vainio-Mattila, K.: User experience evaluation: do you know which method to use? In: CHI 2009 Extended Abstracts on Human Factors in Computing Systems, pp. 2763–2766. ACM (2009)
7. Lallemand, C., Koenig, V.: How could an intranet be like a friend to me?: why standardized UX scales don't always fit. In: Proceedings of the European Conference on Cognitive Ergonomics 2017, pp. 9–16. ACM (2017)
8. Rajeshkumar, S., Omar, R., Mahmud, M.: Taxonomies of user experience (UX) evaluation methods. In: 2013 International Conference on Research and Innovation in Information Systems (ICRIIS), pp. 533–538. IEEE (2013)

9. Bevan, N.: Classifying and selecting UX and usability measures. In: International Workshop on Meaningful Measures: Valid Useful User Experience Measurement, vol. 11, pp. 13–18 (2010)
10. Obrist, M., Roto, V., Vermeeren, A., Väänänen-Vainio-Mattila, K., Law, E.L.C., Kuutti, K.: In search of theoretical foundations for UX research and practice. In: CHI 2012 Extended Abstracts on Human Factors in Computing Systems, pp. 1979–1984. ACM (2012)
11. Hellweger, S., Wang, X.: What is user experience really: towards a UX conceptual framework (2015). arXiv preprint arXiv:1503.01850
12. Rajanen, D., et al.: UX professionals' definitions of usability and UX – a comparison between Turkey, Finland, Denmark, France and Malaysia. In: Bernhaupt, R., Dalvi, G., Joshi, A., K. Balkrishan, D., O'Neill, J., Winckler, M. (eds.) INTERACT 2017. LNCS, vol. 10516, pp. 218–239. Springer, Cham (2017). https://doi.org/10.1007/978-3-319-68059-0_14
13. de Normalisation, O.I.: ISO 9241-11 (2018). Saatavissa: https://www.iso.org/obp/ui/#iso:std:iso,9241(11)
14. Nielsen, J.: Usability Engineering. Elsevier, San Diego (1994)
15. Bargas-Avila, J.A., Hornbæk, K.: Old wine in new bottles or novel challenges: a critical analysis of empirical studies of user experience. In: Proceedings of the SIGCHI Conference on Human Factors in Computing System, pp. 2689–2698. ACM (2011)
16. Schubert, E.: Measuring emotion continuously: validity and reliability of the two-dimensional emotion-space. Aust. J. Psychol. 51(3), 154–165 (1999)
17. Zaman, B.: Introducing a pairwise comparison scale for UX evaluations with preschoolers. In: Gross, T., et al. (eds.) INTERACT 2009. LNCS, vol. 5727, pp. 634–637. Springer, Heidelberg (2009). https://doi.org/10.1007/978-3-642-03658-3_68
18. Law, E.L.C., Van Schaik, P., Roto, V.: Attitudes towards user experience (UX) measurement. Int. J. Hum. Comput. Stud. 72(6), 526–541 (2014)
19. Vissers, J., De Bot, L., Zaman, B.: MemoLine: evaluating long-term UX with children. In: Proceedings of the 12th International Conference on Interaction Design and Children, pp. 285–288. ACM (2013)
20. Väänänen-Vainio-Mattila, K., Roto, V., Hassenzahl, M.: Towards practical user experience evaluation methods. In: Meaningful Measures: Valid Useful User Experience Measurement (VUUM), pp. 19–22 (2008)
21. Law, E.L.C.: The measurability and predictability of user experience. In: Proceedings of the 3rd ACM SIGCHI Symposium on Engineering Interactive Computing Systems, pp. 1–10. ACM (2011)
22. Wohlin, C.: Guidelines for snowballing in systematic literature studies and a replication in software engineering. In: Proceedings of the 18th International Conference on Evaluation and Assessment in Software Engineering, p. 38. ACM (2014)
23. Bevan, N., Macleod, M.: Usability measurement in context. Behav. Inf. Technol. 13(1–2), 132–145 (1994)
24. Agarwal, A., Andrew M.: Beyond usability: evaluating emotional response as an integral part of the user experience. In: CHI 2009 Extended Abstracts on Human Factors in Computing Systems. ACM (2009)
25. Roto, V., Marianna O., Väänänen-Vainio-Mattila, K.: User experience evaluation methods in academic and industrial contexts. In: Proceedings of the Workshop UXEM, vol. 9 (2009)
26. Hassenzahl, M.: The interplay of beauty, goodness, and usability in interactive products. Hum. Comput. Interact. 19(4), 319–349 (2004)
27. Ganglbauer, E., et al.: Applying psychophysiological methods for measuring user experience: possibilities, challenges and feasibility. In: Workshop on User Experience Evaluation Methods in Product Development (2009)

28. Ng, Y., Khong, C.W., Nathan, R.J.: Evaluating affective user-centered design of video games using qualitative methods. Int. J. Comput. Games Technol. **2018** (2018)
29. Hung, Y.-H., Parsons, P.: Affective engagement for communicative visualization: quick and easy evaluation using survey instruments. In: Visualization for Communication (VisComm) 2018 (2018, to appear)
30. Vermeeren, A.P., et al.: User experience evaluation methods: current state and development needs. In: Proceedings of the 6th Nordic Conference on Human-Computer Interaction: Extending Boundaries, pp. 521–530. ACM (2010)
31. Poels, K., De Kort, Y. A.W., IJsselsteijn, W.A.: D3. 3: Game experience questionnaire: development of a self-report measure to assess the psychological impact of digital games (2007)
32. Karapanos, E., Martens, J.B.O.S., Hassenzahl, M.: On the retrospective assessment of users' experiences over time: memory or actuality? In: CHI 2010 Physiological User Interaction Workshop, Atlanta, GA, 10–15 April 2010, pp. 4075–4080. Association for Computing Machinery, Inc. (2010)
33. Ryan, R.M.: Control and information in the intrapersonal sphere: an extension of cognitive evaluation theory. J. Pers. Soc. Psychol. **43**(3), 450 (1982)
34. Almeida, R., Darin, T., Andrade, R., de Araújo, I.: Towards developing a practical tool to assist UX evaluation in the IoT scenario. In: Anais Estendidos do XXIV Simpósio Brasileiro de Sistemas Multimídia e Web, pp. 91–95. SBC (2018)
35. Granato, M., Gadia, D., Maggiorini, D., Ripamonti, L.A.: Software and hardware setup for emotion recognition during video game fruition. In: Proceedings of the 4th EAI International Conference on Smart Objects and Technologies for Social Good, pp. 19–24. ACM (2018)
36. Kahneman, D., Krueger, A.B., Schkade, D.A., Schwarz, N., Stone, A.A.: A survey method for characterizing daily life experience: the day reconstruction method. Science **306**(5702), 1776–1780 (2004)
37. Gomez, R.E.: The evolving emotional experience with portable interactive devices. Doctoral dissertation, Queensland University of Technology (2012)
38. Russell, J.A., Weiss, A., Mendelsohn, G.A.: Affect grid: a single-item scale of pleasure and arousal. J. Pers. Soc. Psychol. **57**(3), 493–502 (1989)
39. Laviea, T., Tractinsky, N.: Assessing dimensions of perceived visual aesthetics of web sites. Int. J. Hum Comput Stud. **60**(3), 269–298 (2004)
40. Bradley, M.M., Lang, P.J.: Measuring emotion: the self-assessment manikin and the semantic differential. J. Behav. Ther. Exp. Psychiatry **25**(1), 49–59 (1994)
41. Scherer, K.R.: Appraisal considered as a process of multilevel sequential checking. Apprais. Process. Emotion Theory Methods Res. **92**(120), 57 (2001)
42. Schaefer, K.: The perception and measurement of human-robot trust (2013)
43. Van Damme, K., et al.: 360° Video journalism: experimental study on the effect of immersion on news experience and distant suffering. J. Stud. 1–24 (2018)
44. Meijman, T., et al.: The measurement of perceived effort. In: Contemporary Ergonomics, pp. 242–246 (1986)
45. Väänänen-Vainio-Mattila, K., Segerstähl, K.: A tool for evaluating service user experience (ServUX): development of a modular questionnaire. In: User Experience Evaluation Methods, UXEM 2009 Workshop at Interact (2009)
46. Lazar, J., Feng, J.H., Hochheiser, H.: Research Methods in Human-Computer Interaction. Morgan Kaufmann, Burlington (2017)
47. Dillman, D.: Mail and Internet Surveys: The Tailored Design Method. Wiley, New York (2000)

48. Väätäjä, H., Koponen, T., Roto, V.: Developing practical tools for user experience evaluation: a case from mobile news journalism. In: European Conference on Cognitive Ergonomics: Designing Beyond the Product—Understanding Activity and User Experience in Ubiquitous Environments, p. 23 (2009)

49. Sauro, J.: SUPR-Q: a comprehensive measure of the quality of the website user experience. J. Usability Stud. **10**(2), 68–86 (2015)

50. Sales, A., Reis, L., Araújo, T., Aguiar, Y.: Tutaform: a multimedia form for Brazilian deaf users. In: Proceedings of the 24th Brazilian Symposium on Multimedia and the Web, pp. 269–276. ACM (2018)

51. Kirakowski, J.: The software usability measurement inventory: background and usage. In: Usability Evaluation in Industry, pp. 169–178 (1996)

52. Lessiter, J., Freeman, J., Keogh, E., Davidoff, J.: A cross-media presence questionnaire: the ITC-Sense of Presence Inventory. Presence Teleoper. Virtual Environ. **10**(3), 282–297 (2001)

53. Bernhaupt, R., Pirker, M.: Methodological challenges of UX evaluation in the living room: developing the IPTV-UX questionnaire. In: PUX 2011 Program Committee, p. 51 (2011)

54. Calvillo-Gámez, E.H., Cairns, P., Cox, A.L.: Assessing the core elements of the gaming experience. In: Bernhaupt, R. (ed.) Game User Experience Evaluation. HIS, pp. 37–62. Springer, Cham (2015). https://doi.org/10.1007/978-3-319-15985-0_3

55. Saadé, R., Bahli, B.: The impact of cognitive absorption on perceived usefulness and perceived ease of use in online learning: an extension of the technology acceptance model. Inf. Manag. **42**(2), 317–327 (2005)

56. Kennedy, R.S., Lane, N.E., Berbaum, K.S., Lilienthal, M.G.: Simulator sickness questionnaire: an enhanced method for quantifying simulator sickness. Int. J. Aviat. Psychol. **3**(3), 203–220 (1993)

57. Witmer, B.G., Singer, M.J.: Measuring presence in virtual environments: a presence questionnaire. Presence **7**(3), 225–240 (1998)

58. Lewis, J.R., Utesch, B. S., Maher, D.E.: UMUX-LITE: when there's no time for the SUS. In: Proceedings of the SIGCHI Conference on Human Factors in Computing Systems, pp. 2099–2102. ACM (2013)

59. Sim, G., Horton, M.: Investigating children's opinions of games: fun toolkit vs. this or that. In: Proceedings of the 11th International Conference on Interaction Design and Children, pp. 70–77. ACM (2012)

60. Laugwitz, B., Held, T., Schrepp, M.: Construction and evaluation of a user experience questionnaire. In: Holzinger, A. (ed.) USAB 2008. LNCS, vol. 5298, pp. 63–76. Springer, Heidelberg (2008). https://doi.org/10.1007/978-3-540-89350-9_6

61. Zaman, B.: Introduction and validation of a pairwise comparison scale for UX evaluations and benchmarking with preschoolers. In: INTERACT 2009. Springer, Uppsala (2009)

62. Horn, D., Salvendy, G.: Product creativity: conceptual model, measurement and characteristics. Theor. Issues Ergon. Sci. **7**(4), 395–412 (2006)

63. Lasa, G., Justel, D., Gonzalez, I., Iriarte, I., Val, E.: Next generation of tools for industry to evaluate the user emotional perception: the biometric-based multimethod tools. Des. J. **20**(sup1), S2771–S2777 (2017)

64. Stahl, A., Hook, K., Svensson, M., Taylor, A.S., Combetto, M.: Experiencing the affective diary. Pers. Ubiquit. Comput. **13**(5), 365–378 (2009)

65. Robinson, R.B.: All the feels: a twitch overlay that displays streamers' biometrics to spectators. Dissertation, UC Santa Cruz (2018)

66. Hussain, J., et al.: A multimodal deep log-based user experience (UX) platform for UX evaluation. Sensors **18**(5), 1622 (2018)

67. Kujala, S., et al.: UX curve: a method for evaluating long-term user experience. Interact. Comput. **23**(5), 473–483 (2011)
68. Broekens, J., Brinkman, W.P.: AffectButton: a method for reliable and valid affective self-report. Int. J. Hum.-Comput. Stud. **71**(6), 641–667 (2013)
69. Nagel, F., et al.: EMuJoy: software for continuous measurement of perceived emotions in music. Behav. Res. Methods **39**(2), 283–290 (2007)
70. Ntoa, S., Margetis, G., Antona, M., Stephanidis, C.: UXAmI observer: an automated user experience evaluation tool for ambient intelligence environments. In: Arai, K., Kapoor, S., Bhatia, R. (eds.) IntelliSys 2018. AISC, vol. 868, pp. 1350–1370. Springer, Cham (2019). https://doi.org/10.1007/978-3-030-01054-6_94
71. Betella, A., Verschure, P.F.M.J.: The affective slider: a digital self-assessment scale for the measurement of human emotions. PLoS ONE **11**, 2 (2016)
72. Kim, J.H., et al.: Tracking real-time user experience (TRUE): a comprehensive instrumentation solution for complex systems. In: Proceedings of the SIGCHI Conference on Human Factors in Computing Systems, pp. 443–452. ACM (2008)
73. Moura, D., El-Nasr, M.S., Shaw, C.D.: Visualizing and understanding players' behavior in video games: discovering patterns and supporting aggregation and comparison. In: Proceedings of the 2011 ACM SIGGRAPH Symposium on Video Games, pp. 11–15. ACM (2011)
74. Schütte, S., Almagro, L.M.: Development and application of online tools for kansei engineering evaluations. In: KEER2018, Go Green with Emotion. 7th International Conference on Kansei Engineering & Emotion Research 2018, Kuching, Malaysia, 19–22 Mar 2018, no. 146, pp. 20–28. Linköping University Electronic Press (2018)
75. Ayzenberg, Y., Hernandez Rivera, J., Picard, R.: FEEL. In: Proceedings of the 2012 ACM Annual Conference Extended Abstracts on Human Factors in Computing Systems Extended Abstracts - CHI EA 2012 (2012)
76. Mendes, M.S., Furtado, E.S.: UUX-posts. In: Proceedings of the 8th Latin American Conference on Human-Computer Interaction – CLIHC 2017 (2017)
77. Drachen, A., Canossa, A.: Analyzing spatial user behavior in computer games using geographic information systems. In: Proceedings of the 13th International MindTrek Conference: Everyday Life in the Ubiquitous Era on – MindTrek 2009 (2009)
78. Cavalcante, E., Rivero, L., Conte, T.: MAX: a method for evaluating the post-use user eXperience through cards and a board (2015)
79. Hassenzahl, M., Burmester, M., Koller, F.: AttrakDiff: Ein Fragebogen zur Messung wahrgenommener hedonischer und pragmatischer Qualität. In: Mensch & Computer 2003, pp. 187–196. Vieweg+Teubner Verlag (2003)
80. Moreira, E.A., dos Reis, J.C., Baranauskas, M.C.C.: TangiSAM. In: Proceedings of the XVI Brazilian Symposium on Human Factors in Computing Systems - IHC (2017)
81. Law, E., Roto, V., Vermeeren, A.P., Kort, J., Hassenzahl, M.: Towards a shared definition of user experience. In: CHI 2008 Extended Abstracts on Human Factors in Computing Systems, pp. 2395–2398. ACM (2008)
82. Lasa, G., Justel, D., Retegi, A.: Eyeface: a new multimethod tool to evaluate the perception of conceptual user experiences. Comput. Hum. Behav. **52**, 359–363 (2015)
83. Veeneklaas, J.N.: VisUX: a framework of user experience within data visualizations. MS thesis (2018)
84. Desmet, P.: Measuring emotion: development and application of an instrument to measure emotional responses to products. In: Blythe, M.A., Overbeeke, K., Monk, A.F., Wright, P.C. (eds.) Funology, pp. 111–123. Springer, Dordrecht (2003)

85. McDuff, D., Karlson, A., Kapoor, A., Roseway, A., Czerwinski, M.: AffectAura: an intelligent system for emotional memory. In: Proceedings of the SIGCHI Conference on Human Factors in Computing Systems, pp. 849–858. ACM (2012)

86. Isbister, K., Höök, K., Laaksolahti, J., Sharp, M.: The sensual evaluation instrument: developing a trans-cultural self-report measure of affect. Int. J. Hum.-Comput. Stud. 65(4), 315–328 (2007)

87. Mehrabian, A.: Framework for a comprehensive description and measurement of emotional states. Genet. Soc. Gen. Psychol. Monogr. (1995)

88. Watson, D., Clark, L.A., Tellegen, A.: Development and validation of brief measures of positive and negative affect: the PANAS scales. J. Pers. Soc. Psychol. 54(6), 1063 (1998)

89. Law, E.L.C., Van Schaik, P.: Modelling user experience—an agenda for research and practice. Interact. Comput. 22(5), 313–322 (2010)

90. Andersen, E., Liu, Y.E., Apter, E., Boucher-Genesse, F., Popović, Z.: Gameplay analysis through state projection. In: Proceedings of the Fifth International Conference on the Foundations of Digital Games, pp. 1–8. ACM (2010)

Game for PLAYability Heuristic Evaluation (G4H-PLAY): Adapting G4H Gamification to Allow the Use of Playability Heuristics

José Cezar de Souza Filho, Ingrid Teixeira Monteiro,
and Paulyne Matthews Jucá(⊠)

Federal University of Ceará (UFC), Quixadá, CE, Brazil
cezarbx@gmail.com, {ingrid,paulyne}@ufc.br

Abstract. Several initiatives have applied the Collaborative Heuristic Evaluation to minimize the discrepancy between the severity ratings made by different evaluators. G4H (Game for Heuristic Evaluation) is one of these proposals and its a gamification developed to engage and motivate the evaluators in the Heuristic Evaluation process. This gamification was designed considering only the Nielsen's usability heuristics. This article presents G4H-PLAY (Game for PLAYability Heuristic Evaluation), an adaptation of G4H to allow the use of playability heuristics. For the definition of this new gamification, the first step is to select the playability heuristics to support. There are many playability heuristics proposals, but G4H-PLAY uses one study that summarizes a set of playability heuristics into a general set of heuristics. Then, information on the specification and use of the heuristics was extracted, which allowed identifying the necessary adaptations to adapt the G4H to the set of chosen playability heuristics. Finally, solutions were developed for these adaptations, thus achieving the adaptation of gamification. G4H-PLAY enables to obtain the motivation and engagement benefits provided by the G4H with the Playability Heuristic Evaluation. This gamification needs to be validated in future empirical studies to ensure that the benefits of G4H can also be achieved by G4H-PLAY.

Keywords: Playability Heuristic Evaluation · Gamification · Card game · G4H

1 Introduction

Heuristic Evaluation is a usability inspection method widely used to evaluate user interfaces to identify usability problems. In this method, the evaluators inspect the interface considering a set of general usability principles (the heuristics) [1] and classify the severity of the violations found, making possible to analyze the feasibility of the problem correction and the selection of those problems that should be corrected with higher priority. This classification is initially performed in an individual stage and, subsequently, collectively among the evaluators [2].

Although Heuristic Evaluation is a widely used method to evaluate an interactive system, there are serious criticisms regarding its validity and reliability [3]. One of these criticisms is the frequent discrepancy between the individual severity ratings, attributed by evaluators to the problems identified [4].

© Springer Nature Switzerland AG 2019
A. Marcus and W. Wang (Eds.): HCII 2019, LNCS 11586, pp. 68–84, 2019.
https://doi.org/10.1007/978-3-030-23535-2_5

Some solutions have been proposed to support the evaluation process, such as the Collaborative Heuristic Evaluation (CHE) [3], an extension of the Heuristic Evaluation, in which the evaluators act as members of a collaborative group for the execution of the activities of this method. Another initiative is G4H (Game for Heuristic Evaluation) [5], gamification based on the principles of CHE, which aims to increase the engagement and motivation of different evaluators during the consolidation of Heuristic Evaluation results.

In the development and validation of G4H, the authors of gamification [5] considered only the Nielsen's usability heuristics [6]. Thus, the original G4H proposal does not apply to other sets of heuristics, such as playability heuristics.

In addition to the initial usability heuristics set created by Nielsen for the Heuristic Evaluation method [6], other heuristics sets were proposed, including the enable the evaluation of other user interface characteristics. In this context, several heuristics sets have been proposed in the literature to evaluate the playability of digital games [7–11]. Through the use of playability heuristics, the method becomes known as Playability Heuristic Evaluation.

The main goal of this article is to present G4H-PLAY (Game for PLAYability Heuristic Evaluation), an adaptation of the G4H to allow the use of playability heuristics based on the set of playability heuristics proposed by Barcelos et al. [10]. In this way, it is intended to provide the motivation and engagement benefits of G4H as well as G4H-PLAY. In the future, empirical studies should be conducted to validate and ensure that the benefits provided by G4H can also be achieved with G4H-PLAY.

This paper is organized as follows: Sects. 2, 3 and 4 present, respectively, the Heuristic Evaluation method, the concepts of gamification and the G4H proposal. Section 5 describes the related works, which deal with games developed for the improvement of methods of the Human-Computer Interaction (HCI) area, as well as the similarities and differences with the present paper. Section 6 presents the methodology steps used for the G4H-PLAY development; and finally, Sect. 7 discusses the conclusions obtained with this research.

2   Heuristic Evaluation

Heuristic Evaluation is "a usability inspection method designed to evaluate user interfaces with the objective of identifying usability problems" [1, 12]. In turn, usability is a quality of use criterion of user interfaces that can be defined as a set of factors that qualify the use of an interactive system by certain individuals. These factors are ease of learning, easy to remember, efficiency, low occurrence of errors and user satisfaction [13].

In the Heuristic Evaluation, the evaluators inspect a previously chosen interface considering usage scenarios and a set of usability principles, also known as usability heuristics [1], to identify problems that violate heuristics. They still need to classify the severity of the problems encountered, to prioritize those that are more serious for the user interaction with the interactive system [2]. Table 1 lists an initial set of 10 usability heuristics proposed by Nielsen [6] to be used in the Heuristic Evaluation method.

Table 1. Nielsen usability heuristics [6]

ID	Heuristic name
H1	Visibility of system status
H2	Match between system and the real world
H3	User control and freedom
H4	Consistency and standards
H5	Error prevention
H6	Recognition rather than recall
H7	Flexibility and efficiency of use
H8	Aesthetic and minimalist design
H9	Help users recognize, diagnose, and recover from errors
H10	Help and documentation

This initial set of heuristics can be expanded to include new guidelines involving the possibility of evaluating other quality of use criteria, not only the usability [2]. In this context, several authors established heuristics to evaluate the playability of digital games [7–11]. Some scientific research [10, 11, 14] apply the Heuristic Evaluation method with playability heuristics that are known as Playability Heuristic Evaluation. There are several definitions for playability in the literature, where each can be considered depending on the purpose of the research being conducted [15]. In this paper, we consider the definition of Sánchez, Zea, and Gutiérrez [16], which defines playability as "the degree to which specific users can achieve certain goals with effectiveness, efficiency and especially satisfaction and fun in a playable context of use."

The classification of severity for each problem found is the result of the combination of three factors [17]:

- Frequency: Does the problem occur constantly or rarely?
- Impact: If the problem occurs, will be easy or difficult for users to overcome it?
- Persistence: Is the problem timely and can be overcome by users, or will it bother users multiple times throughout the interaction?

To facilitate the understanding and comparison of the severity rating performed by the evaluators, Nielsen [12, 17] recommends the use of the following scale:

- 0 - is not a violation: the problem found cannot be categorized as a violation;
- 1 - cosmetic problem: does not need to be corrected, except if there is time available in the project schedule;
- 2 - minor problem: the correction of this problem must have a low priority;
- 3 - major problem: correction of this problem is important, but it has not a higher priority;
- 4 - catastrophic problem: this type of problem can block the user from accomplishing their tasks and reaching their goals and the product cannot be delivered without correcting this problem.

It is also recommended that three to five evaluators participate in the Heuristic Evaluation so that a considerable number of problems are identified in the user interface [1]. This method involves the execution of five activities [2]:

1. Preparation: the evaluators select the screens or prototypes of the system to be evaluated and choose the set of heuristics to use.
2. Data collection: each evaluator individually inspects the selected screens and each of its elements, analyzing whether the heuristics were obeyed or violated, since each violated heuristic is potential usability (or playability) problem;
3. Interpretation of data: each evaluator registers the following information for each identified problem: heuristics violated, place of occurrence (which screens and interface elements are involved), the severity of the problem, the justification for the existence of the problem and recommendations for a solution, when possible;
4. Consolidation of results: Each evaluator shares his /her list of problems identified with the other evaluators so that everyone has an overview of the problems in the interface. Then the evaluators can assign a new degree of severity to each problem encountered. Next, the evaluators should agree on the final classification of the severity of each problem and also select the problems to be reported in the con-solidated report;
5. Reporting of results: the evaluators prepare a report containing the following items: objectives and scope of the evaluation, a brief description of the Heuristic Assessment, set of heuristics used; quantity and profile of the evaluators, and the list of problems encountered.

Although Heuristic Evaluation is widely used to evaluate user interfaces, there are serious criticisms related to its validity and reliability [3]. Among them, we highlight the frequent discrepancy between the individual severity ratings, attributed by evaluators to the problems found in the interface [4]. In this context, CHE (Collaborative Heuristic Evaluation) was proposed, as an extension of the standard Heuristic Evaluation method, in which the evaluators work collaboratively as a group for the execution of all Heuristic Evaluation activities, sharing the challenges and possible frustrations and boredom which may occur in the evaluation process [3].

This paper uses a set of playability heuristics proposed in the literature to elaborate the G4H-PLAY, an adaptation of G4H gamification that only supported Nielsen's usability heuristics [6]. The original G4H proposal and G4H-PLAY are based on the CHE principles.

3   Gamification

Gamification is "the use of game design elements in non-game contexts" [18]. This technique can be applied to "engage people, motivate actions, promote learning and solve problems" [19].

According to Tondello [20], game design elements are components used in game designs to enhance the player experience when interacting with the game. In this way, gamification has an interest in elements such as challenges, badges, levels, points, achievements, avatars (playful representations for certain character profiles) and ranking scores (it allows the player to compare his performance with the other players), rather than focusing on elements such as graphics and audios. Tondello [19] further states that the main purpose of gamification goes beyond the entertaining or fun of the players. For example, gamification can be applied in the areas of business, marketing, education, health, and politics.

According to Werbach and Hunter [21], to develop an appropriate gamification project it is crucial to define how players will be motivated. Motivation is classified into two types: extrinsic and intrinsic. In extrinsic motivation, people perform certain activities because they feel they have to do it, that is, external factors cause motivation. For example, a person may study hard for a test because he knows that the result of that test may impede his graduation. While in intrinsic motivation, people perform specific activities because they want to do it, that is, motivation is self-interest, there are no rewards or other relationships with external factors. For example, a person wants to succeed in a professional career to feel competent and accomplished.

In a gamification project, understanding the difference between these types of motivation is important because the designer can create mechanisms to motivate users for different purposes. Also, it should consider the different profiles of players in the project, and also the factors that can discourage these users [21].

This article intends to develop G4H-PLAY, an adaptation of G4H gamification to allow the use of playability heuristics. The G4H was designed to improve the execution of the Heuristic Evaluation method, specifically in the consolidation of results task. Thus, it is important to know the gamification concepts to understand the proposal of G4H, and consequently, of G4H-PLAY.

4   Game for Heuristic Evaluation (G4H)

Game for Heuristic Evaluation (G4H) is gamification developed in the format of a card game whose main goal is to engage and motivate users in the execution of Heuristic Evaluation method, specifically in the results consolidation task based on the CHE principles (see Sect. 2). In this gamification, the potential users are experts in HCI, and there is also the possibility of use by non-specialists and end users [5].

To reach the established goal, the G4H considers as extrinsic motivation the recognition that a player can obtain from other players for being a good evaluator, and as intrinsic motivation, it is considered the execution of the evaluation and the identification of the precisely violated heuristics. The G4H authors also point out that gamification was developed considering Nielsen's usability heuristics [5].

In G4H, each usability problem found represents a round of the game, in which players need to choose one or more heuristic violations, including the possibility that the problem does not violate any heuristics, and still need to rate the severity grade of the problem. Different evaluators are considered to assign different values of severity because they generally do not have the same level of experience in HCI and the use of heuristics [5].

The game presents negotiation phases, where each player discusses to try to convince others about the violated heuristics and the severity grade chosen for each problem. After this step occurs, players can choose to maintain or to change their selection of heuristic violations and must choose the new severity to be assigned to each problem, considering the justifications presented by the players [5].

At the end of the round, the player who has chosen the correct severity level (selected by most players) is the winner of the round and receives one (1) or two (2) points (see Sect. 4.2). In any round, a player may return three (3) points to buy a new negotiation phase (also called renegotiation), in which the new choices of the players replace previous ones. This mechanics increases the player's chance to convince others with their arguments and win the round, and it represents the competitive character of the gamification, which is especially important to increase the analysis on a certain usability problem, allowing an evaluation end with higher quality. Finally, the player who accumulated the most points during the rounds is the winner of the game [5].

The G4H cards are available in the original proposal of this gamification [5]. The following subsections present the details of G4H.

4.1 Game Setup

For the game start correctly, the following items must be available [5]:

- Heuristic cards: each player must receive a set of 11 cards, where the first ten (10) represent Nielsen's ten usability heuristics, and the last one represents a problem that does not violate any heuristics (referred to grade 0 of the Nielsen's severity scale);
- Severity cards: each player must receive a set of 4 cards. They represent the remaining grades of the Nielsen's severity scale (1–4) used to classify each identified problem;
- Point cards: represent the reward that gamification provides players by assessing the severity of problems correctly;
- Tasks: the actions to be executed, previously and individually, by each player during the inspection of the chosen system, to identify the existing usability problems. The game needs a list of problems discovered during the execution of the tasks, but the evaluation itself is outside the scope of the G4H;
- Access to the system selected for evaluation;
- Heuristics guide: provides a brief description of each Nielsen's usability heuristics, which can be used by players to recall the meaning of each heuristic;
- List of usability problems previously identified by each player;
- Participation of at least three players.

4.2 Activity Cycle Rules

The gamification proposed by G4H presents a simple activity cycle, which involves the execution of ten steps [5]. Figure 1 presents these steps.

1st - Presentation of the problem: the first player selects a problem from his list of problems, which he has worked out previously. The same problems identified by more than one player should not be reevaluated in a new round unless they represent violations of different heuristics. In this step, the round player describes the current

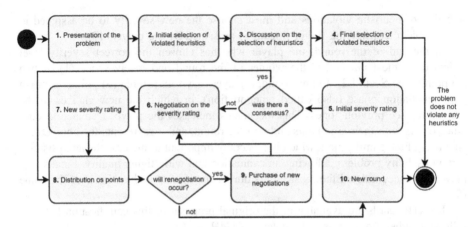

Fig. 1. G4H activity cycle based on [5]

problem for the others. Then, all players discuss the problem by making comments and questions to the player who found the problem in the system. Players can also perform the task again on the system to demonstrate the occurrence of the problem.

2nd - Initial selection of violated heuristics: each player chooses one or more heuristic cards to indicate which heuristics he believes were violated by the round problem. Initially, these cards must be face down so as not to influence the evaluation of the other players. When all players complete their choices, they must turn over their cards at the same time.

3rd - Discussion on the selection of heuristics: all players, one at a time, should argue over how and why they chose certain heuristic cards, which represent violations.

4th - Final selection of violated heuristics: all players vote again on heuristic violations that they consider correct for the round problem. The next steps should considerer the heuristic(s) chosen by most players results in the final selection. An exception occurs when most players decide that the problem does not violate any heuristics, so the round ends in this step and the game returns to step 1.

5th - Initial severity rating: each player chooses a severity card and again keeps it face down to prevent other players' opinions from being influenced until all players complete their selection. Players show their cards at the same time. If the players have agreed to the same classification, the game goes on to distribute the points (step 8). However, if there is any divergence in severity rating, the game proceeds to the negotiation phase (step 6). It is important to remember the choice of each player in this step because it will be used to define the winner of the round and the distribution of points in case of divergence between them.

6th - Negotiation on the severity rating: all players, one at a time, should explain the reasons that led them to choose a certain degree of severity. Players can debate and ask questions about the severity rating. G4H does not specify a fixed amount of time for this negotiation phase but recommends that each player speak at least once. When players agree that enough information already exists to conduct a new classification, the game continues to the next step.

7th - New severity rating: all players re-select a severity card, which may be the same as chosen in step 5 or a new card representing a change of player's opinion. As in the previous steps, the selected card must face down until all players choose their respective cards. The severity card selected by most players represents the severity grade chosen for the current problem. The next step is to define the winner(s) of the round.

8th - Distribution of points: the game rewards all players when there is a consensus in the initial severity rating (step 5), where each player receives 1 point, or also individually rewards players who have guessed the final severity grade (step 7) in your first chance of evaluation (step 5). In this second case, the player who selected the final severity grade (step 7) similar to the one chosen in step 5, receives 2 points. For example, consider a round where 3 players participated: A, B, and C. If in step 5, player A chose the "major" severity, and players B and C chose the "minor" severity grade, and after negotiation (step 7) most players chose "major" severity, only player A earns 2 points. However, if after negotiation the severity grade selected by most players was "minor", only players B and C receive 2 points. The last possibility happens when the final selection of most players is a different severity rating (not mentioned earlier), for instance, "catastrophic". In this case, the player who has selected the severity closest to the final classification gains 1 point. Considering the previous example, player A who chose "major" severity in step 5 would gain 1 point.

9th - Purchase of new negotiations: players can still buy a new trading chance (also called renegotiation), which is interesting when the round decision is balanced, and the player wishes to have a new chance to win the round. For this, this player returns 3 points, which are lost regardless of the results of the new negotiation. The players must also return the points obtained in the last step and must execute steps 6, 7 and 8 again. The G4H allows only one renegotiation purchase per round.

10th - New round: if the player of the round has no further problems to be analyzed in his list of problems, the game proceeds with the player on the left until all problems previously encountered by all the evaluators are discussed and consolidated.

To evaluate the usage of the first version of G4H with potential users, a preliminary study was carried out with the participation of five undergraduate students, who had basic knowledge in evaluating interfaces and in the use of Nielsen heuristics. Participants used G4H to consolidate the results of evaluating a web system, which allows them to compare prices and sell products. During this experiment, it was possible to observe that the participants performed the Heuristic Evaluation with greater satisfaction from the use of G4H [5].

This article uses the G4H proposal to develop G4H-PLAY, an adaptation of this gamification to allow the use of playability heuristics, given that the original G4H proposal considers only the Nielsen's usability heuristics [6].

5 Related Work

The related works present games focused on the concepts and methods of the IHC area, they are UsabiliCity, MACteaching, and UsabilityGame.

UsabiliCity [22] is a serious educational game, developed for the Web platform, to support the teaching and learning of Nielsen's usability heuristics (see Table 1), developed for the Heuristic Evaluation method. This article discusses a game developed for the same method. However, this work proposes a new educational game, while the present article seeks to evolve an existing game: G4H, whose proposal aims to improve the execution of Heuristic Evaluation and is not to teach the method. The main goal of the present paper is to adapt the G4H to allow the use of a set of playability heuristics, while the related work concentrates only on Nielsen Usability Heuristics.

MACteaching [23] is an educational game, developed for the Android platform, with the purpose of supporting the teaching of the Communication Evaluation Method (CEM), a method of the HCI area created to evaluate the communicability of interactive systems [24]. This article also addresses the topic of games aimed at improving HCI evaluation methods. However, this work proposes a new educational game to complement the teaching of CEM, while the present paper seeks to propose a G4H adaptation, as explained before.

The UsabilityGame [25] is an educational simulation game, developed for the Web platform, with the purpose of supporting usability teaching, considering the Usability Engineering Life Cycle [26], which involves the activities of requirements analysis, prototyping, and execution of the Heuristic Evaluation. UsabilityGame also discusses a game developed for the Heuristic Evaluation method. It also proposes a new educational game with the goal of supporting not only the teaching of this method but also the activities of requirements analysis and prototyping, including all stages of the usability lifecycle proposed by Mayhew [26], while the present paper has no focus on teaching the method and uses playability heuristics.

6 Defining G4H-PLAY

This section presents the methodology steps used to develop the G4H-PLAY (Game for PLAYability Heuristic Evaluation).

6.1 Choice of Playability Heuristics

This step consists in selecting a set of playability heuristics proposed in the literature, which will be used to develop the adaptation of G4H, named G4H-PLAY. The goal is to allow to achieve the G4H benefits with the Playability Heuristic Evaluation, and, since that there are many playability heuristics sets defined in the literature, it is necessary to select a playability heuristic set. The heuristics set chosen means only as an application case of this methodology, which has the potential to be replicated with other playability heuristics sets.

In this paper, the playability heuristics set selected was established by Barcelos et al. [10], considering that the heuristics proposed by the authors are refinements of the heuristics sets established by several authors, they are: Desurvire and Wiberg [8], Federoff [7], and Pinelli, Wong, and Stach [9]. The authors also managed to reduce the number of proposed heuristics to 18, since an extensive number of playability heuristics generates difficulty in memorizing for the evaluators, as it was observed in Desurvire, Caplan and Toth work [27] that established 43 heuristics.

Table 2 presents the 18 heuristics defined by Barcelos et al. [10]. According to the authors, the first 8 heuristics are traditional usability principles, which were contextualized for the digital game domain, and the remaining 10 heuristics are specific principles of playability.

Table 2. Barcelos playability heuristics [10]

ID	Heuristic definition
H1	Controls should be clear, customizable and physically comfortable; their response actions must be immediate
H2	The player must be able to customize the audio and video of the game according to their needs
H3	The player must be able to easily obtain information about everything around him
H4	The game should enable the player to develop skills that will be needed in the future
H5	The player must receive a tutorial with clear find a clear training and game familiarization
H6	The player must easily understand all visual representations
H7	The player must be able to save the current state to resume the game later
H8	The layout and the menus should be intuitive and organized so that the player can keep his focus on the game
H9	The story must be rich and engaging creating a bond with the player and the game universe
H10	The graphics and soundtrack should arouse the player's interest
H11	Digital actors and the game world should look realistic and consistent
H12	The main objective of the game must be presented to the player from the beginning
H13	The game must provide secondary and minor goals, parallel to the main objective
H14	The game must have several challenges and allow different strategies
H15	The pace of the game should take into account fatigue and maintenance of attention levels
H16	The game challenge can be adjusted according to the skill of the player
H17	The player must be rewarded for his achievements in a clear and immediate manner
H18	Artificial intelligence should represent unexpected challenges and surprises for the player

6.2 Extracting Information About Heuristics

This step consists of collecting information related to the specification of the playability heuristics set chosen in step 6.1 and its use in the Playability Heuristic Evaluation.

From this information it will be possible to identify the necessary modifications to adapt this G4H gamification to the playability heuristics set chosen, thus elaborating the G4H-PLAY.

As previously mentioned, the playability heuristics set chosen to be gamified was proposed by Barcelos et al. [10], and through this work, the information regarding the proposed heuristics was collected. Table 3 presents the information extracted from Barcelos et al. [10] to identify the necessary modifications for G4H.

Table 3. Heuristics data extracting information

Information	Description
Number of heuristics	The amount of proposed gameplay heuristics
Specification model	The information used to specify the heuristics. Each heuristic must have at least one definition
Does it define categories of heuristics?	An affirmative answer, if the proposed heuristics were classified, or a negative answer otherwise
Does it define severity degrees?	An affirmative or negative answer regarding the classification of severity in the experiment carried out
Is the severity degree rating based on Nielsen's?	If the severity rating is applied, an affirmative response if it is done using the Nielsen severity scale [12, 17], or negative response if the opposite occurs. In the latter case, it is necessary to know the meaning of the scale used, if provided
Number of participating evaluators	The number of evaluators who participated in the execution of the Playability Heuristic Evaluation in the experiment performed

The selected heuristics set contains 18 heuristics, each of which was specified with an identifier (ID) and a definition (see Table 2), representing the specification model. Heuristics were not classified into categories. For each problem identified in the experiment, the severity classification was performed using a six-point scale (0 to 5). It doesn't apply the Nielsen's severity scale [12, 17], and it doesn't provide the meaning of each value of the scale used. It only provides the range of the scale used, which ranges from 0 to 5, and this G4H-PLAY will consider this severity scale. Finally, the participants of the experiment were divided into pairs and the analysis involved the results obtained by three or more pairs, and the analysis of the results of the Playability Heuristic Evaluation involved the participation of at least six evaluators.

6.3   Analysis of the G4H Adequacy

This step consists in analyzing how each information collected in step 6.2 may lead to the adequacy of existing rules and the creation of new G4H cards. For example, each playability heuristics need to be represented into a heuristic card in the gamification. Other information as categories and heuristic definition will also be placed in the card. Each severity level turns into a severity card. Each player needs to receive a set of cards, and all these cards need to be developed for G4H-PLAY. Performing this step is important in identifying what modifications need to be made in G4H to adapt that gamification to the set of chosen gameplay heuristics.

G4H had a fixed number of heuristic cards (11), one for each Nielsen usability heuristic [6], and one last card to represent that the problem that does not violate any heuristics. In the set of chosen playability heuristics, 18 heuristics were established. Thus, for the elaboration of G4H-PLAY, 18 new heuristic cards must be developed (one card for each playability heuristic).

Originally, the G4H heuristic cards presented only name and icon to represent a heuristic. However, the chosen playability heuristics were specified with ID and definition. Thus, it is necessary to adapt the heuristic cards to present this data.

In the G4H proposal, the heuristic guide can be used by players to recall the heuristics definitions during the gamification rounds. However, there is no need to develop a heuristic guide for G4H-PLAY, given that the full information on each heuristic should already be contained in the new heuristic cards.

The playability heuristics set chosen do not classify their heuristics into categories, not causing changes in items or G4H rules. In this case, it was not necessary to modify the heuristic cards template because the original proposal considers Nielsen's usability heuristics [6], which are also not categorized.

Originally, G4H severity cards consider the Nielsen's severity scale [12, 17]. However, in the experiment performed in [10] to validate the playability heuristics set chosen, a different scale (ranging from 0 to 5) was used to classify the severity. Thus, G4H severity cards cannot be used in G4H-PLAY, including also the heuristic card that represents the 0 value (i.e., is not a violation) of the scale suggested by Nielsen. Thus, to develop the G4H-PLAY it is necessary to elaborate six (6) new severity cards (one card for each severity scale value used in the experiment). Changing the severity scale also leads to adjustments in the G4H activity cycle rules, considering that one or more steps in this cycle need to be rewritten to exemplify the use of the new severity scale.

Finally, the participation of six evaluators in the Playability Heuristic Evaluation does not cause adjustments in G4H, since the original proposal of this gamification considers the minimum of three players, but does not define the maximum number of users.

The adaptations necessary to adapt the G4H to the chosen playability heuristics set (G4H-PLAY) are summarized below:

- Adapt the heuristic cards that must present their ID and definition for each playability heuristic. 18 new heuristic cards must be drawn up;
- Adapt the severity cards to represent the six-point severity scale (0 to 5). Six (6) new severity cards must be drawn up;
- Adequate activity cycle rules that should exemplify the use of the six-point severity scale.

6.4   G4H-PLAY Proposal

This step consists in developing solutions for the adaptations identified in step 6.3, which represent the adaptation of G4H to allow the use of the playability heuristics proposed by Barcelos et al. [10]. This adaptation was named G4H-PLAY (Game for PLAYability Heuristic Evaluation), which is presented below.

Cards
Figure 2 presents the 6 severity cards developed from the six-point scale (0 to 5) used by the playability heuristics set chosen. These cards show only the number representing each level of the scale because Barcelos et al. work [10] does not provide the meaning of each number.

Fig. 2. G4H-PLAY severity cards

Point cards were redesigned to adopt the same pattern of heuristic cards and severity cards. Figure 3 shows the new scoring cards.

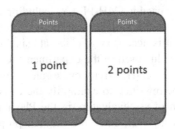

Fig. 3. G4H-PLAY scoring cards

Figure 4 presents the 18 heuristic cards developed from the playability heuristics set chosen for adaptation [10]. Each card represents a heuristic with its ID and corresponding definition.

Activity Cycle Rules
Considering the original activity cycle proposed by G4H (see Sect. 4.2), the only step that needs to be adapted is step eight (8) which deals with the distribution of points, given that only in this step is exemplified the use of severity scale. All other steps can be applied in G4H-PLAY, as originally proposed by G4H.

Step 8 is now written as follows (changes in bold format): the game rewards all players when there is consensus in the initial severity rating (step 5), where each player receives 1 point or individually rewards players who guessed the final severity score (step 7) in their first chance of evaluation (step 5). In this second case, the player who

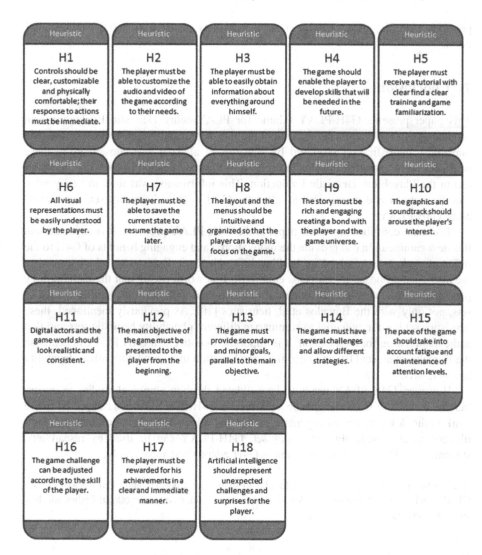

Fig. 4. G4H-PLAY heuristics cards.

selected the final grade (step 7), the degree of severity similar to the one chosen in step 5, receives 2 points. For example, consider a round where 3 players participated: A, B, and C. If in step 5, player A chose **severity grade 3**, and players B and C chose **severity grade 2**, and after negotiation (step 7) most players chose **severity grade 3**, only player A earns 2 points. However, if after negotiation the severity grade selected by most players **was 2**, only players B and C receive 2 points. The last possibility happens when the final selection of most players is a different severity rating (not mentioned previously), for instance, **severity grade 5**. In this case, the player who selected the severity closest to the final classification gains 1 point. Considering the previous example, player A who chose the **severity grade 3** in step 5 would gain 1 point.

7 Conclusion

This paper presents G4H-PLAY (Game for PLAYability Heuristic Evaluation), an adaptation of G4H gamification to allow the use of playability heuristics. For this, the playability heuristics set proposed by Barcelos et al. [10] was chosen. From these heuristics were extracted information related to the specification of each one and their use in the Playability Heuristic Evaluation. This information was used to verify what modifications would be required to adapt the G4H to these heuristics set, thus generating G4H-PLAY.

The main contribution of this paper is the G4H-PLAY proposal. It is expected that this new gamification can provide the motivational and engaging benefits of G4H to the different evaluators involved in the Playability Heuristic Evaluation, which considers the heuristics proposed by Barcelos et al. [10]. It is worth noting that the methodology presented in this work has the potential to be applied with other playability heuristics sets, not only with the Barcelos et al. heuristics [10]. As previously mentioned, these heuristics set has the potential to summarize different playability heuristic sets and that is the main reason for its selection. It is important to notice that G4H-PLAY depends on the Barcelos et al. set [10] and need further adaptation to be used with other playability heuristic sets.

However, G4H-PLAY needs to be validated through empirical studies to ensure that the benefits of G4H can also be achieved by G4H-PLAY. Another expected future work is the development of a generic model that allows the adaptation of G4H gamification to any playability heuristics set. G4H-PLAY can be used by researchers, students, and HCI practitioners to make G4H adaptations more easily.

Acknowledgments. The authors would like to thank the Undergraduate Pro-Rectory (PRO-GRAD) and Quixadá Campus of Federal University of Ceará, through the 50/2017 edict, for their support in conducting the research.

References

1. Nielsen, J.: Finding usability problems through heuristic evaluation. In: Bauersfeld, P., Bennett, J., Lynch, G. (eds.) Proceedings of the SIGCHI Conference on Human Factors in Computing Systems (CHI 1992), pp. 373–380. ACM, Monterey (1992)
2. Barbosa, S.D.J., Silva, B.S.: Interação humano-computador. Elsevier, Rio de Janeiro (2010). (in Portuguese)
3. Petrie, H., Buykx, L.: Collaborative heuristic evaluation: improving the effectiveness of heuristic evaluation. In: Proceedings of UPA 2010 International Conference, Munich (2010)
4. Herr, S., Baumgartner, N., Gross, T.: Evaluating severity rating scales for heuristic evaluation. In: Proceedings of the 2016 CHI Conference Extended Abstracts on Human Factors in Computing Systems (CHI EA 2016), pp. 3069–3075. ACM, San José (2016)

5. Jucá, P.M., Monteiro, I.T., de Souza Filho, J.C.: Game for heuristic evaluation (G4H): a serious game for collaborative evaluation of systems. In: Kurosu, M. (ed.) HCI 2017. LNCS, vol. 10271, pp. 341–352. Springer, Cham (2017). https://doi.org/10.1007/978-3-319-58071-5_26

6. Nielsen, J.: 10 usability heuristics for user interface design. https://www.nngroup.com/articles/ten-usability-heuristics/. Accessed 01 Feb 2019

7. Federoff, M.A.: Heuristics and usability guidelines for the creation and evaluation of fun in video games. Master thesis, Department of Telecommunications, Indiana University, Indiana (2002)

8. Desurvire, H., Wiberg, C.: Game usability heuristics (PLAY) for evaluating and designing better games: the next iteration. In: Ozok, A.A., Zaphiris, P. (eds.) OCSC 2009. LNCS, vol. 5621, pp. 557–566. Springer, Heidelberg (2009). https://doi.org/10.1007/978-3-642-02774-1_60

9. Pinelle, D., Wong, N., Stach, T.: Heuristic evaluation for games: usability principles for video game design. In: Proceedings of the SIGCHI Conference on Human Factors in Computing Systems (CHI 2008), pp. 1453–1462. ACM, Florence (2008)

10. Barcelos, T.S., Carvalho, T., Schimiguel, J., Silveira, I.F.: Análise comparativa de heurísticas para avaliação de jogos digitais. In: Proceedings of the 10th Brazilian Symposium on Human Factors in Computing Systems and the 5th Latin American Conference on Human-Computer Interaction (IHC+CLIHC 2011), pp. 187–196. Brazilian Computer Society, Porto de Galinhas (2011). (in Portuguese)

11. Medeiros, J.F.: Avaliação de Usabilidade e Jogabilidade em Jogos para Dispositivos Móveis. In: Proceedings of the XIV Brazilian Symposium on Computer Games and Digital Entertainment (SBGames 2015—Art & Design Track), pp. 681–690. Brazilian Computer Society, Teresina (2015). (in Portuguese)

12. Nielsen, J.: Enhancing the explanatory power of usability heuristics. In: Adelson, B., Dumais, S., Olson, J. (eds.) Proceedings of the SIGCHI Conference on Human Factors in Computing Systems (CHI 1994), pp. 152–158. ACM, Boston (1994)

13. Nielsen, J.: Usability Engineering. Morgan Kaufmann, San Francisco (1993)

14. Cuperschmid, A.R.M., Hildebrand, H.R.: Avaliação Heurística de Jogabilidade—counter-strike: global offensive. In: Proceedings of the XII Brazilian Symposium on Computer Games and Digital Entertainment (SBGames 2013—Art & Design Track), pp. 371–378. Brazilian Computer Society, São Paulo (2013). (in Portuguese)

15. Mello, V., Perani, L.: Gameplay x playability: defining concepts, tracing differences. In: Proceedings of the XI Brazilian Symposium on Computer Games and Digital Entertainment (SBGames 2012—Art & Design Track), pp. 157–164. Brazilian Computer Society, Brasília (2012)

16. Sánchez, J.L.G., Zea, N.P., Gutiérrez, F.L.: Playability: how to identify the player experience in a video game. In: Gross, T., et al. (eds.) INTERACT 2009. LNCS, vol. 5726, pp. 356–359. Springer, Heidelberg (2009). https://doi.org/10.1007/978-3-642-03655-2_39

17. Nielsen, J.: Severity ratings for usability problems. https://www.nngroup.com/articles/how-to-rate-the-severity-of-usability-problems/. Accessed 01 Feb 2019

18. Deterding, S., Dixon, D., Khaled, R., Nacke, L.: From game design elements to gamefulness: defining "Gamification". In: Proceedings of the 15th International Academic MindTrek Conference: Envisioning Future Media Environments (MindTrek 2011), pp. 9–15. ACM, Tampere (2011)

19. Kapp, K.M.: The Gamification of Learning and Instruction Fieldbook: Ideas into Practice, 1st edn. Wiley, San Francisco (2013)

20. Tondello, G.F.: An introduction to gamification in human–computer interaction. XRDS Crossroads ACM Mag. Students Quantum Comput. **23**(1), 15–17 (2016). https://doi.org/10. 1145/2983457

21. Werbach, K., Hunter, D.: For the Win: How Game Thinking Can Revolutionize Your Business. Wharton Digital Press, Philadelphia (2012)

22. Ferreira, B., Rivero, L., Lopes, A., Marques, A.B., Conte, T.: Apoiando o Ensino de Qualidade de Software: Um Serious Game para o Ensino de Usabilidade. In: VII Fórum de Educação em Engenharia de Software (FEES 2014), pp. 12–21. Brazilian Computer Society, Maceió (2014). (in Portuguese)

23. Queiroz, W., Beltrão, R., Fernandes, M., Bonifácio, B., Fernandes, P.: MACteaching: Um Jogo para o Ensino do Método de Avaliação de Comunicabilidade. In: Companion Proceedings of the 14th Brazilian Symposium on Human Factors in Computing Systems (IHC 2015—Posters and Demos), pp. 70–71. Brazilian Computer Society, Salvador (2015). (in Portuguese)

24. Souza, C.S.: The Semiotic Engineering of Human-Computer Interaction. MIT Press, Cambridge (2005)

25. Sommariva, L., Benitti, F.B.V., Dalcin, F.S.: UsabilityGame: jogo simulador para apoio ao ensino de usabilidade. In: Proceedings of the 10th Brazilian Symposium on Human Factors in Computing Systems and the 5th Latin American Conference on Human-Computer Interaction (IHC+CLIHC 2011), pp. 61–65. Brazilian Computer Society, Porto de Galinhas (2011). (in Portuguese)

26. Mayhew, D.J.: The Usability Engineering Lifecycle: A Practitioner's Handbook for User Interface Design, 1st edn. Morgan Kaufmann, San Francisco (1999)

27. Desurvire, H., Caplan, M., Toth, J.A.: Using heuristics to evaluate the playability of games. In: CHI 2004 Extended Abstracts on Human Factors in Computing Systems (CHI EA 2004), pp. 1509–1512. ACM, Vienna (2004)

Proposal of Usability Metrics to Evaluate E-commerce Websites

Ediber Diaz[(⊠)], Silvia Flores, and Freddy Paz

Pontificia Universidad Católica del Perú, Lima 32, Lima, Peru
{diazr.e,ssflores,fpaz}@pucp.pe

Abstract. Usability form as an important aspect nowadays for software products, even more, when we talk about transactional websites. However, in the present, there are not enough metrics to help us measuring usability level from an E-commerce portal, for this reason, we present a new proposal of metrics of usability. While working on the proposal, we did a research to identify 39 metrics and 10 existing aspects, then we created usability metrics and finally we validated the proposal with five specialists, based on interviews and questionnaires.

Keywords: E-commerce · Metrics · Usability · Human-systems integration · Software metrics · Usability evaluation

1 Introduction

Internet is offering new forms of business to companies, it can be used as a communication tool, to engage the customers and to sell products electronically. Through this tool, companies can spread information, seize opportunities and take advantage over their competitors [1]. The fast growing of E-commerce has created a new way to do transactions globally, because it breaks the geographical barriers and allow the users to get more customers with no great efforts [2]. For companies, electronic commerce is an easy tool to get information about trading, just using website [3].

When we analyzed metrics research sources and other aspects of E-commerce, you can find that, in the present, there are some tools to test usability of transactional websites. Although they are not metrics, they can determinate how they these applications work.

The lack of usability in E-commerce portals such: design, how easy to use and understand they are, the direct influence on users, because they find the portal less "friendly". They do not feel comfortable using the website, so they decided not to use it. It turns into a technological failure, that has become an important market and a financial lost [3]. Due to these new demands, companies have decided to measure the usability level their commercial websites have. The measurement is achieved through techniques that allow an important feedback for companies about the design and the usability standards and interaction with users in the commercial web [4].

For all the reasons mentioned, we propose the elaboration of a group of metrics that can obtain numeric results that allow comparisons between different aspects of usability of E-commerce, starting with the elaborated and current proposals.

© Springer Nature Switzerland AG 2019
A. Marcus and W. Wang (Eds.): HCII 2019, LNCS 11586, pp. 85–95, 2019.
https://doi.org/10.1007/978-3-030-23535-2_6

2 Methodology

In this section, we are presenting the description of the systematic review, the choice of the most relevant articles and the reviews and interviews done with the specialists for the proposal validation.

2.1 Systematic Review

We developed the systematic review of our research sources from previous work [5], which we are using the usability metrics present in the literature. Nevertheless, these metrics are very generic and oriented to general topics, so they can not be used in every domain or software categories, that is the reason why they have to be analyzed and we had to separate those that may be useful for the topic that is being discussed [6]. In addition, the most relevant articles are going to be taken as a source to evaluate the aspects of usability for E-commerce websites.

After analyzing the relevant documents [7–11], we are able of determinate twenty five usability aspects for E-commerce websites which have being compared against the identifying aspect with the existing metrics to know which one of the others is not been taken into account. The results are showed on the Table 1.

Table 1. Comparison of usability aspects for transactional websites.

Usability aspects of metrics found	Usability aspects of literature analysis
Understanding	Accessibility
Learning	User's cultural background
Operability	Attractive
Attractive	Help and documents
Functionality	Information search
Quality of error	Quality of error
Accessibility	Behaviour of the after sale service
Information	Web design consistency
Density of the information	Density of the information
Legibility	Understanding
	Web design standards
	Flexibility and effectiveness
	Functionality
	Information
	Legibility
	Minimize memory load
	Navigability
	Operability
	Transaction status feedback
	Standardized symbology
	Simplicity
	Purchase decision
	Transaction
	Visibility and clarity of elements and status of the system

2.2 Selection

After analyzing the most relevant articles and information of metrics and usability aspects for transactional websites, we made a selection of metrics and the comparison between identifying usability aspects in existing metric and those found in literature.

To proceed with the selection of usability metrics we followed these selection and discard criteria:

1. Domain-oriented: We selected those metrics that let us to evaluate the applications of the E-commerce domain, because it is what this article is orientated to.
2. Metric goal: We selected those metrics with an objective according the website. For example metrics about functionality, errors and others.
3. Target: We select those, which were orientated to the user interaction with software, not the ones focused in developing.

In addition, we discarded the metrics that were too technical, because it is hard to analyze them in a simple way, when the user interacts with the website. For these specific cases, we could use some kind of software that helps to get results with this kind of metrics, for example, how fast the pointer moves, number of pixels used, and others. Likewise, we discard those metrics we cannot apply to the E-commerce, or those that have a similar measuring purpose, or if they are the same as the existing metrics already selected. The results show 25 different usability metrics total that can be used for the proposal.

To compare the usability aspects we found, we identified the aspects being covered with the existing metrics. This way, when compared with other aspects found in literature, we would be able to know which aspects are still not covered, and it would be useful when the new list of usability metrics is proposed.

2.3 Surveys and Interviews

After identifying all metrics and usability aspects, we did surveys and interviewed specialists in the usability subject, so they could review and validate our finds in the literature, and give us their opinion about the matter, so we could notice our possible mistakes and try to improve them. In addition, we did surveys and interviews after we proposed the usability metrics. Since this way our proposal could be validated and know if we directed the proposal to the right field, if they included the usability aspects that allowed to evaluate the transactional websites, and if there was some kind of mistake with the metrics, so we would be able to refine them, and present a completely right proposal.

The surveys and interviews were structured in such a way we could show the specialists the information we found in a clear precise and tidy way, so their opinions and validations would be useful to develop our research.

3 Proposal of Usability Metrics for E-commerce

With the metrics and usability aspects found in literature, we got a group of aspects not considered yet. With this information, we developed a first table with the proposal of usability metrics grouped by aspect. As a result, we created 49 metrics total. We put the metrics on a template that contents the features showed on the Table 2, with an example. We did this way to show them in a clear and tidy way. The results of the consolidated proposal are showed on Table 3 that shows 74 usability metrics, among the existing ones, and the ones created for E-commerce websites.

Table 2. Definition of the metric: "Product Information"

Aspect	Description
Usability aspects	Information
Code	043
Name	Information of the product
Explanation	Required information for customer (stock, description, specifications, etc.) and the purchase
Application mode	Count the amount of labels of information that the user thinks are relevant and found them
Formula	$X = A/B$ A: Amount of labels of information per product the customer finds B: Total of labels of information of a product a user looks for
Result interpretation	$X \geq 0$, the further from 0, the better
Type of result	Value between 0 and 1
Section of application	Product section

Table 3. Consolidated list of usability metrics

Usability aspect	Name	Formula
Accessibility	Loading time	$T = Ti$ where Ti is the loading time of the home page
	Help accessibility	$X = A/B$ where A is the number of correct tasks online found and B the total of tasks evaluated
	Accessibility for users with disabilities	$X = A/B$ is the number of useful functions for disabled users and B is the number of functions implemented
Learning	Easy to learn how to perform a task	$T = Tf$ where Tf is the amount of time a user takes until they achieved the desired result in the task performed
	Average time of component use	$T = Hu - Hi$ where Hu is the final time after the component is used and Hi is the initial time of component use
	Average time to master the component	$T = Hd - Hi$ where Hd is the end time after mastering the component, and Hi is the initial time of the test

(continued)

Table 3. (*continued*)

Usability aspect	Name	Formula
Attractive	Proportion of elements that get the customer's attention (banners, animation, etc.)	X = A/B where A is the number of elements identified by the user and B is the total of elements in the website
	Operation interface density	X = A where A is the number of functions found in a GUI
	Attractive interaction	Questionnaire to evaluate the attractiveness of the interface for users after the interaction
	Appearance and aesthetics of user interfaces	X = A/B is the number of aesthetically pleasing screens for the user and B is the number of screens displayed
Help and documents	Categories in help section	X = A/B where A is the number of categories found by the user and B is the total of help categories
	Help messages understood	X = A/B where A is the number of messages understood by the customer (successfully proved) and B is the total of help messages consulted
	Customer support	X = N where N is equal to 0, if a virtual assistance chat does not exist and equal to 1, if a virtual assistance chat exists
Information search	Proportion of filters by category	X = 1 − A/B where A is the number of filters selected by the user and B is the total of filters in the search section
	Proportion of search boxes	X = A/B where A is the number of search boxes showed and B is the number of sections visited
	Proportion of filters to advanced search	X = A/B where A is the number of filters found and B is the total of search filters
	Products related to the search	X = C where C is the number of products related to the search
Quality of error	Help with errors	X = N where N is equal to 0, if the website does not help the user with their errors, and equal to 1 if the website offers help with errors
	Error messages by the density of functional elements	X = C where C is the total number of errors that show up due to overload
	Proportion of error messages that are correctly understood	X = A/B where A is the number of errors that are understood by users and B is the total number of errors
	Correction of the user's entry errors	X = A/B where A is the number of entry errors for which the system provides a suggested correct value and B is the number of entry errors detected
User's cultural background	Payment methods	X = A/B where A is the number of payment methods that the user found useless and B is the number of payment methods provided by the website
	Affiliates registration	X = N where N is equal to 0, if the website does not offer to affiliate with Facebook, Gmail or others and equal to 1, if the website offers to affiliate with Facebook, Gmail or others

(*continued*)

Table 3. (*continued*)

Usability aspect	Name	Formula
Behaviour of the after sale service	Contact information	X = C where C is the number of means to contact with the customer service
	Purchase confirmation message	X = N where N is equal to 0, if an email confirmation does not exist and equal to 1, if an email confirmation exists
	Tracking order	X = N where N is equal to 0, if the user cannot track its order and equal to 1, if the user can track their order
	Order options (returns, changes, cancellations)	X = A/B where A is the number of order options that the user found useless and B is the number of order options that the website provides
Web design consistency	Design style	X = A/B where A is the number of sections with the same style of design and B is the number of sections navigated by the user
Density of the information	Simplified product information	If, A < B then X = A/B If, B < A then X = B/A Where A is the number of elements of information by product the user needs and B is the total number of elements of information of a product
	Relevant product information	X = A/B where A is the total of aspects that the user wants to know about the product and B is the total of aspects that provides the system about the product
Understanding	Metaphors understood	X = A/B where A is the number of metaphors understood by the user and B is the number of metaphors consulted to the user
	Complete description	X = A/B where A is the number of functions that are understood by the user and B is the total of functions
	Demonstration of accessibility	X = A/B where A is the number of satisfactory cases in which the user achieves to watch the demonstration and B is the number of cases in which the user is requested to watch the demonstration
	Demonstration effectiveness	X = A/B where A is the number of functions correctly performed after the tutorial and B is the total number of demonstration or tutorials reviewed by the user
	Understandable functions	X = A/B where A is the number of interface functions correctly described by the user and B is the number of functions available in the interface
	Understandable inputs and outputs	X = A/B where A is the number of input and output data elements that the user understands successfully and B is the number of input and output data elements available from the interface
	Proportion of exceptions that are correctly understood	X = A/B where A is the number of exceptions that were used correctly and B is the total number of exceptions
	Proportion of returned values that are correctly understood	X = A/B where A is the number of returned values that are understood by the user and B is the total number of returned values
	Hover time	X = T where T is the total time of suspension of a component

(*continued*)

Table 3. (*continued*)

Usability aspect	Name	Formula
Web design standards	Standard iconography	X = C where C is the number of icons identified by the user who do not know their usefulness
Flexibility and effectiveness	Recommended products	X = A/B where A is the number of recommended products satisfactory to the user and B is the number of products that recommend the website
	Selected products	X = A/B where A is the number of sections from where is possible to access to the shopping cart and wish list and B is the number of sections visited by the user
Functionality	Response time	T = Tr where Tr is the response time of the website
	Proportion of functional elements with the appropriate name	X = A/B where A is the number of functions with a correct name and B is the total number of functions
	Proportion of functional elements used without errors	X = A/B where A is the number of functions that were used correctly and B is the total number of functions
Information	Product information	X = A/B where A is the number of information labels per product that the user finds and B is the total of information labels of a product that the user is looking for
	Product quality	X = A/B where A is the number of types of qualification found by the user and B is the total rating types on the website for the product
	Information about the delivery of the product	X = A/B where A is the amount of the information the user needs and B is the amount of information about the delivery of the product
	Product availability	X = N where N is equal to 0, if there is no visibility of the information and equal to 1, if there is a visibility of the information
	Hovers	X = A where A is the number of suspensions of a component
Legibility	Understandable information	X = A/B where A is the number of information labels understood by the user (description, specifications) and B is the number of information labels read by the user
	Understandable labels	X = A/B where A is the number of information labels understood by the user in all their queries (categories, sections, etc.) and B is the number of information labels read by the user
Minimize memory load	Appearance of wish list	X = A/B where A is the number of times the desired list icon is found in the sections visited and B is the number of sections visited
	Desired products	X = N where N is equal to 0, if there is no list of desired products and equal to 1, if there is a list of desired products
	Recent search	X = A/B where A is the number of recent searches displayed by the website and B is the total of searches made by the user

(*continued*)

Table 3. (*continued*)

Usability aspect	Name	Formula
Navigability	Loading time between the different sections	$T = \Sigma \, (Ti)$ where Ti is the loading time in each section
	Proportion of identified product categories	$X = A/B$ where A is the number of categories found by the user and B is the total of categories of the website
Operability	Operational consistency	(a) $X = 1 - A/B$ where A is the number of messages or functions that the user has found inconsistent with what he expected and B is the number of messages or functions (b) $Y = N/UOT$ where N is the number of operations that the user found inconsistent with what was expected and UOT is the user's operating time (during the observation period)
	Correction of error	$T = Tc - Ts$ where Tc is the time to complete the correction of a specified type of errors of the performed task and Ts is the start time of the correction of the errors of the performed task
	Appearance consistency	$X = 1 - A/B$ where A is the number of user interfaces with similar elements but with different appearance and B is the number of user interfaces with similar elements
Transaction status feedback	Number of steps for the purchase process	$X = C$ where C is the number of steps made by customers to make a purchase
Standarized symbology	Standard symbology	$X = A/B$ where A is the number of icons consulted by the user in all the sections that fulfill the same functionality and B is the number of icons consulted by the user
Simplicity	Relative task efficiency	$X = \Sigma \, (Ti * Ni)/\Sigma \, (Ti)$ where Ti is the time it takes for the client "i" to complete the task and Ni is equal to 0, if the task is not completed and equal to 1, if the task is completed
	Register	$X = A/B$ where A is the amount of information that the user considers necessary and B is the amount of information requested by the website
Purchase decision	Proportion of visible offers	$X = A/B$ where A is the amount of visible offers and B is the total of offers on the website
	Existing questions	$X = A/B$ where A is the number of questions found by the user and B is the amount of questions sought by the user
	Comments	$X = N$ where N is equal to 0, if you are not allowed to comment and equal to 1, if you are allowed to comment
	Payments	$X = A/B$ where A is the amount of information regarding the payment found by the user and B is the amount of information regarding the payment necessary for the user

(*continued*)

Table 3. (*continued*)

Usability aspect	Name	Formula
Transaction	Purchase time	T = Tc where Tc is the time it takes to complete a transaction
	Help in the purchase	X = N where N is equal to 0, if there is no guide or purchase tutorial for users and equal to 1, if there is a shopping guide or tutorial
	Purchase summary	X = N where N is equal to 0, if there is no purchase summary for users and equal to 1, if there is a purchase summary
Visibility and clarity of elements and status of the system	Visibility of the number of customers	X = N where N is equal to 0, if there is no visibility of the information and equal to 1, if there is a visibility of the information
	Visibility of the system state	X = N where N is equal to 0, if there is no visibility of the information and equal to 1, if there is a visibility of the information
	Visibility on the status of the purchase in all sections of the purchase process	X = N where N is equal to 0, if there is no visibility of the information and equal to 1, if there is a visibility of the information

4 Validation of the List of Usability Metrics

This proposal was validated carefully with opinions from five usability experts. Each of these were shown and explained to them so they can give us an opinion and recommendations. All this process was developed based on interviews and questionnaires, where each expert evaluated each usability metric and rated them according to the importance they believed was feasible.

The opinion of the experts was diverse, for example, one of them told us that although the metrics and aspects of usability proposed served to evaluate a transactional website, they prefer to witness what results were obtained when evaluating a website within a real scenario. Another expert mentioned the proposed metrics covered very important aspects within the E-commerce websites, however, there could be more important aspects for a transactional website. In addition, a pattern should be developed to help to automate the evaluation of them, as it would be very useful for other people who would like to evaluate a transactional website using the metrics.

All these opinions served to revisit the proposal of metrics and to refine them. In the same way, we searched for more scientific articles related to usability aspects for E-commerce to cover all helpful information, for more accurate and reliable results when evaluating a transactional website.

5 Conclusion and Future Works

Usability is one of the most important aspects to take into account in e-commerce websites, since it is focused on the ease of use of the website in the face of interaction with users. Although companies use different evaluation methods to obtain usability, they are qualitative and do not provide numerical results to indicate the level of usability they possess. In this sense, a proposal of usability metrics was developed, which unites different perspectives of usability aspects to be evaluated in a website. Because this project is focused on metrics for transactional websites, a thorough analysis was made of the current metrics in the literature and the aspects they covered, in order to focus on those that were not taken into account by transactional websites and because next, there were no usability metrics. This analysis evidenced the relevant aspects that were not taken into account by transactional websites, for example the search by information, the purchase decision making, the post-sale behavior, and others.

As future work, we have to test the proposal within a real scenario, putting forward a method of evaluating usability metrics, evaluating different websites, finding their level of usability and comparing the results, going through a validation of specialists and thus provide the most reliable results possible.

Acknowledgement. The authors would like to thank all the participants involved in the surveys and interviews, especially the members of "HCI – DUXAIT" (HCI, Design, User Experience, Accessibility & Innovation Technologies). HCI – DUXAIT is a research group of the Pontificia Universidad Católica del Perú (PUCP).

References

1. Sexton, R.S., Johnson, R.A., Hignite, M.A.: Predicting Internet/e-commerce use. Internet Res. **12**(5), 402–410 (2002). https://doi.org/10.1108/10662240210447155
2. Rivera, S., Rodríguez, C.: Importancia del comercio electrónico y las TICs en el sector turístico Latinoamericano. In: 9th Latin American and Caribbean Conference for Engineering and Technology, October 2016, pp. 2–4 (2011)
3. Paz, F.: Método para la evaluación de usabilidad de sitios web transaccional basados en el proceso de inspección heurística. Tesis de doctorado en Ingeniería Informática. Lima: Pontificia Universidad Católica del Perú, Facultad de Ciencias e Ingeniería (2017). http://tesis.pucp.edu.pe/repositorio/handle/123456789/9903
4. Kotian, H.: A framework for quality management of E-commerce websites (2017)
5. Diaz, E., Arenas, J., Moquillaza, A., Paz, F.: A systematic literature review about quantitative metrics to evaluate the usability of e-commerce websites (2018). https://link.springer.com/chapter/10.1007%2F978-3-030-11051-2_51?fbclid=IwAR12byZWsCY363rucwVnQg8pVo OJai_KKSvTNw9nWBgwcjO2RKtl1sZE6Vw
6. Santos, C., Novais, T., Ferreira, M., Albuquerque, C., De Farias, I.H., Furtado, A.P.C.: Metrics focused on usability ISO 9126 based. In: Iberian Conference on Information Systems and Technologies, CISTI, July 2016 (2016). https://doi.org/10.1109/CISTI.2016.7521437
7. Majid, E.S.A., Kamaruddin, N., Mansor, Z.: Adaptation of usability principles in responsive web design technique for e-commerce development. In: Proceedings - 5th International Conference on Electrical Engineering and Informatics: Bridging the Knowledge between Academic, Industry, and Community, ICEEI 2015, pp. 726–729 (2015). https://doi.org/10.1109/ICEEI.2015.7352593

8. Paz, F., Paz, F.A., Pow-Sang, J.A., Collantes, L.: Usability heuristics for transactional websites. In: ITNG 2014 - Proceedings of the 11th International Conference on Information Technology: New Generations, pp. 627–628 (2014). https://doi.org/10.1109/ITNG.2014.81
9. Bonastre, L., Granollers, T.: A set of heuristics for user experience evaluation in E-commerce websites. In: ACHI 2014 : The Seventh International Conference on Advances in Computer-Human Interactions, (c), pp. 27–34 (2014)
10. Marcus, A. (ed.): DUXU 2015. LNCS, vol. 9186, pp. 256–266. Springer, Cham (2015). https://doi.org/10.1007/978-3-319-20886-2
11. Paz, F., Paz, F.A., Arenas, J.J., Rosas, C.: A perception study of a new set of usability heuristics for transactional websites. Adv. Intell. Syst. Comput. **722**, 620–625 (2018). https://doi.org/10.1007/978-3-319-73888-8_96

Usability Test Based on Co-creation in Service Design

Xiong Ding[1,3(✉)], Shan Liu[1], Jiajia Chen[2], and Manhai Li[3]

[1] Guangzhou Academy of Fine Arts, Guangzhou 510006, China
dingxiong77@163.com
[2] Nanjing University of the Arts, Nanjing 211815, China
[3] Macau University of Science and Technology, Macau 999078, China

Abstract. Service design often solves complex system problems. The diversity of users' requirements and uncertainty of "interaction" in the service delivery process lead to the uncertainty of service usability. The focus of usability in service on design and test can avoid or minimize the uncertainty of service experience to the maximum extent. The concept and mechanism of "Service Co-creation" in this paper plays an important role in this process, including co-design in service planning activities and value co-creation in the process of service delivery. At the same time, after considering the definition of service design, specificity of service and usability factors of interactive products comprehensively, service usability can be summarized as 8 elements in the paper, including adaptability, standardization, flexibility, learnability, memorability, fault tolerance, efficiency and satisfaction. And then take the "Hotel Family Services Design" project as an example, it carries out usability design and test involved people (stakeholders), events (processes) and objects (touchpoints) in the service system. On the one hand, "multi-role stakeholders" participating in the "co-design workshop" can identify the precise needs of users and develop useful and usable services with more pertinence in the service planning stage. On the other hand, different forms and approaches of "prototype test" (Discussion Prototype, Simulation Prototype) to verify the usability and experience of service systems and processes in the service development and delivery phase help service designers and providers ultimately achieve their goals to improve service usefulness, usability and attraction through service iteration.

Keywords: Service design · Service Co-creation · Usability ·
Multi-role stakeholders · Prototype test

1 Introduction

With the coming of service and experience economy era, the focus of design shifts from "objects" to "behaviors" and then to "experience" [1]. Systems, services and experience have become the essential aim and value measurement criteria of design innovation activities. The usability design in service is a "stakeholder-oriented" systematic design to meet the need of service receivers and providers, to conform to their behavioral habits and perceptions, and simultaneously to fulfil service production and consumption efficiently and pleasantly.

© Springer Nature Switzerland AG 2019
A. Marcus and W. Wang (Eds.): HCII 2019, LNCS 11586, pp. 96–116, 2019.
https://doi.org/10.1007/978-3-030-23535-2_7

Service design often solves complex system problems. Complex systems inevitably involve "multi-role stakeholders" and various needs of users. Meanwhile there are many factors that influence the service experience, from macro to micro, including environmental factors when service occurs, personal factors of the participants (service providers and receivers) in service touch and the interaction between them [2]. The diversity of the first and second one leads to the uncertainty of "interaction" in the service delivery process, so the service usability is also uncertain. The focus of usability in service on design and test can avoid or minimize the uncertainty of service experience. And "co-creation" plays a very important role in this process, which includes co-design in service planning activities and value co-creation in the service delivery process. The integrated concept of "Service Co-creation" is proposed in this paper, taking the "Hotel Family Service Design" as an example, separately carrying out usability test based on personnel for service planning and service delivery in the two phases of "Co-Design Workshop" and "Prototype Test".

2 Service Co-creation and Service Usability

2.1 Service Co-creation

The concept of co-creation originates from the value co-creation theory in the field of service marketing and service management, and has been discussed for some time as well as forms a more mature theory system. In recent years, the field of design has concentrated on co-innovation, especially in the field of service design, where "co-design" is one of the basic principles and important methods of service innovation [3, 4]. Therefore, looking through the whole process of service planning, production and consumption, service co-creation can be discussed from two perspectives.

On the one hand, co-creation in most contexts, is also known as co-design and participatory design, that is, in order to achieve a design goal, two or more design subjects (or experts) respectively achieve this design goal with different design tasks together by means of certain information exchange and mutual cooperation mechanism [5]. As a matter of fact, co-design model is the process of information sharing and collaborative decision-making in phases, which is the process of an open and distributed innovation. Collaboration is sharing; synergy is support and coordination is mechanism. The emerging social innovation design [6] in recent years also extraordinarily concerns and emphasizes "co-innovation", "co-creation" and "co-design", according to the method, which can be summarized as "professional designer oriented, social organization supportive and public or individual spending their or his own spare time and ideas to make a difference with the purpose of ameliorating the problems that cannot be solved from top to bottom" [7]. Participatory design and social innovation design are "co-design" with the characteristics of "new era", which are all "bottom-up" designs. Co-design is not a simple design method, but a design concept, process, composition and organization mode.

On the other hand, from the perspective of service, co-creation is to describe the characteristics of services, that is, service providers and customers create value together. Without the resources provided by customers, services cannot be carried out [8].

According to the theory of value co-creation, producers are no longer the only value creators and consumers are no longer pure value consumers, but value co-creators interacting with producers. There are two branches of value co-creation theory: One is based on the value co-creation of consumer experience, emphasizing that co-creating consumer experience is the core of value co-creation between consumers and enterprises and the interaction between members of value network is the basic form to realize value co-creation [9, 10]. The other is on the basis of value-creation theory that service dominates logic, highlighting that the process of value co-creation occurs when consumers use, consume products or services and is the sum of the value created by producers and consumers [11, 12]. The co-creation of service value happens in the process of service delivery and service touch.

Therefore, service co-creation should contain two levels of meaning: one is the co-design of service system, that is, the co-creation in the process of service planning; the other is the co-creation of service value, that is, the co-creation in the process of service delivery (production and consumption). Both co-design and value co-creation need the common involvement of multi-role stakeholders. The overall concept of organic integration and combination between them in the context of service innovation and experience is the real "Service Co-creation" (see Fig. 1). In simple terms, service co-creation occurs among stakeholders; it happens in service planning (design); it comes up in service delivering (touch).

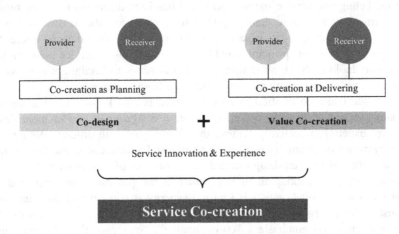

Fig. 1. Definition and framework of Service Co-creation.

2.2 Usability of Service

Birgit Mager, president of the Service Design Network, points out that from the perspective of customers, service design is dedicated to making service interface more useful, usable, and needed. From the perspective of service providers, service design is to make service that they provide more effective, efficient and distinctive [13]. Utility and effectiveness are the foundations of usability and efficiency, being needed and distinctive is the aim of design.

Service usability is a concept used to describe the extent of if services are available. Usability has been studied for many years in the field of interactive design. Usability expert Nielsen believes that usability covers elements such as learnability, memorability, faults' frequency, severity, efficiency and satisfaction [14]. The standard of ISO FDIS 9241211 (Guidance on Usability, 1997) proposes that usability refers to the effectiveness, efficiency and satisfaction of an interaction process when a user uses a product to complete a specific mission in a particular environment. Hartson pointed out that product usability has two implications: usefulness and usability [15]. It can be found that the description of usability factors and meaning becomes more and more general. But in the process of actual operation, the comparatively refined elements proposed by Nielsen are most commonly used because of its better operability. The above concepts are mainly used to describe the usability of products, especially interactive products. There are some differences between services and products, so the description of service usability should have some special attributes of service. Compared with products, services have the following characteristics:

(a) Unstable Quality. The process of service involves materials and personnel of service providers, which are non-standardized, especially personnel. Even the same personnel cannot guarantee the same service per unit time. So, usability will be affected to some extent. How to reduce this impact is what needs to be considered in the design, that is, try to ensure that the interaction process between customers and service providers is relatively standard.

(b) External Influence Factors. Uncontrollable external factors such as temperature, weather and signals may affect the process of service, which leads to unavailable service.

(c) Differences of Customer Resources [16]. Service is the process that service providers act on customer resources. Therefore, differences of customer resources have a significant effect on service efficiency, such as customers' perception, expression, skills and emotions. Take the differences of customer resources into account, prepare a reasonable plan and react flexibly, which will contribute to improving service efficiency.

(d) Customer Intensity [16]. During peak service time, the customer intensity is high, the pressure of service personnel is relatively high, and the rate of faults may increase, the satisfaction of customers may decrease or customers may be lost due to the slow speed of reaction. Therefore, measures should be taken to reduce customer intensity during the peak time in the design, like bringing forward or postponing some service steps.

Consequently, after considering the definition of service design, specificity of service and usability factors of interactive products comprehensively, service usability can be summarized as eight elements:

(a) Adaptability. When external factors change, service is less influenced. Is the service susceptible to uncontrollable factors such as weather and temperature?

(b) Standardization. Does service process, tangible display and so on have a fairly high degree of standardization? Can materials keep a stable condition for a certain period of time? Is there a relatively low requirement for the comprehensive capability and resilience of the staff?

(c) Flexibility. Does service has different response scripts for customers with great difference in resources? Is a plan prepared to raise efficiency for peak time?

(d) Learnability. Does the user (both service receivers and service providers, the same hereinafter) need to learn the steps of service? Is it easy to learn? Does it require users to have relevant knowledge reserve?

(e) Memorability. Does the user need to memorize the steps? Do they know what to do after completing one step? Do they still remember the steps/procedures of service after a period?

(f) Fault Tolerance. Can the user continue when a selection/operation/expression error occurs during the service? Is it easy to correct? Is it possible to have irreparable results?

(g) Efficiency. The efficiency that users complete the steps of service.

(h) Satisfaction. Users is satisfied subjectively in the process of service (with products, personnel, process, themselves, etc.).

3 Service Usability Test Scheme Design Based on Co-creation

The procedure of universal service design is the "Double Diamond Model" provided by the UK Design Council, including four stages: discover, define, develop and deliver [17]. It specifically contains steps such as competitive products analysis, user position, service value proposition, service system map, customer journey map, touchpoint innovative design, service blueprint, prototype test and so on.

According to the theory of service co-creation, innovative service content is based on the joint participation and co-design of multi-role stakeholders. At the same time, the realization of the innovative service system value requires the participation and delivery of all stakeholders (that is, production and consumption of service). Therefore, there is an inseparable relationship between co-creation and service usability design and test. The usability test scheme for service (design) also needs to be designed and generally consists of three steps:

(a) In the phase of exploration and definition, enhance the usability of service planning concept through co-design workshop;

(b) In the phase of development, testing the usability of the specific service design scheme by discussion prototype, making test lists, building test prototypes and arranging staff are basic steps;

(c) In the phase of delivery, carry out service prototype tests multiple times, including participation prototype, simulation prototype and pilot prototype to obtain service effect and quality feedback through observation records, interviews, questionnaires and enhance service usability via service iteration.

3.1   Co-design Workshop

"User-centered" and "co-design" are the basic principles of service design. However, the "users" in the service system design are not only receivers like consumers or customers, but also providers like staff or suppliers. Compared with traditional product design, service design requires more various stakeholders to participate in the early stage of research and planning. Co-design workshop is a common method used in the early stage of service planning. The pros and cons of co-creation results will have a crucial impact on subsequent service development and design. Thus, in this stage, the effectiveness and reliability of the co-design method also need to be improved through "design" to ensure that the co-creation results can be smoothly educed. The procedures in detail are as follows:

First, invite and select different types of co-creators based on co-creation theme. The first category is service receivers, that is, the target customers, consumers or users; the second category is service providers, including bosses, business or department managers and front-line service staff [18]. Both two types of co-creators belong to "primary stakeholders" that must be invited to co-design workshops. The third type of co-creators that can be invited are "secondary stakeholders", such as government departments, industry associations, residents, media, etc. [19]. Whether they are invited or not depends on the needs of the co-creation theme. It should be noted that the selection of co-creators should cover factors like gender, age, occupation or position and industry. Because service design thinking and its methods are still relatively new and have a certain degree of professionalism. Co-design teams composed entirely of public (non-professional designers) may sometimes be at a loss faced with some service co-creation tools. As a result, in the co-design workshop with the aim of service innovation, there is a participant with certain specificity, that is, service designers. Most of them are arranged by the workshop organizer to each co-design team, mainly responsible for the interpretation of service design tools, the advancement of the co-creation process and ensuring that each participant can fully express their ideas, that is to say, service designers in the co-design workshop are the guider of co-creation procedure and method. Their existence greatly improves the efficiency and reliability of co-creation.

Second, these stakeholders are grouped according to different combinations of roles and co-design activities are carried out on the same theme with a unified procedure and method. Specifically, the co-creators discuss interactively about "a certain bad experience or experiences in the past" and "a certain experience in the ideal" under the guidance of service designers and "express" their own demands, ideas and creativity with the help of relevant tools for service design. There are many co-design tools that can be used, such as empathy maps, role-playing, personas, customer journey maps, brainstorming, affinity diagrams, LEGO serious play, etc. [3]. Which methods are specifically adopted, depending on the requirements of co-creation content and the individual factors like the educational background, occupation and personality of the involved co-creators. Workshop organizers should make prediction and choice of method after co-creator's selection. Also, tools need to used flexibly during the course of the workshop and can be changed according to the situation if necessary.

3.2   Discussion Prototype and Service Prototype Test

After completing the major stages, such as "exploring and understanding the precise needs of users", "defining users, service and products", "designing service value, procedures and touchpoints", the last step based on co-creation of service innovation, is a very important step, that is "experience prototype verification and service delivery".

The objects of service design and co-creation are system, procedures, behaviors and corresponding experience. Hence, service experience prototype test cannot be separated from the construction of service scene or service situation. Situation construction in service design is a tool that used in the future service scenarios in visualized form. It simulates the future situation through a presupposed story, including service users, events, physical displays and the relationships of service providers, to show new service [19]. The purpose of constructing the situation is to provide a scenario for the situation experience, and methods and tools for the test of service co-creation. Through the creation and simulation of service scene, the designer is involved in attitude experience as a user, so as to better understand various service interfaces and touchpoints in the service process, discover service idea and verify whether the idea meets user's needs or not.

According to the difference of the situation construction's content, place, and participants, the experience prototypes are usually divided into four categories: semistructured discussion with low cost (Discussion Prototype), participants' walk-through (Participation prototype), a more refined simulation (Simulation Prototype), and a comprehensive pilot (Pilot prototype), the latter three are generally called service prototype [20]. Both discussion prototype and service prototype aim to simulate an overview of innovative products or service in a reasonable way and they are used for user experience and test as a way of situation construction. These four types of prototypes are set up for the advancement of service project. The service and service usability can be tested according to the requirements in different stages of the service design procedures with relevant prototype tools.

Discussion prototype defines user's journey and demonstrates it by empathy, that is, sympathetic thinking and then defines the role and goal of participants, that is, prototype test script or list; situation construction requires the design of real prototypes or touchpoints, and the arrangement of extra tools and facilities; experience the service through role-playing in a real situation, in order to find the bottleneck in the implementation of the service and improve it in the subsequent design stage [19]. Therefore, discussion prototype test is a fictitious process of experience and an indispensable part and a key step to verify service usability in service design process.

The difference between discussion prototype and service prototype is that the former is mainly a method of service designer's internal test, while the latter generally needs the participation of real users in real place. Discussion prototype test is relatively simple, generally used in the early stage of service co-creation, while service prototype test is complicated, which can usually be done in the later service co-creation process.

How to improve the reliability and persuasiveness of test results and make the test results have a rational meaning? A combination of observational records, interviews and questionnaires is needed. In addition to multi-role stakeholders, prototype test includes intangible service procedures and physical touchpoints such as places, facilities and service instructions. Specifically, the objects of observation are direct stakeholders, such as customers and staff, to record their specific behaviors of the whole participation process (before, during and after the service); the content of the interview is consistent with the observation, but it focuses more on the subjective feelings and experience of the individual as well as the objective and deep reasons behind. The questionnaire is a synthesis of the above contents and feelings. By quantifying the experience through the participants' scores, superimposing and calculating the data of all participants (in the case of enough data), we can get the comprehensive evaluation of the "service prototype" usability by various stakeholders, including the specific service usability problems designed at different levels, and on this basis, improve the design and improve the service usability continuously.

4 Test Case: Usability Test of the Family Service Design for Hampton Hotel

4.1 Case Background

The hotel providing the service usability case study for this paper is located in Guanxin Town, at the foot of Xiqiao Mountain, Nanhai district, Foshan city, Guangdong province. As the core project of Lingnan Culture & Tourism RBD in Nanhai district, Guanxin Town's development vision is to create an urban light holiday destination for middle and upper-class people, and integrate the new holiday lifestyle into the natural landscape of Xiqiao Mountain to form an elegant "neighborhood with light resort quality experience". The hotel is subordinate to Hilton Group's Hampton brand and it is a business hotel, but because of its location, according to the type of guests and the resources around the hotel, it is necessary to implant family service content and regional culture elements in the hotel's original service system, and take this as the core to develop service innovation and design.

The entire service planning, design and delivery process of the Hampton's family service design project and the usability test of the service process will be carried out around the concept of "co-creation" and the appropriate and necessary service design tools will be selected at each stage to advance the procedure of innovation. Because of the need to discuss "co-creation-based service usability test," this article will simplify the specific design content, and focus on the "co-creation" process and "service usability" test.

4.2 Online Questionnaire Survey on the Hotel Family Service

In the online survey on the hotel's family service, 395 valid feedback questionnaires are received, of whom 71.1% are mothers, 50.6% the post-80s generation, and 38.0% the post-70s, 49.4% of the respondents have experience of staying at family hotel, which is basically in line with the market big data and the project positioning of people. As for participant composition, one-child family accounts for 65.8% and two-child family 32.7%. The age in average is 0–3, 3–6, 6–9 and 9–12 years old on the distribution; 61.3% of the family is the family of three staying at the hotel. On the whole, the core elements of the family hotel in the minds of the user include the hotel's own environment and theme features (69.4%), a variety of children's entertainment facilities (68.6%), well-equipped children's room supplies (61.3%), etc. Besides, the demand for characteristic children experience courses also accounts for 34.7%. Among these courses, the most popular projects include nature exploration (76.0%), culture and sports (55.4%), art education (49.4%) and science experiments (46.8%). Nearly 70% (68.4%) of the users accept the hotel's childcare service; the time span that it is from one to three hours (56.0%) is suitable, and the most popular content (69.6%) covers comprehensive education and sports. The above data and conclusions provide a potent reference for user selection in the next co-design workshop.

4.3   The Specific Process of the Co-design Workshop

(a) Selection of co-creators. The project team invite 15 stakeholders to participate in the co-design workshop, who are divided into three groups. Among them, there are 6 people in group A, including 3 parents in nuclear family (one father & two mothers), 2 hotel operators and 1 service designer; there are 5 people in group B, including 3 hotel operators (one of them is the president of the hotel), 2 service designers (one of them is an art design teacher, who can be assigned to the role of an art course teacher); there are 5 people in group C, including 2 parents in the nuclear family (one father & one mother) 2 hotel operators (one of them is the general manager of five-star hotel with years of management experience) and 1 service designer. The co-creator of group A and group C are almost the same, considering the combination of users, operators and service designers. The difference is that group C has a hotel executive. Group B is different, mainly composed of hotel operators, including an executive.

(b) Workshop specific steps and output. Before the official start, there is an ice-breaking step (10 min). At first, the host introduces the co-creators to each other through some small games or self-introduction, including family and work background, and then briefly introduces the project that need co-design so that all stakeholders can participate in co-creation based on an initial understanding in the same context. The entire process of co-design is divided into three steps (see Fig. 2). Step one is customer journey map (20 min). Each co-creator writes some of the bad experiences (including behaviors, touchpoints, moods, and pain points) encountered throughout the whole process (including before, during, and after service) of staying at the hotel down on their own or with children on the sticky notes, share it with the team members and post the notes in the diagram. Step two is brainstorming (20 min). Through discussion, the team members select three typical, resonating, or most painful pain points from the previous step. Through brainstorming, analyze the pain points and discuss service innovation direction, attach interesting or meaningful "ideas" to the service creation deduction form and summarize the innovative value proposition. Step three is LEGO series play (20 min). Choose one or several solutions from the previous stage, use LEGO as a tool to tell a small story about family service and share the results.

The specific co-creation results are as follows: Group A uses "story substitution & role-playing" as a breakthrough for family service, with the "task book" as the main line, and develops innovative ideas around game tools, children's gifts, sense of ritual and family interaction; Group C emphasize the "South Lion IP", and take this image in-depth into the hotel's public areas and rooms to create a real sense of "South Lion Country". It shows that the composition of the co-creators in the group A and C are similar and relatively comprehensive, and the derivative service creation solutions are also based on the perspective of users, grasping the needs of users, however, its implementation will face cost and management challenges in existing service. Group B's co-creators are partial to operational management, and the results of co-creation are more concerned with the details of service, such as the concept of "heart-to-heart chamberlain" online and offline, for children, especially special children (allergies, vegetarians, patients etc.), offering more detailed service guideline including room supplies and food. The innovation of this part of service is optimized on the existing service, so the usability is better, but creativity and imagination are not enough.

Fig. 2. Three steps of Co-design Workshop.

(c) The results of co-design workshop test. Through the comparison of co-creation results among groups in the workshop, we can find that there are significant differences between the results of different combinations of co-creators. The key factors include co-creator selection method, the formation and performance of the opinion leader in co-design team, the ability of service designer as the coordinator who controls the co-creation process. Therefore, before organizing a co-design workshop, the project manager, director or service designer needs to have suffi-cient thinking and discussion on user selection and grouping, and make relatively reasonable arrangements according to the needs of specific project.

From this case, the initial "co-design workshop" phase is mainly to complete the task of service planning, and there is no detailed content of service procedures. Some elements of service usability may not be reflected at this stage. However, due to the involvement of multi-role stakeholders, its usability will inevitably improve, such as service providers and customers' awareness of their own resources, which will help them to judge the results. Therefore, each group has different considerations on adaptability, standardization and flexibility, thus leading to different directions of development. In general, due to the participation of multi-role stakeholders, service designers can accurately grasp the focus and feasibility of service innovation from multiple perspectives, thereby improving the usability of service design.

4.4   Hotel Family Service System Design

The design of service system involves a lot of contents. Take this project as an example, including the proposition of the value proposition of "a wonderful journey with Lion Sum", the design of IP image of Lion Sum, the design of a series of family service processes from reservation, check-in, dining, entertainment to check-out, and the design of tangible touchpoints within the whole hotel, etc.

Through the "Service System Map" (see Fig. 3), the hotel's family service system and how it works can basically be clarified and visualized. First of all, the core of the system is the family service in Hilton's Hampton Hotel, that is, "what is"; secondly, the user is targeted at the nuclear family, including parents and children, that is, "for whom"; thirdly, the content of this system or service should include specific content or touchpoints in three sections of "food", "accommodation" and "entertainment", that is, "what is" or "what it has", such as family dining area, children's tableware, family room and children's supplies, children's picture books, lion park (outdoor playground), a series of experience courses, etc. Finally, which departments or suppliers need to support the realization of these services, that is, "how to do", including manufacturers of children tableware and supplies, manufacturers of amusement facilities, software providers for online booking system, providers of experience courses, or full-time teachers. In general, the hotel family service is based on the story of Lion Sum, "learning skills from the master" and taking part in the "lion dance competition", to enhance the "interaction" between parents and children through the form of "children picture books & task cards" around the "lion park" and various courses, to perfect the experience of staying and to achieve the goal of "education and fun".

The design of different kind of touchpoints in the system is also very important. These touchpoints can be divided into three categories: The first category is digital touchpoints, such as the standardization of design for booking hotel and responding to mails, children's picture books, etc. The second category is people's touchpoints, including receptionists, room service staff, course teachers and supportive staff. The design content includes service operation procedure, quality standard, words, emergency mechanism, etc., presented by service manual. The third category is many tangible physical touchpoints, such as the lobby environment, room supplies, restaurants, amusement park and facilities, task cards, family courses and tool kits.

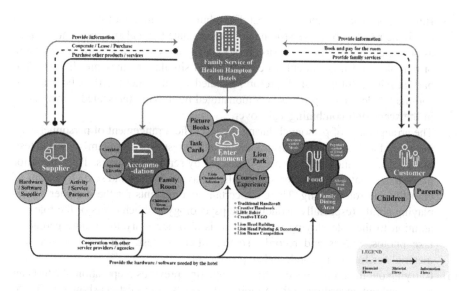

Fig. 3. The family service system map of Hilton Hampton Hotel.

4.5 Discussion Prototype Test of the Hotel Family Services

(a) Making a list for test. The list for test is usually made by the designer of service, including the aim, content, requirement of scenario, materials, arrangement of personnel and detailed procedures of test. The more detailed list is, the clearer guidance for testers is and the smoother test process is. For instance, this project's list of discussion prototype test clearly points out that five scenarios and specific contents of this round of test. They are hotel reservation and family picture books (by email), the reception in the hotel lobby, lion head building course, lion head painting & decorating course, space and procedures of lion park (see Fig. 4).

Fig. 4. Discussion prototype test list.

Fig. 5. Discussion prototype test of the hotel family services.

(b) Building or making a model for test. First, build a 1:1 model of the scene, such as the living room, lobby, classroom, etc. and simulate the real environment as much as possible. Second, for discussion prototype, some service scenarios are too large or complex and it is difficult to construct and simulate as they are, like the lion park in this prototype test. Therefore, a scaled-down model (1:20) is built to test, and the whole service process is demonstrated by moving the scaled-down model in the scene and combining voiceover.

(c) The arrangement of personnel during the test. The arrangement of personnel is an uncertain factor in the test. Discussion prototype test is design team's internal test. Stakeholders in the service process are acted by service designers. Thus, the actor needs to simulate the real user's thoughts, behaviors, words and so on by means of empathy and role-playing. There are certain requirements for the designer's role-playing ability (especially deducing the psychology and behaviors of the role). In addition to the role-playing personnel, it is also necessary to arrange people to take photos, videos and records, so that after the test, there is evidence and material for further research and improvement.

(d) Carrying out the prototype test. After completing previous preparation, the test can be carried out according to the established process of the list, as shown in Fig. 5.

(e) The results and optimization of discussion prototype test. In fact, more or less problems will be found during the above five stages of test. For example, the procedure of check-in is not simple and convenient enough; the procedure for distributing task cards is not reasonable; the rules of the game are not clear enough; the lion head building course is too difficult to inspire the enthusiasm of children; the tools to paint and decorate the lion head is not ideal; the discrepancy between the overall shape of the lion head and the original version is quite evident, and so on. Almost all of these problems arise in the course of test during the co-creation process of service delivery between service providers and receivers and it is quite difficult to find these problems in service system map, the customer journey map and the service blueprint. This is exactly the main reason why service design pays much attention to scenario construction and prototype test.

In the process of discussion prototype, there are enough details about service to specifically examine the factors that affect service usability. This case reflects some problems exist in the aspects of learnability, memorability, efficiency, standardization, satisfaction, etc. And hence the design team mainly optimizes the design of material package, toolkit and instructions for the test results of the above discussion prototype (see Figs. 6 and 7).

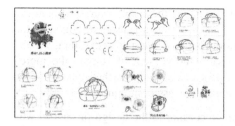   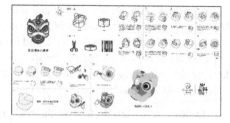

Fig. 6. Optimized manual of lion head building.

Fig. 7. Optimized manual of lion head painting & decorating.

4.6   Simulation Prototype Test of the Hotel Family Services

According to the content and progress of the project, we carry out simulation prototype test for scene 3 (lion head building course, hereinafter called course 1) and scene 4 (lion head painting & decorating course, hereinafter called course 2) in the test mentioned earlier.

(a) Recruitment, training and interview of teachers for the course. According to the principle of authenticity in simulation prototype test, the design team recruits an art graduate of the Guangzhou Academy of Fine Arts who has experience in teaching children's art courses (painting, handcrafting), but hasn't taken part in family courses that parents and children attend together. The service designer first trains her on the course being tested, including the content of course, procedures and tools. And then interviews her about the results of training. The main content is shown in Table 1.

Table 1. The record of interview after the teacher of course being trained

Question	Feedback
Do you know about lion head building and lion head painting & decorating? How well you know them?	I don't know about them in detail but have seen it in the TV program. There is lion dance performance in my hometown during the festival and I have also seen the lion head being built
Do you feel it difficult when listen to the trainer's explanation?	It doesn't sound difficult
Can you perfectly remember the content of work in the entire process after training?	I can remember most of it, but there are so many steps in the middle part of building, so I need to read the manual
Is there any difficulty in the actual operation? Which steps are easy to make mistakes or fail?	It's a little bit difficult, for example, to fix three wires at the same time and attach skin to the lion head during lion head building
Are you a competent candidate for this job? What abilities do you have that will help in this job?	Yes, I am. As a patient person, I have relevant experience and can liven up the atmosphere and I am good at handcrafting

According to the training effect and interview content, the design team has obtained the following enlightenment: It is very important to recruit a teacher of course with relevant experience in family course and art or design professional background, which helps to accurately understand, grasp and convey the content of course; the more detailed the manual is, the better it is; from the perspective of the teacher, the course is a little bit difficult; using some props can activate the classroom atmosphere.

(b) Inviting real users to test on the real site. According to the design of course, we invite four groups of real family users to experience the parent-child course. One of them is a family of four (two children, the brother is younger than the sister) and the others are families with three members. Among the five kids, there are two boys and three girls. The oldest is 7.5 years old, in the second grade of primary school; the youngest is 4 years old, in the middle class of kindergarten; the others are 6.5–7 years old, in first grade of primary school. The mothers of these four families are researchers or administrative staff of Guangdong Museum, while the fathers are from technology companies, universities and news agencies. This type of family activity between colleagues or friends is a common phenomenon in cities of China.

As for the site, the location of course in the plan is the semi-outdoor space (with sunshades) on the eighth floor of the hotel, but on test day, because of the low temperature (7 °C), the course is transferred to a conference room of the hotel temporarily, which inspires the design team that the weather factor (especially in Guangdong, where it is hot and rainy in summer and wet and cold in winter) is an unpredictable and uncontrollable factor in the process of service delivery, which will have a great impact on service operation. The existing course design is extremely unreasonable to carry out in a semi-outdoor space.

(c) Making relevant observation records during the test. During the test, in addition to taking videos and photos (as Fig. 8 shows), there is someone (service designer) in charge of observation and recording in details throughout the process. The content includes what the observer sees and hear–the words and deeds of the teacher, service personnel, children and parents and the solution from the perspective of service design (see Fig. 9).

From the overall effect of the course, it is smooth, active and joyful; as for the final handworks, they are beyond expectations. On the one hand, almost all families can do their work quite well, even to the youngest child. Of course, we have to give credit to the assistance of parents. On the other hand, some handworks are beyond the imagination of the teacher and the team of project. Users do not completely follow the manual and the guidance of teacher to create, but to add their own ideas, which makes works more stunning and outstanding. It is exactly the value of service co-creation and service uncertainty.

Fig. 8. Simulation prototype test of the family courses.

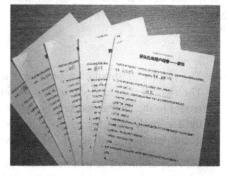

Fig. 9. Observation and record of the courses.

Fig. 10. The questionnaires filled by parents after the courses.

(d) Interviews and questionnaires for users after the test. Interviews with children and parents after the course are the most direct feedback on the effectiveness of the course. Interviews (see Table 2) and questionnaires (see Fig. 10 and Table 3) focus on the difficulty, steps, tools, children's interests, satisfaction and other indicators that are closely related to service usability. It should be pointed out here that interviews with children are a little bit difficult. First, they don't always answer every question; second, their answers may be self-contradictory. But the interview is still able to judge intuitively the children's feelings about the course as a whole.

Table 2. Making a record of interviews with children after the course

Question	Feedback (5 persons)
Do you like handcrafting? Do you like handcrafting with mom and dad?	Like (5), like (5)
Is the course interesting? Which part is the most interesting?	Interesting (5), sticking decoration (2)/building the framework (2)/coloring & cutting the paper (1)/attach the skin (1)
Can you understand when the teacher talks? Do you feel it difficult? Which part is the most difficult?	Can understand (2)/can't understand (1, 4 years old boy), not difficult (1)/a little bit difficult (1)/difficult (2), difficult to find the framework (2)/difficult to stick the skin (2)
Have you read the instructions? Can you understand?	Course 1: have read (5), can understand (4) Course 2: have read (2), can understand (1)/can't understand (1); haven't read (3)
Which steps are the easiest and you can finish the fastest?	Course 1: building the framework (2)/find the position (1)/cutting the tape (1) Course 2: coloring (4)/decorating (1)/cutting the tape (1)/paper cutting (1)
Is there any wrong step?	None of them (a group mistakes two wires with the same shape but different position marks at the beginning of lion head building, but it doesn't affect the effect of the building)
Do you like this lion head? Do you feel that you are doing well? Is it ease to use these tools for you?	Like (5), good (5), easy to use (2)/the other 3 persons don't answer

(e) The results of simulation prototype test and advice for subsequent optimizing. Throughout the teacher training and interview before the course, the observation record in the course and the interview and questionnaire after the course, most of the feedback from the users is consistent. In general, the test results and subsequent optimizing advice are as follows:

Poor adaptability. The planned site is particularly vulnerable to weather conditions, which leads to the unavailable service. It is suggested that the permanent site of the course be changed to indoors.

High degree of standardization. Although the course design has certain requirements for teachers' ability to respond and communicate, the method of teaching the course can be mastered via simple training and all steps are basically controllable on time and effect.

High flexibility. In this case, the customer resources that have a great impact on the results are parents and children's handicraft skills and ability to understand. In the end, regardless of competence, they all finish the work with satisfaction.

Low index of learnability. According to children's general feedback, it's difficult. Considering it is family service, the degree of difficulty can be decreased by cooperation with parents, or the age of children moving up to 9–12 years old.

Table 3. Doing a parent questionnaire survey after the course

Question	Feedback (5 persons)
Course 1: Lion Head Building	
Do you know about lion head building before participating in the course? Is this theme attractive to you?	Don't know, but attractive (3)/have a knowledge of it, attractive (2)
Do you feel difficult after listening to the instruction and getting the material toolkit? In your judgement, whether the course is difficult for your kid?	It's easy, but it can be a little bit difficult for kids (4) It's very easy, and it's not difficult for children (1)
Are there any operations that make you feel difficult during the process?	Distinguishing wires (2)/binding the paper tape (1)/no (2)
Is there any step that you feel is not doing well enough and affects the effect of the entire work?	No (4)/yes (1, binding the paper tape)
Can your child keep up with the teacher's rhythm during the process? If he can't keep up, in which step he can't?	Yes (2)/no (3, step 14 to 16, step 4)
Have you read the manual? If so, to what extent does the graphic symbol of the manual help your understanding? Please rate it, out of ten	Yes (5)/(9.8)
Please rate the difficulty of the course, the most difficult (1)/the easiest (10)	(7.6)
Please rate the satisfaction of the whole course from the following aspects, very dissatisfied (1)/very satisfied (10)	schedule and procedure (9.6)/the atmosphere of course (9.8)/tools provided (9.8)/the degree of relaxation (9)/kid's or your own handwork (9)/the final effect of works (9.2)/ overall performance of the child in the course (9.4)
Course 2: Lion Head Painting & Decorating	
Do you feel difficult after listening to the instruction and getting the material toolkit? In your judgement, whether the course is difficult for your kid?	It's easy, but it can be a little bit difficult for kids (5)
Which steps have you spent a long time to understand or felt that the teacher/manual hasn't expressed clearly?	No (4)/yes (1, sticking the tape and doing it inside as support)
Are there any operations that make you feel difficult during the process? why?	Sticking the tape (4)/judging the length of the paper tape (1)
Is there any step that you feel is not doing well enough and affects the effect of the entire work?	No (4)/yes (1, sticking the tape)
Can your child keep up with the teacher's rhythm during the process? If he can't keep up, in which step he can't?	Yes (2)/no (3, ticking the tape, basically done by parents)

(*continued*)

Table 3. (*continued*)

Question	Feedback (5 persons)
Have you read the manual? If so, to what extent does the graphic symbol of the manual help your understanding? Please rate it, out of ten	Yes(5)/(9.4))
Please rate the difficulty of the course, the most difficult (1)/the easiest (10)	(8.4)
Please rate the satisfaction of the whole course from the following aspects, very dissatisfied (1)/very satisfied (10)	schedule and procedure (9.4)/the atmosphere of course (9.8)/tools provided (9.8)/the degree of relaxation (9.2)/kid or your own handwork (8.6)/the final effect of works (9)/ overall performance of the child in the course (9.2)

High efficiency. All users can complete all the steps within time. Even though some children or parents fail to keep up in some steps, they can complete it on their own according to the manual.

High memorability. Basically, there is no need to remember, and in each step, staff or instructions will offer guidance.

Good fault tolerance. The teacher makes a mistake when teaching step 2. Two wires are mistaken, but the work is still completed smoothly. Except that, all children show that no wrong operation occurs and the work is finished well.

High satisfaction. The whole process is relaxed. Despite some difficulties, children and parents are satisfied with the final work and have a high evaluation of the course.

It can be seen that the optimizing suggestions at this stage mainly focus on the course's objects, place, time control, service quality, etc., and there is no major adjustment in the core content of the course, such as course's content, procedure and tools. That is to say, the design of the whole system has a good performance at all levels of usability, which confirms that the co-design workshop in the early stage of service planning correctly guides service usability design and the necessity of discussion prototype test in the phase of service design.

5   Conclusion

"Multi-role stakeholders" are the most uncertain factors in service design activities and service delivery process, both in the phase of co-design and process of service contact, but this uncertainty is not completely uncontrollable and unchangeable. Start from two important stages of service co-creation and carry out usability test involved people (stakeholders), events (processes) and objects (touchpoints). On the one hand, "multi-role stakeholders" participating in the "co-design workshop" can identify the precise needs of users and develop useful and usable services with more pertinence in the service planning stage. On the other hand, different forms and approaches of "prototype test" to verify the usability and experience of service systems and procedures in the service development and delivery phase help service designers and providers ultimately achieve their goals to improve service usefulness, usability and attraction.

Finally, it should be pointed out that the process of usability test is dynamic, reciprocating and it can and must be tested multiple times according to the project's advancement and needs. Each test of discussion prototype or service prototype is a good chance to improve and optimize service procedures and touchpoints. By comprehensively comparing the results of different test methods and testing multiple times with the addition to service iteration, service usability can be effectively verified and improved before carrying out the service. Besides, even though the service is already carried out, the production and consumption of each service can still be regarded as a prototype (pilot prototype) test to collect, to organize and to comprehensively analyze more users' needs, which can provide the most reliable evidence for a new round of service iteration.

References

1. Ding, X., Liang, Z.: New ideas about public design in the era of service and experience economy. Art J. **4**, 90–95 (2016)
2. Xin, X., Wang, X.: Co-creation and uncertainties of experiences in service design. Zhuangshi **4**, 74–76 (2018)
3. Service Design Tools. http://www.servicedesigntools.org. Accessed 2009
4. Stickdorn, M., Schneider, J.: This is Service Design Thinking: Basics-Tools-Cases. BIS Publishers, Amsterdam (2010)
5. Zhao, N.: Return to origin: constructing participatory design method. Design **7**, 183–185 (2013)
6. Manzini, E.: Design, When Everybody Designs: An Introduction to Design for Social Innovation, 1st edn. Publishing House of Electronics Industry, Beijing (2016)
7. Manzini, E.: Public services and collaborative people: how social innovation and design can change public services. Creat. Des. **5**, 6–9 (2011)
8. Dai, F., Xin, X.: Research on the definition of service design based on phenomenological method. Zhuangshi **10**, 66–68 (2016)
9. Prahalad, C.K., Hamel, G.: The core competence of the corporation. Strateg. Learn. Knowl. Econ. **3**, 3–22 (2000)
10. Prahalad, C.K., Ramaswamy, V.: Co-creation experiences: the next practice in value creation. J. Interact. Mark. **18**(3), 5–14 (2004)
11. Vargo, S.L., Lusch, R.F.: Evolving to a new dominant logic for marketing. J. Mark. **68**, 1–17 (2004)
12. Payne, A.F., Storbacka, K., Frow, P.: Managing the co-creation of value. J. Acad. Mark. Sci. **36**(1), 83–96 (2008)
13. Mager, B., Evenson, S.: Art of service: drawing the arts to inform service design and specification. In: Hefley, B., Murphy, W. (eds.) Service Science, Management and Engineering Education for the 21st Century. Springer, New York (2008)
14. Jakob, N.: Usability Engineering. Academic Press, Boston (1993)
15. Hartson, H.R.: Human–computer interaction: interdisciplinary roots and trends. J. Syst. Softw. **43**, 103–118 (1998)

16. Scott, E.S.: Essentials of Service Design: Developing High-value Service Businesses with PCN Analysis, 1st edn. Createspace Independent Publishing Platform Publication, Charleston (2013)
17. Design Council. https://www.designcouncil.org.uk/news-opinion/design-process-what-double-diamond. Accessed 17 Mar 2015
18. Freeman, R.E.: Strategic Management: A Stakeholder Approach. Shanghai Translation Publishing House, Shanghai (2006)
19. Chen, J.: Service Design: Definition, Language, Tools, 1st edn. Jiangsu Phoenix Fine Arts Publishing, Ltd, Nanjing (2016)
20. Polaine, A., Lovlie, L., Reason, B.: Service Design: From Insight to Implementation, 1st edn. Tsinghua University Press, Beijing (2015)

Exploiting the meCUE Questionnaire to Enhance an Existing UX Evaluation Method Based on Mental Models

Stefano Filippi[(✉)] and Daniela Barattin

DPIA Department, University of Udine, Udine, Italy
filippi@uniud.it

Abstract. Several definitions of User eXperience (UX) are present in the literature, representing the references for different UX evaluation methods and tools. Among these methods and tools, the irMMs-based method and the meCUE questionnaire show different peculiarities and seem good candidates to speculate on their integration, aiming at improving applicability, completeness and effectiveness of UX evaluation activities. The goal of this research is indeed to integrate the irMMs-based method with the meCUE questionnaire in order to enhance the former by exploiting the stronger points of the latter. To achieve this, we analyze the lacks of the irMMs-based method and verify the meCUE questionnaire capabilities in overcoming these lacks. Once verified, we proceed with the integration by modifying the evaluation activities of the irMMs-based method. Finally, we perform a first validation of the enhanced release by comparing it to the old one in the field. Researchers can exploit the same procedure to integrate other methods and tools in order to improve them; on the other hand, industrial practitioners can use the enhanced release for their UX evaluations since it is ready to be applicable even by non-developers.

Keywords: UX evaluation · irMMs-based method · meCUE questionnaire

1 Introduction

Nowadays, User eXperience (UX) is a key factor in designing, developing and managing interactive products and services [1]. Nevertheless, a clear and universal UX definition is still missing. UX fundamentals vary in terms of scopes and objects/elements considered; researchers and industrial practitioners seem to have different opinions about UX [2]. According to the ISO 9241-2010, the UX includes users' emotions, beliefs, preferences, perceptions, physical and psychological responses, behaviors and accomplishments that occur before, during and after the use of a product, system or service [3]. The hedonic/pragmatic model of Hassenzahl [4] assumes that people perceive interactive products along two dimensions, pragmatics and hedonics. Pragmatics refers to the perceived product ability to support the achievement of specific "do-goals" connected to users' behaviors like "making a call", "choosing a dress", etc. The assessment of pragmatics focuses on the usefulness and usability of a product relating to potential tasks. Hedonics refers to the perceived product ability to support the achievement of specific "be-goals" connected to the user

© Springer Nature Switzerland AG 2019
A. Marcus and W. Wang (Eds.): HCII 2019, LNCS 11586, pp. 117–133, 2019.
https://doi.org/10.1007/978-3-030-23535-2_8

himself/herself like "being expert", "being special", etc. The assessment of hedonics focuses on human needs considering three different facets: "stimulation" (novelty and change, personal growth), "identification" (communication of identity to relevant others, relatedness) and "evocation" (provoking memories, symbolizing). Users, products and contexts of use influence pragmatics and hedonics; specific emotions and behaviors are generated consequently. The UX framework of Kort, Vermeeren and Fokker [5] considers UX as based on three aspects influenced by the design elements of products: the compositional aspects focusing on usability and on pragmatic and behavioral aspects of the experience, the aspects of meaning representing the symbolic significance of the experience and the aesthetic aspects addressing the capability of the products to satisfy one or more senses. Emotions are the results of the interactions among these three aspects. Other theories consider emotions as a direct component of UX instead of as consequences of other things. The product experience framework of Desmet and Hekkert [6] considers UX as composed by the aesthetical experience - the product capability to delight one or more human sensory modalities, the experience of meaning - personal and/or symbolic significance assigned to a product by a user, and the emotional experience - appraisal of an event or a situation as potentially beneficial or harmful. In the CUE model [7], the UX components are the perception of instrumental product qualities (usability and usefulness), the perception of non-instrumental product qualities (aesthetic, symbolic and motivational aspects) and the emotional reactions. These components generate the overall judgment of the product, usage behavior, user preferences between alternatives and intention to use.

The literature offers different UX evaluation tools based on these definitions. The AttracDiff 2 [8], based on the hedonic/pragmatic model, is a questionnaire that measures the perceived pragmatic qualities and a part of the perceived hedonic qualities (stimulation and identification). Based on the same model, the User Experience Questionnaire (UEQ) measures the pragmatic (perspicuity, efficiency and dependability) and hedonic (stimulation and novelty) qualities through the evaluation of 26 items [9]. Among the methods and tools that consider emotions as a direct UX component, the irMMs-based method [10], based on the product experience framework, provides a qualitative UX evaluation by exploiting mental models and emotions. This evaluation occurs thanks to the comparison of the users' expectations about the interaction with a product and the users' evaluation after the real interaction. The meCUE questionnaire [8], referring directly to the CUE model, quantifies the UX of a product by exploiting question-like statements about instrumental and non-instrumental product qualities, emotional reactions and consequences of use of the product.

The irMMs-based method and the meCUE questionnaire show different peculiarities. For example, the former provides a qualitative UX evaluation while the latter a quantitative one; the latter considers product aspects not covered by the former like aesthetics, consequences of use, etc. This makes the two tools good candidates to speculate on their integration, aiming at improving applicability, completeness and effectiveness of UX evaluation activities. The goal of this research is indeed to integrate the irMMs-based method with the meCUE questionnaire in order to enhance the former by exploiting the stronger points of the latter. To achieve this, we analyze the lacks of the irMMs-based method and verify the meCUE questionnaire capabilities in overcoming these lacks. Once verified, we exploit the meCUE questionnaire to modify the irMMs-based method by highlighting the phases to affect and the way to intervene. Finally, we perform a first validation of the enhanced release by comparing it to the old one. The outcomes of this research can be useful for both researchers and industrial practitioners. The former can exploit the same procedure adopted here to integrate other methods and tools in order to improve them; on the other hand, the latter can use the enhanced release for their UX evaluations since it is ready to be applicable even by non-developers.

2 Background

2.1 The irMMs-Based UX Evaluation Method

The irMMs-based UX evaluation method (irMMs method, hereafter) evaluates the experiences of users interacting with products by exploiting interaction-related mental models (irMMs). The irMMs are cognitive processes that users generate in their mind before to act in order to satisfy a specific need in a specific situation of interaction. They consist of lists of users' meanings and emotions, including users and products' behaviors determined by these meanings and emotions [10]. The generation of an irMM develops through five steps, based on the Norman's model of the seven stages of the action cycle [11]. In the first step, the user perceives and interprets the need. Thanks to this interpretation, in the second step the user recovers previous irMMs and selects those ones that could be suitable to satisfy the need. The presence of one or more real products could influence this selection. The selected irMMs allow the user to establish the goals in the third step. Goals represent intermediate and time-ordered results to achieve; they help in defining the path to follow to satisfy the need. In the fourth step, the user assigns expected meanings and emotions to the need. These come from the elaboration of meanings and emotions belonging to the irMMs selected before. Positive meanings and emotions tend to remain as they are; negative ones could change into their positive correspondences depending on the amount of previous experiences that report those negative meanings and emotions. In the fifth step, the user defines his/her behavior and the related product behavior in order to achieve those expected meanings and emotions. These behaviors come again from elaborating the behaviors present in the irMMs selected before.

The adoption of the irMMs method happens through user tests. Users generate their irMMs respect to a specific need to satisfy and compare these irMMs to the real interaction with the product. The adoption generates two lists of positive and negative UX aspects that describe the strong points and the criticalities of the experience, respectively. More specifically, the irMMs method consists of three sections that differ in the knowledge about the product of the users who undergo the tests. The first section considers users who do not know the product at all; they generate their irMMs based on previous experiences with different products only. This is the absolute beginners (AB) section. The second section considers again users who do not know the product; nevertheless, before the generation of the irMMs (and before to know the need to satisfy) they are allowed to interact freely with the product for some time. This is the relative beginners (RB) section. Finally, the third section considers users who already know the product. This is the relative experts (RE) section. Figure 1 summarizes the adoption of the irMMs method. The tests for the three sections can run in parallel, providing that no influences among them happen in the meantime.

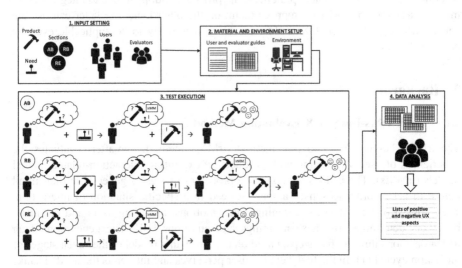

Fig. 1. The irMMs method adoption.

Phase 1. Input Setting. This phase defines five inputs. The features of the product to evaluate are the first input; the need to satisfy is the second one. Features can be functions, procedures, physical components, etc. and users will try to satisfy the need by exploiting these features. The third input is the sections of the irMMs method to adopt. Their selection depends on the expectations about the evaluation outcomes, on the resources available, etc. For example, aiming at investigating about the learnability of a feature, AB and RB sections would be the best candidates because RE users - those users involved in the tests of the RE section - already know the product and cannot give indications about learnability. The fourth input are the users who undergo the tests. Their selection comes by obeying to several requirements. For example, AB and RB users must not know the product before the evaluation; on the contrary, RE users must know the product and have used it at least for a given period (its duration varies time by time, depending on the product complexity, on the required reliability of the evaluation results, etc.). Another requirement, valid for every section, is "users must have similar knowledge about the field the product belongs to". More requirements can apply due to specific evaluation characteristics. Finally, the fifth input concerns the evaluators. Regarding AB and RB sections, evaluators can be almost any, from skilled and knowledgeable ones about the product to those barely aware of it; contrarily, for the RE section, evaluators must know the product very well because, in case of users running into very specific problems, they must be able to overcome these problems quickly and easily.

Phase 2. Material and Environment Setup. The second phase prepares material and environment to perform the tests. Material consists of two documents for each section, the user and the evaluator guides. The user guide helps users in generating the irMMs and in performing the interaction with the product. Its first part reports the need to satisfy and the instructions to generate the irMM, together with examples. The second part shows suggestions to perform the interaction with the real product and to compare it to the irMM. This document contains tables and empty spaces to describe the irMM and to comment the comparison. In the case of the AB section, the user guide is free of references to the product to evaluate in order to avoid bias. On the contrary, the user guides for the RB and RE sections contain precise information on the product under evaluation to make the users' attention focusing on it rather than on products that the users could know and/or have used in the past. The evaluator guide allows evaluators collecting data classified against their type (meanings, emotions, etc.) and tagged with the references to the users who generate them; moreover, this document contains instructions to analyze the data. The test execution phase also requires the setup of a suitable environment reflecting the common use of the product under evaluation. Depending on the characteristics of the specific evaluation, this phase selects a UX lab where the equipment to collect data is already present or identifies a real environment to perform the tests and moves the equipment there.

Phase 3. Test Execution. The third phase starts with the RB users freely interacting with the product. The evaluators invite them to focus on the product features selected in the input setting phase. Once this free interaction comes to the end, every user generates his/her irMM. Then, he/she tries to satisfy the need by using the product. The user must behave as described in his/her irMM; in the meantime, he/she checks if the product allows performing his/her behavior and if he/she gets the expected reactions/feedback (behavior) from the product. Of course, problems can occur anytime; these problems are addressed as gaps. If a gap shows up, the evaluators suggest the way to overcome the problem in terms of user and product behaviors. The user reports the reasons for the gap from his/her point of view and judges if the allowed behaviors are better or worse than those described in his/her irMM. Once finished the interaction, a debriefing where the user reasons about his/her experience and expresses further comments about it takes place. In particular, the evaluators invite the user to reconsider meanings and emotions expressed during the generation of the irMM in order to highlight and comment any change.

Phase 4. Data Analysis. Three rules lead the evaluators' analysis of the data collected during the tests. These rules allow generating the positive and negative UX aspects from the expected and real meanings and emotions as well as from the gaps. These rules are as follows.

- First rule. Every expected meaning and emotion expressed by the RB and RE users generates an UX aspect. This aspect will be positive or negative depending from the positivity/negativity of the meaning or emotion it comes from. For example, consider the need "washing delicate clothes with a washing machine". One meaning associated to this need can be "temperature", with a positive judgment because of the reason "since it is difficult to know the best temperature for washing any type of clothes, the washing machine has predefined programs where all parameters are already set, temperature included". This meaning and the related reason would allow generating the positive UX aspect "the washing machine offers predefined programs where all parameters are already set; the user must only select the right program according to the type of clothes to wash". This rule does not consider the AB users because their expected meanings and emotions refer to products different from the one under evaluation.

- Second rule. Every gap generates an UX aspect. Even in this case, the UX aspect will be positive or negative depending from the positivity/negativity of the gap it comes from. For example, consider again the need about washing delicate clothes. A gap related to the expected product behavior "all parameters of the washing program shown in the display" could raise during the real interaction because the product shows only washing time and temperature. The judgment about the gap would be negative, with the reason "when a washing program is selected, all washing parameters should be shown on the display to be sure to wash the clothes in the right way and safely. Unfortunately, the spin dryer speed is not shown". This gap would allow generating the negative UX aspect "the information reported on the display about the selected washing program is incomplete because spin dryer speed is missing".

- Third rule. Every change between the expected meanings/emotions and the corresponding real ones generates one or more UX aspects. If the change shows a positive trend, the UX aspect(s) will be positive, negative otherwise. This generation occurs considering the reasons of the changes expressed by the users. These reasons can refer to the interaction in general or they can point at specific gaps. In the first case, only one UX aspect arises; in the second case, also the UX aspects generated starting from the pointed gaps are considered as responsible for the change. For example, consider always the need of washing delicate clothes. The expected emotion "happy" can become "very happy" once the real interaction has occurred. There is a positive trend between the expected emotion and its real mate. The reason for this change could be "programming the washing time to work at nighttime is very interesting because, in this way, the risk to forget switching on the washing machine highly decreases as well as money are saved (at nighttime, electricity is cheaper)". This reason would allow generating the positive UX aspect "the washing machine is smart in choosing the right time to launch the washing program". Nevertheless, also the positive gap "the display proposed to the user a washing time to launch the washing program, expecting just a confirmation" could be responsible for this change; therefore, also the UX aspect "the washing machine suggests the best time to launch the washing program automatically" derived from that gap would be associated to this change.

As soon as the application of the rules comes to the end, the comparison of all the UX aspects takes place in order to delete doubles. Then, the UX aspects are classified against the interaction topics they refer to (specific procedures, product components, etc.) and, for each topic, the UX aspects are split into positive and negative and ordered against the number of occurrences and the impact. If an UX aspect refers to product characteristics rarely involved in the interaction, its impact will be low; on the contrary, if the UX aspect deals with core procedures determining the cognitive compatibility of the product with the users' problem solving processes, the impact will be higher.

2.2   The meCUE Questionnaire

The meCUE questionnaire 2.0 (meCUE, hereafter) provides a quantitative UX evaluation starting from the Components model of User Experience (CUE model) of Thuring and Mahlke [12]. As shown in Fig. 2, this model considers the perceptions of instrumental and non-instrumental product qualities and the emotional reactions as main components of the UX.

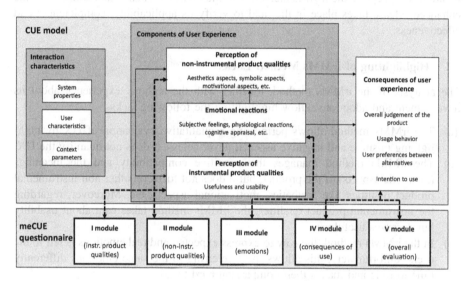

Fig. 2. CUE model and meCUE questionnaire.

The perceptions of non-instrumental product qualities consider aesthetics, symbolic and motivational aspects (visual and/or haptic qualities, associative or communicative symbolics, and personal growth, respectively). The emotional reactions consider aspects like subjective feelings, physiological reactions, cognitive appraisal, etc. Finally, the perceptions of instrumental product qualities include aspects like usefulness and usability. System properties, user characteristic and context parameters, all of them addressed in the figure as interaction characteristics, influence these three components. The consequences of the user experience, i.e., the overall judgement of the product, the usage behavior, the user preferences between alternatives and the intention to use, represent the outcomes of the main components. The meCUE questionnaire covers the CUE model thanks to five modules describing the perception of instrumental and non-instrumental product qualities, emotional reactions, consequences of use and the overall evaluation [8]. The first four modules contain question-like statements (thirty-four in all) that are evaluated using a 7-point Likert Scale reaching from 1 (strongly disagree) to 7 (strongly agree). The fifth module contains only the statement "finally, how would you rate the product overall?" and users rate it using values between -5 (bad) and 5 (good). All users' answers are collected separately for each module in order to compute specific mean values. Any combinations of modules can be selected to match the goal of the evaluation at best.

3 Activities

In order to achieve the goal of the research, we analyze possible lacks of the irMMs method and verify the meCUE capabilities in overcoming these lacks. After this verification, we integrate the irMMs method with the meCUE. Then, a first adoption of the enhanced release takes place in the field to verify its applicability, completeness and effectiveness.

3.1   Highlighting of irMMs Method Lacks

The analysis of the irMMs method, together with the authors' experience about its development and adoptions, allow highlighting the following lacks.

(a) The irMMs method allows performing a qualitative evaluation of UX by highlighting positive and negative aspects; nevertheless, it does not quantify the UX.

(b) The irMMs method manages the cognitive compatibility and the meanings (symbolic aspects) of the product, but it does not focus on other non-instrumental product qualities like aesthetics, motivational aspects, etc. Moreover, regarding the instrumental product qualities, the irMMs method takes care about usability but deserves usefulness.

(c) In the irMMs method, the way to express expected and real emotions is left to the users; unfortunately, this allows users referring to the same emotions differently time to time and makes their comparison hard to do.

(d) The irMMs method does not take care about possible changes in the users' opinions after the real interaction regarding usage behavior, user preferences between alternative products and intention to use.

3.2   Verifying the meCUE Capabilities in Overcoming the irMMs Method Lacks

The strongest point of the meCUE is the quantitative evaluation of the UX. This assures the overcoming of the first lack of the irMMs method (labelled as 'a' in the previous paragraph). The first two meCUE modules regard instrumental and non-instrumental product qualities; this can help overcoming the lack 'b' of the irMMs method since they deal with all those UX components deserved by the irMMs method now. The meCUE provides a fixed set of generic statements to define emotions; this makes their quantification and comparison easier, overcoming the lack 'c' of the irMMs method. Finally, the fourth module of the meCUE focuses on the consequences of use by collecting users' opinions about usage behavior, user preferences between alternatives and intention to use while the fifth module performs an overall evaluation of the whole experience by referring to the overall judgment of the product. Indeed, all of this can help in overcoming the lack 'd' of the irMMs method because it allows a deeper investigation of users' evaluation after the real interaction.

3.3   Integrating the irMMs Method with the meCUE

Once assessed the meCUE suitability to the research goal, the integration of the irMMs method takes place. Figure 3 shows the result of this. White boxes represent those activities of the irMMs method that remain as they are; four grayed boxes contain activities modified and seven grayed boxes with bold text indicate the new activities added by the integration.

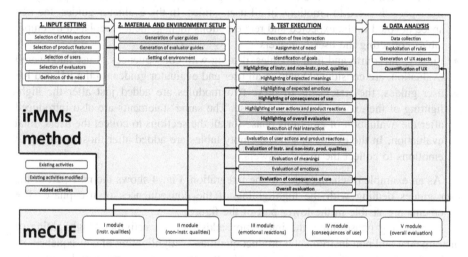

Fig. 3. Integration of the irMMs method with the meCUE.

The integration implies changes in phase two (material and environmental setup), changes and additions in phase three (test execution) and additions in phase four (data analysis).

Changes in phase two affect the existing activities "generation of user guides" and "generation of evaluator guides"; they occur as follows.

- The statements of the first meCUE module, dealing with the instrumental product qualities, are considered in all user and evaluator guides. Referring to the RB and RE user guides, these statements are introduced after the goal identification and before the highlighting of the meanings phases in order to collect the expectations about the product. The same statements are also introduced after the real interaction for all the sections to collect the users' final evaluation. The evaluator guides are modified to collect the users' answers classified by section and to compute the final mean values. In order to obtain this, empty tables are introduced after the free space devoted to the generation of the UX aspects.

- The second module, dealing with the non-instrumental product qualities, is considered in all user and evaluator guides as well. Its statements are inserted in the RB and RE user guides just after those of the first module. The same statements are also introduced again after the real interaction after the statements of the first module for all the sections. The presence of the meanings in the irMMs method suggests adding two statements not appearing in the meCUE. These statements are "the product evokes in my mind many different past experiences" and "I can identify the product in many situations of my life". The new statements are added to quantify the contribution of the meanings while reasoning about non-instrumental product qualities. In the evaluator guides, empty tables are added after those focused on the instrumental product qualities to collect and manage the users' answers.
- The statements of the third module, dealing with emotions, replace completely the free space devoted to emotions in all user guides. In the evaluator guides, the free space devoted to the expected and real emotions management is replaced by empty tables collecting the users' answers.
- Finally, the fourth and fifth modules, dealing with consequences of use and overall evaluation, are considered again in all user and evaluator guides. In the RB and RE user guides, the statements of these two modules are added just after the highlighting of the expected emotions phase. The same statements are also introduced after the evaluation of emotions phase for all the sections to collect the users' final evaluation. In the evaluator guides, empty tables are added after those referring to emotions to collect the users' answers.

As an example of changes due to the integration, Fig. 4 shows the new part of the user guides dealing with the highlighting of the consequences of use phase. The statements are visible in the lower part of the figure.

Considering phase three, the integration adds the new activities "highlighting of instrumental and non-instrumental product qualities", "highlighting of consequences of use", "highlighting of overall evaluation", "evaluation of instrumental and non-instrumental product qualities", "evaluation of consequences of use" and "overall evaluation". Moreover, the integration introduces changes to the existing activities "highlighting of expected emotions" and "evaluation of emotions". These additions and changes correspond to the answering to every statement just introduced in all the user guides.

Finally, considering phase four, the integration adds the new activity "quantification of UX". The new empty tables added by the integration allow the evaluators collecting the users' answers divided by section. Considering each section separately, evaluators compute the mean values two times. The first computation is on the answers of the RB and RE users about the highlighting of their expectations on the product; the second computation refers to the answers of all the users about the final evaluation of the UX. Finally, the evaluators compute the overall mean value considering the sections altogether. This new activity enriches the evaluation outcomes from two points of view: first, quantitative data appear along with the qualitative ones; second, the granularity of this computation allows comparing the results of the sections to each other.

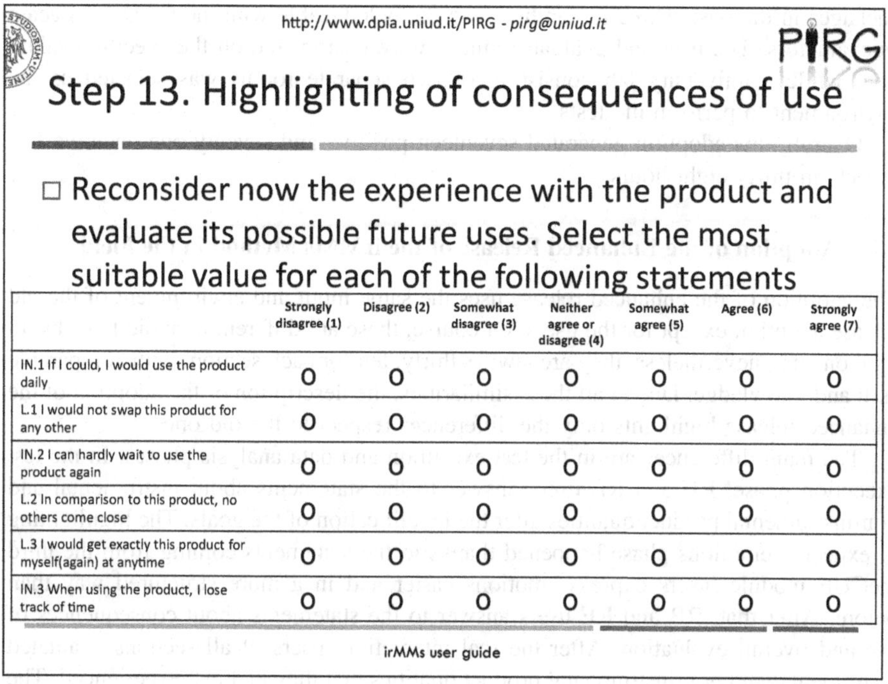

http://www.dpia.uniud.it/PIRG - pirg@uniud.it

PIRG

Step 13. Highlighting of consequences of use

□ Reconsider now the experience with the product and evaluate its possible future uses. Select the most suitable value for each of the following statements

	Strongly disagree (1)	Disagree (2)	Somewhat disagree (3)	Neither agree or disagree (4)	Somewhat agree (5)	Agree (6)	Strongly agree (7)
IN.1 If I could, I would use the product daily	O	O	O	O	O	O	O
L.1 I would not swap this product for any other	O	O	O	O	O	O	O
IN.2 I can hardly wait to use the product again	O	O	O	O	O	O	O
L.2 In comparison to this product, no others come close	O	O	O	O	O	O	O
L.3 I would get exactly this product for myself(again) at anytime	O	O	O	O	O	O	O
IN.3 When using the product, I lose track of time	O	O	O	O	O	O	O

irMMs user guide

Fig. 4. The new part of the user guides related to the highlighting of the consequences of use phase.

4 First Validation of the Enhanced irMMs Method

What follows describes the adoptions of the old and of the enhanced releases of the irMMs method. These adoptions evaluate the UX of a state-of-the-art CAD software package developed by a well-known software house working in the engineering research and application field. This choice comes from the availability of past adoptions of the old release with the same product as well as of that of the users and evaluators to involve.

4.1 Adoption of the Old Release of the irMMs Method in the Field

The adoption of the old release occurred as described in Filippi and Barattin [10]. Only a summary of that experience is reported here.

The 3D modeling tool of the CAD software package was selected as product feature to evaluate and the need was "use the CAD software package available on the PC to generate the 3D model of the socket shown in the enclosed figure. This model will be for production. Please respect the assigned dimensions". All the sections of the irMMs method were selected and thirty users (ten for each section) took part to the tests; they were students of mechanical engineering university courses with good skill and knowledge about 3D modeling since they used one or more CAD software packages in the past. Three researchers very knowledgeable with the CAD field acted as evaluators. The user and evaluator guides were customized on the specific evaluation, while a university lab consisting of two separate rooms was selected as the environment to perform the tests.

Overall, this adoption generated seventeen positive and seventy-one negative UX aspects in thirty-eight hours.

4.2   Adoption of the Enhanced Release of the irMMs Method in the Field

The adoption of the enhanced release uses the same input and environment of the old release adoption except for the users. Of course, these are different to avoid bias due to fixation, etc.; nevertheless, they are always thirty, ten for each section, with comparable skill and knowledge. Due to all these similarities, the description of the adoption of the enhanced release highlights only the differences respect to the old one.

The main differences are in the test execution and data analysis phases. In the test execution phase, RB and RE users answer to the statements about instrumental and non-instrumental product qualities after the identification of the goals. The highlighting of expected emotions phase happened thanks to the statements coming from the third meCUE module; users express emotions easier and in a more structured way than before. After that, RB and RE users answer to the statements about consequences of use and overall evaluation. After the real interaction, users of all sections evaluated instrumental and non-instrumental product qualities that they had just experienced. The same statements to highlight expected emotions allow expressing the emotions after the real interaction. Then, users state the consequences of use and overall evaluation of the product. In the data analysis phase, the evaluators perform the quantitative analysis by exploiting the answers to the statements and compute the mean values for each meCUE module.

No problems arise all along the tests and this starts assessing the applicability of the enhanced release.

Overall, this adoption generates twenty-six positive and eighty-seven negative UX aspects in forty hours.

4.3   Results of the Two Adoptions

Table 1 reports the results of the two adoptions. AB, RB and RE columns contain the values corresponding to the three sections, separately; the ALL columns contain the results independently from the sections the data come from. The first row of the table reports the numbers of positive and negative UX aspects, without doubles. Next, gaps are classified as positive and negative as well, doubles excluded again. The Goals row contains the mean values of the goals the users think as necessary to satisfy the need. The Expected meanings and Expected emotions rows contain the numbers of them, doubles excluded. It must be noticed that the number of expected emotions highlighted by the enhanced release is considered differently than before. Now, the set of emotions is fixed and users just rate them. If a user does not feel one or more emotions, he/she rates them with the neutral value 4, "neither agree nor disagree", because the user guides do not allow marking those emotions as "not applicable". For this reason, the enhanced release considers as expected all those emotions scoring differently from 4. The Changes of meanings and Changes of emotions rows contain the numbers of positive and negative changes, doubles excluded. The rows from Instrumental product qualities to Overall evaluation contain the mean values of the scores given by the users to the corresponding statements before and after the real interaction. Obviously, these rows apply only for the enhanced release; moreover, the mean values consider RB and RE sections only (except for the module devoted to the emotions that considers AB users too) because AB users cannot be asked for opinions about a specific product that they cannot know in advance. Finally, the last row reports the time to conduct each adoption.

Table 1. Results of the adoptions of the old and of the enhanced releases.

Results		Old release				Enhanced release			
		AB	RB	RE	ALL	AB	RB	RE	ALL
UX aspects (#; no doubles)	Positive	4	8	11	17	9	10	13	26
	Negative	36	24	22	71	40	31	22	87
Gaps (#; no doubles)	Positive	2	4	4	8	5	7	7	14
	Negative	20	11	9	36	20	14	15	39
Goals (mean)		6.0	4.7	3.3	4.7	5.2	5.0	4.7	4.9
Expected meanings (#; no doubles)		5	10	8	14	9	5	8	16
Expected emotions (#; no doubles)		8	5	5	8	10	12	11	12
Changes of meanings (#; no doubles)	Positive	0	0	2	2	2	0	1	3
	Negative	3	1	4	8	2	1	2	4
Changes of emotions (#; no doubles)	Positive	4	8	6	12	13	4	6	9
	Negative	17	10	5	22	4	2	4	6
Instrumental product qualities (means)	Before	N/A	N/A	N/A	N/A	N/A	5.89	5.11	5.50
	After	N/A	N/A	N/A	N/A	5.33	5.89	5.17	5.53
Non-instrumental product qualities (means)	Before	N/A	N/A	N/A	N/A	N/A	4.39	3.53	3.96
	After	N/A	N/A	N/A	N/A	3.89	4.36	3.26	3.81
Emotions (means)	Before	N/A	N/A	N/A	N/A	2.97	3.72	3.58	3.42
	After	N/A	N/A	N/A	N/A	3.39	3.86	3.58	3.61
Consequences of use (means)	Before	N/A	N/A	N/A	N/A	N/A	4.33	3.56	3.95
	After	N/A	N/A	N/A	N/A	3.06	4.78	3.22	4.00
Overall evaluation (means)	Before	N/A	N/A	N/A	N/A	N/A	2.33	2.67	2.50
	After	N/A	N/A	N/A	N/A	2.67	4.00	2.67	3.34
Time for adoption (hours)		16	13	9	38	17	15	10	42

The enhanced release generated the 153% of positive UX aspects and the 123% of negative ones of the old release. A similar situation occurred for the gaps, where the enhanced release found more positive and negative gaps than the old one, considering both each section separately and in general. The mean values related to the goals as well as the numbers of expected meanings are similar for the two releases, in general. The numbers of expected emotions in the enhanced release are higher than in the old one, considering both each section separately and in general. Changes of meanings decreased from the old (10) to the enhanced (7) release and the same occurred for the changes of emotions (34 vs. 15). Among the general mean values of the data collected thanks to the statements, the instrumental product qualities show the highest mean values before and after the real interaction (5.50 and 5.53, respectively) while the overall evaluation shows the lowest mean values before and after the real interaction (2.50 and 3.34, respectively); the non-instrumental product qualities, emotions and consequences of use report quite low mean values, all of them in the range [3.42, 4.00]. Finally, the time to adopt the enhanced release was slightly higher (42 h) than that of the old release (38 h).

Qualitatively speaking, the most of the positive and negative UX aspects identified by the enhanced release were highlighted also by the old one. Examples of them are the positive UX aspects referring to the intuitiveness of some menu icons and to the possibility of modeling parts and assemblies in the same environment and the negative UX aspects about the functionality to create square holes, about the setting of the model view and about the dimensioning command. Nevertheless, the enhanced release reported thirty fresh UX aspects; some examples of them are the negative UX aspects referring to the low number of options in the main menu bar and to the missed command to generate construction lines and the positive UX aspect referring to the presence of the local menu in the extrusion functionality. On the other hand, the old release reported only five fresh UX aspects; one example of them, positive, consists of the availability of different file formats to export the model.

5 Discussion

The adoptions in the field of the two releases of the irMMs method and the comparison of the results start assessing the applicability, completeness and effectiveness of the enhanced release. Its adoption occurred without problems and this supports its applicability. Completeness is witnessed by the presence of both quantitative and qualitative evaluations; moreover, these evaluations consider all the UX components (instrumental and non-instrumental product qualities and emotional reactions), as well as the consequences of use and the overall evaluation of the product. Finally, two elements assess the effectiveness of the enhanced release. The first element is the presence of thirty fresh aspects against the five of the old release; the most of them refer to the usefulness, usability and appearance of the product and are mainly due the different number of gaps and to the richer final users' comments. The second element is the capability of the quantitative analysis to identify precisely the weak points of the product features to improve (lower-scoring modules than the others) and the strong points to strengthen (modules showing higher mean values). Clearly, all of this happens because of the integration with the meCUE. The following two reasons seem to be responsible for it. First, the statements seems to push the users towards paying attention to other aspects than those strictly connected to the cognitive compatibility. For example, an RB user wrote as a final comment "to me, this CAD software package is not suitable for professionals; it is more for education because of the coarse way commands are shown (many commands are hidden), because of the unique way to save models (in the cloud only), etc." As the user reported, this aspect came to his mind thanks to the statements about aesthetics and consequences of use. The second reason supporting the effectiveness of the enhanced release seems to be the ability of the meCUE to encourage users focusing on the positive characteristics of the products under evaluation. For example, an RB user and two RE users reported that they appreciated the icons of the main menu as well as the labels of the local menus of different functionalities because they were clear and easy to interpret without further explanations. One of the RE users also wrote that his considerations were evoked by answering to the statements focused on usability (instrumental product qualities module). None of the users exploiting the old release reported similar reasons in their final comments, nor these comments were so focused on positive characteristics of the product under evaluation.

Currently, this research shows some drawbacks. Some statements appear as too generic against the way the irMMs method conducts the evaluation where all the elements (the need, the request for meanings, user actions and product reactions/feedback, etc.) are customized on the product. All of this makes the user guides uneven; sometimes users asked for changing the statements to make them referring more precisely to the CAD software package because they did not know how to interpret them. Unfortunately, this customization is not allowed by the enhanced release now. The enhanced release does not ask the users the reasons why they give specific scores to the statements. This is a problem because UX aspects can be generated only starting from the reasons that support those scores. Some users just wrote their reasons as final comments but the most of them did not report anything. Therefore, precious pieces of information got lost. The possible benefit of the UX quantification has only been mentioned (weak and strong points identification); there is not any discussion about this. The enhanced release requires more time to conduct the tests and to analyze the data because of the presence of many new activities. Sometimes users were annoyed or almost upset because of this. Finally, the enhanced release has not been validated with adoptions involving different products and users as well as against other UX evaluation methods and tools.

6 Conclusions

The research described in this paper aimed at enhancing the existing irMMs-based UX evaluation method. This was achieved by analyzing its lacks and verifying if the meCUE questionnaire capabilities could overcome these lacks. Once assessed this, the irMMs-based UX evaluation method has been integrated with the meCUE by modifying materials and activities. Finally, a first validation of the enhanced release took place to assess the improvement in terms of applicability, completeness and effectiveness.

Some research perspectives are as follows. The statements in the user guides should be customized against the product under evaluation. All of this would avoid users misunderstanding them during the tests. The reasons why users give specific scores to the statements should be asked and collected in suitable tables or free spaces, all of this in order to allow generating new UX aspects from them. Possible exploitations of the UX quantification should be deeply addressed because they could give precious hints and suggestions for product redesign. For example, the strong point of the CAD software package concerning the instrumental product qualities module can be strengthened by turning those appreciated images that appear now on menu buttons into short videos showing the correct use of the functionalities. Because of the addition of the statements, the activities of all sections of the irMMs method should be optimized to avoid time-consuming tests. For example, the same statements should not appear in two separate tables because this forces the users to jump back and forth in the user guides to compare their expectations (before the real interaction) to what happens for real (after it). There should be unique tables only, containing both the spaces to fill before and after the real interaction. Users would be more concentrated and the results less affected by annoyance and/or tiredness. Finally, a deeper validation of the enhanced release should take place in order to demonstrate its completeness and effectiveness. This validation must involve different products, situations and users (not all recruited from university courses), as well as other UX evaluation methods and tools, like the Valence method [13] or the Tracking Real-Time User Experience [14].

References

1. Law, E.L.C., Roto, V., Hassenzahl, M., Vermeeren, A.P.O.S., Kort, J.: Understanding, scoping and defining user eXperience: a survey approach. In: Greenberg, S., Hudson, S.E., Hinckley, K., Morris, M.L., Olsen, D.R. (eds.) Conference on Human Factors in Computing Systems, CHI 2009, pp. 719–728. ACM, New York (2009)
2. Park, J., Han, S.H., Kim, H.K., Cho, Y., Park, W.: Developing elements of user experience for mobile phones and services: survey, interview, and observation approaches. Hum. Fact. Ergonom. Manuf. Serv. Ind. 23(4), 279–293 (2013)
3. International Standard ISO 9241-210.: Ergonomics of human-system interaction. Part 210: Human-centred design for interactive systems (2010)
4. Hassenzahl, M.: The hedonic/pragmatic model of user experience. In: Law, E., Vermeeren, A., Hassenzahl, M., Blythe, M. (eds.) Towards a UX Manifesto. COST294-MAUSE Affiliated Workshop 2007, pp. 10–14 (2007)
5. Kort, J., Vermeeren, A.P.O.S., Fokker, J.E.: Conceptualizing and measuring user eXperience. In: Law, E., Vermeeren, A., Hassenzahl, M., Blythe, M. (eds.) Towards a UX Manifesto. COST294-MAUSE Affiliated Workshop 2007, pp. 57–64 (2007)
6. Desmet, P.M.A., Hekkert, P.: Framework of product experience. Int. J. Des. 1(1), 57–66 (2007)
7. Minge, M., Thüring, M.: The meCUE questionnaire (2.0): meeting five basic requirements for lean and standardized UX assessment. In: Marcus, A., Wang, W. (eds.) DUXU 2018. LNCS, vol. 10918, pp. 451–469. Springer, Cham (2018). https://doi.org/10.1007/978-3-319-91797-9_33
8. Hassenzahl, M.: The interplay of beauty, goodness, and usability in interactive products. Hum. Comput. Interact. 19, 319–349 (2004)
9. Rauschenberger, M., Schrepp, M., Cota, M.P., Olschner, S., Thomaschewski, J.: Efficient measurement of the user experience of interactive products. How to use the user experience questionnaire (UEQ). Example: Spanish Language Version. Int. J. Artif. Intell. Interact. Multimed. 2(1), 39–45 (2013)

10. Filippi, S., Barattin, D.: Considering users' different knowledge about products to improve a UX evaluation method based on mental models. In: Marcus, A., Wang, W. (eds.) DUXU 2018. LNCS, vol. 10918, pp. 367–378. Springer, Cham (2018). https://doi.org/10.1007/978-3-319-91797-9_26

11. Norman, D.: The Design of Everyday Things. Revised and Expanded Edition. Basic Book, New York (2013)

12. Thuring, M., Mahlke, S.: Usability, aesthetics and emotions in human-computer technology interaction. Int. J. Psychol. **42**(4), 253–264 (2007)

13. Burmester, M., Mast, M., Kilian, J., Homans, H.: Valence method for formative evaluation of user experience. In: Halskov, K., Petersen, M.G. (eds.) Designing Interactive Systems Conference 2010, pp. 364–367. ACM, New York (2010)

14. Kim, J.H., Gunn, D.V., Schuh, E., Phillips, B.C., Pagulayan, R.J., Wixon, D.: Tracking real-time user experience (TRUE): a comprehensive instrumentation solution for complex systems. In: Burnett, M., et al. (eds.) International Conference of Human-Computer Interaction, CHI 2008, pp. 443–451. ACM, New York (2008)

A User Study to Examine the Different Approaches in the Computer-Aided Design Process

Chen Guo[1(✉)], Yingjie Victor Chen[2(✉)], and Zhenyu Cheryl Qian[2(✉)]

[1] James Madison University, Harrisonburg, VA 22801, USA
guo4cx@jmu.edu
[2] Purdue University, West Lafayette, IN 47907, USA
{victorchen, qianz}@purdue.edu

Abstract. The computer-aided design process is in a complicated non-linear structure involving selections from a pool of configurations with optimized parameters. In order to understand and improve this decision-making process, this paper conducted a user study on students and expert professionals with more than three years of computer-aided design experience. The study revealed the common design problems and challenges faced by CAD designers. The findings also showed that the design approaches students and expert professionals used were different. Additionally, we found that computer-aided designers expect the system to be able to understand vast quantities of multivariate data, control high-quality products for low costs, manage the knowledge personalization and codification within the company, as well as prevent the design mistakes at the design stages. Our findings may lead to the future development of new approaches to improve the computer-aided design process and close up the gap between student and expert professionals in computer-aided design. This paper provides initial support for this future approach.

Keywords: User study · Computer-aided design · Design process

1 Introduction

Situated in the highly competitive industry markets, companies are facing many challenges such as reducing design time length and lead-times, quick design turnovers, and significant quality improvements. Computer-aided design (CAD) must be optimized to reduce development time while satisfying constraints and improving manufacturability. The engineering design process is a complicated non-linear model involving selections from a set of configurations. Thus, a deep understanding of design problems in computer-aided design is very important for researchers and practitioners to build a decision-making tool to assist the process.

Poli [1] introduced three basic engineering design problem types: conceptual, parametric and configuration designs. Conceptual design involves the gathering of customer requirements and transforming these statements into parameters [2]. The parametric design achieves optimal values for parameters and satisfies a set of

© Springer Nature Switzerland AG 2019
A. Marcus and W. Wang (Eds.): HCII 2019, LNCS 11586, pp. 134–142, 2019.
https://doi.org/10.1007/978-3-030-23535-2_9

requirements [3]. Configuration design selects and combines a set of pre-defined components to meet unique requirements [4]. Many design tasks that aim to solve these problems involve selection from a set of configurations followed by parametric optimization of the chosen configuration [5]. However, we see people use different ways to solve these design problems although they mostly follow the same general approach. In order to better understand this complicated design process, we conducted a user study to gather participants' descriptions of their design experience from both students and professionals in the CAD field.

2 Related Work

2.1 Scientific Foundations of Design

Many design problem can be informally described as a problem in which a set of needs and desires is given and where the solution is a description of some structure that satisfies these needs and desires [6]. Often, the needs and desires are specified in an informal way and leave much unsaid. The designer has to perform an analysis process that transforms the needs and desires into a more formal and complete set of requirements and constraints.

Some researchers utilized an input-output model to describe the design process [7]. The design process is to compute a set of performance parameters from a set of input parameters, based on a mathematical model. The design task is to specify a set of inputs that yield outputs satisfying specified criteria. These inputs typically include a configuration choice as well as values for the parameters associated with that configuration, called design parameters. Values for design parameters must satisfy constraints among variables arising from specialized engineering and other disciplines. The form of the constraints varies in complexity from heuristics to logical relations, to partial differential equations.

Some researchers are particularly interested in developing tools to assist the designer in the preliminary phase of engineering design, by making more information available on the performance of design alternatives than is available using conventional design techniques [8]. This technique calculates the approximate output quantities from the imprecise input parameters for each of the design alternatives and determines the qualitative relations between the input parameters and the performance parameters (outputs). The designer is able to rank the input parameters according to their impact on the performance parameters and to rate a design alternative according to its merit in relation to the others under consideration.

2.2 Computer-Aided Design in the Design Process

Computer-aided design (CAD) has been widely used to create 2D and 3D graphic representations from conceptual design to manufacturing. In addition to traditional drawing and sketching, both novice designers and highly experienced designers complete the concept design, embodiment design, and detail design phase through CAD tools [9]. However, as CAD tools are sophisticated, it still remains unanswered how CAD application affects the cognitive aspects of problem-solving in the design process and the final design. Veisz, Namouz, Joshi, and Summers [10] investigated the CAD design process through a case study of a senior design project. The researchers found that CAD tools positively contribute to design efficiency and effectiveness in the later design process. The use of CAD at the earliest stage of design may lead to a loss of design efficiency and effectiveness. Häggman et al. [11] asked eighteen experienced engineers and designers to generate concepts and address design task using sketches, prototypes, or CAD. The study aims to examine how designers generate and represent ideas, as well as the interplay between the choice of the design tool, design attributes, and user evaluations of design quality. Pei, Campbell, and Evans [12] conducted empirical research to reveal the inter-disciplinary collaboration pattern during new product development. They found that inspiration sketches were never employed by engineering designers. Sketches and drawings are mainly used at the concept design and development stage. Models and prototypes are commonly used at the embedment design and detail design stages.

Research has shown that the CAD design process demands the appropriate design tools and methods. In turn, different design tools affect the design exploration and final outcome. To better understand the impact of design tools on the design process, further empirical research on understanding CAD designers' design approach and strategy is recommended.

2.3 Knowledge-Based Capturing for CAD Design

In this paper, we also explore the formal foundations of methods to solve a class of design problems that require the assignment of values to a set of design parameters (parametric design). A general approach is to use knowledge-based systems to assess product design, determine tooling needs, complete their process designs and deliver products on time [13].

Rocca [14] provides a comprehensive review of Knowledge Base Engineering (KBE) in the purpose of extending the level of understanding of its technology fundaments. KBE system is developed towards the specific needs of the engineering design, which comes from a cross point of diverse fundamental disciplines of artificial intelligence (AI), computer-aided design (CAD) and computer programming. Some of the KBE features are caching and dependency tracking. KBE product model represents a generative design that it doesn't make up of fixed geometric entities, with fixed dimensions, in a fixed configuration, but it contains the engineering rules that at run-time we will determine the design of the product.

Bermell-Gracia and Fan [15], conduct a searching survey of a large international engineering consultancy firm and a leading PLM/KBE software vendor in order to understand the needs for future PLM-base Knowledge-based system and their associated interoperability issues. Due to the small data sample, the study focuses on a qualitative analysis of the data, which considering the background of the participants and the value of their inputs provide useful insights. All practitioners who are involved in functions of KBE/PLM integration were given a literature survey as initial data collection, and unstructured interviews as further data collection. The analysis of interview transcripts and meeting notes helps narrow down the selected practitioners for the final set of data. The final outcome of the study is a ranked set of business functionalities that the interviewed participants expect to be fulfilled from the KBE/PLM integration.

Toussaint, Demoly, Lebaal, and Gomes [16] developed an approach to accelerate routine processes in engineering design. In industrial companies, approximately 80% of the time spent in engineering is devoted to routine engineering activities and the remainder 20% is dedicated to innovation. The process from design to manufacturing requires important amounts of data and information, which mostly relies on the experience gathered from the development of previous projects. This knowledge often does not get captured or managed properly for future uses. Because only a limited number of "experts" have the information, organizations will run into time-wasting project delays. Product Lifecycle Management (PLM) approach integrates knowledge base on engineering features, such as expert rules definition or design experience feedbacks, in order to reduce costs, lead time, and also improve product qualities and values.

3 Methodology

3.1 The Semi-structured Interview

We aim to identify CAD design problems, especially for configuration and parametric design. The semi-structured interview allowed us to understand designers' attitudes and thoughts during the design process.

The subjects chosen for this study were graduate students, educators from Purdue University, and industrial CAD designers. All the participants have more than three years of CAD design experience. The 17 participants include three professional CAD educator, five CAD professional designers, nine graduate students. One-third of them are female.

A semi-structured interview allows participants to fully describe their personal experiences relating to the CAD design process. Each interview lasted about 30 to 40 min. The participants had the same interviewer and were put through the same interview process with the same interview questions. We started with general questions to gather demographic data about the participants' educational background and work experience (Table 1). Next, we asked open-ended questions focused on their design process, methods, and tools used to design a product, as well as design successes and failure (Table 1).

After gathering enough feedback from respondents, we read the transcripts and transformed the initial notes into emerging themes. A qualitative approach was essential here to capture potentially elusive qualities of individuals' design conceptions, with the goal of rich description. The bottom-up grounded theory was used to analyze our data. In the theme analysis, meanings rely on different design context. We picked up the most prevalent and important issues that contribute most to our analysis and deleted some overlapping items. We referred back to our transcription to reach a consensus that the selective codes are the most important ones affecting the overall user experiences. In the end, we refined the final categories by combining some relevant sub-categories together. The findings are reported in the next section.

Table 1. A list of interview questions.

Question number	Interview question
1	What is your name?
2	What is your role and position in the company/university? (for educator and CAD practitioner)
3	Tell us about your education background
4	How many years of experience do you have as a CAD designer?
5	Can you tell us about a recent CAD project you have been working on?
6	Can you walk through how you design a product?
7	What are your design approach and design strategy adopted in the project?
8	What has been your experience when it comes to planning out the key parameters of your design?
9	Describe the tools and methods used to design a product
10	What makes it difficult for you to design a product?
11	Names the success or failure factors in CAD design

3.2   Findings

There are three levels in our findings: (1) an overview of participants' description, (2) engineers' choices of the most and the least important design activities, and (3) problems and challenges during the engineering design process from both academic and professional practice perspectives.

The General Engineering Design Process
All the participants followed the general iterative design process that contains the steps of problem identification, ideation, design exploration, prototype development, to the refinement of design. Several of the design steps were heavily discussed during the interview.

Identifying Design Problems Through Benchmark, Customer Requirements and Design Research
    The common strategies designers used were conducting interviews with potential customers, organizing focus groups, and observing similar products in use. It was important for them to identify the customer needs and wants, which included problems that customers were unaware of or accepted without questioning.

Brainstorming and Generating Product Concepts
    In this process, engineering designers generated a number of product concepts while considering technical feasibility that matched the requirements of the target group. To narrow down the list, a comparison is made between the ideas based on the best product architecture and layout alternative.

Selecting the Final Product Concept
    Engineering designers assessed the trade-off between various design attributes. The final specification result of the trade-off was made between technical feasibility,

expected service life, projected selling price, and the financial limitations of the project. This specification may keep on changing until all product attributes were satisfied. During this process, a virtual prototype was developed.

Detail Design Process

Figure 1 displays the result of frequently used terms in respondents' description of the design in their interviews. Most of the respondents talked about how to understand the design problem, how to get all the constraints, how to communicate with customers, and how to seek information and make a decision. It is interesting to note that "problems" was ranked higher than others.

Fig. 1. The word cloud of frequently used terms.

For most graduate CAD design students, sketches, drawing, and prototypes were mainly concerned with the design and technical information. Engineering designers often created their own sketches on paper in order to visualize the product. While sketching, they specified the critical dimension according to the product specification and product function. While building a CAD model, they use sketches and spreadsheets for product specification to manage the product information.

For the experienced CAD practitioners and educators, the process is a little different. Instead of creating new parts, the company tends to reuse the CAD models they built before. This model is kept on being modified until it satisfies the requirements. This method saves the company time, effort, and money on designing the product from sketch while providing a boundary of design practices among the company's products. These design boundaries are common company's knowledge and practice base standard, cost, supply chain, material, etc. They always use PDM and PLM systems such as Teamcenter to manage the product information. Table 2 shows the differences in the detail design process between graduate CAD design students and experienced CAD practitioners and educators.

Table 2. The differences in the detail design process between graduate CAD design students and the experienced CAD practitioners and educators.

Categories	Graduate CAD design students	CAD practitioners and educators
How to form design concepts	Use less structured forms of representations such as sketches and models	Reuse the previous product CAD model they have already created
How to specify the critical dimension	Based on product specification and product function	Based on the product requirement and customer needs
How to manage the product information	Sketches and spreadsheets	PDM and PLM systems such as Teamcenter

Common Design Problems and Challenges

We found that CAD designers have some common challenges during the process of designing and managing the product's CAD design.

Understanding Vast Quantities of Multivariate Data

In the CAD design process, there is a huge amount of multivariate data. Multivariate data, also termed hypervariate data, is defined for a high dimensionality of three or above. Modeling the data in a 3D space is the most straightforward way, but problems arise with displaying it in a two-dimensional representation. Mathematicians consider dimension as the number of independent variables in an algebraic equation. Engineers take dimension as measurements of breadth, length, height, and thickness.

As products become complex, it is very difficult for CAD designers to interpret the vast quantity of information. It still requires extensive work to create visualizations to best display the data in a meaningful and comprehensible way.

Controlling the Manufacturing Cost of High-Quality Products

In order to be more competitive, there is a demand to create an expensive product but cheap to manufacture. Creating such a product means to have the best quality while reducing the number of necessary components, streamlining the design, eliminating redundancies, reusing parts from the previous project and promoting standard parts.

Managing the Knowledge Personalization and Codification Within the Company

This refers to the product knowledge that the company has been collected over the years. The information is either stored in the company's databases (product information and knowledge) or personalized (individual's knowledge and experience over years). The biggest challenges are finding the right people who have the resources.

Though codifications are stored in the computer for long-term use, personalize knowledge is not. To access these personalize knowledge, it required different communication methods such as face-to-face conversation, email, CSWS, etc. The biggest challenges are finding the right people who have the answer. When these people are retired or remove from the company, the organization loses the resources from them.

Preventing the Design Mistakes at the Early Design Stages

Engineering designers usually have a difficult time to discover design mistakes until much later in the process, which lead to more costs and more time to recover the product. For example: when a part is designed to a wrong dimension, the designer might not able to discover until the manufacturing process that the part cannot be assembly.

Attitudes to Parametric Modeling

Some designers thought that parametric modeling tools such as Pro/ENGINEER were very hard to learn because it is script-based and requires training. However, almost all the designers loved to use Grasshopper since it uses a very visual plug and plays interface to automate the scripting. Since Grasshopper is very flexible, users can set up almost any kind of relationship they like. The graph visualization platform in Grasshopper is also helpful for engineering to view all the completed relationship. It inspired us to find a solution and provide a visualization way to allow designers to generate models more easily. Experienced designers can re-compute the outputs once the inputs are changed in a reasonable time but are usually unable to generate multiple solutions.

We summarized the features that CAD designers desired to generate parametric models:

- Automatic computation of several sets of inputs that achieve the desired targets.
- Need a reference or standard model for comparison. The configuration will be changed based on different perception.
- Use of an explicit optimality criterion.
- Faster re-calculation of outputs when inputs are changed.

4   Conclusions

The CAD design process is complex and dynamic. We reviewed the current problems and challenges in the CAD design area and presented the students' and professionals' solutions. Our study may benefit the community in two directions. Firstly, educators should fill the gap between students and professional designers by introducing more collected scenarios and strategies. Secondly, we should explore new approaches to handling the complex engineering design problem, especially during this large data era, the product itself and the design process may carry a large amount of information. Handling such information visually may improve engineering design.

References

1. Poli, C.: Design for Manufacturing: A Structured Approach. Butterworth-Heinemann, Oxford (2001)
2. Kroll, E., Condoor, S.S., Jansson, D.G.: Innovative Conceptual Design: Theory and Application of Parameter Analysis. Cambridge University Press, Cambridge (2001)

3. Myung, S., Han, S.: Knowledge-based parametric design of mechanical products based on configuration design method. Expert Syst. Appl. **21**, 99–107 (2001)
4. Mittal, S., Frayman, F.: Towards a generic model of configuration tasks. In: Proceedings of the 11th International Joint Conference on Artificial Intelligence, vol. 2, pp. 1395–1401. Morgan Kaufmann Publishers Inc., San Francisco, CA (1989)
5. Ramaswamy, R., Ulrich, K., Kishi, N., Tomikashi, M.: Solving parametric design problems requiring configuration choices. J. Mech. Des. **115**, 20–28 (1993)
6. Wielinga, B.J., Akkermans, J.M., Schreiber, A.T.: A formal analysis of parametric design problem solving. In: Proceedings of the 9th Banff Knowledge Acquisition Workshop (KAW 1995), p. 37-1 (1995)
7. Ramaswamy, R., Ulrich, K.T., Kishi, N.: Solving Parametric Design Problems Requiring Configuration Choices. Sloan School of Management, Massachusetts Institute of Technology, Cambridge (1991)
8. Antonsson, E.K., Otto, K.N.: Imprecision in engineering design. J. Mech. Des. **117**, 25–32 (1995)
9. Vidal, R., Mulet, E.: Thinking about computer systems to support design synthesis. Commun. ACM **49**, 100–104 (2006)
10. Veisz, D., Namouz, E.Z., Joshi, S., Summers, J.D.: Computer-aided design versus sketching: an exploratory case study. AI EDAM **26**, 317–335 (2012)
11. Häggman, A., Tsai, G., Elsen, C., Honda, T., Yang, M.C.: Connections between the design tool, design attributes, and user preferences in early stage design. J. Mech. Des. **137**, 071408–071408-13 (2015)
12. Pei, E., Campbell, I.R., Evans, M.A.: Development of a tool for building shared representations among industrial designers and engineering designers. CoDesign **6**, 139–166 (2010)
13. Akkermans, H., Wielinga, B., Schreiber, G.: Steps in constructing problem solving methods. In: Aussenac, N., Boy, G., Gaines, B., Linster, M., Ganascia, J.-G., Kodratoff, Y. (eds.) EKAW 1993. LNCS, vol. 723, pp. 45–65. Springer, Heidelberg (1993). https://doi.org/10.1007/3-540-57253-8_47
14. Rocca, G.L.: Knowledge based engineering: between AI and CAD. Review of a language based technology to support engineering design. Adv. Eng. Inform. **26**, 159–179 (2012)
15. Garcia, P.B., Fan, I.S.: Practitioner requirements for integrated knowledge-based engineering in product lifecycle management. Int. J. Prod. Lifecycle Manag. **3**, 3 (2008)
16. Toussaint, L., Demoly, F., Lebaal, N., Gomes, S.: PLM-based approach for design verification and validation using manufacturing process knowledge (2013)

Developing Usability Heuristics
for Recommendation Systems
Within the Mobile Context

Zhao Huang[✉]

School of Computer Science, Shaanxi Normal University,
Xi'an 710119, People's Republic of China
zhaohuang@snnu.edu.cn

Abstract. The rapid development of advanced mobile technologies and wireless Internet services has accelerated the explosion of the mobile service market. Such an extension encourages an increasing number of users engaging in mobile applications. However, the challenge of designing "useful" mobile applications still remains. To overcome this challenge, this study conducts a systematic review of mobile applications, identifying a set of heuristics and relevant features in mobile applications design. More specifically, seven usability heuristics, namely navigation, content, error handling, consistency, functionality, cognitive load and aesthetic design have been developed for mobile applications. The results identify a number of design features based on the proposed usability heuristics, and the associated requirements of usability heuristic to mobile physical constraints are described. The major contribution is to propose a systematic analysis of mobile application usability for mobile developers and designers.

Keywords: Mobile devices · Mobile applications · Mobile usability ·
Usability heuristics

1 Introduction

Advanced mobile technologies have enabled the thousands of applications to be developed that can be used by people on their move [1]. The ability of the mobile applications to quickly learn and easily use is vital to users [2]. Poor usability of those applications might be rejected, not used or even removed from mobile devices [3]. Therefore, usability is an important part of mobile applications, which needs to be carefully considered when developing mobile applications. However, the study of usability in aspects of mobile applications is an emerging research area, facing the significant challenges due to the unique features of mobile devices, such as small screen size, lack of display resolution, limited connectivity, high power consumption rates, different processing capability, single input modalities and complex context of use [4]. To overcome these challenges, the usability heuristics need to be addressed during all the steps of mobile applications development. Some studies have emphasized on the platform-based heuristics in aspects of design issues of mobile applications (e.g. Apple, Android design guidelines [5]). Other studies have focused on extending the

© Springer Nature Switzerland AG 2019
A. Marcus and W. Wang (Eds.): HCII 2019, LNCS 11586, pp. 143–151, 2019.
https://doi.org/10.1007/978-3-030-23535-2_10

existing heuristics for mobile applications design (e.g. [6]), and exploring the impacts of mobile applications design (e.g. [7]) and user engagement by analyzing their task implementation (e.g. [3]). We argued that these heuristics are too general to evaluate usability of mobile applications, especially without necessary considerations of the unique features of mobile applications.

To this end, this research aims to provide a systematic review of mobile applications analysis and design, identifying main heuristics and their associated features in mobile applications design from a user experience perspective. To be more specific, seven usability heuristics, namely navigation, content, error handling, consistency, functionality, cognitive load and aesthetic design have been developed for mobile applications. Our main contribution is to propose a systematic analysis of mobile applications for business managers and designers, providing a better understanding on how important usability design features are.

This paper is structured as follows. In Sect. 2 we provide some background on mobile application design. In Sect. 3 we present mobile usability heuristics development. We then detail and discuss usability heuristics with mobile physical limitations in Sect. 4. Finally, our conclusion, implications and limitations are detailed in Sect. 5.

2　Mobile Application Usability

The concept of usability from the International Standards Organization [25] can be simply defined as the effectiveness, efficiency and satisfaction. Venkatesh and Ramesh [8] further explain the usability in mobility, which is about the degree to which a mobile application can be used by particular users to achieve particular goals with effectiveness, efficiency, and satisfaction in a particular context of use. Some studies interpret the concept of mobile application usability that derives from website usability (e.g. [8]). For example, Joyce et al. [6] conduct a study to evaluate the usability of mobile computing applications, proposing a set of usability heuristics that is mainly developed by Nielsen's website usability guidelines. Similarly, a study conducted by Masooda and Thigambaram [9] who investigate the importance of usability in mobile educational applications design for children. All six heuristics used in usability testing evolve from website usability, including visibility of the system status, match between system and the real world, user control and freedom, consistency and standards, recognition rather than recall, and help and documentation. Although a useful starting point, we argue that they lack of research instructs that fit in the unique characteristics of mobile applications, such as small screen and context of use. This is also supported by Billi et al. [10], stressing that the distinctions between website heuristics and the mobile usability heuristics are the facts that website heuristics assume static desktop location and use, mobile heuristics address mobile usage and context.

Some explore research methods that evaluate usability of mobile applications [11]. For example, Zhang and Adipat [12] analyze two major traditional research methodologies used in mobile application usability testing, including laboratory experiments and field studies. Their results suggest that the selection of an appropriate methodology for a usability study depends on mobile application objectives and usability heuristics. Others develop the theoretical usability frameworks for mobile use. For instance,

Kjeldskov and Stage [13] propose a research framework that focuses on the different ways in which a user could be moving physically while using a mobile system, and users' notion of divided attention. The findings show that the framework supports the identification of usability problems that are experienced in mobile use. Although above mentioned studies provide insights into usability evaluation of mobile systems, it still lacks necessary considerations of multiplatform tests, and also only covers few number of usability heuristics used in mobile applications. To overcome such shortcomings, Mendes and Dias-Neto [14] employ a process-based approach comprised by process, artifacts templates and metrics for compatibility usability testing in multi-platform mobile applications. The results further address the importance of understanding usability by having a close look at relevant usability heuristics. Evidence shows that a variety of usability heuristics are helpful to address multiple aspects of usability. Therefore, seven usability heuristics were developed in our study (see Table 1).

Table 1. Usability heuristics

No.	Usability heuristic	Interpretation
U1	Navigation	To deploy easy navigation support and obvious user control
U2	Content provision	To provide quality content and information
U3	Error handling	To prevent error occurrence and support error correction
U4	Consistency	To keep the consistent design features and schemes
U5	Functionality	To ensure various functions in mobile applications well integrated
U6	Cognitive load	To minimize total amount of mental effort in working memory
U7	Aesthetics design	To grasp user attraction and be aesthetically pleasant

3   Research Method

To conduct a systematic literature review, this study follows the procedure provided by Kitchenham, consisting of searching, electronic source selection, results collection, results selection criteria and relevant paper identification (see Fig. 1). The search was carried out and relevant papers were retrieved based on our research aim. All retrieved papers were read thoroughly and selected based on the inclusion criteria, exclusion criteria and quality assessment criteria. The selected papers cover both journal articles and conference proceedings. Title and abstract of the papers were primarily employed to retrieve relevant journal and conference papers.

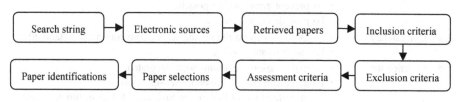

Fig. 1. Research process

Search string aims to search for all results that are related to mobile apps usability from the identified sources. These searching sources include IEEE Xplore, ACM Digital Library, Science Direct, Springer Link, Emerald, Wiley. The search strings used are based on our proposed research aims and have been considered into three different scopes as starting point, which are mobile devices, including mobile phones, smart phones and tablets, applications covering a diversity of mobile applications, and the topic of usability studies.

4 Usability Heuristics Development

Having indicated a high level of usability heuristics, this section describes a set of usability features relating to usability heuristics. Each usability feature is a particular design focus that is used to measure the quality of mobile applications. We argued that such efforts are helpful as a first step towards understanding the concept of usability in mobility, but they are still too general to focus on the specific features in mobile application usability design, which might not allow us to accomplish an in-depth insight. A lack of detail in the analysis would lead to failure in addressing specific needs of todays' mobile application development. It is therefore important to devise a set of associated usability features for each usability heuristics. Such features are devised based on usability research and the interpretation of a wide range of mobile application studies. In the selection, features that are not suitable for the usability of mobile application context are not selected. Features that are found to relate to more than one usability heuristic are grouped into one heuristic based on their key characteristics (see Table 2).

Table 2. Usability heuristics

No.	Usability heuristic	Usability features
U1	Navigation	• To provide clear consistent navigation • To show user position while navigating through the application • To make visible and well defined buttons for easy navigation • To reduce navigation by providing hierarchies and menu • To minimize scrolling through search button
U2	Content quality	• To use terms that are related to real world • To provide rich and accurate content • To avoid use of fast moving objects and animations
U3	Error handling	• To correct mistakes occurred in the first time • To prevent errors where possible • To provide error message
U4	Consistency	• To use a consistent theme and terms, conventions and standards • To use consistent styles
U5	Functionality	• To make various functions well integrated • To make camera, microphone, sensors work well • To provide physical buttons or equivalent for main functionalities

(continued)

Table 2. (*continued*)

No.	Usability heuristic	Usability features
U6	Cognitive load	• To provide little, homogenous information in modules • To provide minimal steps or actions to complete a task • To make objects, actions, options visible
U7	Aesthetics design	• To design a visually pleasing interface • To create an aesthetic and identifiable icon • To provide visible color contrast of background and front content • To avoid fancy font styling • To limit number of screens and providing title for each

5 Usability Heuristics with Mobile Physical Limitations

Having indicated the importance of usability to mobile application design, the unique features of mobile devices and wireless technologies raise a number of significant challenges for mobile application design and development, including small screen size; limited connectivity; limited processing capacity; different display resolutions; storage space; context of use; limited input capabilities; multimodal mobile applications (see Table 3).

Physical constraint of mobile devices, especially small screen size has the significant influence to usability of mobile applications [7]. Unlike putting everything on desktop screen, it is critical that only the necessary content and input options are available on small screen of a mobile device [10]. Small screen size increases the demand for succinct and actionable information [15]. Conversely, excessive information presentation on small screen may cause users difficulty in reading content and orienting their movement through mobile applications [16], creating aesthetically unpleasant experience [17].

Mobile connectivity that uses wireless network connection with limited bandwidth is often getting slow and unreliable [18]. These connection signals vary at different time and locations on users' movement. With such permanent or intermittent network connection, it has a big impact on the performance of mobile applications when connectivity is utilized [1]. In particular, this connectivity significantly influences the speed of data transfer, such as downloading time [12]. Therefore, it is important to consider mobile connectivity in a usability study.

Mobile devices also contain less processing capacity, memory and power. Some mobile applications, such as graphic processing and three-dimension video games require a large amount of memory and fast processing speed. Such limitations may hamper the development of mobile applications that are hard for users to interact [19]. Thus, the way to deal with processing limitations must be addressed into the usability considerations [1].

Display resolutions largely affect the usability of mobile applications since the display capability of mobile devices has low resolution [12]. Such a low level of resolution directly reduces the readability of content, as well as degrades the quality of multimedia display [10], making users' dissatisfaction with mobile applications. Hence, the results of usability are largely influenced by the use of display resolutions.

Mobile devices have limited storage space, which restricts mobile application usefulness. Storage space creates virtual disks from the available capacity in the storage pools [7], helping users to protect data from drive failures [20]. However, the limited storage space in mobile devices decreases the memory usage, obstructing mobile application implementations and relevant capabilities, such as displaying and analyzing of data [21].

Context of use is a critical issue in mobile applications usability [6]. It can widely refer to anything that influences the interaction between users and an application [22]. For example, when users interact with a mobile application, it is vital to eliminate the possibility of the error occurring. When users are in poor lighting conditions, appropriate adjustability need to be available to support users' task completion. Therefore, it is important to reduce the impact of context-of-use on the usability of the mobile applications.

Another big challenge for mobile application development is limited input capabilities. Small buttons and touch screens naturally strain users' effectiveness and efficiency in data entry, which may reduce input capability and increase human errors [12]. Input capabilities available for mobile devices are different from desktop devices and require certain level of aptitude. It makes input more difficult and slower while on the move. In particular, some users who have limited mobility in their upper extremities tend to have high error rates when using touch screens and this may cause unacceptable difficulties with certain small size targets [23].

Finally, multimodal mobile applications pose dramatic challenges to usability of mobile application design [12]. Multimodality combines a variety of internal mobile features, including microphone, camera and sensors to enrich the mobile user experience. However, these internal features of mobile devices may cause some functional conflicts. For example, the codec used to record audio from the microphone was incompatible with the sound codec in many applications used by users, meaning that when audio recording was activated, all other sound was disabled [24]. The aforementioned problems caused by physical restrictions of mobile devices and wireless networks suggest that when designing or evaluating usability for mobile applications, these issues need to be carefully considered.

Table 3. Usability heuristic requirements with mobile physical limitations

Usability heuristic	Mobile physical limitations							
	1	2	3	4	5	6	7	8
U1. Navigation	√	–	–	√	–	√	√	√
U2: Content quality	√	–	–	–	–	√	√	√
U3: Error handling	√	–	–	√	–	√	√	√
U4: Consistency	√	√	√	–	√	√	√	√
U5: Functionality	√	–	–	√	–	√	√	√
U6: Cognitive load	√	–	–	–	–	√	√	√
U7: Aesthetics design	√	–	–	√	–	√	√	√

Note: 1 = Small screen; 2 = Limited connectivity; 3 = Limited processing capacity; 4 = Low display resolutions; 5 = Storage space; 6 = Context of use; 7 = Limited input capabilities; 8 = Multimodal mobile applications; √ means related; – means not related.

Table 3 shows the results of the usability heuristic with various mobile application design limitations. Overall, almost all the identified usability heuristics are necessarily relevant with the constraints of mobile devices in terms of screen size, display resolutions, context of use, input capabilities and multimodal mobile applications. However, for limited connectivity, limited processing capacity and storage space, less identified usability heuristics are required. These findings suggest that mobile devices themselves may play a much more influential role in mobile application usability design compared with desktop computers do in desktop applications. When designing and developing usability for mobile applications, usability and the physical constraints of mobile devices must be considered as whole, minimizing the effect of contextual factors on perceived usability.

Moreover, with respect to each usability heuristic identified, significant differences to a variety of mobile design limitations are also found. As showed in Table 3, for example, simplicity of systems is addressed in screen size, display resolutions context of use, input capabilities and multimodal mobile applications. This result is also reflected in the usability heuristics of consistency, visibility of system status and aesthetics design. A possible reason might be that these usability heuristics are in the areas of design look, which closely support users' visual cognition and understanding when they interacting with mobile applications. However, for the physical constraints of connectivity, processing capacity and storage space, the usability heuristic of functions integration is particularly required. These results imply that mobile application usability design needs to match with the characteristics of the physical constraints of mobile devices.

6   Conclusion

The rapid development of advanced mobile technologies and wireless Internet services has accelerated the explosion of the mobile service market. Except the basic function of telephony, mobile phones enable a variety of mobile services, such as education, health care, entertainment and social networking services through mobile applications. Today, thousands of users are increasingly interacting with mobile applications. Usability is becoming the most important issue for mobile applications design. Users' acceptance and use of mobile applications is determined by whether usability is demonstrated through mobile application design. However, the physical constraints of mobile phones raise a number of significant challenges for mobile application design and development. In this vein, this research aims to provide a systematic review of mobile applications analysis and design, identifying main heuristics and features in mobile applications design from a user perspective. The results focused on seven usability heuristics, namely navigation, content, error handling, consistency, functionality, cognitive load and aesthetic design that need to be carefully considered during mobile application design. More important, relevant design features for each usability heuristic were identified. Furthermore, the links of usability heuristic to mobile physical limitations were found and described. The major contribution is to propose a systematic analysis of mobile applications for business managers and designers. The specific usability features proposed in this research can be used as guidance in the development of mobile applications.

However, these are some limitations in this study. First, this study only conducts a systematic review, which may provide a limited viewpoint from the empirical side. Further study may consider the mobile applications usability evaluation through an experimental work or a field study. Second, this study only considers mobile application usability design in general, which may limit our results. Different categories of mobile applications may be involved in order to provide more comprehensive results.

Acknowledgments. This study was supported by research grants funded by the "National Natural Science Foundation of China" (Grant No. 61771297), and "the Fundamental Research Funds for the Central Universities" (GK201803062).

References

1. Rachel, H., Derek, F., David, D.: Usability of mobile applications: literature review and rationale for a new usability model. J. Interact. Sci. **1**, 1 (2013). https://doi.org/10.1186/2194-0827-1-1
2. Joyce, G., Lilley, M.: Towards the development of usability heuristics for native smartphone mobile applications. In: Marcus, A. (ed.) DUXU 2014. LNCS, vol. 8517, pp. 465–474. Springer, Cham (2014). https://doi.org/10.1007/978-3-319-07668-3_45
3. Asta, T., Shahrokh, N., Rimantas, G.: Mobile application driven consumer engagement. Telemat. Inform. **34**(4), 145–156 (2017)
4. Marco, B., et al.: A unified methodology for the evaluation of accessibility and usability of mobile applications. Univers. Access Inf. Soc. **9**(4), 337–356 (2010)
5. Moumane, K., Idri, A., Abran, A.: Usability evaluation of mobile applications using ISO9241 and ISO25062 standards. SpringerPlus **5**, 548 (2016). https://doi.org/10.1186/s40064-016-2171-z
6. Joyce, G., Lilley, M., Barker, T., Jefferies, A.: Mobile application usability heuristics: decoupling context-of-use. In: Marcus, A., Wang, W. (eds.) DUXU 2017. LNCS, vol. 10288, pp. 410–423. Springer, Cham (2017). https://doi.org/10.1007/978-3-319-58634-2_30
7. Ji, Y.G., Park, J.H., Lee, C., Yun, M.H.: A usability checklist for the usability evaluation of mobile phone user interface. Int. J. Hum. Comput. Interact. **20**, 207–231 (2010)
8. Venkatesh, V., Ramesh, V.: Web and wireless site usability: understanding differences and modeling use. Manag. Inf. Syst. Q. **30**, 181–206 (2006)
9. Masooda, M., Thigambaram, M.: The usability of mobile applications for pre-schoolers. Procedia Soc. Behav. Sci. **197**, 1818–1826 (2015)
10. Billi, M., et al.: A unified methodology for the evaluation of accessibility and usability of mobile applications. Univ. Access Inf. Soc. **9**, 337–356 (2010)
11. Inostroza, R., Rusu, C., Roncagliolo, S., Rusu, V., Collazos, C.A.: Developing SMASH: a set of SMArtphone's uSability heuristics. Comput. Stand. Interfaces **43**, 40–52 (2016)
12. Zhang, D., Adipat, B.: Challenges, methodologies, and issues in the usability testing of mobile applications. Int. J. Hum. Comput. Interact. **18**, 293–308 (2005)
13. Kjeldskov, J., Stage, J.: New techniques for usability evaluation of mobile systems. Int. J. Hum. Comput. Stud. **60**, 599–620 (2004)
14. do Nascimento Mendes, I., Dias-Neto, A.C.: A process-based approach to test usability of multi-platform mobile applications. In: Marcus, A. (ed.) DUXU 2016. LNCS, vol. 9746, pp. 456–468. Springer, Cham (2016). https://doi.org/10.1007/978-3-319-40409-7_43
15. Monkman, H., Kushniruk, A.: A health literacy and usability heuristic evaluation of a mobile consumer health application. Stud. Health Technol. Inform. **192**, 724–728 (2013)

16. Burigat, S., Chittaro, L., Gabrielli, S.: Navigation techniques for small-screen devices: an evaluation on maps and web pages. Int. J. Hum. Comput. Stud. **66**, 78–97 (2008)
17. Kumar, B.A., Mohite, P.: Usability of mobile learning applications: a systematic literature review. J. Comput. Educ. **5**, 1–17 (2018)
18. Longoria, R.: Designing mobile applications: challenges, methodologies, and lessons learned. In: Usability Evaluation and Interface Design: Cognitive Engineering, Intelligent Agents and Virtual Reality. Lawrence Erlbaum Associates, Inc., Mahwah (2001)
19. Silva, D.B., Eler, M.M., Durelli, V.H.S., Endo, A.T.: Characterizing mobile apps from a source and test code viewpoint. Inf. Softw. Technol. **101**, 32–50 (2018)
20. Yang, L., Wei, T., Zhang, F.W., Ma, J.F.: SADUS: secure data deletion in user space for mobile devices. Comput. Secur. **77**, 612–626 (2018)
21. Tsai, C.C., Lee, G., Raab, F., Norman, G.J., Sohn, T., Griswold, W.G., Patrick, K.: Usability and feasibility of PmEB: a mobile phone application for monitoring real time caloric balance. Mob. Netw. Appl. **12**, 173–184 (2007)
22. Maguire, M.: Context of use within usability activities. Int. J. Hum. Comput Stud. **55**, 453–483 (2001)
23. Bergman, J., Kauko, J., Keränen, J.: Hands on music: physical approach to interaction with digital music. In: Proceedings of the 11th International Conference on Human-Computer Interaction with Mobile Devices and Services. ACM, Bonn (2009)
24. Falloon, G.: Young students using iPads: app design and content influences on their learning pathways. Comput. Educ. **68**, 505–521 (2013)
25. International Standards Organization: Ergonomic requirements for office work with visual display terminals, Part 11 – Guidance on usability. ISO 9241-11:1998, Geneva, Switzerland (1998)

The Advent of Speech Based NLP QA Systems: A Refined Usability Testing Model

Diarmuid Lane, Robin Renwick[✉], John McAvoy,
and Philip O'Reilly

University College Cork, Cork, Ireland
{113456738,117223923}@umail.ucc.ie,
{J.McAvoy,Philip.OReilly}@ucc.ie

Abstract. This paper outlines a refined usability testing model, developed for industry specific comparative usability testing of two natural language processor (NLP) based question answering (QA) systems. The systems operate over differing modalities, one through text and the other speech. The revised model combines two existing usability testing frameworks, the System Usability Metric (SUM) and the System Usability Scale (SUS). It also integrates the context-specific determined target user - financial managers working within the financial services industry. The model's metric weightings are determined through key informant interviews. The presented model will be the working framework from which a series of comparative usability tests will be carried out within the target organisation.

Keywords: Natural language processor · Question Answering System · Usability

1 Introduction

As we move further into the 21st century, interaction with automated natural language processor (NLP) based question answering (QA) systems will become commonplace (Levy 2016; Panetta 2017). The trend may be seen emerging through commercially available *zeitgeist* tools such as Amazon's Alexa, Google Assistant, Apple's Siri and IBM's Watson. QA system development may be seen through the seemingly unstoppable adoption of text based 'helper' systems proliferating the internet and mobile applications - colloquially known as 'chat-bots' (López et al. 2017). QA systems are a subfield of natural language processing research, focused on the location and retrieval of specific data points relating to user questions posed in natural language. NLP powered QA systems act as human-computer interfaces; delivering accurate and efficient responses to queries through the modes of text or speech (Lopez et al. 2011). QA systems are becoming increasingly commonplace in contemporary workplaces, carrying out a range of activities - from administrative workplace tasks through to complex human resource functions (Knight 2016). It is estimated that by 2020 over 50% of large enterprises will have internally deployed 'chat-bots' to carry out, or augment, business functions. It is envisioned this will lead to more fluid interactions with Information Systems (IS), whilst correspondingly reducing levels of human-error

© Springer Nature Switzerland AG 2019
A. Marcus and W. Wang (Eds.): HCII 2019, LNCS 11586, pp. 152–163, 2019.
https://doi.org/10.1007/978-3-030-23535-2_11

(Goasduff 2018). It was noted as early as 2001 that speech based interactions would become an accepted mode of communication between human and computer (Hone and Graham 2001), while recent research has indicated a significant upturn in the market penetration of bi-directional speech-based interactions (Moore et al. 2016; Moore 2017a, 2017b; Simonite 2016). However, the question remains which mode of communication is preferred, or more effective for businesses implementation – speech or text.

The design of QA interactions between human and computer will determine the mode and interface through which we engage. Core to the concept of QA interaction design is the measure of usability. Usability is a complex term, with myriad interpretations found in varied, and sometimes disparate, fields: design science; design engineering; information science; human computer interface (HCI) design; user interface (UI) design; and user experience (UX) design (Green and Pearson 2006). Research has highlighted the need for 'usable' NLP based QA systems (Hausawi and Mayron 2013; Ferrucci et al. 2009). However, there remains a paucity of research within the context of modality comparison. With this in mind, this paper proposes a usability testing model to assess NLP QA systems, incorporating specific nuances associated with both speech and text based interfaces. The model is developed by reviewing and extending literature from a number of disciplines, paying particular attention to IS publications, user experience and/or usability literature, and the field of HCI design. The model is refined in the development stage through interaction with key industry informants. This paper describes existing usability testing models, details how these are viewed as inadequate for the specific context of comparative usability testing between speech and text, and outlines the development of a new model within a context led scenario.

2 Usability Literature Review

A definition of usability is set forth by the International Organisation of Standards, through ISO 9241-11. The international standard details usability as "the extent to which a product can be used by specified users to achieve specified goals with effectiveness, efficiency and satisfaction in a specified context of use" (ISO 1998, p. 1). A number of studies base testing metrics on this definition, or encapsulate its importance in defining a testing model (Green and Pearson 2006; Hone and Graham 2001; Möller et al. 2008; Rohrer et al. 2016; Sauro and Kindlund 2005). Criticism has been leveled at the ISO 9241-11 definition from various angles, most notably from within the usability testing profession. Usability is the characteristic of a product that inherently makes it 'usable', but the term may mean different things to different people, and is dependent on contextual, behavioural, and/or situational aspects (Quesenbury 2003; Rohrer et al. 2016). The core criticism aimed at the ISO definition is that specific users will view concepts such as effectiveness and efficiency differently. The lack of flexibility in the ISO definition has previously been noted, as has its suitability as a working base from which to start (Quesenbury 2003). Incorporating project specifics along with the target user into the process of building a revised understanding ensures that any devised model can move away from generality towards specificity.

There are three core criticisms of the ISO based definition (Green and Pearson 2006; Quesenbury 2003). The first is that the model is too focused on well-defined tasks and goals; ignoring the more intangible elements of user experience. The second problem is that the definition foregrounds efficiency and effectiveness, without catering for products where these are of lesser concern; where pleasure and engagement are more relative to any measure of usability. The final criticism focuses on the use of the word 'satisfaction', viewed as too narrow a testing term (Quesenbury 2003). Similar sentiments have been discussed within HCI design and research, where "'usability' is a construct conceived by the community to denote a desired quality of interactive systems and products" (Tractinsky 2018, p. 131). The issues associated with the usability construct are thought to have stemmed from the fact that usability incorporates both subjective and objective dimensions, broadening the distance between the usability construct and its measures (Hone and Graham 2001; Sauro and Lewis 2009; Tractinsky 2018). The context specific nature of usability increases the ambiguity associated with the construct and its measurement (Brooke 2013). In practice this implies a disjunct between how usability is defined, and how it is actually tested.

A model for usability may be drawn in which the construct is understood by its perceived components in a reflective manner, as opposed to a formative model which first understands components and then attempts to define how they drive a specific frame (Tractinsky 2018). The distinction between the two methods is important, as concerns regarding how project specific usability and testing contexts should inform the development of any new usability testing model are incorporated. However, it should be remembered that existing frameworks offer overarching guidance, or reference, from which more exacting project specific models may be developed (Quesenbury 2003).

2.1 ISO 9241-11 Standard Based Frameworks

Green and Pearson (2006) outline an ISO 9241-11 standard based usability testing model, designed for the user-based testing of an e-commerce website. The focus is on the user, with any potential pitfalls encountered while using the system viewed as the measure of whether the product is 'usable' or not. Understanding usability in this context means that it extends "…beyond the issues of ease of use, ease of learning, and navigation…with additional pressure for the design to be intuitive" (Green and Pearson 2006, p. 66). Alternatively, a usability testing model for web-based information systems based on the ISO 9241-11 standard examines the correlation between web-based systems 'quality' and overall usability (Oztekin et al. 2009). Causation is created between the overall 'quality' of a system, or interface, and its measured level of usability.

The single, standardised and summated usability metric (SUM) is based on the ISO 9241-11, and the American National Standards Institute (ANSI) dimensions of usability: effectiveness, efficiency, and satisfaction (Sauro and Kindlund 2005). From these dimensions four usability metrics are derived - time on task, number of errors, task completion, and average satisfaction. The metrics have been selected as base standards for the testing of usability. The four measures show significant correlation; a weighted average of the standardised values convey the maximum amount of information in one combined score (Sauro and Kindlund 2005). One key feature of SUM is the equal weighing denoted to the three dimensions of usability (efficiency, effectiveness, and satisfaction); offering an unbiased overall 'systems usability' score. SUM has been successfully extended for a multitude of purposes: measuring the usability of mobile applications (Avouris et al. 2008), through to the testing of educational software (Lado et al. 2006).

The Practical Usability Rating by Experts (PURE) framework was developed in conjunction with industry representatives at Intel Security (Rohrer et al. 2016). PURE is a framework that includes ratings as given by teams of trained evaluators, testing validity against independent studies completed by specific usability experts. The comparisons offer guidance on the verifiability and accuracy of the testing procedure, as well as the governing framework. PURE derives an understanding of usability from the ISO 9241-11 standard, acknowledging interaction between three standard components of user experience while simultaneously stating its core focus as usability. By integrating knowledgeable evaluators drawn from the target firm, the PURE model fosters a co-opt design process, in which prospective end users engage in the development, testing, and refinement process. This ensures that the target user's understanding of 'usability' is integrated into the framework; a method suggested as being integral to a successful and accurate derivation of a testing model (Quesenbury 2003; Tractinsky 2018). The overall success of the framework is built on the specified outline of what the interface, or product, is going to be used for. Once a specification is detailed, it is possible to outline project specific metrics which will be used within the testing framework.

2.2 Usability Metrics

Employing effective and quantifiable usability metrics reveal important numerically based information pertaining to user experience (Tullis and Albert 2013). There are three distinct categories of measurement in the ISO standard of usability: effectiveness (the act of completing a given task); efficiency (the level of effort needed to compete a given task); and satisfaction (the extent to which a user enjoyed the experience of performing a given task). Within these three categories lies a host of sub-metrics which may be applied by usability practitioners in specific usability study scenarios:

- *Task success* metrics are concerned with whether participants are able to complete a given task associated with an interface, product, or system. When testing for task success, identifying and testing completion rates removes certain aspects of ambiguity.
- *Task time* is concerned with the length of time needed to complete a specific task. In order to test efficiency, a method is set forth by the National Institute of Standards and Technology (NIST): efficiency is based on a combination of the task success metric, and the task time metric (NIST 2001).
- *Learnability* refers to how easy it is for users to complete specific tasks associated with an interface, product, or system the first time they encounter the design (Nielsen 2003). Due to the nature of the design presented in this research, the concept of learnability allows comparisons to be made of two modes of interaction - speech and text.

- *Self-reported metrics* are critical to gaining an understanding of users' perceptions about an interface, product, or system. These metrics give the tester a generalised insight into how a user 'feels' about a system. They also allow a tester to evaluate any differences that may exist between how a user perceives a system, and how the system actually is (Bangor et al. 2008; Hone and Graham 2001; Silvervarg et al. 2016).

Objective usability metrics provide an accurate measure of a systems performance, quantified using usability performance indicators. Self-reported metrics are employed in order to quantify a user's subjective opinion of a system's usability. An adequate model must be employed in order to accurately measure this subjective opinion. A review of such models is necessary prior to integrating subjective metrics into a context specific usability framework.

System Usability Scale (SUS)

The System Usability Scale (SUS) was developed as a quick and effective usability survey scale, developed to assess users' subjective perception of usability with respect to a given system, or design (Brooke 1996). SUS has become a leading model in the usability industry, having been successfully extended to assess interface technologies, novel hardware platforms, and voice response systems (Bangor et al. 2008). The original SUS questionnaire was composed of 10 statements, scored on a Likert scale - measuring responses to answers ranging from 'strongly agree' to 'strongly disagree'. The questionnaire alternates between positive and negative questions concerning the usability of the system being tested. A percentile score is then derived based on the provided responses (Brooke 1996).

There have been some criticisms of SUS, with researchers noting that erroneous answers appear at various stages of the testing response procedure. Respondents have been found to mistakenly agree with negative questions, leading to unreliable questionnaire scores (Sauro and Lewis 2011). Due to the continued reporting of user error, a number of semantic changes have been made to the questionnaire since it first appeared; roughly 90% of tests since its formation have been found to use a revised version (Bangor et al. 2008). When SUS was originally developed it was intended to assess users perceived usability, yielding a single usability score (Brooke 1996). As SUS was designed prior to the proliferation of speech based systems we see today, a review of speech based usability testing is required before the development of a context specific usability testing framework.

2.3 Speech Based Usability Testing

Since the emergence of Siri in 2011, speech based interfaces have become increasingly commonplace in society (Moore 2017a, b). However, overall adoption metrics, usability testing frameworks, and/or specific metrics for evaluating mode of interaction have not been developed. A subjective assessment model for speech-based interfaces has appeared, with the emergence of the SASSI model (Hone and Graham 2001). Work has also been done predicting the quality and usability of spoken dialogue interfaces (Möller et al. 2008). However, it is still not understood if speech based interaction is genuinely demanded, preferred, or if the proposed mode of interaction is capable of providing the type and level of usability demanded from the end user. For mainstream adoption to occur two needs must be met: "the need to align the visual, vocal and behavioural affordances of the system, and second, the need to overcome the huge mismatch between the capabilities and expectations of a human being and the features and benefits offered by even the most advanced autonomous social agent" (Moore 2017a, p. 10).

Usability research of speech based interfaces designed specifically for the elderly has unearthed complex discourse surrounding themes such as privacy, dependency, loss of control, and the affordances of speech based interfaces to tackle psychological and societal issues such as loneliness (Portet et al. 2013). Themes such as these are beyond the bounds of this study, but are worth considering when detailing how speech based interfaces may impact procedures and processes at any level of human computer interaction. Specific issues have also been raised with respect to the interactional abilities of speech interfaces. Differences in use of vocabulary and grammatical structure have been noted as being key determinants in scores for usability, with speech based interfaces responding differently to accents, regional dialects, and sentence syntax - sometimes to the frustration of users or detriment of the system (Portet et al. 2013; Vacher et al. 2015).

Researchers have investigated the functionality and usability of competing proprietary speech based user interface systems (López et al. 2017). Four of the most widely available speech based interfaces were included in the study. The systems were evaluated with respect to a defined task list, offering results against specific operational modes: shopping and buying assistant; care assistant; travel and entertainment assistant; and administrative assistant (López et al. 2017). Similar to the aforementioned SUS model, a 5-point Likert scale was used to assess the 'naturality' of interactions, while 'correctness' was measured with respect to task success. The research concluded that improvements could be made by all interface systems and that further study is needed to understand effectiveness and usability of the available proprietary systems (López et al. 2017; Torres et al. 2017). With this in mind, the research presented in this paper acknowledges the exacting requirements for testing two natural language processor based QA systems operating under two alternative modalities. A refined model is required that encompasses existing models, as discussed, as well as the project specific context that the research addresses.

3 Initial Usability Testing Model

The model presented in this paper is designed to evaluate the usability of two distinct forms of question answering systems, one interfaced through speech, another through text. Similar to the previously outlined models, the foundation definition of usability is that set forth by ISO 9241-11. The paper incorporates the three main dimensions of usability (efficiency, effectiveness, and satisfaction); chosen as base constructs for the usability testing framework. The three dimensions have initially been allocated equal weighting, provisioning for a summated Question Answering System Usability Score. This scoring system is viewed as similar to that of Sauro and Kindlund (2005). The model has been designed to test both objective and subjective indicators of usability, assessing performance and perceived usability of the two alternate QA systems. The objective measures are determined by testing carried out similar to ISO based frameworks, and SUM. Scores are determined through specific usability indicators. The subjective score is determined by metrics as put forward by SUS. The research proposes that alternative score weightings are required for increased accuracy and project specific context. These are determined through interviews with key informants from within the financial services industry.

Internal usability metrics have been selected to measure and quantify dimensions of usability (see Fig. 1). 'Time-on-Task' has been chosen to measure the effort required by a user to complete a given task, referred to as 'Task Proficiency'. It determines the usability dimension of 'Efficiency'. 'Number of Errors', and 'Completion' were chosen to measure the dimension of 'Effectiveness'. The above metrics are based on system performance, and are classed as objective measures (Tullis and Albert 2013). The dimension of 'Satisfaction' is associated with the users' perspective while using a system. An adapted System Usability Scale (SUS) will be used to assess the users' perceived usability of the system, and their overall satisfaction level. SUS will act as a measure of users' subjective view of the system; identifying, analysing, and quantifying the perceived usability associated with the QA system from the users' perspective (Lewis and Sauro 2009). Through the use of both subjective and objective usability metrics, the model builds on previous usability testing models; offering an unbiased and comprehensive view of overall system usability.

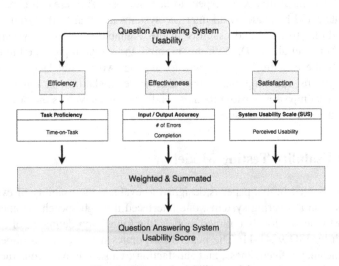

Fig. 1. Proposed usability model

4 Key Informant Interviews

In order to refine the testing model, qualitative interviews were conducted with professionals from the financial services industry, viewed as key informants (KI). The use of key informants as an approach for data collection is beneficial when there is a lack of underlying theoretical understanding (Babbie 1998). This technique has been previously applied in a number of scenarios:

- The study of inter-organisational research when there is a lack of archived data to support such a study (Kumar et al. 1993).
- Developing e-retailing theory when there was a lack of foundational understanding of online retailing (Cowles et al. 2002).
- Using key informants to analyse a groups attitudes and beliefs towards software project reviews (McAvoy 2006).

The user's perception of what is important to them with respect to the usability of question answering systems has not been documented, so key informants were selected to gather this information. Four key informants were chosen from four financial services organisations. The positions held by the key informants are as follows: Chief Operating Officer - Head of Innovation EMEA; Financial Modeling Analyst; Equity Trader; Business Intelligence Analyst. Interviews were conducted on a semi-structured (Myers and Newman 2007; Schultze and Avital 2011) basis. Within their roles, the individuals perform tasks similar to those intended to be completed by the proposed QA system; querying large documents and retrieving answers based on analysis of specified data and data points.

The key informants agreed that the usability dimensions (efficiency, effectiveness, and satisfaction) should have varied weightings based on the specific functional demands associated with the financial services industry. The weighting adjustments suggested by the KIs highlight the specific use case context of QA systems, contrasting strongly with similar usability models devised for alternate contexts. All four interviewees placed significant emphasis on 'Effectiveness', ranking it as the most important dimension of usability. The interviewees stated that correct answers were essential in order for them to "trust" a QA system. Each interviewee stated that QA 'Effectiveness', be it in the context of speech or text is "vital". 'Efficiency' was weighted as the second most important dimension, with one interviewee stating that a QA system must "meet real-world demands of immediate information access". 'Satisfaction' was ranked as the least important usability dimension in all but one case. Consensus formed around the idea of satisfaction being derived only if the system was both efficient, and effective. Satisfaction was perceived to be of least importance; one interviewee stating: "I would be far more concerned with system performance, rather than satisfaction".

5 Refined Usability Weightings from Key Informant Insights

The refined weightings as given by the key informants (see Table 1) highlight the industry specific nuances associated with both speech and text based question answering systems. Consensus formed around 'Effectiveness' taking precedence over both 'Efficiency' and 'Satisfaction'. Based on interviews, 'Effectiveness' accounts for 47.5% of the overall Question Answering System Usability Score. 'Efficiency' is designated an overall contribution of 32.5%, while 'Satisfaction' contributes the remaining 20%. This is reflective of the importance of effectiveness and efficiency as regards the specific QA use case within any given financial services organisation. The layout, and metrics, associated with the model remain unchanged, and are shown in Table 1.

Table 1. Usability dimension weighting.

Usability dimension	Initial weighting	Refined weighting
Efficiency	33%	32.5%
Effectiveness	33%	47.5%
Satisfaction	33%	20%

By combining objective and subjective metrics along with specific refined usability weightings, the question answering usability scoring model attempts to reduce the disjunct between the construct of usability, and its measures (Hone and Graham 2001; Tractinsky 2018). The dimensions of usability have been weighted to incorporate specific nuances associated with the proposed use case, based on the experience of Key Informants; adapting the question answering usability score to more accurately score industry specific QA systems.

6 Conclusion

The research presented in this paper proposes a context specific question answering system usability testing model. It is designed to assess the usability of two alternate natural language processing based question answering systems, operating through alternate modes of communication - speech and text. The weightings associated with the model have been refined through interviews with key informants, applicable to the specific use case context of financial services professionals. The disparity between the original SUM weightings and the Question Answering System Usability Score weightings reflects the view that a 'one size fits all' approach is not always applicable, especially in the case of speech and text. This is evident when testing the usability of natural language processing based question answering technologies within the financial services industry. In order to assess the validity of the model, two natural language processing based question answering proofs of concepts are in development, and a usability testing process will be completed at a future date. The testing procedure will assess a text-based user interface, using IBM Watson Assistant, alongside a speech-based user interface developed using Amazon's Alexa. Comparative analysis will be completed to understand which interface is preferred by the proposed target user, and why this is the case. It is imagined that relative question answering usability scores will reflect user preference. Both proofs of concepts will be tested against the proposed research model in a financial services organisation.

References

Avouris, N., Fiotakis, G., Raptis, D.: On measuring usability of mobile applications. In: International Workshop, p. 38 (2008)

Babbie, E.R.: The Practice of Social Research. Wadsworth Pub., Belmont (1998)

Bangor, A., Kortum, P.T., Miller, J.T.: An empirical evaluation of the system usability scale. Int. J. Hum. Comput. Interact. 24(6), 574–594 (2008)

Brooke, J.: SUS: a retrospective. J. Usability Stud. 8(2), 29–40 (2013)

Brooke, J.: SUS-a quick and dirty usability scale. Usability Eval. Ind. 189(194), 4–7 (1996)

Cowles, D.L., Kiecker, P., Little, M.W.: Using key informant insights as a foundation for e-retailing theory development. J. Bus. Res. 55(8), 629–636 (2002)

Ferrucci, D., et al.: Towards the open advancement of question answering systems. IBM Research Report, IBM, Armonk, NY (2009)

Goasduff, L.: Chatbots will appeal to modern workers, smarter with Gartner (2018). https://www.gartner.com/smarterwithgartner/chatbots-will-appeal-to-modern-workers/. Accessed 6 Mar 2018

Green, D., Pearson, J.M.: Development of a web site usability instrument based on ISO 9241-11. J. Comput. Inf. Syst. 47(1), 66–72 (2006)

Hausawi, Y.M., Mayron, L.M.: Towards usable and secure natural language processing systems. In: Stephanidis, C. (ed.) HCI 2013. CCIS, vol. 373, pp. 109–113. Springer, Heidelberg (2013). https://doi.org/10.1007/978-3-642-39473-7_23

Hone, K.S., Graham, R.: Subjective assessment of speech-system interface usability. In: Seventh European Conference on Speech Communication and Technology, Aalborg, Denmark (2001)

International Standards Organisation (ISO): Ergonomic Requirements for Office Work with Visual Display Terminals (VDT)s-Part II Guidance on Usability, ISO/IEC 9241-11 (1998)

Knight, W.: The HR person at your next may actually be a bot. MIT Technology Review (2016). https://www.technologyreview.com/s/602068/the-hr-person-at-your-next-job-may-actually-be-a-bot/. Accessed 6 Mar 2018

Kumar, N., Stern, L.W., Anderson, J.C.: Conducting interorganizational research using key informants. Acad. Manag. J. 36(6), 1633–1651 (1993)

Lado, M.J., Méndez, A.J., Roselló, E.G., Dacosta, J.G., Pérez-Schofield, J.B.G., Cota, M.P.: R-interface: an alternative GUI for MATLAB. Comput. Appl. Eng. Educ. 14(4), 313–320 (2006)

Levy, H.P.: Gartner's top 10 strategic predictions for 2017 and beyond: surviving the storm winds of digital disruption, smarter with gartner (2016). https://www.gartner.com/smarterwithgartner/gartner-predicts-a-virtual-world-of-exponential-change/. Accessed 2 Feb 2018

Lewis, J.R., Sauro, J.: The factor structure of the system usability scale. In: Kurosu, M. (ed.) HCD 2009. LNCS, vol. 5619, pp. 94–103. Springer, Heidelberg (2009). https://doi.org/10.1007/978-3-642-02806-9_12

López, G., Quesada, L., Guerrero, L.A.: Alexa vs. Siri vs. Cortana vs. Google Assistant: a comparison of speech-based natural user interfaces. In: Nunes, I. (ed.) AHFE 2017. AISC, vol. 592, pp. 241–250. Springer, Cham (2017). https://doi.org/10.1007/978-3-319-60366-7_23

Lopez, V., Uren, V., Sabou, M., Motta, E.: Is question answering fit for the semantic web?: a survey. Semant. Web 2(2), 125–155 (2011)

McAvoy, J.: Evaluating the evaluations: preconceptions of project post-mortems. Electron. J. Inf. Syst. Eval. 9(2), 65–72 (2006)

Möller, S., Engelbrecht, K.P., Schleicher, R.: Predicting the quality and usability of spoken dialogue services. Speech Commun. 50(8–9), 730–744 (2008)

Moore, R.K., Li, H., Liao, S.H.: Progress and prospects for spoken language technology: what ordinary people think. In: INTERSPEECH, San Francisco, California, pp. 3007–3011 (2016)

Moore, R.K.: Is spoken language all-or-nothing? Implications for future speech-based human-machine interaction. In: Jokinen, K., Wilcock, G. (eds.) Dialogues with Social Robots. LNEE, vol. 999, pp. 281–291. Springer, Singapore (2017). https://doi.org/10.1007/978-981-10-2585-3_22

Moore, R.K.: A needs-driven cognitive architecture for future 'intelligent' communicative agents. In: Proceedings of EU Cognition "Cognitive Robot Architectures", vol. 1855, pp. 50–51 (2017b)

Myers, M.D., Newman, M.: The qualitative interview in IS research: examining the craft. Inf. Org. **17**(1), 2–26 (2007)

National Institute of Standards and Technology (NIST). ANSI/INCITS 354-2001: Common Industry Format (CIF) for usability test reports (2001). https://www.irit.fr/ ~ Philippe.Truillet/ens/ens/upssitech/3ASRI/ihm/outils/ANSI_NCITS_354.pdf

Nielsen, J.: Usability 101: introduction to usability. Nielsen Norman Group (2003). https://www.nngroup.com/articles/usability-101-introduction-to-usability. Accessed 23 Feb 2018

Oztekin, A., Nikov, A., Zaim, S.: UWIS: An assessment methodology for usability of web-based information systems. J. Syst. Softw. **82**(12), 2038–2050 (2009)

Panetta, K.: Gartner top strategic predictions for 2018 and beyond, smarter with Gartner (2017). https://www.gartner.com/smarterwithgartner/gartner-top-strategic-predictions-for-2018-and-beyond/. Accessed 4 Apr 2018

Portet, F., Vacher, M., Golanski, C., Roux, C., Meillon, B.: Design and evaluation of a smart home voice interface for the elderly: acceptability and objection aspects. Pers. Ubiquitous Comput. **17**(1), 127–144 (2013)

Quesenbury, W.: Dimensions of usability: defining the conversation, driving the process. In: UPA 2003 Conference, Scottsdale, AZ, pp. 23–27 (2003)

Rohrer, C.P., Boyle, F., Wendt, J., Cole, S., Sauro, J.: Practical usability rating by experts (PURE): a pragmatic approach for scoring product usability. In: CHI 2016 Extended Abstracts, San Jose, CA (2016)

Sauro, J., Kindlund, E.: A method to standardize usability metrics into a single score. In: Proceedings of the SIGCHI Conference on Human Factors in Computing Systems, Portland, Oregan, pp. 401–409 (2005)

Sauro, J., Lewis, J.R.: Correlations among prototypical usability metrics: evidence for the construct of usability. In: Proceedings of the SIGCHI conference on human factors in computing systems, Boston, Massachusetts, pp. 1609–1618. ACM (2009)

Sauro, J., Lewis, J.R.: When designing usability questionnaires, does it hurt to be positive? In: Proceedings of the Conference in Human Factors in Computing Systems, CHI 2011, Vancouver, BC, pp. 2215–2224. ACM (2011)

Schultze, U., Avital, M.: Designing interviews to generate rich data for information systems research. Inf. Org. **21**(1), 1–16 (2011)

Silvervarg, A., et al.: Perceived usability and cognitive demand of secondary tasks in spoken versus visual-manual automotive interaction. In: INTERSPEECH, San Francisco, CA, pp. 1171–1175 (2016)

Simonite, T.: Google thinks you're ready to converse with computers. MIT Technology Review (2016). https://www.technologyreview.com/s/601530/google-thinks-youre-ready-to-converse-with-computers/. Accessed 13 Feb 2018

Torres, J., Vaca, C., Abad, C.L.: What ignites a reply?: Characterizing conversations in microblogs. In: Proceedings of the Fourth IEEE/ACM International Conference on Big Data Computing, Applications and Technologies, Austin, Texas, pp. 149–156. ACM (2017)

Tractinsky, N.: The usability construct: a dead end? Hum. Comput. Interact. **33**(2), 131–177 (2018)

Tullis, T., Albert, W.: Measuring the user experience: collecting, analyzing, and presenting usability metrics, 2nd edn. Newnes, Waltham (2013)

Vacher, M., Caffiau, S., Portet, F., Meillon, B., Roux, C., Elias, E., Lecouteux, B., Chahuara, P.: Evaluation of a context-aware voice interface for ambient assisted living: qualitative user study vs. quantitative system evaluation. ACM Trans. Access. Comput. (TACCESS) **7**(2), 5 (2015)

Research on User Experience Evaluation Model of Smart Jewelry Based on Kansei Engineering

Jinghan Lin[⊠], Jian Shi, and Chao Yu

Jewelry Fashion Industry Research Center, Shanghai Jiaotong University,
Shanghai, China
linjinghan1995@sjtu.edu.cn

Abstract. Kansei engineering is a theory that pays close attention to the emotional experience of users. This paper is based on Kansei engineering theory. The research group collected a certain number of emotional words related to the user experience of smart jewelry, and established a multilevel evaluation model of user experience based on analytic hierarchy process. Then the researchers get the weight of various indicators by calculating the judgment matrix. Thus the researchers can quantify the user experience status of the smart jewelry, and improve the design of the product.

Keywords: Smart jewelry · AHP · Kansei Engineering

1 Introduction

Jewellery refers to jewelry made of gold, silver, or natural materials (minerals, rocks, gem, etc.) and of certain value, such as rings, necklaces, earrings and pendants. When ancient ancestors began to adorn themselves, jewelry was born at that time. The earliest jewelry can trace its history to the Stone Age. With the rapid development of society, economy and culture, the kinds of jewelry become more and more. In recent years, along with the fast growth of Internet technology and digital information, wearable smart jewelry is beginning to enters people's field of vision. Digital information is the only way for jewelry industry to seek development, and it is also a magic weapon to win [1]. Smart jewelry, as same as traditional jewelry, is aesthetical and decorative. In addition to that, it also has the similar function of wearable devices. According to Maslow's hierarchy of needs, abundant material living conditions push the spiritual demand of consumers to a higher level, so people are no longer satisfied with homogeneous and stereotyped jewelry design. Pursuing individuality and showing oneself is becoming the theme of jewelry design at present. User experience design refers to improving the usability, accessibility and pleasure of the product during the process of interaction between the user and the product, so as to improve the usability of the product. It involves complex psychological activity mechanism of the users. Against this background, how can smart jewelry brings unique user experience to users has become the focus of smart jewelry designers.

© Springer Nature Switzerland AG 2019
A. Marcus and W. Wang (Eds.): HCII 2019, LNCS 11586, pp. 164–171, 2019.
https://doi.org/10.1007/978-3-030-23535-2_12

2 Concepts and Research of Kansei Engineering

Sensibility is opposed to reason, and it is composed of people's cognition and five senses. John Locke said that: "I conceive that Ideas in the Understanding, are coeval with Sensation; which is such an Impression or Motion, made in some part of the Body, as makes it be taken notice of in the Understanding" [2]. Kansei, means sensibility in Japanese. The theory of Kansei Engineering was first born in Japan. In 1989, a famous Japanese scholar called Mitsuo Nagamachi published a book entitled "Kansei Engineering", and he defined Kansei engineering as "the technique of translating user's emotional needs to improve product design. When a user chooses a product, he is no longer just satisfied with its utility. The user makes a comprehensive consideration of the product through his own senses. These subjective feelings determine whether or not the product is ultimately purchased. Kansei engineering uses quantitative techniques to analyze and study users' perceptions, and it uses statistical methods to explore which product is better suited to the emotional needs of users. The product design method based on Kansei engineering consists of the following steps: Set goals-Collect emotional words- Evaluating emotional words-Quantify by means of engineering- Get the result. Although Kansei engineering is a relatively new theory, it has been widely used in the fields of automobile, electronic products, architecture and so on.

At present, the research on the application of Kansei engineering in the field of smart jewelry in China is still few. Using Kansei Engineering to establish an evaluation model for the user experience of smart jewelry can help designers and developers to find emotional and cognitive problems of users more efficiently and improve the design.

3 Establishment of User Experience Evaluation Model for Smart Jewelry

After interviewing the users who have used the smart jewelry, the research team of this article divided user experience of smart jewelry into the following three levels: Sensory experience, operation experience and value experience.

3.1 Experimental Method

The main experimental method used in this paper is Analytic hierarchy process (AHP). It is a decision method put forward by American operational researcher Thomas L. Saaty in the early 70 s of the 20th century, and it has particular application in group decision making [3]. Analytic hierarchy process treats a complex decision-making problem as a system, decomposing it into a hierarchy of goals, criteria, alternatives, and so on. By constructing a judgment matrix, we can calculate the weight of each element, the best scheme is the one with the largest weight. Analytic hierarchy process (AHP) has been widely used in economics, management, engineering and other fields.

In the field of design, analytic hierarchy process (AHP) is mainly applied in the evaluation of design plan and usability test. This method divides problems into several hierarchies and decomposes them layer by layer, and using quantitative methods to reduce the risk of subjective judgment of the evaluator. In this paper, combined with literature research and user interviews, analytic hierarchy process (AHP) is finally chosen as the research method of this paper.

3.2   Research Framework

The research framework is shown in Fig. 1

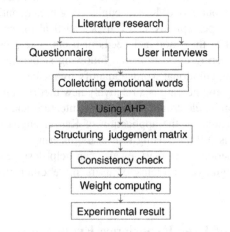

Fig. 1. Research framework

3.3   Collecting and Choosing Emotional Words

Emotional word is generally used to describe users' subjective impressions about products, and it is mainly used in the process of collecting emotion states. In this paper there are three ways to collect emotional words: (1) From relevant literature: Emotion related evaluation in usability test of Interactive products; Research and achievements related to emotional words in psychology literature. (2) User surveys and interviews: questionnaires or interviews conducted online or offline for consumers who have used smart jewelry. (3) Vocabulary expressions and emotional comments in product advertisements, websites and brochures.

Through these three approaches, researchers collected 92 emotional words and eventually chose 20 typical words, as shown in Table 1 below.

Table 1. Twenty emotional words selected in this paper.

No.	Emotional word	Explanation
1	Novel	The shape of the product is creative
2	Comfortable	The product is comfortable to wear
3	Colorful	Color matching of the product is beautiful
4	Natural	The product interacts in a natural way
5	Pleasurable	The product is pleasant to use
6	Easy	The operation of the product is very easy
7	Fashionable	The product conforms to the trend
8	Dazzling	The product is very compelling
9	Convenient	Operation of the product is not redundant
10	Reliable	The product is stable and trustworthy
11	Effective	All functions of the product are effective
12	Delicate	Appearance of the product is not rough
13	Light	Appearance of the product is refined
14	Understandable	Operation of the product is simple
15	Considerate	The product brings the user intimate feeling
16	Warmhearted	Product can bring emotional satisfaction
17	Qualitative	Product can reflect the quality of life
18	Controllable	Operation of the product is controllable
19	Healthy	Products can assist users to live a healthy life
20	Technological	The product has a sense of technology

3.4 Hierarchical Analysis

The team divided user experience of smart jewelry into several levels and then numbered them. User experience of a product (A) as Target layer. Sensory experience (B_1), operation experience (B_2) and value experience (B_3) as criterion layer. Sensory experience refers to the appearance of product appearance, color, material and texture. Operation experience refers to the experience during the interaction between users and products. Value experience refers to emotional and value resonance of the users. 20 emotional words selected are used as the alternatives ($C_1 - C_{20}$). The hierarchy created is shown Table 2 below:

Table 2. Hierarchy

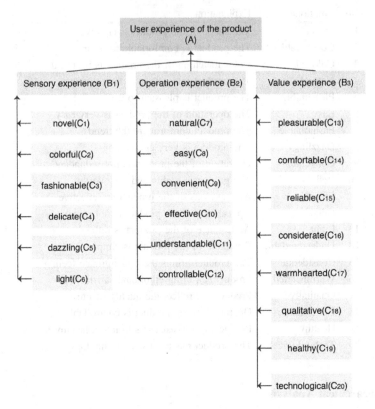

3.5   Establishing Pairwise Judgement Matrices

Researchers invited 24 designers, 12 college students whose major is design and users of smart jewelry to participate in AHP surveys, and then collected the data and built judgment matrices. This method lists all indicators, and form an N × N matrix. In order to quantify the judgment, the researchers used the 1–9 scale proposed by Saaty and the details of 1–9 scale are shown in Table 3. Then, the researchers compared the factors to one another at one time. The evaluation of the factors shows the influence on the factors above them.

Values obtained from pairwise comparisons between different indicators are recorded as a_{ij}, If the ratio of element a_i to element a_j is a_{ij}, then the ratio of element a_j to element a_i is $1/a_{ij}$.

Table 3. Analytic hierarchy measurement scale

Reciprocal measure of intensity of importance	Definition	Explanation
1	Equal importance	Two activities contribute equally to the objective
3	Weak importance of one over another moderate importance	Experience and judgement slightly favor one activity over another
5	Moderate importance	Experience and judgement strongly favour one activity over another
7	Strong importance	An activity is strongly favored, and its dominance is demonstrated in practice
9	Absolute importance	The evidence favoring one activity over another is of the highest possible order of affirmation when compromise is needed
2, 4, 6, 8	Intermediate values between two adjacent judgements	When compromise is needed

3.6 Consistency Check

The research Group used mathematical methods to check the consistency of judgement Matrix in order to ensure that the judgment matrix can evaluate the importance of each index scientifically. The weighting factors of the different index can be computed by calculating vector resemblance-degree of index vector and normalization. The method of calculating the eigenvectors of a judgment matrix is:

$\bar{W}_i = \sqrt[n]{M_i}$ (M_i is the product of each row of the matrix).

Then the eigenvectors are normalized to get the relative weight W_i. The computing method is as follows:

$$W_i = \frac{\bar{W}_i}{\sum_{i=0}^{n} \bar{W}_i}$$

In order to verify whether the matrix constructed is consistent, a consistency checking is needed. "The oldest and most commonly used measures are the consistency index (CI) and consistency ratio (CR)" [4]. Here we need to calculate the value of consistency ratio CR, and the calculating formula is defined as:

$$CR = CI/RI$$

If CR = 0, the matrix created is completely consistent, and if CR = 1, it means that the matrix is completely inconsistent. Base on Saaty's theory, when CR is between 0.1 and 0.15, the consistency of the matrix is acceptable. When CR > 0.15, the evaluation need to be repeated until CR is within the range mentioned above. In this experiment, the value of CR is 0/0.490 < 1, meeting the consistency conditions.

3.7   Calculation of the Index Weight

Calculation process of weight is completed with aid of software Yaahp, and the result is shown as the follows:

Table 4. Weight of the index

User experience of the product (A)	Sensory experience (B_1)	0.312	Novel (C_1)	0.026
			Colorful (C_2)	0.039
			Fashionable (C_3)	0.057
			Delicate (C_4)	0.072
			Dazzling (C_5)	0.061
			Light (C_6)	0.057
	Operation experience (B_2)	0.211	Natural (C_7)	0.019
			Easy (C_8)	0.017
			Convenient (C_9)	0.033
			Effective (C_{10})	0.041
			Understandable (C_{11})	0.054
			Controllable (C_{12})	0.047
	Value experience (B_3)	0.477	Pleasurable (C_{13})	0.069
			Comfortable (C_{14})	0.063
			Reliable (C_{15})	0.047
			Considerate (C_{16})	0.040
			Warmhearted (C_{17})	0.057
			Qualitative (C_{18})	0.076
			Healthy (C_{19})	0.071
			Technological (C_{20})	0.054

4   Result and Conclusion

In this experiment, the researchers combine Kansei engineering and AHP together, and established a evaluation model for the user experience of smart jewelry creatively. The main purpose of Kansei Engineering is to explore the relationship of sensibility and rationality of products. By quantifying user's subjective feelings, designers can find the best combination in product design which can meet the specific sensitivity needs of users. When choosing a smart jewelry, the desire of purchasing is often influenced by user's values, background and culture. Kansei engineering builds a bridge between users and products, and then the user can communicate with the product psychologically. The researchers of this paper take user experience of smart jewelry as the object, but the experimental method mentioned in this paper can also be applied to other fields of design, such as wearable devices design, design evaluation and usability test.

According to the details shown in Table 4, we can clearly see that the value of the weight reflects the influence degree of each perceptual evaluation index on total user experience of the product. Experimental results show that users of smart jewelry pay more attention to the value experience, especially whether the product can improve their life quality. The weight of C_{19}(healthy) and C_{13} (pleasurable) are respectively the second and third largest values. So designers of smart jewelry need to consider that whether the product can lead to a healthy life. In addition, the pleasure brought by the product is also necessary.

In the second place, users tend to pay attention to the sensory experience brought by products. Smart jewelry still has the traditional function of decoration, therefore, the appearance of smart jewelry cannot be ignored. The weight of C_4 (delicate) and C_5 (dazzling) show that consumers still prefer those smart jewelry with fine and shining looking as same as traditional jewelry.

By calculating the weight of B_2, it seems that the users pay less attention to operation experience. It may due to that users of smart jewelry are mostly young people who are no longer new to electronic products. Users tend to focus on understandability and controllability of smart jewelry.

Research and Evaluation of user experience from the perspective of Kansei Engineering can help R & D and designers understand the current situation and improvement direction of the product, so as to enhance the quality of the product.

Through this experiments we can see that it is feasible to create a smart jewelry user experience evaluation model based on Kansei engineering. By applying the theory of Kansei engineering in design process, we can quantify subjective feelings of the user, and give better realization of user's emotional demand. Thus the designers can combine sensibility and rationality together in a product. Due to time, energy, and feasibility of experiment, samples selected in this article are restricted and it may also caused some limitations.

References

1. Shi, J., Ding, Y.: Construction of responsive jewelry brand in the Internet. Ideas Des. (3), 59–63 (2016)
2. Locke, J.: An Essay Concerning Humane Understanding, p. 44
3. Saaty, T.L., Peniwati, K.: Group Decision Making: Drawing out and Reconciling Differences. RWS Publications, Pittsburgh (2008). ISBN 978-1-888603-08-8
4. Brunelli, M., Critch, A., Fedrizzi, M.: A note on the proportionality between some consistency indices in the AHP. Appl. Math. Comput. **219**(14), 7901–7906 (2013)

A Systematic Literature Review of Usability Evaluation Guidelines on Mobile Educational Games for Primary School Students

Xiao Wen Lin Gao[✉], Braulio Murillo, and Freddy Paz

Pontificia Universidad Católica del Perú, San Miguel, Lima 32, Lima, Peru
{x.lin, fpaz}@pucp.pe, bmurillov@pucp.edu.pe

Abstract. Recently, mobile educational games became a trend for primary school students, because it makes children learn in an entertaining way, and since nowadays they spend more time with their mobile devices, especially smartphones, the usage of this games is widespread. This kind of games must consider different aspects so these can cover all the purpose that they want to provide, such as usability, playability, learnability, effectiveness, simplicity, and so on. That is why the usability evaluation plays an important role in it. However, despite the fact that a lot of usability evaluation methods exist, most of them are focused on traditional computer usage and those are not 100% compatible with mobile phone usage. Therefore, a systematic literature review was conducted in order to identify usability evaluation guidelines for mobile educational games, which are concerning primary school students as users. This work is the first step toward making a set of usability guidelines for the evaluation of mobile educational games for Primary school students.

Keywords: Systematic literature review · Usability guidelines ·
Usability evaluation · Mobile educational games · Primary school students

1 Introduction

Usability refers the extent to which a product can be used with efficiency, effectiveness and satisfaction in a specific use context and where the user meets certain goals with the use of this product [1]. This topic is very important in educational applications, given that if it has a high level of usability, it would effectively support learning and cause a positive impact by motivating students to learn, therefore the success or failure of these applications [2].

The challenge of educational games is the fact that the subconsciousness of people normally transmits the feeling that something related to education will not be entertaining even if it is related with any word that sounds fun by itself, as the word "video game", and that discourages people from using them [3]. One of the crucial factors is because usually, it is often to omit characteristics or features related to playability in most of the educational video games, as they pretend to have a strong educational intention [4]. For this reason, usability plays a significant role in those kinds of games,

The original version of this chapter was revised: Second author's family name has been corrected. The correction to this chapter is available at https://doi.org/10.1007/978-3-030-23535-2_46

helping the developers improve the visual aspects or the playability of them, in order to achieve higher acceptance of the players.

In this study, we present a systematic literature review to identify guidelines of usability evaluation on mobile educational games for primary school students and the aspects that are considered relevant in the usability evaluation of mobile educational video games. Through this procedure, we can find out the state of the art of mobile educational games guidelines for usability evaluation. It is intended to serve as a literature base for future work that want to create new set of mobile educational games guidelines of usability evaluation.

The paper has the following structure. In Sect. 2, we describe the main concepts related to our topic. In Sect. 3, we present the methodology used to undertake this study. In Sect. 4, we present the results of our research. Finally, we present the conclusions in Sect. 5.

2 Background

2.1 Usability

According to the ISO/IEC 9126-1 standard [5], usability is defined as "the capability of the software product to be understood, learned, used and attractive to the user, when used under specified conditions."

Another definition of usability is given by Nielsen [6], who defined it as "a quality attribute that assesses how easy user interfaces are to use." This author mentioned that the word usability also refers to "methods for improving ease-of-use during the design process", and defined it by 5 quality components:

- **Learnability:** How easy is it for users to accomplish basic tasks the first time they encounter the design?
- **Efficiency:** Once users have learned the design; how quickly can they perform tasks?
- **Memorability:** When users return to the design after a period of not using it, how easily can they reestablish proficiency?
- **Errors:** How many errors do users make, how severe are these errors, and how easily can they recover from the errors?
- **Satisfaction:** How pleasant is it to use the design?

2.2 Usability Evaluation

An evaluation method is a procedure composed by a series of activities well defined with the purpose of collect user data related to the interaction of a final user with a software product and to understand how specific features of this software contributes to achieve a certain degree of usability [7].

Although there are several taxonomies to classify the usability evaluation methods, these can be classified broadly into two main groups: empirical methods and inspection methods [8].

The empirical methods are based on capturing and analyzing the usage data from a group of representative users. While these users perform a series of predefined tasks, an evaluator, that could be human or a specific software, is registering the results of their actions. From the analysis of these collected results, it can provide us valuable information to detect usability problems [7].

On the other hand, the inspection methods are executed by expert evaluators or designers, which do not require the participation of real end users. These methods are based on examining the usability aspects of the user interface with a set of guidelines. These guidelines not only can review the compliance level of certain usability attributes, but also can predict problems related to software interfaces into a heuristic evaluation [9].

2.3 Game-Based Learning

According to Pho and Dinscore, game-based learning is a trend that has been implemented in many settings including workplace training, education, and social media [10]. It converts users into designers of their own learning environment using video games as a means. Many researches show successful results from innovative educational practices mediated by video games. Also, these studies highlight the positive impact in reasoning ability of children's education and the development of complex capabilities, such as leadership or cooperation using video games in Primary school students [11].

3 Systematic Literature Review

A systematic literature review is a methodology that identify, synthesize and interpret all available studies that are relevant to a research question formulated previously, or topic area, or phenomenon of interest [12]. Although systematic reviews require more effort than traditional reviews, the advantages undertaking this method are greater. It can identify any gaps in current research and summarize the existing evidence in the literature in order to help further investigations. The aim of this work is to identify relevant studies about guidelines of usability evaluation applied to mobile video games of the educational domain focused on primary school children. In addition, to identify educational games aspects that are commonly considered part of usability evaluation criteria. This work was based on the guidelines proposed by Kitchenham and Charters [13] for performing systematic literature reviews in the field of Software Engineering. The steps of this methodology are documented below.

3.1 Research Questions

The research questions formulated to this study are:

RQ1: What guidelines are used to measure the usability of educational video games for smartphones?

RQ2: What aspects of educational video games are considered in the usability evaluation?

In order to elaborate the search string, we defined general concepts using PICOC method. The "comparison" criterion was not considered, because the focus of this research was not comparing "interventions". The definition of each criterion is detailed in Table 1.

Table 1. Definition of the general concepts using PICOC.

Criterion	Description
Population	Educational video games on smartphones for primary school children
Intervention	Usability guidelines
Outcomes	Study cases which contribute usability guidelines of educational video games
Context	Academic context, software industry and all kinds of empirical studies

4   Search Process

Based on our research questions, we determined a set of terms and grouped them according to each criterion of PICOC. In order to get current studies in the review and relevant to the state of the art of usability guidelines for mobile educational games, we only considered studies whose publication year was after 2014. The search string defined was the following one:

("Educational game app" OR "educational video game" OR "mobile educational game" OR "educational game" OR "educational touchscreen application" OR "educational smartphone application" OR "educational smartphone game" OR "mobile games for learning" OR "game app for learning" OR "teaching with mobile games" OR "teaching with game apps") AND ("children" OR "primary school student" OR "primary school") AND ("Usability" OR "Interface" OR "User Interface" OR "UX" OR "User Experience") AND ("Methodology" OR "Method" OR "Framework" OR "Guidelines" OR "Principles" OR "design" OR "evaluation" OR "user interface" OR "study") AND (publication year > 2013)

The search process was performed by using three recognized databases in order to obtain the relevant studies: SCOPUS, Springer y IEEExplorer. The search string was adapted according to the instructions of each search engine. No additional study was considered.

4.1   Inclusion and Exclusion Criteria

Every article that was obtained from the search, was analyzed by its title, abstract and keywords, in order to determine its inclusion in the review, if the proposal presented was focused on educational video games developed in smartphones and had been applied for children of primary school. Additionally, we analyzed whether their content was about guidelines of usability evaluation or usability in general to decide if it had to be included as relevant studies in the context of the systematic review.

Articles that match any of the following items were excluded from this review: (1) *the study is not apply for mobile video games, but for computers or in-person games,* (2) *the study is not about usability,* and (3) *the study is not written in English.*

4.2   Data Collection

After the application of the procedure in the databases, 910 results were found, in which 36 studies were selected for the review process. The obtained studies were filtered based on our inclusion and exclusion criteria. Table 2 shows the summary of the amount of studies that were found in the search process, and Table 3 shows the list of selected studies.

Table 2. Summary of search results.

Database name	Search results	Duplicate papers	Relevant papers
SCOPUS	114	6	34
Springer	223	10	2
IEEExplorer	573	0	0
Total	910	16	36

Table 3. List of selected studies.

ID	Authors	Title	Year
003	Al Fatta H., Maksom Z., Zakaria M.H.	Systematic literature review on usability evaluation model of educational games: playability, pedagogy, and mobility aspects	2018
004	Maqsood S., Mekhail C., Chiasson S.	A day in the life of Jos: a web-based game to increase children's digital literacy	2018
006	Cruz B., Marchesini P., Gatto G., Souza-Concilio I.	A mobile game to practice arithmetic operations reasoning	2018
008	Drosos V., Alexandri A., Tsolis D., Alexakos C.	A 3D serious game for cultural education	2018
009	Tuli N., Gargrish S., Mantri A.	Low-cost learning environment for grass-root education	2018
012	Nascimento, I., Silva, W., Gadelha, B., Conte, T.	Userbility: a technique for the evaluation of user experience and usability on mobile applications	2016
015	Bunt L., Leendertz V., Seugnet Blignaut A.	A heuristic evaluation of the design and development of a statistics serious game	2017
016	Muravevskaia E.	Empathy development in young children using interactive VR games	2017
019	Petri G., Von Wangenheim C. G., Borgatto A.F.	A large-scale evaluation of a model for the evaluation of games for teaching software engineering	2017
021	Duh E.S., Koceska N., Koceski S.	Game-based learning: educational game Azbuka to help young children learn writing Cyrillic letters	2017
022	Gunawan T.S., Bahari B., Kartiwi M.	Development of educational game for primary school mathematics using microsoft kinect	2017
023	Adnan F., Prasetyo B., Nuriman N.	Usability testing analysis on the Bana game as education game design references on junior high school	2017
029	Álvarez-Xochihua O. et al.	Comparing usability, user experience and learning motivation characteristics of two educational computer games	2017
030	Sriharee G.	Software development perspective on game-based learning	2017

(continued)

Table 3. (*continued*)

ID	Authors	Title	Year
031	Alsumait, A., Al-Osaimi, A.	Usability heuristics evaluation for child e-learning applications	2009
033	Xinogalos S., Satratzemi M., Malliarakis C.	Microworlds, games, animations, mobile apps, puzzle editors and more: what is important for an introductory programming environment?	2017
044	Hussain A., Abdullah A., Husni H.	The design principles of edutainment system for autistic children with communication difficulties	2016
055	Martins V.F., Sampaio P.N. M. et al.	Usability evaluation of a gestural interface application for children	2016
064	Yannier N., Koedinger K.R., Hudson S.E.	Learning from mixed-reality games: is shaking a tablet as effective as physical observation?	2015
065	Veeramanickam M.R.M., Radhika N.	A study on educational games application model in E-learning cloud system	2015
066	Ni Q., Yu Y.	Research on educational mobile games and the effect it has on the cognitive development of preschool children	2015
067	Nagalingam V., Ibrahim R.	User experience of educational games: a review of the elements	2015
073	Mozelius P., Torberg D., Castillo C.C.	An educational game for mobile learning - some essential design factors	2015
078	Figueiredo M., Bidarra J.	The development of a gamebook for education	2015
079	Bidarra J., Figueiredo M., Natálio C.	Interactive design and gamification of ebooks for mobile and contextual learning	2015
080	Bidarra J., Natálio C., Figueiredo M.	Designing ebook interaction for mobile and contextual learning	2015
082	Kiili K., Lainema T., de Freitas S., Arnab S.	Flow framework for analyzing the quality of educational games	2014
084	Roscoe R.D. et al.	The writing pal intelligent tutoring system: usability testing and development	2014
085	Hswen Y., Rubenzahl L., Bickham D.S.	Feasibility of an online and mobile videogame curriculum for teaching children safe and healthy cellphone and internet behaviors	2014
090	Malliarakis C., Satratzemi M., Xinogalos S.	Designing educational games for computer programming: a holistic framework	2014
091	Marques D., da Silva A.C., da Silva L.F.	A survey to evaluate educational games designed to teach software engineering	2014
111	Khanana K., Law E.L.-C.	Designing children's digital games on nutrition with playability heuristics	2013
115	Souza-Concilio I.A. et al.	CalcPlusWeb: a computer game to stimulate the reasoning in mathematics	2013
119	Leidi J. Enriquez Muñoz et al.	Graphical user interface design guide for mobile applications aimed at deaf children	2018
160	Débora N. F. Barbosa et al.	Using mobile learning in formal and non-formal educational settings	2016

5   Data Analysis and Results

In order to determine the relevant studies for the present work, we have identified those which have their main topic as educational video games and divide into subtopics that are relevant for our analysis. The selected results are presented below in Table 4.

Table 4. Frequency of topics related to our research.

ID	Related topic	Studies	Number of studies
T1	Mobile applications	160	1
T2	Primary school children	022	1
T3	Usability	029, 030, 082, 084, 091	5
T4	Guidelines of usability evaluation	016, 019, 033, 090, 111, 115	6
T5	Mobile applications + focus on Primary school children	-	0
T6	Mobile applications + usability	012, 023, 065, 067, 073	5
T7	Focus on primary school children + usability	004, 008, 009, 019, 111, 115	6
T8	Mobile applications + focus on primary school children + usability	003, 006, 015, 016, 021, 031, 044, 055, 064, 066, 078, 079, 080, 085, 119	15
	Total		39

5.1   Usability Evaluation Methods

Based on the articles obtained in the systematic review, it was observed that the most common methods for usability evaluation of mobile applications were through heuristics, metrics and questionnaires. Most of the usability evaluations were based on a specific application, with an emphasis on the user interface aspect.

A study reveals that they have found evaluation models specifically for the aspect of playability, such as the *SEEM model* and entertaining factors evaluation metrics proposed by Read, Macfarlane and Casey [14].

USERBILITY model, a model that evaluates the user experience (UX) and usability of mobile applications in general, using generic heuristics based on the Nielsen model. Although this model has been designed for mobile applications, it does not take into account the distinctive characteristics of the mobile environment. For the evaluation of user experience, Userbility uses the *3E model* (Expressions, Emotions and Experiences), this model is also a generic model for evaluating the user experience, and is not designed especially for mobile applications [15].

HECE, a model to evaluate the dimensions of playability for children, that uses the Nielsen model as a basis and adds aspects of usability for children, where it also assesses aspects such as learning ability for children and if it is appropriate for them [16]. The authors use this model to apply it in the development of usability evaluation for m-GBL in primary schools.

A study has established *guidelines for Graphical User Interface* (GUI) for the design and development of mobile application prototypes focused on children with hearing impairment. Additionally, they applied an usability evaluation using the inspection method, taking into account three types of user profiles: specialists in children with hearing disabilities, designers and developers. They take into consideration aspects of identity criteria, design, accessibility and the development of the GUI design guide for mobile applications aimed at children with hearing disabilities [17].

The *MEEGA model* is intended to be used in case studies that begin with the treatment of educational videogames, and after playing the game, the MEEGA questionnaire is answered by the apprentices in order to collect the respective data [18].

The *Usability Testing*, consists in Nielsen's model of evaluating the aspects of ease of learning, efficiency, memorability, errors and satisfaction [19].

5.2   Aspects Considered in the Usability Evaluation of Mobile Educational Video Games

We found that in addition to the five main aspects in the traditional usability evaluation [6], aspects such as visibility, game logic, playability, simplicity and learning capacity are also taken into consideration. Table 5 shows the number of studies found in this research of each aspect that are relevant to our domain.

Table 5. Aspects considered in the usability evaluation of mobile educational video games.

Aspects of usability evaluation	Number of studies
Learnability	12
Efficiency	6
Memorability	3
Errors	3
Satisfaction	10
Visibility	5
Game logic	16
Playability	**30**
Simplicity	6
Learning capacity	29
Mobility	5
Good design	**30**

Below are the studies that substantiate the importance of the aspects selected as relevant:

Since it is about gaming applications, *playability* would be the fundamental characteristic for the usability evaluation. This plays a very important role in children's learning, since their natural way of learning is through experience [14].

Mozelius indicates a set of key factors for the design of mobile educational games, which are: *simplicity, mobility, usability, playability, gradual increase of game levels, practical and conceptual understanding, collaboration, competition*, among others [20].

From Padilla's point of view, it must take into consideration the aspect of *playability* for an educational video game to be really effective, which makes it attractive to users, and the *learning capacity*, which allows users to obtain an educational benefit from the game [3].

According to Maqsood, Mekhail and Chiasson, they take into consideration aspects such as the *length of the game content*, the *relevance of the themes*, the *visual design* and the *learning capacity*, important for an educational game. They mention that the group of children who participated in the study case, preferred designs with characters that look older, because they felt that they can teach them about situations that may be found in the future. In addition, the colors used in the game also play an important role, since they can influence the perceptions that the players have [21].

According to the results of Cruz's study, who applied a questionnaire to evaluate usability in his mobile video game, which involves practicing reasoning of arithmetic operations. It is observed that aspects such as visibility of the system state and the consistency of elements such as buttons are not so relevant for the players. However, aspects such as the competitiveness of multiplayer and sound effects are important factors, as it motivates the player to continue playing and therefore generate *satisfaction* in the players. Another point that highlights the game is that not only has the logical reasoning part, but also has help with strategies, so players can have easier situations to win the game, in which this is related to the appearance of *simplicity* of the game [22].

In a study of Drosos, applied to a serious 3D game, the students who tried the game mentioned that it was very flat and that it did not have characteristics that increased the pleasure of playing it. So, it can be said, that the *playability* plays an important role in educational games. Although, the majority has mentioned that they like the 3D *design of the game*, and that it was a pleasant educational experience learning new concepts about El Greco, which was the central theme of the game [23].

6 Conclusions and Future Works

Based on the information obtained from the systematic literature review, we present the state of the art of usability evaluation methods for mobile educational video games. In addition, we identify the impact that these mobile applications have on primary school children lives nowadays. Studies related to m-learning have been found, either in a general way or applied to a specific educational level. However, there are not many studies that link the importance of m-learning with the game usability. The existing usability evaluation methods seems not to concern all the aspects about a mobile educational game. Some studies about the development of new mobile educational game evaluate it usability adapting general usability heuristics. The results indicate a need for new sets of guidelines of usability evaluation for mobile educational games, especially focused on primary school children, since they are mainly the target audience of this kind of applications.

References

1. Bevan, N., Carter, J., Harker, S.: ISO 9241-11 revised: what have we learnt about usability since 1998? In: Kurosu, M. (ed.) HCI 2015. LNCS, vol. 9169, pp. 143–151. Springer, Cham (2015). https://doi.org/10.1007/978-3-319-20901-2_13
2. Valdez-Velazquez, L.L., Gomez-Sandoval, Z.: A usability study of educational molecular visualization on smart phones (2014)
3. Padilla Zea, N.: Metodología para el diseño de videojuegos educativos sobre una arquitectura para el análisis del aprendizaje colaborativo. Metodología para el diseño de videojuegos educativos sobre una arquitectura para el análisis del aprendizaje colaborativo (2011)
4. González Sánchez, J.L.: Caracterización de la experiencia del jugador en video juegos. Editorial de la Universidad de Granada (2010)
5. ISO/IEC 9126-1: ISO/IEC 9126-1:2001 - Software engineering – Product quality – Part 1: Quality model (2001). https://www.iso.org/standard/22749.html. Accessed 05 Oct 2018
6. Nielsen, J.: Usability 101: Introduction to Usability (2012). https://www.nngroup.com/articles/usability-101-introduction-to-usability/. Accessed 30 Sept 2018
7. Fernandez, A., Insfran, E., Abrahão, S.: Usability evaluation methods for the web: a systematic mapping study. Inf. Softw. Technol. **53**(8), 789–817 (2011)
8. Insfran, E., Fernandez, A.: A systematic review of usability evaluation in web development. In: Hartmann, S., Zhou, X., Kirchberg, M. (eds.) WISE 2008. LNCS, vol. 5176, pp. 81–91. Springer, Heidelberg (2008). https://doi.org/10.1007/978-3-540-85200-1_10
9. Paz, F., Pow-Sang, J.A.: Usability evaluation methods for software development: a systematic mapping review. In: Proceedings of 8th International Conference on Advances Software Engineering and Its Applications, ASEA 2015, vol. 10, no. 1, pp. 1–4 (2016)
10. Pho, A., Dinscore, A.: Game-Based Learning (2015)
11. del Moral Pérez, M.E., Guzmán-Duque, A.P., Fernández, L.C.: Proyecto game to learn: aprendizaje basado enjuegos para potenciar las inteligencias lógico-matemática, naturalista y lingüística en educaciónprimaria. Pixel-Bit. Rev. Medios y Educ., no. 49 (2016)
12. Kitchenham, B.: Procedures for performing systematic reviews. Keele UK Keele Univ. **33**, 1–26 (2004)
13. Kitchenham, B., Charters, S.: Guidelines for performing systematic literature reviews in software engineering version. Engineering **45**(4ve), 1051 (2007)
14. Al Fatta, H., Maksom, Z., Zakaria, M.H.: Systematic literature review on usability evaluation model of educational games : playability, pedagogy, and mobility aspects 1. J. Theor. Appl. Inf. Technol. **31**(14) (2018)
15. Nascimento, I., Silva, W., Gadelha, B., Conte, T.: Userbility: a technique for the evaluation of user experience and usability on mobile applications. In: Kurosu, M. (ed.) HCI 2016. LNCS, vol. 9731, pp. 372–383. Springer, Cham (2016). https://doi.org/10.1007/978-3-319-39510-4_35
16. Alsumait, A., Al-Osaimi, A.: Usability heuristics evaluation for child e-learning applications. In: Proceedings of the 11th International Conference on Information Integration and Web-based Applications & Services – iiWAS 2009, p. 425 (2009)
17. Muñoz, L.J.E., et al.: Graphical user interface design guide for mobile applications aimed at deaf children. In: Zaphiris, P., Ioannou, A. (eds.) LCT 2018. LNCS, vol. 10924, pp. 58–72. Springer, Cham (2018). https://doi.org/10.1007/978-3-319-91743-6_4

18. Petri, G., Gresse von Wangenheim, C., Ferreti Borgatto, A.: A large-scale evaluation of a model for the evaluation of games for teaching software engineering. In: 2017 IEEE/ACM 39th International Conference on Software Engineering: Software Engineering Education and Training Track (ICSE-SEET), pp. 180–189 (2017)
19. Adnan, F., Prasetyo, B., Nuriman, N.: Usability testing analysis on the Bana game as education game design references on junior high school. J. Pendidik. IPA Indones. **6**(1) (2017)
20. Mozelius, P., Torberg, D., Castillo, C.C.: An Educational Game for Mobile Learning-Some Essential Design Factors (2015). books.google.com
21. Maqsood, S., Mekhail, C., Chiasson, S.: A day in the life of JOS. In: Proceedings of the 17th ACM Conference on Interaction Design and Children - IDC 2018, pp. 241–252 (2018)
22. Cruz, B., Marchesini, P., Gatto, G., Souza-Concilio, I.: A mobile game to practice arithmetic operations reasoning. In: 2018 IEEE Global Engineering Education Conference (EDUCON), pp. 2003–2008 (2018)
23. Drosos, V., Alexandri, A., Tsolis, D., Alexakos, C.: A 3D serious game for cultural education. In 2017 8th International Conference on Information, Intelligence, Systems and Applications (IISA), pp. 1–5 (2017)

Using Mobile Eye Tracking to Evaluate the Satisfaction with Service Office

Zai Xing Liu[✉], Yi Liu, and Xun Gao

Guangzhou Academy of Fine Arts, No. 257, Changgang East Road,
Haizhu District, Guangzhou, Guangdong Province, People's Republic of China
392641@qq.com

Abstract. Eye tracking can be applied to a variety of scenarios as a means of measuring visual attention and interpreting visual solution strategies. In this article, we use mobile eye-tracker to collect information to evaluate user satisfaction with the tax service office. Mobile eye tracking can collect precise information concerning the users' visual attention and interactions in authentic environments. Unlike screen-based eye-tracker using a laboratory or stationary computer, mobile eye tracking also can be used effectively in a walk a round scene where users could walk around and interact with diverse resources. In the progress of eye tracking data analysis, fixations and gaze points, areas of interest (AOIs), heat-maps play an important role. This annotation is typically the most time-consuming step of the analysis process. To reduce processing time and human effort, we introduced the latest computer vision techniques (i.e., You Only Look Once, YOLO) based on a convolutional neural network (CNN) to detect and recognize specific objects in recorded video. We propose a new method to evaluate the user satisfaction of a service system by implicating mobile eye tracker. In addition we gave a new idea of using CNN-based object detection technique to annotate video data collected by mobile eye tracker, which could be followed up for further analysis.

Keywords: User experience · Mobile eye tracking · Satisfaction evaluation · Visual analytics · YOLO

1 Introduction

Eye tracker technology can be widely used in a variety of situations related to visual psychology by capturing user gaze information [1]. Fixations and gaze points, areas of Interest (AOI) play an important role because they provide semantic information about the area being surveyed or potentially interested [2]. The measured gaze information can be assigned to the AOI as the basis for many statistical [3] and visual [4] evaluation methods. For static source from screen based eye tracker, defining AOI is easier to perform than using mobile eye tracker. For AOIs (or objects of interest) could move, change their size and shape, and even disappear and regain in dynamic scene. Performing a manual annotation with objects of interest is a time consuming processing.

However, with the continuous development of deep learning technology, a variety of target recognition and detection algorithms have been proposed, gradually replacing

© Springer Nature Switzerland AG 2019
A. Marcus and W. Wang (Eds.): HCII 2019, LNCS 11586, pp. 183–195, 2019.
https://doi.org/10.1007/978-3-030-23535-2_14

traditional objects recognition and Detection algorithm (i.e., You Only Look Once, YOLO). Among these algorithms, YOLO [5] is the fastest while preserves high precision. This model uses a single neural network to predict bounding boxes and class probabilities in one evaluation. Then it became possible to calculate the distance between gaze points and objects recognized in the video frames collected in mobile eye tracking examination. To improve analysis efficiency with computer algorithms, Kuno Kurzhals and his group provide a novel visual analytics approach to accomplish the annotation process by image-based, automatic clustering of eye tracking data integrated in an interactive labeling and analysis system [6]. They demonstrate their approach with eye tracking data from a real experiment and compare it to an analysis of the data by manual annotation of dynamic AOIs. This method provides a good idea for using computer vision to assist in the analysis of eye tracker data.

Our main contribution in this article is giving a new visual analytics approach that allows the efficient comparison of data from multiple videos acquired during experiments with mobile eye tracking. By including unsupervised clustering techniques in the pre-processing and interactive image queries in the labeling step of the analysis process, we achieve annotation results comparable to current state-of-the-art techniques, but with far less human effort and a more efficient annotation process.

2 Related Works

User experience research includes the entire process of users using products, and has become one of the core competitiveness of current industrial design. For user experience evaluation methods, there are many research related. Vermeeren compares multiple user experience methods such as questionnaire assessment, self-report assessment, vocal thinking assessment, and physiology-scientific assessment methods [8]. Virpi Roto conducts retrospective analysis of user experience evaluation methods (UXEM) collected by academia and industry, such as observation, eye movement, heart rate, myoelectricity, questionnaires, etc. evaluate user perception [9]. Marchitto explores the application of cognitive psychology and ergonomics in user experience assessment [10]. Ramakrisnan used the eye tracker experimental method to conduct human-computer interaction evaluation of electronic systems [11]. Shin studies the user experience research model in the 3D virtual environment. The cognitive sensation and usage behavior of the user in the experimental questionnaire are recorded in the experiment, which verifies the important role of user cognition and perception in the overall experience of the user [12]. Vaananen, Obrist, et al. discuss about user experience base on "analysis of behavioral value of usability", "user experience and user acceptance", "experience in product innovation design", "how to choose user experience method" and "user research theory and its practical application" [13–16].

Eye tracking is considered to be the most effective method of visual information recognition and processing for human-computer interaction. Eye tracking is also an important method of assessing the user interface in the field of work. Through the visual cleverness of how to search and locate the user in the determined task, the deep cognitive mechanism of the user's eye movement behavior can be analyzed, and the human behavior of the user interface such as vision, cognition and attention can be deeply studied [7].

In the previous eye tracking research, the user's eye movement behavior indicators are as follows; such as the first gaze time, the first gaze point and the gaze map. For example, Golberg et al. used eye movement data evaluation methods to explore the differences in response of users to different user interface materials. The eye movement data coordinates and the saccade path indicators are used to measure the interface quality [17]. Augustyniak et al. proposed a new interpretation method which using eye tracking characteristics by collecting the visual inspection behavior of expert users. Through the participation of 17 expert participants and 21 students in visual test tasks, the characteristics of eye movement parameters in the estimation of eye movements were revealed [18]. Ito et al. Uses eye movements with an average gaze ratio to visualize the user's visual behavior [19]. On the other hand, Burch et al. used the thermograph, visual trajectory and area of interest (AOI) to describe the cognitive process of three different tree visualization charts [20]. Liu et al. used eye-tracking technology to measure the impact of the residual text information on the screen on the user's perception of the multimedia process. The experiment collected indicators such as the number of fixation points and the duration of fixation, and the average fixation time, to compare the information processing strategies of participants when browsing the web. Participants collected and assessed their cognitive load levels in the task through a self-assessment questionnaire [21]. Zulch studied the relationship between different data expression methods by observing the number of gaze points and the first gaze time. By observing the different behavior strategies of different users in searching data [22]. In general, eye movement data such as Areas of interest (AOI), Heat map, time to first fixation, and fixations before fixation are the main acquisition object of eye tracking research.

The studies presented in this article use mobile eye tracking techniques to evaluate the usability of service systems. Mobile eye tracking is far less constrained, allowing the participants to move freely during an experiment. Nevertheless, mobile eye tracking becomes more and more popular, allowing "in-the-wild" studies that are not possible with restricting experimental settings. Therefore, the development of more efficient analysis methods for these challenging datasets is an important research field. Only few studies investigated how mobile eye tracking techniques can be used in real world scenarios. Schuchard et al. examined the ideal sign placement for patients with dementia in a nursing home [23]. The group of participants was restricted to persons who need special assistance, no navigation aid was used and the study was very exploratory. Similarly, Pinelo da Silva used mobile eye tracking to examine visual cognition and way finding in the city of London but no navigation aid was included [24]. Delikostidis used eye tracking to examine pedestrian navigation systems during his experiments [25]. He conducted a field study in an outdoor area showing different mobile map depictions.

As a summary, eye tracking is a well-established measurement technique in research fields of variety aspects. However, as already stated above, until now it is rarely used to evaluate the usability of a service system (specially, a government service department). In this article, we filled this methodological gap by measuring the users' gazes and objects of interest (or the association mappings between them) during a real-world navigation experiment that examines the suitability of specific task flow in a service system.

3   Domain Problem Characterizations and Design Process

3.1   Government Service Department Task Flow Characteristics

The local taxation and taxation authority is one of the state's public administration institutions. The quality and efficiency of taxation services provided by the taxation administration directly affects the image of the government. More important, the management skills in organizing tax revenue directly affect the government's fiscal revenue [26]. The tax service hall, as the mainly contact to the pubic for the local tax authorities to handle the business externally, its law enforcement ability and performance are related directly to the attraction to taxpayers. However, the public still feeling that there is still a big gap between the attitude and management effectiveness of government agencies and their expectations. They are not only concerned about whether the government has fulfilled its due responsibilities, but also concerned that the government is fulfilling its duties. Whether the responsibility is efficient and convenient, and whether they can get a fast, effective and satisfactory service response when they go to the government department or seek help. In this context, my team cooperated with the Local Tax Service Hall of Yuexiu District, Guangzhou (P.R.CHINA) to use the mobile eye tracker as Experimental instrument. We design a corresponding test plan and performing actual user testing follow the service flow in the tax service hall, aid to objectively evaluate the satisfaction of the taxpayers with the service quality of the service system.

3.2   Implementation Process Introduction and Analysis

After preliminary investigation, we found that the tax administration business could classify with five categories: declaration, correction, tax registration, document acceptance, and punishment. And the applicants are divided into enterprises, private industrials, flexible employment and natural persons. Taxpayers with different identity will involve different types of tax administration business, and related tax business processes would be very different. For example, the process for "tax withholding registration" shows in Fig. 1 and the process for "Examination and approval of VAT deduction vouchers deduction" shows in Fig. 2.

Fig. 1. The steps process in the flow of "tax withholding registration".

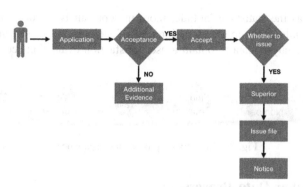

Fig. 2. The steps process in the flow of "examination and approval of VAT deduction vouchers deduction".

Obviously, different business must be carried out according to the established process, and each process is quite different. This is the contradictory two-sided feature of the services provided in the government service hall: on the one hand, the user is required to complete the cumbersome established process to achieve his goal; on the other hand, the user is as a consumer to be serviced, and the service provider wishes to provide better service to increase their satisfaction. In such a special scenario, we must design a reasonable evaluation method to understand the user's pain points more accurately, so as to give reasonable suggestions for how to improving their satisfaction. In this case, mobile eye tracker gave a perfect solution as an instrument to record the whole process with the user's first perspective.

Then, we have to abstract the various business processes of the steps into one unified task process for the following three reasons. First, our purpose is to evaluate the satisfaction of the taxpayers, so the experiment we design should stand on the user experience as the basic dimension, and the detail of business is not our concerned. So we could ignore the difference in detail and merge some steps of those processes. Secondly, for the participants in this experiment are real users, they come to the office to have their own purposes and will not follow the same process. That is, collecting enough statistics for the same process would be very time-consuming and would be too expensive for our budget. Therefore, we need to summarize the task flow of different users into an abstract unified process, in order to calculate the test data from different test samples, and then obtain objective evaluation values. Third, the test data collected by mobile eye tracker is combining with video stream and gaze points' position record, which is some kind of unstructured data. It is one of the methods for effectively extracting structured data by dividing the video stream data into units by their duration. For example, the difference time consumed in stages can be counted and comparison.

3.3 Analysis Process

As mentioned above, to summarize all service processes into a unified interactive task sequence is the footstone of subsequent data analysis. After manual analysis to all recorded data, we summarize the seven key task sequences, shown in Fig. 3. With this task sequence as the statistical latitude, more in-depth analysis could be implement. Basically, we could count up the execution time of each task node and various types of eye movement analysis data to obtain a user satisfaction evaluation score.

| Entrance | Get a Number | Finding Counter | Waiting | At Counter | Tax Collector |

Fig. 3. Tax service process task sequence.

4   Eye Tracker Data Processing

4.1   Experimental Design

We used a head-mounted eye tracker to perform a mobile eye tracking experiment to record eye movement data of participants during business process. Among the people who came to the service hall for tax administration business, we randomly selected four different identities (enterprises, private industrials, flexible employment and natural persons) for testing. During the experiment, participants were asked to wear a head-mounted eye tracker at the entrance and complete their business process with the eye tracker until they are finish. They need to complete the process of taking a number, looking for the counter, and at the counter without any special help. Since the selected head-mounted eye tracker is very light, the participant can subjectively ignore the presence of the eye tracker for a short time and remain relaxed during the experiment. In addition, in order to record the actual fact of how the participants completing the business process, test assistants will not communicate with them at all until the end.

We completed a total of 35 tests in three days. After exporting the eye tracker data, we obtained a total of 1920 * 1080 resolution and a total duration of 892 min of video image data. Some screenshots are shown in Fig. 4, the red circle in the picture is the gaze point.

Fig. 4. Screenshots from video record in the experiment. (Color figure online)

4.2   Apparatus

Wearable eye tracker designed to capture natural viewing behavior in any real-world environment while ensuring outstanding eye tracking robustness and accuracy. It's possible to combine with biometric devices for even deeper insights into human behavior. This experiment used a Tobii Pro Glasses 2 Eye Tracker (www.tobii.com), which Sampling rate is up to 100 Hz. The Tobii Pro Glasses 2 head unit films what the participant sees and records the ambient sound while moving around. The pocket-sized recording unit saves the gaze data onto an SD card. Figure 6 shows the author calibrating the headset eye tracker for the participant in this test project.

Fig. 5. Tobii Pro Glasses 2, image from Tobii Official website. (Color figure online)

Fig. 6. The author is calibrating the mobile eye tracker for the participant in this project.

4.3   Problems and Solution Strategy

Interpretation of Eye Tracking Mode in Usability Testing In view of the past usability tracking mode usability study, the main statistical parameters are: number of gaze points, gaze ratio (time ratio) of each region of interest, average gaze dwell time, The number of points of interest for each region of interest, the average gaze dwell time for each region of interest, and the gaze rate (gaze points) [27]. The "number of fixation points" means that the total number of fixation points is considered to be an indicator related to search performance, and the "average fixation dwell time" is the average value of the fixation stay time in a period of time, "The average gaze dwell time of each interest area" is the average of the dwell time of an object. Long gaze is considered to be difficult for the subject to extract information from the display interface. If the subject's gaze on a particular display element is longer, it indicates that it is difficult to extract or interpret the information on the display element. A larger number of gaze points indicate a low performance search. Can be used to display the poor layout of the elements. At the same time, the large value of these data also represents the psychological impatience and conflict of the data users, which also means that the user's satisfaction begins to decrease [27].

However, as described above, Since the data collected by head-mounted eye tracker are recorded during the user's movement, the AOIs extract from coordinates of the gaze points could be no specific meaning. If we apply hotspot map, focus map, and gaze map to gaze points in the mobile eye tracker testing, the result tending to focus in the center of the picture, which has no practical significance for further analysis. Obviously, in this case, it would consume a lot time to annotation the association of gaze points and region of interest manually. In order to solve this problem, this article introduces the YOLO V3 algorithm based on convolutional neural network, which could quickly identify the objects in the video image and gave the corresponding coordinate regions. By comparing the coordinates with gaze points, it is possible to automatically determine whether user's attention stays on an object, and further statistic to objects of interest with the user's attention.

4.4 YOLO Network Architecture

YOLO (You Only Look Once) is an end-to-end convolution neural network commonly used in object detection recognition. The main features of YOLO include high speed and accuracy. Redmon and others developed The YOLO (You Only Look Once) algorithm at 2016 [5]. It is a regression-based target recognition method. By 2018, it has developed to the third generation YOLO V3 [28]. Just like its name, it only needs to do a forward calculation to detect a variety of objects, so the YOLO series algorithm is super fast. YOLO V3 still maintains the fast detection speed of YOLO V2 [29], and the recognition accuracy is greatly improved, especially in the detection and recognition of small targets. YOLO V3 draws on the idea of residual neural network, introduces multiple residual network modules and uses multi-scale prediction to improve the defect of YOLO V2 for small target recognition. For it has high detection accuracy and high speed, it is one of the best algorithms for target detection. This model uses a number of well formed 3 * 3 and 1 * 1 convolutional layers, and some residual network structures are used later for multi-scale prediction. In the end it had 53 convolutional layers, so the author also called them Darknet-53. YOLO V3 introduces the idea of using anchor boxes [30] in Faster R-CNN, and uses 3 scales for COCO datasets and VOC datasets to predict each scale. There are 3 anchor boxes [30] for each scale, and the feature map uses a small predict box. And the network structure can be modified according to the scale of the prediction of the preparation.

4.5   Processing

Our goal is to design a method and develop related algorithms and build a system to automatically counting the number of gaze points, fixation duration, average fixation duration, gazing objects. First step is to split each video record into sub-records according to the task sequence shown in Fig. 3. Then apply YOLO V3 algorithm on each sub-record and obtain all coordinate of box of object shown out in each frame (technically, sequence of coordinates). Finally, to develop corresponding compare algorithms for different situations, generating statistical data automatically as output. The complete processing steps are shown in Fig. 7. And some screenshots from processed results after applied YOLO V3 algorithm to videos recorded by mobile eye tracker are shown in Fig. 8.

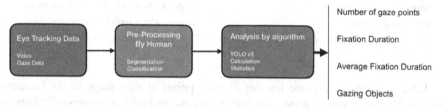

Fig. 7. We create an analysis process for mobile eye tracking data. (Red: video and gaze point coordinate sequence. Yellow: manually segment the video according to the process node, and classify the processing content to give the corresponding statistical algorithm. Green: apply YOLO V3 algorithm and generate statistical data: number of gaze points, fixation duration, average fixation duration, gazing objects.) (Color figure online)

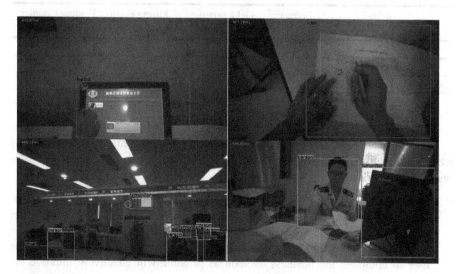

Fig. 8. From left to right, from top to bottom are as follows: get a number, filling a form, finding counter, at counter.

As shown in the bottom left picture of Fig. 8, after the annotation to video contents by the YOLO algorithm, some extra objects were identified. If these objects are given to next step for counting, they will become some kind of interference data. So we need to pre-process (yellow mark in Fig. 5) those videos, mark the objects that need to be counted, and give them to the statistical program for statistics. According to the above evaluation strategy and the actual situation of the experimental process, the data collected and the evaluation criteria are shown in Table 1. The eye tracker automatically collects the experimental data, and all the values are averaged after the data is generated, and the data is retained one decimal place.

Table 1. Data collection and evaluation criteria

Data collection	Evaluation criteria
Number of gaze points	Larger values indicate more attention
Fixation duration	Larger values indicate more attention
Object of interest and average fixation duration	Less value indicates less attention

Table 2 is for the average number of gaze points at each stage of the business process. The data shows that there are higher gaze points in the two stages of "filling in the form" and "waiting". Explain that these two steps have produced significant congestion and is one of the factors that reduce user satisfaction.

Table 2. Duration and average number of gaze points

	Entrance	Get a number	Filling Form	Finding Counter
Number of Gaze Point	25.2	16.9	223.2	34.7

	Waiting	At Counter	Tex Collector
Number of Gaze Point	210.2	134.7	185.8

The user's attention at each stage of the business process and the corresponding average gaze duration are shown in Table 3. By analyzing these data, we can get some interesting conclusions:

(1) When the user is in the "waiting" phase, the attention time for the "mobile phone" suddenly rises, while at other stages it is almost zero. It can be judged that the user is "busy" at other stages, and the user is in a state of psychological tension. Therefore, if the consulting service can be added at various stages, assisting the user to complete the business as soon as possible will effectively improve the user's satisfaction.

(2) From the comparison of the attention values of "display" and "queue ticket", it can be seen that the user pays attention to the "queue ticket" at the same time when paying attention to the "queuing ticket", and the two have the relevance of attention. The reason is that while user is in the stage before the "At Counter", the row number information provided on the "queue ticket" needs to be compared with the calling number information provided on the screen. It is also a design direction to improve user satisfaction by reducing the user's attention time for both of them.

(3) The attention time for "Ad. Material" is obviously unreasonably little, and even insufficient attention has been paid in the "entry" stage. Consider adjusting the slab design or placement of the advertising material to get a higher profile.

Table 3. Object of interest and average fixation duration (s)

	Entrance	Get a number	Filling form	Finding counter	Waiting	At counter	Tex collector
Person	27.1	3.1	23.5	2.1	0.4	54	83.6
Monitor	0	**10.8**	0	**12.4**	**23.8**	1.4	0
Paper	0	0	125.3	0	0	28.1	24.6
Ticket	0	**4.23**	0	10.2	**30.1**	0	0
Chair	0	0	0	2.3	0	132	1.3
Cell phone	0	0	0	2.3	**302.2**	0	0
Ad. material	**0.3**	0	0	0.2	0.1	0	0
Others	2.2	0.4	4.2	8.2	12.4	3.2	1.6

5 Conclusion

User-experience assessment using a mobile eye-tracker (especially in the scenarios that user could walk around) is more objective and more logged than traditional ways, such as user interviews, questionnaires, observations, etc. In addiction, the evaluation of the latitude is more abundant; the test sample is small and so on. However, due to the particularity of the experimental method of the mobile eye tracker, it is necessary to solve the problem of how to analyze the image data with moving object of interest. In this paper, the YOLO v3 object recognition program is used to automatically recognize the coordinates of the objects and compare them with the coordinates of the gaze points. The valuable statistical data could be quickly obtained automatically by the processing method we gave.

This article proposes a new method to evaluate the user satisfaction of the service system. Although it is not rigorous enough from the statics data, but it provides a new idea to analyze data recorded by mobile eye-tracker. With this idea, we could design more automated test methods, for example, pre-position specific patterns in the executed space of each stage, so that the object recognition algorithm could automatically recognize these patterns, to let the analyze system could automatically divide each task phase. Or, training the YOLO algorithm to recognize a specific object (for example, the "person" could divide into "visitor" and "staff"), and the statistic data with marking specific objects could be used for subsequent effective analysis.

References

1. Duchowski, A.: A breadth-first survey of eye-tracking applications. Behav. Res. Method Instrum. Comput. **34**(4), 455–470 (2002)
2. Goldberg, J.H., Kotval, X.P.: Computer interface evaluation using eye movements: methods and constructs. Int. J. Ind. Ergon. **24**, 631–645 (1999)
3. Holmqvist, K., Nystrom, M., Andersson, R., Dewhurst, R., Jarodzka, H., Van de Weijer, J.: Eye Tracking: A Comprehensive Guide to Methods and Measures. Oxford University Press, Oxford (2011)
4. Blascheck, T., Kurzhals, K., Raschke, M., Burch, M., Weiskopf, D., Ertl, T.: State-of-the-art of visualization for eye tracking data. In: EuroVis-STARs, pp. 63–82 (2014)
5. Redmon, J., Divvala, S., Girshick, R.: You only look once: unified, real time object detection. In: Computer Vision and Pattern Recognition, pp. 779–788 (2016)
6. Kuno, K., Marcel, H., Christof, S., Daniel, W.: Visual analytics for mobile eye tracking. IEEE Trans. Vis. Comput. Graph. **23**, 301–310 (2016)
7. Duchowski, A.T.: Breadth-first survey of eye-tracking applications. Behav. Res. Methods Instrum. Comput. **34**(4), 455–470 (2002)
8. Vermeeren, A.P.O.S., Law, E.L.C., Roto, V.: User experience evaluation methods: current state and development needs. In: Proceedings of the 6th Nordic Conference on Human-Computer Interaction: Extending Boundaries, pp. 521–530. ACM, New York (2010)
9. Roto, V., Vermeeren, A., Väänänen-Vainio-Mattila, K., Law, E.: User experience evaluation – which method to choose? In: Campos, P., Graham, N., Jorge, J., Nunes, N., Palanque, P., Winckler, M. (eds.) INTERACT 2011. LNCS, vol. 6949, pp. 714–715. Springer, Heidelberg (2011). https://doi.org/10.1007/978-3-642-23768-3_129
10. Marchitto, M., Cañas, J.J.: User experience as a challenge for cognitive psychology and ergonomics. Hum. Technol. **7**(3), 268–280 (2011)
11. Ramakrisnan, P., Jaafar, A., Razak, F.H.A.: Evaluation of user interface design for leaning management system (LMS): investigating student's eye tracking pattern and experiences. Procardia Soc. Behav. Sci. **67**, 527–537 (2012)
12. Shin, D.H., Biocca, F., Choo, H.: Exploring the user experience of three-dimensional virtual learning environments. Behav. Inf. Technol. **32**(2), 203–214 (2013)
13. Kaisa, V., Virpi, R., Marc, H.: Now let's do it in practice: user experience evaluation methods in product development. In: Proceedings of CHI 2008 Extended Abstracts on Human Factors in Computing Systems, pp. 3961–3964. ACM, New York (2008)
14. Marianna, O., Virpi, R., Kaisa, V.: User experience evaluation: do you know which method to use. In: Proceedings of CHI 2009 Extended Abstracts on Human Factors in Computing Systems, pp. 2763–2766. ACM, New York (2009)
15. Obrist, M., Roto, V., Law, E.L.G.: Theories behind UX research and how they are used in practice. In: Proceedings of the 2012 ACM Annual Conference Extended Abstracts on Human Factors in Computing Systems Extended Abstracts, pp. 2751–2754. ACM, New York (2012)

16. Fuchsberger, V., Moser, C., Tscheligi, M.: Values in action (ViA): combining usability, user experience and user acceptance. In: Proceedings of the 2012 ACM Annual Conference Extended Abstracts on Human Factors in Computing Systems Extended Abstracts, pp. 1793–1798. ACM, New York (2012)
17. Goldbeerg, J.H., Kotval, X.P.: Computer interface evaluation using eye movements: methods and constructs. Int. J. Ind. Ergon. **24**(6), 631–645 (1999)
18. Augustyniak, P., Tadeusiewicz, R.: Assessment of electrocardiogram visual interpretation strategy based on scan path analysis. Physiol. Meas. **27**(7), 597 (2006)
19. Ito, K., Speer, S.R.: Anticipatory effects of intonation: eye movements during instructed visual search. J. Mem. Lang. **58**(2), 541–573 (2008)
20. Burch, M., Konevtsova, N., Heinrich, J.: Evaluation of traditional, orthogonal, and radial tree diagrams by an eye tracking study. IEEE Trans. Vis. Comput. Graph. **17**(12), 2440–2448 (2011)
21. Liu, H.C., Lai, M.L., Chuang, H.H.: Using eye-tracking technology to investigate the redundant effect of multimedia web pages on viewers' cognitive processes. Comput. Hum. Behav. **27**(6), 2410–2417 (2011)
22. Zulch, G., Stowasser, S.: Eye tracking for evaluating industrial human-computer interfaces. Mind **2**(3), 4 (2003)
23. Schuchard, R., Connell, B., Griffiths, P.: An environmental investigation of way finding in a nursing home. In: Proceedings of the 2006 Symposium on Eye Tracking Research and Applications, p. 33. ACM, New York (2006)
24. Pinelo da Silva, J.: Spatial Congruence Theory: Visual Cognition and Way Finding in the Urban Environment. UCL (University College London), London (2011)
25. Delikostidis, I.: Improving the Usability of Pedestrian Navigation Systems. University of Twente, Faculty of Geo-Information and Earth Observation (ITC), Enscheda (2011)
26. Kaplan: Benchmarking Study Report, Serving the American Public: Best Practices in Performance Management, Economics and Management (1997)
27. Pemice, K., Nielsen, J.: Eye-tracking methodology: how to conduct and evaluate usability studies using eye tracking. Nielsen Norman Group Technical report (2009)
28. Redmon, J., Farhadi, A.: YOLOv3: an incremental improvement. In: IEEE Conference on Computer Vision and Pattern Recognition (2018)
29. Redmon, J., Farhadi, A.: YOLO9000: better, faster, stronger. In: IEEE Conference on Computer Vision and Pattern Recognition, pp. 6517–6525 (2017)
30. Dai, J., Li, Y., He, K.: R-FCN: object detection via region-based fully convolutional networks. In: Neural Information Processing Systems, pp. 379–387 (2016)

Information and Experience Visualization: An Analysis Approach and Decision-Making Tool for the Usability Research

Xi Lyu[⊠] and Yang Wang

Sichuan Fine Arts Institute, Chongqing, China
lucy@scfai.edu.cn, 375645209@qq.com

Abstract. With the transformation and development of the age of network, information and digital, information has evolved into the basic exchange in our lives. Information visualization serves as a communication and dialogue interface between people and objects, between human and environments, and between individuals themselves. It emphasizes the context of information application scenarios and the need to effectively convey information oriented to users' needs and purposes, providing users with sound and efficient meaningful behavior guidance as well as experience characterized by cultural metaphors and aesthetic significance. In the usability research of products and services, visualization is a means of external representation of thinking as well as an expression method of cognitive tools or conceptual structures. Based on dematerialized service systems, user behavior and experience, information and experience visualization present quantitative or qualitative usability-related research in an intuitive and figurative manner. In this way, it enables us to objectively understand the operational status of products or services, analyze the effectiveness and adaptability of links between process tasks, functional architectures, system feedback of user behaviors and experience. In addition, it offers guidance and new insights and plays an analytical and decision-making role in solving complex problems. Meanwhile, visualization represents an ideal tool to help the team to promote comprehensive cognition, build consensus to ensure smooth communication in the design research process.

Keywords: Visualization · Usability · Service design ·
Analysis and decision-making

1 Introduction

Whether in the past, the present or the future, in the natural world or the artificial world, whether from micro or macro, and from material or non-material perspective, all existence, each of which has with its own mysterious code, constitute a large and intricate system of human social life. By means of abstract or figurative representations and evolving technologies and media, information, including texts, symbols, messages, sounds, graphics, images, codes, numbers, diagrams, signals, signs, are constantly involved in the process of production and consumption, transmission and reception, and encoding and decoding. Gleick states in A Brief History of Information:

© Springer Nature Switzerland AG 2019
A. Marcus and W. Wang (Eds.): HCII 2019, LNCS 11586, pp. 196–211, 2019.
https://doi.org/10.1007/978-3-030-23535-2_15

"Evolution itself embodies an ongoing exchange of information between organism and environment" [1]. By acquiring and identifying different information in nature and society, human beings are able to distinguish different things and thus understand and transform the world.

With the continuous transformation and development of network, information and digital technologies, "DNA of information" (Nicholas Negroponte, Being Digital) is replacing atoms as the basic exchange in human life at a lightning speed, and massive data clusters and TMI (too much information) have become an important component of social life. In our daily life and or in increasing public and commercial services, the mass production, collection, storage of data and the organization, transferring, sharing and application of information have profoundly changed the way we think, behave, communicate, live and work and have become the source of new inventions, new services and new models.

On the one hand, as the computing power and graphics processing technology of computers spring up, the new field of visualization has emerged as a result of people's unremitting efforts to explore multi-dimensional visualization of the complex relationships between big data and information using computer graphics technology. In fact, information visualization applications, such as annual reports, maps, brochures, popular science, medical illustration, geographic surveys, news reports, public space guides, interactive virtual navigation, website interfaces, Apps etc. have long been available in all aspects of our daily lives. From two-dimension, three-dimension, four-dimension to multi-dimension, from vision to five senses, and from static, dynamic to interactive visualizations, these lead to more diversified forms of visual telling and presentation.

On the other hand, TMI has posed a serious threat to the decision makers of public management and business operations. As information systems generate more and more data, it is a crucial yet arduous task to provide users with useful information to solve problems. After all, information recipients must gain access to a large amount of abstract data before making a decision. Commercial services such as retailing, shopping, communications, and finance have a deluge of raw transaction data, which prove to the precondition for further abstracted market behaviors. Instant information visualization applications facilitate financial analysis and sales decision-making and guide user behavior so as to gain new significance and even direct rewards. In the field of public services, data or information visualization presents huge development potential in such areas as abnormal network detection, real-time urban traffic information, disease monitoring and prediction, monitoring and forecasting of severe weather and geological disasters, public event reporting, etc. Information visualization programs and analytical reports are effective means to assist public decision-making and create social value.

2   Related Concepts

2.1   About DIKW

Data Information Knowledge and Wisdom Hierarchy (DIKW) refers to a classic model widely accepted in such fields as information science, information theory, and knowledge management. Interestingly, DIKW hierarchy was first mentioned in T. S. Eliot's poetry published in 1934, "The Rock" [2]: "Where is the wisdom we have lost in knowledge? Where is the knowledge we have lost in information?" But another interesting thing is that the hierarchy was mentioned by Frank Zappa in album Joe's Garage in 1979 [3]: "Information is not knowledge, Knowledge is not wisdom, Wisdom is not truth, ..." Later, the concept is interpreted differently in Milan Zeleny's (1987) article "Management Support Systems" [4], Michael Cooley (1987)'s article, "Architecture or Bee?" [5], and Russell Ackoff's (1989) article "From Data to Wisdom" [6]. In 1999, Zwaga et al. focused on the shifts from data to information and from information to knowledge [7]. In 1999, Shedroff pointed out that understanding is a continuum that leads from data, through information to knowledge, and ultimately to wisdom [8].

Data itself cannot "inform or transmit data". Instead, it is an objective fact that is non-subjective and raw, but can be discovered, collected, and recorded. Data is the raw material of information that can be generated continuously, and exists in a quantitative or non-quantitative form. It is only through filtering, sorting, collecting and processing that data becomes usable and effective information.

With a plethora of raw data in our daily life, it is impossible for us to understand them one by one. Only when data is organized into information that needs to be informed, and when there is a comprehensive and corresponding relationship between the output and receiving of information about certain object, content, purpose, media and form, can specific and targeted information be transmitted to inform others of what to do. As processed and meaningful data, information has the internal attributes of informing and telling facts, helps users to think and make better decisions and guides their following actions in the context of specific application scenarios.

Knowledge is an elusive concept which is difficult to measure and define. The transformation from information to knowledge is another sublimated and integrated process filled with cognition and communication. The connection and summary between various information and between concepts constitute knowledge, which is designed to help explore and grasp the intuitive information and the nature. Instead of a simple accumulation of data and information, knowledge is information that can be used to guide practice; it is the sum of the understanding and experience gained in the practice of transforming the world; it is a dynamic combination of structured experience, values, and related information and professional insights.

Knowledge eventually evolves into wisdom. Shedroff explained that Wisdom is a kind of "meta-knowledge" of processes and relationships adjusted through experiences [8]. Wisdom refers to the ability to utilize knowledge, experience, understanding, common sense, and insight to guide thinking and actions, thus obtaining a quick, flexible, and correct understanding and judgment. It emphasizes abstraction from the perspective of philosophy, thus, in a sense, it is a more intelligent process. Or the process of making decisions is intelligent, involving meditation, evaluation, interpretation and reflection.

2.2   Brief Analysis of Visualization Types

The report of *Visualization in Scientific Computing* [9] published by the National Science Foundation (NSF) in 1987 emphasized the necessity of applying graphics and image technology into scientific computing, a new computer-based visualization technology. The report has exerted a far–reaching impact on the field of visualization. Visualization is an essential auxiliary tool in the process of scientific research from observing natural phenomena to simulating natural phenomena and to analyzing related results. Based on the principles and methods of computer graphics, scientific visualization is referred to as loop and iterative visualization exploration and analysis (data filtering, mapping, drawing and feedback) about scientific data obtained by measurement and large-scale multi-dimensional data generated by experimental calculation. The purpose of scientific visualization is to graphically illustrate scientific data and objective phenomena to enable scientists to gain insights into them and thus grasp the essence of nature.

Data visualization mainly focuses on data services and warehouses in finance, retail, communications and other business fields. Through visual quantization techniques, it allows researchers to understand the information and rules embedded in data, thus providing material basis for decision-making. Data mining, as a crucial link, involves classification, clustering, predication and association analysis. Classification is a process of categorizing the data with unknown class labels in the database with the help of classification models (classifier). Clustering is a process of organizing samples without classes into different groups and describing the data clusters. Prediction denotes the establishment of models based upon historical data, and the application of data to forecast the future development trend and possible outcomes. Data association refers to important and discoverable knowledge in the database. The purpose of the related analysis is to find out the hidden associations in the database. Data visualization focuses on the close relationship between graphics and statistical modelling, as well as the statistical properties of results. The former enables readers or viewers to understand data structures, while the latter plays an important role in the process [10].

In a general sense, the goal of information design is to allow audience to communicate in a smooth and convenient manner, because clear and intuitive way of visual communication can transcend the barriers among regions, languages and cultures. Information visualization is closely related to information design and usability. In terms of information design, it is defined as "the art and science of preparing information so that it can be used by human beings with efficiency and effectiveness" [11]. Nathan Shedroff pointed out that information design is related to the organization and presentation of data, and that how data is transformed into valuable and meaningful information, which elaborated the attributes of and relationships between information and data. According to International Institute for Information Design (IIID), information design is the defining, planning, and shaping of the contents of a message and the environments it is presented in with the intention of achieving particular objectives in relation to the needs of users." Visualization is defined as "the use of computer-supported, interactive, visual representations of data to amplify cognition" [12]. It focuses on visualization and navigation of abstract data structures using graphics and interactive animation. However, information visualization values the context and user needs in application scenarios, with efficiency and effectiveness of information transmission its ultimate goal. It covers such knowledge fields as graphic design, visual design, cognitive psychology, communication theory and cultural studies and other aspects of knowledge. Therefore, information visualization is more concerned with aesthetic metaphors and pleasures of visual languages and forms.

Eppler and Burkard argue that knowledge visualization designates all (interactive) graphic means that can be used to develop or convey insights, experiences, methods, or skills [13, 14]. In addition to transmitting facts, knowledge visualization conveys insights, experiences, attitudes, values, expectations, perspectives, opinions, and predictions, and thus helps others correctly reconstruct, memorize, and apply related knowledge [13]. These interpretations reflect extended objects, means, goals of the visualization field, whose main purpose is to support users in creating and sharing knowledge with others. Generally speaking, the field of knowledge visualization examines the use of visual representations to improve the creation and transfer of knowledge between at least two people. Knowledge visualization thus designers all graphic means that can be used to construct and convey complex insights [13].

Regardless of different types of visualization, DATA represents raw and unprocessed objective facts and first-hand materials. In comparison, scientific visualization focuses more on the data in physical world and natural science fields, such as the real-time tracking or display of computing results of astronomy, meteorology, medical images, astrophysics, biochemistry, geological survey. The data gained through data visualization is mainly applied in business operations and services such as finance, retail, communications, travel, etc. Although these abstract data do not correspond to the meaning of physical space, they are displayed in perceptible space fields to help people understand, manage, utilize these data and related laws. As the nature of "information" is to inform facts, information visualization values the application scenarios in real life, effective transmission of information about user objects and target needs, and description or storytelling about events related to specific themes or opinions. It can enable users to analyze, judge, and understand phenomena, characteristics, relationships, causes, and trends. Since knowledge denotes cognitively processed information that is integrated into human knowledge structures, knowledge visualization emphasizes the application of visual representation to promote the reorganization, description, dissemination and co-construction of group knowledge.

With the technological advancement of network, big data, information technologies and artificial intelligence, the visualization application has been expanding in breadth and depth in social life, producing greater intertwined coexistence. It is difficult and unnecessary to make a clear distinction between differently described terms, but the objectives and functions of the visual presentation varies in different research, application or user communication scenarios. In spite of different types of visualization, visual exploration is carried out functionally and formally, because there is no absolutely natural mapping between abstract data or information and graphic images. At the same time, the multi-dimensional application of auditory, tactile and other non-visual media has led to more diversified multi-sensory and interactive presentation and communication models in the practice. Therefore, how to maximize the audience's understanding and usability matching remains the biggest challenge facing visualization technologies and design.

3   Information Visualization as a Method and Tool for Usability Research

In the general interaction design and service design centered on user experience, the behavior, activity, process, system and experience have taken place of objects as the dematerialized research and design object. When using specific products or interactive service system, there are various factors concerning the usability evaluation criteria, such as whether the products and services have smooth procedures, reasonable behavior, stable system, and satisfactory experience or not.

The International Organization for Standardization (ISO) 9241-11 defines usability as "the extent to which a product can be used by specified users to achieve specified goals with effectiveness, efficiency, and satisfaction in a specified context of use." Steve Krug states in his book *Don't Make Me Think* that usability really just means making sure that something works well: that a person of average (or even below average) ability and experience can use the thing—whether it's a website, a fighter jet, or a revolving door—for its intended purpose without getting hopelessly frustrated.

Tullis and Albert argue that usability metrics can help reveal patterns that are hard or even impossible to see, and also help you gain new insights and lead toward a better understanding of user behavior [15]. From the perspective of user behavior and experience, usability is an important quality indicator to evaluate and develop user-friendly interactive products or service systems. When using the products and interactive service system in daily life, whether the product is effective, easy to learn and memory, efficient, error-free, satisfactory for the user, whether the product meets the user's needs and expectations, whether it can offer users favorable experience, whether users can use the product to perform their tasks, and how about subjective feelings (i.e. Flow or not? Any problems? Better than other products? Want to use it again? etc.). There are many specific and quantifiable data involved in usability indicators, and also many qualitative data, such as uncertain elements or events difficult to quantify that are related to user perception, emotion, and experience.

For product use or service study, information visualization is a significant method or tool to present usability indicators, to analyze, illustrate, explain and judge usability-related objective facts, and to tell facts logically. In the process of visual design, it is important to identify and mine raw data related to product and service availability, including all objective facts, quantifiable and non-quantifiable. It is more important to truly understand that the data alone do not make sense. Meaning will gradually become clear only when combined with the context through analysis and processing as well as purposeful and logical induction, integration and narration. The process of information visualization mainly includes: (1) collection, mining and correlation exploration of the original data or objective facts; (2) filtering, classification and association of data, and the construction of information organizations and architectures with views and paths; (3) visual coding of related classified information, selection of graphics, images, symbols, colors and their logic; (4) the formal exploration of visualization perception. Its forms should not only correspond to the original objective data and material, but also conform to the cognitive habits and experience of information receivers. In the first two procedures, special attention should be paid to the correlation between quantitative data and non-quantitative facts such as participants' activities, environment, behaviors, actions and emotions, as well as the logical relationship between basic data and the information to be conveyed, so as to intuitively present the usability problems in the practice; The last two procedures are not completely independent of the first two. When adjusting the visualization sketch based on the sorting of data and information, the correspondence among data or information, visualization elements coding and visualization forms has been gradually established. The selection of all abstract or representational elements, such as points, lines, planes, volumes, graphics, images, symbols, texts, colors, and their matching with size, height, thickness, texture, orientation, direction, and lightness, is directly related to quantitative or qualitative data. And the final form of visual presentation bears closer relation to the attributes of the data itself, the logic and narration of the information architecture and its description. For the sake of the final visual presentation of information logic, the visualization process represents an important link and tool of visual thinking centered on the research of product and service availability.

In days when Nokia and Samsung phones dominated, it was somewhat difficult to say which brand was better in terms of usability. The operational comparison of the two brands (Fig. 1), in which the main functions of Nokia (black) and Samsung (blue) phones are stacked, and the process and steps of using mobile phones to complete tasks are visualized through information architecture for usability analysis.

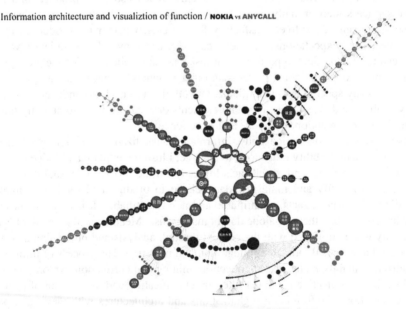

Information architecture and visualiztion of function / **NOKIA vs ANYCALL**

Fig. 1. NOKIA vs ANYALL: information architecture and visualization of function (Color figure online)

The center of the illustration shows the functions, with the size of the circle corresponding to the frequency of usage and steps required to complete a tasking using each function. As shown in the figure, it takes 5 steps to make a phone call with the Nokia mobile phone, and 8 steps with the Samsung mobile phone; it takes 8 steps to edit and send specified text message with the Nokia mobile phone, and 14 steps with its counterpart. Similarly, we can intuitively see from the figure the overall comparison and difference in terms of tasks to steps. This is also the reason why users claimed that Nokia's enjoyed greater usability in previous user experience evaluation.

The Liming daycare center for the disabled in Zhangqi town, Cixi city, Zhejiang province, is a small non-profit organization run by a private community. With government grant as its main funding sources, the center still relies on elderly care service fees to make ends meet. The center hopes to report to the official Civil Affairs Bureau and obtain more financial support. The design service is need to help sort out and visualize the various interests and operation status of the center, understand the needs of different stakeholders, analyze and propose specific projects and contents for service design, help gain more government support and thus build a public service brand platform and service chain. In the previous design survey, we have developed multi-dimensional understanding of the needs of stakeholders, including central managers, care workers, disabled people, volunteers and government. Through various information visualization diagrams, the visual management analysis, judgment and description are carried out in a more intuitive and concise manner in light of the interests of stakeholders, the process of day care, the status of behavior and activities. In this way, the government management department can have a better understanding about challenges facing the center. There are 19 disabled people in the center, including 16 with mental handicap, 3 with polio and physical disability. In terms of day activities, social care enterprises, namely, Bull Power Strip Factory and Xinhai Lighter Factory, provide and assemble working parts, which are paid services. The center offers limited space which has a combination of functions, such as work, eating, rest, activities, and relatively fixed seats for the nursing staff and three physically handicapped people. In the spatial layout map and personnel activity heatmap (Fig. 2), it can be found that the activity area has low utilization rate, with nobody using the treadmill; the space around the work table is the most popular place where a variety of activities have been conducted; two working tables will be temporarily changed into dining tables at noon every day, and the area is in disorder due to the movement of parts on the table; except for 2 couches, there are no other facilities for more people to take a break in the afternoon. The visualization diagram reflects the inconsistency between space, equipment and people's behavior, and provides decision-making basis for later space function division and design, facility design and transformation, and product ordering based on the special needs of disabled people.

4 Information and Experience Visualization in Service Design

Service design involves a variety of interwoven factors that are human or non-human and tangible or intangible. As the subject of service interaction, people has various interactive relations with information, products, equipment, systems and environment in the service process. Usability analysis runs through the whole design process

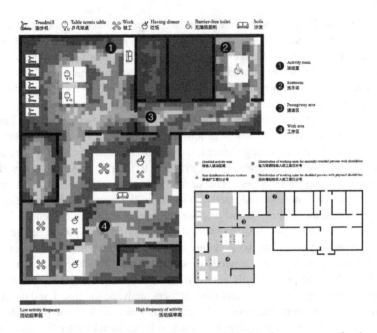

Fig. 2. Spatial distribution and behavioral heatmap of Liming daycare center for the disabled

characterized by gradual and repeated exploration. As one of the user-oriented design methods, usability research aims to design products and services that are useful and easy and pleasant to use, directly influencing and guiding users' behavior and experience in using the products and participating in the service. Conversely, if the user experience is used as the content and goal of designs, it also offers the basis and standard for the usability analysis and testing in the product and service design process. For the visualization of dematerialized service systems and processes, user behaviors and experiences, tools such as service blueprints, service system diagrams, and experience maps are all visually developed for quantitative and qualitative research and analysis. It involves sorting the relationship between processes, tasks, people, behaviors, purposes, and contact points in different contexts of the service process, decomposing tasks and steps in each phase, refining and quantifying actions, time consumption, work intensity, operational results, and emotional changes so as to reveal the relationship between the above aspects and service efficiency, service quality, and user experience, as well as usability-related issues.

4.1   Case 1: Campus Service Design

The purpose is to help the family members of faculty to solve the problem of how to accompany their preschool children to play in the school. The design goal is to carry out more meaningful service design and transformation without damaging and interfering the teaching environment. The pre-design team conducted follow-up observations, interviews and records of typical user households, and observed and recorded their relatively fixed paths and places in school, participants, activity content and methods, and duration. In the user behavior and experience map (Fig. 3), it can be seen that the design team divides the activity into four scenes based on geographical location. c.17-min journey for walking and playing along route 1, c.20-min staying for playing on the site1, c.6-min journey for walking and playing along route 2, and c.35-min c.20-min staying for playing on the site2. That means parents accompany their children to play for c.78 min (excluding return trip). The time on the left represents importance of the behavior with the color and text size. On the right side, pictures and texts are displayed to clearly and briefly reminds the participants of the main behaviors and activities, among which the red image is a sign or warning of problems in relevant places. The team members visualize the presentation ideas and mark the questions to achieve a global view and weighted consensus on the service activities.

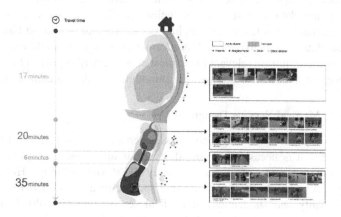

Fig. 3. User behavior and experience map of campus service (Color figure online)

In the concept sketch and interaction model (Fig. 4), the brainstorming conceptual sketch on the left, a means of visual discussion, enables the team to quickly sort ideas and conduct conceptual analysis. It serves as an effective visual dialogue and reasoning, and quickly presents the exploration of uncertainties on the service context. The interaction model on the right, which is based on the original data, the information architecture and visualization, adopts a more rational, abstract and simplified visual organization approach. In this way, it shows the relationship between participants, the exchanges and flows of materials and information, and complex and intertwined relationships in the service system, such as activities and environment interactions, and also directly guides the design logic of the final service design at the process and contact point.

The service activities involve too much content and details. In the design process, especially in the participatory design process, the information or experience visualization at different stages with different goals is not only a useful tool to help the team to analyze the phenomenon, sort ideas and discover problems. At the same time, it is an intuitive way to promote communication between teams, service providers and participants. In the pre-design phased analysis process, it is necessary to conduct valuable

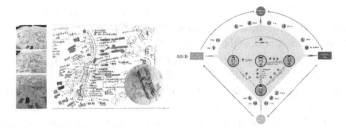

Fig. 4. Concept sketch & interaction model of campus service

information extraction and organization based on the repeated analysis, understanding of participants' behaviors and activities and to construct clear information logic (architecture) during data screening and collation. In this way, we can integrate the scattered understanding of team members into stories that can be told, and into different types of basic data as objective facts. The information logic and simplification mean of visualization description are relevant to the most effective way to present the objectivity of the service site and how to improve the smoothness of design communication.

4.2   Case 2: Medical Service Design

Medical service involves extremely complex systems and relationships. In the design research process, it is necessary to consider various questions, such as how to truly understand the attributes of service, namely IHIP (Intangibility, Heterogeneity, Inseparability, separability, Perishability) in a specific medical service, how to recognize the normality and suddenness of medical service, the difficulty in evaluating service output, and the particularity of doctor-patient relationship, how to understand the complex interwoven and interactive relationship in the medical service system, and how to establish the appropriate design weight and principles and how to guide the detailed design of contact points.

A county-level comprehensive hospital is located in a remote area in western China, with very limited conditions and resources, such as funds, equipment, personnel, all of which are far worse than those of other first-class hospitals in first-tier cities in China. According to the three-year adverse event records in the hospital, the seemingly normal daily care work of infusion has contributed to a majority of such events. Although many medical staff are involved in different stages of the whole process and there are strict, standardized and repeated checks and verification, the process still has a relatively high error rate. Therefore, the infusion-related safety problem put forward by the hospital has become the entry point for the medical care service design. The research subject is the infusion care service of the adult general unit (department of respiration). The department has a total of 10 medical staff, including 8 general administrators, dispensing nurses and responsible nurses, who are the main executives who actually enter the infusion care process. The department has a total of ten medical staff, eight of whom, including the general nurse, dispensing nurse and responsible nurse, are main individuals involved in the infusion care services. During the high incidence period of respiratory diseases in winter, average 50–70 patients are under care per day. If the desired daily dosage for each patient averages 4–6 bottles, nurses need to infuse at least 200–400 bottles per day. At the same time, limited by the overall medical conditions at the county level in western China, there are many prominent problems such as insufficient medical staff, lack of high-tech means and obsolete medical equipment. Through methods and tools such as on-site follow-up observation, nurse interviews, scenario simulation, mind maps, behavioral decomposition maps, and experience maps, quantitative and qualitative research and analysis are carried out to discuss the design weight of the contact point and the specific design solution under the service contact situation. All this is made possible by sorting the relationship between people, processes, and tasks in the service process in different situations.

For infusion care systems, visual exploration with different logic is part of the visual discussion and analysis based on on-site tracking observations and interviews, reflecting different dimensions and perspectives to help understand the systemic relationship of infusion care. The final infusion care system context diagram (Fig. 5) shows overall systemic relationship of infusion care, starting from the doctor's advice to nurse's entering the ward. It covers the main stakeholders (doctors, nurses, patients, care workers), places (pharmacy, warehouse, nursing station, treatment room, ward), nursing methods, work content in order to show and help understand the current status of the infusion care system.

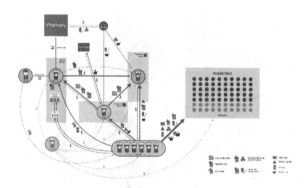

Fig. 5. The relationship of roles and tasks of current infusion care system

The daily infusion process visualization diagram in temporal logic (Fig. 6), presents different nurses, times, tasks, work intensity, and associated emotion changes with the passage of time, as well as gradually refined relationship between time, roles, tasks, and main contact point. The whole process runs from the infusion preparation in the treatment room in the afternoon to the infusion in the ward in the next morning.

According to the role simulation in different stages, the contextual relationships between daily care tasks, operational behaviors, workloads and service touch points, the team simulates the thinking patterns and behavioral habits of nurses after training, decomposes and quantifies the time consumption and operation results of tasks, steps,

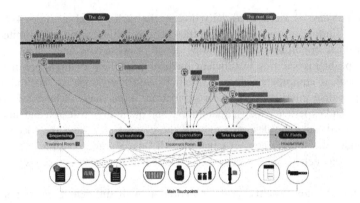

Fig. 6. The procedure and main touchpoints of daily infusion process

and actions in each stage, and presents experience and emotions in the whole nursing process (Fig. 7).

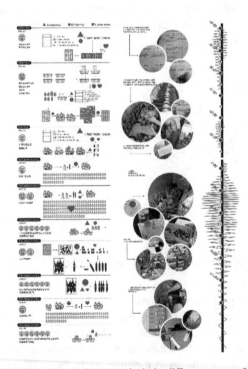

Fig. 7. Contextual details and experience analysis in different steps of infusion care service

With the gradual refinement of the overall relationship and each link of the infusion care service, the visualization abstraction of process, touch points, problems and relationship (Fig. 8) shift the focus on design thinking. Combined with the visualization analysis of different dimensions and the understanding of nursing service in the early stage, visualization abstraction defines the objectives, principles and the design weight of contact points.

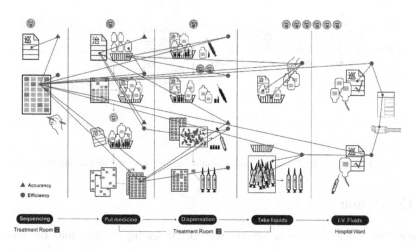

Fig. 8. Analysis of touchpoints and relationship in infusion care process

A case in point is the improvement of medicine baskets design as part of touch point design. The improvement design takes the purpose and behavior of the liquid-taking link (Fig. 9-A) as the design weight (the responsible nurse takes the first three groups of liquid into the ward at one time) and is aligned with the information description and operational behavior (the first three groups of liquid are placed according to the order of that of infusion) in the put-medical link (Fig. 9-B). Therefore, additional partition in the structural design of the medicine basket can be deduced and added (Fig. 9). It is also a example of actively designing and enhancing nurse's behavior and norms in building the interactive relationship between the information contact point and the product contact point.

During the analysis and advancement of infusion care service design research, the design team constantly adjusts and mines different types of data in the practice. With quantitative and qualitative analysis interwoven, data is collated and reorganized ceaselessly. By means of information visualization tools, the design team specifies and visualizes abstract intangible services in practical research, develops an objective understanding about the interactive relationships and weight basis of process, time, places, people, tasks, behaviors, and touch points from different logical dimensions. Based on the understanding of complex motivations, needs and emotions of different stakeholders, final design solution has been put forward in light of design objectives, principles, and weight.

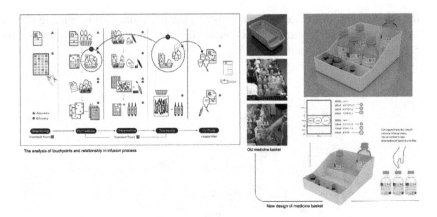

Fig. 9. Context analysis and decision making with the visualization

5 Conclusion

Information visualization is a unique way of presenting information. By mining, analyzing and exploring the laws or connections of various data or information, information visualization transforms these laws and connections into appropriate visual or other perceptible forms. Information visualization serves as a communication and dialogue interface between people and objects, between human and environment, and between individuals themselves. It makes full use of people's natural ability to recognize, understand and remember information. With the help of intuitive visual graphic languages and forms, perceptible materials, sound media, and a variety of interactive means and media, it enables users to observe, analyze, scan, and understand abstract information. Accurate information visualization design can provide users with useful, smooth and efficient guidance on behavior; vivid and creative visual presentation can also show differences in the complicated information-based world, generating physiologically and psychologically aesthetic pleasure. At the same time, visualization is a means of external representation about thinking, a cognitive tool or expression method for abstract concepts and structures. In product and service usability research, it visually describes and interprets objects that is abstract, intangible and non-material, and reflects the usability activities of products or services in a non-textual manner. In this way, it enables us to analyze the effectiveness and adaptability of links between process tasks, functional architectures, system feedback of user behaviors and experiences. Furthermore, it offers users guidance and new insights and plays an analytical and decision-making role in solving complex problems. In addition to providing visual experience, it adds new meaning to define and design new services.

References

1. Gleick, J.: The Information: A History, a Theory, a Flood. Pantheon Books, New York (2011)
2. Cleveland, H.: Information as a resource. Futurist **12**, 34–39 (1982)
3. Zappa, F.: "Packard Goose" in album Joe's Garage: Act II & III (1979)
4. Zeleny, M.: Management support systems: towards integrated knowledge management. Hum. Syst. Manag. **7**(1), 59–70 (1987)
5. Cooley, M.: Architecture or Bee?. The Hogarth Press, London (1987)
6. Ackoff, R.L.: From data to wisdom. J. Appl. Syst. Anal. **16**, 3–9 (1989)
7. Zwaga, H.J.G., Boersma, T., Hoonhout, H.C.M.: By way of introduction guidelines and design specifications in information design. In: Boersma, T., Hoonhout, H.C.M., Zwaga, H. J.G. (eds.) Visual Information for Everyday Use. Design and Research Perspectives. Taylor & Francis, London (1999)
8. Shedroff, N.: Information interaction design: a unified field theory of design. In: Jacobson, R. (ed.) Information Design. MIT Press, Cambridge (1999)
9. McCormick, B.H., DeFanti, T.A., Brown, M.D.: Visualization in scientific computing. Comput. Graph. **21**(6), 247–307 (1987)
10. Chen, C., et al.: Handbook of Data Visualization. Springer, Heidelberg (2008). https://doi.org/10.1007/978-3-540-33037-0
11. Horn, R.E.: Information design: emergence of a new profession. In: Jacobson, R. (ed.) Information Design. MIT Press, Cambridge (1999)
12. Card, S., et al.: Readings in Information Visualization. Morgan Kauffman, San Francisco (1999)
13. Eppler, M.J., Burkard, R.A.: Knowledge visualization. In: Towards a New Discipline and Its Fields of Application, ICA Working Paper 2/2004. University of Lugano, Lugano (2004)
14. Eppler, M.J., Burkhard, R.A.: Visual representations in knowledge management: framework and cases. J. Knowl. Manag. **4**(11), 112–122 (2007)
15. Tullis, T.S., Albert, W.: Measuring the User Experience. Elsevier Inc., Waltham (2008)

Development of a Heuristic Evaluation Tool for Voice User Interfaces

Martin Maguire[(⊠)]

Design School, Loughborough University, Loughborough,
Leicestershire LE11 3TU, UK
m.c.maguire@lboro.ac.uk

Abstract. Voice user interfaces (VUIs) are now a common means of interaction with IT systems. To assist in evaluating the usability of such interfaces, a set of evaluation heuristics assessing speech interfaces was developed by following an existing methodology for defining usability heuristics. Two groups of eight participants conducted an evaluation by inspection of three speech-based systems, a mobile phone assistant, a smart speaker and an in-car hands free phone system. One group used Nielsen and Molich's general heuristics for user interface design while the other group used the VUI heuristics. The second group found, on average, more problems than the first group. However, most heuristics from both sets were rated as useful during the study. This indicates that a mixture of both general and application specific heuristics are needed for a comprehensive evaluation to be performed. Experience from a pilot study, where a smart speaker was set up in a domestic setting, highlighted the need to also consider social and environmental issues to gain a complete picture of user experience when interacting with speech systems.

Keywords: Speech systems · Voice user interfaces · Heuristic evaluation · Smart speakers · Smart homes

1 Introduction

Voice user interfaces (VUIs) are having an increasing an effect in our daily lives. People are now appreciating the potential of a hands-free interface that uses natural language capability rather than requiring keyboard input. While speech-based telephone interfaces, in-vehicle voice recognition, and dictation systems have existed for a long time, the advent of voice-based assistants on a mobile phone or smart speaker has helped to make voice interaction a mainstream technology. This increases the need to provide tools and techniques to evaluate these systems.

This paper reports on a study to define and test whether usability heuristics developed specifically for VUIs, are better able to identify usability problems with VUIs, compared to using general-purpose usability heuristics.

© Springer Nature Switzerland AG 2019
A. Marcus and W. Wang (Eds.): HCII 2019, LNCS 11586, pp. 212–225, 2019.
https://doi.org/10.1007/978-3-030-23535-2_16

2   Literature Review

2.1   Development of Voice User Interface Technology

A voice-user interface (VUI) makes spoken human interaction with computers possible using speech recognition to understand spoken commands and questions and, typically, text-to-speech to play a reply. VUIs are not new, with the first elementary examples such as 'Radio Rex' being produced in the 1920s [1]. Rex was a small celluloid dog set into a wooden dog house. When the dog's name was called, it would jump out of the house to the owner. In the 1950s, Bell Labs built a system called 'Audrey' (Automatic Digit Recognizer) for single-speaker recognition of digits. This achieved a high degree of accuracy. These early systems had small vocabularies and were not much use outside of the lab. In the 1960s and 1970s, the research continued, expanding the number of words that could be understood and working toward "continuous" speech recognition (not having to pause between every word).

Organisations such as IBM and the U.S. Department of Defense experimented with speech recognition in the following decades, but it was only in the 1990s that it became a consumer product with Dragon releasing a consumer speech recognition product, Dragon Dictate, in 1990, and BellSouth launched the first consumer voice portal, VAL, in 1996. Testing by Xiong et al. [2] showed that automated systems performing a transcription task can reach parity or exceed the performance of human transcribers. In terms of recognition accuracy, machine errors are substantially the same as human ones, the main difference being that the machine was less able to identify backchannel utterances such as like "uh-huh" signalling that the speaker should keep talking, and hesitations sounds like "uh" which indicate that the current speaker has more to say and wants to keep his or her turn.

Speech recognition and voice commands also started to be built into operating systems such as Windows Vista and Mac OS X, as well as interactive voice response (IVR) systems for telephone callers. Voice interaction arrived on mobile devices for the first time in 2008 with the release of the Google Voice Search app for iPhones. This technology was later added to Google Search, Maps and the Chrome browser.

Voice recognition apps are now ubiquitous across mobile devices. Apple's Siri virtual assistant processed 1 billion queries per week in 2015, while 20 percent of Google searches on mobile devices are performed through voice recognition [3]. These services and devices depend on data and content assets acquired by these platforms to fulfil user requests. Thus, when a user asks Siri for directions, it can quickly leverage Apple Maps to provide a routing. When they ask Amazon Echo to play a song or read an Audible book, Alexa draws on those Amazon assets to play back the user's content [4].

In recent years, the benefits of speech technology have become more widely recognised since it enables systems to be commanded by voice without keyboard input and while the user is performing other tasks so that their eyes and hands may be busy e.g. when cooking or driving [5]. It uses conversational skills which most people have and apply naturally. A Stanford study showed that speaking (dictating) text messages was faster than typing, even for expert texters. Voice, which includes the characteristics of tone, volume, intonation, speed and emotion, conveys information that a textual message generally does not. Speech interaction can have benefits for people with physical disabilities in controlling household devices such as TVs, lights, window blinds, heating controls, and security cameras, more easily than doing so directly or by using a remote handset.

2.2   Usability of Voice User Interfaces

As VUI systems have developed, researchers have gained experience in the design aspects that determine their usability. The authors Cohen et al. [6], in writing about interactive voice response (IVR) systems, describe many aspects of design e.g. persona, prosody (intonation, tone, stress and rhythm), error recovery, and prompt design, that are still relevant to today's VUIs. Harris [7] also describes a process for designing voice user interfaces including the voice or agent characteristics, dialogue design, scripting and iterative evaluation. In designing voice user interfaces, Harris emphasises the need to craft the interface for voice and not to try to match it to a visual user interface i.e. to create an auditory version of a GUI.

Cohen et al. [6] advises against making design decisions without consideration of the context or environment in which the system operates. In relation to this, Whitenton [8] emphasises the need for the system to be able to distinguish voice from interfering noise such as music or other sounds in the environment, and the ability to detect a voice input from a reasonable distance. Efficiency can be important for repetitive tasks so having to repeat multiple times, "please add milk to shopping list", "please add bread to shopping list", etc. can become laborious. Another principle described is the need to avoid more than 4 or 5 speech-based options as users must keep them in working memory in order to make the correct choice.

Asthana et al. [9] propose three dimensions for studying the usability of IVR design. The first is 'navigation' which is the time spent on announcements and selection of menu and submenu options which should be minimised while making the process clear. Secondly 'relevance' of information delivered to the user. This is determined by the ease with which users can accurately choose the option they want from the menu list. It was found that new callers tended not to select the wrong menu as they listened carefully to the options, while repeat callers tried to guess from previous usage which often led to an error especially if the order of the menu options, or the options themselves changed over time. This is an argument for maintaining consistency are far as possible when menus are updated. Thirdly, 'capacity' should be considered, which is the number of options in a menu balanced against the systems ability to correctly match user utterances to the options. If the number of options is too large, then the chance of an error increases.

Howell et al. [10] studied the use of spatial metaphors within a hierarchically structured mobile phone city guide service. They found that the use of spatial metaphors could lead to improved usability by capitalising on people's well-developed special abilities. The metaphors used were driving on a journey, managing a filing system, and a shopping journey. The study, which employed by first time users, showed that the office filing system metaphor borrowed from graphical user interfaces (GUIs) could be successfully transferred to a speech-based VUI.

Franzke et al. [11] compared a simulated speech recognition interface (using a 'wizard-of-oz' experiment) for a basic voice mail application, with functionally similar touch-tone and operator assisted versions. They found that subjects adjusted their behaviour when using the speech system compared to interacting with a human operator. Participants used less complex grammar when talking to a computer, less words per utterance, did not include the sentence subject as often, and tended to exclude the indirect objects from sentences, than when participants were talking to an operator. This may imply that a sophisticated natural language processing unit is not a necessity for a speech recognition application of the size and structure of a basic voice mail system. Speech was also regarded as generally more time efficient and subjectively easier to handle than key-command combinations since spoken commands are easier and faster to learn.

Damper and Gladstone [12] evaluated the IMAGINE speech-based interaction system to provide universal access to electronic services including disabled users. The system development initially concentrated on the application of an online shop. The system allowed basic shopping steps and speech specific steps. These included: logging on, setting speech output preferences, listing products by letter, browsing the catalogue, putting products in the basket, checking out, etc. Testing showed that users wanted to try out the system first. This idea of checking through the steps of an online process is as likely to be just as useful for a voice user interface as it is for a visual interface. The development and testing of the system identified some design rules that needed to be applied. These included removing the definite or indefinite article e.g. "a tin opener", keeping the list of products spoken below 6, and the need to recognise product codes as well as names. Also, when the user asks to browse all the browse options should be presented. This study shows that both general and specific requirements for a speech system will emerge as the application develops.

In studying IVR systems, Kim [13] states that user satisfaction with these systems is still low. Using a simulator to enable usability testing of speech systems, they identified four types of usability problem: (1) 'term ambiguity', where ambiguous terms and expressions can lead to delayed task completion, (2) 'phonetic deficiency' of speech output including pronunciation, volume and voice speed, (3) 'information navigation' where callers have to return to the root or previous menu to proceed with their task, and (4) 'cognitive overload' which can occur due to loss of concentration e.g. when listening to a list of menu options.

Portet et al. [14] reports a user evaluation study that assessed user acceptance and user concerns related to a smart home voice interface using a 'wizard-of-oz' technique. The study included scenarios for appliance control by voice, communication with the outside, responding to a system interruption to close a door or turn off an oven, and managing a shared calendar. The study included 18 people (8 older people, 7 relatives and 3 caregivers). They found that the issuing commands using keywords is well accepted compared with sentence-based commands. They also found that successful applications using speech recognition tend to have smaller vocabularies, and it is difficult to manage out-of-vocabulary and ill-formed commands uttered by the user. It was also discovered that people would tolerate having to repeat some commands when the VUI did not understand their first attempt, although this might diminish over time. Further findings were that natural voice outputs from the system was preferred to synthetic outputs. Nine participants preferred the system to have a female voice, one preferred a male voice, while the remainder did not mind which gender it was.

Yankelovitch et al. [15] investigated the challenges of conversational interface design by development of a research prototype for voice command and interaction with email, a calendar, weather information and stock quotes. A study with 14 participants found several design challenges. To make the interaction feel conversational, prompting the user for input was avoided where possible, so allowing users to comfortably take the lead in formulating their input e.g. 'read the message' or 'skip this'. Other guidelines from the study were to ground the conversation, avoid repetition, and to handle interruptions. Immediate and informative feedback was also seen as essential so that users would know that the system has heard them and that their command had been recognised correctly. A long pause may result in the user trying to keep their conversational turn by using 'errs' and 'ums' which can result in recognition errors. Interpreting silence from the system is sometimes ambiguous as it may mean that the system is not working or simply that it did not hear the user input. The challenge of converting a visual interface (GUI) into a voice interface (VUI) was also addressed. Using voice, a user won't necessary use the correct menu command, e.g. 'tell me …' rather than 'what is …', and may use relative dates e.g. 'a week from tomorrow'. Numbering messages or tagging them with codes (g. old or new) may be a natural means of managing them visually but becomes awkward in a voice system. Also, when a dialog box is used to control flow with 'yes' and 'no' options, users may try other commands using speech e.g. 'send' or 'read the next message'.

Further aspects of voice interaction are provided by Bernholz [3]. He describes the importance of understanding users' expectations when they interact with a system and the scope of topics that the system covers. System feedback should make it clear what question it is answering. For example, as well as just providing a football score, it should name the teams and the date when the game was played which acts as useful confirmation. Apple Siri helps to solve these needs by listing ideas for possible questions when the users starts using the service and gives both visual and tactile feedback to show when it is listening.

Bernholz also mentions some practices to avoid when building a VUI as part of a mobile application. These include asking the user a question when the application expects a response, not making it clear about how the user should respond, giving the user too many choices, and being too verbose (e.g. "say 'football' for football. say 'basketball' for basketball…") and confirming the user's query too often. Confirmations should be reserved for important actions such as sending a message or making a purchase.

The results from these previous studies show that many findings from the past still apply to current VUIs. At the same time, the development of new voice input technological capability will open up new areas when design guidelines will be required.

2.3   Heuristic Evaluation

The method of heuristic evaluation developed by Nielsen and Molich [16] utilises experts who inspect an interface to identify usability problems. During the inspection, usability heuristics or 'rules of thumb' are used as a checklist to stimulate thinking and to categorise the problems found. The results from all the experts are combined to create a comprehensive list of problems to be addressed by redesign. Nielsen and Molich's 10 usability heuristics are as follows:

1. Visibility of system status
2. Match between system and the real world
3. User control and freedom
4. Consistency and standards
5. Error prevention
6. Recognition rather than recall
7. Flexibility and efficiency of use
8. Aesthetic and minimalist design
9. Help users recognize, diagnose, and recover from errors

As speech-based systems become more common, the question arises as to whether speech as a form of user interaction is distinct enough from traditional screen-based interfaces that heuristics tailored to speech systems are needed to conduct usability inspections of them. A paper by Quiñones and Rusu [17] states that user interface heuristics such as Nielsen and Molich's, developed to evaluate traditional screen-based interfaces, are limited by not being able to evaluate the unique features of an application such as a voice user interface. Johnson and Coventry [18] studied the specific application of a VUI to a self-service automated teller machine (ATM). They question the use of traditional heuristics as their origin and general application concerns conventional screen-based, often desktop, interaction. Usability heuristics for use when evaluating VUIs have been produced by Cohen et al. [6] and Harris [7]. Both sources state the need for the adaptation of traditional heuristics when conducting heuristic evaluation due to their orientation towards screen-based user interfaces.

3 Pilot Study Work

To gain a more direct understanding of how users might interact with current voice interaction technology, a field study was conducted by installing an Amazon Echo/Alexa smart speaker in the kitchen of a student house for one week. The participants were four undergraduate students who were aware of speech-based assistants but stated that they had limited experience of using them. The intention was to see whether the participants used the smart speaker, what they used it for, and how they felt about the technology after one week of usage.

At the start of the week, the participants were shown how to interact with the device by using the wake-up command 'Alexa' and how to issue different commands such as play music or set a timer. They could interact with Alexa during the following week as they wished. The Alexa software app was available to access the user interactions and speaker responses made during the week. It was found that 27 interactions with the speaker were made which included requests to play music or the radio, set a timer (e.g. as a wake-up alarm or for cooking purposes), ask for information or a joke, download a skill or read the news headlines. Possibly more use of the device would have occurred if it had been linked into home devices such as the control of lights or ordering groceries.

Despite the limited use, participants felt that they had interacted with the device effectively. There were comments about the limited accuracy/success rate of interactions, feeling self-conscious when speaking to the assistant with others present, and speculation about the microphone being 'always on' and listening in to their conversations. These results reflect the survey conducted by Milanesi [19] which showed that people's current use of consumer voice-based assistants may be at a basic level but as more services become reliant on them and they become integrated into homes, users will become more familiar with them and less self-conscious about using them.

A recent study by Adobe [20] indicates that smart speakers have led to a growing acceptance of voice interaction with systems. It reported that 72% of smart speaker owners are now comfortable with using voice assistants in front of others. Among people not owning smart speakers, only 29% are comfortable with doing so. Arguably, voice is becoming increasingly interwoven into our cultural fabric and will become a key element in how consumers engage with the world around them.

4 Development and Evaluation of VUI Heuristics

A study was conducted to define and validate a set of usability heuristics specifically for voice user interfaces (VUIs) and to see how effective they were in comparison with general purpose usability heuristics, when evaluating speech-based systems.

The VUI heuristics were developed following the method by Rusu et al. [21]. The method included the key stages of:

(1) Exploration – identify source material on problems related to speech interfaces.
(2) Description – group the problems by theme to create proto-heuristics.
(3) Correlation – refine the proto-heuristics by correlating them with well-established general-purpose sets of heuristics.
(4) Explication – specify the heuristics in a standard way and provide examples.
(5) Validation – comparison of new heuristics with benchmark set of heuristics.

The language used in the enhanced VUI heuristics was explicitly linked to the domain of speech interaction. Heuristics not seen as necessary for 'voice' were removed and new specific VUI heuristics were introduced. The results of each stage are as follows:

Exploration: A systematic review of literature relating to the usability of VUIs was conducted to build a relevant bibliography. Seventeen items of literature were identified including 12 journal papers, 2 books and 3 websites. From this sample, 72 usability related items were found comprising principles, guidelines, ideas and concepts related to usable VUIs.

Description: Athematic analysis was conducted on the items, resulting in 8 themes (see Table 1).

Table 1. VUI usability themes identified from the literature

Theme	Further detail
Cognitive load	• Limited capacity for short term memory • Recognition rather than recall
Speak the user's language	• Setting user expectations • Avoid ambiguity
Efficiency	• Avoid unnecessary words • Interface can be tedious when listing products or items
Feedback	• Visibility of system status • Usability improved with consistency of system-voice and feedback
Accuracy	• Network delays • Speech recognition more prone to error
Tolerant of errors	• Error prevention • Frustration from repetitious prompts adding no information
User control	• Flexibility and efficiency • Option to return to main menu at any time
Consistency	• Consistency in operation of voice system • VUI must be consistent with corresponding screen user interface

Correlation: Three widely used sets of 'traditional usability heuristics' were identified to correlate with the VUI heuristics. These included Nielsen [22] (see Sect. 2.3), Shneiderman and Plaisant [23] and Norman [24] (see Appendix). (The design principles of Shneiderman and Norman are listed in the Appendix. These were compared with the VUI usability themes to help validate them as a basis for final definition.

Explication: the heuristics were described using a standard template including an identifying number, name, definition, explanation and example (see Table 2). Cross-references with the literature are also shown in brackets.

The heuristics were evaluated to measure their effectiveness. Two groups of participants assumed the roles of usability experts, one group of eight was provided with Nielsen's general heuristics while the second group of eight used the VUI-specific heuristics. Participants were asked to complete usage scenarios with three speech-based systems to cover a range of usage contexts and identify as many usability problems with each as possible. The three systems included the Amazon Echo smart speaker, iPhone Siri voice assistant and the VW in-car hands-free kit for call acceptance, phone number selection by voice, and voice control of a media player. The participants then completed a debrief questionnaire asking them to state the advantages and disadvantages of using the heuristics they were allocated (traditional or enhanced) to identify which specific heuristics, in their set, that they found particularly useful.

Figure 1 shows that, on average, 13.5 usability problems per person were identified using Nielsen's general heuristics while 18.25 problems per person were identified with the VUI-specific heuristics.

An independent samples t-test showed that the difference in mean values was significant to the 1% level. This corresponds with the range of problems found by each

Table 2. Developed VUI Usability Heuristics

Number	Description
1	**Minimise short term memory load:** The user's short-term memory load should be kept to a minimum. In the absence of a companion screen display, listed information should be kept short and concise, containing only information necessary to the action being performed. The complexity of concepts the user must understand and the number of things they must learn to use the system must also be kept to a minimum. [12, 13, 22, 23] *Examples: Information that is listed shall be kept short and concise; Allow user to request repetition of previous system output*
2	**Accommodate conversational speech:** The system should speak in a natural way and adopt human-to-human speech conventions. This acts to increase the interaction flow and comprehension. [6, 15] *Examples: Ensure natural conversational flow including turn-taking, following conversation pragmatics and using a friendly tone and manner; Use terms that the user will understand; Be able to understand variations in dialect*
3	**Maximise efficiency:** Users want speed and efficiency. The fewer the number of steps that user-system dialog requires, the greater the perceived efficiency of the interaction with the system. [7, 15, 22] *Example: An action should not be broken into too many steps; Craft the interface for speech rather than try to create an auditory version of a GUI*
4	**Ensure adequate system feedback:** The system should always keep the user informed about what is going on through appropriate feedback within a reasonable time, providing, if necessary, confirmation of actions. [3, 15, 23, 24] *Examples: The system should avoid periods of silence during interaction and should provide confirmation of actions; In response to a user question, give feedback to confirm what question the system is answering; Allow processing of backchannel utterances and background noise*
5	**Ensure high accuracy to minimize input errors:** Recognition is important since errors degrade usability and lead to user frustration. [2, 6, 8, 9, 14] *Examples: The system should be enough to allow for natural speech with few requirements for the user to repeat utterances. Ensure noise in the environment does not interfere with the speech system; Users can tolerate a small amount of repetition of speech input if the system fails to understand it the first time*
6	**Recover from errors:** Users become confused and frustrated when errors occur. The system should enable easy recovery from errors and offer guidance to the user on how they can correct it. [22, 23] *Example: The system should provide error responses relevant to the error which has occurred and provide context to any error*
7	**Provide ability to control and interrupt:** The system should allow the user to interrupt if routed to a path they do not wish to follow. [15, 22, 23] *Example: The user can either interrupt with a new interaction or simply say 'stop'*
8	**Consistency and standards:** Users should be able to maintain their focus on one interface or the link to a second interface (e.g. screen display) should be clear and consistent in operation. [9, 22–24] *Example: The system could take a user's food order and then repeat it back or invite them to review it on screen*

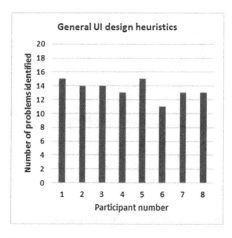
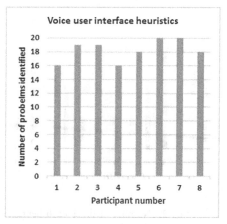

Fig. 1. Total number of problems identified per participant using either General or VUI heuristics

participant for each method: 11 to 15 for the general set of heuristics and 16 to 20 for the VUI-related set.

In a post-test questionnaire, participants were asked what they thought were the advantages and disadvantages for the set of heuristics they used. Interestingly, the benefits for both were similar: making the evaluation process easier and quicker, providing a structure or checklist to work to, and helping to identify problems that would otherwise not have been thought about. Fewer negative comments were received for either set. For the general heuristics, it was said that they were quite broad and could be better phrased to suit voice systems. For the VUI heuristics, the descriptions were thought to potentially limit or to narrow thinking during the evaluation and could include more general aspects of user interfaces.

Participants were asked to identify any heuristics that they had used during the evaluation that they found particularly useful. Figure 2 is a histogram showing the frequency with which each heuristic was selected. Most of the heuristics in both the general and VUI sets were regarded as especially useful by at least one participant. For the general set (Nielsen): (1) 'visibility of system status', and (9) 'help users recognise, diagnose, and recover from errors', were the most frequently cited. This may be an indication that people using VUIs still expect such applications to provide help to overcome errors although they might prefer that the help be integrated into the inter-action dialogue and not be a separate task. This finding was also seen in a study by Bertini et al. [25] when assessing heuristics for use with mobile computing. Heuristic (8) 'aesthetic and minimalist design', was the only one not mentioned by any of the participants. While this might seem appropriate as it is normally applied to screen-based systems, it could be applicable to VUI in relation to the aesthetic qualities of the voice and adopting an efficient and effective conversational style.

Regarding the VUI heuristics, those referred to more frequently were: (2) 'adopt conversational speech', (5) 'achieve high accuracy', (7) 'support user control and interruption' and (8) 'consistency and standards'. Heuristic (4) 'ensure adequate system

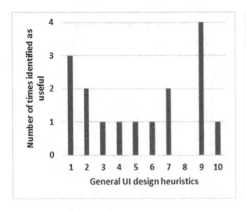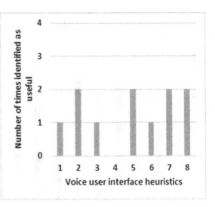

Fig. 2. Number of times each heuristic was chosen as being particularly useful

feedback' was not selected. This is surprising since this is central aspect of conversational interaction.

A limitation of the study was that while all participants did have knowledge of IT and usability, this may have been of variable level, so that some were better able to apply the heuristics evaluation method and identify problems than others.

5 Discussion

The finding that more usability problems were identified by participants who used VUI specific heuristics in comparison with general heuristics is consistent with similar studies looking into the effectiveness of application specific usability heuristics in other domains. For example, Inostroza et al. [26], who studied the use of heuristics for touch screen mobile devices, identified that evaluators using specific heuristics for these devices were able to identify more usability problems than the evaluators that used Nielsen's heuristics. However, the fact that many of the general heuristics were regarded as especially useful during the VUI evaluation study shows that there are other aspects of user interfaces, not necessarily speech specific, that should be included in an evaluation. This may mean that using a combination of the general and application specific heuristics is a more effective approach for conducting an evaluation of an application for a specific domain.

In can be said then that general usability heuristics clearly apply to VUIs e.g. minimising short term memory load and give suitable feedback after user input. However, there are other aspects for which heuristics can be generated e.g. following natural conversational conventions, that should also be covered by heuristics. Since voice interaction is also closely related to intelligent systems using natural language, this raises the issue of whether artificial intelligence related heuristics are also needed, such as whether system outputs show 'common sense' or reflect a knowledge of the real world. The Nielsen and Molistic heuristic 'match between the system and the real world' could be applicable here.

Broader aspects of VUIs that arose from the pilot study conducted in the student house relate to trust and social context. An extension of the heuristics may be needed to address them.

6 Conclusion

This study has investigated and evaluated usability heuristics specifically for auditory VUIs where interaction is conducted solely through voice. The usability heuristics were also generated following heuristic development method in a systematic way. It was anticipated at the start of the study that when conducting the usability evaluations, participants who used Nielsen's general heuristics would find many of them less relevant compared to participants who used the VUI-specific heuristics. However, the findings showed that participants using either set of heuristics found most of the heuristics available to them were useful. This may mean that the optimum design of an evaluation tool for usability inspection is one that combines both general and application specific heuristics. A modular approach could therefore be adopted where subsets of heuristics can be chosen to match a specific evaluation context.

Continuing from this study, further iterative development of the heuristics could be undertaken to reflect new developments in applying speech interfaces to intelligent systems and considering the broader contextual or environmental issues where VUI systems are implemented.

Acknowledgement. The author would like to acknowledge the work of the Loughborough Design School students, Simon Hughes and Daniel Essom, which this paper draws upon.

Appendix

Ben Shneiderman's eight golden rules for interface design:

1. Strive for consistency
2. Enable frequent users to use shortcuts
3. Offer informative feedback
4. Design dialog to yield closure
5. Offer simple error handling
6. Permit easy reversal of actions
7. Support internal locus of control
8. Reduce short-term memory load

Don Norman's principles of interaction design:

1. Visibility
2. Feedback
3. Constraints

4. Mapping
5. Consistency
6. Affordance

References

1. Jurafsky, D., Martin, J.: Speech and Language Processing: An Introduction to Natural Language Processing, Computational Linguistics, and Speech Recognition, 2nd edn. Pearson-Prentice Hall, Upper Saddle River (2009)
2. Xiong, W., et al.: Toward human parity in conversational speech recognition. IEEE/ACM Trans. Audio Speech Lang. Process. **25**(12), 2410–2423 (2017)
3. Bernholz, W.: VUI: Voice user interfaces and the future of voice in mobile apps (2017). https://www.dropsource.com/blog/vui-voice-user-interfaces-and-the-future-of-voice-in-mobile-apps/. Accessed 03 Mar 2019
4. Asher, M.: The history of user interfaces–and where they are heading (2017). https://www.cmo.com/features/articles/2017/7/20/a-brief-history-of-ui-and-whats-coming.html#gs.tcqMwFlo. Accessed 03 Mar 2019
5. Jones, D., Hapeshi, K., Frankish, C.: Design guidelines for speech recognition interfaces. Appl. Ergon. **20**(1), 47–52 (1989)
6. Cohen, M., Giangola, J., Balogh, J.: Voice User Interface Design, 1st edn. Addison-Wesley, Boston (2004)
7. Harris, R.: Voice Interaction Design, 1st edn. Morgan Kaufmann, San Francisco (2005)
8. Whitenton, K.: Voice interaction UX: brave new world…same old story. Nielsen Norman Group (2016). https://www.nngroup.com/articles/voice-interaction-ux/. Accessed 03 Mar 2019
9. Asthana, S., Singh, P., Singh, A.: Assessing designs of interactive voice response systems for better usability. In: Marcus, A. (ed.) DUXU 2013. LNCS, vol. 8012, pp. 183–192. Springer, Heidelberg (2013). https://doi.org/10.1007/978-3-642-39229-0_21
10. Howell, M., Love, S., Turner, M.: Visualisation improves the usability of voice-operated mobile phone services. Int. J. Hum.-Comput. Stud. **64**(8), 754–769 (2006)
11. Franzke, M., Marx, A., Roberts, T., Engelbeck, G.: Is speech recognition usable? ACM SIGCHI Bull. **25**(3), 49–51 (1993)
12. Damper, R., Gladstone, K.: Experiences of usability evaluation of the IMAGINE speech-based interaction system. Int. J. Speech Technol. **9**(1–2), 41–50 (2006)
13. Kim, H.-C.: An experimental study to explore usability problems of interactive voice response systems. In: Pan, J.-S., Chen, S.-M., Nguyen, N.T. (eds.) ACIIDS 2012. LNCS (LNAI), vol. 7198, pp. 169–177. Springer, Heidelberg (2012). https://doi.org/10.1007/978-3-642-28493-9_19
14. Portet, F., Vacher, M., Golanski, C., Roux, C., Meillon, B.: Design and evaluation of a smart home voice interface for the elderly: acceptability and objection aspects. Pers. Ubiquitous Comput. **17**(1), 127–144 (2011)
15. Yankelovich, N., Levow, G., Marx, M.: Designing SpeechActs. In: CHI 1995 Proceedings of the ACM SIGCHI Conference on Human Factors in Computing Systems, pp. 369–376. ACM Press, New York (1995)
16. Nielsen, J., Molich, R.: Heuristic evaluation of user interfaces. In: CHI 1990 Proceedings of the SIGCHI Conference on Human Factors in Computing Systems, Seattle, Washington, pp. 249–256 (1990)

17. Quiñones, D., Rusu, C.: How to develop usability heuristics: a systematic literature review. Comput. Stand. Interfaces **53**, 89–122 (2017)
18. Johnson, G.I., Coventry, L.: "You talking to me?" Exploring voice in self-service user interfaces. Int. J. Hum.-Comput. Interact. **13**(2), 161–186 (2009)
19. Milanesi, C.: Voice Assistant Anyone? Yes please, but not in public! (2016). http://creativ estrategies.com/voice-assistant-anyone-yes-please-but-not-in-public/. Accessed 03 Mar 2019
20. Adobe Digital Insights: State of voice assistants (2018). https://www.slideshare.net/adobe/ adi-state-of-voice-assistants-113779956. Accessed 03 Mar 2019
21. Rusu, C., Roncagliolo, S., Rusu, V., Collazos, C.: A methodology to establish usability heuristics. In: ACHI 2011: The Fourth International Conference on Advances in Computer-Human Interactions, pp. 59–62 (2011)
22. Nielsen, J.: Usability Inspection Methods. Wiley, New York (1994)
23. Shneiderman, B., Plaisant, C.: Designing the User Interface, 1st edn. Addison-Wesley, Upper Saddle River (2010)
24. Norman, D.: The Design of Everyday Things. Basic Books, New York (2013)
25. Bertini, E., Gabrielli, S., Kimani, S.: Appropriating and assessing heuristics for mobile computing. In: Proceedings of the Working Conference on Advanced Visual Interfaces - AVI 2006 (2006)
26. Inostroza, R., Rusu, C., Roncagliolo, S., Jimenez, C., Rusu, V.: Usability heuristics for touchscreen-based mobile devices. In: ITNG 2012 Proceedings of the Ninth International Conference on Information Technology - New Generations (2012)

Web Accessibility Evaluation Methods: A Systematic Review

Almendra Nuñez[1]([✉]), Arturo Moquillaza[1,2], and Freddy Paz[1]

[1] Pontificia Universidad Católica del Perú, San Miguel, Lima 32, Peru
{almendra.nunezc,amoquillaza,fpaz}@pucp.pe
[2] Universidad San Ignacio de Loyola, Lima 12, Lima, Peru
miguel.moquillaza@usil.pe

Abstract. In this paper, we present the results of a systematic review involving the techniques or methods of web accessibility currently used, the domains that have been covered and the disabilities that were focused. The search strategy identified 343 studies, where only 20 were finally selected for the review. We found that automatic tools are the most frequent techniques used to evaluate web accessibility. In addition, most studies performed in the educational domain and the majority of studies do not focus on a special disability.

Keywords: Systematic review · Web accessibility ·
Evaluation methods · Software applications ·
Human-Computer Interaction

1 Introduction

Accessibility represents nowadays an essential aspect to be considered in the development of Web applications [1]. The companies are adopting technologies as one of the main means of dissemination and visibility of the information, which should be accessible to all people, easy to use, accurate and safe [2]. This assertion can also be applied to the web domain, where the technological advance has allowed companies to provide online services through online applications [3]. This digital transformation has led to the identification of four categories of change [4]: (1) the expectations of the customer's experience, (2) the innovation in products and services, (3) the disappearance of barriers between industries and regulation, and (4) the accompaniment by society to the new technologies. Therefore, one of the main concerns of the big enterprises is the development of tools that allow customers to get their goals with satisfaction.

One of the global goals of companies is to provide electronic services that allow all people to access them, regardless of their auditory, movement, visual and cognitive abilities [5]. To achieve this, several factors must be considered in the design of interfaces. The impact of not taking into account web accessibility standards in software products leads customers with visual disabilities to stop using the services due to their inaccessibility [6]. Therefore, it is essential to

A. Marcus and W. Wang (Eds.): HCII 2019, LNCS 11586, pp. 226–237, 2019.
https://doi.org/10.1007/978-3-030-23535-2_17

perform a continuous accessibility assessment of the components of a system to verify if all the interfaces can be accessed independently of the disability of a specific user [7]. The way to determine if a software product meets the necessary compliance of the existing guidelines that would allow it to be accessible, is through evaluation methods [8]. The accessibility is as essential, that companies can win a legal problem if customers can not use the services provided through the interfaces that present accessibility problems [6]. Finally, within the social values adopted by companies, equality, inclusion and social commitment are considered, and in this sense, their web applications must make reflect the values of the organization and help to improve its image further [9]. Therefore, accessibility can be considered as an innovation for the relationship between the organization and all its stakeholders, which becomes a substantial competitive advantage for companies [6].

Given the importance of accessibility in software products, in this paper we describe the process of a systematic literature review that was performed with the purpose of identifying the main accessibility assessment methods that are currently used by the scientific community. The paper is structured as follows. In Sect. 2 we present the essential concepts and definitions that were used to develop the research work. In Sect. 3, we describe the protocol that guided the entire process of systematic review. Likewise, the findings and results are discussed. Finally, in Sect. 4, the conclusions and future works are established.

2   Background

2.1   Web Accessibility

Web accessibility can be defined as a universal access to the Web, which does not depend on the hardware or software used, nor the language, culture or physical or mental abilities of users [10].

The goal of web accessibility is to ensure that the information or services delivered through web sites are available and can be used by the widest possible audience [11].

2.2   WCAG Web Accessibility Guidelines

The WCAG guidelines (Web Content Accessibility Guidelines) are aimed at those who design or develop content for the Web. They consist of specific recommendations, written in a generic way. The objective is to make the content presented in an accessible way. The Web Accessibility Initiative (WAI) of the World Wide Web Consortium (W3C) elaborated annexed guides that exploit each point and detail the steps to follow to implement and comply with them [12].

2.3 WCAG 2.0 Guide

These guidelines provide guidance and examples to meet the guidelines using specific technologies. For this, they have adequacy levels A, AA, AAA that will be applied differently to each one of their criteria. The WCAG 2.0 guidelines are composed of 4 principles, 12 guidelines and 61 compliance criteria, each of which will have different levels of compliance (A, AA, AAA), in addition to a set of sufficient techniques and advisory techniques [11]. The principles are the following:

1. Principle 1: Perceptible: The information and the components of the user interface must be presented to the users so that they can perceive them. It is composed of 4 guidelines and 22 compliance criteria.
2. Principle 2: Operable: The components of the user interface and navigation must be operable. It consists of 4 guidelines and 20 compliance criteria.
3. Principle 3: Understandable: Information and user interface management must be understandable. It consists of 3 guidelines and 17 compliance criteria.
4. Principle 4: Robust: The content must be robust enough to rely on its interpretation by a wide variety of user agents, including assistive technologies. It consists of 1 guideline and 2 compliance criteria.

3 Systematic Mapping Review

A systematic literature review is a method to analyze, evaluate and interpret all relevant studies to a specific research question. In spite of the systematic literature review is frequently used in Medicine, there are proposals to use this methodology in the field of Software Engineering. Kitchenham and Charters [13] establish a set of steps to achieve relevant and rigorous systematic studies for software engineering topics. The steps of this methodology are presented in the subsequent sections.

3.1 Research Questions

The purpose of this systematic review is to explain the current methods and techniques that are used to evaluate web accessibility. Besides, we identified the domains where this evaluation where taken and which disabilities are considered in the evaluation. The main objective of this research is to review the literature and situate it into the current scenario. In this way, we formulated the following research questions:

RQ1: Which methods and techniques are reported in the literature for the evaluation of accessibility in web applications?
RQ2: Which domains are the most evaluated?
RQ3: Which disabilities are considered for the evaluation of web accessibility?

After we have established the research questions, we defined the general concepts based on PICOC. Since our research is not intended to compare interventions, the "comparison" criterion was not considered. Table 1 contains the concepts.

Table 1. Definition of the general concepts using PICOC

Criterion	Description
Population	Web applications for disable people
Intervention	Web accessibility methods and techniques for evaluation
Outcomes	Not concentrated on results
Context	Academic and software context, including any type of empirical study

3.2 Search String

The search strategy was based on the general concepts. To obtain more relevant studies some synonymous were selected. We only considered relevant studies, whose publication date was since 2015, in order to analyze the current state of art.

C1: ("web application*" OR "website*" OR "web site*" OR "web page*")
C2: ("web accessibility")
C3: ("method*" OR "technique*")
C4: ("evaluation" OR "verification" OR "validation")

The resulting string was:
("web application*" OR "website*" OR "web page*") AND ("web accessibility") AND ("method*" OR "technique*") AND ("evaluation" OR "verification" OR "validation").

3.3 Search Process

To perform the search process we use four recognized databases: IEEExplore, ACM Digital Library, SCOPUS and SpringerLink. Grey literature was excluded since it is not peer reviewed.

3.4 Selection of Primary Studies

Each study that was retrieved from the automated search in the databases, was examined by the authors in order to determine its inclusion in this study. The process of evaluation involved a review of the entire document: title, abstract, introduction, background, state of the art, methodology, study case, results and conclusions. Furthermore, we established some inclusion criteria to determine the inclusion of the study.

- Studies that present a web accessibility evaluation a specific domain explaining the method used.
- Studies that present a comparison between two or more web accessibility evaluation methods.

– Studies that present the assessment of the accessibility of a domain focused on a disability.

On the other hand, we established the exclusion criteria:

– Studies that present evaluation of other factors such as usability, user experience, etc.
– Studies where assistive technology for the disabled is presented.
– Articles where algorithms for the development of web pages for the disabled are presented.

3.5 Data Extraction

The information we extracted form the selected studies include the following:

(a) Paper ID
(b) Paper Title
(c) Author(s)
(d) Year of publication
(e) Database in which the study was found.

The automated search for our systematic mapping was performed on December 20th, 2018. We obtained 343 studies from the four consulted databases. After the application of the inclusion and exclusion criteria, 21 of these papers were selected for the analysis. Table 2 shows the results of the search process.

Table 2. Summary of search results

Database name	Search results	Duplicated papers	Relevant papers
IEEE Xplore	21	-	5
ACM Digital Library	119	0	5
Scopus	43	12	7
SpringerLink	160	4	3
Total	**343**	**16**	**20**

3.6 Data Analysis and Results

The list of the selected articles are presented in Table 3.

Table 3. Selected studies

ID	Title	Author	Year	Database
S1	Evaluation of the web accessibility of higher-education websites	Acosta-Vargas, P., Lujn-Mora, S., and Salvador-Ullauri, L.	2016 [14]	IEEExplore
S2	Framework for accessibility evaluation of hospital websites	Acosta-Vargas, P., Acosta, T., and Lujn-Mora, S.	2018 [15]	IEEExplore
S3	Group vs individual web accessibility evaluations: Effects with novice evaluators	Brajnik, G., Vigo, M., Yesilada, Y., and Harper, S.	2016 [16]	IEEExplore
S4	Quality evaluation of government websites	Acosta-Vargas, P., Lujn-Mora, S., and Salvador-Ullauri, L.	2017 [17]	IEEExplore
S5	Towards web accessibility in telerehabilitation platforms	Acosta-Vargas, P., Rybarczyk, Y., Pérez, J., González, M., Jimenes, K., Leconte, L. and Esparza, D.	2018 [18]	IEEExplore
S6	Advancements in web accessibility evaluation methods: how far are we?	Baazeem, I.S., and Al-Khalifa, H.S.	2015 [19]	ACM Digital Library
S7	Crowdsourcing-based web accessibility evaluation with golden maximum likelihood inference	Song, S., Bu, J., Artmeier, A., Shi, K., Wang, Y., Yu, Z., and Wang, C.	2018 [20]	ACM Digital Library
S8	Beyond web content accessibility guidelines. Expert accessibility reviews	Calvo, R., Seyedarabi, F., and Savva, A.	2016 [21]	ACM Digital Library
S9	An approach to make software testing for users with down syndrome a little more pleasant	Mendoza-González, A., Luna-García, H., Mendoza-González, R., Rusu, C., Gamboa-Rosales, H., Galván-Tejada, J.I., ... and Solis-Robles, R.	2018 [22]	ACM Digital Library
S10	The accessibility of administrative processes: Assessing the impacts on students in higher education	Coughlan, T., and Lister, K.	2018 [23]	ACM Digital Library
S11	Website accessibility in the tourism industry: an analysis of official national tourism organization websites around the world	Domínguez Vila, T., Alén González, E., and Darcy, S.	2018 [24]	SCOPUS
S12	Peruvian public universities and the accessibility of their websites	Benites Alfaro, F.D., Zapata Del Río, C.M.D.P.	2018 [25]	SCOPUS
S13	Toward a combined method for evaluation of web accessibility	Acosta-Vargas, P., Luján-Mora, S., Acosta, T., and Salvador-Ullauri	2018 [26]	SCOPUS
S14	Evaluation of the quality and accessibility of available websites on kidney transplantation	Valizadeh-Haghi, S., and Rahmatizadeh, S.	2018 [27]	SCOPUS
S15	Method for accessibility assessment of heading in online editors	Acosta, T., Luján-Mora, S., and Acosta-Vargas, P.	2017 [28]	SCOPUS
S16	Research foci, methodologies, and theories used in addressing E-government accessibility for persons with disabilities in developing countries	Agangiba, M., and Kabanda, S.	2017 [29]	SCOPUS
S17	Methodology for heuristic evaluation of web accessibility oriented to types of disabilities	Orozco, A., Tabares, V., and Duque, N.	2016 [30]	SCOPUS
S18	Using WCAG 2.0 and heuristic evaluation to evaluate accessibility in educational web based pages	Debevc, M., Kožuh, I., Hauptman, S., Klembas, A., Lapuh, J. B., and Holzinger, A.	2015 [31]	SCOPUS
S19	Accessibility and usability of websites intended for people with disabilities: A preliminary study	Zitkus, E., Brigatto, A.C., Ferrari, A.L.M., Bonfim, G.H., Carvalho Filho, I.F., Reis, T. D.,... and Paschoarelli, L.C.	2016 [32]	SCOPUS
S20	Multilevel accessibility evaluation of institutional websites in Tunisia	Gharbi, I., Bouraoui, A., and Saoud, N.B.B.	2018 [33]	SCOPUS

The purpose of the first question was to find the methods or techniques used for the evaluation of web accessibility. Table 4 shows the methods found and the frequency with which they appear in the articles selected for this research. Then we proceed to explain each method more in depth.

Table 4. Methods for evaluating web accessibility

Method	Article
Automatic tools	S1, S2, S4, S5, S6, S7, S11, S12, S13, S14, S15, S16, S19, S20
Expert evaluation	S3, S6
User testing	S3, S6, S7, S8, S9, S10, S13, S17, S18, S19, S20

Automatic Tools: When using automated tools, a methodology followed to evaluate the domains covered by the studies S1, S2, S4 and S6. Figure 1 shows the steps.

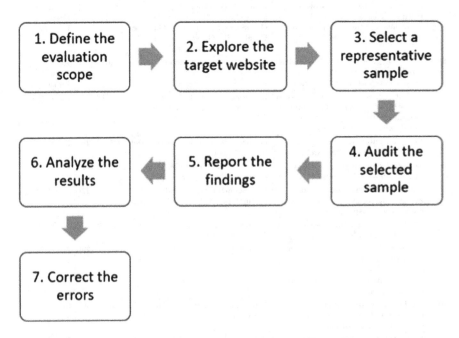

Fig. 1. The seven phases to evaluated web accessibility using automatic tools

(a) Define the evaluation scope: In this phase it is necessary to identify the pages involved in the evaluation. Besides, we must establish the adequacy level (A, AA, AAA), which depends on the domain the study will be evaluated.

(b) Explore the target website: The purpose of this phase is to determine the principal features that are essential for the domain. This include style, designs, structures, functions and processes. In this phase, the evaluator needs to check for broken links.

(c) Select a sample: In this phase, the main page of the website is identified and the future pages that follow the navigability of the website.

(d) Audit sample selected: Each page is tested by the automatic tool in order to meet the adequacy level established in phase 1. The evaluator also must verify if the data is introduced correctly and the notifications and interactions are verified and evaluated.

(e) Report the findings: The results are documented. Generally, most of the automatic tools present reports explained the problems they found and the broken guidelines. In some cases, they present a solution to modify.

(f) Analyze the results: The problems that were identified in the previous phase are discussed in order to decide if these problems will be corrected.

(g) Correct errors: Developers and designer can follow the suggestions of the automatic tools or they can adjust their pages as they consider.

Expert Evaluation: Although the evaluation of experts has not been very approached in the literature, articles S3, S6 refer to web accessibility experts must make an evaluation on the web pages contrasting what is indicated in the guidelines such as WCAG 2.0 and if these are complying depending on the domain. When a methodology is not specified, as in the case of automated tools, the experts consider it important that before specifying the evaluation, the characteristics of the domain to be worked are specified. In the studies found, experts evaluate the page through interaction. When they find an error, this is recorded, as these same classify the severity of this.

User Testing: Manual tests are an accessibility evaluation method. The main advantage lies in the fact that specific accessibility problems and violations can be found directly, because the equation can be designed according to the purpose sought. Within the criteria to consider, you can use international standards or you can establish your own criteria. There is a lot of reference to the team of evaluators that will design the tests. Regarding the participants that are used for the tests, S3 indicates that they must be people who interact frequently with the domain to be evaluated. On the other hand, the specific tasks in user tests are focused on complying with the processes that are embodied in the web page.

Regarding the domains that have been addressed, it can be seen that the education sector has been the most studied, followed by the government sector. Some studies do focus on the importance of the domain and the reason for the study, however, in other studies the study focuses more on the methodology that selects a test domain. Table 5 specifies the domains that have been addressed.

Finally, the disabilities that have been addressed in the literature are presented. Most studies specify what disability is being addressed. This is because

Table 5. Domains evaluated

Domain	Article
Education	S1, S8, S9, S10, S12, S13, S15, S18, S20
Health	S2, S5, S14
Government	S3, S8, S16, S19
Entertainment	S8, S11

the selected method and the work structure used do not emphasize a specific disability. In the case of automated tools, they do not detect accessibility problems according to the type of disability. The S7 study does emphasize having participants who suffer from different disabilities, which does analyze the interaction between the person and the web page in order to detect problems or difficulties in fulfilling the tasks. Table 6 shows the disabilities addressed in the literature.

Table 6. Disabilities worked in the studies

Disability	Article
Mental	S10, S17
Auditive	S7, S10, S17
Visual	S7, S10, S17
Physical	S5, S7, S10, S17
Do not specify	S1, S2, S3, S4, S6, S8, S9, S11, S12, S13, S14, S15, S16, S18, S19, S20

4   Conclusions and Future Works

Some evaluation methods have been proposed to determine the level of web accessibility in web applications. Although automated tools are the most used in studies, they do not always lead to the identification of all web accessibility problems that exist. Expert testing can be the most effective method to ensure compliance with some standards, while user testing seems to work efficiently to verify how people with disabilities could perform certain tasks.

Following a predefined protocol, we identified 343 studies, of which 20 were selected. This work allowed us to determine that: (1) automatic tools, (2) expert evaluation and (3) user tests are the most used techniques according to the literature. In addition, in this study, we have determined the domains in which web accessibility assessments have been carried out, the most frequent being (1) education, (2) government, (3) health, (4) entertainment. Finally, the disabilities in which they have worked were determined, being the most frequent result that the majority of studies do not focus the evaluation on any disability.

As future work, comparisons can be made between accessibility assessment methods to complement each other. On the other hand, you can contrast the accessibility guidelines that several methods follow to contrast them with the needs that each disability needs when interacting with web applications.

Acknowledgement. This study is highly supported by the *Section of Informatics Engineering* of the *Pontifical Catholic University of Peru - Peru* and "HCI, Design, User Experience, Accessibility & Innovation Technologies Research Group, HCI-DUXAIT". HCI-DUXAIT is a research group of the Pontificia Universidad Católica del Perú (PUCP).

References

1. Aizpurua, A., Harper, S., Vigo, M.: Exploring the relationship between web accessibility and user experience. Int. J. Hum.-Comput. Stud. **91**, 13–23 (2016)
2. Vollenwyder, B., Iten, G.H., Brühlmann, F., Opwis, K., Mekler, E.D.: Salient beliefs influencing the intention to consider web accessibility. Comput. Hum. Behav. **92**, 352–360 (2019)
3. Aguirre, J., Moquillaza, A., Paz, F.: Methodologies for the design of ATM interfaces: a systematic review. In: Ahram, T., Karwowski, W., Taiar, R. (eds.) IHSED 2018. AISC, vol. 876, pp. 256–262. Springer, Cham (2019). https://doi.org/10.1007/978-3-030-02053-8_39
4. Martínez, A.B., Andrés, J.D., García, J.: Determinants of the web accessibility of european banks. Inf. Process. Manag. **50**(1), 69–86 (2014)
5. Henry, S.L., Abou-Zahra, S., Brewer, J.: The role of accessibility in a universal web. In: Proceedings of the 11th Web for All Conference, W4A 2014, pp. 17:1–17:4. ACM, New York (2014)
6. Wentz, B., Pham, D., Feaser, E., Smith, D., Smith, J., Wilson, A.: Documenting the accessibility of 100 US bank and finance websites. Univers. Access Inf. Soc. (2018)
7. Nazar, H., Sarfraz, M.S., Shoaib, U.: Web accessibility evaluation of banking website in Pakistan. Int. J. Comput. Sci. Inf. Secur. **15**(1), 642–650 (2017)
8. Chalhoub, G.: Evaluating accessibility and usability for different applications. Technical report, University of Southampton (2018)
9. Katerattanakul, P., Hong, S., Lee, H.M., Kam, H.J.: The effects of web accessibility certification on the perception of companies' corporate social responsibility. Univers. Access Inf. Soc. **17**(1), 161–173 (2018)
10. W3C: Accessibility (2016). https://www.w3.org/standards/webdesign/accessibility. Accessed 23 Jan 2019
11. Navarrete, R., Luján, S.: Accesibilidad web en las universidades del ecuador. análisis preliminar. Revista Politécnica **33**(1), 43 (2014)
12. Valdés, F.F.: Desarrollo de sitios web: la ley, el orden y los estándares. Serie Bibliotecología y Gestión de Información **28**, 1–24 (2007)
13. Kitchenham, B., Charters, S.: Guidelines for performing systematic literature reviews in software engineering. Technical report EBSE 2007-001, Keele University and Durham University (2007)
14. Acosta-Vargas, P., Luján-Mora, S., Salvador-Ullauri, L.: Evaluation of the web accessibility of higher-education websites. In: 2016 15th International Conference on Information Technology Based Higher Education and Training (ITHET), pp. 1–6, September 2016

15. Acosta-Vargas, P., Acosta, T., Luján-Mora, S.: Framework for accessibility evaluation of hospital websites. In: 2018 International Conference on eDemocracy eGovernment (ICEDEG), pp. 9–15, April 2018
16. Brajnik, G., Vigo, M., Yesilada, Y., Harper, S.: Group vs individual web accessibility evaluations: effects with novice evaluators. Interact. Comput. **28**(6), 843–861 (2016)
17. Acosta-Vargas, P., Luján-Mora, S., Salvador-Ullauri, L.: Quality evaluation of government websites. In: 2017 Fourth International Conference on eDemocracy eGovernment (ICEDEG), pp. 8–14, April 2017
18. Acosta-Vargas, P., et al.: Towards web accessibility in telerehabilitation platforms. In: 2018 IEEE Third Ecuador Technical Chapters Meeting (ETCM), pp. 1–6, October 2018
19. Baazeem, I.S., Al-Khalifa, H.S.: Advancements in web accessibility evaluation methods: how far are we? In: Proceedings of the 17th International Conference on Information Integration and Web-based Applications & Services, iiWAS 2015, pp. 90:1–90:5. ACM, New York (2015)
20. Song, S., et al.: Crowdsourcing-based web accessibility evaluation with golden maximum likelihood inference. Process. ACM Hum.-Comput. Interact. **2**(CSCW), 163:1–163:21 (2018)
21. Calvo, R., Seyedarabi, F., Savva, A.: Beyond web content accessibility guidelines: expert accessibility reviews. In: Proceedings of the 7th International Conference on Software Development and Technologies for Enhancing Accessibility and Fighting Info-Exclusion, DSAI 2016, pp. 77–84. ACM, New York (2016)
22. Mendoza-González, A., et al.: An approach to make software testing for users with down syndrome a little more pleasant. In: Proceedings of the XIX International Conference on Human Computer Interaction, Interacción 2018, pp. 5:1–5:8. ACM, New York (2018)
23. Coughlan, T., Lister, K.: The accessibility of administrative processes: assessing the impacts on students in higher education. In: Proceedings of the Internet of Accessible Things, W4A 2018, pp. 5:1–5:10. ACM, New York (2018)
24. Vila, T.D., González, E.A., Darcy, S.: Website accessibility in the tourism industry: an analysis of official national tourism organization websites around the world. Disabil. Rehabil. **40**(24), 2895–2906 (2018)
25. Benites Alfaro, F.D., Zapata Del Río, C.M.D.P.: Peruvian public universities and the accessibility of their websites. In: Marcus, A., Wang, W. (eds.) DUXU 2018. LNCS, vol. 10920, pp. 589–607. Springer, Cham (2018). https://doi.org/10.1007/978-3-319-91806-8_46
26. Acosta-Vargas, P., Lujan-Mora, S., Acosta, T., Salvador-Ullauri, L.: Toward a combined method for evaluation of web accessibility. In: Rocha, A., Guarda, T. (eds.) ICITS 2018. AISC, vol. 721, pp. 602–613. Springer, Cham (2018). https://doi.org/10.1007/978-3-319-73450-7_57
27. Valizadeh-Haghi, S., Rahmatizadeh, S.: Evaluation of the quality and accessibility of available websites on kidney transplantation. Urol. J. **15**(5), 261–265 (2018)
28. Acosta, T., Luján-Mora, S., Acosta-Vargas, P.: Method for accessibility assessment of heading in online editors. In: Proceedings of the 2017 9th International Conference on Education Technology and Computers, ICETC 2017, pp. 243–247. ACM, New York (2017)
29. Agangiba, M., Kabanda, S.: Research foci, methodologies, and theories used in addressing e-government accessibility for persons with disabilities in developing countries. Interdisc. J. Inf. Knowl. Manag. **12**, 245–268 (2017)

30. Orozco, A., Tabares, V., Duque, N.: Methodology for heuristic evaluation of web accessibility oriented to types of disabilities. In: Antona, M., Stephanidis, C. (eds.) UAHCI 2016. LNCS, vol. 9737, pp. 91–97. Springer, Cham (2016). https://doi.org/10.1007/978-3-319-40250-5_9

31. Debevc, M., Kožuh, I., Hauptman, S., Klembas, A., Lapuh, J.B., Holzinger, A.: Using WCAG 2.0 and heuristic evaluation to evaluate accessibility in educational web based pages. In: Uden, L., Liberona, D., Welzer, T. (eds.) LTEC 2015. CCIS, vol. 533, pp. 197–207. Springer, Cham (2015). https://doi.org/10.1007/978-3-319-22629-3_16

32. Zitkus, E., et al.: Accessibility and usability of websites intended for people with disabilities: a preliminary study. In: Marcus, A. (ed.) DUXU 2016. LNCS, vol. 9747, pp. 678–688. Springer, Cham (2016). https://doi.org/10.1007/978-3-319-40355-7_66

33. Gharbi, I., Bouraoui, A., Bellamine Ben Saoud, N.: Multilevel accessibility evaluation of institutional websites in Tunisia. In: Miesenberger, K., Kouroupetroglou, G. (eds.) ICCHP 2018. LNCS, vol. 10896, pp. 43–46. Springer, Cham (2018). https://doi.org/10.1007/978-3-319-94277-3_8

Seeing Potential Is More Important Than Usability: Revisiting Technology Acceptance

Brian Pickering[1]([🖂]), Mariet Nouri Janian[2], Borja López Moreno[3],
Andrea Micheletti[2], Alberto Sanno[2], and Michael Surridge[1]

[1] Electronics and Computer Science, IT Innovation, University of Southampton,
Gamma House, Enterprise Road, Southampton SO16 7NS, UK
{jbp,ms}@it-innovation.soton.ac.uk
[2] Center for Advanced Technology in Health and Wellbeing IRCCS San
Raffaele Hospital, Via Olgettina, 60, 20132 Milan, Italy
{nourijanian.mariet,micheletti.andrea,
sanno.alberto}@hsr.it
[3] Biocruces Bizkaia Health Research Institute, Plaza Cruces 12, Barakaldo,
Spain
BORJA.LOPEZMORENO@osakidetza.eus

Abstract. With ever-increasing technology complexity, there is a need to consider how technology integrates within typical and specific environments. Empirical work with technology acceptance models has to date focused largely on perceived or expected ease-of-use along with the perceived or expected usefulness of the technology. These constructs have been examined extensively via quantitative methods. Other factors have received less attention. There is some evidence, for instance, that technology adoption may depend on how technology contributes to self-efficacy and agency. Less accessible perhaps to standard quantitative instruments, it is time to consider a mixed-methods approach to examine these aspects of technology acceptance. For this exploratory study, we have begun to evaluate a security modeller tool within a healthcare. We asked IT professionals working in hospital environments in Italy and Spain to work with the technology as part of a limited ethnographic study, and to complete a standard ease-of-use questionnaire. Comparing the results, we found that the quantitative measures to be poor predictors of a willingness to explore the affordances presented by the technology. Although limited at this time, we maintain that a more nuanced picture of technology adoption must allow potential adopters to be creative in response to how they believe the technology could be exploited in their environment.

Keywords: Technology acceptance · User expectation · Mixed-methods ·
System usability score · Ethnography · Technology affordance · Self-efficacy ·
Agency

© Springer Nature Switzerland AG 2019
A. Marcus and W. Wang (Eds.): HCII 2019, LNCS 11586, pp. 238–249, 2019.
https://doi.org/10.1007/978-3-030-23535-2_18

1 Introduction

With increasing reliance on ever-more complex technology, it is important to revisit models of technology acceptance. [1] recently reviewed fourteen models and variants. Although his literature review identifies the Unified Theory of Acceptance and Use of Technology (UTAUT) [2], the Technology Acceptance Model (TAM) [3] and the Diffusion of Innovations (DOI) [4] models to be the most frequently referred to, there is no other attempt at empirical or other evaluation. [5] compared TAM initially with the socio-psychological Theory of Reasoned Action (TRA) [6]. Based on quantitative self-reported responses to a relatively simple technology among university students, initial comparison asserts that Perceived usefulness and Perceived ease-of-use, both constructs in the original TAM, and their influence on Behavioral intention from both TAM and TRA to be the most powerful predictors of technology adoption [5]. As well as the restricted demographic of participants casting doubt on the generalisability of results, empirical evaluation was based solely on restricted-item quantitative instruments.

Recognising such procedural limitations, [2] implemented a rigorous quantitative evaluation of eight acceptance models to derive the UTAUT model as an extended and unified version of TAM. Generalisability is more valid, they assert, by using employees rather than just students; timing needs to look at the potential for future adoption rather than analysing an historical intention to use; and voluntary as opposed to mandatory adoption is more illuminating. They do not, however, explicitly look at the type of technology or its complexity, though they identify this as a significant factor. Instead, they seek to introduce contextual variables and the moderating factors. These may resonate with the social norms and subjective factors alluded to in TRA and possibly the Theory of Planned Behaviour [7, 8]. The problem remains though that evaluation and validation are still based on quantitative survey data. Attitude and intention is known to relate to affect [9]. Further, the reported intention to act in a certain way does not necessarily mean that participants would actually behave in that way [10]. Indeed, Chuttur [11] concludes that the evaluation of acceptance models (in his case TAM) may have less relevance and practical application to information systems than claimed. Their evaluation, he concludes, needs greater rigour and relevance.

In parallel to the literature on technology acceptance, some headway has been made with combining attitudinal, contextual, technological and subjective factors specifically for trust in technology at least. McKnight, Thatcher and their colleagues, for instance, evaluated trust constructs in both adoption and post-adoption studies [12, 13]. Their experimental cohort is once again confined to students. Pickering, Engen and Walland [14] extended that model with increased theoretical validation, based on literature review only. Elsewhere, technology adoption has been associated with human adaptation to technology defects [15, 16]. Technology may also be embraced in support of human cognition, not simply via task automation [17, 18]. Recent application of affordance theory to information systems [19] refocuses attention on subjective responses in the acceptance and adoption process. It may well be that affordance perception has a role to play in the decision to adopt a technology.

Evaluation of acceptance models to date have been quantitative and largely theoretical only, therefore. Constructs like social norms and emotional response in general tend to be ignored. Further, there has been little attention paid to responses to complex technologies in a work environment. This exploratory study is a first step to addressing this problem. Two separate cohorts of IT professionals operating in different countries were asked to discuss their experience when evaluating a modelling tool. We compare both quantitative and qualitative measures of their responses to their experience of the tool in an attempt to provide a full indication of their intention to adopt the technology.

2   Method

To investigate usability, we initially used a standard quantitative instrument, the System Usability Score (SUS). In addition, we monitored behaviours and performance qualitatively in a limited ethnographic study. The approach is described in more detail below.

2.1   Research Questions

For the purpose of the studies reported there, we seek to address two research questions:

RQ1: can qualitative methods help re-evaluate existing approaches to technology acceptance?

RQ2: how can qualitative methods improve existing quantitative approaches to technology acceptance?

SUS scores were elicited and analysed to provide some measure of participants' ease-of-use. These scores were compared with the outcome of the ethnographic study.

2.2   Design

We focus initially on two constructs from TAM, namely perceived usefulness and perceived ease-of-use. As highlighted above, they related directly to similar constructs in the more ambitious and rigorously derived UTAUT. In regard to the ease-of-use construct, we rely on a standard quantitative instrument, the original System Usability Scale (SUS) [20] as summarised in the Table 1 below. Participants score each item on a 5-point Likert scale from Strongly Agree to Strongly Disagree. Even-numbered items are reverse coded to maintain attention.

Although [21] claim an 8-item scale gives sufficient reliability, and [22] cautions against its use for non-native speaker, we chose the original instrument for compatibility with other similar studies. This was complemented a small-scale ethnographic study [23] of tool use for the qualitative part of the study. Researcher notes from the ethnographic study were analysed with a simple thematic approach [24]. Following [2], we focus on a pre-adoption scenario to avoid any routinized experience as well as adaptive behaviours. Further, we focus in this exploratory research on a specific IT design-time technology [25, 26] targeted at IT professionals developing and supporting

Table 1. The original 10-item system usability scale

Item	Assertion
1	I think I would like to use this system
2	I found the system unnecessarily complex
3	I thought the system was easy to use
4	I think that I would need the support of a technical person to be able to use this system
5	I found the various functions in this system well integrated
6	I thought there was too much inconsistency in this system
7	I would imagine that most people would learn to use this system very quickly
8	I found the system very cumbersome to use
9	I felt very confident using the system
10	I needed to learn a lot of things before I could get going on this system

systems in the healthcare environment. This represents an important security-sensitive environment where risk, especially to patient care and data, must be minimised not least as a function of privacy by design [27–29]. At this time, the technology is under development within a research environment, though is being evaluated as a proof-of-concept by various commercial partners.

2.3 Participants

Two small cohorts of IT professionals were recruited one in Italy the other in Spain. All participants had between 5- and 20-years' experience in their field, and covered multiple specific roles including design, development and maintenance. Five Italian engineers and developers were recruited from the Ospedale San Raffaele (OSR) in Milan. Each of the five participants was from a different area of the hospital's IT department. The covered the following disciplines: Application Development & Management; Service Desk; Privacy, Procurement & Control; CRM, Business Intelligence & Process; and Enabling Services & Security. Four self-selecting Spanish participants were from the Biocruces Bizkaia Health Research Institute, including a bioinformatics technician, a computer science engineer, a software developer and a database manager. As such, they represent different disciplines associated with the successful development and deployment of IT services. They need to work collaboratively such that individual requirements from each area can be represented and included. All participants in both countries were fully informed of the intention to validate a security modelling tool which provides support in the identification of potential risks to individual components with a design as well as to the overall configuration. All agreed to participate.

2.4 Data Collection Method

The test context involved a scenario familiar to participants. Each cohort interacted with the tool in their respective environment working independently of each other: the

Spanish participants worked together as a single team; the Italian participants interacted in two small groups of two and one working individually. After a brief introduction to the technology, participants were given a relevant task. They were asked to design a human-machine network similar to what they would expect when implementing a specific patient-data sharing service in their environment [25, 26]. The researchers in the two locations (the two co-authors MNJ and BLM) observed participants as they worked on the task, occasionally interacting with participants if specific technology questions came up. Although a limited ethnographic study in the traditional sense, it was nevertheless deemed appropriate at this stage to focus on how those who might use the technology would behave as part of a typical task for their professional role. Participants were encouraged to "think aloud" and verbalise their reaction to the technology. Following their initial experience with the tool completing the task they were presented with, participants were then asked to complete the SUS questionnaire [20]. So the experimental set up was almost identical in the two locations, with the exception of the groupings: in Italy, participants worked in small groups or alone, whereas in Spain they worked together throughout. The order of evaluation (task and ethnographic monitoring followed by SUS) may be significant, as discussed below.

2.5   Data Analysis Method

The scores of the SUS underwent the recommended treatment to provide an overall measure of usability [20]. This was taken as a quantitative measure of the usability (or ease-of-use) for the tool being investigated.

Research notes made during the sessions were reviewed to identify common themes and patterns in how individual participants reported their experience with the technology. The primary constructs of Perceived ease-of-use and Perceived usefulness from the original TAM as initial codes, with the addition of External variables which was defined as:

"… provid[ing] the bridge between the internal beliefs, attitudes and intentions represented in TAM and the various individual differences, situational constraints and managerially controllable interventions impinging on behavior" [5, p. 988]

This latter code was used simply as a catchall for any other observations which may be deemed relevant. In this way, we hoped to capture other factors such as the related Social Influence and Facilitating Conditions proposed by [2]. The results are presented in the following section.

3   Analysis

3.1   Quantitative Results

Initial experience with the modeller tool appears to be poor, with an average SUS score of 41[1] for the Italian cohort and 52.5 for the Spaniards, well below the target score of

---

[1] In a second iteration, the score rose to 65.5.

68^2. Overall, the average across both cohorts was 46.1. The range of individual scores, however, went from 15 to 82.5. This would predict that the modeller would not be adopted, since ease-of-use as measured by the SUS instrument is so low. The item highlighted as problematic for non-native speakers, namely I found the system very cumbersome to use [22], was scored at 1.4 on average by the Italian engineers, and double that at 2.8 by the Spaniards. This is exactly the same, however, for a corresponding item I needed to learn a lot of things before I could get going on this system; and almost the same as I think that I would need the support of a technical person to be able to use this system (scored on average at 1.4 and 2.5 respectively for the Italians and the Spaniards). There appears to be some consistency in the scores, both internally (i.e., participants are consistent in their own judgements) and externally (i.e., the two cohorts report similar results).

One question is what the SUS is actually measuring. Of course, [2] replace the labels Perceived ease-of-use and Perceived usefulness from the original TAM with Effort expectation and Performance expectation. It may well be that the users in these cohorts, as experienced professionals, already have an expectation of how technology should be presented and that this may have influenced their perceptions. Effort expectation, therefore, if not at the level of current user interfaces for office tools might obscure any real Performance expectation. Secondly, it should be remembered that individual participants responded independently to the SUS questionnaire: they did not seek any consensus amongst themselves, but simply gave their own individual response.

3.2 Italian Ethnographic Study

Direct observation of participant interaction with the tool gave a different, more nuanced view. The Italian cohort reported multiple issues and concerns with Perceived ease-of-use. Overall, the researcher noted 27 specific problems from responsiveness to iconography across twelve separate aspects of the user interface. For example, the modeller requires individual components ("assets") within the model to be connected appropriately. So, a connection between a browser and a host machine would identify that the browser runs on the host; a connection between two servers would support data transfer between them. But participants did not find the process of connecting assets obvious. They felt that there needed to be some description, either as a manual or perhaps one or more tooltips to explain the rules and logic behind connections.

The modeller user interface also provides a canvas to draw a model, along with a palette of objects to drag and drop onto the canvas. Participants complained that they couldn't find basic functions like edit and save. In consequence, one participant supported the rationale behind the tool. He felt that the idea of such a tool to help identify risks and mitigation strategies was not wrong per se, but significantly concluded that it was the implementation that was at fault.

---

[2] The assumption in scoring SUS results is that a score of 68 corresponds to a 50% rank. Below 68 is therefore perceived as marginal or poor.

For these participants, then, without a positive response to usability, the TAM would predict negative effects on Perceived usefulness as well as Behavioral intention; UTAUT would similarly predict a negative effect on intention to use. Not surprisingly, therefore, observation of the Italian participants about Perceived usefulness suggested that the security modeller tool as implemented currently seems to make simple operations more obscure. There seemed to be a general feeling that there were other tools that would achieve the same results but better. Clearly, therefore, an implicit comparison was being made with existing technology. This prior knowledge and experience would lead to expectations and obscure the potential usefulness of the modeller.

The *External variables* in TAM or *Facilitating conditions* from the UTAUT for the Italian cohort includes experience with other competing offerings. As such, we can readily explain the poor SUS scores. To evaluate and assess the real potential of a prototype technology, the focus is really on searching out novel affordances which could motivate further investigation. Without a simple and intuitive user interface, the perception of those affordances is impossible [19]. Overall, only one of the five Italian participants reported any desire to continue investigating the technology.

For the Italian cohort, therefore, the SUS score is entirely consistent with a qualitative analysis of the discussion with participants. Evidence was found on specific aspects of *Perceived ease-of-use* which seem to mitigate against any exploration of ultimate technology adoption. This ties in with both the TAM and UTAUT models of technology acceptance.

3.3   Spanish Ethnographic Study

For the Spanish cohort, using the same technology provoked a very different response. Indeed, despite the low SUS scores (ranging from 37.5 to 65, with an average of 52.5), participants reported positive reactions to the user interface. During the ethnographic study, they stated that they had found the user interface intuitive and easy to use. Are they simply struggling with terminology [22] or are there other factors which the SUS score does not capture?

The Italian cohort, working in pairs or alone, reported multiple problems (27 individual issues across 12 areas). By contrast, the Spanish participants reported specific things which they found useful. For example, irrespective of overall system performance, they were pleased that they could develop an architecture relatively quickly (it took them about ten minutes). They also thought that results were provided in a format that made it easier to subdivide risks into different types, which would presumably make their respective jobs much easier. One participant even reported that they found the user interface "friendly": specifically, the modeller tool presented threats directly with a description, making it easier to identify potential outcomes and to develop and implement appropriate control strategies. For the Spaniards, therefore, Perceived ease-of-use was poorly reflected in the SUS results. But the discussions they had among themselves moderated their views somewhat. In the context of Perceived usefulness, they seem to have re-assessed ease-of-use.

Their more positive attitude, although somewhat at odds with the SUS score, therefore, leads to an increased perception of usefulness: three of the four participants stated that they could see specific opportunities for deriving benefit from the tool in their respective roles. For example, the database manager wanted to use the tool to evaluate some of the databases that are hosted in the hospital; the computer science engineer thought it could be used profitably each time the architecture of the servers is changed; and the bioinformatics technician thought it particularly well adapted to be used in structural analysis (access to structural alignment services). Only the software engineer did not see any use for the tool, admitting that it was not so relevant for his job. His peers, therefore, could see beyond the usability of the user interface to identify potential benefits for themselves.

Beyond this, though, the participants in the Spanish cohort also began to explore possible scenarios where they could imagine that the modeller tool would have specific benefits. These may be summarised as follows:

1. *Mitigating enterprise-wide risk*: participants saw potential for the security modeller tool to be able to build up a picture of the whole enterprise security landscape.
2. *Keeping risk exposure status up to date*: further, participants felt the tool would help them responding to unexpected attacks as well as plan for future risk.
3. *Promoting consistent enterprise-wide security policies*: a comprehensive and consistent repository of known (and potential) threats along with appropriate mitigation strategies would help overall management of the site from a security perspective.

Participants have therefore not only looked beyond the specific problems they reported via their SUS scores but are furthermore identifying affordances in the technology. On that basis, they speculate about how to exploit those affordances, what [19] refer to as affordance perception and affordance actualization respectively. Whether these affordances would have been recognised without the Spaniards' positive reaction to *Perceived ease-of-use* is a moot point. What is important is their willingness to explore potential. In effect, they begin to internalise their perception of usefulness to the point where they can see direct benefit to themselves within their own work context.

4   Discussion

In respect of our research questions, it is clear that quantitative methods alone may not be sufficient to capture all aspects of user response when testing technology (RQ1). But in addition, a simple qualitative approach (ethnographic monitoring of technology-focused behaviours) can begin to reveal a much richer and more nuanced interpretation of user responses to technology (RQ2). At the very least, Perceived ease-of-use as measured by the SUS is only part of the overall technology acceptance landscape. Although validated in multiple studies, the individual items encourage a rather broad stroke approach to technology use. Participants, especially IT professionals, may well compare a test technology with their experience or expectations from other technologies. Without specific design and implementation focus on the user interface, this is almost certainly bound to depress the SUS scores.

Other factors may account for these results. Participants in both cohorts carried out the test task first, and then responded to the SUS. In so doing, there is a very real chance that an initially negative reaction to the modeller tool for whatever reason—a user finding the user interface different from what they expect, and so forth—could lead to a negative memory of the technology and therefore a negative judgement. This type of priming has been well-attested for some considerable time [30]. The Italian participants may therefore have become fixed with the sheer number of issues they had found. Working independently or in pairs, there would be no opportunity for any diversionary discussion around the issue. Instead, for the pairs in the Italian study, one of the pairs it was reported would frequently have to provide support to the other.

Given that, though, why would the Spanish cohort react differently. They too report a negative response to the technology via the SUS questionnaire. But they didn't focus on the negative aspects of the user interface. As outlined above, they began to think creatively about what benefit they could derive from the technology. One major difference in set up for the two test sites was, of course, that the Spanish cohort worked together. Although they too responded negatively to the closed set of questions in the SUS, the collaborative nature of the group work may have primed them for increased creativity [31]. They are more open to thinking of different ways that they might exploit the technology in the context of their own jobs. Indeed, consistent with the DOI, as one colleague begins to identify potential, so the others too perceive affordances in the modeller tool.

External variables [5] or *Facilitating Conditions* [2] seem to involve the collaborative environment within which the technology is being tested. Prior user experience and expectation may lead to an exaggerated focus on negative aspects (as seen in Italy) which prevents creative exploration of technology use. But if discussion and collaboration is allowed, perhaps, then all parties begin to see potential and are more positive in their response to the technology under test. There is a mediating effect, therefore, not of Perceived ease-of-use as predicted by the TAM, but of a willingness to think creatively and collaboratively. Such willingness depends on the perception of affordances which through actualisation seem to increase perceived self-efficacy and agency: potential adopters begin to explore how the technology can support them satisfy the requirements of their own responsibilities [14, 32, 33].

5 Limitations and Future Study

It should be noted first and foremost that the cohort of participants has some limitations, beyond the total number who took part. We do not claim saturation at this point, even though recommendations may be ambiguous in this area [34]. This was an opportunity sample, dependent on our access as researchers to colleagues in other areas of our respective institutions. There may well have been some experimenter effect with participants being more positive about a technology introduced to them by a colleague. The results may not therefore be generalizable. Further, because of our familiarity with technology acceptance models, there may have been some bias in our coding scheme to identify common topics in the feedback from the Spanish cohort to provide codes for the analysis of the Italian feedback.

What we believe we are finding here is increased complexity for technology adoption models. The perception and actualisation of affordances is related, we maintain, to a willingness to explore technology both pre- and post-adoption [12]. In turn, this leads to increased self-efficacy and agency [13, 14, 32]. We propose to revisit other validation activities we have been involved with in the past to re-evaluate those results for a larger cohort and in connection with other technology in a different domain. In addition, we will be using qualitative methods in other technology validation exercises to establish what sort of conclusions may emerge with a view to increasing the richness of the data itself [35]. We believe at least that qualitative methods provides a relatively straight forward mechanism to access constructs such as *External variables* and *Facilitating conditions* in a meaningful way. These are connected to self-efficacy and perceptions of agency when exploring technology potential.

6 Conclusion

The mixed methods approach as outlined in this preliminary study has begun to identify significant factors in assessing technology acceptance. In so doing, there is also some indication that the research protocol itself—that is the order of presentation of task and surveys, whether participants work individually or collectively—may influence the outcome of technology acceptance experimentation. Despite the limited scope and coverage reported here, and inconsistent though explainable results for the different cohorts, there is a strong indication that quantitative instruments may be insensitive to important considerations in technology acceptance beyond the initial estimate of *Perceived* or *Expected ease-of-use*. Previous evaluation of TAM and its derivative, UTAUT, as well as the SUS, may well fail to ensure completeness and ecological validity for technology evaluation. In reconsidering technology acceptance research, we maintain that qualitative methods provide a standardised mechanism to access subjective and social norms which have previously been highlighted in promising models such as TRA, TPB and possibly DOI, but left out of TAM/UTAUT as inaccessible.

Acknowledgements. This work was conducted as part of the SHiELD project, which received funding from the European Union's H2020 research and innovation programme under Grant Agreement No. 727301.

References

1. Taherdoost, H.: A review of technology acceptance and adoption models and theories. Procedia Manuf. **22**, 960–967 (2018). https://doi.org/10.1016/j.promfg.2018.03.137
2. Venkatesh, V., et al.: User acceptance of information technology: toward a unified view. MIS Q. **27**, 425–478 (2003)
3. Davis, F.D.: A Technology Acceptance Model for Empirically Testing New End-User Information Systems: Theory and Results. Massachusetts Institute of Technology, Cambridge (1985)
4. Rogers, E.: The Diffusion of Innovations. The Free Press, Mumbai (2003)
5. Davis, F.D., et al.: User acceptance of computer technology: a comparison of two theoretical models. Manag. Sci. **35**(8), 982–1003 (1989). https://doi.org/10.1287/mnsc.35.8.982
6. Fishbein, M., Ajzen, I.: Belief, Attitude, Intention and Behavior: An Introduction to Theory and Research (1975)

7. Ajzen, I.: The theory of planned behavior. Organ. Behav. Hum. Decis. Process. **50**(2), 179–211 (1991). https://doi.org/10.1016/0749-5978(91)90020-T

8. Ajzen, I.: The theory of planned behaviour: reactions and reflections. Psychol. Health **26**(9), 1113–1127 (2011). https://doi.org/10.1080/08870446.2011.613995

9. De Guinea, A.O., Markus, M.L.: Why break the habit of a lifetime? Rethinking the roles of intention, habit, and emotion in continuing information technology use. MIS Q. **33**, 433–444 (2009)

10. Acquisti, A., et al.: Privacy and human behavior in the age of information. Science **347** (6221), 509–514 (2015). https://doi.org/10.1126/science.aaa1465

11. Chuttur, M.Y.: Overview of the technology acceptance model: Origins, developments and future directions. Sprouts Work. Pap. Inf. Syst. **9**(37), 1–21 (2009)

12. Thatcher, J.B., et al.: The role of trust in postadoption IT exploration: an empirical examination of knowledge management systems. IEEE Trans. Eng. Manag. **58**(1), 56–70 (2011). https://doi.org/10.1109/TEM.2009.2028320

13. McKnight, D.H., et al.: Trust in a specific technology: an investigation of its components and measures. ACM Trans. Manag. Inf. Syst. **2**(2), 12 (2011). https://doi.org/10.1145/1985347.1985353

14. Pickering, J.B., Engen, V., Walland, P.: The interplay between human and machine agency. In: Kurosu, M. (ed.) HCI 2017. LNCS, vol. 10271, pp. 47–59. Springer, Cham (2017). https://doi.org/10.1007/978-3-319-58071-5_4

15. Lee, J.D., Moray, N.: Trust, control strategies and allocation of function in human–machine systems. Ergonomics **35**(10), 1243–1270 (1992). https://doi.org/10.1080/00140139208967392

16. Lee, J.D., See, K.A.: Trust in automation: designing for appropriate reliance. Hum. Factors J. Hum. Factors Ergon. Soc. **46**(1), 50–80 (2004). https://doi.org/10.1518/hfes.46.1.50_30392

17. Norman, D.A.: Things that Make us Smarter: Defending Human Attributes in the Age of the Machine. Basic Books, New York (1993)

18. Norman, D.A.: Living with Complexity. MIT Press, Cambridge (2010)

19. Pozzi, G., et al.: Affordance theory in the IS discipline: a review and synthesis of the literature. In: Proceedings of AMCIS 2014 (2013)

20. Brooke, J.: SUS-A quick and dirty usability scale. Usability Eval. Ind. **189**(194), 4–7 (1996)

21. Lewis, J.R., Sauro, J.: The factor structure of the system usability scale. In: Kurosu, M. (ed.) HCD 2009. LNCS, vol. 5619, pp. 94–103. Springer, Heidelberg (2009). https://doi.org/10.1007/978-3-642-02806-9_12

22. Finstad, K.: The system usability scale and non-native English speakers. J. Usability Stud. **1** (4), 185–188 (2006)

23. Hammersley, M., Atkinson, P.: Ethnography: Principles in Practice. Routledge, Abingdon (2007)

24. Braun, V., Clarke, V.: Using thematic analysis in psychology. Qual. Res. Psychol. **3**(2), 77–101 (2006). https://doi.org/10.1191/1478088706qp063oa

25. Chakravarthy, A., et al.: Trustworthy systems design using semantic risk modelling. In: Trustworthy Systems Design Using Semantic Risk Modelling, 1st International Conference on Cyber Security for Sustainable Society (2015)

26. Surridge, M., et al.: Trust Modelling in 5G mobile networks. In: Book Trust Modelling in 5G Mobile Networks, Proceedings of the 2018 Workshop on Security in Softwarized Networks: Prospects and Challenges, pp. 14–19. ACM (2018)

27. Cavoukian, A.: Privacy by design in law, policy and practice. In: A White Paper for Regulators, Decision-Makers and Policy-Makers (2011)

28. Langheinrich, M.: Privacy by design—principles of privacy-aware ubiquitous systems. In: Abowd, G.D., Brumitt, B., Shafer, S. (eds.) UbiComp 2001. LNCS, vol. 2201, pp. 273–291. Springer, Heidelberg (2001). https://doi.org/10.1007/3-540-45427-6_23

29. European Commission: Regulation (EU) 2016/679 of the European Parliament and of the Council of 27 April 2016 (2016)

30. Logan, G.D.: Attention and automaticity in Stroop and priming tasks: theory and data. Cogn. Psychol. **12**(4), 523–553 (1980). https://doi.org/10.1016/0010-0285(80)90019-5

31. Friedman, R.S., et al.: Attentional priming effects on creativity. Creativity Res. J. **15**(2–3), 277–286 (2003). https://doi.org/10.1080/10400419.2003.9651420

32. Thatcher, J.B., et al.: Internal and external dimensions of computer self-efficacy: an empirical examination. IEEE Trans. Eng. Manag. **55**(4), 628–644 (2008). https://doi.org/10.1109/TEM.2008.927825

33. Engen, V., Pickering, J.B., Walland, P.: Machine agency in human-machine networks; impacts and trust implications. In: Kurosu, M. (ed.) HCI 2016. LNCS, vol. 9733, pp. 96–106. Springer, Cham (2016). https://doi.org/10.1007/978-3-319-39513-5_9

34. Marshall, B., et al.: Does sample size matter in qualitative research? A review of qualitative interviews in IS research. J. Comput. Inf. Syst. **54**(1), 11–22 (2013). https://doi.org/10.1080/08874417.2013.11645667

35. Fusch, P.I., Ness, L.R.: Are we there yet? Data saturation in qualitative research. Qual. Rep. **20**(9), 1408–1416 (2015)

DUXU Practice

A Solution Development Model for Industry Based on Design Thinking

Raquel Zarattini Chebabi[(⊠)] and Henrique von Atzingen Amaral

IBM Research, São Paulo, Brazil
{rchebabi,hvon}@br.ibm.com

Abstract. This work presents the program BlueJourney that was created with the objective of identifying problems and challenges of our clients and, in a process of collaboration, develop processes and systems innovation projects. BlueJourney was designed by ThinkLab Brazil, the innovation laboratory of IBM Research that has an environment suitable for co-creation and a specialized team. The program is based on Design Thinking techniques, therefore, innovation is achieved with a focus on people's need, and with technical and business feasibility analysis. With defined steps, we engage industry, technology, business and research experts in activities like co-creation, research, interviews, prototype development and testing. The experts understands and explores the challenges of the subject or area to be transformed and create the most complete solutions. At the end of the program, we have a list of projects to be developed, changes in processes and systems, and people who have learned to seek innovation in a creative, collaborative and engaged way. The most important is a change of mindset, because solutions might be about human needs. In this article, we'll present in detail the steps of BlueJourney applied in a real case.

Keywords: User centered design · Design Thinking · Innovation

1 Introduction

Since companies began to use internet-related solutions for their business, the corporate environment has changed dramatically. Technological evolution has brought new digital tools that can increase sales, lower costs, improve operational efficiency and, above all, improve the customer experience. To develop and implement these new technologies in companies is essential to have a process in order to direct the results to the end customer, internal or external. And it was not different in our company, it was urgent to use a methodology to generate innovation in the corporate environment to create projects based on these new technologies.

We have an experience from years working with some methodologies like Organizational Semiotic [1], Ethnography and Learning Communities [2], so that we believe that Design Thinking [3] brings together several techniques that allow the best design for project development.

ThinkLab has been working since 2015 with Design Thinking techniques to connect customers, IBM researchers and other technical areas. We have a specific space for

© Springer Nature Switzerland AG 2019
A. Marcus and W. Wang (Eds.): HCII 2019, LNCS 11586, pp. 253–262, 2019.
https://doi.org/10.1007/978-3-030-23535-2_19

immersion and co-creation and a team with professionals specialized in software development, business, engagement, design, ecosystem, education, marketing and content production. With the experience gained from the projects carried out so far, we decided to create the BlueJourney program in 2018, that it is a project model that meets the transformation needs of our clients from the deep knowledge of their challenges. In this way we have viable solutions that truly meet the needs and expectations of people.

In the next sessions, we will explain the BlueJourney application and present a real case.

2   Method and Materials

BlueJourney uses Design Thinking techniques to carry out all the steps necessary to develop a new project by understanding the problems and opportunities of clients and studying ideas to create a transformation process. It's a deep journey, an immersion, an opportunity to join all the people with necessary skills to think and work together. As we work with this concept of immersion, we started creating the visual identity for BlueJourney by using the diving dress image (Fig. 1).

Fig. 1. The BlueJourney identity represents the deep immersion on the problems and challenges.

BlueJourney is a model based on Design Thinking methodology, so we defined the steps by using the concept of Inspiration, Ideation and Implementation. The Inspiration step is to understand the problems and challenges from our clients with them; the Ideation is when we create possible solutions. In the end of this process, the Implementation step, we have real projects to select, implement and test. Figure 2 is the Design Thinking approach from IDEO.org [3], this human-centered design method that brings to us the concept of co-creation. The cycle merges diverge and converge phases that organize the thoughts during the collaboration process.

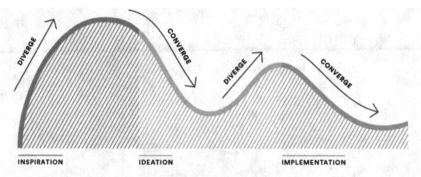

Fig. 2. Design Thinking approach by IDEO.org.

Another approach that we are inspired by is the IBM Design Thinking Framework [4]. This framework defines principles like:

- Focus on the user outcomes (to achieve the users goals);
- Restless reinvention (treating everything as a prototype);
- Diverse empowered teams (to be fast and efficient).

The Fig. 3 is the Loop, that represents an infinite process to Observe, Reflect and Make. The idea is to understand deeply the problems and challenges from people how knows about that; to create solutions based on this knowledge and to make solutions, keeping in mind that as fast we test and observe and reflect again, as fast you have the best solution.

Observe >   Reflect >   Make >

Immerse yourself in the   Come together and look   Give concrete form to
real world.   within.   abstract ideas.

Fig. 3. IBM Design Thinking loop.

BlueJourney has a general model with well-defined steps. The steps have a suggested timeline and people who should be involved. But for each project, we customize all details. In Fig. 4, we present the general steps, Investigation, Ideation, Prototype and Pitches and Selection.

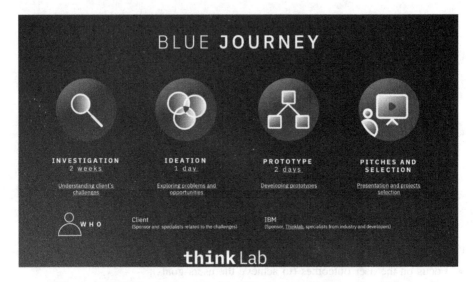

Fig. 4. The BlueJourney model with 4 (four) steps and who will participate.

In the Investigation, we understand why the client company came to us, what they want to improve and what they think when talk about innovation. Through meetings and interviews, we organize the information and highlight the real challenges of this client. With interviews and ethnographic method, we approach the people who really understand about the outstanding challenges, and explore the problems and opportunities of transformation in more detail. At this moment, everyone in the client company is already aware that the process must be participatory, that the more the experts are engaged and dedicate time to the project, the greater are the possibilities of transforming their processes and systems. This steps usually takes two weeks and we need people who really understand about the business involved.

In the stage of Ideation, we bring who understand most from the challenges listed in the Investigation, for a day of co-creation in the ThinkLab space. On this day, we work with selected tools according to the challenges like Personas, Empathy Map, Scenery Map, Hopes and Fears, Map of Stakeholders, Ideation etc. At the end of this day, we have a list of prioritized solution ideas to develop in the next step. Usually this step takes one entire day and it's on our lab to have the real immersion.

In the Prototyping stage, the prioritized ideas are developed by a team formed by client team and IBM specialists. Usually we divide the group in teams to develop the projects. Ideas are transformed into prototypes and this development may or may not involve software coding. Depending on the need of each prototype, specialists are chosen to participate in this stage that takes two entire days.

In the Pitches and Screening step, the participants present their prototypes in pitches format (quick presentation technique), usually in 5 (five) min, for client executives who will evaluate them. This evaluation will consider mainly, the technical and business viability so that the winning solution (or more than one) is really a project that will be implemented in the company. This step can takes some hours in the end of Prototype step.

For each client, we adapt the times and techniques of the mentioned steps so that we can meet their needs and create an adequate scope. In the next session, we will present a real case with a Telecommunication company.

3   A BlueJourney Case

In this section, we will describe a case of BlueJourney that was developed at ThinkLab in 2018. This project shows how the time and schedule of a BlueJourney varies according to the scope and challenge of the client, since it was our most extensive project in 2018 and lasted 3 (three) months. It's quite different time from our basic model described in the last session, but the steps and fundamentals are exactly the same.

In order to maintain the confidentiality of the project and the customer information, we can mention that the customer is from the Telecommunication industry, without identifying it. For this reason, we will name Company. This customer came to us with the need to improve the relationship of their collaborators with the company's Human Resources (HR) area, especially in digital relations. It is very common for BlueJourney to develop solutions for the customers of our customers, but in this case, the project was completely internal for the Company.

This project involved the entire Human Resources area and its collaborators throughout Brazil, so the project was very extensive, and this was the main reason why the BlueJourney was adapted to be realized in more time than usual. At each stage, people and techniques were chosen so that the partial and final results were achieved.

3.1   Investigation

In May 2018, we began the first meetings with the Company's executive team to understand their main needs, why they came to us, and how to design the project steps in accordance with the principles of Investigation. Thus, we were able to plan the project agenda, to choose the participants of each phase, and we had full knowledge about the final result they expected.

In June, we started to involve the main areas with an opening event to align the understanding of the project. This event was attended by managers from the Company's HR area and an IBM project management team with HR background. We executed an immersion day in our lab by using techniques such as Personas, Empathy Map and Scenario Map to identify the current journey of the employee from the perspective of the relationship with HR. About 30 (thirty) HR managers, the IBM project management team and the ThinkLab team participated in this stage. As a result, we identified 4 (four) personas to represent all employees, built the journey for each persona and identified all pain points to know exactly where were the opportunities to improve the employee's lives within the Company. Figure 5 is Empathy Map from

IBM design thinking [5] and shows how to represent the personas in the project context.

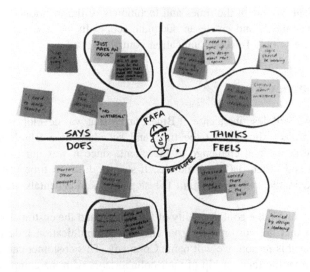

Fig. 5. This is an example of a empathy map that illustrates the persona's feelings, thoughts, speech and actions on the journey investigated.

As the scope was quite complex, we continued in the Investigation stage to conduct a survey with the company's employees to identify if the perception of HR managers was correct. Given that we had HR managers dealing with the journey and the pains of their employees, we needed to ensure that the information worked on the immersion was completely correct, and the only way was talk to the employees themselves.

For this reason, we developed two types of research, interview and online survey. We selected representatives from several areas for the interview, and participation was voluntary. The interviews were conducted in groups mediated by the IBM team. A very careful communication work was done by the Company so that the collaborators had complete tranquility of exposing their thoughts about the subject. We ensured that everyone involved was aware that this was a project to improve employee relations with HR. About 20 (twenty) interviews were conducted with groups of up to 10 (ten) people.

The online survey was sent with the same kind of communication and we had the voluntary participation of approximately 3 (three) thousand employees, so we had participants from many cities and we were able to know the reality of each place.

So that, with this research, it was possible to validate the information raised during the immersion with the HR managers. More than that, we have identified a lot of detailed information that has greatly enriched by research. As much data was collected, it was consolidated by the IBM data analysis tool, Watson Analytics. All online survey data was anonymized.

With these results, it was possible to review the personas journeys, validating and including information identified in the surveys. This investigative work involving a large number of people has created a sense of importance to employees, because they were not just represented, but they could express their feelings and experiences. Figure 6 is the example of a map. It was designed and validated with information from surveys and contains the speech and mood from the persona in each step of journey.

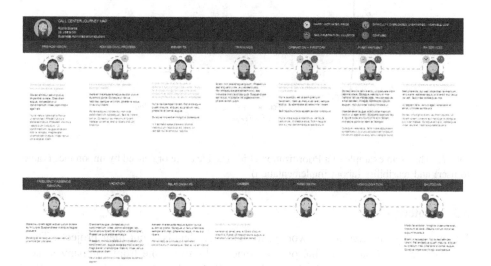

Fig. 6. This is an example of a journey map that illustrates the persona's mood and speech. The sentences are not real to protect the company information.

3.2 Ideation

In Ideation step, we performed another immersion in our lab, with the same team of HR managers from the Investigation stage. This time, we worked based on the journeys designed for each persona as the example in Fig. 6. We also used all the data consolidated by the IBM tool, Watson Analytics. It was possible to query in many formats and access an organized data.

Thus, knowing the Company's employee journey and all the problems and opportunities in which to improve the lives of its employees, it was possible to create innovative project ideas. At this stage, we use tools to create solutions ideas and prioritize them according to the identified pains and the feasibility of deployment at Company. IBM's experts participated to evaluate the technical feasibility of projects. Five teams were created to develop in the next step, Prototyping, more details for each project. Figure 7 represents a Prioritization Grid of ideas for decision making, from IBM Design Thinking [6].

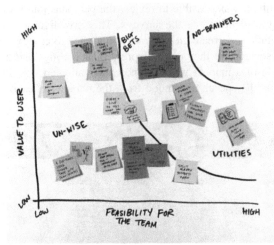

Fig. 7. This is an example of a Prioritization Grid. The ideas are organized by importance (value to user) and feasibility (about implementation).

3.3 Prototype

Following this, the five teams worked to define all details about their projects. They searched for information online or even made calls to people from company to add more information to create the best solution. IBM and customer technicians participated to build together workable solutions from a technological and business point of view. The ThinkLab team realized a prototype training so they were capable to prototype their projects. We used some sketches, software and building blocks to represent the sequence, phases and interface from each solution. In Fig. 8, we have an example how to prototype a process. Sometimes, the solution is not about technology, but is about improve processes. In these cases, we can use sketches and building blocks.

3.4 Pitches and Selection

After this work, ThinkLab team trained the groups to present their projects by using the Pitch format. This is a model to present ideas in a simple and efficient way and in a short time, like three or five minutes.

Like an event, at the same day, we invited the executives from the Company to evaluate and choose some projects to win. These projects are now, part of a transformation schedule to be developed by Company and IBM. This moment is not just a selection time, but it's a celebration because we have many ideas, great projects to develop and people looking forward to think and create innovation always.

Fig. 8. This is an example of a prototype process. Building blocks were used to represent some processes and how to improve them.

4 Conclusion

BlueJourney is a model that brings together people, knowledge, creativity, solutions and a change of mindset. We have great feedbacks from our clients as in a short time, we figure out exactly where are their problems and in a very planned agenda we have viable ideas and solutions. The environment is about a lot of work and the same time, is nice, constructive and inspiring. Not less important than design solutions to implement, is the learning process for all, like important concepts: explore the problems before create solutions; join the people how really understand about it; create possible and fast projects and test as soon as possible; solutions are about people's needs so talk to them.

In 2019 we expect to create great BlueJourney projects and discover many other techniques to improve our model, always using co-creation and focus on people.

Acknowledgement. BlueJourney was created by a professional team from ThinkLab that developed the method and media content. They are the authors, and Flavia Roberta Silva, Paula Fernanda Pereira; Pedro Pavanato and Victoria Perfetto.

References

1. Chebabi, R.Z., Baranaukas, M.C.C.: Mediando Processos de Comunicação em Organizações e Desenhando Interfaces. In: Latin American Conference on Human-Computer Interaction, CLIHC, Cuernava, México (2005)
2. Chebabi, R.Z.: Cidade Aprendente: um modelo de desenvolvimento de cidades que associa a valorização da aprendizagem às tecnologias de informação e comunicação. Thesis, Instituto de Artes, Universidade Estadual de Campinas, Campinas (2011)
3. IDEO. https://www.ideo.org/approach. Accessed 01 July 2019
4. IBM. https://www.ibm.com/design/thinking/page/framework/. Accessed 01 July 2019

5. IBM. https://www.ibm.com/design/thinking/page/toolkit/activity/empathy-map. Accessed 01 July 2019
6. IBM. https://www.ibm.com/design/thinking/page/toolkit/activity/prioritization. Accessed 01 July 2019

Overcoming Organizational Barriers to the Integration of UX Methods in Software Development: A Case Study

Vincent Kervyn de Meerendré$^{(\boxtimes)}$, Luka Rukonić,
and Suzanne Kieffer

Institute for Language and Communication, Université catholique de Louvain,
Louvain-la-Neuve, Belgium
{vincent.kervyn, luka.rukonic,
suzanne.kieffer}@uclouvain.be

Abstract. Despite User Experience (UX)' increased popularity, the willingness of organizations to integrate it into their processes and UX practitioners still encounter challenges in integrating UX methods. Research in HCI has presented theoretical and pragmatic models. Most of the time, these models lack presenting validation in practice, documentation or support for their use when difficulties appear. Even if difficulties could be expected. In this paper, we present a categorization of organizational barriers extracted from the relevant literature: lack of UX resources, lack of UX literacy, poor use of UX artifacts and communication breakdowns. Then, we propose a 4-step procedure to identify and overcome organizational barriers with a case study describing how this procedure helped us to anticipate and overcome organizational barriers encountered in a project. With a UX Capability/Maturity (UX CM) assessment conducted at the beginning of the project, we were expecting organizational barriers and constant readjustment of our UX strategy. We Communicated about findings and readjustment to stakeholders in order to increase their awareness about problems along the way of the project and we had prepared remediation strategies for the emergence of barriers.

Keywords: User Experience · UX process · UX barrier · UX methods integration · Software development

1 Introduction

Over the last two decades, User Experience (UX) has become a core concept of Human-Computer Interaction (HCI), extending the perspective on usability to less pragmatic, more hedonic and non-task-oriented considerations about interactive systems [6–8]. This phenomenon has led to the proliferation of UX methods intended to support and improve both UX activities and software development [21]. However, the literature consistently reports the emergence of organizational barriers standing in the way of the integration of UX/usability into software development models [4, 5, 9, 13, 17, 18, 20, 22]. Table 1 synthesizes organizational barriers extracted from the relevant literature.

© Springer Nature Switzerland AG 2019
A. Marcus and W. Wang (Eds.): HCII 2019, LNCS 11586, pp. 263–276, 2019.
https://doi.org/10.1007/978-3-030-23535-2_20

Table 1. Organizational barriers to UX

UX resources	Lack of time to perform UX activities	[13, 18, 20]
	Lack of UX budget	[17, 18, 22]
	Lack of trained UX staff	[4, 17]
UX literacy	UX mistaken for look and feel of products	[20]
	UX informally performed by developers	[4, 5, 13, 20]
	Lack of understanding of the return on investment (ROI) of UX	[9, 13, 17, 18, 20, 22]
UX artifacts	Focus on UX design at the expense of UX analysis and/or evaluation	[4, 5, 9, 20, 22]
	UX activities performed too late in the development lifecycle and important late design changes	[9, 17, 18, 20, 22]
Communication breakdowns	Limited access to users	[9, 18, 20, 22]
	Reluctance of user involvement	[9, 18, 22]
	Conflicts between management and managers	[18, 20, 22]
	Resistance to User-Centered Design	[17]

These organizational barriers prevent the implementation and achievement of UX activities. Worse, they reduce the benefits, or Return on Investment (ROI), usually associated with UX/usability: increased sales and revenues, increased user efficiency and satisfaction, reduction of development time and costs, etc. [3]. Nevertheless, barriers to UX appear to be insufficiently studied and discussed in the literature, which focuses almost exclusively on reactive solutions to these barriers rather than on means to anticipate their emergence and be adequately prepared to overcome them. This paper presents a case-based procedure and recommendations to identify and overcome barriers to the integration of UX in software development organizations. To this end, we propose the following 4-step procedure:

1. Conduct UX Capability/Maturity (CM) assessment to identify barriers to UX
2. Communicate findings to stakeholders to increase their awareness about potential problems along the way of the project
3. Prepare remediation strategies
4. At the emergence of a barrier: apply strategies.

The contribution of this paper is twofold:

- Clarification of the barrier concept through a targeted literature review;
- Documentation of case study that illustrates how to use the 4-step procedure presented above to identify barriers to UX and how we attempted to overcome them.

2 Background

Table 1 summarizes the organizational barriers to UX identified in the relevant literature. To identify the relevant literature, we conducted a targeted literature review using the following keywords: organizational barrier, usability barrier, UX barrier, development, barrier UX integration. Next, to classify the organizational barriers, we used a systematic mapping study of HCI practice research [16]. This, in turn, allowed us to distribute the organizational barriers among four categories:

1. Lack of UX resources
2. Lack of UX literacy
3. Poor use of UX artifacts
4. Communication breakdowns.

2.1 Lack of UX Resources

This category refers to the cases where organizations cannot achieve the goals of UX processes because of a lack of UX resources. UX resources include time, allocation of a UX budget and trained staff. Lack of time occurs when teams are put under pressure to deliver work products. Typically, lack of time is characterized by design changes that happen too late in the development lifecycle [9, 20]. Related works document cases where UX/usability evaluation was integrated neither into the development process nor into the project schedule [13, 20].

Budget-related barriers occur in organizations that have not integrated UX in a sustainable manner yet: typically, such organizations focus on fixing UX flaws rather than on using UX as a strategic asset [18, 20]. Lack of budget and lack of time can be interrelated when a person, not necessarily someone knowledgeable in UX, is in charge of both UX budget and scheduling [22].

Barriers related to lack of staff occur when UX positions are not filled by trained staff with a background in UX, and when UX activities are informally performed by a another project team member, typically a developer [11, 13].

2.2 Lack of UX Literacy

Lack of UX literacy refers to situations where the staff performing UX misunderstands or underestimates the value or the return-on-investment of UX [18]. In such situations, the preference is given to design at the expense of usability, to look-and-feel at the expense of the interaction, which tends to let developer, who are experts in coding, believe they can be substituted to UX experts [20]. Related work documents some case where UX experts are excluded from the decision-making processes and not acknowledged by stakeholders [9].

2.3   Poor Use of UX Artifacts/Methods

If UX is misunderstood, UX methods may not be properly planned, properly executed and may not produce the expected outcome. If not properly planned, UX methods end up at the bottom of the list of prioritized items [22]. In a similar way, UX evaluations may not performed in a robust manner and/or standardized [20]. Another issue is the tendency to want to obtain visible results quickly, at the expense of the robustness of user requirements analysis. By rushing into UX design without any prior knowledge about user needs, expectations and limitations, software organizations increase the risk of late design changes, consequently significantly reducing the ROI of UX [4, 5].

2.4   Communication Breakdowns

Communication breakdowns refers to interaction problems within an organization (e.g. group, department, company, etc.) or between several parties [9, 22]. For example, let us assume that UX expert E works for company A, which provides services to company B, within a Business to Business (B2B) prospect. B is the client of A, which is the client of E. From E's perspective, this corresponds to a B2B2C relation. In such relations, E needs to go through these two commercial relationships to get access to end-users. This distance from users causes a lack of knowledge about them. Limited access to the user (top-down) and lack of user feedbacks (bottom-up) are the most frequent organizational barriers to UX integration [11]. In this communication scheme, both users and E are located at the extremity of the communication flow, and internal problems could be found between them. Internal problems occur when top management or C-level executives' opinions have more impact on decisions regarding UX than those of UX staff [5, 22]. If top management or C-level executives do not have any commitment to UX, it can lead to resistance to User-Centered Design (UCD). Figure 1 depicts an example of such situation.

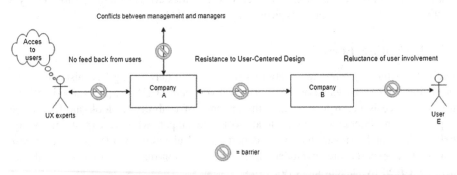

Fig. 1. Location of breakdowns in the communication flow

3   Proposed Procedure

We propose a 4-step procedure to identify and overcome organizational barriers to UX:

1. Conduct UX Capability/Maturity (CM) assessment to identify barriers to UX;
2. Communicate findings to stakeholders in order to increase their awareness about potential problems along the way of the project;
3. Prepare remediation strategies;
4. At the emergence of a barrier: apply strategies.

The next section reports a case study that describes how we applied this procedure in a project with an industrial partner.

4   Case Study

4.1   Context

This project is funded by Service Public de Wallonie (SPW) under convention n° 7767 and intended to support the growth of a company—also referred to in the following as "our partner" or "organization"—whose core business is the sector of the energy. Specifically, the company develops software solutions for distribution system operators and energy suppliers in the gas and electricity market. Thanks to the SPW funding, the company intends to expand its market to neighboring countries and to increase its workforce and revenues by 2021. It is interesting to add that the company operates on a "home-shore" system: it does not have offices and its members work from home most of the time. Besides, it follows and agile approach for software development, which by its nature, implies frequent changes in project requirements.

The project was officially launched on February 26, 2018 in the presence of all partners: the organization, its subcontractors and the sponsor. The first author is the primary UCLouvain researcher on this project and was hired on September 15, 2018.

4.2   Mission and approach

Our primary mission in this project is to improve the UX of existing products. Our secondary mission consists of supporting the integration of UX in the company's software development model. To fulfill our mission, we rely on earlier work on UX Process Reference Model (UXPRM) [10] in the two following ways. On the one hand, we use the UX lifecycle proposed in this paper to communicate about primary UX lifecycle processes, especially to advocate for the integration of (user requirements) analysis activities as early as possible in the product development lifecycle. On the other hand, we use the classifications of UX methods and artifacts for roughly assessing the UX capabilities of our industrial partners.

It is worth mentioning that the mission takes place in a similar model than the B2B2C one depicted in Fig. 1. In other words, we (the UX experts) need to go through these two commercial relationships in order to access users (Fig. 2).

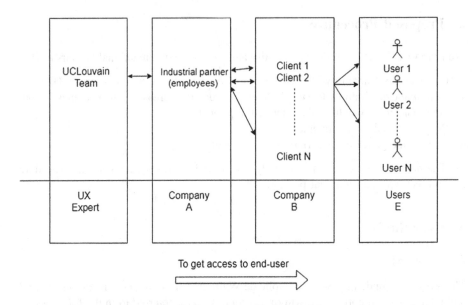

Fig. 2. Project organization model

4.3 Conduct UX Capability Assessment (Step 1)

In March 2018, the third author carried out in-person, prospective interviews with two employees. The objectives were (1) to identify the business goals of our partner in order to turn them into UX goals; (2) to assess the UX CM of our partner in order to produce a subcontracting offer that would fit the partners' business/UX goals; and (3) to identify potential organizational barriers to the integration of UX in their software development model. Table 2 summarizes the results regarding UX resources, Table 3 the results regarding UX literacy, Table 4 regarding UX artifacts and methods and Table 5 regarding the communication breakdowns.

Table 2. UX resources

Barriers	Indicator
Time	Percentage of time spent on UX: <1%
	Enough time to conduct UX: no
Budget	Percentage of the UX budget within the IT budget: <1%
	Formal UX budget allocated to ongoing project: no
Staff	Designer-developer ratio: 1/100
	UX staff: no (UX informally performed by developers)

Table 3. UX literacy

Barrier	Indicator
Understanding of the ROI of UX	UX does helps reduce development time and costs: no
Understanding of UX analysis	UX analysis is conducted before design and development: never
UX prioritization	UX activities performed too late in the development lifecycle: yes
	Summative UX is systematically employed before product release to make sure UX goals are met: never

Table 4. UX artifacts and methods

	Preliminary interview
Artifacts	
Persona	Never
Work models	Never
UX goals	Never
User story	Always
Task models	Never
Low-fi prototype	Never
High-fi prototype	Never
Design principles	Never
Methods	
Survey research	Never
Experience sampling	Rarely
Experiment	Never
Hierarchical task analysis	Never

Table 5. Communication breakdowns

Barrier	Indicator
Limited access to users	Users are involved as stakeholders throughout the product development lifecycle: never
Reluctance to user involvement	Survey research involving questionnaires is conducted to collect self-reported user satisfaction: never
Resistance to UCD	Contextual task analysis is conducted to elicit user requirements: never

4.4 Communicate Findings (Step 2)

The UX capability assessment allowed us to raise awareness about the following:

- Organization's UX goals/our mission: to improve the UX with their products;
- Barriers: difficult access to users; uncertainty about the sustainability of a UX budget; lack of time to implement UX; potential conflict of some UX methods with current software development model;
- Opportunities: public funding of this research, which will serve as a business case for UX in the organization; the significant size of projects under development in the company; important user needs for technical support and assistance; important user needs for a better UX with their products.

To communicate the previous findings to company's stakeholders and increase their awareness about potential problems along the way of the project, we had several meetings with our privileged contact person. He is a manager dedicated by the company to our project. He was also one of the two interviewees at the beginning of the project. During t meetings, we also presented our progress and needs for the current project. We set up a next meeting where he reported back to us on the organization's feedback and any new requests. Based on these new elements, we adapted our strategy.

4.5 Prepare Remediation Strategies (Step 3)

We believed that making a business case for UX would help to overcome the barriers related to UX budget, time constraints, and conflict with the development model. Regarding the difficult access to users, we opted for the following strategy (step 3):

A. Try to access to users in-person within a user-centered design approach,
B. If strategy A failed, try to access to users remotely,
C. If strategy B failed, use expert-based (without users) methods and techniques.

Our "Deluxe usability evaluation" (called "Strategy A") is trying to access to users in-person within a user-centered design approach. It regroups methods of contextual ethnography (contextual inquiry, work model, etc.), experiments with users (with calibrated instruments, A/B testing, etc.) and artifacts (affinity diagram and task model).

"Strategy B" represents the methods and artifacts producible without mobilizing users or going to the field.

Our "Strategy C" is using expert-based (without users) methods and artifacts. Nielsen's "Discount usability engineering" theory taught us that a good quality usability evaluation can be performed with few users, but with user nevertheless [1].

Discount Usability Engineering [14] is based on three components:

- Simplified user testing (think-aloud)
- Narrowed-down prototypes
- Heuristic Evaluation

The three components are based on both inspection and test methods. Inspection methods (heuristic evaluation) do not use end-users during the tests, whereas test methods use them. Better results are reached mixing these two kinds of methods [10, 12], but when the access to users is limited, inspection methods still remain the best option. We conducted a heuristic evaluation using UX guidelines in order to complete the spectrum of methods used and provide the organization with an artifact that can be used in the future.

4.6 Apply Strategies (Step 4)

Figure 3 describes how our objectives have changed over time: three different contexts of use (design of a dashboard, redesign of feature 1, redesign of feature 2) which corresponds to three different uncompleted iterations as highlighted by the red and orange symbols. The first line of each project specifies the context of use: users, tasks, platforms and environments [13]. As can be seen from Fig. 3, the goal of Project 1 was

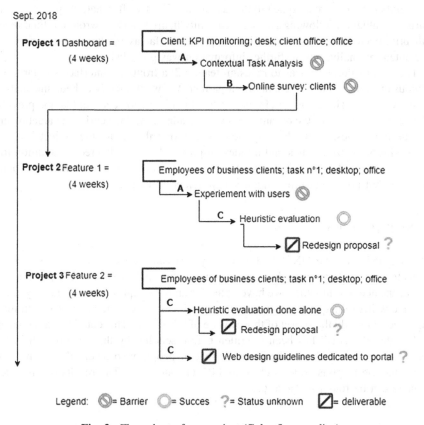

Fig. 3. Flow chart of our project (Color figure online)

to design a dashboard for clients. We first intended to gather client needs and expectations about this dashboard by means of context-meeting (strategy A). Context-meeting is a group discussion similar to a focus group with the emphasis on the context-of-use of the future product. Our industrial partner answered that it was impossible to gather representatives from different clients together at once. Therefore, we decided to conduct remote survey research using an online questionnaire (strategy B). We were told that the questions would not be understood by the clients as they were too technical, and that the survey approach would damage our partner's image. A few days later, we were assigned to Project 2.

The goal of Project 2 was to redesign feature1: a front-end interface allowing users to consult gas and electricity consumption and invoicing. We first intended to conduct a controlled experiment with real users (strategy A). We were told that gathering the real users is too difficult because they are geographically spread out. Instead, we decided to conduct a heuristic evaluation (Strategy C). To do this, we asked to involve and train members of the company in this technique. We have prepared a short training for the two members who were assigned to this technique. Shortly after that, we performed the heuristic evaluation following Nielsen's usability heuristics [15], wrote the final report with prioritized issues and a redesign proposal. As far as we know, the report was distributed internally, but no further information was provided to us.

The goal of Project 3 was to redesign feature 2: a front-end interface similar to the previous one but for another client of our partner. We went directly to heuristic analysis (Strategy C) to evaluate the wireframes of this interface. However, unlike the previous analysis, no members of the organization were available, so the heuristic evaluation and the redesign proposal were done by the main author only. As for the project 1, a final report with prioritized issues and a redesign proposal were delivered, in addition to a set of pragmatic design guidelines. As far as we know, the report was distributed internally, but no further information was provided to us neither.

5   Next Iteration

After we had used the UXPRM for roughly assessing the UX capabilities, we had conducted a new iteration to draw an accurate picture of our partner UX practices. In view of the above difficulties, we have opted for an online questionnaire send by email. We have written the questionnaire and the introductory text. The email was sent to all employees, but only the subset of those aware of UX did so. This could be explained by the fact that the email has been rewritten before sending by the organization in this regard. As we do not know the exact number of people who received the email, we assess that the response rate is close to 14% (11 answers). The results of this questionnaire can be found in Table 6.

Table 6. Frequency of use of UX methods/artifacts (1: never; 2: rarely; 3: sometimes; 4: often; 5: always; ?: do not know how often; X: do not know this artifact)

Artifacts	1	2	3	4	5	?	X
Customer journey map	1	4	2	0	0	1	3
Persona	5	3	1	0	0	0	2
Service blueprint	0	2	2	3	1	0	3
Work models	0	3	3	3	1	0	1
UX goals	2	3	2	1	1	0	2
Affinity diagram	3	2	1	0	0	0	5
Concept map	2	1	2	1	0	0	5
Card sort	1	1	1	0	0	1	7
User scenario	0	2	5	1	1	1	2
User story	1	1	1	4	0	2	2
Task models	0	0	3	3	0	0	5
Low-fi prototype	1	6	2	0	0	0	2
High-fi prototype	2	2	2	1	0	1	3
Design principles	0	1	5	1	1	2	1
Methods	**1**	**2**	**3**	**4**	**5**	**?**	**X**
Group interview	0	2	6	1	0	1	1
Individual interview	1	2	4	2	0	1	1
Survey research	5	3	0	0	0	2	1
Experience sampling	5	1	1	0	0	0	4
Experiment	5	0	1	0	0	1	4
Instrument-based experiment	7	0	1	0	0	0	3
Observation	5	2	0	0	0	2	2
Simulation	3	1	2	0	0	1	4
GOMS	0	0	1	0	0	0	10
Hierarchical task analysis	0	1	2	1	0	0	7
Inspection	2	1	2	0	0	0	5
Literature review	0	2	3	0	0	3	3

In Table 7, we compare the result of the frequency of use of UX methods/artifacts collected with the online questionnaire and the statements made in preliminary interviews. For example, in the preliminary interview, Persona was categorized as never realized and five people answered the same in the questionnaire, three answered "rarely" and one answered "often". Table 8 compares the preliminary interview statements with the most frequent answer in the questionnaire. Only one artifact (persona) and two methods (survey research and experiment) present corresponding statements between the preliminary interview and the questionnaire, described as never used. This leads us to think that most of UX activities were not well understood and or not very perceivable within our partner.

Table 7. Frequency of use of UX methods/artifacts and preliminary interview (1: never; 2: rarely; 3: sometimes; 4: often; 5: always)

Artifacts	Interview	1	2	3	4	5
Persona	Never	5	3	1	0	0
Work models	Never	0	3	3	3	1
UX goals	Never	2	3	2	1	1
User story	Always	1	1	1	4	0
Task models	Never	0	0	3	3	0
Low-fi prototype	Never	1	6	2	0	0
High-fi prototype	Never	2	2	2	1	0
Design principles	Never	0	1	5	1	1
Methods	**Interview**	**1**	**2**	**3**	**4**	**5**
Survey research	Never	5	3	0	0	0
Experience sampling	Rarely	5	1	1	0	0
Experiment	Never	5	0	1	0	0
Hierarchical task analysis	Never	0	1	2	1	0

Table 8. Preliminary interview and most frequent answer about frequency of use of UX methods/artifacts

Artifacts	Interview	Most frequent answer
Persona	Never	Never
Work models	Never	Rarely, sometimes, often
UX goals	Never	Rarely
User story	Always	Often
Task models	Never	Sometimes, often
Low-fi prototype	Never	Rarely
High-fi prototype	Never	Never, rarely sometimes
Design principles	Never	Sometimes
Methods		
Survey research	Never	Never
Experience sampling	Rarely	Never
Experiment	Never	Never
Hierarchical task analysis	Never	Sometimes

6 Discussion

With the aim of understanding organizational barriers and why they occur, we sought after relevant literature. Few references cover the subject, even fewer attempt to present some explanations. However, one explication is presented by Lewis [11] with the "peanut butter theory of usability": *A spread that can be smeared over any software model, however dreadful, with good results if the spread is thick enough. If the underlying functionality is confusing, then spread a graphical user interface on it... If the user interface still has some problems, smear some manuals over it. If the manuals are still deficient, smear on some training which you force users to take* [19]. In other words, this would be due to a lack of understanding among companies of what UX is and confusion between UX and User Interface (UI). This misunderstanding leads to a poor use of UX methods and artifacts.

7 Conclusion

Typically, design and evaluation are intertwined within an iterative and incremental test-and-refine process that aims to improve the product. But organizational barriers can slow down or prevent iterative processes. To contribute to identifying and overcoming these organizational barriers, we proposed:

- A categorization of organizational barriers
- and a case study to present a proposed procedure to overcome these barriers.

Thanks to the rough UX CM assessment conducted in the beginning of the project, we were expecting such constant readjustment of our UX strategy. We suggest that regularly interviewing employees of the company would allow to check for potential changes in the UX CM of the organization. However, mostly employed by the UX community [2], interviews lead to meaningful data but are time-consuming. This leads us to consider other tools for UX CM assessment in the future.

Acknowledgements. The authors acknowledge the support by the Projects HAULOGY 2021 and VIADUCT under the references 7767 and 7982 funded by Service public de Wallonie (SPW), Belgium.

References

1. Discount Usability: 20 years. Nielsen Norman Group (2009). https://www.nngroup.com/articles/discount-usability-20-years/
2. Bargas-Avila, J.A., Hornbæk, K.: Old wine in new bottles or novel challenges? A critical analysis of empirical studies of user experience, p. 10 (2011)
3. Bias, R.G., Mayhew, D.J.: Cost-Justifying Usability: An Update for an Internet Age, 2nd edn. Elsevier, Amsterdam (2005)
4. Bornoe, N., Stage, J.: Active involvement of software developers in usability engineering: two small-scale case studies. In: Bernhaupt, R., Dalvi, G., Joshi, A., Balkrishan, D.K., O'Neill, J., Winckler, M. (eds.) INTERACT 2017. LNCS, vol. 10516, pp. 159–168. Springer, Cham (2017). https://doi.org/10.1007/978-3-319-68059-0_10
5. Gulliksen, J., Boivie, I., Göransson, B.: Usability professionals: current practices and future development. Interact. Comput. **18**(4), 568–600 (2006). https://doi.org/10.1016/j.intcom.2005.10.005
6. Hassenzahl, M., Tractinsky, N.: User experience-a research agenda. Behav. Inf. Technol. **25**(2), 91–97 (2006)

7. Hassenzahl, M.: The thing and I: understanding the relationship between user and product. In: Blythe, M.A., Overbeeke, K., Monk, A.F., Wright, P.C. (eds.) Funology. HCIS, vol. 3, pp. 31–42. Springer, Berlin (2003). https://doi.org/10.1007/1-4020-2967-5_4

8. Hassenzahl, M.: User experience (UX): towards an experiential perspective on product quality. In: Proceedings of the 20th Conference on l'Interaction Homme-Machine, pp. 11–15. ACM (2008)

9. Jokela, T., Abrahamsson, P.: Modelling usability capability – introducing the dimensions. In: Bomarius, F., Oivo, M. (eds.) PROFES 2000. LNCS, vol. 1840, pp. 73–87. Springer, Heidelberg (2000). https://doi.org/10.1007/978-3-540-45051-1_10

10. Kieffer, S., Rukonić, L., Kervyn de Meerendré, V., Vanderdonckt, J.: Specification of a UX process reference model towards the strategic planning of UX activities, p. 12 (2019)

11. Lewis, C., Rieman, J.: Task-centered user interface design, p. 190 (2001)

12. Maguire, M.: Methods to support human-centred design. Int. J. Hum. Comput. Stud. **55**(4), 587–634 (2001). https://doi.org/10.1006/ijhc.2001.0503

13. Metzker, E., Reiterer, H.: Integrating usability engineering methods into existing software development processes via evidence-based usability engineering, p. 17 (2004)

14. Nielsen, J.: Guerrilla HCI: using discount usability engineering to penetrate the intimidation barrier, p. 18 (1994)

15. Nielsen, J.: Applying discount usability engineering. IEEE Softw. **12**(1), 98–100 (1995). https://doi.org/10.1109/52.363161

16. Ogunyemi, A.A., Lamas, D., Lárusdóttir, M.K., Loizides, F.: A systematic mapping study of HCI practice research. Int. J. Hum.-Comput. Interact. (2018). https://doi.org/10.1080/10447318.2018.1541544

17. Rosenbaum, S., Rohn, J.A., Humburg, J.: A toolkit for strategic usability: results from workshops, panels, and surveys, p. 10 (2000)

18. Rundqvist, D.: A case study about integrating UX practices within a UX-immature organization, p. 31 (2018)

19. Seffah, A., Eduard, M.: Adoption-Centric Usability Engineering: Systematic Deployment, Assessment, and Improvement of Usability Methods in Software Engineering. Springer, London (2009). https://doi.org/10.1007/978-1-84800-019-3

20. Van Kuijk, J., Van Driel, L., Van Daan, E.: Usability in product development practice; an exploratory case study comparing four markets. Appl. Ergonom. **47**(March), 308–323 (2015). https://doi.org/10.1016/j.apergo.2014.10.007

21. Venturi, G., Troost, J., Jokela, T.: People, organizations, and processes: an inquiry into the adoption of user-centered design in industry. Int. J. Hum. Comput. Interact. **21**(2), 219–238 (2006)

22. Winter, J., Rönkkö, K., Rissanen, M.: Identifying organizational barriers—a case study of usability work when developing software in the automation industry. J. Syst. Softw. **88** (February), 54–73 (2014). https://doi.org/10.1016/j.jss.2013.09.019

Analysis the Impacting of "User Experience" for Chinese Mobile Phone's Brands Market Changing

Hui Li[(⊠)] and Yi Wei

Shandong Management University, No. 3500 Clove Road,
Changqing, Jinan, Shandong, China
Leehui-1@163.com

Abstract. Entering the 21st century, the transition of the economic form and the "people-centered" design of the force of the trend of combining people show a strong preference blurs aesthetic inclination, and experience design attention; and highlights the importance of user perception value. The mobile phone market is not exceptional also, under the lead of apple, each of big mobile phone brands have set up the user experience department, to introduce the relevant personnel. Not only in terms of visual image, interaction design, through the visualization image visual summary, show the characteristic of enterprise spirit and enterprise culture. More vivid, specific, sensitive to product characteristics, brand value, corporate philosophy, and other information to the audience. For consumers the most direct and most users and vivid brand image, create a better experience for the foundation. And, in the process of enterprise overall brand management, are often based on user experience, a good user experience has become a brand is the key to improve the image of the market. This paper mainly focuses on China's current mobile phone market, respectively for major brands, such as Apple, Huawei, Xiaomi, Samsung, … etc., to analyze the change course of brands, and to discuss the user experience in brand building and the important role and significance in the process of communication.

Keywords: User experience · UX design · Market · Brand image · Design psychology

1 Changes in China's Mobile Phone Market in the Last Years

According to Suning.com released by the second quarter of China's smartphone 2018 physical retail report: Huawei for many months to win the offline mobile phone brand TOP1, market share accounted for 28.1%, and the iPhone fell to fourth place, at any time may be surpassed by Xiaomi. Apple's new iPhone XS and iPhone XS Max are officially on sale in China 8 o'clock in the morning September 21, 2018. However, the crowd queuing at the Apple store was a lot colder than in previous years. Compared with the iPhone4 when the sale of the year, is already momentary taekwondo. At the Apple Experience store, you can pay for the goods at the scene, even if you don't have an appointment. A scalpers said, "Do not need to wait, now the number of machines is

© Springer Nature Switzerland AG 2019
A. Marcus and W. Wang (Eds.): HCII 2019, LNCS 11586, pp. 277–287, 2019.
https://doi.org/10.1007/978-3-030-23535-2_21

enough, basically want to have." "On the iPhone sale day of previous years, this is largely impossible. Not only that, Apple after the sale of various channels prices have fallen below the offer price, even the sale of mobile phone cattle, but also shouted "big loss." And as consumer buying enthusiasm began to dissipate, the entire smartphone industry began to enter a "cold winter" (Table 1).

Table 1. The top 10 of mobile phone

Source of data: Suning.com

In the third quarter of 2018, Vivo, OPPO, Huawei, Glory and Xiaomi became the top five mobile phone makers in China's smartphone market. Among them, vivo with 20.62 million sales, accounted for 19.2% of the market share, oppo sales of 20.58 million, the market share of 19.1%, Huawei sales of 17.11 million, the share of 15.9%, the glory sales of 13.62 million, the market share of 12.7%, Xiaomi sales of 12.61 million, Market share 11.7%. Earlier, Huawei's Internet mobile phone brand Glory announced the departure from the Huawei system, the establishment of independent companies in the country. With Huawei releasing the mate 20 flagship phone series, revealing a strong signal that Huawei will focus on the high-end brand market, although Huawei is not yet able to compete with Apple and Samsung in sales, but in this move, the anti-Apple meaning is self-evident. In addition, with Oppo, Vivo this "brother Ming reckoning" data statistics are different, Huawei and glory of the main and sub-two brands are also the use of separate statistics. Also said, if Huawei and the glory of the two brands add up sales and share, the entire Huawei sales will be 30.72 million, the market share of 28.6%, more than vivo become the industry's first.

At the same time, from the Cylon Q3 According to the China smartphone market report, we can also see that the mobile phone industry Matthew effect more and more serious. In contrast to the OV Glory of these head manufacturers against the trend, the processing of domestic mobile phone brands in the two-tier echelon has become increasingly difficult. For example, in this year's Q3, Meizu sales slipped 53% and Jinli slipped 82%; So, The top six rankings largely accounted for 90% of the nearly domestic market share. 4%), and this gap should grow in the future. Still, domestic brands continue to sell low-end handsets, and profit margins are still far inferior to those of Samsung and Apple. As far as market capitalisation is concerned, even Huawei is less than one-fifth of Apple's (Table 2).

Table 2. Sano 2018 Q3 overall market sales ranking.

	Brand	2018 Q3 (10,000)	18 Q3 compared to the previous year	The market share
1	Vivo	2062	15%	19.2%
2	Oppo	2058	−4%	19.1%
3	HUAWEI	1711	32%	15.9%
4	HONOR	1362	19%	12.7%
5	MI	1261	1%	11.7%
6	Apple	1054	−16%	9.8%
7	Meizu	189	−53%	1.8%
8	Samsung	123	−39%	1.1%
9	Gionee	71	−82%	0.7%

Source of data: Cylon

Specifically, in the Chinese market, Apple and Samsung, the two major industry giants have seen a decline in sales, Apple slipped 16%, while Samsung has slipped 39%.

1.1 Samsung: China has a Market Share of Less Than 1%

Recently, well-known research institutions Strategy Analytics announced South Korea's Samsung phone 2018 third quarter results of the year. Samsung phones shipped only tens of thousands in the third quarter of China, according to the report. It also says that one months of shipment of thousands of units. This is surprising compared to the total shipment of Samsung mobile phones in the world 7230 million parts!

In the third quarter of 2018, Samsung's share of mobile phones remained at the forefront of the global market, according to Counterpoint, another research institute.

But at the same time, Huawei, from China, has ranked second in shipments that have overtaken Apple by 14%. In the Chinese market, Huawei is well ahead of the market share of 23%, while Samsung is largely classified as the "other" item in the statistical table. Far less than the vivo, OPPO, millet behind Huawei. A serious 39% percent decline year earlier.

Gaodongjin, head of Samsung's mobile business, has acknowledged Samsung's failure in the Chinese market in an interview with android.ru in response to the virtual lack of presence of Samsung phones in the Chinese market. Gaodongjin to the interviewer: "In the Chinese market, Samsung in the entry-level and midrange smartphone market, can not compete with Chinese brands such as Xiaomi, Huawei and other Chinese companies, because China's domestic brands of mobile phones, whether in pricing or marketing strategy more flexible." But on the international market, entry-level and mid-tier smartphones remain one of Samsung's most important revenues, precisely because of the sales of these entry-level and midrange smartphone devices on the international market, Samsung remains the industry leader, surpassing Apple and Huawei in global sales."

Samsung in China in two years has been defeated to the status of no sense of existence, there are the following reasons:

1. Note 7 after the explosion door, because of arrogance and prejudice and the difference between Chinese consumers, after the incident, Samsung is not to reshape the Chinese consumer trust in the brand, but to dump the pot to the consumer's behavior hit Samsung hard.
2. Samsung mobile phone products themselves lack of innovation, localization and cost-effective are not as good as domestic brands, although Samsung has repeatedly designed models for the Chinese market, trying to rely on "brand superiority" to let consumers pay for high-priced low-energy products, take Chinese consumers as fools, has long been China's consumption through.
3. the most important is the domestic mobile phone camp no matter in the design, innovation of rapid progress, and Samsung prides itself on the photo advantage is also being overtaken by domestic mobile phones.

1.2   Apple Phone Market Sales in China

According to market research institutions IDC of data, 2018 in the second quarter of the year, Apple's market share in China was 6.7%, down a year earlier, 5%, behind Huawei, OPPO, vivo and Xiaomi, ranks fifth in the country. The report also noted that Apple's high product prices have already led some users to retreat, with Apple's sales in China continuing to decline year-on-year. In fact, even on a global scale, IPhone sales have stagnated. It has been overtaken by Huawei in the third quarter of this year. For the first time in seven years, the pattern of joint dominance between Samsung and Apple has been broken (Tables 3 and 4).

Table 3. In the global smartphone market in the second quarter of 2018, the top five companies saw their shipments, market share and sales grow year-on-year

Brand	2Q18 sales volume/10,000	2Q18 The market share	2Q17 sales volume/10,000	2Q17 The market share	Compared to the previous year
Samsung	7150	20.9%	7980	22.9%	−10.4%
HUAWEI	5420	15.8%	3850	11.0%	40.9%
Apple	4130	12.1%	4100	11.8%	0.7%
MIUI	3190	9.3%	2140	6.2%	48.8%
Oppo	2940	8.6%	2800	8.0%	5.1%
Else	1137	33.2%	13950	40.1%	−18.5
Total	34200	100.0%	34820	100.0%	−1.8%

Source of data: IDC

Table 4. Global handset profit share by brands-Q2 2018

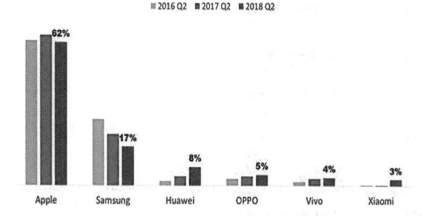

Source of data: Counterpoint

Market Research Institutes Counterpoint released by 2018 the global smartphone brand's profit distribution, data shows that Apple is still the world's most profitable company, 2018 the smartphone market was taken down in the second quarter 62% profit, followed by Samsung 17%, while Huawei, which is ranked first in the profits of domestic mobile phone brands, accounts for only 8%.

8 o'clock in the morning September 21, 2018, Apple new products officially sold in China. However, compared with previous years, Apple's new products are not very popular, From Apple's official delivery time, the iPhone XS/XS Max's delivery time is generally 1–2 weeks, and including Tmall, Jing Dong, and other third-party licensors, basically has a full spot sales, completely no previous machine difficult, fare increase to buy the scene.

Apple New product cold, one reason is the price rise, expensive iPhone XS Max 512 GB price of 12799 yuan, entry-level products are in the 6000+ range; Cutting kidney can not afford; another reason is that the main dual-card dual-stay, double-photography and other technological innovations, the market has been a long time.

Long-term accumulation of brand effect, so that Apple even if the price is high, there are always consumers willing to pay. With this underpinnings, the price increase is reasonable. It's just that I don't know how long it's going to last. Since the iPhone xs/xs Max was sold, it has been exposed to a variety of product quality issues, such as some models of screen display failure, mobile phone and WiFi signal is not bad. Early apples, the pursuit of perfect products, however, after jobs, there was no subversion (Table 5).

Table 5. How much have iPhones cost since 2010?

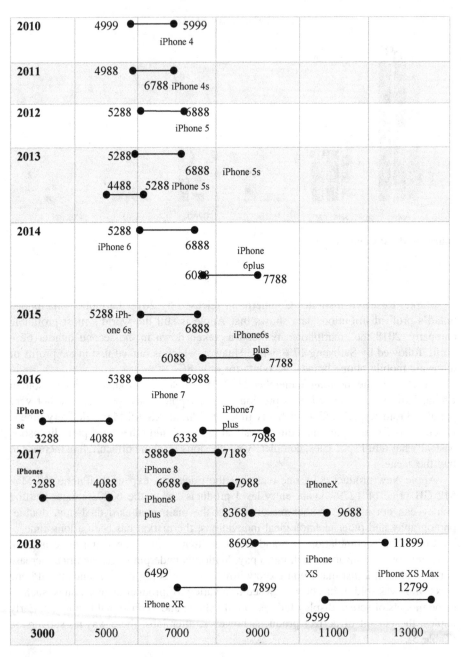

| 3000 | 5000 | 7000 | 9000 | 11000 | 13000 |

Source of data: Curiosity daily

Today's apples, but not so harsh on the product, the loss of innovative genes of the apple, only from the price to show their unique identity, but also the pursuit of the perfect market. It is understood that the iPhone X/iPhone X signal problems, may be with the iPhone and Qualcomm patent dispute, abandon the industry's best performance of the Gotongki belt chip, from iPhone7 began to use Intel's baseband chip. Obviously, in the above reasons, Apple's new iPhone wants not to encounter sales Waterloo, is a very difficult thing.

A few days ago, Mobdata released the third quarter of China's smartphone market research report, said that Apple is still the user's awareness of the first brand of mobile phones, but when Apple's three new machines released this year, the number of old models has shown a state of non-decline. This means that consumers are not too happy with the new iPhone after sidelines, and instead start the old model. Among them, the iPhone 6s, 6s Plus and iPhone 7 Plus, the three old models stand out.

In terms of Apple's specific model sales, the iPhone 6 series accounted for 16.1% of the iPhone, which currently has the highest holdings, while the iPhone 6s series accounted for 26.9% of the share. In other words, the two models together account for an astonishing proportion of almost half of Apple mobile phone users.

On the other hand, most of the Android phones released by the same era have now been shelved. At the same time, there are reports of various smartphone user portraits analyzed:

Apple users are the largest number of young people aged 18–34, with the largest number of unmarried women, high school and below and bachelor's degree, belong to the invisible poor;

Huawei's age level is 25–34 years old, college degree is the majority, male married ethnic group, monthly income between 5000 yuan to 20000 yuan, belongs to high-end business people.

In addition, Oppo is the majority of female married people, is also 25–34 years old, college degree, monthly income of 3000 yuan to 10000 yuan, belongs to the housewife.

Vivo's user base is about the same as the Oppo group. Xiaomi is an entry-level white-collar, male married people, 25–34 years old, bachelor's degree, monthly income of 5000 yuan to 10000 yuan.

2 The Theory and Development of User Experience

Today's internet industry, including all aspects of people's lives, social, gaming, search, e-commerce, payment, television, advertising, reading, and with the development of various types of mobile products, scope and use is still expanding, has a very large market space and development scope. The continuous progress of the Internet industry can inject a steady stream of vitality into the society and provide a broad world for economic reform, scientific and technological innovation and social development.

Under the impetus of people's daily needs and other positive factors, smartphones, as the basic carrier of mobile Internet, have quickly replaced the popularization of traditional mobile phones after several years of renewal, not only to realize the basic functions of traditional mobile phone calls and text messages, but also to meet people's material and cultural needs. Convenient for people to surf the internet anytime, anywhere to communicate, entertainment, reading, shopping and so on. Accelerate the progress of the industry while promoting the continuous innovation of mobile phone hardware and software technology. A good product, in order to have market competitiveness and development prospects, improve the number of users at the same time to increase user viscosity, the need to optimize the user experience to achieve product goals. As users' standards for cell phone evaluation extend from functional and technical requirements to the need for a product experience, the concept of product design centered on the user experience begins to receive widespread attention in the industry.

The user experience (UE or UX) refers to "the parts of a product or service that users can experience, involving all aspects of the user's knowledge of the product, search, classification, purchase, installation, service, support, and upgrade".

The meaning of the user experience in a narrow sense represents the user's function of the product and the appearance of the sensory experience, in a broad sense refers to the user's use of a product before and when the use of the psychological feelings and experience, as well as the subsequent impression and evaluation of the product, but also the brand and products are compatible with the needs of ideological experience.

Scholars of different disciplines have different definitions and studies of the user experience.

Jess James Garrett, an American interaction design expert, defines the user experience in his book Elements of user experience: The user experience refers to "how the product connects and works with the outside world," that is, how people "touch" and "use" it. He believes that user experience refers to the way products are expressed and used in the real world, including the user's experience of brand characteristics, information availability, content, functionality, and so on.

Donald Norman, a cognitive psychologist in the United States, extends the concept of user experience to every level of interaction between users and products Donald Norman. He believes that in order to better understand the user's technical experience, emphasis should also be placed on emotional factors, including enjoyment, aesthetics and entertainment, including three basic dimensions: physical, cognitive and emotional.

Bernd H. Schmitt in "experience marketing" through the "Human brain Module analysis" and psychological sociology said that the user experience is divided into 5 Categories: sensory, emotional, thinking, behavior, association. The user experience involves a variety of disciplines, including user psychology, behavioral science, marketing, and aesthetics, which are difficult to quantify. At present, the concept of user experience has been widely used in the field of human–computer interaction research and application, but the definition is not yet certain, scholars from their respective fields of study, put forward different theories and viewpoints, in which there are intersections and there are great differences, Uniform standards have not yet been developed.

With the rapid development of computer technology and Internet, the form of technological innovation, which is closely related to people's life, has changed, and more and more attention has been paid to the concept of user-centered and people-oriented design. Measuring the standard of a product is not only functional and usability, but also determined by the user's own psychological feelings and behavior. User experience is a pure subjective feeling that users build up in the process of using products. The user's usage habits, sensory experiences, and possible modes of operation need to be incorporated into the design of the product's use steps, information structure, and interactive approach. Although each user's subjective feeling is different, but after defining the consumer object, through the design experiment can realize the user group's experience commonality.

3 The Important Role of User Experience in the Change of Mobile Phone Market

The coming of the 5G era means that the speed of mobile networks can be comparable to that of wired networks. Mobile phones and mobile internet have been completely integrated with people's lives, in the early days of the internet because of the small variety of software, pay attention to the function of software, do not pay too much attention to the user experience. But now is very different, the same kind of function has many kinds of apps to choose from, users must pay more attention to mobile phone interface design, interactive design. In modern commercial design, user experience is gradually becoming the core competitiveness of merchants in the market competition, which is also increasingly hot.

Apple has always been the IT industry in the user experience design pioneer and leader, product design everywhere reflects the user-centric, people-oriented design ideas, is the user experience as the advantage, in order to enhance the brand image of the typical. Enterprises through the establishment of user experience Department, the market and user research, so that product development to better meet people's needs, for corporate image and brand have a good improvement. At present, other mobile phone brands by virtue of the needs of users continue to pay attention to and continuous progress in technical performance cost-effective, market competitiveness is also increasing.

At present, in China, the perception of the user experience is relatively late, but the development is very fast. Because merchants can recognize that a product user experience is better, on behalf of the company's industry is reasonable and successful. The success of the user experience directly related to product sales, user stickiness, consumer strength and promotion, is the key to determine the life and death of businesses. Other mobile phone brands by virtue of the user's needs of continuous attention and continuous progress in technical performance cost-effective, market competitiveness is also increasing.

From the use of mobile phone users to analyze the benefits, although it involves price, performance, appearance ... And many other aspects, but the most directly related to it is nothing more than two aspects: on the one hand, it is the consideration of its price factors, on the other hand, the consideration of user experience. This requires that in the communications and Internet industry, on the basics of consideration of value for money, but also to consider as far as possible to meet the user experience.

As a result, most of the domestic mobile phone brands focus on the following aspects, thus greatly improving the level of sales.

3.1   The Visual Interface Design of Innovative

Interface can be understood as a medium for the interaction of information exchange in human–computer interaction between man and smartphone and application software. Includes the way to interact with mobile apps, the operation process, and the design of visual effects. Excellent interface design for the product, not only to make the application stylized and branded, but also to increase the professional, usability, operational and ease of use of mobile phones and software, can give users a good first impression, can also be users to buy mobile phones, download mobile apps (application, short app) app, The reason for using the app can be one of the factors that increase the user's stickiness.

Interface design is an important part of product design and development, mobile phones, tablets, computer systems and software interface vision, can obtain the user's most intuitive visual experience, is the product to the user's first impression, is the user experience with the user's most closely integrated parts, is the product and user communication between the bridge. Interface Vision design, large to style, layout, color, text, small to every icon, button, spacing, are based on the user as the starting point, is based on the user's psychological, perceptual, emotional and behavioral analysis. Good interface visual design, can reduce the user's learning costs, improve user productivity, increase user stickiness, create a natural and comfortable operating environment, to optimize the user experience.

3.2   Guide User Needs

User-centric, to cater to and guide user needs. Break the user's favorite, inherent use habits, in order to enhance the user experience, enlighten the needs of users, so that users of the use of habits in the case of inadvertently imperceptible, natural transformation, to achieve breakthroughs and innovation.

3.3   Saving the Development Cost

In the market of mobile application products, there is a lot of software in the design process, is technically very professional but lack of user interface design based programmers designed, such software often lack of user interface experience considerations, resulting in design errors and the failure of the user experience, The increased development costs that lead to the redesign of the product. For the research of mobile application Interface visual design, we can sum up some design errors, design taboos, provide design rules that designers should follow to avoid errors, help GUI designers and developers learn to design a better user vision interface, for enterprises or development teams, can save development time and cost.

3.4   Shaping and Disseminating Brand Culture

People mainly through the visual to accept external information, users through the interface vision to accept the information transmitted by the product. For enterprises, brand-based design can improve brand diversity and quality stability, but also can convey brand positioning, values, culture and other factors, so that consumers have the trust and loyalty to them, effectively strengthen the competitiveness and influence with other brands [26]. As one of the powerful media of mobile application brand communication, a good user experience has put forward high requirements for its performance and interface vision. Enterprises have recognized this point, so in the interface visual design are very important to the brand core value, brand concept and brand image into the mobile application interface of the overall design of the visual style and visual symbols to go, which is of great significance for shaping and disseminating brand culture.

3.5   Improve Overall Design Capabilities

With the development of mobile internet industry, domestic mobile Internet enterprises are very concerned about the interface design profession, has set up a product interface design department, and has the user experience designer, interaction Designer, visual designer clear function Division of functions. In the field of interface vision design, most of the research on the web side, the research on the mobile side is relatively few, has not yet formed a complete set of design process and design methods. In the process of interface visual design of APP, there is no corresponding theoretical basis. For designers engaged in the visual design of the App interface, it is of reference value and significance for the design to improve the design ability, study and summarize the design process and methods in practice. Process and method, which has reference value for future design, can improve the design ability, and is of great significance for the formation of complete design process and method.

References

1. Hai, Y.: Co-construction alliance platform collaborative industry development. China's Manuf. Inf. **7**, 21–23 (2004)
2. Reimann, R.: Aboutface 3: The Essence of Interactive Design. Electronic Industry Press, Beijing (2014)
3. Zhang, K.: On the pros and cons of the age of Big data. Comput. CD Softw. Appl. Date (6), 123–123
4. Liu, H.: Research on the Interaction Behavior of Apple Application Software. Shanghai Jiaotong, Shanghai
5. Wu, Q.: Domains and boundaries of interactive design. Decoration (2010)
6. Zhou, J.: Visual design analysis and cognitive research of mobile phone interface. Northwestern University (2013)
7. Chen, K.: Research on interface experience design of mobile application software. Harbin University (2013)
8. Hu: Research on humanized design in the interface design of smartphone. Nanjing Forestry University (2008)
9. Chen, F.: Research on mobile internet resource management for user experience. China University of Science and Technology

Making Meaning: How Experience Design Supports Data Commercialization

Manhai Li[1(✉)], Xiangyang Xin[1], and Xiong Ding[2]

[1] Macau University of Science and Technology, Macau 999078, China
1393101@qq.com
[2] Guangzhou Academy of Fine Arts, Guangzhou 510006, China

Abstract. The work aims to analyze the different stages of data commercialization and explore the research paradigm of making meaning through the experience process. Based on the cases of data-driven products, a classification study was conducted through induction and summary, and the characteristics of four stages of data commercialization was illustrated. In the era of big data, data is not just about extra output or subsidiary force or core competency, but raw materials in the process of commercialization, which is an inevitable trend. The goal of data commercialization is to make meaning by the way of experience design. At different stages of data commercialization, the methods of experience design have to adjust as consumers' demands for meaning are various. With the development of internet technology, the correlation and connection between people's daily life and data will be strengthened unconsciously, and the appeal to meaningful experience of data products will become more common. When data is treated as a kind of raw material in the fourth stage of data, the mode of experience design is: data infrastructure as theater, data-driven services or products as the stage, data as props, and engaging data consumers as actors in a way that creates some memorable and meaningful events.

Keywords: Making meaning · Experience design · Big data · Data-driven · Data commercialization

1 Introduction

1.1 Demand for Meaning

Theoretically, Clifford Geertz, one of the preeminent thinkers in contemporary anthropology, regarded that meaning is our mind's construction of reality, the translation of existence into conceptual form. Why do we construct meaning in the first place? Aside from reflexes and instincts, human beings require an explanation of the world that helps us decide how to act. Meaning helps us understand the world and ourselves, learn, and make sense of what's around us. It provides a framework for assessing what we value, believe, condone, and desire. Anything that supports a sense of meaning supports the basis for understanding and action, making it extremely valuable to us [1]. For example, millions of downloadable songs are not just because of fickle consumers, but because each of these items is a building block in the reality which we increasingly prefer they fit our concept of self. As we selectively purchase or

© Springer Nature Switzerland AG 2019
A. Marcus and W. Wang (Eds.): HCII 2019, LNCS 11586, pp. 288–299, 2019.
https://doi.org/10.1007/978-3-030-23535-2_22

reject these items, they become inextricably part of how we construct meaning in our lives.

As a matter of fact, it is common in advanced consumer markets that products and services have been already designed to meet sophisticated emotional or identity needs. The new generation of consumers who have grown up with the smart phones and instant messaging are talking more frequently and passionately about meaning in their lives, expressing a desire for—even expecting—meaningful experiences from daily necessities. The emotions of young people are easy to light up when they learn about something capable of making their friends develop a stronger sense of community. Take iPod as an instance, what makes the iPod an overwhelming success is the union of invention, design, and marketing into a seamless whole that evokes meaning in the enjoyment of music by concentrating on the customer's experience. It goes beyond simply selling digital-music to selling the sensation of freedom, wonder and control. This wildly popular product integrated and reinforced a desirable musical experience, meeting the customer's demand for meaning.

Not only because of the demand for meaning may even be the defining characteristic of what makes us human [2], but also there are some objective reasons for meaningful consumption, such as social trends, economic forces, and technological advances [3]. Take WeChat as an example for the factor of social trends, it is a kind of communication software or platform that connecting more than a billion people with calls, chats, and more, profoundly affecting the process of people's interactions. Just as its slogan says, it has been a way of life, which means it is changing the way people socialize, like paying with WeChat Pay instead of cash when people go to the supermarket. The phenomenon of more and more people becoming smartphone addicts illustrates this point. The economic ability of consumers has to be considered, when it comes to the factor of economic forces. Alibaba's turnover was 213.5 billion yuan on the Double Eleven Shopping Festival in 2018, which shows excess income that people perceive they have, or that they expect to have, to give them purchasing power. As social factors change, where and how people spend their money changes. And along with the material life being satisfied, more and more people are tending to pursue spiritual needs. Technological factors refer to the potential value of direct or indirect use of new technologies and research results for the design of data products, including communication technology, space technology and engineering technology. As for the factor of technological advances, the technology of virtual reality must be mentioned, which has the potential to integrate natural human motions into the computer aided assembly planning environment. This would allow evaluations of an assembler's ability to manipulate and assemble parts and result in reduced time and cost for product design [4]. These advanced technologies make customized and personalized production available to provide meaningful experiences for different kinds of consumers simultaneously.

1.2 Meaningful Data Commercialization

Nowadays, data is accompanied by people anytime and anywhere, bringing lifestyle changes to all fields and society as a whole. From the agricultural society to the industrial society, data was generated in every manufacturing process. While in the information age, as the amount of data has exploded, data is becoming more and more popular to discuss. At different times, people had different views on data. In the beginning, the data was irrelevant and ignored, while now the identity and emotion play momentous roles in the ultimate success of data commercialization, at the same time, the customer's experience of interacting with data is a positive one (Fig. 1).

Fig. 1. Data is recorded and designed to conveys the rhythm of Tai Chi [5].

For example, combining camera technology, data processing and artistic creation, Tai Chi's movements of hands and feet, including position coordinates and dwell time, are digitized and saved into data as the material of multimedia art creation. These limb's location data manually are collected and processed through the artistic processing of data visualization, such as changing the point where the hands and feet stay longer, and converting them into grayscale changes, which not only reflects the movement of the body in the most basic way: with visual motion akin to Chinese ink brush painting, but also conveys the rhythm of Tai Chi and the operation of "Qi" in Chinese traditional culture, gathering invisible power from universe and balancing inner turbulences to harmonization.

Another example, if you choose the location of Hangzhou in the electronic map (https://sou-yun.com/poetlifemap.html), you can see all the names and works of poets related to Hangzhou in history will be displayed, which is a wonderful experience, expecially combined with live video and specific music. If anyone wants to feel the literary charm of Hangzhou, he can use the map to find out which ancient poets ever come to Hangzhou, what verses they had written. This system with a good experience benefits from meaningful processing of the data. That is, the literary materials left by ancient poets and writers in every location in China were organized, categorized, and then presented on an electronic map, so that the viewer only needs to select a certain place on the electronic map to feel the rich stereoscopic poetry charm of the place.

It is important for data-driven companies to evoke meaning through user experiences. As we've suggested, the experience people have with products, services, and events is only partly due to what a company might envision and endeavor to provide. The bulk of the experience is actually created by the consumers; that's how it becomes highly relevant for the individual.

2 Experience Design

2.1 A Meaningful Experience

A meaningful experience is any process we're conscious of and involved in as it happens. As an individual, all of those things happen in the course of daily life express parts of your identity and define you in significant ways, including the tasks you do, the responsibilities you hold, the relationships and decisions you make etc. Specifically, you would rather get up early to walk through a beautiful park to go to work, instead of choosing to take the subway to work in a hurry, which means "harmony" is the meaning you prefer to experience. You are in pursuit of harmony by seeking a work/life balance. The meaning of what you do is reflected in the process of experience.

Sample:
Drawings is an effective means for children to explore and communicate their understandings about the world, which means drawing is a constructive process of thinking in action, rather than a developing ability to make visual reference to objects in the world [6]. It is quite important for children to freely use their imagination, including scribbling and expressing without unwanted constraints, which is nearly the most important meaningful experience for children in the drawing process. As some scholars have mentioned, the meaning of drawings resides most significantly in the ways that participants interpret those images, rather than as some inherent property of the images themselves [7]. It is necessary to care about children's narratives and interpretations during their drawings, so that their views are able to be presented clearly and their contexts are capable of being understood correctly. Several studies show that the best way for children to construct and convey meaning is drawing while talking at the same time, and both the drawing and the narrative that accompanies the drawing has proven to be a powerful combination [8]. Focusing on drawing as meaning-making moves away from the discourse of drawing as representation. The discourse of drawing as meaning-making recognizes the importance of context in children's drawings. Context includes the availability of resources and materials as well as social and cultural elements. In the eyes of adults, the results of drawing maybe are not so favored, while more importantly, the importance of drawing as a process, rather than the drawing product. Many researchers have done much to extend the understanding of drawing as a tool for constructing and sharing meaning.

Apart from the impossibility of completely controlling all touch points in an experience, there's positive value in intentionally relinquishing some control and encouraging customers to participate in co-creating experiences. Some of companies, like Disney and Apple are well recognized for the success of their total customer experience. Combining the power of invention, design, and marketing to create meaningful experiences for their customers provides a blueprint to achieving sustained and stable growth. The companies that recognize the importance of these experiences and provide them to become the cocreators of consumers' lives. This type of bond between a company and a consumer goes beyond customer satisfaction and brand building. Rather than being a component of marketing or design, designing experiences that evoke meaning is the heart and soul of innovation.

2.2   Data and Experience

As symbols, Data is the storage of intrinsic meaning, a mere representation. The main purpose of data is to record activities or situations, to attempt to capture the true picture or real event [9]. Data commercialization is not unique in the information age. Humans have been using data for a long time. Throughout the historical process of data applications, the relationship between data and design can be divided into four stages. Here we use small dot to represent data and big circle to represent design (see Fig. 2).

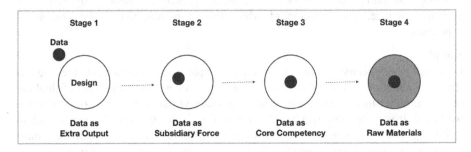

Fig. 2. Four stages of data commercialization.

In the first stage, data as extra output is usually used to deepen the perception of experience, for example, designers can make a graph of how many players have lost in the game and let the players feel his achievements in an intuitive way after experiencing a wonderful game. In the second stage, when data becomes the subsidiary force of design, data is capable of helping designers to build a good fragmented experience. For example, based on user preferences, a precise advertising system has the ability to allow users to receive useful information and avoid interference from spam ads, which partially enhance the user experience. In the third stage, as data becomes the core competency of organization, the application of data is used throughout all aspects of manufacturing and marketing to create an integrated user experience. In the fourth stage, when data becomes a kind of raw material, many companies can purchase these universal materials to make a wide variety of data products, just as garment companies buy common fabrics to produce different styles of clothing, which means a revolution that you can create a meaningful and complete experience.

In order to figure out how user experience design supports data commercialization, the Table 1 gives a summary of the relationship between data applications and impact on experience in the different stages of data commercialization.

Table 1. The relationship between data applications and impact on experience.

Stage	Data applications	Impact on experience
1	Data as extra output	Deepen perception of experience
2	Data as subsidiary force	Build a good fragmented experience
3	Data as core competency	Build a good whole experience
4	Data as raw materials	Build a meaningful whole experience

3 Four Stages of Data Commercialization

3.1 Stage 1: Data as Extra Output

In the process of using products, users may temporarily leave down some data such as numbers or words in the system, most of which will be forgotten or destroyed because these data are additional outputs. At this stage, the relationship of data and design can be considered to be irrelevant or interrelated.

Whether or not these data are used depends on the designer. For example, knowing the rise and fall of Chinese dynasties helps understand the critical transitions of Chinese history and study the tradition of specific manageable history segments. Based on the overall data of social stability, economic power, technological advancement, ideological development and geographical span, scholars are able to draw a picture to show dynasties over time versus the evaluation of their strength. At times when the country was geograophically unified, political strong, culturally influential and with social stability and prosperous economy, its overall success is represented through the high raised curve line. Viewer can easily find out the regular pattern through the picture.

Another example, they can be used to deepen the player's perception of game performance, through data visualization (see Fig. 3). The processing of data helps achieve a sense of accomplishment benefiting from intuitive data presentation and user experience. Through this interface, players can see the medals and rewards they have received this time. Although these things are all intangible spiritual incentives, players will get excitement and have the desire to continue to participate in the game.

At this stage, data is considered as extra output, which does not mean that data is unuseful. Actually data is still valuable, depending on how to use the data.

3.2 Stage 2: Data as Subsidiary Force

In today's Internet products arena, as the User Experience Professional Association mentioned in a research report, nearly 70% of respondents underlined the importance of data-driven design [11]. This survey shows that data will effectively help designers learn to understand consumers' habits and meet their needs accurately, because the behavior log can restore consumers' online access path and discover the specific page

Fig. 3. Data visualization in the case of data as extra output [10].

that causes confusion during the transaction process. In the field of natural sciences, physicists and chemists have been experimenting with data to improve their experimental programs for hundreds of years. At this stage, data is used to improve or optimize the design inseparably, in order to give users a better experience with the product.

Kansei engineering is a typical example, which quantifies users' various sensations by transforming their perceptions of products into data, such as heartbeat, blood pressure, sound decibel and etc. The quantification allows designers to be more rational in optimizing products, in order to increase the comfort of the product experience. Kansei Engineering is a proactive product development methodology, which translates customers' impressions, feelings and demands on existing products or concepts into design solutions and concrete design parameters [12]. Kansei data collection and analysis is often complex and connected with statistical analysis, most of them require good expert knowledge and a reasonable amount of experience to carry out the studies sufficiently.

3.3   Stage 3: Data as Core Competency

With the right mindset, data can be cleverly commercialized to become a fountain of new services and innovation, such as Google Flu Trends [13], using data to predict the future in advance. Another example, Alibaba is evolving into a more strategic and sustainable brand-building platform, called Brand Databank, which analyses live data from consumers across its vast ecosystem by combining its massive data, which will provide brands insights into consumer behavior and, in turn, brands can use this data to segment audiences, which affects the life and death of the company. At this stage, data is the object of design, decisively influencing the quality of design results.

In the field of science and technology, self-driving car is a good case of showing the core competency of data. The challenge for driverless car designers is to produce control systems capable of analyzing sensory data in order to provide accurate detection of other vehicles and the road ahead [14]. These self-driving cars combine a variety of sensors to perceive their surroundings, such as radar, computer vision, lidar, and sonar, to collect data from different dimensions. Some of these sensors that keep an eye out for you while you can do something such as text somebody, shave, put your makeup on, watch a video, anything but pay attention to your driving. Advanced control systems fuse data from multiple sensors and interpret sensory information to identify appropriate navigation paths, which requires a lot of calculations on the data. These data are core competency undoubtedly.

In the field of humanities and arts, the core competency of data is reflected in social computing, which is based on creating or recreating social conventions, capable of outlining possible changes in human environments that could be brought about. For example, a team of social scientists in Facebook is hunting for unprecedented insights about human behavior and reshape the understanding of how our society works [15].

3.4 Stage 4: Data as Raw Materials

As data has been becoming a torrent flowing into every area of the global economy, data can be seen as the oil of the information economy [16], which means data becomes intangible corporate asset and raw material of new business models. There is strong evidence that data can play a significant economic role to the benefit not only of private commerce but also of national economies and their citizens, like creating momentous value for the economy of the world. For the entrepreneurs, in the new context of big data, when the data-driven emerging business ecosystems such as Alibaba's Sesame Credit, China Unicom's Wisdom Footprint, and new retail are gradually maturing, the industrial environment, product attributes, and design processes that designers serve are quite different from traditional product designs. For the artists, they can use data directly to express ideas. Through a computational process, artworks can be produced by an autonomous system based on an algorithm designed by the artist, with data sources used as raw materials. Such as Shan Shui in the World presents landscape paintings of selected places in the world generated by a computational process based on geography-related data [17]. At this stage, the world we live in today can be described by countless data sources, and design process is based on data inputs.

Many researchers argued that products and services should be encouraged to go beyond the limitations of traditional "features-and-benefits" marketing and move to a more holistic model of delivering integrated and meaningful experiences, especially for the data products. According the mode of experience economy [18], when a person buys an experience, he pays to spend time enjoying a series of memorable events that a data-driven company stages—as in a theatrical play—to engage him in a personal way. Here we propose an experience design mode: user experience in the data commercialization occurs when a company intentionally uses data infrastructure as theater, data-driven services or products as the stage, and data as props, to engage data consumers as actors in a way that creates some memorable and meaningful events (see Fig. 4).

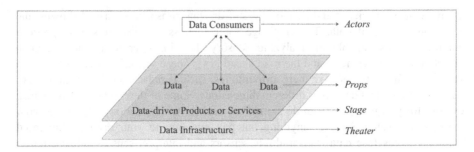

Fig. 4. Experience design mode in the case of data as raw materials.

Sample 1:

For example, the Arena of Valor, an international adaptation of Wangzhe Rongyao, is a multiplayer online battle arena mobile-game, having more than two hundred million players who are willing to pay for fictitious heroes in the game. Since all parts of the game are made with data, in a non-material form, they can be reused by many people without loss. Just by selling these virtual heroes' virtual clothes in the game, Tencent company could account for more than 100 million yuan a day once before, which is the most prominent way to generate profits. The reason is that Tencent provides the staged experiences of the theme games based on the stable data infrastructure, free of charge for any player. In this case, the game players are data consumers, like an actor, playing the role of heroes in the game; different fictitious heroes made by data are like different props waiting on the stage to pick according to the need of the game scenes, which are data-driven; the environment of theater built by the data infrastructure is invisible but vital, capable of supporting hundreds of thousands of players simultaneously online.

Speaking of meaningful experience, players can manage to accomplish the game task together with friends from different places in the world through online voice chat, which is the most important meaning that the game can bring to the game players. Accomplishment is what they pursue, which is a sense of satisfaction that can result from productivity, focus, talent, or status by achieving goals and making something of oneself. Some player would rather endure bad food and prefer to save money to buy heroes' virtual clothes, because they are not just buying practical functions and visual effects, but more importantly, satisfying the sense of accomplishment.

Sample 2:

Another example is TikTok mobile app, also known as Douyin in China, which is a media app for creating and sharing short videos, allowing users to create a short video of themselves which can be sped up, slowed down or edited with a filter and then upload it to share with others. All parts of the app are made with data, and it is well-known that video is also a type of data. While users are attracted to participate in the data commercialization, one of the reasons is because of the user-friendly video editing tools as well as the convenient social platform, the other is benefit of users' demands for the sense of unity and connection with others. In this case, data consumers as actors use the App to deal with different props such as short videos and other type of data. Those video filters are driven by data, which can be considered as stage. The data infrastructure of App platform is like a theater, providing basic data application capabilities.

When it comes to the meaningful experience, these interactions among users make important meanings. And the offerings of this App are underlined by the sharing and enjoying of community, which is a sense of unity with others around us, a deeper desire for belonging, and a general connection with other human beings.

The following Table 2 gives a summary of these two samples.

Table 2. Experience design samples in data commercialization.

Data commercialization	Arena of Valor	TikTok
Data consumers as actors	Game players	App users
Data as props	Fictitious heroes	Short videos
Data-driven products as stage	Game scenes etc.	Video filters etc.
Data infrastructure as theater	Game platform	App platform
Making meaning	Accomplishment	Community

Whether it is a game product, or a social product made by data, they need to provide a series of memorable events—as in a theatrical play—to engage every distinctive user in a personal way. The experience itself has a satisfying emotional quality because it possesses internal integration and fulfillment reached through ordered and organized movement [19]. Designers are responsible for creating opportunities for users to participate in the performance process, making it possible for users to accomplish certain things. Take TikTok as an example again, a video can be viewed and forwarded by tens of millions of people, not because some designer helps push, but the designer creates opportunities for tens of millions of users to participate in forwarding. The consumer is the main role, not the object to be observed and studied. Consumers can make his own decisions according to personal preferences and personalized needs instead of passively accepting the arrangement. Consumers creates new value of the data through interaction with others in the process of using the data.

After the data is commercialized as raw materials, the data products have five basic characteristics: 1. Data products exist in a non-material form and do not have the physical characteristics of appearance, size and material. Although the existence and circulation of data products need to be attached to material carriers, they are independent of material carriers. 2. The initial input cost of the data product is high, but the later replication cost is very low. Different users can have the same piece of data products at the same time. As the number of users expands, the average cost per unit of data products continues to decline, and the marginal cost of the data product tends to zero. 3. Before using the data product, the user cannot recognize and understand the content owned by the data product and must be understood by the user after a period of experience. 4. The consumption of data products does not result in any change in the content of the data. The main factor in measuring whether a data product is scrapped is the value and timeliness of the data product. 5. The process of using data products by users will further increase the value of data products, because the related operations performed in conjunction with their existing knowledge and experience will generate new data that can be developed to form new data products.

4 Conclusion

We are still at the dawn of big data, those new technologies like motion-based-simulators, virtual-reality and artificial-intelligence particularly encourage whole new genres of meaningful experience. As a series of technology trends accelerate and converge, it is necessary and urgent to do some research about how to make meaning through the experience process in the data commercialization.

Based on the case studies of data-driven products, data commercialization can be divided into four stages, namely: data as extra output, data as subsidiary force, data as core competency, and data as raw materials. The goal of the data was initially used to deepen perception of experience, gradually shift to build a good fragmented experience. With the production of amounts of data, designer should become an enabler, using data to build a good whole experience, and then further to build a meaningful whole experience, to make data possible for consumers to enjoy the meaningful process.

References

1. Geertz, C.: The interpretation of cultures (1973)
2. Diller, S., Shedroff, N., Rhea, D.: Making meaning: how successful businesses deliver meaningful customer experiences (2005)
3. Cagan, J., Vogel, C.M.: Creating breakthrough products: innovation from product planning to program (2002)
4. Seth, A., Vance, J.M., Oliver, J.H.: Virtual reality for assembly methods prototyping: a review. Virtual Real **15**, 5–20 (2011). https://doi.org/10.1007/s10055-009-0153-y
5. Z Lab Homepage. https://cargocollective.com/zeelab/Taichi-Motion. Accessed 20 Jan 2019
6. Cox, S.: Intention and meaning in young children's drawing. Int. J. Art Des. Educ. **24**, 115–125 (2005). https://doi.org/10.1111/j.1476-8070.2005.00432.x
7. Stanczak, G.C.: Introduction: images, methodologies, and generating social knowledge. In: Visual Research Methods: Image Society, and Representation, pp. 1–21. Sage Publications, Thousand Oaks (2007)
8. Einarsdottir, J., Dockett, S., Perry, B.: Making meaning: children's perspectives expressed through drawings. Early Child Dev. Care **179**, 217–232 (2009). https://doi.org/10.1080/03004430802666999
9. Liew, A.: DIKIW: data, information, knowledge, intelligence, wisdom and their interrelationships. Bus. Manag. Dyn. **2**, 49–62 (2013)
10. Screenshot from the game named The Arena of Valor, by Manhai Li. 20 Jan 2019
11. UXPA: User Experience Practice in the Internet Age. uxpachina.org (2014)
12. Schütte, S.T.W., Eklund, J., Axelsson, J.R.C., Nagamachi, M.: Concepts, methods and tools in kansei engineering. Theor. Issues Ergon. Sci. **5**, 214–231 (2004). https://doi.org/10.1080/1463922021000049980

13. Ginsberg, J., Mohebbi, M.H., Patel, R.S., Brammer, L., Smolinski, M.S., Brilliant, L.: Detecting influenza epidemics using search engine query data. Nature **457**, 1012–1014 (2009). https://doi.org/10.1038/nature07634

14. Zhu, W., Miao, J., Hu, J., Qing, L.: Vehicle detection in driving simulation using extreme learning machine. Neurocomputing **128**, 160–165 (2014). https://doi.org/10.1016/j.neucom.2013.05.052

15. Simonite, T.: What Facebook knows. Technol. Rev. **115**, 42–48 (2012)

16. Mayer-Schonberger, V., Cukier, K.: Big data: a revolution that will transform how we live, work and think (2013)

17. Shi, W.: A generative approach to Chinese Shanshui painting. IEEE Comput. Graph. Appl. **37**, 15–19 (2017). https://doi.org/10.1109/MCG.2017.13

18. Joseph Pine, B., Gilmore, J.H.: Welcome to the experience economy. Harv. Bus. Rev. **76**, 97–105 (1998). https://doi.org/10.1080/00076799800000334

19. Dewey, J.: Having an experience. In: Art as Experience, pp. 39–40. Penguin Group, New York (1934)

New Intelligent Information Technology-Assisted Design Innovation Entrepreneurship Course Potential for User Experience Economy in China

Zhen Liu[1], Zhichao Liu[2,3], Ruiqiu Zhang[1], and Minfang Shen[4(✉)]

[1] School of Design, South China University of Technology,
Guangzhou 510006, People's Republic of China
[2] School of Business Administration, South China University of Technology,
Guangzhou 510641, People's Republic of China
[3] School of Entrepreneurship Education, South China University of Technology,
Guangzhou 510641, People's Republic of China
[4] Institute Office, Harbin Institute of Technology,
Shenzhen 518055, People's Republic of China
shenminfang@hit.edu.cn

Abstract. Currently, there are a number of experience economy and experience design research in China, but it is lack of user experience economy course for design innovation entrepreneurship education. Moreover, using new intelligent information technology has been more considered for business model innovation, and little attention is paid to the discussion of entrepreneurial process. Furthermore, carefully considered experience design is aiming for promising value proposition resulting in entrepreneurial success in experience economy. There is a need for considering new intelligent information technology for user experience design and economy to entrepreneurship education. Therefore, this paper is focused on exploring the potential aspects, such as a business model architecture and an entrepreneurial process model architecture in terms of design innovation and entrepreneurship, a new intelligent information technology approach architecture for entrepreneurship, and a experience design and economy approach architecture for design innovation entrepreneurship, which have been used for establishing a proposed new intelligent information technology-assisted design innovation entrepreneurship course framework for user experience economy. The proposed framework has a triangle structure with three interactive modules, namely, new intelligent information technology module, entrepreneurial module, and experience economy and design module, which contains all the above investigated aspects.

Keywords: User experience · Experience economy · Experience design · Design innovation · Entrepreneurship education · Creative thinking · Intelligent information technology

© Springer Nature Switzerland AG 2019
A. Marcus and W. Wang (Eds.): HCII 2019, LNCS 11586, pp. 300–317, 2019.
https://doi.org/10.1007/978-3-030-23535-2_23

1 Introduction

On May 4, 2015, the General Office of the State Council of China issued the "Implementation Opinions on Deepening the Reform of Innovation and Entrepreneurship Education in Colleges and Universities" that includes the promotion of innovative talent training mechanism and the improvement of the curriculum of innovation and entrepreneurship education [1]. It requires colleges and universities to establish interdisciplinary courses to explore a new mechanisms for cross-disciplinary, and interdisciplinary training of innovative and entrepreneurial talents, and also to promote the transformation of talent cultivation from a single discipline to a multi-disciplinary integration. In response to the opinions of the General Office of the State Council of China, on March 29, 2018, the General Office of the Ministry of Education of China announced the "Notice on Excellence in Deepening the Construction of Reform and Entrepreneurship Education Model Universities in 2018" [2]. The notice calls for the full use of modern information technology to accelerate the construction of innovative entrepreneurship education courses.

Recently, KPMG, the world's leading accounting firm, surveyed nearly 800 technology industry executives and released the 2018 Global Technology Innovation Report [3]. The report points out that the world is currently in an era of technological innovation, which the Internet of Things (IoT), artificial intelligence (AI) and robots will inevitably affect global businesses, where the enterprises that do not take the initiative to seize future trends will be eliminated. Global technology leaders believe that revenue growth has replaced patents and has become the primary indicator for measuring the success of a company's technological innovation. Patents have fallen out of the top three, with market share and return on investment ranked second and third. Meanwhile, they believe that the role of the Chief Information Officer is responsible for promoting innovation within the company rather than the Chief Innovation Officer. However, Chinese respondents most often talk about chief innovation officers.

The collaboration between the key elements of the new intelligent information technology, such as IoT, data analysis, and AI, will create a huge network of intelligent machines in the world, enabling massive business transactions without human intervention. The data they create and share will bring a new information revolution to human work and life. People will be able to use the information from the IoT to deepen their understanding of the world and their lives, and make more appropriate decisions to achieve the best user experience and its economy. The experience economy is based on a developed service economy. In the era of information technology, it is gradually and even large-scale, and called, the fourth stage of economic development after the agricultural economy, industrial economy and service economy stage, or the extension of the service economy. Good product design often means better entrepreneur business performance, especially as the boundaries between hardware, software and services become increasingly blurred.

Lately, McKinsey, the world's leading consulting company, spent five years tracking the design behavior of 300 listed companies in different countries and in different fields, and released a report on the Business Value of Design [4]. The report emphasizes that design requires cross-industry capabilities that break the boundaries between physical, digital, and service design. At the same time, the design is not only about the product, it is an experience.

Therefore, the aim of this paper is to explore the potential of establishing cross-disciplinary, and interdisciplinary design innovation and entrepreneurship education course for achieving user experience economy by implementing new intelligent information technology.

2 Innovation and Entrepreneurship Education

Innovation is building a new production function. Entrepreneurship is essentially establishing a new production function plus a new organization, that is, innovation plus the establishment of a new organization [5]. Innovation education and entrepreneurship education are interlinked in essence. Innovation is the foundation of entrepreneurship. Entrepreneurship is the carrier and realization form of innovation. Usually, the success or failure of a startup depends on the degree of innovation. From the perspective of the relationship between innovation education and entrepreneurship education, the two have the same goal orientation, which aims to cultivate students' innovative spirit and practical ability. The two functions are of the same effect. Entrepreneurship education integrates innovation education into the requirements of entrepreneurship quality. Innovation education focuses on the overall grasp of human development, while entrepreneurship education focuses on how to realize people's self-value [6]. For example, in the United States, innovation education emphasizes that schools should pay more attention to the development of students' individuality, originality and innovation ability while cultivating their comprehensive development [7]. In the UK, under the model of tutorial system, innovation education attaches great importance to cultivating students' self-learning ability, hands-on ability and innovation ability. And that's exactly what entrepreneurs need to start a business.

China's innovation and entrepreneurship education originated from the wave of reform and opening up in the late 1970s. There are eight characteristics of innovation and entrepreneurship education [8]: (1) The government attaches great importance to it; (2) The beginning of the series of courses; (3) The teaching methods are becoming more and more perfect; (4) Some schools have set up special innovation and entrepreneurship teaching projects; (5) Teaching materials Construction has begun to take shape and scale; (6) Under the impetus of the Ministry of Education, many schools have a strong planning and innovation in entrepreneurship education; (7) Many schools have established practical teaching institutions for innovation and entrepreneurship; and (8) Focus Academic research supports the system and depth of innovation and entrepreneurship teaching.

There are also some shortcomings in innovation and entrepreneurship education in China, such as: (1) Marginalization of the discipline status of innovation and entrepreneurship education; (2) Lack of practical teaching in teaching methods; (3) Teaching objects vary from school to school; (4) Teaching content varies from teacher to teacher; (5) Academic research on innovation and entrepreneurship supporting teaching needs to be systematic and deepened; and (6) The degree of curriculum system needs to be improved.

Hence, educators should pay attention to their characteristics and weaknesses when carrying out innovation and entrepreneurship education. At the same time, they should have a detailed understanding of the key factors of innovation and entrepreneurship, i.e. business model and entrepreneurship process.

2.1 Business Model

In order to create new markets and wealth, entrepreneurs first need to consider the innovation of a whole business concept or business model that is a framework for figuring out how to start a company, sell a product, and make a profit [9]. Instead of tweaking existing business models, entrepreneurs create entirely new ones in unconventional ways.

The term business model first appeared in the computer science journal of the 1970s and was used to describe the relationship and structure between data and processes [10], which originally came from the widespread use of spreadsheet software that allows planners to easily modify parameters based on different assumptions to produce different plans [11]. After the rise of e-commerce, a large number of new companies have used their business in different ways in the past, and widely used the term business model in order to distinguish them from traditional operations [11]. However, there is no uniform definition of business model in academia. It can be:

- Operational innovation [12]. It involves using an entirely new operational approach to complete tasks, develop products, provide customer service, or complete other operational activities;
- An activity undertaken to help customers create value [11]. It is the enterprise structure and its partner network formed by enterprises for value creation, value marketing and value provision, so as to generate profitable customer relationship capital that can maintain income flow [13]; and
- The mixture of value streams, revenue streams, and logistics [14]. Business model is the focus of enterprise innovation and the decisive source of value created by enterprises for themselves, suppliers, partners and customers.

In addition, the structural dimension is an endogenous variable of the business model, reflecting the intrinsic characteristics of the business model, which has following eight issues [15]:

Value Proposition. A value proposition is a statement of what the company is addressing for its customers. What kind of value does the company want to offer its customers? With the different value positioning among manufacturers, the activities of manufacturers will also have different differences. Through the design and implementation of all activities of manufacturers, manufacturers will transfer their value proposition to customers and create value for manufacturers and individuals.

Core Strategy. A core strategy is one in which a firm decides how to transform its assets and resources into meaningful value for customers.

Resource Allocation. It refers to the arrangement made by a manufacturer for its assets, resources and processes in order to realize its claim of providing value to customers.

Organizational Design. It refers to the work that a manufacturer may adjust its organizational structure to suit its resource allocation and core strategy.

Value Network. When the manufacturer decides that some operational activities need to be outsourced, it can create value for customers through external business partners.

Product and Service Design. No matter how the manufacturer defines its value proposition, what consumers can feel is the products and services provided by the manufacturer. Therefore, product and service design is very important. The manufacturer shall ensure that its products and services are consistent with its value proposition, and even the supporting measures of the whole product and service shall be consistent with its value proposition. The feeling of consistency will improve customers' perception of the value of products or services, while ignoring any link will result in the loss of the value provided by manufacturers to customers.

Business Revenue Mechanism. The design of a manufacturer's business revenue mechanism determines how fees and charges are charged to customers.

Profit Potential. The purpose of business model innovation is to help manufacturers gain wealth, so profit potential is the most critical factor in business model design.

Further, a business model should has four main elements [16]: (1) the value proposition. A business model describes what value an enterprise provides to its customers and business partners; (2) product or service. Products and services determined by value proposition will link the manufacturer and the customer. They must meet the company's commitment to customer benefits; (3) value architecture. It includes three modules: market design, internal architecture and external value architecture; and (4) revenue model. Revenue model to explain how the firm get her earnings. They can have different sources of profit sources of revenues. When these sources combine, they form a revenue model for the firm.

Business models emphasize value creation. It is an activity to create new value in order to bypass competitors [17]. Business model innovation is an extension of the product, which requires entrepreneurs to dramatically increase existing strategic changes and create thousands of new ideas that allow us to find new themes and directions [9].

In terms of business model innovation, product design should consider following aspects [17]: (1) performance and support, which means how the company contacts customers, what channels it uses, what forms of customer support it provides, and what level of service it provides; (2) information and insight, which refers to the information obtained by the company from customers and the ability to gain insight into information, through which the company can provide customers with unique value; and (3) relationship dynamics, which refers to how the company interacts with customers and through which indicates what kind of customer loyalty the company can cultivate. Moreover, products and services are used for connecting manufacturers with customers. This is determined by value proposition and the company must satisfy the commitment to the customer. When deciding what to offer to satisfy the customer, it also determines what the company should do. The customer interface includes vendor-to-customer, customer-to-vendor, and among customers, which is often with distribution channels and information that the company use to create value for customers [16]. Furthermore, when conducting product design, entrepreneur must consider the following issues [18]: the interests of stakeholders that the company must meet or influence; the benefits and disadvantages of the commodities provided to all stakeholders; capturing the timing of the firm's impact on stakeholders; and Identifying where the company is delivering value. As such, in terms of business model innovation, it is important to consider what kind of customer relationships can be promoted through product and service design activities, and how should vendors apply these relationships [15]? This requires thinking about the impact of product and service design on stakeholders, when and where they are provided. What are the products and what information they can get? This kind of thinking can enable the company to better use this information and create more value for customers. However, creating value for customers does not mean that the company can make profits. Profits can only be determined by the game among suppliers, customers, competitors, substitutes and complements. In order to determine the profit of a company, it is necessary to consider specific resources, resource scarcity, resource substitution, resource imitability, capability unpredictability, network externality, time difficulty, the use of strategy against imitation and the integration of related resources [19].

Therefore, as shown in Fig. 1, in terms of design innovation and entrepreneurship, business model is defined as: taking value proposition as the design goal and forming revenue model with profit potential as the entrepreneurial goal through value architecture design taking product and service design activities as the starting point.

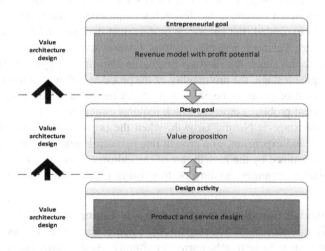

Fig. 1. The business model architecture in terms of design innovation and entrepreneurship (devised by the authors based on the literature).

2.2 Entrepreneurship Process

Entrepreneurship is a complex phenomenon across multiple disciplines. Different disciplines, including economics, psychology, sociology, anthropology and management, observe and study entrepreneurship from their unique research perspectives by using concepts and relevant terms in this field [20]. The entrepreneurial process involves all the events in the process of making a business plan into a real business organization [21]. However, the entrepreneurial process is not only the creation of an organization, but also the process of grasping opportunities, that is, opportunity is the core issue of entrepreneurial research, and the entrepreneurial process is a series of processes centering on the identification, development and utilization of opportunities [22]. Further, the entrepreneurial process is more of a rational, nonlinear and repeatedly revised practical process, including initial opportunity identification, product line construction, organization creation, market transactions and customer feedback [23].

The entrepreneurial process is a dynamic and complex process that needs to be presented in the form of a theoretical model of the entrepreneurial process, which has been recognized in following three types of theoretical models [24]: a linear model of enterprise growth based on the new product development process, a linear model of complex enterprise growth aiming at the staged success of the enterprise, and a dynamic adjustment dominated by the most important driving factors of the model.

A Linear Model of Enterprise Growth Based on the New Product Development Process. It has five stages [25]. The first stage is the Proof-of-principle Stage. In this stage, new organizations have not appeared yet, and the main task of entrepreneurs is to verify the feasibility of innovative technologies. In the second stage, the Prototype Stage, the product has been produced and the organizational structure has also formed its prototype. The third stage is the Model-shop Stage, in which mainly tests the market response of products to improve the feasibility of products. The scale of the organization has been expanded, the necessary professional division of labor has emerged, and the necessary business activities such as finance and marketing have begun to appear. In the fourth stage, the Start-up Stage, the start-up enterprises have entered a mature development stage, the profitability of the products is further improved, and the second generation of products begin to appear. As the organization expands further, more management problems emerge, which requires entrepreneurs to put more energy into it. The fifth stage is Natural Growth, when the organization enters the stage of Natural Growth and expansion. The growth rate is much lower than the start-up stage, and is more determined by the growth rate of the industry. Entrepreneurs start thinking about new strategic changes, holding on to existing market share, or entering a new start-up cycle.

A Linear Model of Complex Enterprise Growth Aiming at the Staged Success of the Enterprise. It consists of five stages [26]. Stage 1: Existence. The main objective of the entrepreneur is to form a business opportunity. At this time, the organizational structure is simple, and the entrepreneur must deal with almost all the affairs. Stage 2: Survival. The goal of investors and entrepreneurial teams is how to make the enterprise larger and enter the next stage. Otherwise, they can only continue to stay in the survival period. If the stagnation period is too long, the cash flow of the enterprise may dry up and the enterprise may go bankrupt. Stage 3: Success. The enterprise has obtained a good income and its organizational scale has begun to take shape. At this time, there may be differences between investors and managers of the enterprise, and some investors hope to withdraw their investment at this time. Another challenge for enterprises at this stage is whether they can timely adjust their strategies in the face of external changes. If they cannot make adjustments smoothly, their development is likely to go backwards. Stage 4: Take-over. The enterprise maintains rapid growth and its organizational function has been quite perfect. At this time, investors begin to look for opportunities to sell the enterprise. Voluntary or involuntary management changes may occur in the enterprise restructuring, which may have a great impact on the operation of the enterprise and even may reverse the development of the enterprise. Stage 5: Resource Maturity: enterprises have obtained enough resources to support the operation of enterprises and achieve economies of scale. However, at this time, enterprises are likely to fall into the misunderstanding of traditional large enterprises, such as lose initiative, be satisfied with the status quo, and be eager to avoid risks, until the market environment changes significantly and forced to change.

A Dynamic Adjustment Dominated by the Most Important Driving Factors of the Model. Entrepreneurial process is a highly dynamic process, in which business opportunities, resources and entrepreneurial team are the most important driving factors [27]. Business opportunity is the core element of the entrepreneurial process. Resources are necessary support for the entrepreneurial process. In order to rationally use and control resources, entrepreneurs often have to try their best to design a delicate and prudent strategy for entrepreneurship, which is often extremely important for new enterprises. Entrepreneurial team is a key component of a new enterprise. The basic qualities necessary for entrepreneurial leaders and entrepreneurial teams are: strong learning ability, ability to deal with adversity freely, integrity, reliability, honest quality, determination, perseverance and creativity, leadership, and communication skills. The model features three core elements forming an inverted triangle with the entrepreneurial team at the bottom of the triangle. In the initial stage of entrepreneurship, the triangle will be inclined to the left due to the large business opportunities and the lack of resources. With the development of enterprises, enterprises will have more resources, but then the original business opportunities may become relatively limited, which leads to another imbalance. Entrepreneurial leaders and teams need to constantly explore greater business opportunities and make rational use of resources to maintain a proper balance in the development of enterprises. It is the actual process of the development of the new enterprise to adjust the three constantly and realize the dynamic equilibrium.

Therefore, as shown in Fig. 2, for design innovation and entrepreneurship, the entrepreneurial process is a the dynamic process to grasp business opportunities, resources, entrepreneurial team advantages, through the new product and service development process, to achieve success of each stage of the enterprise development.

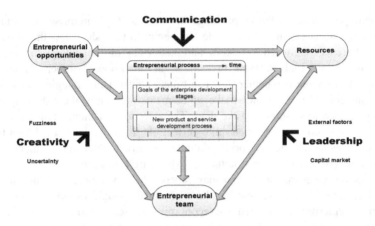

Fig. 2. The entrepreneurial process model architecture in terms of design innovation and entrepreneurship (devised by the authors based on the literature).

3 New Intelligent Information Technology Potential for Entrepreneurship

Intelligent information technology is jointly constructed by information technology and intelligent theory [28]. Information technology is a multi-level, multi-disciplinary integrated technology, which refers to the whole of sensing technology, communication technology, intelligent technology (including computer hardware, software, and AI, artificial neural networks) and control technology. Among them, sensing technology includes sensor technology and measurement technology, such as remote sensing and telemetry technology, which are technologies that enable people to better obtain useful information from the outside world. Communication technology is the technology that transmits information. Intelligent technologies, including computer hardware technology, software technology, artificial intelligence technology and artificial neural networks, can better process and reproduce information. The control technology can intervene the movement state and mode of external things according to the input instruction information (decision information), that is, the technology that utilizes information. The theory of intelligence is a science to explore the mysteries and laws of human intelligence and to reproduce human intelligence in machines. It is the frontier of modern scientific research. At present, the theory and technology of intelligence are mainly in two aspects, of which one is the direct research on the generation, formation and working mechanism of intelligence; the other is to study how to simulate, extend and expand intelligence with artificial methods and how to improve the intelligence level of machines, especially computers, so that machines can become intelligent machine systems with perception, reasoning and decision-making.

With the proliferation of emerging online and web-centric technologies, the intelligent information technologies are gaining increasing attention, and these technologies are designed to make it relatively easy for users to perform complex tasks in fields such as information systems, intelligent agents, AI, and web engineering [29]. In addition, emerging emerging intelligent information technologies, such as the internet plus,

Internet of Things, blockchain, and big data and their analytics, bring new vitality and direction to intelligent information technology. Hence, Fig. 3 summarizes an approach architecture of new intelligent information technology for entrepreneurship potential, which has three levels, namely, intelligence theory, information technology, and entrepreneurship. However, at present, for these new intelligent information technology entrepreneurship researches in China, the focus is on the discussion of business model innovation, and little attention is paid to the discussion of entrepreneurial process.

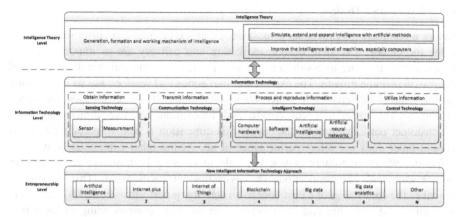

Fig. 3. New intelligent information technology approach architecture for entrepreneurship potential (devised by the authors based on the literature).

4   The Experience Economy

Throughout the history of the development of human society, human society has evolved from the product economy era to the service economy era, and now to the experience economy era [30]. As an extension of service economy, experience economy is the fourth type of economy after agricultural economy, industrial economy and service economy, which emphasizes the sensory satisfaction of customers and attaches importance to the psychological experience of customers when consumer behavior occurs [31]. Experience economy is different from agricultural economy, industrial economy and service economy in terms of production behavior and consumption behavior [32]:

Agricultural economy: the production behavior is based on the production of raw materials; Consumer behavior is based solely on self-sufficiency.

Industrial economy: the production behavior is based on goods manufacturing; Consumer behavior emphasizes functionality and efficiency.

Service economy: emphasize division of labor and product function in production behavior; Consumer behavior is service-oriented.

Experience economy: the production behavior is led by the improvement of service, and the goods are used as props; Consumer behavior pursues the appeal of sensibility and situation, creates activities worth recalling by consumers, and pays attention to the interaction with goods.

The traditional economy mainly focuses on the powerful functions, beautiful appearance and price concessions. The current trend is to shape the sensory experience and thinking identity from the perspective of life and situation, so as to capture the attention of consumers, change consumer behavior, serve as products, and find new survival values and spaces. That is to say, the company focuses on service, and uses goods as the material to create a memoryworthy feeling for consumers to be economically successful.

4.1   Experience Design

Before a company gets revenue, it must design an experience that customers consider value for money. Excellent design, marketing and delivery are as important to the experience as they are to goods and services. Design and innovation will always lead the way in revenue growth. The experience, like goods and services, has its own unique qualities and characteristics, and presents its own unique design challenges. As shown in Fig. 4, The experience for design and innovation has two dimensions [31]: (1) customer participation. At one end of this dimension is passive participation, and the customer does not affect performance at all. At the other extreme is active participation, where customers play a key role in creating performance or generating experiences; and (2) connection, or environmental relationship. This dimension describes the connection of a customer to an activity or performance, that is, one end is absorption and the other end is immersion. In addition, corresponding to these two dimensions, the experience can have a broader four realms, namely, entertainment, Educational, escapist, and esthetic.

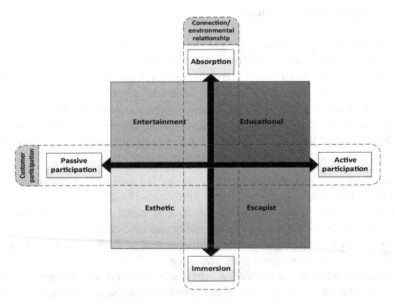

Fig. 4. The characteristics of experiences for design and innovation: two dimensions and four realms (devised by the authors based on the literature).

Further, experience design has become a commercial art like today's product design and process design, with five key experience design principles:

(1) Theme the experience;
(2) Harmonize impressions with positive cues. Although the theme is the foundation, experience must be presented in an indelible impression. The impression is the "takeaway" of experience, which is used to help complete the theme. In order to leave the impression customers wants, the company must give the guest some cues to confirm the nature of the experience. Each cue must support the topic, and any clues should not be inconsistent with the topic;
(3) Eliminate negative cues. Ensuring the integrity of the customer experience requires more than just positive cues. At the same time, it is necessary to eliminate any weakening, contradictory or decentralized subject matter;
(4) Mix in memorabilia. People buy certain goods, mainly for the memories they convey; and
(5) Engage all five senses. Accompanied by a sensory stimulus from experience should support and strengthen its theme. The more senses involved in an experience, the more effective and memorable it is.

However, the use of these five design principles is not a guarantee of success, but also need to consider the law of supply and demand. If companies fail to provide a consistently engaging experience, overprice the value of the experience, or overpay for it, they will certainly face pressure from demand, pricing, or both. Design is an important means for enterprises to adapt to the new trend of social, economic and technological development and meet the new needs of consumers. As a new design concept emerging in the era of experience economy, experience design marks that design has entered a new stage of humanization from standardization and customization, and that design has evolved from product as the core to consumer experience as the core, and from paying attention to the function and economy of things to providing consumers with delightful experience.

Therefore, as indicated in Fig. 5, for design innovation entrepreneurship, the contribution that experience design and economy can offer is to center on the dimension of design services for business services guided by entrepreneurial economic factors, throughout the entire process of commodities, goods, services, and experiences (i.e. extract, make, deliver, and stage), while referring to the five key principles, and two dimensions and four realms of experience design (refer to Fig. 4), to realize the economic value of innovation and entrepreneurship.

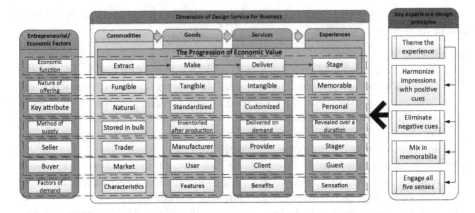

Fig. 5. The experience design and economy approach architecture for design innovation entrepreneurship potential (devised by the authors based on the literature).

4.2   Current Experience Economy and Experience Design Research in China

At present, as the economy grows, there is a boom in experience economy and experience design in China. As shown in Table 1, research on experience economy and experience design covers a number of design-related fields, as well as its related categories and subjects. Design-related fields mainly focus on spatial design, visual communication and product and industrial design. In addition, they also cover fashion design, emotional design and creative culture industry design, interaction experience design, game design, public art design and design management. Spatial design focuses on public space, including commercial and non-profit public spaces, and the discussion of related categories and subjects. The design categories related to the company's branding are the focus of visual communication, including brand website, brand strategy, brand advertising, and brand visual identity. Interestingly, the experience economy and experience design associated with the tourism industry covers many design-related fields, categories and topics.

4.3   Current User Experience Economy Course for Design Education in China

The era of experience economy is coming, and the design education about experience economy and experience design in China is gradually emerging. Unlike the research and applications mentioned above, which have covered a number of aspects of design, the current research on design education of experience economy and experience design in China involves several fields, such as space design [33], visual communication design [34], industrial design [35, 36], and clothing design [37]. Among them, there are only three design courses that respectively cover topics on commercial building interior design [33], industrial design [35], and garment design [37].

5   Discussion and Conclusion

The modern society based on information technology has led to fundamental changes in people's life style. Information culture has swept the whole world and stepped into the era of experience economy. In the era of experience economy, with the continuous innovation of information technology and the development of network, the product is no longer the only important link in the business process [38]. Since the service is mainly a kind of experience, designer needs to consider people's spiritual experience and pay attention to the high-level demand of people's self-realization. To meet personalized needs, designer is required to not only focus on innovating products, but also realize innovative services through design, so as to bring better services to consumers, realize business value and achieve entrepreneurial success. The designer's responsibility shifts from designing good products to achieving better services and experiences through design, satisfying the value propositions of enterprises, consumers and stakeholders, and obtaining commercial benefits. The original concept of design education has been unable to meet the social demand for design talents and such entrepreneurship [39]. From the day of its birth, the design discipline is an interdisciplinary subject of various disciplines such as art, psychology, materials science, aesthetics, literature, engineering, and sociology. With the development of social economy, it continues to absorb more disciplines. Innovation and scientific and technological achievements have led to design innovation that has led to the emergence of design thinking, technological innovation, and business model innovation.

However, currently, there are a number of experience economy and experience design research in China, but it is lack of user experience economy course for design innovation entrepreneurship education. moreover, using new intelligent information technology has been more considered for business model innovation, and little attention is paid to the discussion of entrepreneurial process. Furthermore, carefully considered experience design is aiming for promising value proposition resulting in entrepreneurial success in experience economy. There is a need for considering new intelligent information technology for user experience design and economy to entrepreneurship education. Therefore, this paper is focused on exploring the potential aspects, such as a business model architecture and an entrepreneurial process model architecture in terms of design innovation and entrepreneurship, a new intelligent information technology approach architecture for entrepreneurship, and a experience design and economy approach architecture for design innovation entrepreneurship, which have been used for establishing a proposed new intelligent information technology-assisted design innovation entrepreneurship course framework for user experience economy, as shown in Fig. 6. The framework has a triangle structure with three interactive modules, namely, new intelligent information technology module, entrepreneurial module, and experience economy and design module, which contains all the above investigated aspects. Further research will focus on the creation and demonstration of the course content.

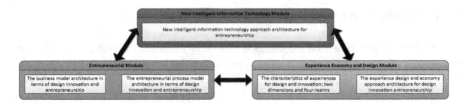

Fig. 6. A proposed new intelligent information technology-assisted design innovation entrepreneurship course framework for user experience economy (devised by the authors).

Table 1. Current experience economy and experience design research in China (devised by the authors based on the literature).

Design-related fields	Design-related category	Design related subject
Interaction experience design	Digital interaction	
Product and industrial design	Industrial product	
	Toy design	
	Ceramic product design	
	Furniture design	
	Campus cultural products	
	Design aesthetic	
	Tourism products	The hotel product
		Tourist souvenir
		Catering products
Emotional design	Product design	
	Packaging design	
	Vegetable market design	
Spatial design	Architectural design	
	Landscape design	
	Interior design	
	Commercial public space	The mall
		Restaurant
		Theater
		Urban commercial complex planning
	Non-profit public space	Public environment facility
		Historical and cultural district
		Museum
	Exhibition Design	Science and technology museum
		Traditional furniture
Fashion design	Experiential clothing	
	Experiential design	
	Clothing brand new retail	

(*continued*)

Table 1. (*continued*)

Design-related fields	Design-related category	Design related subject
Visual communication	Interface design	
	Brand website	
	Brand strategy	
	Brand advertising	
	Brand visual identity	
	Visual culture	
	Packaging design	
	Book design	
	Tourism information communication	Scenic guidance system
		Travel Information
Game design	Digital game	
Public art design	Sculpture	
Design management	Design management process	
Creative culture industry design	The film and television	
	Tourism industry	Film and television tourism
		Sports and leisure
		Marketing

Acknowledgements. The authors wish to thank all the people who provided their time and efforts for the investigation. This research is supported by "Guangdong University Students Innovation and Entrepreneurship Education Research Center" (Project Number 2018A100402), and South China University of Technology (SCUT) project funding x2sj-K5180600.

References

1. China General Office of the State Council: http://www.gov.cn/xinwen/2015-05/13/content_2861327.htm. Accessed 26 Jan 2019
2. Ministry of Education of the People's Republic of China: http://www.moe.gov.cn/srcsite/A08/s5672/201804/t20180411_332854.html. Accessed 26 Jan 2019
3. KPMG Global Technology Innovation: https://info.kpmg.us/techinnovation.html. Accessed 26 Jan 2019
4. McKinsey Business Value of Design: https://www.mckinsey.com/business-functions/mckinsey-design/our-insights/the-business-value-of-design. Accessed 26 Jan 2019
5. Drucker, P.: Innovation and Entrepreneurship. Routledge Classics, New York (1985)
6. Kuratko, D.F.: The emergence of entrepreneurship education: development, trends, and challenges. Entrep. Theory Pract. **29**(5), 577–598 (2005)
7. Wilson, F., Kickul, J., Marlino, D.: Gender, entrepreneurial self-efficacy, and entrepreneurial career intentions: implications for entrepreneurship education. Entrep. Theory Pract. **31**(3), 387–406 (2007)
8. Zhang, Z.: Enlightenment of American University entrepreneurship education to China. Sci. Res. Manag. 26 (2005)

9. Hamel, G.: Innovation as a deep capability. Lead. Lead. **27**(1), 19–24 (2003)
10. Konczal, E.F.: Models are for managers, not mathematicians. J. Syst. Manag. **26**(1), 12–14 (1975)
11. Magretta, J.: Why business models matter. Harv. Bus. Rev. **80**(5), 86–92 (2002)
12. Hammer, M.: Deep Change: How operational innovation can transform your company. Harv. Bus. Rev. **82**(2), 85–93 (2004)
13. Dubosson, M., Osterwalder, A., Pigneur, Y.: Deep change: e-business model design, classification and measurement. Thunderbird Int. Bus. Rev. **44**(1), 5–23 (2002)
14. Amit, R., Zott, C.: Value creation in E-business. Strateg. Manag. J. **22**(6/7), 493–520 (2001)
15. Luo, M.: A review of the theoretical framework of business models. Contemp. Econ. Manag. **31**(11), 1–8 (2009)
16. Stahler, P.: Business Models as an Unit of Analysis for Strategizing. International Workshop on Business Models, Lausanne (2002)
17. Hamel, G.: Leading the Revolution: How to Thrive in Turbulent Times by Making Innovation a Way of Life. Harvard Business School Press, Boston (2000)
18. Mitchell, D., Coles, C.: The Ultimate Competitive Advantage: Secrets of Continually Developing a More Profitable Business Model. Berrett-Koehler Publishers, San Francisco (2003)
19. Afuah, A.: Business Models: A Strategic Management Approach. McGraw-Hill, Boston (2004)
20. Zhang, J., Jiang, Y.: Research and development of entrepreneurship theory. Econ. Dyn. **5**, 71–74 (2003)
21. Carter, N., Gartner, W., Reynolds, P.: Exploring start-up event sequences. J. Bus. Ventur. **11**, 151–166 (1996)
22. Shane, S., Venkatamman, S.: The Promise of entrepreneurship as a field of research. Acad. Manag. Rev. **25**(1), 217–226 (2000)
23. Bhave, M.P.: A process model of entrepreneurial venture creation. J. Bus. Ventur. **9**, 223–242 (1994)
24. Lin, G., Zhang, W., Qiu, Q.: Research review and development trend of entrepreneurial process. Nankai Manag. Rev. **7**(3), 47–50 (2004)
25. Galbraith, J., Venkatamman, S.: The stage of growth. J. Bus. Strategy **3**(1), 70–79 (1982)
26. Churchill, N.C., Lewis, V.L.: The five stages of small business growth. Harv. Bus. Rev. **5**, 30–50 (1983)
27. Timmons, J.A.: New Venture Creation, 5th edn. McGraw-Hill, Irwin (1999)
28. Li, Y.: Discussion on intelligent information technology. Sci. Inf. **14**, 603 (2010)
29. Sugumaran, V.: Intelligent Information Technologies and Applications. IGI Global Snippet, Hershey (2008)
30. Pine II, B.J., Gilmore, J.H.: The Experience Economy: Work Is Theater & Every Business a Stage, 1st edn. Harvard Business School Press, Harvard (1999)
31. Pine, II. B.J., Gilmore, J.H.: Welcome to the experience economy. Harv. Bus. Rev. 98407 (1998)
32. Pine II, B.J., Gilmore, J.H.: The Experience Economy, Updated edn. Harvard Business Review Press, Harvard (2011)
33. Li, M.: Teaching exploration on the interior design for commercial building in the age of experience economy. Huazhong Archit. **10**, 55–57 (2017)
34. Meng, G.: Visual communication design education under the influence of experience economy. Packag. World **5**, 34–35 (2010)

35. Jiang, Z., Liu, X.: Exploration on the reform of industrial design courses in the age of experience economy. Curric. Educ. Res. **20**, 223 (2015)
36. Wang, K.: The development of industrial design education in the era of experience economy. Bus. Inf. **17**, 153–154 (2012)
37. Lu, Y., Ni, W.: The course of "ready-to-wear design" under the background of experience economy. Text. Garment Educ. **31**(1), 53–56 (2016)
38. Pine II, B.J., Korn, K.C.: Infinite Possibility: Creating Customer Value on the Digital Frontier, 1st edn. Berrett-Koehler Publishers, San Francisco (2011)
39. Liu, Q.: Research on the cultivation of design professional innovative talents under the experience economy. Art Educ. **329**(13), 146–147 (2018)

Research on Automatic Fault Diagnosis Technology of IT Equipment Based on Big Data

Xiaomei Liu[(⊠)]

Shandong University of Finance and Economics, 7366 East Second Ring Road,
Lixia District, Jinan, Shandong, China
18660115199@163.com

Abstract. This paper studies the automatic diagnosis technology of large data-based IT equipment faults. By combining traditional IT equipment operation and maintenance system with mobile terminal, users can receive alarms and important performance indicators of network equipment in real time at any time, understand the operation status of network equipment clearly and intuitively, and maintain network equipment remotely through mobile terminal. Now IT equipment centralized operation and maintenance management. The knowledge base of IT equipment is formed by integrating the experience, knowledge, skills, reasoning and synthesizing of many experts in fault diagnosis of IT equipment. A set of general fault diagnosis platform is constructed. The equipment fault can be diagnosed automatically by computer. The normal index of the knowledge base of IT equipment expert is retrieved by the expert system of IT equipment through the technical parameters of the tested equipment, and the reasoning and judgment are carried out. Output of failure components, test results of indicators, causes of failure, treatment measures, etc.

Keywords: IT equipment failure · Big data · Automatic diagnosis · Real-time reception

1 Introduction

With the rapid development of IT technology, the functions and types of IT equipment on-line are increasing day by day, and the popularization scope of automated and intelligent office is becoming wider and wider. For enterprises with IT equipment as the main body, their equipment management level has a direct impact on the development of enterprises [1]. With the increasing scale of enterprise equipment, the proportion of IT equipment in the total fixed assets of enterprises continues to increase. As far as the operation efficiency of the whole enterprise is concerned, the effect of IT equipment management will have a direct impact on it [2]. IT equipment management system can reduce the cost of enterprise equipment management, so as to improve the efficiency of equipment utilization and management, and improve the competitiveness of enterprises in the market [3]. Nowadays, with the rapid development of society, enterprises pay more attention to the construction of information systems. Hardware system and software system are two indispensable parts in the construction of enterprise informationization.

© Springer Nature Switzerland AG 2019
A. Marcus and W. Wang (Eds.): HCII 2019, LNCS 11586, pp. 318–328, 2019.
https://doi.org/10.1007/978-3-030-23535-2_24

Firewall, storage device and switch belong to hardware system equipment. OA, ERP and CRM belong to information application software system. The core of enterprise informationization system is composed of these software and hardware systems, which play a supporting role in the normal operation of enterprises. However, in today's society where science and technology are constantly updating, the characteristics of production equipment are not unchanged. There are significant differences in the level of intelligence, automation and high-speed of equipment. Therefore, it needs to be maintained by manual means, which requires a lot of manpower and material resources. Therefore, once problems arise, it will cause unpredictable losses [5–7]. Therefore, the construction of intelligent equipment maintenance system is of great urgency. In the era of big data, IT equipment expert system can be applied to large-scale and complex dynamic systems with normative knowledge sources, and can collect expert instructions from various aspects, to a large extent, to ensure the scientific rationality of the final conclusions. Therefore, collecting and sorting out the contents of fault diagnosis of IT equipment, building a perfect knowledge base of IT equipment, so as to realize the automatic diagnosis of equipment faults by computer, and realizing the retrieval, reasoning and judgment of IT equipment expert system with equipment technical parameters. Based on this, this paper studies the automatic diagnosis technology of IT equipment faults based on large data.

2 Problems in IT Equipment Management and Maintenance in the Big Data Ages

In the era of big data, the business of enterprises is becoming more and more extensive and needs large-scale and complex information applications. Therefore, it is very important to maintain these software and hardware systems, and the difficulty is increasing. From traditional decentralized IT operation and maintenance management mode to centralized IT operation and maintenance management, user-perceived IT operation and maintenance management replaces machine-oriented IT operation and maintenance management. All of them are the key problems to be solved urgently at present. Therefore, it is urgent to build a scientific and perfect IT operation and maintenance model.

The equipment maintenance and management of IT equipment redundancy enterprises mainly includes three aspects. The first problem is the low efficiency of operation and maintenance. In the actual process of IT operation and maintenance, when events occur and cause impact, it can be found and processed, which causes the quality of user experience can not be improved. Event failures are repetitive and simple problems, resulting in a large amount of energy and time consumed by IT operation and maintenance personnel. The second problem is the lack of efficient mechanism for IT operation and maintenance. It is difficult to find the main reasons accurately and quickly when problems arise due to the diversification of IT failures. It is impossible to contact relevant personnel in time for processing, repairing, or lack of feedback records after solving problems. The third problem is the lack of efficient tools for IT operations and maintenance. IT systems are becoming more and more complex in the era of big data. Network servers, equipment, key business and middleware systems make IT operations and maintenance personnel difficult to deal with. Even deploying and maintaining frequent equipment failures in time will cause business disruption, partly because of the lack of diagnostic tools, event monitoring and automatic system diagnosis.

3 Requirement Analysis of Automatic Diagnosis for IT Equipment System

3.1 IT Equipment Monitoring Objects

The object of automatic diagnosis and monitoring of IT equipment includes software and hardware, as well as various monitoring indicators of software and hardware. The monitoring indicators of device host server include IO load ratio, connectivity, disk utilization, memory utilization, network card sending flow, etc. CPU load and port sending flow are the key contents of router monitoring indicators; the monitoring indicators of three-tier switch include port receiving flow, memory utilization rate, CPU load and port sending flow; besides, there are firewalls. Monitoring indicators, database monitoring indicators, storage equipment monitoring indicators and application system monitoring indicators.

3.2 IT Equipment Monitoring and Early Warning, User Perception and Equipment Value Output

Monitoring indicators of IT equipment are the basis and prerequisite for the realization of early warning indicators. Therefore, it is necessary to include interval early warning, upper limit early warning and off-line early warning, which can automatically generate system alarm information and timely inform relevant leaders and managers. Change the traditional IT operation and maintenance system currently used, build a user-oriented IT equipment operation and maintenance system, enhance user perception, real-time understanding of the operation status of equipment under the support of mobile terminals and other means. Through the monitoring of a large number of performance data by IT equipment, data mining and analysis, so that the value output of IT equipment operation and maintenance system can be effectively formed.

4 Model of SOM Neural Network Based on Large Data Artificial Intelligence

The self-organizing feature map neural network consists of two layers: input layer and output layer. The input layer of the network belongs to the one-dimensional matrix of the input mode, and the number of neuron nodes is determined by the dimension of the input eigenvector. Through weights, the competition layer and neurons of the input layer are connected. When the input signal is received by the network, the corresponding output layer neurons of the mapping will be excited.

When learning SOM neural network, the weights ω_{ij} of network connection are assigned to random values in the [0,1] interval, and input vectors $X = [x_1, x_2, \ldots, x_n]^T$ are provided to the network.

There is unit C which is the best matching of input neurons. Neurons which are laterally connected with the best matching unit C in its neighborhood N_c to be excitatory C, while the other neurons outer of N_c are inhibited and the output is 0. Specific application steps include:

The first step is to set the input vector, i.e. the set of fault symptoms $X = [x_1, x_2, \ldots, x_n]^T$, which corresponds to the weight coefficient i of the neuron to form a weighted vector $W_i = [w_{i0}, w_{i1}, \ldots, w_{in}]^T$. In the absence of feedback, the steady output value of the neuron can be seen in formula (1):

$$y_i = \sum_{j=1}^{n} w_{ij} x_j = W_i^t X \tag{1}$$

The second step is to find the neuron i when the maximum value y_i is obtained, then it is the best matching unit. The third step is to define a topological neighborhood N_c of the best matching unit C, so that the output of N_c's outer unit is 0 and the output of N_c's inner unit is 1, so that the network has a clustering function. The fourth step is to train the weights by formula (2):

$$\begin{cases} w_{ij}(t+1) = w_{ij}(t) + \alpha(t)[x_i(t) - w_{ij}(t)]; & i \in N_c \\ w_{ij}(t+1) = w_{ij}(t); & i \notin N_c \end{cases} \tag{2}$$

In the formula, $0 << 1$ is the learning factor. After weight training, return to the second step and stop when the requirement $\alpha(t)$ or the r N_c is met. The fifth step is to input the next input vector into the first step for the next round of learning, and stop when all the samples are finished.

5 Overall Design of IT Equipment Management and Monitoring System in Five Data Ages

IT equipment management monitoring system follows the following technical development route: reliable and mature software system is the prerequisite for system operation, through mature and advanced object-oriented third-party software and development tools. The system is based on DWR + SSH framework to build a scalable and highly reliable system. Based on the core server operating system, the database server uses AIX operating system to ensure the reliability, security, convenience and stability of the server. The Sql Server database is used in the database. RAID technology is used in the information data storage system, which can prevent the loss of key data and enhance the reliability of the storage system.

5.1 Architecture Design of IT Equipment Management Monitoring System

Unified monitoring application layer: unified alarm platform, unified report platform, unified display platform, decision-making analysis platform; unified monitoring analysis layer: unified monitoring analysis platform, business monitoring and analysis of each monitoring system; large data layer, which is essentially integrated data cleaning, processing system, including cleaning raw data through ETL tools, storage and calculation of large data platform; According to the acquisition layer, the raw data collected in this layer include bypass, agent, log capture, SNMP, Flume, Agent. Mobile terminals can maintain channels, monitor important performance indicators and so on, so as to fully grasp the operation status of users'IT equipment. Figure 1 shows the architecture of IT equipment management monitoring system.

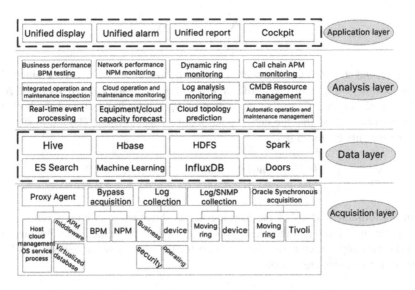

Fig. 1. IT equipment management monitoring system architecture

5.2   Network Design of IT Equipment Management Monitoring System

Wide area network interconnection mainly provides access system for mobile terminal users; internal local area network can connect local area network users, control the operation of business processing application software, and access external mobile terminal network; firewall can connect internal LAN core switching system to ensure the connection and access of internal and external networks, and open part of resources in accordance with certain rules. Restrict the unsafe access objects and support VPN, so that the outgoing personnel can access the internal LAN through NPM network traffic collected by hard probes at the front-end of business, application host, server, middleware, etc., through the existing data warehouse and the collection of network traffic for business, application, etc., and complete the end-to-end real-time network traffic by combining the two data acquisition to achieve the end-to-end real-time network traffic. Analysis and performance prediction; Provide real-time network KPI analysis and alarm; Provide historical traffic backtracking analysis, accurate fault location; Provide virtual machine and cloud network performance monitoring and analysis; Fig. 2 is the network design of IT equipment management monitoring system.

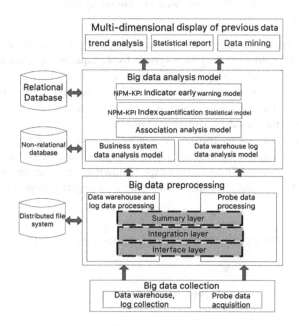

Fig. 2. Network design of IT equipment management monitoring system

5.3 Module Design of IT Equipment Management Monitoring System

Performance indicators monitoring, mobile terminals, data analysis, topology display, alarm centralized monitoring, maintenance channels and other modules are the key components of IT equipment management monitoring. Topology display can provide information in the form of topology and use multiple topology maps to intuitively grasp the use and relevance of current equipment. Centralized alarm monitoring can centralize the alarm information issued by the equipment; performance indicators monitoring can analyze and monitor the performance parameters of the equipment, and provide intuitive performance data; combined with historical data, a comprehensive analysis and exploration is carried out, and a dynamic baseline analysis model is built to predict the trend of future performance indicators, when the predicted value deviates from the actual collected value. When it exists, there will be performance event alarms, which will reduce the number of false alarms and missed alarms and improve the accuracy of alarms. Through this function maintenance channel, network equipment can be maintained and connected. Mobile terminal receives all kinds of important network indicators and alarm information in real time, and maintains network devices through maintenance channels on mobile terminal.

6 Analysis and Design of 6 IT Equipment Expert Automatic Diagnosis System

6.1 Architecture of Expert Automatic Diagnosis System for IT Equipment

Fault diagnosis knowledge system and manual computer program are two key modules to construct expert automatic diagnosis system for IT equipment. They can accurately judge fault problems and take appropriate measures to deal with them. Generally, the problem that the fault diagnosis expert system of IT equipment can solve is reasoning on the basis of incomplete information and incomplete conditions, and finally comes to a conclusion. Integrating database, inference engine, human-computer interaction interface, knowledge management, knowledge acquisition and database management are the main contents of building the structure of fault diagnosis expert system for IT equipment. Inference engine and IT equipment expert knowledge base are the core parts of the system. Figure 3 shows the structure of fault diagnosis expert system for IT equipment.

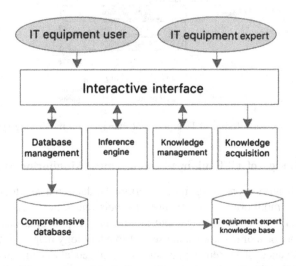

Fig. 3. The structure of fault diagnosis expert system for IT equipment

6.2 Construction of Expert Knowledge Base for Automatic Diagnosis of IT Equipment

The experience judgment knowledge of fault diagnosis experts is stored in the expert knowledge base of IT equipment, which can play a significant role in the process of fault diagnosis conclusion and problem solving [9]. Knowledge management, knowledge acquisition and knowledge representation are the main contents of constructing IT equipment expert knowledge base. Knowledge acquisition is to extract equipment technical parameters and expert fault diagnosis knowledge, summarize and summarize them, encode them to meet the application needs of computers, and carry out automatic fault diagnosis operation on the basis of computers. Generally speaking, its acquisition mode is manual operation, first of all, it needs to obtain preliminary instructions to sort out and improve the original diagnostic instructions; then it needs to process and process the original knowledge, which is executed by IT equipment experts; the third stage IT equipment experts need to judge the knowledge. In fact, knowledge representation can describe fault diagnosis knowledge, symbolize and deal with knowledge situationally. Knowledge representation method is the main content of the research and design of data structure, while storing and describing computer knowledge code. Knowledge management is based on the knowledge of man-machine interaction section control and control system.

6.3   Inference Machine for IT Equipment

In the computer program, the reasoning machine of IT equipment can be divided, and the reasoning process can be completed according to the corresponding steps. When determining the available rules, it is necessary to use IT device inference engine and select the verified control strategy to execute the available rules. Rules can be used to complete the task reasoning of IT equipment inference engine. Rule reasoning is based on rules in the expert knowledge base of fault diagnosis of IT equipment.

7   Design of Automatic Fault Diagnosis System for IT Equipment

7.1   Hardware Composition of IT Equipment

The tested equipment, computer, printer and display are the main components of the hardware of the automatic fault diagnosis system for IT equipment. Figure 4 shows the hardware composition of the system for IT equipment.

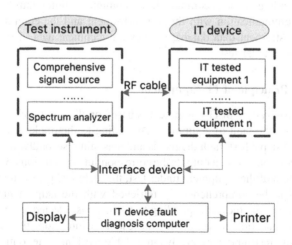

Fig. 4. Hardware composition of IT equipment system

7.2   IT Equipment Software Composition

The software of automatic fault diagnosis system for IT equipment includes instrument control module, equipment control module, man-machine interface, communication control module, expert system, etc. Figure 5 shows the software structure of the automatic fault diagnosis system for IT equipment.

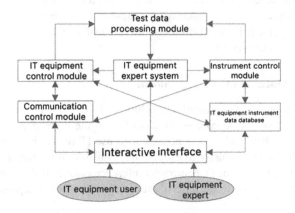

Fig. 5. Software structure of automatic fault diagnosis system for IT equipment

The control module of IT equipment can stabilize the working parameters of the equipment under test so as to make it stable in the corresponding working state; the test data processing module mainly collects the information of the instrument control module and the equipment control module, and provides information input for the expert system of IT equipment; the instrument control module mainly controls the instruments used in the test process, and according to the use status of the instrument according to the test indicators. In addition, the instrument is automatically adjusted and the corresponding work is completed; the communication control module mainly completes the communication with the test instrument and the equipment under test; the equipment instrument data database stores the technical data of the device under test and the device under test.

7.3   Working Principle of IT Equipment

The fault diagnosis system of IT equipment is based on the ability of computer to automatically diagnose the fault of equipment. According to the implementation, it can be divided into three steps: first, fault diagnosis and reasoning; secondly, it needs to test the technical indicators; and third, it outputs the corresponding conclusions. When testing the technical indicators of the equipment under test, the technical parameters of the current equipment need to be comprehensively retrieved with the help of human-computer interaction interface, and the corresponding test scheme is selected to ensure the correct communication connection mode. Starting the test of the indicators, the equipment under test and the testing instrument are always in a stable working state, outputting effective results, and summarizing and sorting out the test results. As a result, we can get scientific and reasonable technical parameters under test. The second step is to retrieve the normal indexes of expert knowledge base in the IT equipment expert system based on the technical parameters of the equipment under test, and output diagnostic conclusions through reasoning and judgment. If the test scheme is not completed, we need to continue testing the next index to ensure that the test scheme can be completed eventually. It is necessary to record and print the detection time and the related content of the whole process. Figure 6 shows the process of fault diagnosis expert system for IT equipment.

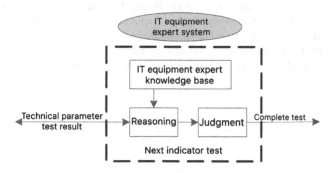

Fig. 6. Processing process of fault diagnosis expert system for IT equipment

8   Conclusion

In this paper, based on large data, the automatic diagnosis technology of IT equipment fault is studied. By combining traditional IT equipment operation and maintenance system with mobile terminal, users can receive alarms and important performance indicators of network equipment in real time at any time, understand the operation status of network equipment clearly and intuitively, maintain network equipment remotely through mobile terminal, and realize IT establishment. Centralized operation and maintenance management. The contents of fault diagnosis of IT equipment are collected and sorted out, and a complete knowledge base of IT equipment is constructed to realize computer automatic fault diagnosis. The retrieval, reasoning and judgment of the expert system of IT equipment are realized by combining the technical parameters of the equipment. The fault components, index test results, fault causes and treatment measures are output.

References

1. Delayed Spring: Design and practical value of IT equipment maintenance system. Inf. Syst. Eng. **11**(20), 111–112 (2016)
2. Kebin, C., Li, B., Xu, X., et al.: Automatic diagnosis and location of thermal faults of electrical equipment based on image enhancement technology. Infrared Technol. **36**(2), 162–168 (2014)

3. Jing, E., Li, K., Meng, F., et al.: China Financ. Comput. **4**, 35–41 (2018)
4. Wang Hui, L.: Research on fault diagnosis and prediction of key components of rotating machinery equipment. Silicon Valley **23**, 54–55 (2014)
5. Taoyuan, L.: Design and Implementation of Enterprise IT Equipment Operation and Maintenance Management System Based on ITIL. Liaoning University, Shenyang (2016)
6. Si, J., Ma, J., Niu, J.: Intelligent fault diagnosis expert system based on fuzzy neural network. Vib. Impact **36**(4), 164–171 (2017)
7. Feng, S.: Design and Implementation of Web-based Integrated Monitoring System for IT Services. Xiamen University, Xiamen (2014)
8. Wenbo, G.: Application of fault diagnosis technology in maintenance of modern mine mechanical and electrical equipment. Mech. Manag. Dev. **32**(11), 52–53 (2017)
9. Research on Intelligent Management System Architecture of IT Equipment of Li Zhongxu. BYC Company. Beijing Jiaotong University, Beijing (2015)
10. Xu, P.: Data Center floor air supply and IT equipment cabinet heat dissipation CFD simulation methods summary and comparison. Build. Energy Sav. **42**(8), 38–43 (2014)

The Purpose Quadrant: A Collaborative Workshop Method to Brand UX Teams and Raise Their Reputation in Organizations

Alexandra Matz[1]([⊠]) and Anja Laufer[2]([⊠])

[1] ICD User Experience, SAP SE, Walldorf, Germany
alexandra.matz@sap.com
[2] Products and Innovation GRC, SAP SE, Walldorf, Germany
anja.laufer@sap.com

Abstract. Design and User Experience (UX) of products and services today are recognized as key differentiators. Accordingly, the respective teams in organizations have grown both in size and relevance.

However, UX and other creative teams are often included too late in projects. Sometimes they are only called in to fix a user interface at the last minute before shipment and without thoroughly researched user needs or problems. Even though the Return of Investment of UX work can be determined [28] and the value of design and UX in businesses manifested [39], the reputation of these teams still has the potential to improve.

Purpose has become an integral element in branding. Purpose-led companies perform better and products designed with a purpose resonate with customers as they match their quest for the product which does the job they need to get done [2]. Our research shows that UX teams often cannot clearly communicate how they are adding value to their projects, organizations or society. However, a purpose, a raison d'être, and an understanding of everybody's contribution to a larger whole is key to a successful, recognized and valued team. We argue that by closing the 'purpose gap', the reputation and success of UX teams can be increased. This paper discusses a new method enabling UX teams to jointly develop their purpose statement and thus raise their standing and reputation.

Keywords: User Experience · Purpose · Design Thinking · Collaboration · Branding · User centered design · User research

1 Introduction

Creative professionals in agencies and organizations today are more valued and recognized than ever before [27]. The number of UX professionals in large enterprises started to grow significantly [5]. As devices became smaller and more efficient over the last years, mobile productivity tools, software and apps do not only have to work but also need to be easy to use and beautiful to look at. Therefore, UX was put into the spotlight and became more important. UX can no longer be passed by if a company wants to launch commercially successful products. The advent and penetration of Design Thinking throughout businesses underpinned the importance of diverse teams

© Springer Nature Switzerland AG 2019
A. Marcus and W. Wang (Eds.): HCII 2019, LNCS 11586, pp. 329–345, 2019.
https://doi.org/10.1007/978-3-030-23535-2_25

working together, creating empathy for users, prototyping and iterating throughout the design and development process.

Yet, the day-to-day practice shows that UX and creative teams are not always at the forefront when new projects are launched or during the early definition phases when UX also could add value. There are reports of User Experience professionals being referred to as "pixel-pushers", making things nice at the last moment [3] or, especially in the context of Design Thinking, being labelled "post-it heroes" whose main skill is to cover walls and walls with sticky notes [16]. These examples indicate that, even though the value of design work [28] and the Return of Investment (ROI) of UX can be communicated [39], the reputation of the teams has room for improvement. In our research we noted that UX teams do work on so-called mission statements, for example, defining them in all-hands meetings, sometimes deriving them top-down, sometimes in the groups themselves. Yet, we discovered that most of the times the teams did not communicate these statements regularly nor were they known to their stakeholders, which triggered our research question why this is the case.

This paper discusses a method which enables UX teams to collaboratively define a purpose statement and use this to communicate their added value to their Lines of Business, company, stakeholders and customers. In this way, they brand their team by laying out what makes them special and what their key differentiating benefits are. Typically, UX teams are made up of individuals with diverse qualifications and experiences. This diversity is why it is even more important for a UX team to find and formulate a common purpose with which everybody in the team can identify.

The Purpose Quadrant method is based on a collaborative, interactive workshop set-up and uniquely combines elements of Design Thinking, cognitive psychology, UX as well as experience marketing, specifically branding. The collaborative and interactive set-up is essential. We discovered that a normal meeting, e.g. with everybody sitting down in a meeting or conference room to discuss a team's purpose would not result in a statement which (a) all team members would feel they have contributed to, (b) uncovers the key differentiating attributes of the team and (c), connects the team with a 'higher purpose'.

The method is composed of four main steps, to allow for small and incremental buckets of work and to stimulate both emotional and functional ideas: (1) Building the purpose quadrant, (2) adding benefits and impacts, (3) composing the purpose statement and (4) voting for the final purpose statement.

The Purpose Quadrant consists of four cluster areas which all participants need to embrace as they build up the Quadrant. With a focus on their current job, each participant is asked to brainstorm and note down on sticky notes (a) what they really like doing, (b) what they as a team can do really well, (c) what makes them happy in their everyday job as a team, (d) what only they as a team and nobody else in the organization can do. These four categories build the Purpose Quadrant. The participants write down as much data as possible and then present their items to the group, all under strict timekeeping on the part of the moderators. After a clustering the group votes on the three most important items from all four quadrants to take forward.

In the second step, all participants are instructed to brainstorm and write down what benefits these quadrant items create for their organization, company, customers or the society, and what their larger-scale impacts are.

Third, with all the data collected and visible, the teams start to compose their purpose statement, based on the impacts, benefits and top-rated items from the Purpose Quadrant. The statement must adhere to certain characteristics such as: be inspirational, authentic, empowering and future-oriented.

Finally, all groups present their purpose statements and the entire team votes to select a single, joint one.

This workshop method was successfully applied with several teams of the User Experience and Innovation organizations at SAP SE (a provider of enterprise software in the cloud and on-premise), as well as with individuals at the Design District Festival 2018 in Zagreb, Croatia. All workshops were completed successfully within 2.5 h even those conducted simultaneously with teams spread across the globe.

Our findings are based on post-workshop feedback through interviews with individual workshop participants. In these interviews, participants pointed out that their purpose statement represents them as a team member as well as the team itself. All interviewees indicated that they use their purpose statement e.g. in presentations or email-signatures. Further, participants stated that the method helped them to understand their team's current and future role and that their teams benefit both in terms of team-building and a stronger confidence in their added value to their organization and beyond.

The method can be regarded as new, as - to the best of our knowledge - we have combined multiple creative and group dynamics techniques in a step-by-step approach for best results. The method paces the group through the process of collaboratively brainstorming and generating their very own purpose statement rather than trying to come up with a purpose statement in an unstructured discussion or working on a predetermined statement (e.g. a purpose statement handed down from management level).

Further research needs to include a larger participant sample and extended pre- and post-workshop surveys and interviews. This will enable us to compare a team's condition and ability to use their purpose statement to create and grow their brand both before and after applying the method.

In the following we present the importance and context of purpose, the detailed process and elements of the "Purpose Quadrant" method and related findings of our study.

2   Purpose and Its Relevance to Branding UX Teams

There is no singularly applicable and accepted definition for "purpose". Instead, plenty of explanations and definitions are in use for the term, like 'The reason for which something is done or created or for which something exists' [34]. Émile Durkheim specified that 'Life is said to be intolerable unless some reason for existing is involved, some purpose justifying life's trials' [9]. It can also mean to give personal meaning to all experiences. Purpose is not only relevant for individuals but also can bring together a group of people. This is particularly true for teams of professionals expected to achieve defined business objectives for a company or institution. Without a defined purpose, short-term goals lead nowhere and people start to engage in undirected and indiscriminate activities [9]. Investing time and effort in meaningless and unimportant activities is something to be avoided, especially in a professional environment. Or to put it another way: A common purpose can help set the team on their path, gives direction and engenders the energy needed to perform successfully. It also results in better contributions to a company's goals and priorities [18]. The team leaders play a crucial role in this: if they embrace the purpose-driven approach and are able to illustrate how important the team's purpose or the company's purpose is to their own daily work and decision making, they inspire their teams to think about their purpose and their contributions as well [14].

2.1 Purpose, Vision, Mission and Branding

When discussing purpose, the terms "mission" and "vision" also need to be discussed as these words are sometimes confused. A mission statement defines why a company or organization exists and what it does, thus giving management and employees a focal point for the near future. A vision statement, in contrast, explains where a company imagines itself to be long term [19].

Moreover, it is crucial not to confuse brand with purpose but consider purpose being an elemental part of a company's business success as it strongly correlates with trust of consumers, customers and employees [13]. A brand is meant to be a unique attribute of a specific product or service, such that people easily recognize it as belonging to the company and quickly remember its values [31].

There are strong indications that branding and usability go hand in hand. Branding is one of the essential parts of a website and must provide engaging usability for the user [15]. Ritter and Winterbottom [35] state that 'UX gives a brand the edge to really stand out against competitors'. Good UX influences the brand and can help to push it to new heights.

It seems ironic that the very people (i.e. UX professionals) who are pivotal for the success of a product or service suffer from their own brandlessness within their organizations. This triggered our methods research: Why not get UX teams to use purpose as an element to brand their work and values?

2.2 Business Value of UX Teams

Before the turn of the century UX Design was not seriously considered or known to contribute to business value, or to have a serious effect on it [40]. While this has improved since, in some business sectors UX is still not seen as being essential to the success of the company. Some business areas do not know the advantages and benefits of good UX design or are not convinced of its added value. Thus, it is important to involve stakeholders and managers at an early stage – at best long before a project starts - to get them to understand how UX can support their work. If the UX professional is able to 'translate UX activities into stakeholder goals' managers and stakeholders are much more likely to involve UX and thus raise the awareness of UX within their organization [21, 36]. Once awareness has been created, it is necessary to include UX in the entire life cycle of a product [6]. However to 'truly transform the enterprise experience, it must become part of the larger organization's DNA which means weaving UX into its culture, its standard operating procedures, and decision making' [32]. Fortunately, nowadays the impact of UX Design is being noticed and appreciated more and more. Large, well-known companies like Google and Apple consider UX to be one of their key factors for success [29].

2.3 Individual Purpose and Purpose-Driven Organizations

People spent most of their time at work, and so it is not surprising that employees demand recognition for their work and contribution to the company's success [1]. In large corporations in particular, it is hard for employees to identify their own contribution in the organization's overall achievements and to reflect where and how they managed to influence their company's performance. This is also true for UX teams and professionals - especially in large companies it is difficult for them to detect their wide range of influence [10]. If people don't see that they add value, they do not feel related to the organization and its purpose, and this potentially leads to a deterioration of trust [13]. The global purpose of a company usually is quite broad and tends to be phrased in rather a general way. This makes it difficult for individuals to see their own values represented. Consequently, we recommend that employees and teams both actively work to understand their company's purpose and come up with their own purpose which reflects their values and benefits.

SAP's CEO Bill McDermott confirmed the importance of a company purpose for employees by stating in an interview [22] that SAP was purpose-driven even before a purpose-driven brand became more popular. 'Not just because it is the right thing to do but because it's the smart thing to do. This is a generation that is inspired by purpose, and our purpose is to help the world run better' [11]. He emphasizes the importance that people feeling personally connected with the company's purpose. This is underpinned by the fact that employees are five times more likely to stay with an employer that is guided by a convincing purpose. Furthermore, research shows that purpose-driven companies perform ten to fifteen times better in Standard & Poor's ratings than companies which are not [11].

Another factor to consider is that in today's business environments many employees and freelancers work remotely or in distributed teams from different locations all over the world. And these numbers are increasing, as per Luk and Brown who state that 'The global mobile workforce is set to increase from 1.45 billion in 2016, accounting for 38.8% of the global workforce, to 1.87 billion in 2022, accounting for 42.5% of the global workforce' [25]. This fact makes it even more necessary to have a common purpose that keeps the teams and their members motivated to work collaboratively and push product design and development into the right direction [12].

3 Purpose Quadrant: The Method

The request which triggered the development of the Purpose Quadrant came from a UX team manager from SAP SE. She/he? wanted us to facilitate a 30-min slot in her/his weekly team meeting to help the team devise a purpose statement. Based on the findings from the research outlined above it was obvious that a simple 30-min discussion would not deliver an ambitious and reputation-changing purpose statement for the team. This is when we decided to meet this challenge in a systematic way, which resulted in the Purpose Quadrant Method.

In this chapter we will outline this method in more detail.

3.1 Study Group Setup

We will document the Purpose Quadrant method as used for two exemplary teams at SAP. These teams are good representations of other SAP teams with regard to team size, knowledge and skills set, as well as professional and locational diversity. The first team (study group A) consisted of 25 UX specialists distributed across three locations (Germany, India and Canada). The 10-member team of study group B was based in one location (Germany), and had a diverse mix of UX specialists, marketeers, innovation experts as well as developers.

Study group C consisted of 5 voluntary participants of a workshop at the Design District Festival in Zagreb, Croatia. The participants had backgrounds in various design disciplines, and all worked for different agencies or companies. This gives a clear variance to teams A and B, as the participants did not attend the workshop as part of a team but as individuals in their own right. As such the results from study group C are not comparable to those of study group A and B. However, as the method was applied successfully for this "individualistic" setup, we will discuss these results as well, especially as they document that the method can also be applied to individual creative professionals such as freelancers. Moreover, this aspect offers an outlook and opportunities for further research.

Both study groups A and B were randomly subdivided into smaller groups of 5–7 members each. Study group A's Canadian team members formed a group of only two. A set of basic rules was agreed upon with the team members, that is: regardless of their hierarchy level, seniority or any other factor, all team members, their opinions and concerns are treated and valued equally. This was to avoid a purpose statement being handed down or influenced from management, which could result in the purpose developed by the team not being accepted. In contrast to top-down management approaches, a non-hierarchical environment is required to ensure that everyone feels listened to and valued, and that every input is equally appreciated [26]. Only then does the result reflect the opinion and ideas of all members, both locally and remotely, and participants identify with the purpose statement generated. This workshop setup, with its parallel workstreams in the different locations, proved to be one key success factor of the method.

The individuals in study group C were not part of a team and thus no groups were formed. This allowed everyone to develop their own purpose statement.

3.2 Preconditions and Preparations

In Design Thinking projects and (User Experience) Design activities, conducting user research is a widely used and important approach at the beginning of a project. The goal of this research is to get an understanding of, and empathy for, the needs and pain points of the people for whom a team designs and develops. These might be end-users of software, or stakeholders and clients who are involved in processes or are the recipients of services. UX teams often act as an internal agency between an organization's various departments, for example consulting, marketing, and development. Therefore, as the end users of the team's UX services, a UX team's stakeholders and clients need to be interviewed to understand their needs and expectations for services around UX design or research. Hence, for the "Purpose Quadrant method", these research activities must be executed before, and the results be available and visible, during the workshop. Any ideas and findings derived in the workshop must be reviewed against the impact they might have on a team's (internal) customers and end-users. It must be clear to the team which job they are hired and paid for by their stakeholders [2]. The research results and an understanding of the Jobs-To-Be-Done are the basis that supports the bottom-up, team-internal activity of creating a purpose statement that the team identifies with and that also resonates with the team's audience. The topic of researching the stakeholder group is not part of this research paper as this is thoroughly discussed in the respective body of knowledge. Nevertheless, it is important to note that both study group A and B (and some individuals in study group C) reported that, in particular, their acceptance and standing within their organizations and stakeholders could be improved. For study group A and B, this was one of the key factors mentioned in their workshop briefing.

While study group A had conducted research interviews with several stakeholders about a year before the actual workshop, study group B conducted a small survey to understand their stakeholders' expectations of their team shortly before the workshop. As no communication ahead of the workshop was possible with the members of study group C, upfront research with these participant's stakeholders was not an option.

Our review of the manager's initial briefs revealed that a meeting or round table discussion would not work for generating a team purpose. Therefore, we decided to dedicate 2.5-h in a workshop setting to this task, with all team members expected to participate in person at their respective location. As mentioned before, integrating remote teams is of utmost importance for the success of the method and for a purpose statement that is embraced by all teams at all locations. The goal must be for all team members to be included in the activity, regardless of their office location. Yet, there are limitations due to time zone differences, and these also affected study group A. With our guidance, this team formed 5 sub-groups, two each in Germany and India, and one in Canada. In preparation, each location had reserved a room for the duration of the workshop, with additional buffer time before and after. The teams in Germany and India were connected live via video conferencing, with additional video cameras and screen-sharing facilities installed. While the team in Canada could not be synched into the same session due to the vast time zone stretch, they were instructed and facilitated by us in a separate session a few hours later the same day. They conducted the Purpose Quadrant method just as the other teams did, with the only difference that they could not live-share their intermediate results with the German and Indian groups. These multi-location workshop settings need to be planned and tested thoroughly in advance, to avoid delays and technical problems during the actual workshop.

3.3   Method Considerations and Implications

We used different methods based on creative problem-solving techniques such as documented by Oswald [33] and the design thinking methodology. These include brainstorming to generate as many items and ideas as possible, and clustering (affinity diagrams) to give the items a structure and enable prioritization. By voting individual items and ideas up and down in priority, the vast amount of ideas is condensed, thus providing guidance and direction for the team on their move forward.

To avoid lengthy discussions and the possibility of dominant team members overruling others during the activities, 'silent' brainstorming was applied as a key method. Silent in this context refers to people noting down on sticky notes as many of their ideas as possible (one idea per note), without talking to each other during the brainstorming. Afterwards, each team member has a set amount of time (monitored by the workshop leads) to share their ideas with the others and pin the sticky notes to the board.

In general, brainstorming is meant to trigger creative, unexpected and great ideas. But this is only one of the advantages brainstorming offers on the way to a new or better solution or while solving a problem. Brainstorming does not only help create an idea but encourages people to generate as many ideas as possible in a defined time slot. In addition, it enables participants to build on the ideas of others. That way participants come up with new ideas even after they thought they had written it all down before [20].

To achieve the best outcome from a brainstorming session, it is recommended to work in a diverse team and group setup, ideally mixing people from different locations, professions or disciplines, and of various ages and genders. In brainstorming together, they can illuminate the problem from different perspectives, rather than all taking the same angle on it. Diverse teams develop more creative solutions [7, 23].

Brainstorming is not only about solving problems and creating new, fresh ideas. A well-facilitated brainstorming session can 'help your team build consensus, recognize common goals, and [...] have positive outcomes on attitudes and relationships. Participants feel included, respected, and valued for their input' [24]. The high number of data points (visible in the form of sticky notes) in each of the activities and across all our study groups proved it.

3.4   The Purpose Quadrant Process During the Workshop

Phase 1 – Setting Up the Groups and Introducing the Method
In the study groups A and B, we collaborated with the team managers. They welcomed the team to the workshop and introduced its goal. Following on from this, we outlined the Purpose Quadrant method and explained the importance of purpose. Using a team building warm-up exercise, the teams of study groups A and B were split up in diverse sub-groups (Fig. 1).

We did not form groups for study group C, as the participants were individual design professionals and wanted to develop their own personal purpose statement.

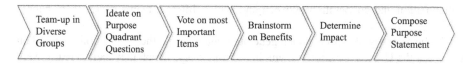

Fig. 1. Process overview of the Purpose Quadrant method.

Phase 2 – Ideating on the Purpose Quadrant Questions
Following the group setup, the key step of the method, the Purpose Quadrant Questions, is explained to the participants. The Purpose Quadrant contains four questions that are designed to nudge participants away from the overall workshop goal (i.e. the work towards a team's purpose) and to writing down as many data points as possible for each individual question during a silent brainstorming.

While the Purpose Quadrant questions are oriented on various techniques from personal [32] and workplace coaching [17] which focus, for example, on self-reflection, goal setting and reaching clarity about one's personal strengths and abilities, we developed four questions which we grouped into motivational aspects and aspects which reflect a participants' pride in their work (Fig. 2).

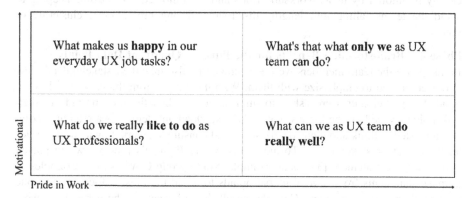

Fig. 2. Visualization of the Purpose Quadrant questions and their relation to motivation and pride in work.

The Purpose Quadrant visualizes the relationship between motivational aspects and aspects that generate pride in one's work (see Fig. 2). The lower of the motivational aspects quadrants collects ideas about what UX professionals really like to do in their daily business. In one workshop a participant mentioned that he likes to generate wild and crazy ideas. Someone else noted down that he likes to 'flash' (inspire) people or customers with their products and ideas. Additionally, it was stated that it is fun to put oneself into the shoes of the customer. Then, the teams were asked to note down things that make them happy as a UX team. In this category participants highlighted, for example, that they appreciate the diversity of their work, and that topics are changing on a regular basis, resulting in many learning opportunities. It became obvious that the collaboration and cooperation between and across different teams makes them happy, too.

In the category of aspects which generate pride in work, the groups brainstormed on tasks that the UX team completes with high proficiency, which they can do really well. It turned out that they considered themselves very good in creative problem solving, and in thinking outside of the box. Afterwards, the focus was put on things that only the (their) UX team can do. For example, team members mentioned skills like the ability to create end-to-end products which hardly anybody else in the organization would be able to in the same way. Or the unique ability to represent complex things in an easy and consumable way. The later especially is a key success factor of UX teams and should not be underestimated.

Phase 3 – Voting for the Work Group's Most Important Purpose Quadrant Items

Subsequently, all participants in each group presented their data points to their group members who were prompted to ask questions and to add ideas, building on those of the others. Following the presentation of the data points, the groups clustered them by topic. Finally, the participants used voting stickers to rank their most important data points. These were carried forward to the next phase of the method. The exercise was closely monitored by us as workshop leads and we followed a strict time-keeping to avoid the teams falling into lengthy discussions during presentation, clustering or voting.

Phase 4 – Brainstorming Benefits for the Purpose Quadrant Data Points

In this phase the team members were encouraged to also take their stakeholders' view into account and to emphasize with them. With the results from the previous phase in mind, the participants were asked to think about the benefits they provide to their stakeholders based on the highest voted Purpose Quadrant items. As a reference point we suggested to think about customers, users and consumers, marketing as well as sales teams and other stakeholders. To aid teams A and B in this process, we displayed SAP's purpose statement [37] as an example. Study group C was shown examples of purpose statements from several global brands to avoid too close a focus on just one company's purpose statement. Considering all this information, the participants were asked to do another silent brainstorming to come up with as many benefits as possible. During this process they listed with benefits like adding future-oriented approaches to their organizational DNA, easy to use products, or a shift to more consumer-oriented and cheaper development.

Phase 5 – Assigning Impacts to the Benefits

The following phase was entirely dedicated to the larger impact that the team's work has on their organization, company or the society. In another round of brainstorming, the participants noted down how the benefits defined earlier impact their work ecosystem all the way to their customers and end-users as well as business partners and the society. For example, using the SAP company purpose which defines its impact as 'At SAP, our purpose is to help the world run better and improve people's lives' [37]: The claimed impact in this example is that 'people's lives are improved'. Example responses for impacts created by the workshop teams ranged from 'happy employees', 'creating a leading advantage in the market' to 'helping to manifest a creative and innovative image'.

Phase 6 – 'Pitch Your Purpose': Developing and Presenting the Group's Purpose and Voting for the Team's Final Purpose Statement
The next phase is the most important one as the groups (or individuals in study group C) were tasked to develop their purpose statements. A central point was to connect to a 'higher purpose', that is, to define the team's own purpose, but basing it also on the company's stated purpose. The participants were asked to create a statement that encompassed all of the following characteristics: inspirational, clear and challenging, differentiating, empowering, future-oriented, clear and concise as well as authentic [8].

In a final step, each group's purpose statement proposals were presented to the entire team, followed by a direct voting on the team's final purpose statement. As one group (based in Canada) of study group A did not attend the workshop at the same time, each group's presentation was recorded on video and stored on a team server. This allowed a final, anonymous voting by all team members using a digital voting tool. Study group B was able to vote directly in the workshop session. For study group C there was no need for a cross 'team' voting as all five participants presented their final personal purpose statement.

4 Discussion

The results of the workshops have shown that it is possible to develop a team purpose statement within a relatively short timeframe of up to 2.5 h, in a cross-locational team-setup as well as for individuals. The main findings which will be discussed are based on our qualitative notes and observations from study groups A and B. These are teams at SAP SE from which we collected non-standardized feedback through short individual interviews after the workshop which describes a limitation to the results which need to be confirmed by further research. A questionnaire for collecting both qualitative and quantitative data is currently being developed, as described in Sect. 5, but could not yet be used as either post- or pre-workshop data was missing. At this stage our data represents an initial collection of data items which we will further examine for construct validity and internal consistency upon availability of the data. The same is true for study group C.

Finding A – The Purpose Quadrant Method's Modular and Interactive Approach Supports the Fast Creation of Coherent Purpose Statements that are Generated Bottom-Up
When we presented the process, the teams interested in creating a purpose statement initially had some reservations against dedicating a whole workshop and several activities to this method. Yet, it quickly turned out that the Purpose Quadrant method and the workshops are highly effective in generating a common purpose statement, faster than traditional discussion and moderation techniques can. A comparison group who was not part of this study needed several meeting iterations over several weeks and the result was generated more or less top-down by management, not bottom-up from within the team.

The essential techniques in our proposed method, along with a clear focus on developing a whole framework of a team's unique skills and diverse qualities are key to successful purpose statements: (a) Brainstorming to create as many data points as possible (diverging) with the voice of each participant, be it manager or employee, carrying the same weight, (b) the Purpose Quadrant questions which aim for the positive, motivating and empowering aspects the participant's work, and (c) voting techniques by which the teams choose the most important items (converging).

Finding B – Carving Out Benefits and Impacts Helps Refine a Purpose Statement and Adds to Participants' Self-recognition of Their Work Impact

Brainstorming benefits and impacts did not result in as many data points as the Purpose Quadrant questions generated in the previous phase. However, it was apparent that especially in this phase the participants were much more engaged in discussions. They started to make statements about the larger effects and influences their work can deliver. Further, getting the participants to consider their stakeholders' viewpoints and Jobs-To-Be-Done helped them to define the benefits and impacts through identification and empathy with the stakeholders.

Finding C – The Purpose Quadrant Method can be Applied to Various Team Set-Ups

As the practice showed, the method is transferable. Thus, practitioners can use this method within their teams and organizations, as well as with individuals.

After we developed and applied the method with the team from which we had received the initial brief, we were able to use the method with different team setups, from other professional areas, and with diverse backgrounds. The Purpose Quadrant method only needed to be slightly adapted to each team in terms of focusing it on their particular stakeholders, customers and users in phases 4–6. All workshops were also executed within the 2.5-h timeframe. It is recommended to have one workshop lead for every 10–12 people to manage the team interactions and dynamics as well as timekeeping.

The workshop setup in Zagreb was different, yet the method proved successful in this situation, too. Working with individuals rather than teams requires much more information and introduction as well as individual guidance. The participants cannot work in groups during the phases, however, they still benefit from the cross-presentation of each person's intermediate results between the phases. As there is no common company purpose applicable to all the participants, the activities in phases 4 and 5 needed to be explained in more detail. Purpose statements of several brands were required so the participants were able to find an example they could relate to. While for the teams at SAP the result was one team purpose statement to which the whole group subscribed, the individual workshop setting resulted in five naturally diverse purpose statements. All participants indicated these to be very personal and were happy and proud to go forward with them.

Finding D – Diverse Teams and Participation of All Team Members Increases the Identification with the Generated Purpose Statement

In all our study groups the teams were complete to a large extend. Single drop-outs (e.g. a participant had to leave the workshop earlier) led to those participants questioning the final purpose statement of his group. Bringing this participant back to the level of discussion of the workshop created additional effort for the other group members.

Feedback given to us in the post-workshop interviews positively highlighted the fact that all team members actively and jointly contributed to the team's purpose statement in a collaborative fashion. Frequently a marked improvement of team-spirit was mentioned, indicating a team building effect. Hence, the method can be used as part of a team building activity. We recommend it to be set up as described in this paper to avoid conflicts with other elements of the team building.

The companies that the participants in study group C worked for had no explicit purpose statement. Interestingly, these participants showed a stronger identification with their work, and had more knowledge about how their work influences their company's achievements. This might be due to the fact that these participants worked for smaller companies, agencies or were working as freelancers. In a direct feedback gathering session after the workshop (using the 'I like I wish' method [4]) participants indicated that they strongly identified with their personal purpose statement for their work and were confident in efficiently communicating it to their work peers.

Finding E – Authenticity is Key for the Acceptance of the Purpose Statement by the Team and Its Stakeholders

In each workshop, all groups generated one purpose statement, and from these proposals the final statement was chosen by vote. Thus, it was possible to monitor how the different statement proposals resonated across the groups and teams. If a purpose statement was precise and meaningful as well as honest we noted a higher appreciation in voting results.

In phase 6, most of the individual workshop groups created more than one alternative for their purpose statements. These drafts were subject to strong discussions in the group, especially in how far a statement should have an advertising character which precisely matches the known needs of the stakeholders. Most notably, these more constructed draft versions usually did not make it to the finish line and were rejected as a group's purpose statement.

This also became apparent during the final voting process after phase 6, where the purpose statement proposals of all workshop were presented to the entire team and then anonymously voted for. Statements which were less original, and which tried to 'please' stakeholders or to communicate very sophisticated team abilities (i.e. technical skillsets) received fewer votes than more personal, engaging and authentic statements.

The manager's manager of study group A released the team's final purpose statement for global internal use at SAP SE, commenting favorably on the authenticity, meaningfulness and clarity of their purpose statement.

Finding F – Branding a Team with a Purpose Statement Helps the Team's Standing

This finding is based primarily on observed and reported statements from participants and their managers. We have not yet collected enough data, nor has enough time passed to evaluate a mid- to long-term impact (see Sect. 5).

Both study group A and B have used and are still using their purpose statements in numerous ways. The statements are included in e-mail signatures, in presentations for (potential) stakeholders, they are shown on their landing pages in the internal Web portal or on WIKI pages, as well as team productivity tool's cover page. We noticed that the purpose statement became a part of the team's identity, positioned as a tagline next or below the team's name. The team managers stated that the purpose statement helped them communicate their service offering and the value of their team to stakeholders or customers. Internal stakeholders who approached the managers of both study groups claimed that the content of the purpose statement encouraged them to request project support in the first place. The manager of study group A also mentioned that the purpose statement helped him to communicate the team's charter in a short and precise manner when talking to applicants for jobs or internships.

5   Limitations and an Outlook to Further Research

There are a number of limitations in the research on the Purpose Quadrant method.

While the sample variation in the participant's cultural, biographical and professional profiles was significant, especially in study groups A and B, the number of experienced creative professional to experts was much higher than the number of novice participants.

An important limitation is the small amount of qualitative data and the lack of quantitative data. It is possible to evaluate the applicability and validity of the Purpose Quadrant method through the existing qualitative data [30]. However, only by collecting and analyzing quantitative data will we be able to express to what degree a team's standing in an organization has improved by using and promoting their purpose statement. We are planning further research to quantify the validity of our method.

As long-term observations are still missing we plan to evaluate how a participant's identification with the purpose statement develops both midterm (3-month post-workshop) as well as longer-term (after 6 months). That way we can determine (a) in which way and how often the purpose statement is used and (b) how the perception of the team changes over a longer period. The data will be collected from both participants and their stakeholders before and after the workshop activity to obtain a holistic view and to detect potential changes in the perception and appreciation of the team and its services. The research before and after the workshop will contain questions to collect qualitative data as well as quantitative data. In addition to Likert-scale questions this will also include several Semantic Differential questions. These questions aim to capture the attitude of the participants as well as stakeholders towards the team's standing and reputation. We prepared the category pairs, for example "trust worthy" and "not trust worthy" or "creative" and "not creative", headed by the question 'How do you feel that others perceive your team?' for the participant version and 'How do you perceive the services, attitude and experience of team xy' for the stakeholder version.

Determining the value of a team's brand in metrics is of a complex nature and could not be examined in the study. Measuring a team's brand value and brand contribution requires comparable data from other teams and, hence, requires the existence of a companywide framework for measuring the metrics. While study group A and B's company, SAP SE, receives rankings for brand value and brand contribution by external analysts such as the BrandZ [38], we are not aware of companies collecting this data for teams within their organization. Future areas of research are to explore methods for re-designing existing team rankings and performance evaluations to enable a brand characteristic and purpose-driven results evaluation.

6 Conclusion

The purpose of this paper was to examine the interaction of various discipline's method strengths and their utilization to improve a UX team's and individual creative professionals' standing with their stakeholders, in their organizations, agencies or with customers. In a quasi-experimental group comparison setup, we conducted workshops with a total of 40 participants in three study groups. The two study groups A and B consisted of permanent teams within a high-tech company. For the duration of the workshop, these teams were divided into sub-groups by the authors. The participants in study group C were not formed into sub-groups as they participated in the workshop as individuals. The results of the study are based on subjective and objective observations and data, with the latter offering interesting aspects for further research.

The findings indicate that combining and cascading aspects and methods from marketing, group dynamics, creative problem solving/innovation techniques, as well as from personal/work-place coaching creates synergies and benefits in a workshop setting. The participants were guided through the Purpose Quadrant method step-by-step, using a mix of techniques and methods from the abovementioned areas (as opposed to asking them to define a purpose statement straight away). Using this method, they successfully and sustainably branded their teams by means of a purpose statement.

Branding and directing companies with a purpose is widely discussed in literature and in practice. We discussed how the importance and positive effects associated with purpose in the context of a company's success [13] can be leveraged for UX teams and individual creative professionals.

This paper contributes to the body of work for researchers, scholars, User Experience staff as well as workshop leads and Design Thinking coaches. Emphasizing the many interwoven experiences and strengths of various professional disciplines and discussing their potential when combined, it adds to cross-discipline research. With the Purpose Quadrant method, we have identified and outlined several actionable steps which can be replicated and carried forward in workshops to come.

Acknowledgments. We would like to thank the following colleagues at SAP SE: Our managers, Matthias Berger, Andreas Stier and Thomas Uhl for trusting us to develop the method and apply it in co-located team settings. Clarissa Götz and Dr. Theo Held for their continuous and detailed feedback as well as Sigrun Junge and Heather Morrison for their expertise and input on innovation and brand experience which allowed the method to become a truly cross-disciplinary work. Further we thank Sanda Voloder, for her wonderful support at our workshop during Design District Festival Zagreb, Croatia. Our special thanks go to all participants of our workshops, for their great and open contribution allowing us to further evolve the method.

References

1. Allmon, W.D., Allmon, J.T.: The Worth of the Individual, the Value of Work, and the Power of the Mind: An Unconventional Southerner on Business, Race, Religion, and Self. Xlibris, Bloomington (2010)
2. Christensen, C.M., Anthony, S.D., Berstell, G., Nitterhosue, D.: Finding the right job for your product. MIT Sloan Manag. Rev. **48**(3), 38–47 (2007)
3. Cooper, A.: When Companies Question the Value of Design. User Friendly (2018). https://medium.com/s/user-friendly/whats-the-roi-of-ux-c47defb033d2. Accessed 30 Jan 2019
4. d.school: I like, I Wish, What If. d.school Design Thinking Method Cards. https://dschool-old.stanford.edu/wp-content/themes/dschool/method-cards/i-like-i-wish-what-if.pdf
5. Dear, M.: The Ebbs and Flows of UX Teams in Large Organizations (2018). https://www.uxmatters.com/mt/archives/2018/08/the-ebbs-and-flows-of-ux-teams-in-large-organizations.php. Accessed 30 Jan 2019
6. Degen, H., Yuan, X.: UX Best Practices. McGraw-Hill Publishing, Emeryville (2011)
7. Ehrlenspiel, K., Hundal, M.S., Kiewert, A., Lindemann, U.: Cost-Efficient Design. Springer, Berlin (2007). https://doi.org/10.1007/978-3-540-34648-7
8. Roberts, E.: A Guide to Writing Your Team's Charter Statement (2002). https://minds.wisconsin.edu/bitstream/handle/1793/44769/Documents/PDF_FILES/A%20Guide%20to%20Writing%20your%20Team's%20Charter.pdf. Accessed 1 Feb 2019
9. Froese, P.: On Purpose: How We Create the Meaning of Life, 1st edn. Oxford University Press, New York (2015)
10. Hartson, R., Pyla, P.S.: The UX Book: Process and Guidelines for Ensuring a Quality User Experience. Elsevier, Amsterdam (2012)
11. Harty, P.: The American Dreamer (2018). https://irishamerica.com/2017/12/the-american-dreamer/. Accessed 16 Jan 2019
12. Hendricks H.: 5 Things A Remote Team Needs To Be More Effective (2018). https://www.forbes.com/sites/drewhendricks/2015/05/07/5-things-a-remote-team-needs-to-be-more-effective/#ce6ac7c3c0cb. Accessed 12 Oct 2018
13. Hollensbe, E., Wookey, C., Hickey, L., George, G., Nichols, C.V.: Organizations with purpose. AMJ **57**(5), 1227–1234 (2014). https://doi.org/10.5465/amj.2014.4005
14. Izzo, J., Vanderwielen, J.: The Purpose Revolution: How Leaders Create Engagement and Competitive Advantage in an Age of Social Good. Berrett-Koehler Publishers, Oakland (2018)
15. Jamison, S., Hanley, S., Cardarelli, M.: Essential SharePoint 2010: Overview, Governance, and Planning. Pearson Education, London (2010)
16. Jen, N.: Design Thinking Is Bullsh*t (2017). https://99u.adobe.com/videos/55967/natasha-jen-design-thinking-is-bullshit. Accessed 30 Jan 2019
17. Jones, R.J., Woods, S.A., Guillaume, Y.R.F.: The effectiveness of workplace coaching: a meta-analysis of learning and performance outcomes from coaching. J. Occup. Organ. Psychol. **89**(2), 249–277 (2016). https://doi.org/10.1111/joop.12119
18. Katzenbach, J.R., Smith, D.K.: The Discipline of Teams: A Mindbook-Workbook for Delivering Small Group Performance. Harvard Business Review, Boston (2002)
19. Kenny, G.: Your Company's Purpose Is Not Its Vision, Mission, or Values (2014). https://hbr.org/2014/09/your-companys-purpose-is-not-its-vision-mission-or-values. Accessed 21 Sept 2018
20. Kliem, R.L.: Creative, Efficient, and Effective Project Management. Taylor and Francis, Hoboken (2013)
21. Kuusinen, K., Väänänen-Vainio-Mattila, K.: How to Make Agile UX Work More Efficient: Management and Sales Perspectives (2012). ACM. http://dl.acm.org/ft_gateway.cfm?id=2399037&type=pdf

22. Leaders Magazine, Inc.: The Power of Purpose. An Interview with Bill McDermott, Chief Executive Officer, SAP. http://www.leadersmag.com/issues/2018.2_Apr/Purpose/LEADERS-Bill-McDermott-SAP.html. Accessed 18 Jan 2019
23. Levi, D.: Group Dynamics for Teams. SAGE Publications, Thousand Oaks (2015)
24. Lillicrap D.: The Value of Brainstorming. Build Consensus, Recognize Common Goals, and Avoid Groupthink (2011). https://5by5design.com/advice/value-brainstorming. Accessed 15 Oct 2018
25. Luk G., B.A.: The Global Mobile Workforce is Set to Increase to 1.87 Billion People in 2022, Accounting for 42.5% of the Global Workforce. Continued Globalization will Drive the Growth of Mobile Workers in All Regions (2016). https://www.strategyanalytics.com/strategy-analytics/news/strategy-analytics-press-releases/2016/11/09/the-global-mobile-workforce-is-set-to-increase-to-1.87-billion-people-in-2022-accounting-for-42.5-of-the-global-workforce. Accessed 1 Feb 2019
26. Lupton, T.: Organisational Change: "Top-Down" or "Bottom-Up" Management? Pers. Rev. 1(1), 22–28 (1971). https://doi.org/10.1108/eb055191
27. Marcus, A.: User-experience planning for corporate success. Interactions 11(3), 24–27 (2004). https://doi.org/10.1145/986253.986266
28. Marcus, A.: User interface design's return on investment. In: Bias, R.G., Mayhew, D. J. (eds.) Cost-Justifying Usability: An Update for an Internet Age, 2nd edn, pp. 17–39. Morgan Kaufmann, Amsterdam (2005)
29. Chapman, L., Plewes, S.: A UX maturity model: effective introduction of UX into organizations. In: Marcus, A. (ed.) DUXU 2014. LNCS, vol. 8520, pp. 12–22. Springer, Cham (2014). https://doi.org/10.1007/978-3-319-07638-6_2
30. Mays, N., Pope, C.: Qualitative research: rigour and qualitative research. BMJ 311(6997), 109–112 (1995). https://doi.org/10.1136/bmj.311.6997.109
31. McCoy, J.L., Anema, M.: Fast Facts for Curriculum Development in Nursing: How to Develop & Evaluate Educational Programs in a Nutshell. Springer, New York (2012). https://doi.org/10.1891/9780826109996
32. Megginson, D., Clutterbuck, D.: Techniques for Coaching and Mentoring, vol. 523. Taylor & Francis, Hoboken (2012)
33. Osborn, A.F.: Applied Imagination: Principles and Procedures of Creative Problem-Solving, 3rd edn. Scribner, New York (1979)
34. Oxford University Press: English Oxford Living Dictionaries. https://en.oxforddictionaries.com/definition/purpose. Accessed 21 Sept 2018
35. Ritter, M., Winterbottom, C.: UX for the Web, 1st edn. Packt Publishing, Birmingham (2017)
36. Rohn, J.A.: How to organizationally embed UX in your company. Interactions 14(3), 25–28 (2007). https://doi.org/10.1145/1242421.1242440
37. SAP SE: Our Purpose and Promise. https://www.sap.com/corporate/en/vision-purpose.html. Accessed 2 Feb 2019
38. Schept, K.: BrandZ™ Top 100 Most Valuable Global Brands 2018 Flipbook Report (2018). http://online.pubhtml5.com/bydd/rxhd/#p=257. Accessed 2 Feb 2019
39. Shappard, B., Sarrazin, H., Kouyoumjian, G., Dore, F.: The Business Value of Design (2018). https://www.mckinsey.com/~/media/McKinsey/Business%20Functions/McKinsey%20Design/Our%20insights/The%20business%20value%20of%20design/The-business-value-of-design-vF.ashx. Accessed 25 Oct 2018
40. Trenner, L., Bawa, J.: The Politics of Usability: A Practical Guide to Designing Usable Systems in Industry. Springer, London (2012). https://doi.org/10.1007/978-1-4471-1530-4

Measuring UX Capability and Maturity
in Organizations

Luka Rukonić(✉) ⓘ, Vincent Kervyn de Meerendré ⓘ, and Suzanne Kieffer ⓘ

Institute for Language and Communication, Université catholique de Louvain,
Louvain-la-Neuve, Belgium
{luka.rukonic,vincent.kervyn,suzanne.kieffer}@uclouvain.be

Abstract. Measuring organizational UX Capability/Maturity (UXCM) has been difficult or inaccurate. Moreover, the lack of empirically developed maturity models, models validated in practice, studies demonstrating their benefit and poor documentation or support for their use, has made this measurement even more problematic. To date, there is no straightforward and efficient method to assess UXCM although such assessment is a prerequisite for the improvement of UX processes. UX artifacts, methods and resources contribute toward the execution of UX processes: the production of UX artifacts demonstrate the execution of a process, whereas the use of UX methods demonstrates the implementation of specific UX processes with specific UX resources. In this paper, we present a measurement structure aiming at assessing organizational capabilities to implement UX processes. This structure consists of a capability scale, a maturity scale, a rating scale and a set of process attributes as measurable characteristics of UX processes. The contribution of this paper is threefold: a description of the measurement structure for the UXCM assessment, a questionnaire for the capability assessment by means of online survey or remote interviews and the documentation of a case study demonstrating the efficiency of the proposed model in an industrial project.

Keywords: User Experience · UX process ·
Capability maturity assessment · Process Assessment Model

1 Introduction

Many organizations have integrated User Experience (UX) processes into their formal software development model because UX processes help improving the user experience with their products and increasing organizational efficiencies [1]. User-Centred Design (UCD) is a methodological approach for product development which places users and their needs at the core of the development process [11]. It is by now generally accepted that UCD should integrate UX processes [15]. Moreover, organizations in sectors such as automotive industry, education,

© Springer Nature Switzerland AG 2019
A. Marcus and W. Wang (Eds.): HCII 2019, LNCS 11586, pp. 346–365, 2019.
https://doi.org/10.1007/978-3-030-23535-2_26

entertainment, health or retail could benefit from the integration of UX processes into their software development model in order to develop products that better fit user needs and expectations [24,25].

This growing interest for UX has resulted into numerous ad-hoc approach variations for integrating UX into software development models [19], making it difficult or even impossible to assess the UX capability/maturity of an organization. The UX capability/maturity of an organization is the extent to which this organization consistently achieves UX processes. UX Capability/Maturity Models (UXCMMs) have generally been associated with the assessment of UX capability/maturity, as these models also provide support for increasing UX organizational efficiencies [12,14]. However, the assessment of UX capability/maturity remains a challenge because of the lack of UXCMMs validated in practice, lack of empirical data demonstrating their benefit for organizations and lack of documentation or support for their use in practice [14].

Capability/Maturity Models (CMMs) include a Process Reference Model (PRM) and a Process Assessment Model (PAM). A PRM describes a set of processes and their interrelations within a process lifecycle, whereas a PAM is a measurement structure for the assessment of the capability or performance of organizations to implement processes [9]. Following Paulk's pioneer model [20], CMMs typically include five maturity levels: initial (level 1), repeatable (level 2), defined (level 3), managed (level 4) and optimized (level 5). The purpose of CMMs is to support organizations moving from lower to higher maturity levels. In a CMM, both base practices and work products serve as indicators of the capability/maturity of processes.

Our previous work [13] focuses on the specification of a UXPRM describing primary UX lifecycle processes and a set of supporting UX methods and artifacts. In this paper, we present a UX Process Assessment Model (UXPAM) for measuring the UX capability/maturity of organizations. The proposed UXPAM consists of a capability scale, a maturity scale, a rating scale and a set of process attributes as measurable indicators of the achievement of UX processes. In particular, we use UX artifacts, methods and resources as indicators as we argue that UX artifacts, methods and resources contribute to the execution of UX processes as follows: the production of UX artifacts demonstrates the execution of UX processes, whereas the use of UX methods demonstrates the implementation of specific UX processes with specific UX resources. The contribution of this paper is threefold:

1. The description of a complete measurement structure for assessing UX capability/maturity in organizations;
2. A questionnaire that serves as tool for measuring UX capability/maturity in organizations by means of survey research or interview;
3. The documentation of a case study demonstrating the efficiency of the proposed UXPAM in a project conducted with four industrial partners.

2 Background

2.1 Capability/Maturity Model

CMMs address both generic and specific contexts such as Usability Engineering (UE) [5], healthcare [24] and software development [20,23]. They were introduced to evaluate an organization's maturity and capability. The maturity refers to the ability to consistently implement processes, while the capability of processes refers to the ability to achieve the required goals of a process [3,14]. CMMs describe the organization's evolution from a less ordered to a more structured state. The maturity of an organization can be assessed by measuring the capability of processes [14]. In addition, CMMs give recommendations for improving processes by adopting base practices and help organizations to achieve their business goals. Only a few evaluations of CMMs have been published because they are resource-intensive. Goldenson and Gibson [7] document 12 case studies that show how the implementation of the Capability Maturity Model Integration (CMMI) framework [23] increases the performance of organizational processes (e.g. reduction of costs and delays) and brings benefits such as increased customer satisfaction. Typically, CMMs include a PRM and a PAM.

2.2 Process Reference Model

PRMs describe a set of processes and their interrelations in a process lifecycle [9, 10,14]. Additionally, they describe the objectives, expected outcomes and related work products that demonstrate the execution of a specific process. Usually, PRMs are refined into base practices that contribute to the production of a work product. In turn, PRMs define a set of process-related indicators to evaluate for assessing the capability/maturity of an organization. Indicators allow the comparison between current and desired capability of processes [14].

2.3 Process Assessment Model

PAMs are measurement structures intended for measuring the capability of processes, more specifically for assessing how well organizations comply with a prescribed PRM [8]. Major CMMs such as Paulk's CMM [20] or CMMI-DEV [23] comply with the principle of defining a measurement structure in CMMs, which is also recommended by ISO 15504 [9]. The measurement structure contains three elements: process attributes, a capability/maturity scale and a rating scale.

Process attributes are measurable characteristics of a process which are directly related to its maturity and/or capability [5,14,23]. A maturity scale is a scale that describes Maturity Levels (ML) where each level builds on top of the level below and includes a set of characteristics that reflect the level of UX maturity [24]. A capability scale contains Capability Levels (CL) and represents an evolutionary order of stages to measure the achievement of processes. A rating scale is an ordinal scale used to rate the capability of processes. Typically, MLs are expressed as a set of Process Areas (PA) that have achieved a certain CL, whereas CLs relate to the capability of individual PAs or even processes [14,23]. A PA is a group of related activities that together contribute to the achievement of a common goal [14,23]. The structure of a PAM is shown in Fig. 1.

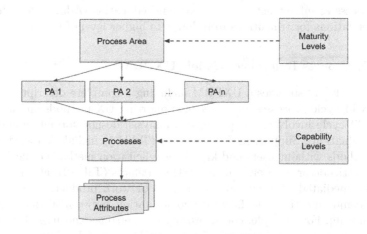

Fig. 1. A structure of a Process Assessment Model

3   Related Work

3.1   UX Capability/Maturity Model (UXCMM)

A Systematic Literature Review (SLR) reported in [14] identifies 15 CMMs which focus on UX and usability. The authors raise the question of the validity of generic CMMs when applied to specific domains such as UX and usability by making the following statements about the identified CMMs:

- They do not describe in sufficient details the methodology that was adopted to develop them;
- Only a third of them (5 out of 15) includes a UXPRM;
- Although they all include a UXPAM, they do not provide any method or tool to perform the process assessment, which in turn decreases the possibility of their adoption in practice;
- Their validation remains questionable due to a lack of scientific rigor of their validation.

The relevant literature often refers to the following CMMs: Schaffer's usability CMM [22] including six MLs but which has not been validated [24]; Nielsen's usability/UX CMM [17,18] including 8 MLs, which makes it difficult to distinguish between levels [14]; Earthy's usability CMM [4] including 6 MLs together with detailed documentation about its application.

The Healthcare Information and Management Systems Society (HIMSS) proposes a Healthcare Usability Maturity Model (UMM) in order to increase the awareness about usability in healthcare organizations. The paper describes wake-up calls such as failed products, competitive pressure or important needs for increasing patient's safety that serve as triggers for the adoption of UCD. The model includes 5 MLs described across five dimensions: focus on users, management, process & infrastructure, resources and education. Additionally, it gives recommendations for transitions from lower to higher level of maturity.

3.2   UX Process Reference Model (UXPRM)

Previous work [13] specifies a UXPRM including a complete description of primary UX lifecycle processes and a set of supporting UX methods and artifacts. The UX lifecycle involves four processes (analysis, design, formative and summative evaluation). Supporting UX methods (Table 1) include knowledge elicitation methods without users and knowledge elicitation methods either focused on users' attitude or on users' behavior. UX artifacts (Table 2), also referred to as artifact-mediated communication methods or work products, are means to increase communication and facilitate collaboration between distinct development teams [6]. For example, coded-prototypes, personas and user stories facilitate the communication between agile and UCD teams [6], while paper prototypes are most frequently used artifacts when performing usability inspection [2].

Table 1. Supporting UX methods

Category	Methods (related techniques)
Without users	GOMS (CMN-, CPM-GOMS,NGOMSL, Keystroke-Level Model)
	Hierarchical task analysis (hierarchical task analysis)
	Inspection (cognitive walkthrough; expert review; heuristic evaluation)
	Literature review ((systematic) literature review; systematic mapping)
Attitudinal	Cards (cards; emocards; emotion cards)
	Experience sampling (daily or repeated-entry diary)
	Group interview (brainstorming; focus group; questionnaire)
	Prospective interview (questionnaire; role-play; twenty questions)
	Retrospective interview (cognitive or elicitation interview)
	Survey (interview; questionnaire)
	Think-aloud (co-discovery; (retrospective) think-aloud protocol)
Behavioral	Automated experience sampling (automated interaction logs)
	Experiment (A/B testing; controlled experiment; remote experiment)
	Instrument-based experimentation (experiment with
	Calibrated instrument (biometrics, eye tracker, sensors, etc.)
	Observation (field observation; systemic observation)
	Simulation (paper-and-pencil evaluation; WoZ experiment)

Table 2. Supporting UX artifacts

Category	UX artifacts
About user needs	Customer journey map; service blueprint; persona; work models; UX goals
About products	Affinity diagram; concept map; card sort; user scenario; user story; task model; low- and high-fidelity prototype; design principles

3.3 UX Process Assessment Model (UXPAM)

The UXCMM presented in [21] includes an assessment tool based on a survey of UX professionals about their use of existing CMMs. The paper identifies the integration of UX within the organization, the UX budget, the researcher-designer-developer ratio, the UX buy-in throughout organization and the frequency of UX evaluations as key indicators of UX capability/maturity. In a similar way, Jokela and Abrahamsson [12] suggest three dimensions of usability capability, which are also applicable to UX capability: infrastructure to implement UCD in projects (e.g. prototyping tools or usability lab), efficiency, effectiveness and quality of the planning and implementation of UCD, and the commitment of the management to support UCD.

4 Proposed UX Process Assessment Model (UXPAM)

4.1 Model Development Method

Maturity models have to be developed systematically, mention the sources used and have to be developed to address a specific domain or have a more general scope. We decided to adopt the maturity model development methodology by de Bruin [3]. This methodology has six phases, whose order is important to follow, and decisions made in each phase have an impact on the later phases. Namely, the phases are Scope, Design, Populate, Test, Deploy and Maintain. Also, the development methodology supports iterative design, especially in phases such as Populate, Design and Test. In this paper, we present the work we did in the first four phases.

4.2 Scope Phase

In the Scope phase, we determined the focus of our CMM and its domain. This allowed us to set its target definition and characterize the difference between existing models. As a result, we aimed at developing a domain-specific CMM, whose stakeholders are academics and practitioners [3], to support the integration of UX processes in software development models. Our model aims to help organizations assess the capabilities of their UX processes through a set of process attributes. Moreover, the model provides a basis for the UX process improvement. First, we used the available literature to identify the relevant domain issues and the shortcomings of the existing models. Our model documents its development methodology, provides an assessment tool and covers non-process elements such as resources, culture and management attitude [14].

4.3 Design Phase

In the Design phase, we made decisions related to the needs of our model's target audience as well as decisions related to the model's architecture. According to the SLR [14], most reviewed models use the 6-level capability scale adopted from ISO 15504 [9], whereas the maturity scales range between three and six levels. Capability levels are shown in Table 3. Regarding maturity scales, we opted for the most common one, a 5-level scale as it is detailed enough to describe the evolutionary stages of organization's maturity, and simple enough to distinguish the differences between levels. Our maturity levels are shown in Table 4. Also, having in mind the audience that will typically perform the self-assessments, we chose to develop a questionnaire as an effective assessment tool. Respondents to this questionnaire will mostly consist of management and employees of the assessed organization, including UX staff, developers, researchers and managers.

Table 3. Capability levels description from ISO 15504 [9]

Level	Description
0: Incomplete	The process is not implemented, or fails to achieve its purpose
1: Performed	The implemented process achieves its process purpose
2: Managed	The Performed process is planned, monitored and adjusted, and its work products are appropriately established, controlled and maintained
3: Established	The Managed process is implemented using a defined process, tailored from a set of standard process assets, that is capable of achieving its process outcomes
4: Predictable	The Established process operates within defined limits to achieve its process outcomes
5: Optimizing	The Predictable process is continuously improved to meet relevant current and projected business goals

4.4 Populate Phase

In the Populate phase, we extracted the relevant domain components of our UX PAM from the literature, that are mutually exclusive and collectively exhaustive. This allowed us to identify which process attributes are good candidates for the measurement of capability/maturity. A core part of the PAM are the PAs. We clustered process attributes into PAs, depending on their relatedness. Based on relevant literature [12, 16, 24, 25], we have realized the importance of UX resources, culture and literacy as fundamental for the UX process improvement.

Table 4. Maturity levels

Level	Characteristics
1: Unrecognized	UX not considered
	A wake-up call is needed
2: Initial	Low/late user involvement
	Individuals perform UX processes
	Ad-hoc management of UX
	Unpredictable quality of products (processes often changes)
3: Tactical	Insufficient support from top executives
	UCD is accepted, but sometimes traded off for development
	Lack of formal UX literacy
4: Strategical	Full understanding of UX ROI
	UX ROI is linked to the business goals
	UX is controlled and predictable
5: Optimal	Continuous improvement of UX processes
	UX culture established
	The leadership is user-centered

Besides, according to an in-depth analysis reported in [11], these non-process elements were regularly excluded from CMMs focused on UCD. However, according to [14], recent CMMs seem to put more emphasis on the management issues, management of UX/usability resources, processes and their integration. They serve as indicators of the effectiveness of UX processes [11,12] and enable the measurement of UX capability and maturity. Table 5 shows PAs and process attributes we use in our PAM. The structure of our PAM is depicted in Fig. 1.

4.5 Test Phase

In the Test phase, we conducted a survey among our partners in the industry. The survey consisted of an online questionnaire and remote interviews. We interviewed some participants to cross-check their survey answers and to gather information related to their UX literacy and the ways they think UX can facilitate the development of their products. Specifically, we checked their understanding of the UX Return On Investment (ROI) and their organization's attitude towards UX discipline. ROI is demonstrated through increased organizational efficiencies, reduced development time and costs or reduced need for technical support [1].

4.6 The UXCM Questionnaire

The proposed questionnaire is divided into five blocks. The first three blocks focus on the frequency of use of UX artifact and UX methods and the availability

Table 5. Process areas and process attributes

Process area	Process attributes
PA1 Product development	High-fidelity prototypes
PA2 Visual design	Design principles (icons, font, colors, look & feel)
PA3 Stakeholders involvement	Stakeholders analysis; context meeting; focus group
PA4 Discount UX evaluation	Inspection; think-aloud; low-fidelity prototypes
PA5 Experts involvement	Inspection (heuristic evaluation; cognitive walkthrough); GOMS; hierarchical task analysis
PA6 User involvement	Regularly throughout development lifecycle
PA7 Iterative design	Creation of redesign solutions; formative UX testing
PA8 UX resources	UX skills; infrastructure (prototyping tools; labs)
PA9 User research	Experience sampling; surveys; interviews; personas
PA10 Contextual design	Context of use analysis and specification (A1-A5); UX goals setting; work modelling
PA11 UX culture	Perception of UX; management support of UX; lifecycle integration; link to business goals
PA12 Continuous improvement	Link to business goals; UX training;
PA13 Monitoring of UX	UX KPIs; UX effectiveness data collection;

of UX resources. The two remaining blocks focus on UX literacy and UX culture. These blocks correspond directly to the indicators of UX process capability described previously in the paper. The blocks 1–3 are shown in Table 6 and blocks 4–5 are presented in Table 7.

5   Preliminary Questionnaire Validation Results

We performed the initial validation study of our questionnaire. We used the questionnaire presented in Tables 6 and 7 to perform a two-round assessment. In total, four companies were involved in the survey. We distributed it to our industrial partners working on a project in automotive sector. Our role in the project is to provide support for the integration of UX activities and lead the UX-related tasks.

5.1   First Round

In the first round, we conducted an online survey containing questions from Table 6, that had been opened to participants to respond for two weeks. Additionally, the online survey contained a section related to participants' personal

Table 6. Questionnaire for the UXCM assessment - part 1

Block 1. UX artifacts

How often are these artifacts used in the projects you have been involved in? (never; rarely; sometimes; often; always; I don't know how often; I don't know this artifact)

Describing user needs	About product design and evaluation
A1 Customer journey map ___	A6 Affinity diagram ___
A2 Service blueprint ___	A7 Concept map ___
A3 Persona ___	A8 Card sort ___
A4 Work models ___	A9 User scenario ___
A5 UX goals ___	A10 User story or epics ___
	A11 Task models ___
	A12 Low-fidelity prototype ___
	A13 High-fidelity prototype ___
	A14 Design principles ___

Block 2. UX methods

How often do you use the following methods with **real end-users** in the projects you have been involved in? (never; rarely; sometimes; often; always; I don't know how often; I don't know this method)

M1 Group interview (brainstorming, focus group, stakeholder interview) ___
M2 Individual interview (in person, remote, elicitation) ___
M3 Survey research (online questionnaire) ___
M4 Experience sampling (repeated-entry diary) ___
M5 Experiment (A/B testing, controlled/remote experiment, think-aloud) ___
M6 Instrument-based experiment (biometric, eye-tracker, face reader, sensors) ___
M7 Observation (field observation) ___
M8 Simulation (paper-and-pencil, Wizard of Oz)

How often do you use the following methods **without real end-users** in the projects you have been involved in? (never; rarely; sometimes; often; always; I don't know how often; I don't know this method)

M9 GOMS ___
M10 Hierarchical task analysis ___
M11 Inspection (cognitive walkthrough, heuristic evaluation, expert review) ___
M12 Literature review (background study, SLR, systematic mapping) ___

Block 3. UX resources

How many full-time equivalent developers (analysts; developers; testers) work in your organization? ___

How many full-time equivalent UX positions (i.e. people doing only UX activities) work in your organization? ___

Who is performing UX activities in your organization?
Nobody ☐ Developers ☐ Analysts ☐ UX consultants ☐ UX consultants ☐

What is the range of duties of the UX designers employed in your organization?
Information Architecture Design ☐ Interaction Design ☐ Prototyping ☐
User Testing ☐ Visual Design ☐ I don't know ☐

Table 7. Questionnaire for the UXCM assessment - part 2

Block 4. UX literacy

Please indicate your level of agreement with the following statements
about UX ROI.
(1: strongly disagree; 2: disagree; 3: neutral; 4: agree; 5: strongly agree)

In my opinion, UX helps to:

Improve products' look and feel ___
increase user efficiencies ___
increase user satisfaction ___
reduce user needs for training and technical support ___
increase organizational efficiencies ___
reduce development time and costs ___

Please indicate your level of agreement with the following statements
about the attitude towards users.
(1: strongly disagree; 2: disagree; 3: neutral; 4: agree; 5: strongly agree)

In my opinion, users:

---

do not need enhanced usability, they just need training ___
are unable to express what they want ___
expectations are difficult to manage ___

Block 5. UX culture

Please indicate the way employees are being educated about UX, through training.
None ☐ Gained at work ☐ One-shot UX training ☐
Internal awareness programme ☐ Regular corporate UX training ☐

How is UX perceived in your organization?
We don't need it ___ We are already experts in the domain ___
UX could improve the success of our products ___ UX could facilitate development ___

How do managers see UX?

How do employees see UX?

Who should be doing UX?
Nobody ☐ Developers ☐ Project Managers ☐ Visual Designers ☐ UX staff ☐

When do you think UX designers should be involved in the project?
Never ☐ When needed ☐ During evaluation ☐ From the beginning ☐ Always ☐

Please indicate the level of agreement with the following statements.
(1: strongly disagree; 2: disagree; 3: neutral; 4: agree; 5: strongly agree)

Your organization links UX to its business goals. ___

UX is often discussed during meetings. ___

UX is supported by C-level executives. ___

information, asking them to provide their job title or their function, their highest educational degree level, and the title of their degree (i.e. field of education). The goal of a survey was to assess the UX capabilities of UX processes. We used the project's mailing list to reach the participants. Altogether, 20 respondents took the survey and fully completed it, 4 participants only partially submitted their answers, and 10 did not enter any data but only opened the questionnaire's homepage. Thus, we had a response rate of 57%, based on 35 invitations sent. Participants mostly work in business, management, engineering and telecommunications fields, but their roles are broad, ranging from managers and directors to researchers and engineers. None of them had an educational background in HCI. Figure 2 shows capability scores for each partner company in terms of the two UX capability indicators, UX artifacts and methods, and their overall capability score.

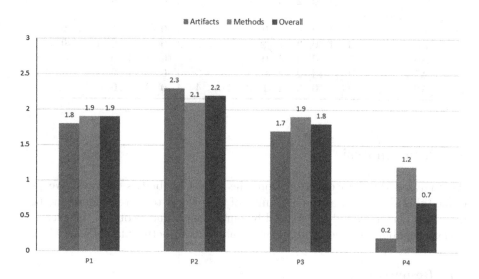

Fig. 2. Capability scores per company

5.2   Second Round

In the second round, we have conducted phone interviews with 6 participants, in order to find out more about their organizational practices and debrief their survey answers. We used the set of questions shown in Table 7. The findings allowed us on one hand to assess the UX literacy and UX culture of our partners, and on the other to double-check their answers with the goal to validate the measurement tool, i.e., the questionnaire. During interviews, we described each artifact and method to interviewees and allowed them to change their answers. This is shown in Table 8. We noticed a small number of changed answers, mostly at the degree of change equal to one, and twice at the degree of two. This suggests that our questionnaire is robust enough to support the assessment of UX capabilities and that participants' answers are reliable. Most commonly, answer changes resulted from participants' misunderstanding of what a method/artifacts is.

Table 8. Round 1 vs Round 2 differences (blanks mean "I don't know")

		S1			S9			S15			S17			S18			S20		
ID	Methods	R1	R2	Δ	R1	R2	Δ	R1	R2	Δ	R1	R2	Δ	R1	R2	Δ	R1	R2	Δ
M4		1	1	0	2	1	-1	1	1	0	1	1	0	3	3	0	1	1	0
M5		1	1	0	3	2	-1	1	1	0	3	3	0	1	1	0	1	1	0
M6		1	1	0	2	1	-1	1	1	0	3	1	-2	1	1	0	1	1	0
M7		1	1	0	2	3	1	1	1	0	2	2	0	1	1	0	1	1	0
M12		1	1	0	2	3	1				2	2	0	3	3	0			
	Artifacts																		
A3		1	1	0	4	4	0				3	3	0	2	3	1	1	1	0
A5		1	1	0	3	1	-2				2	2	0	1	1	0	1	1	0
A6		1		-1	3	3	0						0	1	1	0			
A7		1		-1	2	2	0				3	3	0	1	1	0			
A9		1	1	0	3	4	1	3	3	0	4	4	0	3	3	0			

6 Data Analysis

We analyzed the data collected from the "UX Capabilities Survey". We performed this assessment at the beginning of the project to better understand how the UX is perceived and understood by our partners and to obtain the overview of their capabilities which will, in turn, enable us to better plan UX activities.

6.1 Resources

UX resources represent the necessary infrastructure for the organization to effectively plan and implement UX processes in their development projects. It is essential to have the UX staff with the right amount of UX skills who will perform the UX activities. The Designer:Developer (D:D) ratio is a good indicator of the potential capability to perform UX activities. We present D:D ratio as a range between best and worst-case scenario given that the provided number of UX staff and developers varied among respondents. We could only calculate it for P1, and it ranges between 1:4 and 1:40. It is clear that the resources are scarce, UX staff exists in only one company (P1) and there are no dedicated labs or tools to perform UX tests. Therefore the resources can hardly support the effective UX work. Figure 3 shows who is performing UX work in each company.

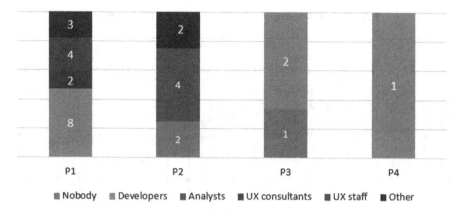

Fig. 3. Distribution of UX activities by role

6.2 Methods and Artifacts

Tables 9 and 10 present results from the first round of the survey, blocks 1 and 2, respectively. The heat map clearly shows the most used methods and artifacts. Blanks represent the answer "I don't know this method/artifact". Zeros indicate the answer "I don't know how often". In the last column an average capability score for each method and artifact is given. Numbers in the table correspond to the answers on the rating scale: I don't know how often (0), never (1), rarely (2), sometimes (3), often (4) and always (5).

Table 9. UX artifacts (blanks mean "I don't know")

	P1										P2					P3			P4		
ID	S1	S2	S3	S4	S5	S6	S7	S8	S9	S10	S11	S12	S13	S14	S15	S16	S17	S18	S19	S20	Score
A1	1	4	4	4					2		2	2	2	3		2	2	1	3		2.5
A2	1	4	3						1				3	5		3	1	1	1		2.3
A3	1	4	4	4			3		4		4	4	4	2		3	1	2	3	1	2.9
A4	1	4	3						1			3	5	4	5	4	1	3	3	1	2.9
A5	1	4	3	3				3	3		3		4	4		2	1	1	3	1	2.6
A6	1	3	3					3	2				3	3			1	1	3		2.3
A7	1	3	3		4				2	2	2	3	3	5		3	1	1	3		2.6
A8	1	3	4						2	2			2	3	3		1	1	2		2.2
A9	1	5	5	4	5		3		3	3	4	5	5	5	3	4	3	3	4		3.8
A10	1	5	5	5	5	4	4	3	4	3	4	5	5	5		3		3	4		4
A11	1	3	3	0					1		3	2		3	4	3		3	3		2.4
A12	1	3	4		3		3		4	1	1	1	5	3		2		1	3		2.5
A13	1	4	4		4		4		4	1	1		4	2		3		4	5		3.2
A14	1	5	4		3				4	1	2		4	3		2		2	3		2.8

Table 10. UX methods (blanks mean "I don't know")

ID	P1										P2						P3			P4	Score
	S1	S2	S3	S4	S5	S6	S7	S8	S9	S10	S11	S12	S13	S14	S15	S16	S17	S18	S19	S20	
M1	1	4	4	4	3	3	3	4	4	4	5	5	5	4	1	3	2	2	4	2	3.35
M2	1	4	4	3	3	3	4	2	3	2	5	5	5	4	1	2	1	2	4	1	2.95
M3	1	4	4	3	3	3	3	4	3	1	3	5	4	4	1	3	1	2	5	1	2.9
M4	1	3	3		2			3	2	1	2		3	1	1	1	1	3	5	1	2.06
M5	1	3	2		1			1	3	1	1		3	1	1	3	1	1		1	1.6
M6	1	2	2	1	1		2	1	2	1	1	1	3	1	1	3	1	1		1	1.44
M7	1	3	4	2	5		0	3	2	1	2	1	4	3	1	2	1	1	4	1	2.16
M8	1	2	4		3			2	3	1	1	1	2	3	1	1	1	3	5	1	2.06
M9	1	1	1						1				1				3	1			1.29
M10	1	1	1	3				4	2	3		1	3	4		2	0	1			2
M11	1	2	2		3			1	3	1	1	1	3	3		3	0	1			1.79
M12	1	4	2	5	4			5	1	4	4	5	1	4		1	0	3	5	5	3.29

6.3 Literacy

Knowledge of the UX artifacts and UX methods is considered essential in order to properly plan and perform UX activities. UX literacy refers to the knowledge and skills of an organization regarding UX. We decided to put the "I don't know this method/artifact" answer in our questionnaire so that we can properly distinguish the knowledge of a particular method or artifact and its unknown frequency of use from being unfamiliar with it. The latter feeds into the UX literacy dimension and therefore allows us to calculate the literacy scores, based on participants' answers. Last two rows in Table 11 present the literacy percentage scores for UX methods and UX artifacts per company. They are calculated as an average of percentage shares between two categories: a sum of all answers on the frequency rating scale and all "I don't know this method/artifacts" answers for each method/artifact, where higher means better. Furthermore, our model addresses the understanding of UX ROI, attitude towards users and UX training as fundamental to UX literacy. In the second round, we asked participants the questions from Block 4. Results are presented in Table 11.

6.4 UX Culture

This is a summary of questions from Block 5. Generally, all partners see the value UX could bring to their projects, but fail to integrate it properly into their software development models. They generally think UX comes as an additional work which might generate delays in development. The positive side is that they understand that UX processes should be employed from the beginning of the development process. From the management's perspective, UX is only slightly supported and they don't seem to be much aware of it. For employees, on the other hand, UX is either not a concern, or they see it as beneficial to the

Table 11. UX literacy assessment

Category	Statement	P1 S9	P2 S15	S17	P3 S18	P4 S20
UX ROI	Improve products' look and feel	3	5	5	5	5
	Increase user efficiencies	4	5	5	4	5
	Increase user satisfaction	4	5	4	5	4
	Reduce user needs for training and tech. support	4	4	5	5	4
	Increase organizational efficiencies	4	4	3	5	2
	Reduce development time and costs	3	5	4	3	2
Attitude towards users	Do not need enhanced usability, they need training	5	2	5	2	3
	Are unable to express what they want	3	1	3	2	3
	Expectations are difficult to manage	3	3	2	3	2
Training	UX training is offered to employees	1	1	4	1	1
			3.5	4		
	Literacy score	**3.4**	**3.75**		**3.5**	**3.1**
Knowledge	Literacy score for UX methods	77%	84%		83%	75%
	Literacy score for UX artifacts	58%	71%		69%	21%

development of high-quality products that meet user needs. P2 agrees that UX could be a way to achieve business goals, whereas P1 is not sure how can UX be offered from the business perspective.

6.5   Summary

Table 12 shows the summary of UX process capability by PA. Overall, the highest capability was measured in Product Development, User Research and Contextual Design in descending order. First one does not come as a surprise because high-fidelity prototypes closely resemble the finished product and summative evaluation can be easily performed on them. The second and the third PAs are closely related because artifacts describing user needs and the context of use often stem from the user research activities (interviews, surveys, personas creation). On the other hand, partners overall score is low in Stakeholders and Experts Involvement, and Monitoring of UX PAs. Again, for these to score better, UX should be more deeply integrated into their organizations and UX culture established. Finally, the Score column indicates the overall capability score for each partner across PAs and it could be considered an initial overall maturity score.

Table 12. Process areas assessment per partner company (red = 1 SD below average; orange = 1 SD above average), M = 1.71, SD = 0.5498

	PA1	PA2	PA3	PA4	PA5	PA6	PA7	PA8	PA9	PA10	PA11	PA12	PA13	Score
P1	3.1	3	1	2.1	1.7	1	2.5	2	2.6	2.8	2	2	1	2.06
P2	2.5	2.8	1	2.1	1.9	2	2.2	1	2.7	3.3	3	2	1	2.12
P3	4.5	2.5	1	1.2	1	1	2.7	1	2.3	1.9	2	2	1	1.85
P4	0	0	1	0.3	0	1	0.8	1	1.8	1.3	1	1	1	0.78
	2.53	2.08	1	1.43	1.15	1.25	2.05	1.25	2.35	2.33	2	1.75	1	

6.6   Discussion

Conducting the case study allowed us to learn the following:

Use of UX Methods. Most often used UX methods are those that require less effort and resources to be implemented such as literature review or user interviews. Most used artifacts are user stories, user scenarios and personas. We noticed a lack of formative UX evaluations, but none of the companies have dedicated UX teams that could work in parallel with development teams. This is indicated with the high tendency to use high-fidelity prototypes for evaluation. Furthermore, during interviews in second round, we noticed that participants did not always understand the correct meaning of UX artifacts or methods, which led to change of answers in the second round. This suggests that further refinement is needed to remove any eventual ambiguity.

Identify Barriers. The findings allowed us to improve our UX activity plan and to anticipate bottlenecks in product development, such as lack of motivation for user requirements analysis (product-oriented versus user-centered mindset), which demonstrates a low level of UX capability. This does not come as a surprise as they have expressed the need for UX expertise in their project, but have claimed that they already do some UX work.

Insights. P2 consistently performed best among four companies. Surprisingly, it is a technologically-oriented and research-driven company, but they showed knowledge of a majority of UX methods. As a matter of fact, their results demonstrate the highest capability scores in all dimensions. Their perceived value of UX was made clear during interviews where all interviewees had a similar vision of the benefits of UX as well as confirmed the regular implementation of UX activities when the project demands it. P1, as a main project stakeholder, scored less than expected, despite their high interest in the implementation of UX processes. Other two companies P3 and P4 scored relatively low, due to their focus on technological development and delivering software to other providers. Generally, they don't have the connection to end-users.

7   Conclusion

The assessment of UXCM is a prerequisite to the UX process improvement. To bridge this gap, this paper presented a UXPAM accompanied with an efficient method to assess UXCM, using a questionnaire as a data collection method supporting the use of online surveys and remote interviews. Building on top of previous studies, we assess the UXCM across five UX dimensions: artifacts, methods, resources, literacy and culture. We performed an initial case study demonstrating the use of our UXPAM. The results seem to accurately capture the current UX capability of an organization. However, further work is required to provide the assessment feedback in a more systematic way.

8   Future Work

Future research will further evaluate and validate our UXPAM. Concretely, we aim to conduct a longitudinal study to test its usefulness and ability to improve the UX processes in an organization. We will implement the phases five and six of de Bruin's [3] methodology, Deploy and Maintain. Additionally, we intend to merge our UX PAM with the UXPRM into one UX Capability Maturity Model (UXCMM). To achieve this, we need to establish a mapping between the PAM and the PRM, as required per ISO 15504. In addition, more empirical analysis is needed to establish the relation between CLs that each PA must meet to achieve a certain ML. We also aim to provide a structured approach toward the increase of organizational maturity and deliver empirical results demonstrating the model's applicability in practice. Finally, we intend to allow practitioners to make justified choices when selecting the UX methods and provide support to successfully integrate UX activities in the software development model.

Acknowledgements. The authors acknowledge the support by the projects VIADUCT and HAULOGY 2021 under the references 7982 and 7767 funded by Service Public de Wallonie (SPW), Belgium.

References

1. Bias, R.G., Mayhew, D.J.: Cost-Justifying Usability: An Update for an Internet Age, vol. 2. Morgan Kaufmann, Burlington (2005)
2. Da Silva, T., Silveira, M., Maurer, F.: Usability evaluation practices within agile development. In: Proceedings of the Annual Hawaii International Conference on System Sciences, vol. 2015, pp. 5133–5142 (2015). https://doi.org/10.1109/HICSS. 2015.607
3. De Bruin, T., Freeze, R., Kaulkarni, U., Rosemann, M.: Understanding the main phases of developing a maturity assessment model. In: Australasian Conference on Information Systems (ACIS) (2005)
4. Earthy, J.: Usability maturity model: human centredness scale. INUSE Proj. Deliverable D5 **5**, 1–34 (1998)

5. Earthy, J.: Usability maturity model: processes. Lloyd's Reg. Shipp. **2**, 84 (1999)
6. Garcia, A., Silva da Silva, T., Selbach Silveira, M.: Artifacts for agile user-centered design: a systematic mapping. In: Proceedings of the Annual Hawaii International Conference on System Sciences, pp. 5859–5868 (2017)
7. Goldenson, D.R., Gibson, D.L.: Demonstrating the impact and benefit of CMMI: an update and preliminary results. Special report, Carnegie Mellon Software Engineering Institute, Pittsburgh, USA (2003)
8. ISO: Information Technology — Software Process Assessment - Part 2: Performing an Assessment. Standard, International Organization for Standardization, Geneva, Switzerland (2003)
9. ISO: Information Technology — Software Process Assessment - Part 1: Concepts and Introductory Guide. Standard, International Organization for Standardization, Geneva, Switzerland (2004)
10. ISO: Information Technology — Software Process Assessment - Part 5: An Assessment Model and Indicator Guidance. Standard, International Organization for Standardization, Geneva, Switzerland (2012)
11. Jokela, T.: Usability capability models-review and analysis. In: McDonald, S., Waern, Y., Cockton, G. (eds.) People and Computers XIV-Usability or Else!, pp. 163–181. Springer, London (2000). https://doi.org/10.1007/978-1-4471-0515-2_12
12. Jokela, T., Abrahamsson, P.: Modelling usability capability – introducing the dimensions. In: Bomarius, F., Oivo, M. (eds.) PROFES 2000. LNCS, vol. 1840, pp. 73–87. Springer, Heidelberg (2000). https://doi.org/10.1007/978-3-540-45051-1_10
13. Kieffer, S., Rukonic, L., Vincent, K.D.M., Vanderdonckt, J.: Specification of a UX process reference model towards the strategic planning of UX activities. In: Proceedings of the 14th International Joint Conference on Computer Vision, Imaging and Computer Graphics Theory and Applications (VISIGRAPP 2019) - Volume 2, HUCAPP. vol. 2, pp. 74–85 (2019)
14. Lacerda, T.C., von Wangenheim, C.G.: Systematic literature review of usability capability/maturity models. Comput. Stand. Interfaces **55**(C), 95–105 (2018)
15. Law, E.L.C., Roto, V., Hassenzahl, M., Vermeeren, A.P.O.S., Kort, J.: Understanding, scoping and defining user experience: a survey approach. In: CHI 2009, vol. 23, no. 1, pp. 23–32 (2009)
16. Mayhew, D.J.: Business: strategic development of the usability engineering function. Interactions **6**(5), 27–34 (1999)
17. Nielsen, J.: Corporate UX Maturity: Stages 1–4. Nielsen Norman Group, Silicon Valley (2006)
18. Nielsen, J.: Corporate UX Maturity: Stages 5–8. Nielsen Norman Group, Silicon Valley (2006)
19. Ovad, T., Larsen, L.B.: The prevalence of UX design in agile development processes in industry. In: Proceedings 2015 Agile Conference, pp. 40–49 (2015)
20. Paulk, M.C.: Capability maturity model, version 1.1. IEEE Softw. **10**(4), 18–27 (1993)
21. Sauro, J., Johnson, K., Meenan, C.: From snake-oil to science: measuring UX maturity. In: CHI 2017 Extended Abstracts, pp. 1084–1091 (2017)
22. Schaffer, E.: Institutionalization of Usability: A Step-by-Step Guide. Addison Wesley Longman Publishing Co., Inc., Redwood City (2004)

23. Software Engineering Institute: CMMI for Development, Version 1.3. Carnegie Mellon University (2010)
24. Staggers, N., et al.: Promoting usability in health organizations: initial steps and progress towards a healthcare usability maturity model. In: 11th International Congress on Nursing Informatics, p. 56 (2011)
25. Venturi, G., Troost, J., Jokela, T.: People, organizations, and processes: an inquiry into the adoption of user-centered design in industry. Int. J. Hum.-Comput. Interact. **21**(2), 219–238 (2006)

A Value-Centered Approach for Unique and Novel Software Applications

Björn Senft[✉], Florian Rittmeier, Holger Fischer, and Simon Oberthür

Paderborn University, SICP, Fürstenallee 11, 33102 Paderborn, Germany
{b.senft,f.rittmeier,h.fischer,s.oberthuer}@sicp.upb.de

Abstract. It is difficult to make accurate predictions about what delivers value for users, especially in innovative contexts. The challenge lies in the lack of understanding of the problem and solution space. Design Thinking helps here with its converging and diverging thinking in which different solutions are tried out in practice and compared with each other. Design thinking becomes challenging when using software as a medium, since software development is usually not designed to implement several alternatives simultaneously. Therefore, we present in this paper the outline to an approach how this can be realized with software which we call *Insight Centric Design & Development* (ICeDD). The special aspect of *ICeDD* is the combination of Design Thinking as a front–end technique with non–software and the conducting of field experiments with several software alternatives. The idea behind *ICeDD* has been developed iteratively and incrementally by acting in real–world contexts, observing the effects and reflect on them with the help of a literature research.

Keywords: Design Thinking · Agile development ·
Value–Based Software Engineering · Field experiments · DevOps ·
Evolutionary IT Systems

1 Introduction

Implementing unique and novel software applications contains the great challenge that designers can only build on existing knowledge to a limited extent. This limits the designer in accurately predicting what delivers value for the users. To illustrate how difficult it is to make accurate predictions, have a look at the following real–world example.

The default experience for the *Netflix Frontpage* (see Fig. 1a) is a simple page with a *Sign In*–Button and a *Start Your Free Month*–Button offering three information: Their basic offering, the costs, and their promise to be able to use it everywhere.

This work was partially funded by the German Federal Ministry of Education and Research (BMBF) within the project Zentrum Musik Edition Medien (funding code: 01UG1714AB). Icons are from flaticon.com.

(a) default experience   (b) example prototype

Fig. 1. Example from *Using A/B Testing To Inform Your Designs* by Netflix [3].

Our intuition tells us that we can convince more people to sign up and to use the service if we give them more information. This is the way Netflix thought [3]. Thus, they implemented a prototype where users could browse the library without logging in (cf. Fig. 1b). They tested it against the default experience (cf. Fig. 1a) and were surprised that the default experience still has a better conversion rate.

Their first guess was that their intuition is right, but their implementation was not good enough. They implemented four more prototypes that they tested against the default experience. The other four prototypes were inferior to it as well. However, Netflix learnt during their tests why their default experience is better than their supposed improvement (cf. Blaylock and Iyenga [3]).

Although it was only a moderate change, Netflix was unable to predict that it would deteriorate. This in turn coincides with the experience others have had with unique and novel ideas. Kohavi et al. [20] give an overview of the figures of some companies such as Microsoft, Netflix or Web Analytics. Between 66% and 90% of their implemented ideas fail to show value. This means that in most cases experts have suggested to implement a certain feature but had been wrong in estimating its value.

Current development approaches like *agile software development* (e.g. scrum) or *human–centered design* are only of limited help in this challenge if used on their own. As Norman and Verganti [30] argue, these approaches only fit incremental innovations as they optimize along a known solution path. But they do not try to understand the problem and find more suitable solution paths. Approaches like *Design Thinking* with its *diverging and converging thinking* can help to understand underlying problems and suitable solutions (cf. Plattner et al. [32]). Hence, *Design Thinking* can help to better estimate the value. However, it is unclear how it can be applied successfully in software development [23].

Lindberg et al. [23] see two ways in which *Design Thinking* can be applied to software development. On the one hand as *Front–End Technique* and on the other hand as *Integrated Development Philosophy*. In case of the *Front–End Technique*, *Design Thinking* would be placed as a phase prior to the development process. The output of the *Design Thinking* phase would be a single solution that would then be implemented as software. *Design Thinking* as *Integrated Development Philosophy* is implemented as a one–team approach. This means that all core members (e.g. software developer, designer, lead user) are involved throughout the development process.

In this paper we are proposing a mixture of *Front–End Technique* and *Integrated Development Philosophy* to take creativity of the team and the underlying challenge of the Netflix example (cf. Sect. 2 for further details) into account. Hence, to take a user centric approach and to be sure that we deliver the value also in the actual context of use, we describe a software development approach with the following key aspects:

- A special role called *Value Designer* that ensures that the solution is aligned with the problem and that the knowledge of the *Design Thinking* stage is taken into the software development stage (cf. Sect. 4.6).
- *Design Thinking* as *Front–End Technique* that ends before there is only one possible solution left (cf. Sect. 4.2).
- A kind of continuation of the *Design Thinking* stage into software development through the simultaneous development of at least two solution paths and validation of these through field experiments (cf. Sect. 4.4).
- An intermediate stage to prepare the results of the *Design Thinking* stage for the Software Development stage (cf. Sect. 4.3).

Although design thinking is a methodology that does not limit the medium with which prototypes are produced, software as a prototype medium, especially used in the actual context of use, has special features (cf. Sect. 2) that need to be considered.

2 Challenges of Developing Innovative Software Applications

As already mentioned in the introduction, current approaches only fit incremental innovations. In this paper, the focus is on radical innovations. But what is it and how do they distinguish themselves?

To define it, we look at the technological radicalness that is characterized by Dahlin and Behrens [7] with three criteria:

- Criterion 1. The invention must be novel: it needs to be dissimilar from prior inventions.
- Criterion 2. The invention must be unique: it needs to be dissimilar from current inventions.
- Criterion 3. The invention must be adopted: it needs to influence the content of future inventions.

As can be seen in Criterion 3, the term successful radical invention implies that something must be adopted. But it can only be ex post determined whether something has been adopted and influenced the content of future inventions. This makes this criterion inapplicable in a development approach.

Criterion 1 is a comparison with the past and Criterion 2 with the present. If both criterions apply, we have created a radical invention that potentially can become a successful radical invention. If all three criteria have been fulfilled an invention can be considered as a successful radical invention.

We will continue to use the definition of a successful radical invention as a synonym for a radical innovation. Since Criterion 3 does not allow us to guarantee that the development process will lead to radical innovation, we limit ourselves to the first two criteria. Hence, we are not talking about radical innovations in this paper, but unique and novel software applications.

If our software application is unique and novel, which is a prerequisite for radical innovations, we can neither rely on data from the past nor the present. Hence, constraints and interacting dependencies must be uncovered instead of analyzing or categorizing observations. This in turn is only possible by probing or acting and observe the effects, which is what Netflix did as well in the *Sign–Up* example, described in the introduction.

Decision Making

The need for such a different approach is outlined by Kurtz and Snowden [21] in the *Cynefin* framework, which is developed to address "[...]the dynamics of situations, decisions, perspectives, conflicts, and changes in order to come to a consensus for decision–making under uncertainty". Instead of following a one size fits all approach [24], it's advocating different decision–making approaches according to the context/domain. Very briefly, in *Cynefin* we have clockwise (see Fig. 2) the domains *Chaotic, Complex, Complicated*, and *Obvious*. In the *Chaotic* domain, we know the least about the context and its constraints including interacting dependencies. The more we get to the *Obvious* domain, the more we know about the constraints and the better we can predict future states. Therefore, the closer we get to the *Obvious* domain, the better we can plan. The less we know, the more we must try out, to uncover and understand dependencies and constraints.

Unique and novel inventions are related to the unordered domains *Chaotic* and *Complex* that are the domains of *novel* and *emergent* practices, whereas according to Kurtz and Snowden [21], incremental innovations are mainly located between the boundary of *Obvious* and *Complicated*. The classification into these two domains also means that a mere selection of solutions is not enough, but that problem and solution understandings must be developed creatively. Therefore, the basic principles of creativity must be respected in the approach.

Creativity

The creative performance is determined by *domain knowledge* and *cognitive flexibility* as the two central factors on the cognitive level [8]. This has to do with the fact that creativity means combining the existing into something new. In case of humans, they are dependent on their knowledge and the flexibility to

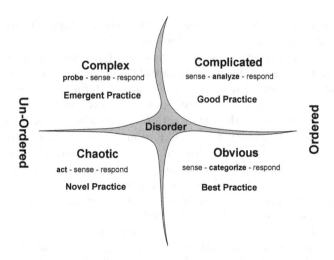

Fig. 2. The Cynefin Framework and its five domains *Obvious, Complicated, Complex, Chaotic, and Disorder*. Own representation based on [21]

combine it. The more knowledge they have and the more flexible they are, the more possibilities exist for novel recombinations.

Experts have a lot domain knowledge. But it is memorized in a quite stable scheme. Therefore, they lose cognitive flexibility. Engaging in a dynamic environment within one's domain attenuates the relationship between domain expertise and cognitive entrenchment [8].

What does that mean for software development? In SD we have at least the implementation and application domain. The standard case for software development is to have an expert from each of these two domains. Since the expert essentially has the domain knowledge for his domain, but not for the application domain, his creative performance for the application domain is limited.

Having knowledge from both domains is important to align the implementation to the core values of the application domain. But it takes a lot of effort for the implementation expert to dig deep into the application domain.

Especially, if you take a cross–project perspective, it becomes clear that a lot of effort is put into getting the implementation expert to learn about the application domain.

Preparing for Adoption

In addition to the first and second criteria (past and present perspective), the third criterion (future perspective) for radical innovations should also be considered in the approach. Even if an innovation cannot be predicted, it is important to know the attributes that influence the adoption of innovations. According to Rogers [35], innovation means that something is considered new by an individual or a group. It is irrelevant whether individuals or groups already exist who no longer regard it as new. Not even the time is important for this. It is only about the subjective perception of individuals or groups, whether something is regarded as innovation/new or not. Innovations do not spread arbitrarily or abruptly but are subject to a certain lawfulness. The process that describes this is defined by Rogers as *Diffusion of Innovations* and consists of four main elements. An (1) innovation is communicated through certain (2) channels over (3) time between the members of a (4) social system. In our paper, the first main element is particularly interesting, as it describes five attributes which have an influence on the product and the development process:

1. *Relative Advantage* is the degree to which an innovation is perceived as better than the idea to be replaced. At this point, it is not important whether the innovation provides objectively large advantages, but whether it is perceived as advantageous by the individual. The more advantageously an innovation is perceived, the faster it is accepted.
2. *Compatibility* is the degree to which an innovation is perceived to be compatible with the current value system, past experiences and needs of the adopters. If an innovation is incompatible, an adoption often requires a new value system, which is a relatively slow process. Therefore, compatible innovations are accepted faster than incompatible ones.
3. *Complexity* is the degree to which an innovation is perceived as difficult to understand and use. Innovations that are easier to understand spread more rapidly than innovations that require the adopter to learn new skills and knowledge.
4. *Trialability* is the degree to which an innovation is experimented with to some extent. An innovation that can be experimented with represents less uncertainty for the individual.
5. *Observability* is the degree to which the results of an innovation are visible to others. The easier it is for individuals to see the results of an innovation, the more likely they are to adopt them.

Regarding the development of unique and novel software applications, this means that the more tangible they are, the better these innovations can be assessed. Depending on the compatibility, it could take a longer time till people accept and give positive feedback. The more incompatible it is, the longer it can be acceptable that people don't like it. Therefore, the goal must be to build tangible prototypes or software applications as quickly as possible so that the relative value can be assessed at an early stage and with less bias.

Special Features of Software for Prototyping

As Boehm [5] points out in his summary of past software experiences, software development has always been in the continuum between *"engineer software like you engineer hardware"* and *software crafting*. The former means a process where everything is preplanned to ensure the quality before the first execution in the actual context of use. The second corresponds to a process of experimenting and working with rapid prototypes even in the actual context of use.

Focus of the development was from the 1970's to the early 2000's, especially the first part of the continuum. There were many reasons for this, such as contract design or infrastructure costs (e.g. testing, operation, distribution). The result, however, was an environment that is not beneficial for experimentation.

Traditional software is written in one technology and made to run on a system with shared libraries and fixed hardware. This leads to side effects if for example several versions of a shared library are required, or multiple applications require the same resource. Because multiple applications share a not isolated operating environment, changes can result in an unstable system. Therefore, changes are seldom made on such a system. In addition, a manual distribution, as is usual with such systems, leads to higher effort and higher risk (cf. Knight Capital's bankruptcy due to incorrect deployment [39]).

Depending on the complexity of the already implemented code, it could be that a switch in technology becomes too expensive, because everything must be transferred at once. In addition, polyglotism is usually not possible in relation to technologies. This leads to the fact that despite more suitable concepts in other technologies, the concepts and constraints of the initially selected technology must be preferred.

Using sequential, phase–oriented software development, software is usually implemented with a point–based engineering approach (cf. Denning et al. [9]) that results in a large overhead compared to set–based concurrent engineering as soon as changes must be communicated (cf. Ward et al. [44]). This overhead resulting from changes can make it seem unfeasible to integrate insights from experiments. In combination with figures about the relative cost of changing software (cf. Stecklein et al. [42]), it has also manifested the image that it is only possible to implement one solution at a time.

In summary, this inhibits experiments as follows:

- Risk to change a running system is high
- High effort to host several alternatives at the same time
- Integrating findings is associated with a high level of effort
- Technology decisions from the past limit the ability to make decisions in the future

Fortunately, this has changed since the advent of agile software development in the early 2000s. Also, technologies and approaches like Cloud Computing [1], Containerization [31], DevOps [40] and Microservices or Evolutionary IT Systems [9] have a positive impact here.

We provide further details how we encourage to use these for experiments in Sect. 4.4.

3   Foundations for Our Solution

From the previous section it becomes clear how important *Design Thinking* is for the development of unique and novel software applications. Above all, diverging and converging thinking (cf. Transitions in Cynefin [21]) as well as working with prototypes (cf. Preparing for Adoption in Sect. 2) are essential in order to find yet unknown interacting dependencies and constraints. However, once we enter the ordered domains (*Obvious* and *Complicated*) according to the Cynefin Framework, it is better to make decisions based on analysis or categorization than probing and acting (cf. Fig. 2). Therefore, the solution should be limited to the transition from the unordered domains to the ordered domains in order to give priority to the established methods there.

Transition means a continuous improvement of the understanding, whereby at the beginning there is a very incomplete understanding. Therefore, less properties of the final product are needed at the beginning, but more probing with different cheap solutions is needed. As a result, other media are more suitable as functionally integer software for use in the early phases. For example, paper prototypes can be produced much faster and cheaper if they are not to be all–inclusive or if interaction is less important. This is also pursued in set–based concurrent engineering in automotive engineering, where clay models instead of finished car bodies are the starting point [44].

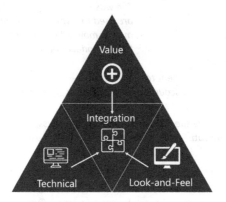

Fig. 3. Prototype Levels. Own representation based on Mayhew et al. [18]

Which general properties a prototype can have and how they can be reduced are described by Houde et al. [18] (cf. Fig. 3). The levels of prototypes they describe are *Value, Technical, Look & Feel,* and *Integration.* Houde et al. called *Value Role* in their paper, which translates to "what an artifact could do for a user". We find that a better description for this is *Value,* according to the idea of Value–Based Software Engineering [4]. In this context *Value* is not a financial term, but is meant as "relative worth, utility, or importance". The *Technical* or *Implementation* Level is for "answering technical questions about how a future artifact might actually be made to work". And the *Look & Feel* Level to "explore and demonstrate options for the concrete experience of an artifact". The last level is *Integration,* which can be an integration of properties of two or all three levels.

Unfortunately, Houde et al. [18] do not describe how to navigate through the levels. Therefore, we use the recommended user experience design process proposed by Mayhew [27] (cf. Fig. 4). They suggest that the first thing to be determined is the utility as it is the prerequisite of a "great [...] user experience". This allows a goal–oriented development and minimizes the risks of changes on the functional or technical level (cf. Stecklein et al. [42] and point–based engineering [44] for the cost effects of changes on those levels.). It also coincides with the basic ideas of Value–Based Software Engineering, which sees value (e.g. utility) as guidance providing and a shortening of the consideration of value as the cause of most software project failures (cf. Boehm [4]). For this reason, our approach also starts at the value level, which includes usability and persuaviness (cf. Sect. 2).

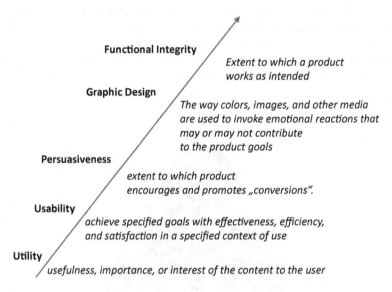

Fig. 4. Recommended user experience design process. Own representation based on Mayhew [27]

In contrast to the recommended user experience design process, we do not see the need that *Functional Integrity* must follow subsequently *Graphic Design*. Due to the greater adoption of the Model–View–Presenter (MVP) architecture pattern (cf. Potel [34] and Fowler [12]) in software technologies (e.g. .NET or Angular) the presentation layer got more separated from the logic layer (e.g. in comparison to MVC). This allows a largely independent development of these levels (*Technical* and *Look & Feel* related to the prototype levels), which is why they can be developed in parallel.

As a result, for navigation through the prototype levels, *Value* must first be identified. In the next step, *Technical* and *Look & Feel* integrated with *Value* can be examined in parallel. Finally, integration is achieved across all three levels.

4   Solution Idea: Insight Centric Design and Development

It is from the combination of considerations from the previous sections that we ultimately developed our software development approach *Insight Centric Design and Development* (ICeDD) (cf. Fig. 5) to handle the challenge of developing unique and novel software applications.

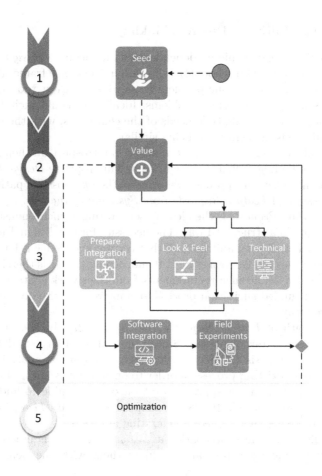

Fig. 5. Integrated Process for *ICeDD* based on [18, 19, 21, 23, 27]

Insights is intended to emphasize that this approach, like qualitative research, is mainly concerned with the reconstruction of meaning and the understanding of the problem and solution space. The focus is on creating unique and novel software applications in terms of *Value* and not *Technical* or *Look & Feel* (cf. Sect. 3). Incremental improvements like in human–centered design (cf. Sect. 1) and reliable measurement is outsourced to the (5) Optimization stage, which is the final stage. The other four stages in *ICeDD* are *(1) Initialize Design*

Thinking, (2) Execute Design Thinking with Non–Software, (3) Prepare Design Thinking with Software, and *(4) Execute Design Thinking with Software.* We have divided *Design Thinking* into *(2) Execute Design Thinking with Non–Software* and *(4) Execute Design Thinking with Software* in order to take advantage of the non–software benefits, especially at the beginning when the problem and solution space is expanded by building many different solutions.

4.1   Stage (1): Initialize Design Thinking

The result of the process is highly dependent on an adequate *Design Challenge.* According to the Stanford d.school [41], the *Design Challenge* frames the process and should not constrain to one problem to solve nor leave it too broad which gives troubles in finding tangible problems. Ideally, it should include multiple characters, problems, and multiple needs of the characters, with the characters, problems, and needs in themselves being similar.

This is good to evaluate a *Design Challenge* in retrospect but helps only to a limited extent in finding such a challenge. To find appropriate *Design Challenges* and therefore initialize our approach we propose the two possible paths *On–Site Feature Requests* and *Feature Requests from Systematic Analysis.*

On–Site Feature Requests is the idea of users stating asynchronously requests for improvements in a structured way. The necessity for this lies in Tacit Knowledge (cf. Gervasi et al. [14]) and the fact that certain knowledge is hard to recall without specific cues (cf. Gervasi et al. [14] and Benner [2]). It is therefore important that users can define such requirements from their work context. In [38] we proposed a tool–guided elicitation process to empower users to do such requests in a structured way.

The other path of *Feature Requests from Systematic Analysis* is based on the analysis by an external person. Since our context does not allow a mere categorization or analysis (cf. Sect. 2), a traditional systems analysis with the aim to examine an existing process in order to optimize it is not useful. Instead, we need a theory–generating approach that makes it possible to find unknown problems or solutions as well. In [28] we adopted *Grounded Theory* for software development to create such a theory generating approach.

With results from these two paths, a *Design Challenge* is created to start swarming by finding attractors and evaluate them with the help of *Design Thinking.*

4.2   Stage (2): Execute Design Thinking with Non–Software

In this stage *Design Thinking* with the help of non–software prototypes and *Design Challenges* from the previous stages is carried out. The goal is to explore the problem and solution space with non–software prototypes to get a better understanding before software is used as a medium. Since *Design Thinking* is a methodology, it must be initiated according to the conditions (e.g. duration or stakeholders).

In our projects we have initiated *Design Thinking* as a one–day workshop format in which both developers and users participate. This workshop sensitizes the various stakeholders to each other and generates initial ideas. In a further step, these ideas are refined by the *Value Designer* (cf. Sect. 4.6) in coordination with the respective stakeholders.

The possible solutions should be reduced in this stage to at least two, but not more than five solutions. Result of this stage are non–software prototypes optimized on a *Value* Level and their documentation. Since the prototypes are more abstract than it is necessary for an implementation, they still must be prepared for implementation.

4.3   Stage (3): Prepare Design Thinking with Software

Overall goal of this stage is to refine the prototypes on a *Technical* and *Look & Feel* Level and transfer them into requirements that can be used in a software development process (*Prepare Integration*). The task of the refinement on the *Technical* and *Look & Feel* Level is not to come up with novel solutions regarding these levels, but to align already existing solutions to the discovered value propositions from the previous stage. The *Value Designer* (cf. Sect. 4.6) supports the designer (*Look & Feel*) or the software developer (*Technical*) to ensure that the value is not lost.

The next step is to integrate all three levels (*Value, Technical,* and *Look & Feel*) on the requirements level (cf. Fig. 5). The requirements should be specific and understandable but not include all underlying decisions to not overburden the developer. Nevertheless, it should be possible to understand the underlying incentives if necessary, in order to understand freedoms and make adjustments. Therefore, the requirements should be linked to the sources to allow traceability.

4.4   Stage (4): Execute Design Thinking with Software

Using *Design Thinking* means evolution of the problem and solution understanding, experimenting with alternatives, and short learning cycles. Challenges in software development that arise from these have been listed in Sect. 2. In order to overcome these, an adapted software development approach is required. To adapt such an approach, the 4P's (cf. Fig. 6) described by Jacobson et al. [19] are quite useful:

"The end result of a software *project* is a *product* that is shaped by many different types of *people* as it is developed. Guiding the efforts of the *people* involved in the project is a software development *process*, a template that explains the steps needed to complete the *project*. Typically, the *process* is automated by a *tool* or set of *tools*."

This means that it is not appropriate for a solution to consider only the process or only the product characteristics, since all the 4P's depend on each other. For example, product properties to enable incremental development may represent an overhead when a strictly sequential process is required (e.g. for legal reasons). Furthermore, tools can be needed to make a process practicable at all.

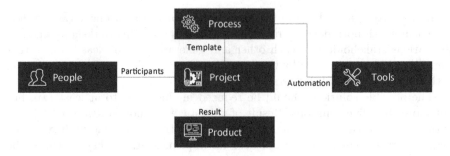

Fig. 6. The 4P's People, Project, Product, Process, and Tools from the Unified Software Development Process [19]. Own representation.

Or people carry out processes differently because they do not match with their mindset. Therefore, we describe in this section for all 4P's the characteristics, which makes *Design Thinking with Software* possible.

People. It is important for the persons involved to understand that the artefacts created in this stage do not necessarily remain as they are and are partly discarded. Since at this stage the development of an understanding of the value comes first, people must be able to concentrate on the properties of the application that are necessary for the valuation of this application. A mindset with which the perfect application is to be developed immediately is not beneficial at this point. There should be a basic understanding of experimenting. Otherwise the same requirements apply as in agile software development.

Product. As Denning et al. [9] emphasize, traditional preplanned development focus on architectures that meet specifications from knowable and collectable requirements, do not need to change before the system is implemented, and can be intellectually grasped by individuals. This is not compatible with our requirements for *Design Thinking*, which is why we need evolutionary architectures instead.

Evolutionary architectures are designed for continuous adaptation through successive rapid changes or through competition between several systems [9]. Ford et al. [11] describe how evolutionary architectures can be achieved through appropriate coupling and allowing for incremental change. Patterns like Model–View–Presenter [34] separate the UI logic from the business logic and therefore enable an independent development of the UI from the Backend. Event–driven architectures and Microservices allow more loosely coupled smaller components that can be polyglot regarding technology.

Event sourcing [13] is particularly interesting in this context, as it enables parallel models, reconstruction of model states, and synergy effects, e.g. for the collection of interaction data. With parallel models the operation of different versions can be enabled on the one hand. On the other hand, data models can be adapted with less consideration of side effects. Model state reconstruction is useful for troubleshooting, preparing test environments, and data recovery.

In summary, evolutionary architectures help to provide fallback variants, increase reliability, develop individual components independently, and reduce the complexity of the individual components. By using synergies with event sourcing, it reduces the effort for data collection in experiments.

Process. The requirement for this stage is the rapid implementation of software alternatives and conducting of field experiments. In the previous stages an understanding of interacting dependencies, constraints, problem space, and solution space has been deepened. Therefore, the requirements at this stage should be stable to the extent that changes no longer occur in such a likeliness that cycles of several hours are useful and necessary. For this reason, these cycle lengths do not have to be supported in this stage and longer cycles can be considered, as in agile software development (cf. Terho et al. [43]).

DevOps including Continuous Deployment in combination with Agile Software Development is very suitable for this. According to Sharma et al. [40], DevOps' goal is to accelerate and increase the frequency with which production changes are made available in order to receive feedback from real users as early and frequently as possible. Consequently, these processes ensure the timely availability of alternatives for experiments.

If you compare the Build–Measure–Learn Cycle from Lean Management (cf. Poppendieck and Poppendieck [33]) with the principles of the Agile Software Development (cf. Meyer [29]) it stands out that Agile Software Development is focused on an acceleration of the Build step to increase the frequency of user feedback. The parts Measure and Learn and their expression are missing. However, these are indispensable in order to learn from their use.

To improve this situation, the implementation is embraced by a process for conducting experiments. At this stage, field experiments are to be used instead of controlled experiments. The advantage of field experiments is the high external validity. We need this as we are still in a state where our mission is understanding and for that we need to reconstruct meaning or subjective perspectives from the usage in production. The disadvantage of field experiments is the usually lower reliability compared to controlled experiments. At this point, however, controlled experiments would not be appropriate, since they require a good knowledge of dependencies and interfering variables.

Project. For each *Design Challenge* that ran through the third stage, a project is initialized. The aim is to understand which of the problems and solutions found lead to a value.

Tools. In order to make experimentation with software solutions more feasible, automation and assistance tools are needed. The use of evolutionary architectures, as described in product, in combination with containerization [31], cloud architectures [1] and a build server for the continuous deployment pipeline enables independent automated deployment as well as roll–back of the individual alternatives, versions or components.

To make them available during an experiment a user specific online orchestration tool should be present. Its task is to orchestrate (e.g. by rerouting or feature toggles) the different alternatives, versions or components individually for each user. An opt–out for the user is essential so that he can continue to work productively with the system in the event of errors or malfunctions.

Since data (e.g. interaction data, surveys or free annotations) accumulate in experiments, a tool is required in which these can be stored, aggregated, and analyzed.

Finally an experiment management system is needed, that guides the users of *ICeDD* through the experiment design and controls the tools for orchestration and data accordingly.

4.5   Stage (5): Optimization/Incremental Improvement

The main objective of *ICeDD* is to better understand the problem and solution space in cases of little or no knowledge. Once the fundamental interacting dependencies and constraints have been understood, it is possible, for example, to design a controlled experiment to learn in detail how the solution can be further optimized. Without this, it would not be possible to eliminate interfering factors and explain why the experiment has a valid operationalization. Of course, other methods that are suitable for incremental innovation (cf. Norman and Verganti [30]) can also be used for optimization.

4.6   Roles

In *ICeDD* we have the normal software development team as in Scrum as well as users. The difference is that instead of a product owner we have a role called *Value Designer*. Her main purpose is to ensure that intentions of the stakeholders are met, and value is delivered with the software application. In terms of Value Based Software Engineering [4] the *Value Designer* is responsible to identify all success critical stakeholders and to mediate between them. Therefore, she neither must be a domain expert nor a technology expert but needs considerable knowledge of both sides. She is the only role involved in all stages as well steps of *ICeDD*.

5   Research Method

Inspired by the ideas of *Action Research* from Lewin [22] and *Grounded Theory* from Glaser and Strauss [15] the concept of ICeDD was developed iteratively and incrementally by acting in a real–world context, observing the effects and reflect on them with the help of a literature research. The foundations for this are the three practical projects *Firefighter Training System* [36], *History in Paderborn App (HiP–App)* [37], and *Zentrum Musik Edition Medien* (ZenMEM) [28].

The *Firefighter Training System* was a one–year project from which it was realized that the *Trialability* and *Observability* of an innovation is important for the assessment of its value by users (cf. Rogers [35]).

HiP–App and *ZenMEM* have been running in parallel since 2014. While the *HiP–App* is developed by a group of constantly changing students (up to 20), *ZenMEM* is developed by a group of up to five permanent developers.

The setting of the *HiP–App* makes it particularly suitable for trying out processes and process changes. Therefore, every semester new building blocks (e.g. Scrum, Scaling Scrum to two teams, Continuous Deployment) were introduced in the *HiP–App* to identify possible challenges from their use and to explain and resolve them with the help of a literature search in corresponding fields. The concepts developed here were transferred to the tool development in *ZenMEM* in order to test them in an additional context. This has allowed us to move step by step closer to the *ICeDD* approach presented here.

6 Related Work

There are some approaches that use *Design Thinking* as a *Front–End Technique* (cf. [16,17,26,46]). They stop with the milestone *x–is finished prototype* and use only one solution for the software development. The limitation of this approach is that there are no experiments in the real world with software, especially not with several alternatives like in our approach. To uncover certain dependencies or constraints like in the Netflix example in the introduction, at least two alternatives must be compared in an experiment in production.

This leads to controlled online experiments. Lindgren and Münch [25] surveyed the state of experiment systems in software development and list several examples for controlled online experiments. The goal of such experiments is as well as in Continuous Software Engineering to get to small incremental quality improvements [10]. The overall goal of *ICeDD* is to find unique and novel software applications regarding value. Therefore, *ICeDD's* research mission is to build understanding of the problem and solution space in order to find such a software application. For this reason, the focus is not on a mainly quantitative, but on a qualitative approach to the subject.

7 Discussion and Further Work

In this paper we presented the outline of a value–centered approach for unique and novel software applications called *Insight Centric Design & Development* by adapting *Design Thinking* into a mixture of *Front–End Technique* and *Integrated Development Philosophy*. This is not solely based on considerations but has been created iteratively and incrementally by acting in real world contexts, observing the effects and reflect on them with the help of a literature research. It has turned out that a consideration of *Design Thinking* with software on a purely process–related level is not enough. Rather, for a successful application, the product properties, people and tools must also be considered. Otherwise, too many factors can inhibit the necessary experimentation with software alternatives in production.

Some parts of the approach have already been partially implemented by us. In order to be able to evaluate the feasibility, we still lack above all tools which makes experimenting with software more viable. Therefore, the mentioned experiment management system, user–specific online orchestration, and feedback collecting and analysis system will be investigated in future work.

References

1. Armbrust, M., et al.: A view of cloud computing. Commun. ACM **53**(4), 50–58 (2010)
2. Benner, P.: From novice to expert. Menlo Park (1984)
3. Blaylock, A., Iyengar, N.: Art vs. Science: Using A/B Testing To Inform Your Designs (Netflix at Designers + Geeks) (2016). https://www.youtube.com/watch?v=RHWVWiiW8DQ. Accessed 20 Apr 2018
4. Boehm, B.W.: Value-based software engineering: overview and agenda. In: Biffl, S., Aurum, A., Boehm, B., Erdogmus, H., Grünbacher, P. (eds.) Value-Based Software Engineering, pp. 3–14. Springer, Heidelberg (2006). https://doi.org/10.1007/3-540-29263-2_1
5. Boehm, B.: A view of 20th and 21st century software engineering. In: Proceedings of the 28th International Conference on Software Engineering, pp. 12–29. ACM, May 2006
6. Corbin, J., Strauss, A., Strauss, A.L.: Basics of Qualitative Research. Sage, Thousand Oaks (2014)
7. Dahlin, K.B., Behrens, D.M.: When is an invention really radical?: defining and measuring technological radicalness. Res. Policy **34**(5), 717–737 (2005)
8. Dane, E.: Reconsidering the trade-off between expertise and flexibility: a cognitive entrenchment perspective. Acad. Manag. Rev. **35**(4), 579–603 (2010)
9. Denning, P.J., Gunderson, C., Hayes-Roth, R.: The profession of IT Evolutionary system development. Commun. ACM **51**(12), 29–31 (2008)
10. Fitzgerald, B., Stol, K.J.: Continuous software engineering and beyond: trends and challenges. In: Proceedings of the 1st International Workshop on Rapid Continuous Software Engineering, pp. 1–9. ACM, June 2014
11. Ford, N., Parsons, R., Kua, P.: Building Evolutionary Architectures: Support Constant Change. O'Reilly Media, Inc., Sebastopol (2017)
12. Fowler, M.: GUI Architectures (2006). https://www.martinfowler.com/eaaDev/uiArchs.html. Accessed 10 Jan 2019
13. Fowler, M.: Event Sourcing (2005). https://martinfowler.com/eaaDev/EventSourcing.html. Accessed 10 Jan 2019
14. Gervasi, V., et al.: Unpacking tacit knowledge for requirements engineering. In: Maalej, W., Thurimella, A. (eds.) Managing Requirements Knowledge, pp. 23–47. Springer, Heidelberg (2013)
15. Glaser, B.G., Strauss, A.L.: Discovery of Grounded Theory: Strategies for Qualitative Research. Routledge, Abingdon (2017)

16. Gurusamy, K., Srinivasaraghavan, N., Adikari, S.: An integrated framework for design thinking and agile methods for digital transformation. In: Marcus, A. (ed.) DUXU 2016. LNCS, vol. 9746, pp. 34–42. Springer, Cham (2016). https://doi.org/10.1007/978-3-319-40409-7_4

17. Häger, F., Kowark, T., Krüger, J., Vetterli, C., Übernickel, F., Uflacker, M.: DT@Scrum: integrating design thinking with software development processes. In: Plattner, H., Meinel, C., Leifer, L. (eds.) Design Thinking Research. UI, pp. 263–289. Springer, Cham (2015). https://doi.org/10.1007/978-3-319-06823-7_14

18. Houde, S., Hill, C.: What do prototypes prototype. In: Handbook of Human-Computer Interaction, vol. 2, pp. 367–381 (1997)

19. Jacobson, I., Booch, G., Rumbaugh, J.: The Unified Software Development Process, vol. 1. Addison-Wesley, Reading (1999)

20. Kohavi, R., et al.: Online experimentation at Microsoft. In: Data Mining Case Studies, vol. 11 (2009)

21. Kurtz, C.F., Snowden, D.J.: The new dynamics of strategy: sense-making in a complex and complicated world. IBM Syst. J. **42**(3), 462–483 (2003)

22. Lewin, K.: Action research and minority problems. J. Soc. Issues **2**(4), 34–46 (1946)

23. Lindberg, T., Meinel, C., Wagner, R.: Design thinking: a fruitful concept for IT development? In: Meinel, C., Leifer, L., Plattner, H. (eds.) Design Thinking, pp. 3–18. Springer, Heidelberg (2011). https://doi.org/10.1007/978-3-642-13757-0_1

24. Linders, B., Snowden, D.: Q&A with Dave Snowden on Leadership and Using Cynefin for Capturing Requirements (2016). https://www.infoq.com/articles/dave-snowden-leadership-cynefin-requirements. Accessed 27 Jun 2018

25. Lindgren, E., Münch, J.: Software development as an experiment system: a qualitative survey on the state of the practice. In: Lassenius, C., Dingsøyr, T., Paasivaara, M. (eds.) XP 2015. LNBIP, vol. 212, pp. 117–128. Springer, Cham (2015). https://doi.org/10.1007/978-3-319-18612-2_10

26. Lucena, P., Braz, A., Chicoria, A., Tizzei, L.: IBM design thinking software development framework. In: Silva da Silva, T., Estácio, B., Kroll, J., Mantovani Fontana, R. (eds.) WBMA 2016. CCIS, vol. 680, pp. 98–109. Springer, Cham (2017). https://doi.org/10.1007/978-3-319-55907-0_9

27. Mayhew, D.J.: Usability + persuasiveness + graphic design = eCommerce user experience. In: Jacko, J.A. (ed.) Human Computer Interaction Handbook: Fundamentals, Evolving Technologies, and Emerging Applications. CRC Press (2012)

28. Meise, B., et al.: Von implizitem Wissen zu nachhaltigen Systemanforderungen. In: Tagungsband der Forschungsdaten in den Geisteswissenschaften (FORGE) (2016)

29. Meyer, B.: Agile. The Good, the Hype and the Ugly. Springer, Heidelberg (2014). https://doi.org/10.1007/978-3-319-05155-0

30. Norman, D.A., Verganti, R.: Incremental and radical innovation: design research vs technology and meaning change. Des. Issues **30**(1), 78–96 (2014)

31. Pahl, C.: Containerization and the PaaS cloud. IEEE Cloud Comput. **2**(3), 24–31 (2015)

32. Plattner, H., Meinel, C., Leifer, L.: Design Thinking Research. Springer, Heidelberg (2012)

33. Poppendieck, M., Poppendieck, T.: Lean Software Development: An Agile Toolkit: An Agile Toolkit. Addison-Wesley, Boston (2003)

34. Potel, M.: MVP: Model-View-Presenter the Taligent programming model for C++ and Java, p. 20. Taligent Inc. (1996)

35. Rogers, E.M.: Diffusion of Innovations. Free Press, New York (2003)

36. Senft, B., Sudbrock, C., Fischer, H.: IT-Unterstützung im praktischen Ausbildungsbetrieb der Feuerwehr. In: Mensch & Computer Workshopband, pp. 111–116, September 2014
37. Senft, B., Oberthür, S.: Auf dem Weg zu einer experimentellen und evidenzbasierten Softwareentwicklung in den Digital Humanities. In: Konferenzabstracts der 3. Tagung des Verbands "Digital Humanities im deutschsprachigen Raum e. V." (2016)
38. Senft, B., Fischer, H., Oberthür, S., Patkar, N.: Assist users to straightaway suggest and describe experienced problems. In: Marcus, A., Wang, W. (eds.) DUXU 2018. LNCS, vol. 10918, pp. 758–770. Springer, Cham (2018). https://doi.org/10.1007/978-3-319-91797-9_52
39. Seven, D.: Knightmare: A DevOps Cautionary Tale (2014). https://dougseven.com/2014/04/17/knightmare-a-devops-cautionary-tale/. Accessed 10 Jan 2019
40. Sharma, S., Coyne, B.: DevOps for Dummies, 3rd Limited IBM edn (2017)
41. Stanford d.school: Create Design Challenges Guidelines (2016). https://dschool-old.stanford.edu/groups/k12/wiki/613e8/Create_Design_Challenges_Guidelines.html. Accessed 10 Jan 2019
42. Stecklein, J.M., Dabney, J., Dick, B., Haskins, B., Lovell, R., Moroney, G.: Error cost escalation through the project life cycle (2004)
43. Terho, H., Suonsyrjä, S., Systä, K., Mikkonen, T.: Understanding the relations between iterative cycles in software engineering (2017)
44. Ward, A., Liker, J.K., Cristiano, J.J., Sobek, D.K.: The second Toyota paradox: how delaying decisions can make better cars faster. Sloan Manag. Rev. **36**, 43–43 (1995)
45. Yin, R.K.: Case Study Research and Applications: Design and Methods. Sage Publications, Thousand Oaks (2018)
46. Ximenes, B.H., Alves, I.N., Araújo, C.C.: Software project management combining agile, lean startup and design thinking. In: Marcus, A. (ed.) DUXU 2015. LNCS, vol. 9186, pp. 356–367. Springer, Cham (2015). https://doi.org/10.1007/978-3-319-20886-2_34

The Construction and Practice of Risk Control Model in User Research

Yan Wang and Junnan Ye[✉]

School of Art Design and Media,
East China University of Science and Technology (ECUST),
M. BOX 286, No. 130 Meilong Road, Xuhui District, Shanghai 200237, China
54756432@qq.com, yejunnan971108@qq.com

Abstract. The importance of user research has been fully recognized by the design industry. However, user research is a project that requires a lot of resources. How to control the risk in the process of user research is very important to the success of the project. Based on the theory of "node control", this paper constructs a risk control model for user research, and analyzes the design process and organizational structure from six indicators: redundancy, one-time, openness, dynamics, isolation and full participation. On this basis, it puts forward three major risk control principles: joint innovation, landmark management and full participation. The risk control of user research was applied on a well-known sports brand's user research. Through the comparative study, it was found that the risk of user research has been effectively controlled. This risk control model of user research is becoming more and more popular and in-depth application in the process of user research, which will greatly improve the cost-effectiveness and success rate of user research.

Keywords: User research · Risk control · Node control · Full participation · Landmark management · Joint innovation

1 Introduction

In recent years, a large number of outstanding enterprises have emerged in China. All of them have make great efforts on the user research. Many small or later-coming enterprises also hope to gain core competitiveness through user research. However, they find that user research not only has a high demand for technology and team, but also has high risk. "Exploratory fieldwork requires researchers to plan for a range of outcomes" [1]. Therefore, whether the risks in user research can be controlled well determines that whether user research can be done well.

"The best companies often work closely with their customers to uncover needs and wants that can be translated into new or improved product or service offerings" [2]. First of all, two kinds of understandings shall be clarified. First, it is also risky without performance of user research. As everyone knows that the market is changing while the consumer demand is also changing, so it is impossible to try to take the fixed approach for the changing market. Then, the first-mover advantage will be grasped by the manufacturers who have conducted user research and successfully developed new

A. Marcus and W. Wang (Eds.): HCII 2019, LNCS 11586, pp. 385–393, 2019.
https://doi.org/10.1007/978-3-030-23535-2_28

products. Moreover, these manufacturers who take the first-mover advantage will use their dominant position to set a high standard for the later-coming manufacturers to make them attend the brutal homogeneous competition. As a result, the manufacturers who have not conducted user research will be forced to compete at a low price, resulting in loss of profits and unsustainable operation ultimately.

Second, user research will be performed with a certain cost. Although it can bring high revenues, such as gaining the initiative of market and excess profits and accumulating the core competitiveness, etc., the enterprise is required to understand that user research is possible to fail due to the constantly changing external factors. "Circumstances that can make it difficult to involve users in the research process include poor health, the time involved, and the challenges of travelling from home to various activities" [3]. When these problem cannot be solved, the mission of user research fails. However, it is impossible to recover the manpower, material resources and financial resources which have been invested in the user research.

2   Risk Control

The risks can be controlled from two aspects for user research. One aspect is that risk can be avoided by the model of node control, which includes three principles: Joint study; Landmark management; full participation. The transfer of risk also means the output of benefits. The large nodes in the user research process are set to conduct as landmarks. Risk assessment should be performed at these landmarks during the user research process. So the previous knowledge can be accumulated and the following risk can be effectively foreseen. As mentioned above, the process of user research is an evolutionary process, so it is impossible to accurately foresee the risks that will be faced later at the beginning of project. However, we can effectively break down the risk, or stop the project midway to avoid greater risk through dividing the whole research process into several relatively independent processes to perform risk assessment (Fig. 1).

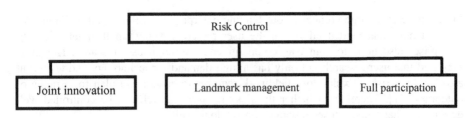

Fig. 1. The model of node control

2.1   Joint Innovation

"Employ a crossdisciplinary team, bringing in perspective from various parts of the organization" [2]. As far as joint innovation is concerned, performance of user research can be performed with the cooperation of several enterprises in the same industry. The results of user research are shared by every attending enterprise. In addition, each enterprise can conduct suitable in-depth research based on the results of the research since each one has different development directions. Now, the concept of competition is different from the past. Different enterprises seek cooperation in the process of competition. Enterprises should pay more attention to diversified competition, while each of them has its own key directions. As a corporate citizen in the society, the enterprise should think about how to seek its own development instead of how to bring down other enterprise. So it is possible to conduct joint user research among different enterprises.

From the perspective of internal organization of enterprise, it is also a very risky business to conduct user research. The enterprise is very weak in the period of reforming because it leaves its most familiar and most competitive product field but steps in a new product field that it is not very good at. The enterprise should adjust the resources resource allocation according to the external environment it is in and the internal resources that it controls.

2.2 Landmark Management

Landmark management also can be used in the process of user research. The process of user research can be divided into several distinct stages, risk assessment is conducted for each stage and different departments are required to reach a certain consensus at certain key points. This way can reduce the conflicts in the future team work and also can make everyone understand what problems will occur in the later stage and what measures should be taken for these problems. In addition, it can play the role of both risk aversion and risk warning.

Some people think that if a consensus can not be reached on a large node, each department should study the solution of existing problems until they reach a consensus. They believed that only when the entire research team has reached a consensus on this key node can they go forward to the next stage. However, we have different viewpoint on this idea. User research can not always reach a complete consensus in every step. As long as the team has a certain understanding of the problem, they can continue to carry out the next step and keep thinking about the existing problems. In fact, the answer will automatically emerge in subsequent research in many cases. If we stop moving forward, all of us may fall into endless quarrels and can not find a specific solution.

2.3 Full Participation

Full participation means that the designer shall participate in the whole process of user research. What role to play is important for designers. Designer s should research needs of the users and provide the final product simultaneously on the base of the research results. Again, the designer is the key person to finally integrates various elements and relationships into the specific product. Therefore, the designer should participate in the whole process of user research.

Besides, the designer should be involved from the beginning of the project approval because he/she has had a lot of understanding of the user's needs in the previous projects. "It is worth adding that the research discussed here is empirical research. This is in contrast to theoretical research" [4]. The knowledge of the entire research team is constantly enriched and the understanding is gradually clear in this process, while the designer can obtain a large amount of explicit and implicit knowledge which constructs the basis of the designer's own design.

In addition, the designer should track the using of new product after the product is launched in the market. The new product cannot be a fully mature product after launched in the market, so its shortcomings will be exposed more fully at this stage. The new product will face a wider range of users. Different consumers may purchase this product for different reasons, while the various living environments faced by consumers are more complicated than those covered by user research.

In real life, most consumers will make more or less adjustments to the products after purchasing them. "A common example of HCI research following the observational method is a usability evaluation" [4]. At this time, the designer is required to have an open mind, who should not set a standard for the use of product and force buyers to learn this standard, but should fully observe the consumers' operation during the using process. So we will enter another stage of user research, that is, from creating something out of nothing to seeking the better solutions. The designer can ask questions directly about a product in this stage. The mission of the user research will be over when the product is improved to a certain extent. When will we end the user research is related to the aim of the user research mission that was originally set.

Since the design is not performed only by the designer, but by a team. If the designer can not participate in the whole process, the designer and other team members will have a big gap in the accumulation of knowledge and understanding of the research objectives in the later design process. The whole team and team members have accumulated a lot of implicit knowledge in the process of user research. It is difficult for the designer who has not participated in the whole process to communicate with other team members on the same knowledge platform.

3   Case Study

3.1   Introduction of the Company

X Company was founded in the early 1990s, which has become a well-known sports goods company in China. Its main businesses include selling sports shoes and sportswear, as well as other related businesses. The types of shoes mainly include soccer shoes, basketball shoes, tennis shoes and running shoes, etc.; Sportswear mainly includes basketball uniforms and soccer uniforms, etc. Today, the market situation faced by this company is that it still can gain generous profits in the market due to its early access to markets. However, this company has a sense of incompetence when facing the internationally renowned manufacturers, such as Nike and Adidas, etc., and has a strong unsafe sense when facing the rise of many domestic sports goods manufacturers.

3.2   Introduction of the Design Department

Shoe design department and clothing design department are the two main design departments of the company. The design department has developed a design process (see Fig. 2 for details). Production Design Direction refers to the product plan issued by the company product planning department. Color Flow refers to a table about the base colors, the popular colors (seasonal colors) and sports-specific colors of the product. The design department will confirm whether the colors used in this season are harmonious and whether there are color conflicts between the categories according to the table. Collection Map refers to the overall design idea based on the division of the categories, which is presented by pictures, such as classical and youth, etc. Fabric Pages refers to the use of specific manufacturing materials to express the specific design scheme.

The shoe design process is similar to the costume design process. The designers will discuss the overall design at first, while each design will be always managed by a same designer. A shoe designer thinks that they will learn from the advanced craft of Nike and Adidas, but they do not learn from their design ideas. Designers believe that the design of the shoes with low price more relies on the designer's design experience. They rarely do user testing during the design process. Generally speaking, the test of the product is carried out in the Order-placing meeting. The advantages and disadvantages of the design will be judged according to the order quantity of the dealer.

They believe that the quality of design is mainly relied on two factors: 1. China's large and diverse consumer groups, which enable the sales of any kinds of products; 2. Design experience and intuition that designers have formed over the years, while they believe that the price but not the design is the first competitiveness in the Chinese market. Besides the ordinary task, the company will also set up special groups for special events, such as the Olympic.

There are four people in the R&D department of the company, two of which collect information, one of which is engaged in bio-mechanical research and the other is engaged in mould research. There is a market research department inside the company, but most of the research work is performed by outside professional companies. There are flagship stores in the bustling streets of the important cities. The different layout is used to distinguish the product categories. There are a focus booth and a historical review area in the store, and the male and female products are distinguished by the background color. In addition, the company participates in Sporting-goods Fair every year.

3.3   Description of Problems

The designers believe that the problem lies with the persons who executed the process instead of the process itself. Everyone has different understanding of the process. In addition, it is impossible to operate in full accordance to the planed process due to the limited number of designers and insufficient time and effort.

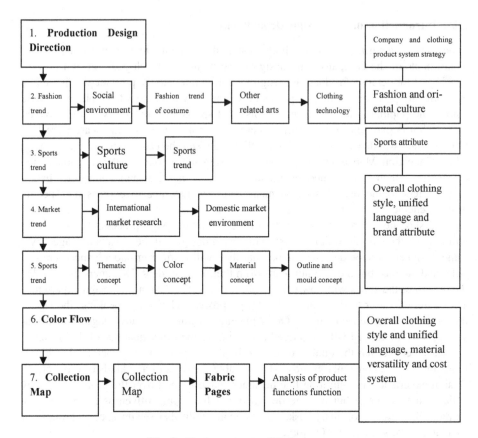

Fig. 2. Design process of X Company

The clothing design department and the shoe design department are not integrated. So good shoe designs can not be penetrated into the clothing design while the good clothing designs can not match the shoe design. Most communications between designers rely on private communication since there are few formal communication channels.

The supervisor of the clothing design department believed that clothing products are also the psychological products and instant products. Moreover, intuitive design accounts for 80% in clothing design. There is a lack of communication with users and a lack of research on users in the process of design. They said that they also needed do some user research during the design process, such as taking some photos and doing some simple conversations, but all of which were superficial.

According to the design process, the product planning group formulates a product planning and submits it to the design department to complete. The product planning group includes product manager and analysis group. However, the design department thinks that they are in a passive situation because the upstream product planning team constantly vetoes their design, while the downstream development department (responsible for making samples) often believes that their design planning can't be realized.

The market research department thought that inter-departmental coordination is not smooth enough- market research sometimes intervenes too early and sometimes too late.

There are three problems of the flagship store:

1. The highlights of design can not be expressed from the shop design;
2. The design of the store is ordinary with low sense of grade;
3. The store layout is dominated by graphic design and lacks interactive design.

4 Problem Analysis and Suggestions

In view of the above problems, we put forward six suggestions according to the risk control model of user research.

4.1 Sufficient Resources

All designers complain about the situation of under-staffing. However, according to further survey, sometimes the designers are very busy and sometimes very idle, which is related to the launch schedule of the products. In view of this, two suggestions are proposed:

a. The company is advised to deeply understand the characteristics of the designers' work and make good use of their redundant time. For example, the designers should put the main energy into the product design if the design time is very urgent, while conduct user research in the idle time;
b. The company should recruit more employees, so as to conduct user research at any time according to the needs of product development. Actually, user research is a kind of work with high accumulation.

4.2 Landmark Management

Different task of user research demands different knowledge background. Different User research have different aim and schedule. For an example, the Olympic project should cost a long time to communicate with the Olympic Organizing Committee. And it also cost a long time to understand the real need of the athletes. According to the model of the "Nude control", it will bring huge risk if the team cannot reach a consensus at some important landmarks. We advised them to clarify the logic of the project an sum up the all nudes.

4.3 Joint Innovation

The employees of this company are very young, with an average age of less than 30. There should have a quite relaxed atmosphere in the company and everyone can express his/her own opinions. Moreover, a Continuous learning department should be established. Many experts and scholars from various institutions should invited to communicated. According to Joint Innovation, the shoe design department should cooperated with the clothing design department to share the risk and the achievement of the user research.

In addition, in terms of the research process of user research, user research necessarily involves different aspects of users, which requires people from different disciplines to participate in the research. It is impossible to get useful research results if different disciplines can not be integrated. There is always a dispute between qualitative research and quantitative research when conducting user research. This dispute can be solved through forming a interdisciplinary team.

4.4 Full Participation

The design department, product planning department and product planning department have a close relationship, but have a poor relationship with other departments in this company. In the study, we found a fact that the market research department had conducted a market research on a new style of shoes and had already had results, but the design department knew nothing about it. In addition, the market research department believed that the research should be completed by them and tended to invite the other professional companies to conduct the research due to the problems of concept and manpower of the department. In this regard, two suggestions are given to the company: a. The communication between various departments should be strengthened if the personal of these departments can not form a team to work together under the current conditions. Moreover, the design department should participate in the entire operation of the company, including advertising and the design of the display store, etc.; b. The designers must participate in the user's field research, which can help them deeply understand the user. "Making conscious use of user participation in research, the researchers develop increased understanding of their own research field, acquire more respect for the users, and form stronger contacts with the groups of users with whom they conduct the research" [2].

5 Conclusion

After we analyzed the design department, we reached a census with the company. Firstly, if they did not invest enough resources in the user research, they couldn't get valuable results, which was a huge waste of resources. So they agreed to recruit new employees. Secondly, different projects had different aims. If the company used the same user research workflow and divided different project into a same landmark framework, it is also dangerous. So we planned a new landmark framework for their ongoing projects. Last, but definitely not least is to re-understand the effect of designers. "As many of these products offer the satisfaction of different and sometimes even contradictory needs, any direct conclusion from the features of such a product as to the effects it may have on its users would be shortsighted" [5]. The company agreed to let the designers to attend more meeting and do a lot more work in the process of the user research.

Acknowledgment. This research was supported by the project of "Industrial design aiming to better life in the new era" supported by shanghai summit discipline in design (Granted No. DB18304).

References

1. Haney, L.: Contextual and cultural challenges for user mobility research. Commun. ACM **48**, 37–41 (2005)
2. Eisenberg, I.: Lead-user research for breakthrough innovation. Res. Technol. Manag. **54**, 50–58 (2011)
3. Kylberg, M., Haak, M., Iwarsson, S.: Research with and about user participation: potentials and challenges. Aging Clin. Exp. Res. **30**, 105–108 (2018)
4. MacKenzie, I.S.: User studies and usability evaluations: from research to products. In: Graphics Interface Conference, pp. 1–8 (2015)
5. Vorderer, P., Reinecke, L.: From mood to meaning: the changing model of the user in entertainment research. Commun. Theory **25**, 447–453 (2015)

DUXU Case Studies

Challenges in Evaluating Efficacy of Scientific Visualization for Usability and Aesthetics

Julie Baca[1], Daniel W. Carruth[2(✉)] [iD], Alex Calhoun[2],
Michael Stephens[1], and Christopher Lewis[1]

[1] U.S. Army Corps of Engineers Engineering Research and Development
Center, Vicksburg, MS 39180, USA
{julie.a.baca,michael.m.stephens,
christopher.m.lewis}@usace.army.mil
[2] Center for Advanced Vehicular Systems, Mississippi State University,
Starkville, MS 39759, USA
{dcarruth,abc352}@msstate.edu

Abstract. This paper presents the results of a study to evaluate the efficacy of scientific visualization for multiple categories of users, including both domain experts as well as users from the general public. Efficacy was evaluated for understanding, usability, and aesthetic value. Results indicate that aesthetics play a critical, but complex role in enhancing both user understanding and usability.

Keywords: Scientific visualization · Usability · Aesthetics

1 Introduction

Evaluating the efficacy of scientific visualization has long presented challenges to those working in the field, whether users, creators, or providers. Early research focused on honing specific visualization techniques and underlying algorithms [1, 2]. As the technology matured, higher level user-centered efforts to evaluate scientific visualization began to appear [3–6].

A recent comprehensive review of evaluation practices in scientific visualization is given in [7]. The review encodes papers from 10 years of IEEE Visualization conferences to assess their evaluation practices. While reports of evaluation per se steadily rose during the review period, the same did not hold true with respect to user involvement in evaluations. Of the encoded papers, over 95% (955/1002) did not include users in a structured evaluation, but instead either (1) presented readers of papers with image or algorithm enhancements, asking them to assess any improvements for themselves or (2) relied on reports of feedback at informal demos to expert users [7].

Our study seeks to address these gaps by engaging multiple categories of potential actual users in formally evaluating the efficacy of scientific visualization.

A. Marcus and W. Wang (Eds.): HCII 2019, LNCS 11586, pp. 397–407, 2019.
https://doi.org/10.1007/978-3-030-23535-2_29

2 Background

2.1 Evaluation Test Bed

Our work providing visualization services to scientists in the DoD High Performance Computing Modernization Program (HPCMP) motivated the need to evaluate scientific visualization from our users' many potential perspectives. We offer support to scientists analyzing large volumes of complex data in a variety of ways, including but not limited to assistance in using a visualization technique, as well as choosing which technique to use for a particular problem. Support may also involve a visualization specialist collaborating with the scientist in the use of the visualization program to extract data or images that highlight problems with an original computation.

Our users often need the visualization results to communicate and collaborate with other experts in their field to solve problems, but also to convey the results of their work to non-expert users who function as sponsors or liaisons to funding agencies. In addition, they must share their research for the purposes of outreach and education of the general public not trained in their research areas.

Hence, the two basic informational and communicative needs of our direct users can be broadly categorized as:

- Collaborating with other experts in their fields to conduct research;
- Communicating results to non-expert sponsors or public consumers

We designed our study to include both of these categories of users.

2.2 Related Research

Three types of evaluations conducted in the field of information visualization are relevant to our study and informed our approach:

1. Usability-centered
2. Aesthetic
3. Iterative, generative designed-based

Usability-centered evaluations assess ease-of-use through objective measurement of user task performance, as well as subjective measures of user satisfaction [8, 9]. Aesthetic evaluations focus specifically on measuring the user's perception of aesthetic quality of a graphic element or visualization, either through objectively quantifiable metrics, such as the number of bends or edges in a graph [10] or through personal judgments of beauty [11].

Iterative, designed-based evaluations use any results gained in an iterative feedback loop to refine or enhance a visualization or other UI as it is being developed [12, 13].

Any of these categories of evaluations may overlap or be used in parallel in a given study, as for example in [14, 15] to examine effects of aesthetics on usability. Of particular relevance to our research, the aesthetic evaluations in these studies based certain key hypotheses of expected user responses on the work of Tufte [16] who argued that the human eye finds nature's palette most harmonious, and that blues, greens, and browns would have the most desirable impact in information display. Additionally, the presence of any organic, lifelike movement or animation, such as that found in nature, would provide further benefit.

Our study uses aspects of evaluation types 1 and 2, with the goal of using the results going forward in the type 3 designed-based evaluations that allow enhancement of a visualization as it is developing.

3 Methods

Approximately 30 users from each category, expert and non-expert, participated in the study. Participants were recruited from among faculty, general staff and students at a university research center. They were asked to watch videos of a scientific visualization, answer questions about its content, and to evaluate its aesthetic quality. They were also asked to rate their perception of the impact of the work visualized for science and the military.

3.1 Visualization Description

The Army is studying heavy fuel engines relying exclusively on direct injection fuel delivery systems. To meet requirements, the engines must significantly advance current fuel flexibility and fuel conversion efficiencies. In propulsion systems, energy conversion by combustion relies on the use of jet fuel in the compressed liquid form. The initial step in the energy conversion process is the atomization, or disintegration of the coherent liquid core, which significantly impacts the droplet-size distribution and fuel conversion efficiency. In combusting scenarios, the liquid fuel must be fully atomized, evaporated and mixed with the carrier gas-phase environment. Hence, the interaction of liquid atomization and spray vaporization is critical, as it determines the level of energy and fuel supplied to the flame.

Also relevant to our work were emails exchanged with the visualization staff regarding the principal investigator's intent for his audience in creating the visualization, as shown in the excerpt below:

> "In the visualization, I'd like to highlight the atomization breakup features of the spray, that is, surface instability corrugations, ligament formation, spray development. Perhaps a transparent media (color) would also show the internal flow structure. I'm open to your expert suggestions as well."

Users in the study were shown an animation of the visualization of the atomization spray that was subsequently created iteratively with our visualization team and the researcher. Key frames of the animation illustrating the atomization process are shown in Figs. 1, 2, 3, 4 and 5.

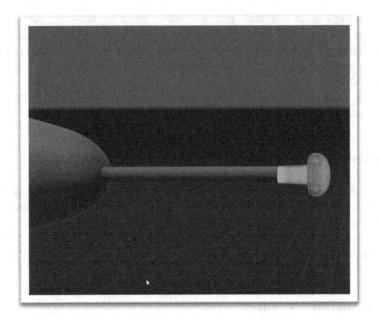

Fig. 1. Early frame in energy conversion process

Fig. 2. Atomization spray droplets beginning to form

Fig. 3. Atomization spray mid-animation

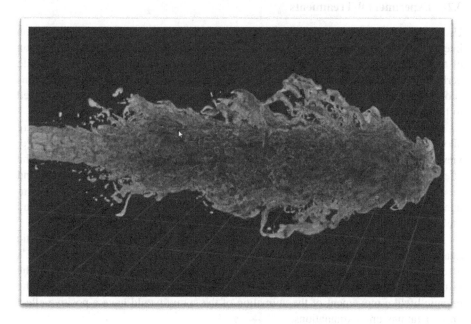

Fig. 4. Atomization spray later in animation

Fig. 5. Atomization spray droplets final animation frame

3.2 Experimental Treatments

Users viewed the set of visualizations of the atomization and spray vaporization interactions shown in Figs. 1, 2, 3, 4 and 5. They were also given a textual description of the entire process on the first screen shown. There were no "tasks" for users to perform in the traditional usability sense; however they were asked to answer questions about what they viewed regarding content, impact and aesthetics. They were also asked to rate their confidence in their answers.

Once they advanced beyond the first screen to answer questions, users were allowed to view the visualizations as many times as they wished, but could no longer view the textual description for the remainder of the experiment in order to isolate the effectiveness of the visualization itself. The relative completeness of their answers, and their confidence ratings, functioned as measures of task completion. The survey contained 8 questions regarding scientific content, its potential importance to science and the military, with 3 questions regarding users' confidence in their answers.

Users were asked in 2 additional questions to rate their perceptions of aesthetic quality of the visualizations and to give an explanation of their rating. Based on Tufte's assumptions [16], tested in [15], we expected that the spectrum of blues used in the visualization of the atomized spray, its similarity to the appearance of water, and the organic lifelike movement of the animation of the spray, would have a positive effect on user ratings and explanations.

4 Results

4.1 Scoring Answers

Scoring understanding of textual answers (i.e., non-numeric) involves a subjective element. Multiple readers (3) provided scores for each answer. Inter-rater reliability for the 3 readers was calculated using Gwet's AC2 [17] and is reported in Table 1. A final score was calculated by taking the average of the 3 scores.

Answers were scored on the following 3-point scale:

0 Wrong, absent, or irrelevant
1 Correct undetailed
2 Correct detailed

Overall results for accuracy of textual answers for the central problem, the main idea, and the impact of the research, as well as the user's confidence in their own answers and ratings is given in Table 1.

Table 1. Overall results for accuracy and user confidence.

	Accuracy (0–2)	Confidence (1–5)	Gwet AC2
Central problem	0.89	2.55	.49
Main idea	1.08	2.78	.63
Impact	0.85	2.48	.39

Overall scores for other questions with numeric ratings that did not require users to write a descriptive answer included significance to science, importance to military, and perceived aesthetics. These scores are shown in Tables 2 and 3.

Table 2. Overall results for significance to science and importance to military

	Least to highest (1–5)
Significance to science	3.63
Importance to military	4.3

Table 3. Overall results for perceived aesthetics

	Ugly to beautiful (0–100)
Perceived aesthetics	72.7

4.2 Analysis

Several key questions motivated our research and guided our analysis of the results. Discussion and analysis for each question are presented below.

1. Does perceived aesthetics predict perception of the significance of the research to science?

Perceived aesthetics was correlated with individuals' assessment of the significance of the research to science, rho = .432, p < .01. Participants who perceived the animation as more attractive were more likely to perceive the research as significant to science. An analysis of variance indicated that for every point towards beautiful, there was a .37 increase in significance, $F(1,39) = 6.05$, p < .05.

2. Does perceived aesthetics affect understanding?

Participant understanding of the impact of the research was also correlated with their perception of the aesthetics of the video, rho = −.356, p < .05. Participants that felt the visualization was less attractive were more likely to provide an accurate assessment of impact.

3. Does perception of aesthetics affect confidence in responses?

The analysis revealed no evidence of a relationship between the aesthetics of the animation and participant self-reported confidence in their responses.

4. Does self-reported prior knowledge of underlying science or modeling and simulation predict accuracy of answers?

Participant self-reported prior knowledge did not predict understanding of the central problem (p = .34), impact (p = .31), or the main ideas presented (p = .78).

5. Does self-reported prior knowledge of underlying science or modeling and simulation predict confidence?

An analysis of variance indicates that self-reported knowledge of modeling and simulation combined with their understanding of the central problem does predict self-reported confidence in their understanding of the central problem $F(4,39) = 2.92$, p < .05). By itself, there was no relationship between self-reported knowledge and the accuracy of their responses. There was no evidence that this relationship also applied to confidence in their understanding of the impact of the research, $F(4,39) = 1.13$, p = .36), or of the main ideas presented in the video, $F(4,39) = 1.98$, p = .12.

6. Is understanding related to confidence in responses?

Participant confidence in their understanding of the central problem was correlated with accuracy, rho = −.342, p < .05, but participants with higher confidence in responses were actually less accurate. However, the analysis did not provide support for a relationship between confidence in understanding of the main ideas and the impact and accuracy in responses.

7. Does understanding predict perceived importance to the military?

Understanding of the central problem was negatively associated (B = −.64) with the perceived importance to the military (better understanding led to less perceived importance), $F(3,39) = 3.29$, p < .05.

In contrast, understanding of the main ideas presented in the visualization was positively associated (B = .48) with perceived importance of the research to military.

8. Does understanding predict perceived significance to science?

The accuracy of participants' understanding of the central problem, main ideas, and impact were not significant predictors of how significant the participants perceived the research to be to science.

9. Will adherence to Tufte's guidelines on the use of organic qualities and colors found in nature positively affect user perceived aesthetics?

Users' explanations for their aesthetic ratings contained a relatively high number of positive comments (18/41, roughly 43%) related to the color choice (blue) and/or the realistic, lifelike quality of the animation of the liquid, including its similarity to water. Given the relatively high overall aesthetic rating of (72.7 points out of 100) this appears to support Tufte's recommendations. Examples of user comments are presented below:

> U1: "...easy on the eyes to visually understand where the fuel is going. It has good colors."
> U2: "The graphical imagery was realistic and the colors popped. The last shot of the up-close visualization was stunning."
> U3: "I liked how the fuel was shot in slow motion and the many different views of that process given. ...The coloring was also nice."
> U4: "...the blues and 3D patterns were cool."
> U5: "...the colors and detail of the liquid are attractive.
> U6: "...the blue colors of the fuel were fairly visually pleasing and seemed to demonstrate the atomization and injection."
> U7: "...the color choices help to distinguish the different regions of density process well."

5 Conclusions

The expectation that aesthetics might play a critical role in both user understanding of the content of the visualization as well as its usability was confirmed, but in more complex patterns than expected. Perceived aesthetics proved a predictor of user perception of the significance of research to science, i.e., "uglier" aesthetic ratings were correlated with lower user perceptions of research significance. In addition, perceived aesthetics affected user understanding of the impact of the research; however, higher or "more beautiful" aesthetic ratings were correlated with less accurate assessments of impact. However, aesthetics were not a significant predictor of user confidence in their ratings. Finally, tracking with Tufte's assertions [16], users' explanations for higher aesthetic ratings included a relatively high number of comments (18/41, roughly 43%) related to the choice of natural, lifelike movement, i.e., water, and/or the colors from nature, i.e., the color blue.

Other key questions of the research regarding self-reported prior knowledge proved complex as well. While this factor did not predict user understanding, it was a predictor of user confidence, i.e. those with self-reported prior knowledge or expertise were more likely to report a high level of confidence in their ratings.

We plan to continue the research by expanding the study in several ways. First we plan to conduct another study using visualizations providing more contextual information such as conceptual animations, and musical tracks to assess the level at which these factors may affect the key questions regarding usability and understanding. Second, we plan to include comparison studies of the original researcher's visualization, which did not adhere to Tuft's guidelines, against the visualization created in collaboration with our visualization team.

Our long-term goal is to use the results of these studies during design and development to enhance the quality of visualizations provided to researchers, scientists, and the general public. This research will enable a more explicit formulation of a visualization usability process to follow to attain our goal.

Acknowledgements. This material is based upon work supported by the U.S. Army TACOM Life Cycle Command under Contract No. W56HZV-08-C-0236.

References

1. Wong, C., Bergeron, D.: 30 years of multidimensional multivariate visualization. In: Hagen, H., Muller, H., Nielsen, G. (eds.) Scientific Visualization. IEEE Computer Society, Los Alamitos, CA, USA (1997)
2. Rheuter, L., Tukey, P., Maloney, L.T., Pani, J.R., Smith, S.: Human perception and visualization. In: Proceedings of the 1st Conference on Visualization 1990 (Viz 1990), pp. 401–406. IEEE Computer Society Press, San Francisco (1990)
3. Herndon, K., Dam, A., Gleicher, M.: The challenges of 3D interaction: a CHI '94 workshop. SIGCHI Bull. **26**(4), 1–9 (2007)
4. Komlodi, A., Rehingans, P., Ayachit, U., Goodall, J., Joshi, A.: A user-centered look at glyph-based security visualization. In: IEEE 2005 Workshop on Visualization for Computer Security, pp. 21–28. IEEE, Minneapolis (2005)
5. Santos, B.S., Silva, S., Teixeira, L., Ferreira, C., Dias, P., Madeira, J.: Preliminary usability evaluation of PolyMeCo: a visualization based tool for mesh analysis and comparison. In: Geometric Modeling and Imaging 2007, pp. 133–139. IEEE, Zurich (2007)
6. Tory, M., Moller, T.: Evaluating visualizations: do expert reviews work? IEEE Vis. Viewpoint Comput. Graph. Appl. **25**, 8–11 (2005)
7. Isenberg, T., Isenberg, P., Chen, J., Sedlmair, M., Moller, T.: A systematic review on the practice of evaluating visualization. IEEE Trans. Vis. Comput. Graph. **19**(12), 2818–2827 (2013)
8. Nielsen, J.: Usability Inspection Methods. Wiley, New York (1994)
9. Norman, D.A., Draper, S.W.: User Centered System Design: New Perspectives on Human Computer Interaction. Erlbaum, Hillsdale (1986)
10. Purchase, H., Allder, J.A., Carrington, D.: Metrics for graph drawing aesthetics. J. Vis. Lang. Comput. **13**, 501–516 (2002)
11. Hartmann, J.: Assessing the attractiveness of interactive systems. In: CHI 2006 Extended Abstracts on Human Factors in Computing Systems, pp. 1755–1758. ACM Press, Montreal (2006)
12. Preece, J., Rogers, Y., Sharp, H.: The process of interaction design. In: Interaction Design: Beyond Human-Computer Interaction. Wiley, New York (2002)

13. Jackson, B., et al.: Towards mixed method evaluations of scientific visualizations and design process as an evaluation tool. In: BELIV 2012, Seattle Washington, USA (2012)
14. Cawthon, N., Vande Moere, A.: Qualities of perceived aesthetic in data visualization. In: CHI 2007, pp. 1–11. ACM Press, San Jose (2007)
15. Cawthon, N., Vande Moere, A.: The effect of aesthetic on the usability of data visualization. In: 11th International Conference Information Visualization (IV 2007), pp. 637–648. IEEE Computer Society, Washington D.C. (2007)
16. Tuft, E.: Envisioning Information. Graphics Press, Cheshire (1990)
17. Gwet, K.L.: Handbook of Inter-Rater Reliability, 3rd edn. Advanced Analytics, LLC, Gaithersburg (2012)

Evaluating Response Delay of Multimodal Interface in Smart Device

Xiantao Chen[✉], Moli Zhou, Renzhen Wang, Yalin Pan, Jiaqi Mi,
Hui Tong, and Daisong Guan

Baidu AI Interaction Design Lab, Beijing, China
chenxiantao@baidu.com

Abstract. Multimodal interface based on natural language processing (NLP) technology is becoming more and more popular. Many studies show that response delay is a key factor to evaluate multimodal interface performance that can influence naturalness and fluency of interaction experience. However, few studies have been conducted to define the optimum response delay time. Focused at multimodal interface with voice as dominant modality, in this paper, we built a research framework to evaluate response delay according to user perception during the voice interaction, in which the system output process was divided into three successive stages. We carried out two experiments to evaluate the influence of response delay time in different stages, a smart speaker with screen and a smart TV were involved in the experiments. The first experiment focused on automatic speech recognition (ASR) feedback delay time, and the second experiment was designed to investigate the influence of both query response delay time and loading response delay time. We defined the satisfying and acceptable delay time for each stage respectively, which could be used as the references to improve corresponding technical performance.

Keywords: Smart device · Multimodal interface · Voice interaction ·
Response delay · Performance

1 Introduction

With the development of artificial intelligence technology, interaction between human and devices is changing profoundly, and more natural and efficient multimodal interface is becoming increasingly prevalent. Multimodal interface enables people to interact with devices through voice, touch, face expression and other modes, which is considered to be more intuitive and easier to learn for people. Comparing to unimodal interface, multimodal interface makes full use of human's natural ability to interact with devices, and the weaknesses or deficiencies of the unimodal interface can be compensated by combination the various modes [1].

In recent years, multimodal interface based on natural language processing (NLP) technology has been widely used in the world, especially in smart home, vehicle, wearable equipment, robots and other fields. Take smart home as an example, Amazon and Baidu have released the smart speakers with screen that enable multimodal interaction. In addition to touch, users can also instruct the devices to play video,

© Springer Nature Switzerland AG 2019
A. Marcus and W. Wang (Eds.): HCII 2019, LNCS 11586, pp. 408–419, 2019.
https://doi.org/10.1007/978-3-030-23535-2_30

play music and search information using human natural language. Voice has become the dominant modality for people to interact with device, to exchange information or to express their intentions [2]. During the process of voice interaction, there are usually two basic interaction stages: voice wake-up and voice dialogue. People need to first trigger the automatic speech recognition system through voice wake-up, and then input voice queries to start dialogue with the device [3, 4].

There are many studies indicating response delay is a key element for evaluating the quality of multimodal interface, and the long response delay can seriously reduce naturalness and fluency of the interaction, and even affect people's willingness to use the device [5–7]. Meanwhile, some researchers suggest that response delay is the most important factor to determine user satisfaction [8]. Although the importance of response delay has been proved, unfortunately, most researchers only focused on providing qualitative descriptions and rarely investigated the specific optimum response delay time or an acceptable range. Moreover, the reasons for response delay of voice interactive devices may be related to the efficiency of ASR, quality of language model, network conditions [9–11]. Continuously improving the responsiveness of voice interaction and reducing response delay time are critical to enhance the usability of voice interactive devices [12].

Targeted at multimodal interface with voice as dominant modality, this paper evaluated response delay of two smart devices with screen, a smart speaker with screen and a smart TV. Compared with the voice input and voice output interaction of smart device without screen, the smart device with screen becomes richer in output interaction, for example, the device can directly display the results of the voice recognition or voice search on screen. In this paper, firstly, we built a research framework for multimodal interface according to users' perception of the voice interaction process, in which the system output process was divided into three successive stages. Secondly, two experiments were conducted to evaluate and quantify response delay time in each stage, the purpose of the first experiment was to measure automatic speech recognition (ASR) feedback delay, and the second experiment was to measure query response delay and loading response delay. Finally, discussions and conclusions of this study would be described.

2 Literature Review

Many researchers have suggested several typical parameters for describing multimodal human-computer interaction including Accuracy (words, gestures, etc.) [13, 14], Delay [15], Efficiency [16], Appropriateness [17, 18], etc. Weiss [5] distinguished system output delay into two types: feedback delay and response delay. Feedback delay refers to the delay when the system successfully receives user input, which is described as average delay from the end of user input to the beginning of system feedback, for example from button press to display of loading status in terms of clock. Response delay refers to the delay of system responding to user input, it is described as average delay of a user response, from the end of user input to the beginning of system output. For example, the system starts to display a new GUI. In addition, Bernsen [17] proposed another time-related parameter named lag of time, which refers to the asynchronism between corresponding modalities.

Many studies have shown that response delay has a negative effect on user satisfaction towards device or service [19–22]. To measure delay time and its impact on user attitudes, behavior and psychological state, a lot of work has been done in graphic user interface (GUI) domain. Galletta and colleagues [23] examined the impact of different website delay times of 0, 2, 4, 6, 8, 10, and 12 s in an experiment, and the findings suggested that the tolerable waiting time was around 4 s. Nah [24] reviewed the literature on computer response time and assessed web user's tolerable waiting time in information retrieval, the results from the study suggested that the tolerable waiting time for information retrieval was approximately 2 s. Wang [25] explored optimal system response time which would make human-information system (HIS) interaction most efficient and found that the interaction efficiency of HIS was the highest when the response time was in the range of 0.25–0.75 s, while a response time less than 0.25 s was likely to make users feel stressed and nervous. Research on response delay time of voice user interface (VUI) is limited, McWilliams [26] studied the impact of voice interface turn delays on drivers' attention and arousal levels in vehicles settings, the results showed that a delay time longer than 4 s was associated with decreased attention to the driving task. This suggested that system delay time under 4 s may be optimal.

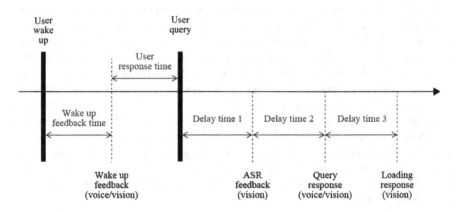

Fig. 1. Four types of system output delay time in voice wake-up and voice dialogue stage.

So far, there are few studies that focus on measuring delay time of multimodal voice user interface. Moreover, no research is identified that investigated response delay in scenarios other than vehicles or driving scenarios, such as in smart home. This study aimed to measure delay time of multimodal voice user interface in two smart home devices with different screen sizes, a smart speaker with 7-in. screen and a smart TV with 55-in. screen were involved in this study. First, according to the user's perception of system output in both wake-up stage and dialogue stage, the system output delay was divided into four types (See Fig. 1): wake-up feedback delay in voice wake-up stage, and ASR feedback delay, query response delay and loading response delay in voice dialogue stage. There are usually differences in wake-up between smart speaker with screen and smart TV. The former mainly uses voice wake-up, while the latter uses button wake-up. Response delay under different wake up modes should be studied separately. Therefore, this study focused on the delay times of voice dialogue stage, and according to user perception, we can divide the voice dialogue stage into several aspects. On the one hand, ASR feedback delay maybe happen when user input voice query. On the other hand, system output delay maybe happens after ASR feedback had finished, which included query response delay and loading response delay. Their descriptions and operational definitions were as follows:

ASR feedback delay time: the delay time from the end of user's input voice query to the beginning of the display of ASR feedback on the screen, for example from the end of user saying "I want to see movie" to the beginning of the text "I want to see movie" displaying on the screen.

Query response delay time: the delay time from the end of ASR results display to the beginning of system output, for example from the end of the screen displaying "I want to see movie" to the beginning a new GUI displays the movie information on the screen.

Loading response delay time: the delay time from the beginning of a new GUI displays on the screen to the end of all results being displayed completely, for example all movie information being shown on the screen.

Next, we conducted two experiments to evaluate the impact of different delay time on users' satisfaction in all three stages mentioned above. The first experiment is designed to investigate ASR feedback delay, which to some extent could reveal the performance of automatic speech recognition technology. And the second experiment mainly focused on system output delay after ASR feedback completed, which could indicate the performance of the system output for user's query or need.

3 Experiments

3.1 Experiment 1: ASR Feedback Delay Time Experiment

Objectives
When having a dialogue with smart device with screen, the query that user input will be displayed on the screen. Currently, display mode of query is mainly real-time, and words recognized by the devices will be shown immediately on the screen while user is inputting. The aim of this experiment was to explore the satisfying and acceptable delay time of ASR feedback in the real-time display mode.

Subjects
In total, 30 subjects participated in the experiment (M = 25.8 years old, SD = 4.37), all of them were employees of internet companies. The sample consisted of 15 females and 15 males, and half of them reported previous experience with smart speaker or smart TV.

Tasks and Materials

We developed an experimental program with Java, which could run on a smart speaker (7 in.) and a smart TV (55 in.), display mode of ASR feedback in the program is real-time way. In the experiment, we arranged movie searching tasks to subjects. In order to cover different length queries as far as possible, three length queries in Chinese were provided in the experiment. They were short query with four Chinese words "Kungfu movie", middle query with ten Chinese words "I want to see movie rating above nine score" and long query with twenty Chinese words "I want to see Andy Lau's Hong Kong movie before 2010 year". Subjects first need to say queries in various delay time conditions and pay attention to when the queries were recognized and displayed on the screen, and then give their scores of satisfactions for the ASR feedback delay time. In order to balance the learning effect and fatigue effect in the experiment, we randomized the sequences of tasks for each subject, the three query lengths were grouped and randomized, and then the delay time was completely randomized. An interview was conducted to collect qualitative data, such as reasons of their evaluations and other comments.

Experimental Variables

The independent variables of the experiment included device screen size (smart speaker with 7-in. screen and smart TV with 55-in. screen), query length (short, middle, long) and ASR feedback delay times (0, 200, 400, 600, 800, 1000, 1200, 1400, 1600, 1800, 2000 ms), and the levels of independent variables referred to the range of relevant parameters of current smart devices. Dependent variables were user's satisfaction evaluation (1-Very Dissatisfied, 2-Dissatisfied, 3-General, 4-Satisfied, 5-Very Satisfied). We used a 2 (screen size) *3 (query length) *11 (ASR feedback delay time) three-factor mixed design.

Results

Descriptive results of the ASR feedback delay time experiment are shown in Table 1. The results of Repeated Measures ANOVA showed that the main effect of screen size was not significant ($F(1,28) = 0.162$, $p = 0.639$), the main effect of different length queries was not significant ($F(2,27) = 1.198$, $p = 0.317$), the main effect of delay time was significant ($F(10,19) = 12.180$, $p < 0.001$), the interaction effect between different length queries and delay time was not significant ($F(20,9) = 1.911$, $p = 0.159$), and the interaction effect between screen size and delay time was not significant ($F(10,19) = 1.424$, $p = 0.243$). Multiple Comparative Analysis showed that there were no significant differences ($p > 0.05$) between 0&200 ms, 0&400 ms, 200&400 ms, 600&800 ms, 800&1000 ms, 1200&1400 ms, 1200&1600 ms, 1200&1800 ms, 1400&1600 ms and 1600&1800 ms, the others were significant differences($p < 0.05$). These results indicated that subjects felt very fast when the ASR feedback delay time was less than 400 ms, and subjects began to feel slow when the delay time was more than 1200 ms.

Table 1. Mean and standard deviation of satisfaction scores for ASR feedback delay time.

Delay times	Mean satisfaction	SD	95% confidence interval	
			Lower	Upper
0 ms	4.24	0.12	4.01	4.48
200 ms	4.12	0.11	3.90	4.35
400 ms	4.22	0.11	3.99	4.45
600 ms	3.87	0.10	3.66	4.07
800 ms	3.72	0.12	3.47	3.97
1000 ms	3.56	0.12	3.32	3.79
1200 ms	3.26	0.13	2.99	3.52
1400 ms	3.21	0.13	2.94	3.48
1600 ms	3.10	0.14	2.82	3.38
1800 ms	2.99	0.13	2.73	3.48
2000 ms	2.67	0.14	2.38	3.38

Table 2. Regression equation of satisfaction to ASR feedback delay time.

Regression equation	F	R^2	Satisfying delay time	Acceptable delay time
Satisfaction = −0.000805 * delay time + 4.347	321.511***	24.5%	431 ms	1673 ms

In this experiment, we regarded satisfaction score "4-Satisfied" as the lower limit of satisfying delay time, and "3-General" as the lower limit of acceptable delay time. We further had a Linear Regression Analysis of ASR feedback delay and user satisfaction, and the results as shown in Table 2. The final results suggested that subjects were satisfied when the delay time was less than 431 ms, and subjects felt acceptable when it was less than 1673 ms, and ASR feedback delay time of more than 1673 ms might dissatisfy users.

3.2   Experiment 2: Query Response Delay Time and Loading Response Delay Time Experiment

Objectives

After the first experiment, we conducted the second experiment. The aim of the second experiment was to measure users' satisfying and acceptable delay time respectively in both query response stage and loading response stage respectively, and further explored the total response delay time of the two stages.

Subjects

32 subjects participated in the experiment (M = 27.0 years old, SD = 3.21), all of them were employees of internet companies. The sample consisted of 16 females and 16 males, and half of them reported previous experience with smart speaker or smart TV.

Tasks and Materials

We developed a program for the second experiment, which could run on a smart speaker (7 in.) and a smart TV (55 in.). As the experiment mainly focused on measuring query response delay and loading response delay, we fixed the feedback delay time of ASR and the search query in this experiment. We arranged movie searching tasks and a short query with four Chinese words was provided which was "Kungfu Movie". Before the experiment, there was a warm up session to introduce about the query response delay and loading response delay. In the experiment, subjects were asked to say the query in various delay time conditions. After subjects finished input the query and it was displayed, a new GUI would be shown on the screen by dynamic loading way and the movies information obtained would be displayed one by one. Subjects need to pay attention to the query response delay time, the loading response delay time, and total delay time, and then gave their scores of satisfactions for the above three delay times respectively. In order to balance the learning effect and fatigue effect in the experiment, we randomized the sequences of tasks for each subject, the query response delay time and the loading response time were completely randomized in the experiment. After the experiment, an interview was conducted to explore the reasons of their evaluations.

Experimental Variables

The independent variables of the experiment included device screen size (smart speaker with 7-in. screen and smart TV with 55-in. screen), query response delay time (200, 600, 1000, 2000, 3000, 4000, 5000 ms), and loading response delay time (200, 600, 1000, 2000, 3000, 4000, 5000 ms), and the levels of independent variables referred to the range of relevant parameters of current smart devices. Dependent variables were user's satisfaction evaluation of query response delay, loading response delay and total response delay (1-Very Dissatisfied, 2-Dissatisfied, 3-General, 4-Satisfied, 5-Very Satisfied), the total response delay time was the sum of the above two kinds of delay time. We used a three-factor mixed design of 2 (screen size) *7(query response delay time) *7(loading response delay time).

Results

Query Response Delay Time

From the descriptive analysis, we found the relationship between query response time and user satisfaction, as shown in Table 3. The results of Repeated Measures ANOVA with satisfaction as dependent variable showed that the main effect of screen size was not significant ($F(1,29) = 0.00$, $p = 0.987$), the main effect of query response delay time was significant ($F(6,24) = 122.674$, $p < 0.001$), the interaction effect between screen size and query response delay time was not significant ($F(6,24) = 0.796$, $p = 0.582$), and Multiple Comparison Analysis suggested that there were significant differences in different query response delay time ($p < 0.05$). We regarded satisfaction score "4-Satisfied" as the lower limit of delay time to satisfy users, and "3-General" as the lower limit delay time acceptable to users. Further Linear Regression Analysis of query response delay time and user satisfaction, as shown in Table 4, the final results indicated that subjects were satisfied when the delay time was less than 867 ms, and subjects felt it was acceptable when the delay time was less than 2537 ms.

Table 3. Mean and standard deviation of satisfaction scores for query response delay time.

Delay times	Mean satisfaction	SD	95% confidence interval	
			Lower	Upper
200 ms	4.47	0.61	4.39	4.55
600 ms	4.16	0.70	4.07	4.25
1000 ms	3.91	0.91	3.79	4.04
2000 ms	3.37	0.98	3.24	3.5
3000 ms	2.57	0.97	2.44	2.69
4000 ms	1.98	0.94	1.85	2.1
5000 ms	1.71	0.87	1.59	1.82

Table 4. Regression equation of satisfaction to query response delay time.

Regression equation	F	R^2	Satisfying delay time	Acceptable delay time
Satisfaction = −0.000599 * delay time + 4.519434	20187.18***	57.1%	867 ms	2537 ms

Loading Response Delay Time

The mean satisfaction scores in different delay time conditions are shown in Table 5. The results of Repeated Measures ANOVA showed that the main effect of screen size was not significant ($F(1, 29) = 0.050$, $p = 0.825$), the main effect of loading response delay time was significant ($F(6, 24) = 69.772$, $p < 0.001$), the interaction effect between screen size and query response delay time was not significant ($F(6, 24) = 2.163$, $p = 0.083$). Multiple Comparison Analysis found that in different loading response delay time condition, there were significant differences of subjects' satisfaction scores ($p < 0.05$). We regarded satisfaction score "4-Satisfied" as the lower limit of delay time to satisfy users, and "3-General" as the lower limit delay time which was acceptable to users. Further Linear Regression Analysis for loading response delay time and user satisfaction, as shown in Table 6, the final results indicated that subjects were satisfied when the delay time was less than 564 ms, and subjects felt it was acceptable when the delay time was less than 2353 ms.

Table 5. Mean and standard deviation of satisfaction scores for loading response delay time.

Delay times	Mean satisfaction	SD	95% confidence interval	
			Lower	Upper
200 ms	4.43	0.67	4.34	4.52
600 ms	4.13	0.72	4.03	4.22
1000 ms	3.62	0.81	3.51	3.72
2000 ms	2.96	0.74	2.86	3.05
3000 ms	2.43	0.71	2.33	2.52
4000 ms	2.04	0.69	1.95	2.14
5000 ms	1.77	0.63	1.69	1.86

Table 6. Regression equation of satisfaction to loading response delay time.

Regression equation	F	R^2	Satisfying delay time	Acceptable delay time
Satisfaction = −0.000559 * delay time + 4.315371	2533.5***	61.8%	564 ms	2353 ms

Total Response Delay Time

The results of Repeated Measures ANOVA with overall satisfaction as dependent variable showed the main effect of screen size was not significant ($F(1,23) = 0.978$, $p = 0.333$), the main effect of query response delay time was significant ($F(4,23) = 76.557$, $p < 0.001$), the main effect of loading response delay time was significant ($F(4,23) = 122.844$, $p < 0.001$), the interaction between query response delay time and loading response delay time was significant ($F(16,8) = 3.849$, $p < 0.05$), and the interaction between the other variables was not significant ($p > 0.05$). Simple Effect Analysis was further conducted since the interaction effect between query response delay time and loading response delay time was significant, as shown in Fig. 2. The results indicated that subjects were not satisfied with the short query response delay but long loading response delay, or the long query response delay but short loading response delay. We further had a Linear Regression Analysis for total response delay and user satisfaction, and the results as shown in Table 7.

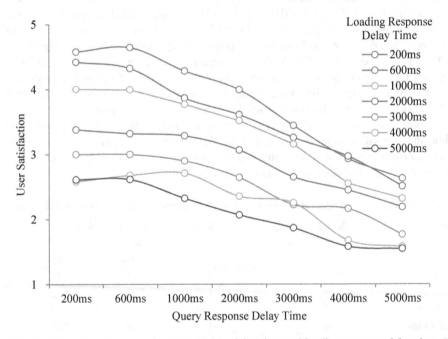

Fig. 2. Interaction diagram of query response delay time and loading response delay time.

Table 7. Regression equation of satisfaction to total response delay time.

Condition	Regression equation	F	R^2
Non-standardized regression equation	Satisfaction = −0.000403 * query response delay time−0.000449 * loading response delay time + (4.08E^{-8}) * query response delay time * loading response delay time + 4.4428	598.209***	53.4%
Standardized regression equation	Satisfaction = −0.613 * query response delay time − 0.683 * loading response delay time + 0.22 * query response delay time * loading response delay time	598.209***	53.4%

4 Discussion

Different from previous studies on response delay [23–26], this paper decomposed the system output into several key response delay stages according to user perception, which included ASR feedback delay, query response delay and loading response delay. In order to support corresponding technical optimization, we measured satisfying and acceptable delay time for users.

The results of ASR feedback delay experiment showed that users' perception of delay time was not influenced by screen size or the length of queries subjects input. From the end of users' input to the being query displayed on the screen, subjects were satisfied when the ASR feedback delay time was less than 431 ms and thought it was acceptable when the delay time was less than 1673 ms. It should be noted that in addition to the real-time display mode, there is also non-real-time display mode, in which the query will be displayed integrally on the screen until all speech recognition is finished. Based on Barnett's [27] and Tom's [28] research, the perception of delay time was affected by user's subjective factors, so the ASR feedback display mode might affect user's subjective perception. We suggest that the satisfied and acceptable delay time under non-real-time display mode should be further investigated.

The results of query response delay and loading response delay experiment showed that the screen size of smart devices still did not affect the perception of response delay time. In query response stage, subjects were satisfied when delay time was less than 867 ms and felt it was acceptable when the delay time was less than 2537 ms. In loading response stage, subjects were satisfied when delay time was less than 564 ms and feel acceptable when the delay time was less than 2353 ms. Comparing with query response delay time, subjects showed higher requirement of faster for loading response delay, that was, the delay time in loading response stage needed to be shorter than in query response stage for them to feel satisfied. Combining the interviews after the second experiment, subjects generally thought that there were different reasons for the response delay in the two stages. Some participants thought that the delay time of query response time was mainly affected by the performance of the product, specifically it was related to search algorithm and efficiency, while the delay time of loading response time was mainly affected by network conditions. Subjects were more tolerant of search algorithm and efficiency than network condition. In addition, it should be mentioned that only video search scenario was involved in the second experiment, and the system output usually included a large amount of multimedia information such as pictures, graphs and texts. For Encyclopedia queries, weather queries and other text-based output scenarios, the response delay should also be further studied.

5 Conclusion

This paper targeted at multimodal interface with voice as dominant modality, we built a research framework to evaluate response delay according to user perception during the voice interaction, in which the system output process was divided into three successive stages. We conducted two experiments to evaluate the response delay in each stage, a smart speaker with screen and a smart TV were involved in the experiment, the first experiment was designed to measure automatic speech recognition (ASR) feedback delay time. Results indicated that, from the end of user input to query displayed on the screen, users were satisfied when the ASR feedback delay time was less than 431 ms and felt it was acceptable when the delay time was less than 1673 ms. In the second experiment, we aimed to measure query response delay time and loading response delay time. We found that users were satisfied when delay time was less than 867 ms and felt it was acceptable when the delay time was less than 2537 ms in query response stage. In loading response stage, users were satisfied when delay time was less than 564 ms and felt it was acceptable when the delay time was less than 2353 ms.

Acknowledgements. We thank R&D engineers in Baidu for supporting our research and developing the experimental programs. This research was supported by Baidu Duer Business Unit (BU) for smart devices and parameters.

References

1. Kühnel, C., Weiss, B., Möller, S.: Parameters describing multimodal interaction-Definitions and three usage scenarios. In: Eleventh Annual Conference of the International Speech Communication Association (2010)
2. Amrutha, S., Aravind, S., Mathew, A., Sugathan, S., Rajasree, R., Priyalakshmi, S.: Voice controlled smart home. Int. J. Emerg. Technol. Adv. Eng. 5(1), 596–600 (2015)
3. Wang, X., Guo, Y., Ge, F., Wu, C., Fu, Q., Yan, Y.: Speech-picking for speech systems with auditory attention ability. Sci. China 45(10), 1310–1327 (2015)
4. Pearl, C.: Designing Voice User Interfaces: Principles of Conversational Experiences, pp. 1–10. O'Reilly Media, Newton (2016)
5. Weiss, B., Scheffler, T., Möller, S.: Describing multimodal human computer interaction. In: Proceedings of Workshop at NordiCHI: Assessing Multimodal Interaction (aMMi), Copenhagen, Denmark, pp. 33–36 (2012)
6. ITU Supplement 25 to P-Series Rec: Parameters describing the interaction with multimodal dialogue systems. In: International Telecommunication Union, Geneva (2011)
7. Shriberg, E., Wade, E., Price, P.: Human-machine problem solving using spoken language systems (SLS): factors affecting performance and user satisfaction. In: Proceedings of the DARPA Speech and NL Workshop, pp. 49–54 (1992)

8. Johnson, J.: Designing with the Mind in Mind: Simple Guide to Understanding User Interface Design Guidelines, pp. 129–146. Morgan Kaufmann, Waltham (2010)
9. Chen, S., Jiang, Q.: Ergonomic study on the performance of speech recognition system. Space Med. Med. Eng. **3**(3), 216–221 (1990)
10. Zhong, W., Xu, B.: Performance evaluation criteria and affecting factors of speech input system. In: NCMMSC1994, pp. 452–456 (1994)
11. Cui, S.: Strategies for improving efficiency of speech recognition. Master's degree thesis of Beijing University of Posts and Telecommunications, pp. 16–18 (2018)
12. Chen, Y., Li, K., Zhou, J., Liu, J., Liu, R.: Novel efficient algorithms in speech/speaker recognition. Comput. Eng. **30**(15), 1–3 (2004)
13. Simpson, A., Fraser, N.M.: Black box and glass box evaluation of the SUNDIAL system. In: Proceedings 3rd European Conference on Speech Communication and Technology (Eurospeech 1993), DE-Berlin, vol. 2, pp. 1423–1426 (1993)
14. Nigay, L., Coutaz, J.: A design space for multimodal systems: concurrent processing and data fusion. In Proceedings of INTERACT & CHI, pp. 172–178 (1993)
15. Price, P.J., Hirschman, L., Shriberg, E., Wade, E: Subject-based evaluation measures for interactive spoken language systems. In: Proceedings of DARPA Speech and Natural Language Workshop, US-Harriman CA, pp. 34–39 (1992)
16. Perakakis, M., Potamianos, A.: Multimodal system evaluation using modality efficiency and synergy metrics. In Proceedings of IMCI, pp. 9–16 (2008)
17. Bernsen, N.: From theory to design support tool. In: Multimodality in Language and Speech Systems. Kluwer, Dordrecht, pp. 93–148 (2002)
18. Bernsen, N., Dybkjær, L.: Multimodal Usability. Springer, London (2009)
19. Weinberg, B.D.: Don't keep your internet customers waiting too long at the (virtual) front door. J. Interact. Mark. **14**(1), 30–39 (2000)
20. Pruyn, A., Smidts, A.: Effects of waiting on the satisfaction with the service: beyond objective time measures. J. Int. Res. Mark. **15**(4), 0–334 (1998)
21. Thompson, D.A., Yarnold, P.R., Williams, D.R., Adams, S.L.: Effects of actual waiting time, perceived waiting time, information delivery, and expressive quality on patient satisfaction in the emergency department. Ann. Emerg. Med. **28**(6), 657–665 (1996)
22. Lee, Y., Chen, A.N., Ilie, V.: Can online wait be managed? The effect of filler interfaces and presentation modes on perceived waiting time online. MIS Q. 365–394 (2012)
23. Galletta, D.F., Henry, R., McCoy, S., Polak, P.: Web site delays: how tolerant are users. J. Assoc. Inf. Syst. **5**(1), 1–28 (2004)
24. Nah, F.: A study on tolerable waiting time: how long are web users willing to wait. In: Americas Conference on Information Systems, pp. 2212–2222 (2003)
25. Wang, H., Yi, S., Yang, W., Di, J.: The influence of system response time on human-information system interaction efficiency. China J. Ergon. **13**(3), 4–13 (2007)
26. McWilliams, T., Reimer, B., Mehler, B., Dobres, J., McAnulty, H.: A secondary assessment of the impact of voice interface turn delays on driver attention and arousal in field conditions. In: Proceedings of the Eighth International Driving Symposium on Human Factors in Driver Assessment, Training and Vehicle Design, pp. 414–420 (2015)
27. Barnett, A., Saponaro, A.: Misapplications reviews: the parable of the red line. Interfaces **15**(2), 33–39 (1985)
28. Tom, G., Lucey, S.: A field study investigating the effect of waiting time on customer satisfaction. J. Psychol. **131**(6), 655–660 (1997)

Developing QR Authentication and Fingerprint Record in an ATM Interface Using User-Centered Design Techniques

Diana Chumpitaz[1](✉), Kevin Pereda[1], Katherine Espinoza[1], Carlos Villarreal[1], William Perez[1], Arturo Moquillaza[1,2], Jaime Díaz[3], and Freddy Paz[1]

[1] Pontificia Universidad Católica del Perú, San Miguel, Lima 32, Peru
{diana.chumpitaz,kevin.pereda,k.espinoza,amoquillaza,fpaz}@pucp.pe
{c.villarreal,william.perez}@pucp.edu.pe
[2] Universidad San Ignacio de Loyola, Lima 12, Lima, Peru
miguel.moquillaza@usil.pe
[3] Universidad de la Frontera, 4780000 Temuco, Chile
jaimeignacio.diaz@ufrontera.cl

Abstract. ATMs are widely used around the world, which leads to the development of new functionalities that need to consider usability. For this reason, the following article presents the development of graphical interfaces for ATM of BBVA Continental Bank, which follows a user-centered process design. In the first place, we gathered information about our target user. Then, we developed a prototype based on the previous information and the needs of the bank, which also took into account expert's feedback. Finally, real users in the bank itself validated the prototypes.

Keywords: Human-Computer Interaction · User-Centered Design · Usability · Automated-Teller Machine

1 Introduction

An Automated-Teller Machine (ATM) is a computer-based interactive machine that offers several banking services. It allows consumers to make deposits, obtain cash from bank accounts, pay bills, transfer money between accounts, print statements and do many other routine transactions as they would at a normal bank teller window [1].

According to ATMIA [2], the automated teller machine is one of the devices that improved the financial services among people. Currently, these machines are acquiring new features different to the classical money delivery.

In this context, the BBVA Continental, one of the leading financial entities in Peru, started an improvement process of its ATM applications in order to offer a better experience to its final user [3].

To contribute with this goal, the BBVA Continental requested master's degree students the design of a usable interface that would permit the following

© Springer Nature Switzerland AG 2019
A. Marcus and W. Wang (Eds.): HCII 2019, LNCS 11586, pp. 420–430, 2019.
https://doi.org/10.1007/978-3-030-23535-2_31

functionality: To get a new credit card being a new user or get a duplicate of the credit card being a known user using secure methods such as QR authentication or fingerprint recorder.

The development of the proposal included the following techniques: personas, empathy maps, storyboards, prototypes, individual interviews, and user testing. The prototypes were analyzed by experts in the field in order to get feedback and improve the prototypes in an initial stage.

The validation took place at the BBVA Continental with real users, which allowed taking feedback and improving the prototypes.

2 Background

2.1 Usability

According to Nielsen [4], usability is a quality attribute that assesses how easy user interfaces are to use. Nielsen proposes five quality components to define usability:

- Learnability, which measures the facility for users to accomplish basic tasks the first time they encounter the design.
- Efficiency, which measures how quickly users perform tasks once they have learned the design.
- Memorability, which measures how easily users can re-establish proficiency after a period of not using the interface.
- Errors: which measures how many errors the user makes and how easily it is to recover from those errors.
- Satisfaction: which measures how pleasant is the design itself.

2.2 User Experience

User Experience (UX) is considered a much broader aspect than usability, and is defined by the ISO 9241-210 standard as a "person's perceptions and responses resulting from the use and/or anticipated use of a product, system or service" [5]. This aspect is not only related to the ease of use of a graphical user interface, but also to the satisfaction degree, emotions, and perceptions that a user can feel during and after the interaction with the system.

2.3 User-Centered Design

The User-Centered Design is a multidisciplinary approach that invites end users to participate in the design of a product. Initially, it focuses on deepening the understanding of users and requirements. Then, an iterative process of design and evaluation is carried out considering the observations that the users could point out [6].

The importance of this collaboration lies in obtaining high value information which will be used to improve and focus the developers work. A UCD design process applied will carry some benefits for the company for example a better ROI (Return on investment) [7].

Personas. Personas allow creating a fictional, yet realistic, description of a typical or targeting user of product [8,9]. Effective personas:

- Represent the important needs of a group.
- Express the user expectation about the system and how likely they are to use the system.
- Describe people with goals, values, general background.

Empathy Map. In user-centered design, empathy maps are best used from the very beginning of the design process. According to Gibbons [10], an empathy map is a "collaborative visualization used to articulate what we know about a particular type of user. It externalizes knowledge about users in order to (1) create a shared understanding of user needs, and (2) aid in decision making".

Prototyping. According to Affairs [11], a prototype is a draft version of a product that allows you to explore your ideas and show the intention behind a feature or the overall design concept to users before investing time and money into development. A prototype can be anything from paper drawings to something that allows click-through of a few pieces of content to a fully functioning site.

User Testing. According to Paz et al. [12], user testing is a method in which a representative amount of end users interacts with the software following a list of predefined tasks. Exhaustive observations of these human-system interactions allow the identification of usability issues related to the system.

3   BBVA ATM Interfaces Design

3.1   Demand

With our approach, we want to design usable interfaces that can be used for BBVA ATMs, keeping in mind that we will design the interfaces for a new requirement: to get a credit card. From a meeting with BBVA representatives, all related information about the requirement was obtained, of said information the following is highlighted:

- The requirement has two kind of users: BBVA clients and non-clients, so specific interfaces must be developed for both.
- Clients could get a duplicate of a lost credit card.
- Non-clients could receive a new credit card.
- Security controls must be employed to assure user identity.
- Find and try to distinct alternative mechanisms to reduce possible implementation cost of interfaces.
- Optimize time spent on getting a credit card.

Also, as a result of the meeting, the acceptance criteria for interfaces was established:

- Clients find appropriate the way the new requirement is presented.
- Clients find appropriate the security controls used in their corresponding interfaces.
- Clients show a positive reaction from interaction with the new requirement.

3.2 Design Process

Interfaces design was developed following a user-centered process. According to disciplines and methods reviewed in the previous section, the next process was followed:

Metaphors Design. In this step, metaphors were designed to help user to find the new requirement through ATM interface and also as guide in the process. Figures 1 and 2 are part of the group of metaphors developed.

Fig. 1. A metaphor to represent the requirement of get a credit card

Fig. 2. Metaphors to distinct process between get a new credit card or duplicated one

Identify User Profiles. The activity consisted of an interview using a ten question questionnaire where a user was asked about common and relevant information like:

- Name, age and gender.
- Expertise level using ATMs.
- Reasons to use ATMs.

From all data collected, target user profile was developed. Persona method is applied in this step obtaining two profiles: a experienced person with technology and a person less experienced with technology. However, both profiles show some concerns about the security and speed of the interaction with ATM. Figure 3 shows details about the experienced person with technology specifying their goals and concerns.

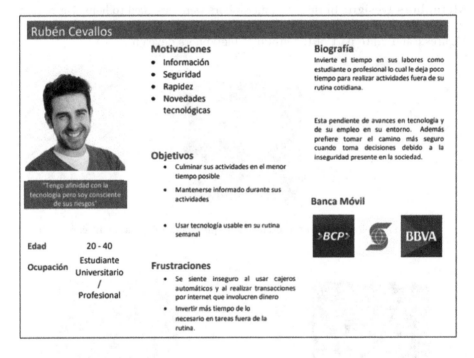

Fig. 3. Persona: Experienced person with technology

Deepen Vision of Target User. In this step, the goal was to contrast the knowledge of the development team about the target users before and after the interview mentioned above. The result of this activity allowed to design interfaces oriented to both target users, organized and presented according to all information collected through the process.

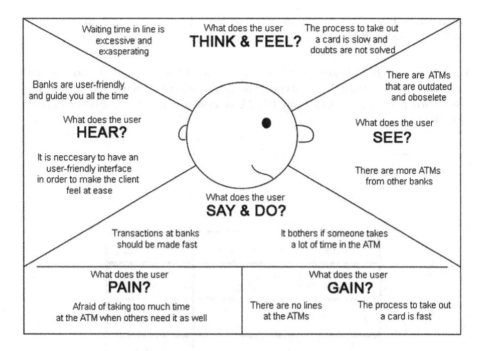

Fig. 4. Empathy map about person experienced with technology

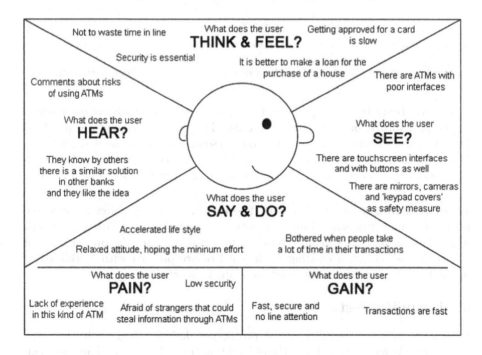

Fig. 5. Empathy map about team knowledge about target users

Brainstorming. The development team looked for a way to represent both workflows (for each target user) by brainstorming (Figs. 4 and 5).

Prototyping. In this step, all ideas were placed into a paper prototype and then improved as digital prototype. The improvement of paper prototype was done with feedback receive from BBVA representatives and usability experts (Fig. 6).

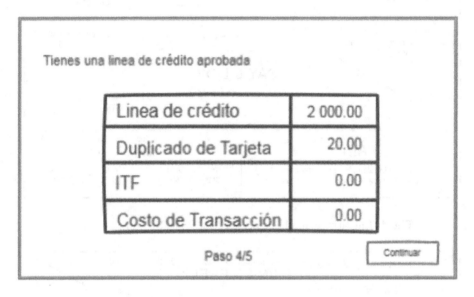

Fig. 6. Paper prototype: Details of new credit line (Non-client workflow)

Usability Test. In this step, a user testing was performed with five users which were representative of our two target profiles. The test environment was provided by BBVA Continental bank, however, due to some features of the designed solution could not be emulated as real as the team wished, users interaction with ATM was affected negatively. More detail about this evaluation on next section.

Improve Prototypes with Users Feedback. Last step, after analyze the feedback from users, some improvements were done to the solution proposed. These improvements, basically, consisted of organize better the presentation of a specific task (block a existing credit card before proceed with workflow) or highlight a specific need to proceed (activate a checkbox).

4   Usability Test

In order to test the usability of the prototypes designed, a usability test was performed. As mentioned above, the objective of this activity is find any problem a user could deal while is interacting with the ATM interface (Figs. 7, 8 and 9).

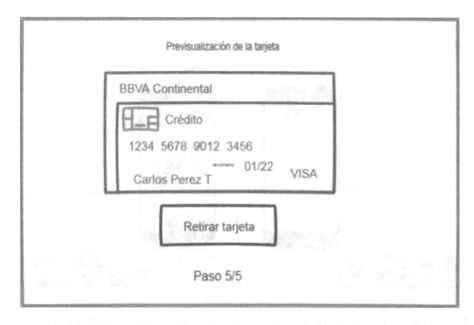

Fig. 7. Paper prototype: Preview of duplicate credit card. (Client workflow)

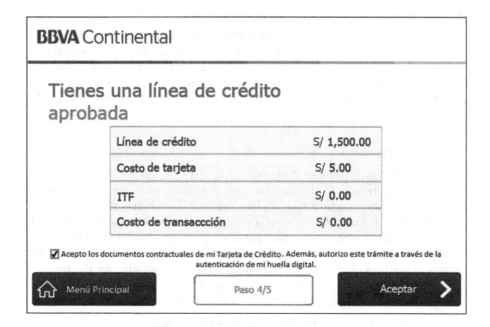

Fig. 8. Digital prototype: Details of new credit line (Non-client workflow)

Fig. 9. Digital prototype: Instructions to continue the process of duplicate a credit card (Client workflow)

4.1 Planning

Some materials were made to use during the execution of the test, a pre-test questionnaire, a task list, scenarios, a post questionnaire and a evaluation tool to track user interaction with developed ATM interfaces. Also, a document to assure the confidentiality of any information given by users was made. All of these materials were prepared to be used by five users which match with the target profiles identified on design process.

4.2 Execution

Test were made on November 29th and 30th, 2018 in San Isidro, Lima. After receiving the users and explaining the test workflow, each one was given all prepared materials necessary to complete the test. In the first place, each user had to sign a Confidentiality Agreement and a pre-test questionnaire. Then, with a list of task, one by one, users where performing each task while a monitor was in charge to take notes about any problem that could happen. Regrettably, due to inherent features of the proposed solution, it was not possible for the team to reach a hundred percent of similarity between the environment test and a real situation. Some of these lacking features to test were:

- Blocking a credit card with BBVA application mobile.
- Automatic response from ATM when a fingerprint is scanned correctly.
- Automatic response from ATM when a evaluation task is completed.

4.3   Results Analysis

From the obtained results, we can confirm that:

- 70% of the users were able to perform the first task with no issues, which consisted in obtaining a credit card duplicated. These users (70%) had a positive attitude towards the QR functionality because they considered it innovative or something they have not seen before in an ATM. The remaining 30% of the users felt that the missing experience, due to the lack of QR software in the ATM, did not satisfied them and that changes can be made.
- 75% percent of the users in the second task considered it was easier than the first one due to the fact that they have already interacted with the application, and that although it is not the same task, task 2 is about getting a new credit card, they felt that the last steps, about confirming the process was similar. The missing 25% percent expressed that it could not be that easier, that we had to be more explicit in the details, because it is an important transaction.

From the feedback of the users, the defects identified are:

- The message about blocking your lost credit card before proceeding to get a duplicate was unclear due to the fact that it did not have a clear button to continue. Users understood this message as a step and not as an advice
- The acceptance text to proceed with the new credit card was small, so important information as this needs to be highlighted

The defects identified were corrected and sent to BBVA Continental in order for them to take into consideration.

5   Conclusions and Future Work

From results obtained from the usability test, we can assure that most of users completed all tasks without any major difficulty, but also due to inconveniences to simulate both process (specially the one about getting a new credit card), users expressions reflected confusion at moments when the workflow could not continue naturally. We can conclude that the deep analysis of our users led us to not make many mistakes.

For future work, we want to improve the test environment used in this test or prepare a one by ourself to gain a better feedback from users, because with the current limitations our results have been affected in a way that at first impression was negatively reflected but could even be positively. Similarly, take into account the feedback provided by the users after the experience.

Acknowledgement. The authors thank to all the participants involved into the experience required to perform the presented study, especially the BBVA Continental Bank. The study is highly supported by the Human-Computer Interaction, Design, User Experience, Accessibility & Innovation Technologies Research Group (HCI-DUXAIT) from Pontifical Catholic University of Peru (PUCP).

References

1. Al-Saleh, K., Bendak, S.: An ergonomics evaluation of certain atm dimensions. Int. J. Occup. Saf. Ergon. **19**(3), 347–353 (2013)
2. ATMIA: ATM benchmarking study 2016 and industry report (2016). https://www.accenture.com/_acnmedia/PDF-10/Accenture-Banking-ATM-Benchmarking-2016.pdf. Accessed 15 Jan 2019
3. Moquillaza, A., et al.: Developing an ATM Interface Using User-Centered Design Techniques. In: Marcus, A., Wang, W. (eds.) DUXU 2017. LNCS, vol. 10290, pp. 690–701. Springer, Cham (2017). https://doi.org/10.1007/978-3-319-58640-3_49
4. Nielsen, J.: Usability 101: introduction to usability (2012). https://www.nngroup.com/articles/usability-101-introduction-to-usability/. Accessed 15 Jan 2019
5. ISO: Ergonomics of human-system interaction - Part 210: Human-centred design for interactive systems. Standard, International Organization for Standardization, Geneva, CH (2010)
6. Mao, J.Y., Vredenburg, K., Smith, P.W., Carey, T.: The state of user-centered design practice. Commun. ACM **48**(3), 105–109 (2005)
7. Usability.gov: benefits of user-centered design (2017). https://www.usability.gov/what-and-why/benefits-of-ucd.html. Accessed 15 Jan 2019
8. Haikara, J.: Usability in Agile Software Development: Extending the Interaction Design Process with Personas Approach. In: Concas, G., Damiani, E., Scotto, M., Succi, G. (eds.) XP 2007. LNCS, vol. 4536, pp. 153–156. Springer, Heidelberg (2007). https://doi.org/10.1007/978-3-540-73101-6_22
9. Pruitt, J., Grudin, J.: Personas: practice and theory. In: Proceedings of the 2003 Conference on Designing for User Experiences, DUX 2003, pp. 1–15. ACM, New York (2003)
10. Gibbons, S.: Empathy Mapping: The First Step in Design Thinking (2018)
11. Usability.gov: Prototyping (2014). https://www.usability.gov/how-to-and-tools/methods/prototyping.html. Accessed 15 Jan 2019
12. Paz, F., Pow-Sang, J.A.: Usability evaluation methods for software development: a systematic mapping review. In: 2015 8th International Conference on Advanced Software Engineering Its Applications (ASEA), pp. 1–4, November 2015

Enhancing the Usability of Long-Term Rental Applications in Chinese Market: An Interaction Design Approach

Jing-chen Cong[1]([⊠]), Chun-Hsien Chen[2], Chao Liu[3], Yang Meng[4], and Zhi-yuan Zheng[5]

[1] School of Mechanical Engineering, Tianjin University, Tianjin 300350, China
congjingchen@tju.edu.cn
[2] School of Mechanical and Aerospace Engineering,
Nanyang Technological University, Singapore 639798, Singapore
[3] Baidu Online Network Technology (Beijing) Co., Ltd., Beijing 100085, China
[4] Lianxian Education Institute (Tianjin) Co., Ltd., Tianjin 300000, China
[5] School of Design and Arts, Beijing Institute of Technology,
Beijing 100081, China

Abstract. At present, there are numerous usability problems in the long-term rental application in Chinese market, including unreasonable interaction design problems and irregular interface design problems. The usability elements and the interaction design principles of the long-term rental application are proposed to support the usability improvement. The usability elements, namely effectiveness, efficiency, satisfaction, learnability, security, and versatility, and the interaction design principles include meeting user mental models; focusing on the analysis and design of different touchpoints; completing information searching path; reasonable information display methods. User behaviors and usage preferences are explored through focus group, non-participant observation and questionnaire survey. One long-term rental application is redesigned to follow the interaction design principle. For usability testing, the measured person uses the application before and after the improvement, counting the usability score and level to determine whether the redesign has been improved. The principle of interaction design can improve the interaction design level and achieve the goal of improving usability of the long-term rental application.

Keywords: Interaction design · Usability goals · Long-term rental application

1 Introduction

With the rapid development of mobile Internet, the long-term rental application is the combination of traditional rental agency service and mobile Internet, integrating large-scale housing into the online comprehensive platform. It makes up for the shortcomings of information asymmetry, high intermediary cost, cumbersome procedures and insufficient service standardization of traditional Chinese rental agency services. After the long-term rental industry entered an accelerated development period, many innovative business models have emerged in the segmentation field. The long-term rental

© Springer Nature Switzerland AG 2019
A. Marcus and W. Wang (Eds.): HCII 2019, LNCS 11586, pp. 431–441, 2019.
https://doi.org/10.1007/978-3-030-23535-2_32

application is a business model, through which the business landlord (individual or company) with legal charter rights provides users with institutional supply, management and operation services. Users can complete online searching, offline viewing, and online signing through the application. The long-term rental application attracts a large number of users because of its easy operation, low cost to find an apartment, large number of apartments and more standardized services.

Chinese long-term rental industry market is huge, but compared with the developed countries such as the United States, there is still a big gap in the maturity of the long-term rental service system. The Chinese rental industry is still in an accelerated development stage. According to the report released by National Health Commission P. R. China in July 2018, as of 2017, Chinese mobile population reached 244 million, occupying 17.55% of the total population [1]. According to the report released by iResearch, the scale of Chinese long-term rental market in 2017 has reached 1.43 trillion RMB, and is expected to reach 3.01 trillion RMB by 2025 [2]. However, at present there are still many usability problems in Chinese long-term rental application, including the lack of uniformity of the page logic, labels which affect attention of users, incomplete screening criteria, and so on [3].

The goals of interaction design include usability goals and user experience goals [4]. The long-term rental application matches the apartments and users through the network channel, the long-term rental apartments play a decisive role in satisfying the user's physiological needs. Moreover, the limited cognitive ability of the public users and the high loss of decision-making failure also make the usability goals become the core goals of the interaction design of the long-term rental application. This paper intends to achieve the goal of improving product usability by studying the interaction design of long-term rental application.

2   Methodology and Results

2.1   Overall Procedures of Proposed Methodology

As shown in Fig. 1, through the focus group, non-participant observation and questionnaire survey, the experiment explored the user demand preferences and the user usage habits of long-term rental application. Summarizing the results of three steps, and proposed interaction design principles to assist long-term rental application to improve the interaction design level, so that the final presentation of the interface can effectively improve the application usability.

2.2   Focus Group

A focus group is a group of individuals selected and assembled by researchers to discuss and comment on, from personal experience, the topic that is the subject of the research [5]. In order to determine the user focus of the interaction design of the long-term rental application based on usability goals, this study firstly explored the needs and suggestions for the usability of products when users used an existing long-term rental application through focus groups. The focus group targeted new graduates or newcomers from 21 to 26 years old who had rental needs in first-tier and second-tier cities. The focus group consisted of 13 users and they were discussed in two separate groups.

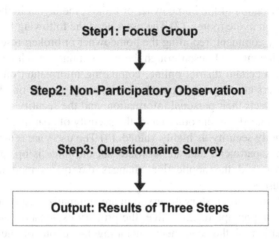

Fig. 1. The framework of the methodology

2.3   Non-participatory Observation

The non-participant observation has much potential for capturing social action and interaction as it occurs. And the objectivity of the non-participant observation makes it more acceptable as a research method [6]. Combining the results of the focus group with the usability goals, this paper conducted research through non-participatory observation. Observing and recording in the real environment that two users used two existing long-term rental applications, effectively discovering the real behaviors and psychological expectations of users in the real environment.

2.4   Questionnaire Survey

Combining the conclusions of the focus group and the non-participatory observation, this paper collected users' views and perceptions through questionnaires [7]. The questionnaire adopted two methods: online distribution and offline distribution, and was distributed in three stages: pre-distribution, formal distribution, and supplementary distribution. The trap question was set. When the user triggered trap question and gave a wrong answer in the system, the questionnaire would be classified as an invalid one. And the questionnaire designed two questions to ensure that all valid respondents had rental requirements. Finally, 389 valid questionnaires were returned.

2.5   Results

The results of focus group are summarized as follows: (1) The users pay attention to the following information: the subway station and supermarket information around the apartment; the contract payment period; the information of other rooms when the house is shared; the information of the homeowner or broker; the layout in the rooms and the facilities information in the rooms. (2) The users need the following functions: viewing the visitor's review comment; reporting the homeowner or broker; reserving the line to view the house; viewing the house through the video online; searching and viewing all the apartments in a certain district online; comparing information on two apartments online. (3) The users attach great importance to security. On the one hand, they hope that the system protects their personal information, and the security of rent and service fees online is guaranteed. On the other hand, the security of apartments, including door locks and community security, is highly valued. (4) The users are sensitive to the price information of the apartment, and are worried that the price is opaque due to infor-mation asymmetry, and the application changes the prices randomly and causes financial loss of users.

The results of non-participatory observation are summarized as follows: (1) During the process of finding an apartment online, the primary expectation of users is to find the basic information of the apartment, including the photo of the apartment, the geographical location, the rent of the apartment, the hardware of the apartment, and the orientation of the apartment. The deep expectation is to find an apartment that meet their own rental requirements, including the commuting time from apartment to their company, the payment methods, and the information of sharing roommates. (2) When looking at the apartment in the real scene, the users pay more attention to the time of the reservation, the authenticity of the apartment, the housekeeper information, the surrounding environment of the community, the safety of the apartment, the sanitation of the apartment, and the match degree between photos online and the real situation. (3) When users sign the contract online, they pay more attention to the contract reg-ulations, the rental fee descriptions, the default statements, the rent payment channels, the payment amount details users' and the fund transfer process.

The results of questionnaire are summarized as follows: (1) The users pay attention to the geographical location and traffic situation of the apartment, and the application should assist the user checking the traffic situation through the core operation. When searching for apartments, 66% of users tend to find apartment near the subway station, 63% prefer to locate houses through company position; 81% of users pay more attention to traffic problems. When comparing the information about the apartments, 69% of users care about the distance from the house to the subway station. (2) The users who focus on the shared apartment are different from that of the whole apartment. In the page displaying the shared apartments, the information displayed should be increased according to the users' needs. The survey found that 77% of users are concerned about the basic information of shared roommates; 55% of users pay attention to whether there is a separate bathroom; 37% pay attention to the problem of water and electricity sharing; 24% of users pay attention to whether other rooms have been rented. (3) The introduction of the apartment in the long-term rental application can be based on short videos, panoramic pictures and photos, combined with live video and text in appropriate scenes. As the form of video is more intuitive than the picture, users are more inclined to understand the listing through short videos. The data shows that the proportion of users who prefer to browse the listing through short videos, panoramic pictures, and photos is 71%, 62%, and 55% respectively. (4) Users are concerned about security issues. Users want an apartment which security can be guaranteed. 58% of users think that security issue is the most important thing when selecting an apartment listing. 60% of users who choose to share an apartment are most concerned about personal security issues.

3   Usability-Based Interaction Design Principles of Long-Term Rental Application

The International Standardization Organization (ISO) defined usability as: "The extent to which a product can be used by specified users to achieve specified goals with effectiveness, efficiency and satisfaction in a specified context of use." in ISO 9241-11 (1998) [8]. Preece et al. (1993) characterized six attributes of usability: feasibility, effectiveness, security, versatility, learnability, and memorization [9]. Arbran et al. (2003) established an enhanced usability assessment model, including five factors: effectiveness, efficiency, satisfaction, security, and learnability [10]. Being different from other applications, the long-term rental application has the characteristics of wide user scope, high capital relevance, and long trading period. Therefore, this paper proposes six usability elements, namely effectiveness, efficiency, satisfaction, learnability, security, and versatility, and these six elements are defined as their usability goals for the long-term rental application.

According to the availability target and experimental research results of the long-term rental application proposed above, this paper proposes the following long-term rental application interaction design principles, so that the products can improve their usability through designing according to the interaction design principles.

Meeting User Mental Models. The user mental model is a simple way for the users to understand the interface through self-creating [11]. According to the report "2018 Young People Renting House Big Data Report", 69% of the current Chinese rental population is a young group born after 1990 [12]. The rental experiences of these users started from their graduation. The long-term rental application is a new system for them, which can improve the users' acceptance degree by simulating users' mental model to their common system. The traditional offline rental mode has some problems in renting service system, apartment management system and credit evaluation system. Therefore, the user mental model of long-term rental application can simulate the user mental model of the mobile shopping application with a larger number of users, instead of the user mental model of the traditional offline model. There are some similarities between mobile shopping and online rental transactions, for example, users find their targeted products and trade online. The long-term rental application can be referred to the user mental model of the mobile shopping platform during designing, including searching products, viewing product details, and collecting products.

Focusing on the Analysis and Design of Different Touchpoints. Touchpoints occur whenever a customer "touches" a system across multiple channels and at various points in time [13]. The user use process of long-term rental application is complicate, and the touchpoints which distributed throughout the system are numerous. As shown in Fig. 2, the information touchpoint is formed between the user and the information platform, the interpersonal touchpoint is formed between the user and the housekeeper, the physical touchpoint is formed between the user and the apartment, and the hidden touchpoint is formed between the user and the landlord. At the beginning of the design, designers need to analyze the touchpoints of different functions in the application and give targeted design plans. Take the most important rental service as an example: (1) It will form a hidden touchpoint between the landlord and the user before the user uses the rental service. Users will not be in direct contact with the landlord, and they can only communicate with the application. The application renovates and shows the apartment information online. Applications should pay attention to that the information published online must be in completely matched to the real situation information of the apartment. (2) At the beginning of using the rental service, the information touchpoint will be formed between the user and the application. The user will be anxious when filtering an apartment from massive information. At this stage, the application should assist the user in making decisions more efficiently through many means, such as filtering information based on user preferences, optimizing information hierarchy, distinguishing information category and so on. (3) When finding an appropriate apartment, the user will make an appointment to view it. During the appointment processing, the user and the housekeeper will form a human touchpoint. Language, behaviors and dressing of the housekeepers will affect the overall evaluation of the application. This part also should be intervened by design. (4) When the user views the house offline, it will form a physical touchpoint between the user and the apartment. The application should guarantee the apartment is consistent with the online descriptions, including the apartment facility information, the roommate information and so on. Information about whether the house has been rented or not, online information needs to be synchronized with the offline situation. At this time, there is an interpersonal touchpoint between the user and the housekeeper. The housekeeper should maintain a friendly attitude and respond to users' questions in time. (5) When the user signing the contract, the information touchpoint with the application is formed through the online system. Application should provide clear feedbacks for different time points in the process of fund transfer. (6) When the user successfully enters the house after signing the contract, there is a physical touchpoint with the house, an interpersonal touchpoint with the housekeeper (when the housekeeper transfers the materials of the apartment to the users), and an information touchpoint with the application (the door lock password information is obtained by the application). The application needs to provide assistance when the users complaint or give feedbacks on issues.

Completing Information Searching Path. The long-term rental application should provide a corresponding path for directed browsing, semi-directed browsing, and undirected browsing [14]: the search bar is the main path provided to the directed browsing behavior; the apartment classification list entrance is the primary path provided to the semi-directed browsing behavior; and the recommended apartment list is the primary path provided to the undirected browsing behavior. It is known from the experiments that the users attach great importance to whether the house is suitable for daily commuting. The application should provide the function of searching the apartment based on commuting. The users can directly find the apartment which is nearest to their companies, or the traffic routes of the apartment meet the users' requirements. Application should minimize the search paths to avoid the anxiety of users when using the application.

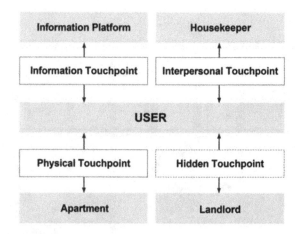

Fig. 2. The touchpoints between user and long-term rental application

Reasonable Information Display Methods. When displaying information, you should select an appropriate form according to the users' requirements. For example, in the apartment detail page, application can increase the form of short video viewing, and play it automatically when the telephone is in the Wi-Fi environment. Adding the apartment comparison function, the user can compare all dimensions of the apartment information to make a satisfied decision. Showing more relevant information of the shared apartment, including the basic information of the shared roommates, whether there is a separate toilet or not, the sharing method of utilities, whether other houses have been rented. In addition, the long-term rental application should also provide a reasonable way to display information, such as using artificial intelligence technology to transform passive information into active information [15], and providing users with personalized recommendations to assist users in decision-making efficiency. User-generated data stands for those acquired from online reviews/comments, audio or video-based text [16]. After obtaining the user's personal data and renting demand, the long-term rental application establishes the user's personal demand model and uses the demand model to recommend actively. After receiving the recommendation result, the user will have operational behaviors (such as browsing, collecting, ignoring an apartment, etc.). The system updates the model according to the user behavior, and quickly uses the updated model for recommendation.

4   Usability Testing

The main purpose of the usability test is to verify the interaction design principles proposed and observe whether the interaction design principles can improve the usability of the application by redesigning a long-term rental application to make it more consistent with the interaction design principles. Usability testing is used to inspect if the improved application has improved its usability (the improved high-fidelity model is shown in Fig. 3).

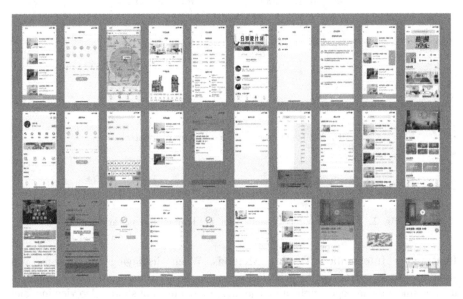

Fig. 3. The improved design prototype (Interface Designers: Jia-xin Lu, Jia-yi Fu, Qi Zhao, Ruo-lun Yang, Shi-qi Zhou, Zhi-yuan Zheng, Zi-you Qiu)

Jakob Nielsen proposed that measured person can find 80% of the usability problems of the design when the number of samples is 5 in the usability test [17]. Based on the predictions using the observed data with a variety of experimental conditions, a general rule for optimal sample size would be '10 ± 2' instead of '4 ± 1' [18]. This experiment selected the number of samples as 13. The test first required the measured person using the online version and the improved design prototype to experience separately, and observed whether the user could successfully complete the entire operation process, then required the measured person filling in the system usability scale.

In order to facilitate the understanding of the users, a slight improvement was made for the system usability scale compiled by the scholar John Brooke by replacing 'system' with 'application'. As shown in Table 1, the scale is a 5-level Likert scale, giving 10 attitude statements. The first, third, fifth, seventh, and seventh statements are forward description statements, and the second, fourth, sixth, eighth, and fourth statements are reverse description statements. The user chooses the degree of recognition of the statements [19]. The fourth and fourth statements in the scale measure the learnability of the application [20].

Table 1. The usability scale

		Strongly disagree				Strongly agree
		1	2	3	4	5
1	I think that I would like to use this system frequently					
2	I found the system unnecessarily complex					
3	I thought the system was easy to use					
4	I think that I would need the support of a technical person to be able to use this system					
5	I found the various functions in this system were well integrated					
6	I thought there was too much inconsistency in this system					
7	I would imagine that most people would learn to use this system very quickly					
8	I found the system very cumbersome to use					
9	I felt very confident using the system					
10	I needed to learn a lot of things before I could get going with this system					

To calculate the SUS score, for items 1, 3, 5, 7, and 9, the score contribution is the scale position minus 1. For items 2, 4, 6, 8 and 10, the contribution is 5 minus the scale position. Multiply the sum of the scores by 2.5 to obtain the overall value of usability [19]. The learnability score is the sum of the 4th and 10th scores multiplied by 12.5.

After calculation, the average usability score of online version is 49.423, and the average learnability score of it is 59.615. The average usability score of improved design prototype is 70.962, and the average learnability score of it is 75.962. According to the average score, usability and learnability can be divided into six levels from A to F from high to low [21]. As shown in Fig. 4, the online version usability and learnability are Level F and Level D. The improved design prototype usability and learnability are Level C and Level B. The usability and learnability level of prototype are both significantly higher than the online version, indicating that the redesigned interaction design has improved usability and learnability, and verified the correctness and usability of the interaction design principles.

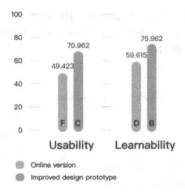

Fig. 4. The average score and the level between the online version and the improved design prototype

5   Conclusion

Starting from the usability of the long-term rental application, combining with focus group, non-participatory observations and questionnaire survey, the principles of interaction design are summarized. Through design practicing and usability testing, it is found that adherence to the interaction design principles can effectively improve the usability and learnability of the long-term rental application and will lay a theoretical foundation for the interaction design of the long-term rental application. For the one thing, the usability goals of the long-term rental application are proposed, including effectiveness, efficiency, satisfaction, learnability, security, and versatility. For another thing, the interaction design principles of the long-term rental application are proposed, including meeting user mental models, focusing on the analysis and design of different touchpoints, completing information searching path and reasonable information display methods. The limitation of this study is that the measured person is all working or studying in metropolis cities of China. In future, the collection of person from small and medium-sized cities are necessary in order to increase the sample size and representative of the entire population of China. Due to the limitations of this study, i.e. time and resource constraints, a collection would be conducted to gather more samples in the future.

References

1. National Health Commission P. R. China. Statistical Data Table of Permanent Residents, Floating Population, and Migrant Workers from 1978 to 2017 [EB/OL]. http://www.chinaldrk.org.cn/wjw/#/home
2. IResearch. 2018 China Long-term Rental Service Industry Research Report [J/OL]. http://report.iresearch.cn/report/201809/3271.shtml
3. Sun, X., Zhong, X., Ren, W.W.: The usability study of rental website: taking 58.com for example. Design **7**, 138–139 (2016)

4. Lu, X.B.: Research on interaction design methods in information design. Sci. Technol. Rev. **25**(13), 18–21 (2007)
5. Powell, R.A., Single, H.M.: Focus groups. Int. J. Qual. Health Care **8**(5), 499 (1996)
6. Caldwell, K., Atwal, A.: Non-participant observation: using video tapes to collect data in nursing research. Nurse Res. **13**(2), 42 (2005)
7. Garrett, J.J.: The Elements of User Experience: User-Centered Design for the Web, United States of America (2011)
8. Bevan, N., Carter, J., Harker, S.: ISO 9241-11 revised: what have we learnt about usability since 1998? In: Kurosu, M. (ed.) HCI 2015. LNCS, vol. 9169, pp. 143–151. Springer, Cham (2015). https://doi.org/10.1007/978-3-319-20901-2_13
9. Preece, J., Rogers, Y., Sharp, H.: Interaction Design: Beyond Human-Computer Interaction, pp. 2839–2841. Wiley, London (2007)
10. Abran, A., Khelifi, A., Suryn, W., Seffah, A.: Usability meanings and interpretations in ISO standards. Softw. Qual. J. **11**(4), 325–338 (2003)
11. Cooper, A., Reimann, R., Cronin, D.: About Face 3: The Essentials of Interaction Design. Wiley, London (2007)
12. CBNData. 2018 Young People Renting House Big Data Report [J/OL]. https://www.cbndata.com/report/1161/detail?isReading=report&page=1
13. Zomerdijk, L.G., Voss, C.A.: Service design for experience-centric services. J. Serv. Res. **13**(1), 67–82 (2009)
14. Marchionini, G.: Information Seeking in Electronic Environments. Cambridge University Press, Cambridge (1995)
15. Qin, J.Y.: Impaction of artificial intelligence on interaction design. Packag. Eng. **38**(20), 27–31 (2017)
16. Zheng, P., Lin, T.J., Chen, C.H., Xu, X.: A systematic design approach for service innovation of smart product-service systems. J. Clean. Prod. **2018**(201), 657–667 (2018)
17. Nielsen, J.: Estimating the number of subjects needed for a thinking aloud test. Int. J. Hum Comput Stud. **41**(3), 385–397 (1994)
18. Hwang, W., Salvendy, G.: Number of people required for usability evaluation: the 10 ± 2 rule. Commun. ACM **53**(5), 130–133 (2010)
19. Brooke, J.: SUS-A Quick and Dirty' Usability Scale. Usability Evaluation in Industry, pp. 189–194. Taylor & Francis Ltd., London (1996)
20. Lewis, J.R., Sauro, J.: The factor structure of the system usability scale. In: Human Centered Design, First International Conference, Hcd, Held As. DBLP (2009)
21. Sauro, J., Lewis, J.R.: Quantifying the User Experience. Elsevier, Amsterdam (2012)

A Usability Evaluation of Privacy Add-ons for Web Browsers

Matthew Corner[1], Huseyin Dogan[1(✉)], Alexios Mylonas[1],
and Francis Djabri[2]

[1] Bournemouth University, Bournemouth, UK
{i7241812, hdogan, amylonas}@bournemouth.ac.uk
[2] Mozilla Corporation, San Francisco, USA
zerodegreedesign@me.com

Abstract. The web has improved our life and has provided us with more opportunities to access information and do business. Nonetheless, due to the prevalence of trackers on websites, web users might be subject to profiling while accessing the web, which impairs their online privacy. Privacy browser add-ons, such as DuckDuckGo Privacy Essentials, Ghostery and Privacy Badger, extend the privacy protection that the browsers offer by default, by identifying and blocking trackers. However, the work that focuses on the usability of the privacy add-ons, as well as the users' awareness, feelings, and thoughts towards them, is rather limited. In this work, we conducted usability evaluations by utilising System Usability Scale and Think-Aloud Protocol on three popular privacy add-ons, i.e., DuckDuckGo Privacy Essentials, Ghostery and Privacy Badger. Our work also provides insights into the users' awareness of online privacy and attitudes towards the abovementioned privacy add-ons; in particular trust, concern, and control. Our results suggest that the participants feel safer and trusting of their respective add-on. It also uncovers areas for add-on improvement, such as a more visible toolbar logo that offers visual feedback, easy access to thorough help resources, and detailed information on the trackers that have been found.

Keywords: Usability · Privacy · Browser add-ons

1 Introduction

Currently, the web is a life-changing service that users visit on a daily basis. The web affects every aspect of our life such as the way we do business, interact with others, entertain ourselves and access information. However, the web comes with a number of vectors that might compromise users' privacy. One of the prominent ways in which privacy is compromised is through tracking. Specifically, there is an incessant effort from most services on the web to track the behaviour of their users. These services collect data in order to find out as much as they can about their user base, including who they are in contact with, and their online purchases [1]. Moreover, trackers nowadays use a number of client-side technologies for tracking users, other than cookies [2].

© Springer Nature Switzerland AG 2019
A. Marcus and W. Wang (Eds.): HCII 2019, LNCS 11586, pp. 442–458, 2019.
https://doi.org/10.1007/978-3-030-23535-2_33

Tracking web users can take place for legitimate purposes (e.g. analytics, personalised user experience, etc.). However, extensive user tracking can lead to behavioural profiling, which provides unauthorised access to a user's personal data. The notion of constructing a 'profile' of a user through collected personal data is also highlighted in [3] and [4]. Roesner et al. [5] found more than 500 unique trackers in a corpus of 1000 websites (from very popular to lesser-used websites). Similarly, Schelter and Kunegis [6] found third-party trackers on more than 3.5 billion websites. This suggests that the sites users visit are most likely not the only entities tracking their behaviour. In the past, tracker blocking has not been offered as an out-of-the-box browser privacy mechanism [7]. However, currently two popular desktop browsers (i.e. Opera and Firefox) enable it by default. Firefox blocks by default if the user is browsing in a private window, but this is not default behaviour for the normal browser window. Furthermore, a variety of privacy add-ons are now available in the add-on repositories of web browsers, which offer protection against web tracking [8].

However, studies suggest there is room to improve the usability of privacy add-ons [9–11]. Schaub et al. [9] found in a privacy add-on study that whilst people tend to be aware of tracking, they do not know the specific details. This holds as the add-ons offered only a limited amount of information regarding who is running the trackers and for what means the data is collected. The use of an add-on increased the users' awareness of online tracking. Marella et al. [10] studied the effectiveness of privacy add-ons in communicating awareness of privacy risks. Their findings suggest users feel a sense of security just from installing the add-on, but generally they remained unsure as to why their data was being collected. A usability study by Leon et al. [11] found that participants had trouble configuring their privacy add-ons, and wrongly assumed they were blocking trackers due to not understanding the user interface or receiving much feedback from it.

Studies in this area show that concern towards online privacy is existent [12–14]. According to [12], nearly 90% of Internet users in Britain are concerned about their online privacy. McCoy et al. [13] found that the intrusiveness of online advertisements can reduce the users' desire to return to a website, due to increased irritation with advertisements. Additionally, according to [14], web users who consider online privacy protection measures are targeted by the NSA for surveillance.

In this context, this work uses a survey with 30 participants in order to evaluate the usability of three popular privacy add-ons with varying user interface styles, namely: DuckDuckGo Privacy Essentials, Ghostery and Privacy Badger. With regard to their Firefox user base, Privacy Badger has more than 500,000 users, DuckDuckGo Privacy Essentials has more than 700,000 users, and Ghostery has more than 1,000,000 [15].

The aim of the work is also to understand users' awareness along with their feelings of trust, concern, and control towards the add-ons. Participants interacted with one of the three add-ons through task-based scenarios whilst thinking aloud during a video screen capture. Further insight was gathered through three questionnaires, which the participants completed themselves at different points during the exercise.

The structure of the paper is as follows: Sect. 2 focuses on the user interface analysis of the privacy add-ons, Sect. 3 presents our methodology and Sect. 4 presents our findings. Finally, Sect. 5 concludes the paper and provides suggestions for future work.

2   User Interface Analysis of the Privacy Add-ons

This section compares interface elements for three popular privacy add-ons, namely:
(i) DuckDuckGo Privacy Essentials,[1] (ii) Ghostery,[2] and (iii) Privacy Badger.[3] Testing
the effectiveness of the add-ons' tracker detection is not within scope for this study.
Instead, its focus is on the usability of the add-ons and the feelings of the users towards
them. In this regard, this section compares for each of the aforementioned add-ons:
(a) its toolbar icon, (b) its main interface panel, and (c) its help support (online web-
pages, help resources).

Fig. 1. Toolbar Icons for DuckDuckGo Privacy Essentials (Logo & Grade), Ghostery and
Privacy Badger

Figure 1, shows the toolbar icons for the three add-ons that are in scope of this
work. The toolbar icon for DuckDuckGo Privacy Essentials displays either the
DuckDuckGo logo or a letter to represent the visited website's privacy grade, which
will be covered later in this section. If the add-on is calculating the grade, or the user
has the browser settings or a new tab open, the logo will be displayed in the toolbar
icon. The toolbar icon for Ghostery displays only the number of trackers detected on
the website the user is currently visiting. Similarly, Privacy Badger shows the number
of trackers blocked. The count on the Privacy Badger icon will turn amber when it goes
above zero.

Figures 2 and 3 show the main interface panel of each add-on, which appears when
the user clicks the toolbar icon. DuckDuckGo Privacy Essentials has a search bar at the
top for the user to use the DuckDuckGo search engine. The privacy grade below is
calculated based on: (a) a rating of the site's privacy practices, (b) the presence of
trackers, and (c) whether an encrypted connection is available. Data for the aforementioned appear below the grade and clicking on their widgets will reveal a more
detailed screen (see Fig. 2a).

In the green area below 'Privacy Practices', the user can disable privacy protection
for that website, which will add it to the whitelist. Moreover, the 'Manage Whitelist'
link allows the user to add sites to the whitelist, and 'Report Broken Site' lets the user
contact the developer if the add-on has impaired the functionality of the website. At the
bottom of the home screen the 'top offender' trackers are displayed, i.e. the ones the

---

[1] https://duckduckgo.com/app.

[2] https://www.ghostery.com/.

[3] https://www.eff.org/privacybadger.

user has encountered most across the websites they have visited. 'All Tracker Networks' takes the user to a new screen listing all the trackers the add-on has encountered.

(a)

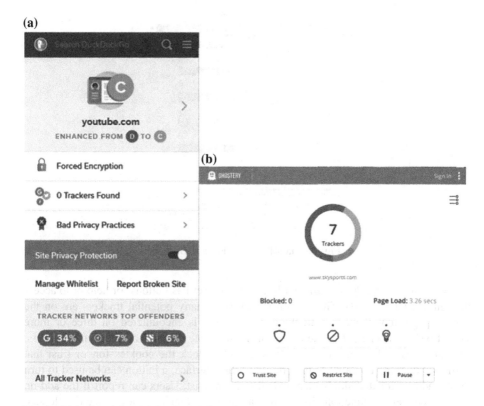

Fig. 2. Main Panel for: (a) DuckDuckGo Privacy Essentials, and (b) Ghostery (Simple View)

Figure 2b, shows Ghostery's main panel in simple view, which displays the number of trackers found, the number of trackers blocked and the time that the visited site took to load. More advanced features can be interacted with via the purple symbols, as can the buttons to trust or restrict a site and pause the add-on. A more detailed view can be accessed by clicking on the list symbol in the top-right of the simple view, shown in Fig. 2b, which has a compressed version of the simple view to the left and a list of the found trackers to the right. The trackers are categorised based on their purpose; for example, Analytics, Essential or Advertising. More information for each tracker can be displayed by clicking on them, with the option to follow a hyperlink to a full tracker profile. Trackers can also be trusted or blocked on an individual basis.

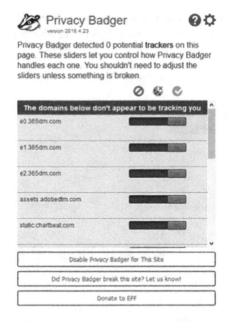

Fig. 3. Main Panel for Privacy Badger

At the top of the Privacy Badger interface the user has buttons for help or to access the settings (see Fig. 3). The add-on shows how many potential trackers are on the current page, it will block a tracking domain if it is encountered on three or more visited websites. The list in the centre of the interface displays all the found trackers. The slider bars allow the user to block entirely, block the cookies for, or trust that particular tracking domain. At the bottom of the interface, a button can be used to turn off the add-on for that site, which adds it to a whitelist. Users can report if the add-on has broken website functionality or click a button to donate money to the developers.

All three privacy add-ons have an introductory webpage that opens in the browser once the add-on is installed, with varying levels of detail. Further help can also be accessed within the add-ons themselves. Ghostery has the options of either a one-click or custom setup during installation.

In DuckDuckGo Privacy Essentials, the introductory webpage can be reopened by clicking on 'Learn More' within the add-on's settings menu. From this webpage, it is possible to navigate to a help library. Ghostery has a help button within its options menu, where the user can access frequently asked questions (FAQs) and support. Privacy Badger's help button, in the top-right of the main interface, reopens the add-on's introductory webpage. By clicking on the hyperlinked 'trackers' text an FAQs page can be accessed.

Finally, Table 1 summarises the comparison of the graphical interface features available across the add-ons used in this study.

Table 1. Comparison of Add-on features

Add-On Feature	DDG Privacy Essentials	Ghostery	Privacy Badger
Enable / Disable for this Site	✓	✓	✓
Report Broken Site	✓	✓	✓
Count of Detected Trackers	✓	✓	✓
List of Found Trackers	✓	✓	✓
Allow / Block Individual Tracker Domains	✗	✓	✓
Specifically Block Cookies for a Domain	✗	✗	✓
Access to FAQs / Help Pages	✓	✓	✓
Domain Whitelist	✓	✓	✓
Donate to Developer	✗	✗	✓
Add-on Settings Menu	✓	✓	✓
Choice of Simple or Detailed Interface	✗	✓	✗
Page Load Time	✗	✓	✗
Sign in with Account	✗	✓	✗
Pause Add-on Protection	✗	✓	✗
Submit a New Tracker	✗	✓	✗
Default or Custom Installation Setup	✗	✓	✗
Choice of Advanced Features	✗	✓	✗
Search Engine Bar	✓	✗	✗
Force Encrypted Connection	✓ (if available)	✗	✗
Website Privacy Practices	✓	✗	✗
Website Privacy Grade	✓	✗	✗

3 Methodology

A survey was carried out to evaluate the usability of the privacy add-ons through a comparative analysis, as well as to understand users' awareness of online privacy and attitudes towards the add-ons. The attitudes focused on were those of trust, concern, and control. The participants were introduced to three scenarios related to their designated add-on, whilst thinking aloud, and the completion of three questionnaires.

Think aloud encourages participants to vocally share their thoughts and feelings whilst interacting with the user interface of a product [16]. We carried out a pilot run-through before commencing the study with the participants, to allow any potential issues to be found and corrected [17].

For the survey, 30 participants were recruited in total and were assigned one of the add-ons via round-robin. However, the very first allocation was randomised. The participants were evenly allocated with 10 individuals per add-on, they were given a £10 Amazon voucher as an incentive to participate. Participants were not computer science students, nor did they have an educational background in this field. They were older than 18 and there was no bias towards age, gender, educational background, web browser preference, or current level of online privacy awareness when recruiting.

Most participants fell into the 18–24 age bracket, with 19 (63%) participants being in this age range. 9 (30%) were in the 45–54 group and the remaining 2 (7%) fell into the 55-64 age bracket. The majority of participants were male, forming 57% of the participant group, which consisted of 17 males and 13 females. 11 participants (37%) held a bachelor's degree, whilst another 11 (37%) held GCSEs (General Certificate of Secondary Education) or equivalent. 7 individuals (23%) possessed A-Levels or equivalent and 1 participant held a master's degree. A-levels are the traditional qualifications that are offered by schools and colleges for students aged between 16 and 19 in the UK. Most participants were Google Chrome users, with 21 of 30 participants (70%) preferring this browser. 4 participants (13%) preferred Safari. Mozilla Firefox was the choice of 3 participants (10%) and 2 of the 30 (7%) chose Internet Explorer as their preferred browser.

The tasks were completed using Mozilla Firefox or Google Chrome within an Ubuntu Linux Virtual Machine. A video screen capture and an audio recording of task completion were taken, due to the use of think-aloud. Recordings were deleted once they had been analysed and transcribed. Within the browser, either the DuckDuckGo Privacy Essentials, Ghostery or Privacy Badger add-on was used. The add-on was uninstalled once each participant had completed their tasks and questionnaires.

Participants were given information sheets and consent forms prior to the testing commencing. They were also given an instruction sheet. The three questionnaires were constructed in Google Forms. A Pre-Task questionnaire was used to gather demographic information and the level of agreement with privacy-related statements. A System Usability Scale (SUS) questionnaire was given to the participants upon completion of the tasks. A final Post-Tasks questionnaire was also given to gather responses to measure perceived concern, trust, and control when using the selected privacy add-on. Participants could share any other thoughts, feelings, or suggestions they had.

3.1 Pre-tasks Questionnaire

Prior to installing the add-on, this initial questionnaire asked participants for some basic demographic information: age, gender, highest completed level of education and preferred web browser. They were also asked how strongly they agreed or disagreed with three statements using a 5-point Likert scale, which were used to classify their attitude towards privacy with Westin's Privacy Index [18]. To get an idea of awareness, participants were asked to define 'web cookie', 'tracker' and 'browser add-on'.

3.2   Scenarios and Tasks

After completing the first questionnaire and asking any questions, the video screen capture and audio recording started. The participants' first task was to install the assigned add-on and quickly familiarise themselves with it-the add-on store page was open for them in the web browser. All participants were instructed to read the introductory webpage, which opens in the browser once installation is complete.

Then, participants completed tasks that were split into three scenarios focusing on (i) government surveillance, (ii) price discrimination, and (iii) social stigma. More specifically, the three scenarios were: (i) 'Imagine that you want to update yourself with recent news on "Brexit". Using the Buzzfeed website, browse and examine pro-Brexit articles', (ii) 'Imagine that you want to book a two-week holiday to a destination of your choice in September of this year. Using the TravelSupermarket website, browse the possibilities they have on offer', and (iii) 'Using the Boots website, search for sexual health and browse the products and advice available'. Tasks incorporated interactions with features common across the add-ons. Participants spent 1–2 min browsing as per the scenario, then completed the specific tasks given to them.

For the first scenario, participants had to whitelist the Buzzfeed[4] website, meaning the trackers present on the site will not be blocked. Then, DuckDuckGo Privacy Essentials and Privacy Badger users had to navigate to the help page, whilst Ghostery users had to find the FAQs.

In the second scenario, the participants were asked to find how many trackers were blocked on the TravelSupermarket[5] website by their assigned add-on. They also had to look for a list to investigate what trackers were found, and what information the add-on gives about them.

Prior to commencing the third scenario, DuckDuckGo Privacy Essentials and Privacy Badger users had to disable their add-on, Ghostery users had to pause it for 30 min. Participants then had to find the number of trackers present on the Boots[6] website before searching for sexual health as part of the scenario. The video screen capture and audio recording was stopped and saved once the third scenario had been completed.

After completing the three scenarios, participants completed a System Usability Scale questionnaire for their assigned add-on via a Google Forms link [19]. At the end of the form, participants were asked to share any further thoughts, comments, or suggestions they had regarding the add-on's usability. An examination of 500 studies into SUS found the average score to be 68 out of 100 [20].

---

[4] Buzzfeed is an internet media and news website: https://www.buzzfeed.com/.

[5] TravelSupermarket is a website for comparing travel deals: https://www.travelsupermarket.com/.

[6] Boots is a health, beauty and pharmacy retailer that is popular in the UK: https://www.boots.com/.

3.3 Post-tasks Questionnaire

The final questionnaire gathered responses to collate participants' feelings of trust, awareness, concern, and control towards their online privacy when using their assigned add-on. Participants were also asked to elaborate on what they think makes the add-on trustworthy or untrustworthy. They were asked how strongly they agree or disagree with the below statements, using a 5-point Likert scale:

1. 'I would feel safer browsing the Internet when using a privacy add-on'
2. 'I would trust the legitimacy of a website more if the privacy add-on reflected it'
3. 'The privacy add-on informed me about the purpose of the trackers it identified'
4. 'I would be reluctant to use a website if it asked me to disable my privacy add-on'
5. 'Overall, the add-on is trustworthy'

Participants were then asked to explain what makes the add-on trustworthy, or untrustworthy.

4 Findings

4.1 Westin's Privacy Index

Most participants fell into the Pragmatist category, 23 of the 30 (77%) had this initial attitude towards privacy. 5 participants (16%) were categorised as Unconcerned and the remaining 2 (7%) were Fundamentalists [18].

4.2 Awareness of Related Terms

When asked to define a 'web cookie', overall the participants appeared to understand the notion. Whilst not all offering full definitions, most participants defined part of what cookies can do and seemed to have a general understanding. Potentially due to the connotations of the word 'tracker' itself, participants were generally aware of the fact that a tracker watches, or monitors, online behaviour. First-party and third-party trackers were mentioned in the responses from the participants. 18 out of the 30 users appeared to have awareness of browser add-ons. Out of these 18 participants, 4 made specific mention of encountering them in the form of an ad-blocker or a VPN. It was generally understood that an add-on is a supplemental software installation for a web browser, to perform a desired set of functions.

4.3 System Usability Scale Scores and User Comments on Usability

System Usability Scales Scores. Ghostery received the highest usability score from participants, with an average of 79. DuckDuckGo Privacy Essentials and Privacy Badger both scored below average, with scores of 60 and 62 respectively. Participants were also asked to give qualitative comments on the usability of the add-on they interacted with.

Out of the 10 DuckDuckGo Privacy Essentials users we found that: 6 somewhat or strongly agreed that they would like to use the add-on frequently, whilst 2 somewhat or strongly disagreed. Just under half (i.e. 4) found the add-on to be unnecessarily complex and another 4 disagreed with this statement, the remaining 2 stayed neutral. 3 participants agreed that the add-on was easy to use, however the majority (i.e. 8) disagreed that there was too much inconsistency in the add-on. Moreover, when asked whether they needed to learn a lot of things before they could get going with the add-on, 6 participants disagreed with the statement whilst 4 somewhat or strongly agreed that they did. Finally, 4 out of 10 participants agreed that they felt very confident using the add-on.

Out of the 10 Privacy Badger users: 7 agreed that they would like to use the add-on frequently, with the other 3 disagreeing. No participants agreed that they found the add-on unnecessarily complex; 6 somewhat or strongly disagreed and 4 were neutral to this statement. Less than half (i.e. 4) agreed that they thought the add-on was easy to use, 3 somewhat or strongly disagreed and 3 did not agree nor disagree. The majority (i.e. 7) agreed that they would imagine most people learning to use the add-on quickly. Just over half (i.e. 6 users) agreed that they felt very confident using the add-on, with 2 disagreeing and 2 answering neutrally. Finally, 4 out of 10 participants agreed that they needed to learn a lot of things before they could get going with Privacy Badger, 5 disagreed with this statement.

Regarding the 10 Ghostery users, our results suggest that: the majority (i.e. 7 users) agreed that they would like to use the add-on frequently. Nearly all (i.e. 9 users) disagreed that they found the add-on unnecessarily complex, the same number of participants agreed that they thought the add-on was easy to use. All 10 participants disagreed that they would need the support of a technical person to be able to use the add-on and disagreed that they found the add-on cumbersome to use. 9 participants agreed that most people would learn to use the add-on quickly, but just over half (i.e. 6 participants) somewhat or strongly agreed they felt very confident using the add-on. Finally, most (i.e. 8 users) disagreed that they needed to learn a lot of things before they could get going with Ghostery.

System Usability Scale Comments. Participants were able to offer comments or suggestions for usability improvements as part of the SUS questionnaire.

For DuckDuckGo Privacy Essentials, P12 said 'When looking for a help page, I'd want to be taken to a different page from the introduction, one with more information.' P30 commented 'the help section was not obvious' and P21 thought 'it was not easy to find the help page'. P27 answered that 'help and explanations need to be clearer'. These thoughts were echoed by comments made during the think-aloud exercise. P1, who used Ghostery during this study commented that 'the only difficulty was finding the FAQs page' but felt that navigating to it made more sense in hindsight. P10 also used Ghostery and thought the 'FAQs was harder to find, but hardly necessary as the add-on was so easy to use'. One of the Privacy Badger users, P8, commented that they 'would have preferred the help link to go to an FAQs website, then have some step by step guides'.

P15 felt the toolbar icon for DuckDuckGo Privacy Essentials needed to be more visible. Also, P18 commented in their SUS questionnaire that the icon is also grey, and they felt it gave no visual feedback, expecting help when hovering the mouse over elements of the user interface. P26, who interacted with Privacy Badger, suggested 'visual aids that could make the usability easier for people who are not tech-minded'.

P10 commented that in Ghostery it was 'simple to see the results'. In terms of the interface layout, P19 thought the button to swap from the simple view to the detailed view 'was a little too close the drop-down setting menu and was a little confusing'. P25 similarly commented that 'the menu bar needs to be more clear'. P10 did appreciate the breakdown of the found trackers and P13's awareness was increased by using Ghostery, they were 'impressed with how many trackers there are when you use the web'. P14 also commented on the information for trackers that Privacy Badger found, they thought the add-on 'could have been a little clearer when breaking down the tracking service'.

4.4 Perceptions of the Privacy Add-ons

Figure 4, presents the results from the post-tasks questionnaire. All three add-ons averaged a score of 4.5 when participants were asked if they would be reluctant to disable the add-on at a website's request, signifying that a site would be deemed unsafe and untrustworthy if it made any attempt or request to turn off the add-on. Participants deemed Privacy Badger to be the least informative regarding the purpose of the trackers it found, receiving an average score of 2.1. DuckDuckGo scored 2.8 and Ghostery was considered the most informative with 3.8.

When participants were asked if they would trust the legitimacy of a website more if the privacy add-on reflected it, DuckDuckGo received an average of 4.3. Ghostery and Privacy Badger averaged at 3.7 and 4 respectively. DuckDuckGo received the highest average of 4.2 when participants had to express if they feel safer browsing the internet with the privacy add-on. Ghostery and Privacy Badger both averaged at 4.

Participants were also asked what made the add-on they interacted with trustworthy, or untrustworthy. For DuckDuckGo Privacy Essentials, P3 'didn't feel especially trusting of it' due to a lack of awareness of the add-on itself, mentioning it may even be a 'ploy to access my data'. On the other hand, P12 said 'the add-on explains its purpose simply, it seems good for a novice to get to grips with'. P6 was unsure of the add-on's trustworthiness as there was not enough to 'give the user any useful information'. P19 was also unsure as they felt there was 'no visual feedback...or severity of the tracker being blocked'. P9 and P30 both felt the add-on was trustworthy; P9 felt it 'goes into frank detail about the potential privacy breaches' and P30 said the add-on is 'very to-the-point'.

A number of participants who interacted with Ghostery felt trusting due to the information given to them by the add-on. P22 said 'it told me which trackers there were and how many'. P10 felt it 'clearly shows what it does' and is 'well-presented and written'. P25 thought the add-on was reliable as it 'gives you a lot of information on the trackers', and P28 trusted Ghostery as 'it helps the user identify unwanted trackers and block them straight away'. However, P16 was neither trusting nor distrusting of Ghostery as they 'don't fully know whether they have listed all the possible trackers'. P7 did not trust Ghostery due to the 'product introduction, marketing, and image'.

P8, who used Privacy Badger, trusted the add-on as it 'helps to identify numerous trackers'. They also commented 'it would help to have more information on why they were blocked though'. P17 found the add-on trustworthy because they felt 'it gave a list of most, if not all, trackers'. P23 and P26 neither trusted nor distrusted Privacy Badger. P23 said 'it shows the trackers but does not give enough information about the trackers'. P26 thought there was 'not enough explanation of the trackers it was identifying and disabling'.

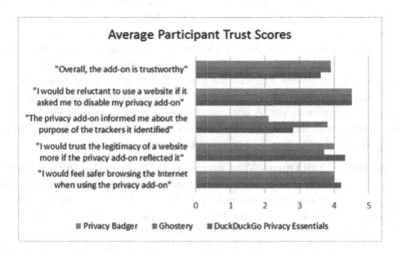

Fig. 4. Average Participant Trust Scores. Scores of 1 indicate strongly disagree, whilst scores of 5 are for strongly agree

4.5   Think-Aloud Findings

Accessible for Less IT-savvy Users. After installing their assigned add-on, participants read the introductory webpage which opens once installation is completed. P9 and P12, who both used DuckDuckGo Privacy Essentials, felt the introductory page was sufficient and simple; P12 said 'it is pretty straightforward to follow'. P21 was unsure whether the add-on was fully installed at this stage, but commented the introduction was 'explaining things at a human level' which they found helpful as they described themselves as 'not IT-literate'. P27 believed some definitions of related terms would be beneficial for inexperienced users and P30 praised the images on the page for 'showing exactly where certain aspects are', in terms of the user interface.

P25, who interacted with Ghostery, also commented that some definitions of terms on the introduction page would be beneficial. P16 felt step-by-step instructions for using the add-on would help, as they thought the page had enough information but lots to read. P7 said the introduction was 'way too full of jargon for your normal person'. P13 praised the use of images to show the layout of the add-on's user interface.

On Privacy Badger's introduction page, P8 said the prompt to 'take the tour' should 'almost slide across like a PowerPoint instead of coming down to read'. They felt the introduction improved their awareness of trackers, commenting 'there is the advertising stuff, and then a lot more deeper that I wasn't aware of before'. P14 was content with the information, saying 'it has broken everything down for you'. P20 commented 'I like the little pictures... I like visual things', praising the use of images to introduce the user. However, P26 felt the page 'doesn't really tell you a lot about what is going on' and would want to see a breakdown of what exactly the add-on does.

When attempting to whitelist the site using DuckDuckGo Privacy Essentials (i.e. during the first scenario), P6 commented 'it is not obvious to me how I would add that as a novice... you'd just want to press a button that is immediately visible to you'. This can be achieved with the 'Site Privacy Protection' toggle on the main interface, possibly suggesting a lack of awareness of related terms, which has also been highlighted by other participants. When P12 saw the green 'Site Privacy Protection' toggle, they comment that 'it is already set' as trusted, when this actually meant the add-on was enabled for that particular site. A site can also be trusted by adding it to the whitelist. P21 was familiar with the concept of a whitelist and commented 'that is a clunky way of having to add it' once they had completed the task.

Keep the Options Tab Open. When navigating to DuckDuckGo Privacy Essentials' whitelist, it opens in a new browser tab. A few participants commented on this tab closing itself as they navigated between it, the Buzzfeed website, and the add-on. P3 went to copy the Buzzfeed URL into the whitelist and exclaimed 'oh it has gone' as they navigated to a different tab. When the tab closed for P12, they said 'that is annoying, you lose everything if you click off'. P18 commented 'oh it went away... I would have expected it to stay open, so I can copy and paste'.

Visible Toolbar Icon with Visual Feedback. A number of users commented on DuckDuckGo Privacy Essentials' toolbar icon. P9 was looking for a duck logo to access the add-on and felt the icon displaying the privacy grade did not stand out. P18 said 'doesn't look like it is active... I would expect something other than mono'; P27 commented 'Is it on? It is not coloured'. During the second scenario, P3 commented on receiving no prompts from the add-on whilst browsing. They said 'because it has not said anything to me, I don't know what it is up to... I've just the assumption it is making what I'm doing safer'.

When P10 whitelisted the Buzzfeed website using Ghostery, they commented 'well that was super easy'. P1 saw the add-ons toolbar icon go grey and said, 'I assume that is trusted', they rechecked the add-on and confirmed with 'yeah, it is trusted'.

During the first scenario, P2 commented on Privacy Badger's toolbar icon. They said 'I've noticed there is a green box with a zero...not quite sure what that means'. Upon seeing how many trackers the add-on had identified, they exclaimed 'wow, 46 potential trackers on this page...that is a lot'. P5 also commented on the toolbar icon, saying 'so there is none there... that is what the little zero is telling me... there is nobody tracking me'. However, this number in the toolbar icon represents the number of trackers blocked, rather than the number found.

Obvious Access to Thorough Help Resources. There were comments related to a perceived lack of visible help for the DuckDuckGo Privacy Essentials add-on. P6 commented they were looking for a help page 'which is not very helpful because it is not there straight away…unless I am being stupid'. Upon being navigated back to the introduction page whilst searching for help, P12 asked 'Nope, why has it sent me there? I would expect something more detailed'. P21 believed 'there is not an obvious place to go for help'. P27 said that 'the whole point of help, you shouldn't have to look for help'.

P4 felt the FAQs page for Ghostery was quite hidden and thought the buttons for the detailed view and options menu were too similar visually. P19 had the same opinion on this. P28 commented 'that is really hidden away' with regard to the FAQs page.

When P26 was navigated back to Privacy Badger's introduction page after clicking the help button they said, 'I guess it does sort of help you…but it is not very clear'. P17 did not like the fact they were sent back to the introduction page and wanted to see definitions for what specific terms meant. P11 thought they had made a mistake at this point, they thought 'for help it feels like it needs a little more information, or something different to what I've already learnt from using it'.

Detailed Tracker Information. When scrolling through the list of trackers found by the DuckDuckGo Privacy Essentials add-on, P3 saw some they did not recognise the names of and said, 'it would be nice if there was more to say what they are, and what they are up to'. P6 wanted more information, commenting 'it is not telling me what those trackers would be tracking'. P21 did not understand why a tracker would be identified but not described, P24 said 'it does not feel entirely adequate'.

Whilst they were examining the list of trackers found by Ghostery, P10 said 'I like this breakdown' and praised the amount of detail when navigating to the full tracker profile. P22 said 'for me, it is enough' and P25 commented 'oh, it gives you a little description. That is good'.

Whilst they scrolled through the list of found trackers in Privacy Badger, P8 said 'Some of them I recognise, some of them I don't…it would be nice to know where they are coming from and what they are doing'. P11 thought it would be interesting to hover over the name of the tracker to get more information on it, P26 also wanted more information on them. P23 commented 'I don't know what these trackers are, it is just a name, that is it'. Similarly, P17 said it 'tells you the name, not what it is'.

Clear Differentiation Between Blocked and Found. For the second scenario, participants had to identify the number of trackers blocked by the add-on and find a list showing what trackers were found. All participants using DuckDuckGo Privacy Essentials correctly identified the number of blocked trackers from information shown on the main user interface. P6, P9 and P30 commented on finding that task easy.

When examining the Ghostery add-on to identify the number of trackers that had been blocked, 4 out of the 10 participants thought the count of found trackers was the number that had been blocked. The rest of the participants identified the number of trackers that Ghostery had blocked. P22 and P25 both commented that they would have expected more trackers to be blocked out of what had been found. P4 commented on the toolbar icon causing confusion during this task, as 'the 13 up there was quite distracting, but it is actually 0 blocked'. P1 incorrectly said 'I assume its four' when looking at the toolbar icon to identify the number of trackers blocked.

Out of the 10 participants interacting with Privacy Badger, half correctly identified the number of trackers blocked. P26 was expecting a more obvious confirmation of how many trackers had been blocked. P29 referred to the toolbar icon saying, 'don't like it says zero up there, I wouldn't know unless I purposely clicked on it'.

Invasiveness of Tracking. The third scenario asked participants to pause or disable their relative add-on prior to browsing for sexual health on the Boot's website. At the end of the browsing time, they had to identify the number of trackers present on the site.

As P9 disabled DuckDuckGo Privacy Essentials they said, 'Oh that is a lot of trackers'. P21 commented 'I am not clicking on Viagra, I will have all sorts of stuff on my IP address'. P9 noticed the tracker count increasing, 'I would be more cautious... I'd definitely think about getting something like this that protects you'. P12 said that whilst 'searching sensitive, private details, I would not want adverts appearing on my social media'. P15 commented 'it is really concerning...that is just unbelievable, you don't know what is going on in the background', and P18 referred to it as 'quite scary'. Most participants seemed to feel quite strongly about privacy during this part of the task, with some commenting that the exercise had increased their awareness.

Out of the 10 participants who used Ghostery, 7 paused for 30 min whilst the other 3 just clicked the pause button without modifying the time. When identifying the number of trackers present, P13 said 'I like the fact I now know...I can block trackers'. P22 commented 'it has opened my eyes a bit... I am more concerned now than I was before doing this'. P28 initially said the tracker amount doesn't bother them too much as 'I don't really care what people think' before stating 'actually no, I wouldn't want that coming up on my Facebook'. Likewise, P19 said 'you don't really want those ads appearing'.

During this exercise, P5 said 'what I am finding more disturbing...I wasn't aware how many people could potentially be tracking you... that has been quite an eye opener for me'. After P5 had disabled Privacy Badger, they commented 'the more personal something becomes, I'm thinking oh gosh how many people are going to be out there tracking me'. During the exercise they shared thoughts on their experience with targeted ads, 'The one thing I find so frustrating...it drives me absolutely nuts'. Comments were also made on the ethics of the trackers. P8 thought 'there is a lot of stigma around people collecting information they shouldn't be'. P11, another Privacy Badger participant, said 'I'm fairly against all this information being tracked and stored...if people are doing it, I like to know they're doing it and why'. P17 commented 'considering I haven't made an account, I haven't given them permission'.

5   Conclusions

With the proliferation of web tracking the importance of privacy preserving add-ons, which extend the out-of-the-box protection offered by web browsers, increases. However, whilst preserving and increasing the efficacy of blocking trackers is of paramount importance, so is the usability of the add-ons and user awareness. In this regard, this work mounted a survey which aimed to gain thoughts and feelings towards three popular anti-tracking add-ons (i.e. DuckDuckGo Privacy Essentials, Ghostery and Privacy Badger) from participants, and to measure their usability. The websites and tasks chosen sought to encourage interaction with the common features of the add-ons whilst using predominately realistic scenarios.

Based on participant responses, the level of information given by the add-on, including on the trackers it has found, may influence their level of trust towards it. There were also comments from participants on the inclusion of definitions or terminology to improve their understanding. A possible improvement could come from their wish of having a help button always visible on the main interface, or it being one of the first options visible when clicking to open the options menu. A glossary of related terms could potentially be included here. Ensuring this button is distinguishable from others would reduce potential confusion of functions. Rather than the help link going back to the introduction page, it should navigate to an FAQs page or some sort of knowledge bank. Users felt that being navigated back to an introductory web page was not helpful. Help resource suggestions from users included a glossary of online privacy related terms, a search function for questions, and step-by-step guides.

Additionally, information on the trackers should be given. Participants were curious as to the purpose and origin of the trackers they found. Not knowing the identity of certain trackers caused concern.

It may be beneficial for the toolbar logo to contain colour and be immediately visible, for the user to know the add-on is functioning by offering visual feedback.

For future work we plan to investigate: (a) producing a prototype for a more usable privacy add-on, (b) the proposition of an initial set of usability heuristics for online privacy add-ons, and (c) the proposition of a perceived user threat model and potential ways of countering them.

References

1. Bujlow, T., Carela-Español, V., Solé-Pareta, J., Barlet-Ros, P.: A survey on web tracking: mechanisms, implications, and defenses. Proc. IEEE **105**(8), 1476–1510 (2017)
2. Belloro, S., Mylonas, A.: I know what you did last summer: New persistent tracking mechanisms in the wild. IEEE Access **6**, 52779–52792 (2018)
3. Liu, D., Gao, X., Wang, H.: Location privacy breach: apps are watching you in the background. In: IEEE 37th International Conference on Distributed Computing Systems, pp. 2423–2429 (2017)
4. Sipior, J.C., Ward, B.T., Volonino, L.: Privacy concerns associated with smartphone use. J. Internet Commerce **13**(3–4), 177–193 (2014)
5. Roesner, F., Kohno, T., Wetherall, D.: Detecting and defending against third-party tracking on the web. In: Proceedings of the 9th USENIX Conference on Networked Systems Design Implementation, pp. 1–12. USENIX, San Jose (2012)
6. Schelter, S., Kunegis, J.: Tracking the trackers: a large-scale analysis of embedded web trackers. In: Proceedings of the Tenth International AAAI Conference on Web and Social Media, pp. 679–682 (2016)

7. Mylonas, A., Tsalis, N., Gritzalis, D.: Evaluating the manageability of web browsers controls. In: Accorsi, R., Ranise, S. (eds.) STM 2013. LNCS, vol. 8203, pp. 82–98. Springer, Heidelberg (2013). https://doi.org/10.1007/978-3-642-41098-7_6

8. Tsalis, N., Mylonas, A., Gritzalis, D.: An intensive analysis of security and privacy browser add-ons. In: Lambrinoudakis, C., Gabillon, A. (eds.) CRiSIS 2015. LNCS, vol. 9572, pp. 258–273. Springer, Cham (2016). https://doi.org/10.1007/978-3-319-31811-0_16

9. Schaub, F., et al.: Watching them watching me: browser extensions impact on user privacy awareness and concern. In: NDSS Workshop on Usable Security (2016)

10. Marella, A., Pan, C., Hu, Z., Schaub, F., Ur, B., Cranor, L.F.: Assessing privacy awareness from browser plugins. In: Poster at the Symposium on Usable Privacy and Security (SOUPS) (2014)

11. Leon, P.G., Ur, B., Balebako, R., Cranor, L.F., Shay, R., Wang, Y.: Why johnny can't opt out: a usability evaluation of tools to limit online behavioural advertising. In: Proceedings of the SIGCHI Conference on Human Factors in Computing Systems, pp. 589–98. ACM, New York (2012)

12. Moth, D.: Econsultancy. https://econsultancy.com/89-of-british-internet-users-are-worried-about-online-privacy-report/. Accessed 10 Dec 2018

13. McCoy, S., Everard, A., Polak, P., Galletta, D.: An experimental study of antecedents and consequences of online ad intrusiveness. Int. J. Hum. Comput. Interaction 24(7), 672–699 (2008)

14. Vincent, J.: Independent. https://www.independent.co.uk/life-style/gadgets-and-tech/news/nsa-reportedly-tracking-any-internet-users-who-research-privacy-software-online-9585250.html. Accessed 10 Dec 2018

15. Mozilla Firefox Privacy & Security Add-ons. https://addons.mozilla.org/en-GB/firefox/search/?category=privacy-security&sort=users&type=extension. Accessed 19 Feb 2019

16. Nielsen, J.: Nielsen norman group. https://www.nngroup.com/articles/thinking-aloud-the-1-usability-tool/. Accessed 10 Dec 2018

17. Preece, J., Rogers, Y., Sharp, H.: Interaction Design: Beyond Human–Computer Interaction, 4th edn. Wiley, Chichester (2015)

18. Kumaraguru, P., Cranor, L.F.: Privacy Indexes: A Survey of Westin's Studies. Institute for Software Research International. Carnegie Mellon University, Pittsburgh (2005)

19. Brooke, J.: SUS-A quick and dirty usability scale. Usability Eval. Ind. 189(194), 4–7 (1996)

20. Sauro, J.: Measuring U. https://measuringu.com/sus/. Accessed 10 Dec 2018

Identifying Psychophysiological Pain Points in the Online User Journey: The Case of Online Grocery

Caroline Giroux-Huppé[(✉)], Sylvain Sénécal, Marc Fredette,
Shang Lin Chen, Bertrand Demolin, and Pierre-Majorique Léger

HEC Montréal, Montréal, Canada
caroline.giroux-huppe@hec.ca

Abstract. The objective of this study is to identify implicit psychophysiological pain points during an e-commerce interaction. In this article, we propose a method that allows to identify implicit pain points in the user's experience, by targeting moments when the user has both a high level of arousal and a negative emotional valence, compared to his baseline state; which means that the user feels an intense negative emotion. Identifying those pain points and combining them with eye-tracking data gives key insights into the user journey and helps identify implicit pain points shared among users. It also allows to gain a deeper understanding of pain points that users may fail to identify during the post-task interview. Our results show that the temporal occurrence of psychophysical pain points can be accurately identified and that it is more reliable than pain points explicitly mentioned by users. This study contributes to the user experience literature and practice by proposing a reliable method to visualise peak emotional reactions experienced by users while performing a task. Thus, providing more precision and reliability in identifying pain points when compared to pain points mentioned by users after the task.

Keywords: User journey · Visualisation method ·
Psychophysiological pain points · Online grocery shopping

1 Introduction

User experience is a user's perceptions and responses resulting from the use of an interactive system, including emotions, beliefs, preferences, physiological responses and much more [16]. To measure these responses, most UX research focuses on explicit methods such as questionnaires and interviews. For example, emotions, or user's feelings regarding a system, have previously been measured using a self-report scale developed by Hassenzahl et al. [22]. However, it is difficult for users to precisely report on their own experience. Prior research shows that there is an important difference between what users felt during the experience and how they recalled it afterwards [11, 18]. Recent findings suggest the influence of multiple biases, such as the peak effect, where the user tends to remember the most intense moment better, and the peak-end rule, where the user's impressions toward the experience tends to be influenced by the final moment [10]. Furthermore, it has been shown that the intensity of

© Springer Nature Switzerland AG 2019
A. Marcus and W. Wang (Eds.): HCII 2019, LNCS 11586, pp. 459–473, 2019.
https://doi.org/10.1007/978-3-030-23535-2_34

emotions felt plays an important part in the recalling process [3] and that negative memories tend to be better remembered than good ones [5].

Considering the lack of proper methods to accurately identify implicit pain points in the UX literature, we propose a systemic method that uses physiological data to identify pain points in a user online journey. Pain points can either be explicit, implicit, or both. An explicit pain point, usually derived from qualitative data, is defined as the negative emotion consciously felt by the participant during a particular moment in the task and mentioned by the participant during or after the task. It is commonly used in marketing research [47]. An implicit pain point, however, is defined here as a moment, in reaction to an event during the interaction, during which the user experiences an automatic physiological activation characterized by a high level of emotional arousal and a negative emotional valence. Building upon previous research on peak loads, that identifies the exact moments users approach or pass their cognitive capacities [36], we use psychophysiological measures of emotional valence and arousal to build a metric that identifies pain points in the online user journey. We then illustrate the results using a journey map representation that allows a better understanding of the reasons behind those pain points as well as an easier comparison, either between different tasks or systems.

Gaining a deeper understanding of the reasons behind pain points contributes to HCI literature and practice by providing insights on peak emotional moments in users' experiences. It also allows UX designers to significantly improve their design by knowing precisely and accurately where the pain points are located, without interrupting users' authentic interactions with the website.

2   Literature Review

2.1   Current Methods to Assess Customer Experience

Customer experience contributes to the success of e-commerce websites and thus to a company's viability. Indeed, understanding customers and meeting their needs have been shown to be keys to success [23]. There is therefore a vast amount of literature focusing on analyzing the customer experience, using a variety of methods, such as personas, experience maps, blueprints, and walk-through audits [27]. However, these methods usually focus on a portion of customer experience, failing to give an overall picture. It has therefore been suggested that combining complementary methods offer a deeper understanding of user experience, while adding implicit measurement, such as physiological tools, allows for a more precise measure of the emotional journey of the participant [26].

A first method, Customer Experience Modeling, has been developed in the service sector to better synthesize the whole customer journey and the sequence of the different touchpoints by using customer-centric soft goals [46]. Soft goals are part of a goal-oriented analysis that allows problem detections in interactions by taking into account the subjective nature of the experience in the customer's evaluation of their different levels of satisfaction [39]. It allows to discover pain points that emerge from interactions. Methods such as Customer Experience Modeling derive pain points from qualitative data. For example, the analysis of common words and sentences while completing a task [47].

Another method, the Customer Job Mapping, also known as the customer centered innovation map, consists of breaking down, step by step, every task customers face, in order to find new ways to innovate. Certain tasks or parts of tasks can bring difficulties for customers and are thus classified as pain points. The main difference between this method and Customer Experience Modelling is that this method focuses on what customers are trying to achieve at every step, instead of looking at what they are doing [6].

The Customer Journey Map, a more recent method, is a diagram, illustrating every touchpoint a consumer has with the company, every step of the way and through every channel used across the company [44]. An example of a Customer Journey Map for grocery shopping can be found in Fig. 1. It is used both in the design service field, to help design the experience, and in the user experience field, to better understand the customer experience [37]. Customer Journey Maps allow companies to focus on the entire customer experience rather than individual interactions [42]. However, recent research suggests that this method is still far from flawless, as it assumes all touchpoints are equally important to every customer, which is not the case [45]. In order to identify the most important touchpoints, Customer Journey Maps should be linked with consumer research by using explicit measures such as self-administered questionnaires and interviews [45]. Another problem with Customer Journey Maps is that although they are now used in various industries, no clear process to design journey maps has been established, which makes it extremely difficult to compare across websites or interfaces, leading to inconsistent and non-generalizable results [37].

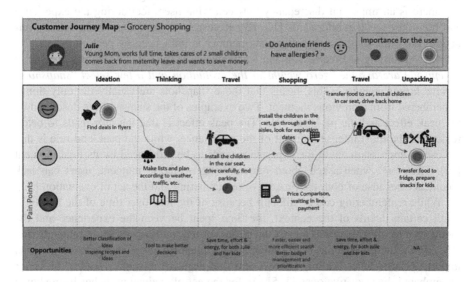

Fig. 1. Example of a customer journey map

As seen from the above-mentioned methods, customer experience measurement has mainly been observed from a qualitative angle, using focus groups or observations, with the exception of surveys, which can include both qualitative and quantitative data [37, 40, 42]. To understand the consumer's complete experience, data driven, quantitative analysis must be combined with qualitative, judgement driven evaluations [42]. There is currently a lack of methods that combine both these approaches [42], as well as a lack of quantitative methods that would make experiences comparable across websites [35]. To this day, there is no agreement on a method that would allow to evaluate all aspects of customer experience while reflecting reality, particularly when the user is completing complex tasks [32]. A recent study highlights the importance of using implicit measures to validate the data obtained from the participant's perceived emotions, to make sure all users emotions and reactions are considered [2]. Another recent study used electroencephalography (EEG) and eye tracking to explore customer experience in order to develop new visualization methods [2]. The authors quantified user experience with data such as attention levels, eye blinks, and pupil size. This study's difference compared to the previous ones is that the data collected comes from implicit, quantitative measures and can therefore be less bias indicators of customer experience, when compared to explicit or qualitative methods [2]. This leads to the next section, explaining why consumers responses are sometimes biased.

2.2   Biases in Consumer Responses

A user's perception towards a system is commonly measured through self-reported measures. However, it is difficult for users to precisely report on their own experience as they may be influenced by multiple biases, often unwillingly. Prior research shows that there is an important discrepancy between what users feel during the experience and how they recall it afterwards [11, 18]. Research suggests that retrospective evaluations are often biased and that human memory is influenced by peak moments [28, 29, 43]. According to Fredrickson and Kahneman [28] (p. 46), "*[...] most moments of an episode are assigned zero weight in the evaluation and a few select "snapshots" receive larger weights*". This means that those snapshots are usually the only things remembered from a previous moment. Two examples of the snapshots are described by the peak effect and the peak-end rule. The peak effect is that the user tends to better remember the most intense moment of the experience, while the peak-end rule is that the user's impression about the experience tends to be influenced by its final moment [10]. Therefore, when asked about remembering a precise moment, users can lack confidence because of both the process of remembering and the act of evaluation [29].

While remembering can be difficult because of the loss over time of the ability to recall certain details of the context, the time spent between the experience and the moment of recalling can also impact the biases related to the operation of remembering [18, 28]. Furthermore, it has been shown that the intensity of the emotions felt plays an important part in the recalling process and that negative memories tend to be better remembered than positive ones [3, 5]. As for the act of evaluation, is has been shown that hedonic and utilitarian moments are remembered differently, but that both are influenced by effects that could bias their retrospective evaluation [33]. Therefore, current methods used to measure and map user experience may be subject to multiple biases, as they are based on human retrospective evaluation. Using implicit physiological measures is a potential way to get around those biases.

2.3   Advantages and Disadvantages of Using Psychophysiological Measures

Over the years, many physiological and psychophysiological measures have been developed to evaluate users' responses such as electrocardiography (ECG), respiration rate, skin-based measures (EDA), blood pressure, ocular measures and brain measures (EEG) [8]. With the increase popularity of e-commerce, it has become necessary to take into account users' emotions when interacting with an interface, as users' decisions are often based on hedonic motivations rather than utilitarian ones [7]. However, research shows that interrupting users during a task negatively affects their affective states, therefore biasing results [4]. Hence, to improve human-computer interaction in e-commerce without interfering with the interaction, using physiological measures can be extremely useful [17]. In domains such as entertainment technologies, physiological measures are far most robust in finding differences between participants and tasks than current subjective methods [34]. Another advantage is that data is collected in real-time, which allows to precisely identify peaks without relying on user's memory. For example, a study on mental workload on air traffic controller operations showed that using real-time eye movement data allowed for deeper insights that subjective ratings might not have discovered, therefore allowing designers to detect problems earlier in the design process [1]. Moreover, capturing data can often interfere with the validity of the results, as users can be obstructed or distracted by the settings or methods used. Using unobtrusive tools to capture psychophysiological data allows users to use a given technology in a realistic way, giving more reliable insights while reducing biases of explicit measures as well, as it can be used in a complimentary way to give more validity to the results [15].

Furthermore, using implicit psychophysiological measures allows to test multiple new factors that can not be accurately reported by the users at any given moment in time. Many of those measures are constructs related to user experience, such as valence, arousal, and cognitive load [14]. For example, a study on equipment installation found that success was negatively impacted by the level of the user's arousal [26]. This result could not have been found with the same accuracy without the help of psychophysiological implicit measures. Another recent study, where users were asked to retrospectively review their previous interaction with a website at every moment in time, show that the user's accuracy of the evaluation of their previous emotions was extremely low and often completely incorrect [24], therefore showing the utility of more accurate measures.

Although physiological measures open new ways for researchers to understand user behavior, it also comes with some disadvantages. Since it is a relatively new area of application, definitions and ways of measuring physiological constructs such as workload or arousal often vary between studies. This makes it difficult to compare results across studies, and to replicate and validate findings [8]. Also, physiological measurement tools can be sensitive to extraneous noise, further complicating comparison between studies. For example, EDA, a skin-based measure of change in electrodermal activity varies with temperature, level of humidity, time of the day and season, which are all difficult to control [30]. Furthermore, in some cases, participants do not react the same way in a laboratory setting as in a real-life setting. For example, a study measuring mental workload for plane pilots showed that measures taken during a real flight tasks were completely different from measures taken during the same task done in a laboratory setting [48]. Another study using cardiovascular responses also showed a weak correlation between laboratory and real-world contexts [27]. Moreover, recent research has shown that a single measure is not sufficient to satisfy validity requirements and therefore, triangulation is necessary in order to obtain valid results [8]. Triangulation is also necessary because a same physiological reaction can be elicited for different reasons, depending on the context and the user's previous experiences [8]. Basically, triangulation allows for better data interpretation and therefore more useful insights.

3   Method

We collected data in order to identify psychophysiological pain points during an e-commerce interaction. The goal was to develop a method that would accurately identify pain points and combine them with eye-tracking data in order to gain key insights into the user journey. A second goal was also to compare the pain points identified using psychophysiological data with the ones identified qualitatively by the users retrospectively. To increase the generalization of our results, we used three different websites in order to obtain different sources of pain points. This allowed us to compare pain points both across websites and between participants using the same websites.

3.1   Context

We used online grocery shopping as the study context. This context has numerous advantages. First, it involves high complexity arithmetic tasks for multiple items, as users need to figure how much they need of each product [13]. This need for multiple items forces the customer to accomplish multiple tasks in a single visit and choose between a vast product assortment, which makes a session longer than a traditional e-commerce session, even if more convenient than a trip to the grocery store [38]. Second, online grocery shopping also generates risk as users need to trust the website regarding both the freshness and the quality of products as well as confidential data such as credit card and phone information [9]. This lack of trust can cause pain points, as users are already potentially opposed to buying fresh products online or filling out their personal information, making them more sensitive towards potential problems. Third, online grocery shopping is an uncommon or unusual transaction for users, as in 2016, only 21% of consumers globally have already bought fresh online groceries [41]. Finally, in this specific context, consumers were more involved in the task as they were buying their own groceries rather than having a simulated goal, compared to other studies where the nature of the task is artificial [25].

3.2 Design, Sample and Procedure

Twenty-one students and young professionals (mean age: 23) were recruited via our institution's panel and were divided between three equal groups of seven participants, each group shopping on a different online grocery website. Using three different websites allowed to illustrate possible comparisons between websites as well as determine if the results were generalizable. Participants had one task: they were asked to do their grocery shopping online, buying items they really needed and paying using their own credit card to maximize ecological validity. The task was the same for all three groups. It lasted between forty-five minutes and an hour, excluding the baseline measures. Participants had to spend at least 50$ and were asked to select the store where they would go pick up their order in the following days. They had to buy at least one fruit, one vegetable and one piece of meat to make sure they would navigate sufficiently on the website. Participants had to fill a questionnaire before the task, right after the task, and after picking up their order from the store. An interview was also conducted right after the task by an experienced moderator, in order to know qualitatively how the user felt about the task. In that interview, the user was specifically asked about the positive and negative aspects of his online grocery shopping experience. Every participant received a $60 cash compensation to reimburse their groceries. Each participant completed a consent form beforehand and this project has been approved by the Institutional Review Board (IRB) of our institution.

3.3 Measures

During the interaction with the assigned website, non-intrusive tools were used to capture the users' reactions in real time. A Tobii X-60 eye-tracker (Stockholm, Sweden) sampled at 60 Hz, as suggested by Laeng et al. [31], was used to capture eye-tracking data and Tobii Studio was used to record the experience. The use of eye tracking data allowed to identify precisely where the participant was looking at every second and the recording allowed to go back afterwards, without interfering with the interaction. Arousal was measured using electrodermal activity (EDA) with the Acqknowledge software (BIOPAC, Goleta, USA). EDA is a precise indication of physiological arousal and its variation throughout time [21]. Emotional valence was measured using facial emotion recognition with the FaceReader™ software (Noldus, Wageningen, Netherlands). FaceReader™ was used to observe facial movements to calculate emotional valence, from negative to positive [12]. The Observer XT (Noldus, Wageningen Netherlands) software was also used to synchronize apparatus and event markers.

At the end of the experiment, a qualitative interview was conducted with each participant, where users we asked explicitly about the positive and negative aspects of the task, in order to verify what pain points were noticed by the participants. Qualitative data was analysed using Reframer from Optimal Workshop to find trends between participants. This was done in order to compare the added value of the implicit and explicit measures in the construction of the journey map.

Calculations of pain points using a specific threshold was done using statistical software SAS 9.4 and results were then illustrated as a journey map using Tableau®. In this particular context, to be qualified as a pain point, the data point needed to be both in the ninetieth percentile of EDA (i.e., high arousal) and in the tenth percentile of valence (i.e., large negative valence). Each pain point was validated manually using the time code of the recording in Tobii Studio. It was also used to put markers at the beginning and ending of each subtask, in order to color code them in Tableau®.

These tools allowed to identify and label the emotional peaks. In sum, the visualization method allowed us to accurately and precisely identify the psychophysiological pain points using non-intrusive tools and ensure that our insights were representative of what the users really felt by comparing the results of the quantitative data (implicit pain points) with the qualitative data (explicit pain points).

4 Results

Our results show that the temporal occurrence of psychophysical pain points can be accurately identified. Using a journey map representation, the evolution of valence (y axis) and arousal (size of dot) over time (x axis), was sampled for every single second (see Fig. 2). We color-coded each subtask, i.e., shopping, account creation, payment, time selection, and store selection to better visualize the order as well as the number of times the participant came back to that subtask. As an optimized journey is expected to be linear (i.e., no coming back to a previous subtask), this allows us to see where potential problems could be as well. For example, in Fig. 2, we can see that the participant started with shopping, then switched to time and store selection, before returning to the shopping task. He then returned to time selection, before proceeding with account creation and payment. As the journey is relatively linear, there are not many pain points along the way. Pain points were identified using a different shape and colour as the other dots, in other to distinguish them. Pain points are illustrated by red squares (Fig. 2) and calculated using a specific threshold. In Fig. 2, most pain points are toward the end of the interaction, in the payment and account creation subtask, except for one located in the shopping subtask. It can also be noticed that some pain points are successive, as they come one second after the other. We called those pain periods, as they usually have the same source. For example, there is a pain period labeled "Enters his last name". This means that this specific task was painful for successive seconds, therefore showing the importance of improving this specific task compared to other single pain points. Finally, the visualization method allows to add labels to the online user journey, to identify the reason behind the pain points visually, so that with one glance, one can understand what is wrong for a specific participant. For the participant below (Fig. 2), we can see that the experience was relatively painless until the end, where s/he experienced many pain points during the payment and account creation subtasks, mainly when entering personal information, such as first name, last name, postal code, and credit card information.

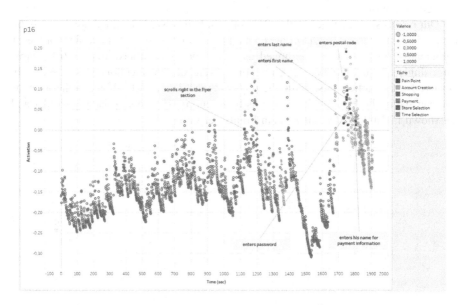

Fig. 2. Visualization of the online user journey for one participant

Furthermore, the visual representation of the user journey allows for an easier comparison between participants. This allows to compare the duration of consumer journeys, as well as the order and duration of the different subtasks and the location of the pain points. In the example below (Fig. 3), one can see that the 6th participant took more than twice the time of the 1st one to complete the same task. All participants started with the shopping subtask, probably because it is the most intuitive way to start. The 2nd participant made his store selection early in the process and that did not cause any pain points, compared to three other participants, that did the same subtask later and experienced pain points doing it. A possible reason explaining those results could be that choosing your store at the beginning shows you only the food items available at the store chosen. If you chose later, some of the products in your cart could become unavailable, causing pain points to the participants because they either had to find a substitute or delete the item from their cart. This method can also be used to compare journeys between different companies. For example, comparing how many pain points were related to shopping or payment for different competitors is a good way to benchmark how well the company is performing in different areas.

Labelling those pain points also allowed us to compare the experience truly felt by the participants with that users mentioned afterwards. This gave additional insights by identifying pain points that were not mentioned qualitatively by the participants afterwards but most importantly, showed us specific moments where the participant clearly mentioned that a specific subtask went well, while the pain points identified clearly showed otherwise. For example, Fig. 4 shows that the participant reported that he had no problems filling out his credit card information. However, its body reactions showed otherwise.

Our results showed that less that 25% of pain points were identified qualitatively by the participant afterwards. Out of the 65 pain points or pain periods identified for the 21 participants, only 16 were mentioned as a negative point afterwards (24,6%). Most surprisingly, 5 out of those 65 pain points were clearly mentioned as specifically positive by the participants, while the physiological data clearly showed otherwise, as you can see in the Fig. 3 below. Results between grocers are surprisingly similar and are shown in Table 1. Details of Pain Points per Grocer 1.

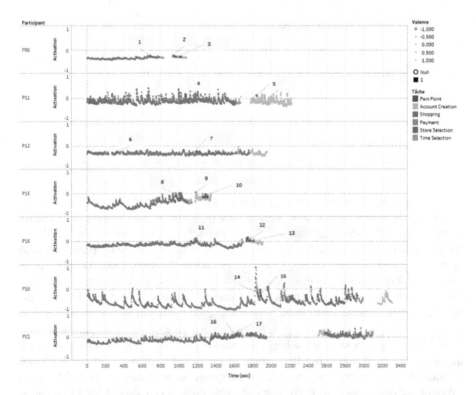

Fig. 3. Comparison of different participants. Legend: Numbers indicate the pain points number.

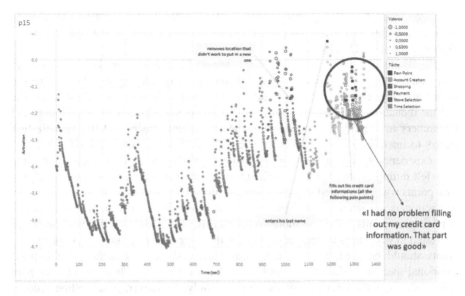

Fig. 4. Comparison of qualitative and quantitative data for one participant: pain points not identified

Table 1. Details of pain points per grocer

	Grocer 1	Grocer 2	Grocer 3	Global
# of total pain points	72	47	43	162
# groups of pain points	17	27	21	65
Pain points identified verbally	4/17 (24%)	7/27 (25,9%)	5/21 (23,8%)	16 24,6%
Pain points mentioned as strengths by user	2/17 (12%)	0/27 (0%)	3/21 (14%)	5 8,7%

5   Discussion and Concluding Comments

Our results show that the temporal occurrence of implicit psychophysical pain points can be accurately identified and that the visual representation of the user journey allows for an easier comparison between participants. Moreover, results showed that less that 25% of pain points were identified qualitatively by the participant afterwards and that some pain points were clearly mentioned as specifically positive by the participants, while the physiological data clearly showed otherwise.

This study contributes to the existing user experience literature by proposing a reliable method to visualise peak emotional reactions experienced by users while performing a task. Thus, providing more precision and reliability in identifying pain points when compared to pain points mentioned by users after the task (Fang et al. [19]). It also introduces the notion of implicit psychophysiological pain points, which, compared to explicit pain points previously used in the literature, allows to identify more pain paints and gives more reliable insights by potentially reducing biases of explicit measures [15, 25].

The results also have managerial implications. First, prior work by Georges et al. [20] explained the importance of several factors when developing new UX evaluation tools using physiological measures, such as the ability to locate issues, the ease of use, and the reduction of the analysis time. This new method allows both practitioners and researchers to identify psychophysiological pain points easily and the visualization allows to interpret and analyze more efficiently the results. This study contributes to user experience's evaluations tools by using physiological data to assess how users truly felt during an online task, providing more precision and accuracy in identifying pain points when compared to pain points mentioned by users after the task. Therefore, if practioners are interested in identifying pain points in order to improve interfaces, implicit pain points provide a more comprehensive list. However, if practitioners are interested in what users remember or think of their interface (e.g. attitude), explicit pain points should be used. Second, this study clearly shows that without the implicit emotional measures of users, it would have been extremely difficult to identify pain points, showing the relevance of this current study. Moreover, in an online grocery shopping context, pain points need to be identified in a much more precise way. The new visualization method presented in this study acknowledges this need, so companies can not only identify the "painful" steps, but the exact moment the pain point happened. Moreover, this new method is useful to benchmark user experience across interfaces, which can be used in prototype comparisons or competing interfaces.

Furthermore, some limitations need to be acknowledged. First, this visualization has so far only been applied to an online grocery shopping context and has not been tested in a hedonic context or a context that has a lot of arousal variations. Secondly, the experiment was about forty-five minutes to an hour long, excluding the baseline measures. This can be a limitation, as participants could have gotten tired and the pain points found in the final parts could be related to participant's fatigue rather than actual problems with the interaction. Finally, as they were only 7 participants per grocery website, this was not a large-scale study, mostly due to the high cost of obtaining the data. Hence, additional studies in different contexts as well as of different durations of time and with a greater number of participants could help with the generalization of these results.

In conclusion, using this new visualization method allows to identify implicit psychophysiological pain points in the user's experience, by targeting moments where the user had both a high level of arousal and a negative valence, compared to his baseline state, which meant that s/he felt an intense negative emotion. Identifying those pain points and combining them with eye-tracking data gives key insights into the online user journey and helps identify common negative moments between users. It also allows to gain a deeper understanding of the pain points that participants failed to identify during the post-task interview as well as compare the experience felt by the participants, either between tasks or between companies.

References

1. Ahlstrom, U., Friedman-Berg, F.: Using eye movement activity as a correlate of cognitive workload. Int. J. Ind. Ergon. **36**, 623–636 (2006)
2. Alves, R., Lim, V., Niforatos, E., Chen, M., Karapanos, E., Nunes, N.: Augmenting customer journey maps with quantitative empirical data: a case on EEG and eye tracking, https://arxiv.org/abs/1209.3155
3. Ariely, D.: Combining experiences over time: the effects of duration, intensity changes and on-line measurements on retrospective pain evaluations. J. Behav. Decis. Mak. **11**, 19–45 (1998)
4. Bailey, B.P., Adamczyk, P.D., Chang, T.Y., Chilson, N.A.: A framework for specifying and monitoring user tasks. Comput. Hum. Behav. **22**(4), 709–732 (2006)
5. Baumeister, R., Bratslavsky, E., Finkenauer, C., Vohs, K.: Bad is stronger than good. Rev. Gen. Psychol. **5**, 323–370 (2001)
6. Bettencourt, L.A., Ulwick, A.W.: The customer centred innovation map. Harvard Bus. Rev. **10**(1), 93 (2008)
7. Bradley, G., LaFleur, E.: Toward the development of hedonic-utilitarian measures of retail service. J. Retail. Consum. Serv. **32**, 60–66 (2016)
8. Charles, R., Nixon, J.: Measuring mental workload using physiological measures: a systematic review. Appl. Ergon. **74**, 221–232 (2019)
9. Citrin, A., Stem, D., Spangenberg, E., Clark, M.: Consumer need for tactile input. J. Bus. Res. **56**, 915–922 (2003)
10. Cockburn, A, Quinn, P, Gutwin, C.: Examining the peak-end effects of subjective experience. In: Proceedings of the 33rd Annual ACM Conference on Human Factors in Computing Systems, pp. 357–366 (2015)
11. Cockburn, A., Quinn, P., Gutwin, C.: The effects of interaction sequencing on user experience and preference. Int. J. Hum Comput Stud. **108**, 89–104 (2017)
12. Den Uyl, M.J., Van Kuilenburg, H.: The FaceReader: online facial expression recognition. In: Proceedings of Measuring Behavior, pp. 589–590 (2005)
13. Desrocher, C., Léger, P.M., Sénécal, S., Pagé, S.A., Mirhoseini, S.: The influence of product type, mathematical complexity, and visual attention on the attitude toward the website: the case of online grocery shopping. In: SIGHCI 2015 Proceedings. 16. (2015)
14. de Guinea, A., Markus, M.: Why break the habit of a lifetime? Rethinking the roles of intention, habit, and emotion in continuing information technology use. MIS Q. **33**, 433 (2009)
15. de Guinea, A., Titah, R., Léger, P.: Explicit and implicit antecedents of users' behavioral beliefs in information systems: a neuropsychological investigation. J. Manag. Inf. Syst. **30**, 179–210 (2014)
16. ISO: ISO 9241-210:2010. Ergonomics of human system interaction - Part 210: Human-centred design for interactive systems (formerly known as 13407). International Organization for Standardization (ISO), Switzerland (2010)
17. Dufresne, A., Courtemanche, F., Tep, S.P., Senecal, S.: Physiological measures, eye tracking and task analysis to track user reactions in user generated content. In: 7th International Conference on Methods and Techniques in Behavioral Research, p. 218 (2010)
18. Eich, E., Schooler, J.W.: Cognition/emotion interactions. In: Eich, E., Kihlstrom, J.F., Bower, G.H., Forgas, J.P., Niedenthal, P.M. (eds.) Cognition and Emotion. Oxford University Press, Oxford (2000)

19. Fang, Y., Qureshi, I., Sun, H., McCole, P., Ramsey, E., Lim, K.: Trust, satisfaction, and online repurchase intention: the moderating role of perceived effectiveness of e-commerce institutional mechanisms. MIS Q. **38**(2), 407–427 (2014)

20. Georges, V., Courtemanche, F., Sénécal, S., Léger, P.-M., Nacke, L., Pourchon, R.: The adoption of physiological measures as an evaluation tool in UX. In: Nah, F.F.-H., Tan, C.-H. (eds.) HCIBGO 2017. LNCS, vol. 10293, pp. 90–98. Springer, Cham (2017). https://doi.org/10.1007/978-3-319-58481-2_8

21. Hassenzahl, M., Tractinsky, N.: User experience: a research agenda. Behav. Inf. Technol. **25** (2), 91–97 (2006)

22. Hassenzahl, M., Burmester, M., Koller, F.: AttrakDiff: Ein Fragebogen zur Messung-wahrgenommener hedonischer und pragmatischer Qualität. In: Szwillus, G., Ziegler, J. (eds.) Mensch and Computer 2003, vol. 57, pp. 187–196. Vieweg + Teubner Verlag, Wiesbaden (2003). https://doi.org/10.1007/978-3-322-80058-9_19

23. Forrester Research: Mapping the Customer Journey (2010)

24. Lourties, S., Léger, P.M., Sénécal, S., Fredette, M., Chen, S.L.: Testing the convergent validity of continuous self-perceived measurement systems: an exploratory study. In: Nah, F. H., Xiao, B. (eds.) HCI in Business, Government, and Organizations. HCIBGO 2018. Lecture Notes in Computer Science, vol. 10923, pp. 132–144. Springer, Cham (2018). https://doi.org/10.1007/978-3-319-91716-0_11

25. Juanéda, C., Sénécal, S., Léger, P.M.: Product web page design: a psychophysiological investigation of the influence of product similarity, visual proximity on attention and performance. In: Nah, F.H., Xiao, B. (eds.) HCI in Business, Government, and Organizations. HCIBGO 2018. Lecture Notes in Computer Science, vol. 10923, pp. 327–337. Springer, Cham (2018). https://doi.org/10.1007/978-3-319-91716-0_25

26. Maunier, B., Alvarez, J., Léger, P.-M., Sénécal, S., Labonté-LeMoyne, É., Chen, S.L., Lachize, S., Gagné, J.: Keep calm and read the instructions: factors for successful user equipment setup. In: Nah, F.F.-H., Xiao, B.S. (eds.) HCIBGO 2018. LNCS, vol. 10923, pp. 372–381. Springer, Cham (2018). https://doi.org/10.1007/978-3-319-91716-0_29

27. Johnston, D., Anastasiades, P., Wood, C.: The relationship between cardiovascular responses in the laboratory and in the field. Psychophysiology **27**, 34–44 (1990)

28. Kahneman, D., Fredrickson, B., Schreiber, C., Redelmeier, D.: When more pain is preferred to less: adding a better end. Psychol. Sci. **4**, 401–405 (1993)

29. Kahneman, D., Wakker, P., Sarin, R.: Back to Bentham? Explorations of experienced utility. Q. J. Econ. **112**, 375–406 (1997)

30. Kramer, A.: Physiological Metrics of Mental Workload: A Review of Recent Progress. Defense Technical Information Center, Ft. Belvoir (1990)

31. Laeng, B., Sirois, S., Gredebäck, G.: Pupillometry. Perspect. Psychol. Sci. **7**, 18–27 (2012)

32. Lallemand, C., Gronier, G.: Méthodes de Design UX. Eyrolles, Paris (2018)

33. Langer, T., Sarin, R., Weber, M.: The retrospective evaluation of payment sequences: duration neglect and peak-and-end effects. J. Econ. Behav. Organ. **58**, 157–175 (2005)

34. Mandryk, R., Inkpen, K., Calvert, T.: Using psychophysiological techniques to measure user experience with entertainment technologies. Behav. Inf. Technol. **25**, 141–158 (2006)

35. Mangiaracina, R., Brugnoli, G., Perego, A.: The eCommerce customer journey: a model to assess and compare the user experience of the eCommerce websites. J. Internet Bank. Commer. **14**(3) (2009)

36. Mirhoseini, S.M.M., Léger, P.-M., Sénécal, S.: The influence of task characteristics on multiple objective and subjective cognitive load measures. In: Davis, F.D., Riedl, R., vom Brocke, J., Léger, P.-M., Randolph, A.B. (eds.) Information Systems and Neuroscience. LNISO, vol. 16, pp. 149–156. Springer, Cham (2017). https://doi.org/10.1007/978-3-319-41402-7_19

37. Moon, H., Han, S., Chun, J., Hong, S.: A design process for a customer journey map: a case study on mobile services. Hum. Factors Ergon. Manuf. Serv. Ind. **26**, 501–514 (2016)
38. Morganosky, M., Cude, B.: Consumer response to online grocery shopping. Int. J. Retail Distrib. Manag. **28**, 17–26 (2000)
39. Mylopoulos, J., Chung, L., Yu, E.: From object-oriented to goal-oriented requirements analysis. Commun. ACM **42**, 31–37 (1999)
40. Nenonen, S., Rasila, H., Junnonen, J.M., Kärnä, S.: Customer Journey–a method to investigate user experience. In: Proceedings of the Euro FM Conference Manchester, pp. 54–63 (2008)
41. Nielson: What's in store for online grocery shopping- Omnichannel strategies to reach crossovers shoppers (2017)
42. Rawson, A., Duncan, E., Jones, C.: The truth about customer experience. Harvard Bus. Rev. **91**(9), 90–98 (2013)
43. Redelmeier, D., Kahneman, D.: Patients' memories of painful medical treatments: real-time and retrospective evaluations of two minimally invasive procedures. Pain **66**, 3–8 (1996)
44. Richardson, A.: Using customer journey maps to improve customer experience. Harvard Bus. Rev. **15**(1), 2–5 (2010)
45. Rosenbaum, M., Otalora, M., Ramírez, G.: How to create a realistic customer journey map. Bus. Horiz. **60**, 143–150 (2017)
46. Teixeira, J., Patrício, L., Nunes, N., Nóbrega, L., Fisk, R., Constantine, L.: Customer experience modeling: from customer experience to service design. J. Serv. Manag. **23**, 362–376 (2012)
47. Wang, B., Miao, Y., Zhao, H., Jin, J., Chen, Y.: A biclustering-based method for market segmentation using customer pain points. Eng. Appl. Artif. Intell. **47**, 101–109 (2016)
48. Wilson, G.: Air-to-ground training missions: a psychophysiological workload analysis. Ergonomics **36**, 1071–1087 (1993)

The Relationship of the Studies of Ergonomic and Human Computer Interfaces – A Case Study of Graphical Interfaces in E-Commerce Websites

Marly de Menezes[✉] and Marcelo Falco

Universidade Anhembi Morumbi, Design Digital, Rua Jaceru, 247,
São Paulo 04705-000, Brazil
arqmarlydemenezes@gmail.com, mfalco@gmail.com

Abstract. The concept of the Human-Computer Interaction - HCI - has contributed to create several tools and interaction devices that allow to perform the tasks of day to day with greater ease, efficiency and intelligence. It provides optimization of energy consumption, agility in mobility and accessibility, performing actions that promote the improvement of people's quality of life. Digital Design course has as main objective the search of solutions for digital interfaces and focus on the value of the users. This article will present the result of the heuristic evaluation related to the ergonomic quality of graphical interfaces of websites, through the Ergonomic Aspects developed by Scapin and Bastien, carried out along the discipline of Ergonomics.

Keywords: Ergonomics · Human Computer Interfaces · Education

1 Introduction

1.1 The Education of the Discipline of Ergonomics in the Digital Design Course

The discipline of Ergonomics in the Digital Design course aims to study the adequacy of cultural objects to man, considering the ergonomic studies of physiology, perception, cognition and memory, dynamic and static anthropometry, control and display management, searching analyze the cycles of interaction and perception, usage scenarios, routines and interpretations of the digital interfaces through user-centered design project evaluations.

The general objectives are: to make students aware of the relevance of the study of ergonomics, especially in relation to the interface; understand the field of ergonomics from the point of view of the user; to know and apply the ergonomic criteria pointed out by several authors; create and contextualize the project, taking into account the principles of ergonomics and usability, deriving from the user experience; and to develop low fidelity prototypes, discussing ergonomic and cognitive issues.

© Springer Nature Switzerland AG 2019
A. Marcus and W. Wang (Eds.): HCII 2019, LNCS 11586, pp. 474–484, 2019.
https://doi.org/10.1007/978-3-030-23535-2_35

The work developed during the second semester of 2018, with the students from the 5th semester of the course, allowed to elaborate a study, where the students were able to put into practice the concepts of ergonomics necessary to understand the importance of the heuristic evaluation, using the Criteria Ergonomic of Bastien and Scapin.

1.2   The Criteria Ergonomic of Bastien and Scapin

The program content of the discipline of Ergonomics for the Digital Design course at Anhembi Morumbi University is based on the criteria of different authors such as: Jakob Nielsen's Usability Heuristics, Ben Shneiderman's Gold Rules and Scapin's Ergonomic Criteria and Bastien, as a resource to evaluate the graphical interfaces of digital projects.

In this research on the graphical interfaces of e-commerce sites, the Ergonomic Criteria developed by the French Dominique Scapin and Christian Bastien, elaborated in 1993, at the Research Centre INRIA in Paris, were used to facilitate the understanding of interactive software, reducing conflicts generated by the user's ignorance (Cybis 2010).

Scapin and Bastien subdivided into 8 criteria: Guidance, Workload, Explicit Control, Adaptability, Error Management, Consistency, Significance of Codes and Compatibility. In this item, each criterion will be presented briefly for a better understanding of the research carried out on the analysis of e-commerce sites:

1. Guidance is the criterion that seeks to help the user navigate the interface through the location of titles, menu options, format of labels, readability of information and immediate feedback. In this way, if the presentation of the interface "the invitation" is carried out properly, the user will have a good experience to understand its operation.
2. Workload is the criterion that allows mitigating and facilitating the actions to be performed by the user insofar as these events are part of the daily routine of the user and, therefore, it is not necessary to memorize them.
3. Explicit Control is the criterion that provides the user with the domain of their intentions to perform a procedure or not, such as canceling or deferring a long-lasting download.
4. Adaptability is the criterion that seeks to facilitate the action to be performed by the user, considering the degree of their experience, allowing the execution of an action of different forms and, in this way, reach a greater number of users of different levels of interaction.
5. Error Management is a criterion that guides the user when some data is inserted in a way incompatible with the action to be performed, informing him about the lack of some information or a typo, for example.
6. Consistency is a criterion, based on the visual identity of a product, that homogeneously displays the elements that make up the interface and that have the same properties. In this way, the user perceives the environment between the various digital pages as belonging to a unit, just as a volume of a book belongs to a collection.

7. Significance of Codes is the criterion that is concerned with the cultural aspects of the user insofar as it establishes the functionality of the system through the basis of the cognitive, perceptual and expectations of the user. This criterion in conjunction with the Adaptability criterion is directly related to the previous experience of the user.
8. Compatibility is the criterion that adjusts the action to be performed by the user with the inherent needs of the interface data processing, such as the logic of completing a form in a certain sequence: name and address, not the other way around.

1.3 Methodology

The methodology used in Digital Design classroom is based on Active Methods, using Problem-Based Learning, in which the teacher provides the class with a daily situation, instigating the student to reflect on the reality in which he lives. In this context, seeks to focus in the learning process to the student, placing him in an active position to search for knowledge through research, discussion, planning and collaboration within the group.

Therefore, the methodology applied was data collection in theoretical references on the ergonomic aspects studied by Dominique Scapin and Christian Bastien, and a case study of graphical interfaces websites related to the e-commerce.

1.4 Development

Within the Constructivist concept guided by Piaget, the practice of evaluating a product through theoretical analysis is inserted in the discipline of Ergonomics, of the course of Digital Design. By the same token, seeks to study the suitability of objects and workspaces to man, seeking to analyze the usage scenarios through user-centered product evaluations.

Each group of students chooses e-commerce websites to verify different criterion studied matches with the user's needs and desires. Throughout the analysis process, students should carry out a heuristic evaluation addressing the user's objectives, the interface objects and the qualities to be performed by the interfaces.

This activity allows the student to understand the importance about criteria of an ergonomic in the evaluation of digital projects facilitating the Human Computers Interactions. Besides that, the discipline of Ergonomics employing the qualities of efficacy, agility and insight of the Human-Computer Interaction in order to question, understand, relate and share information such as accessibility, mobility, sustainability. Through teaching processes influence the professional's practice of the future designer in different areas related to human life.

2   The Application of the Heuristic Evaluation of the Ergonomic Criteria

2.1   Preparation of the Work

In the discipline of Ergonomics, teachers have worked on a constructivist pedagogical practice, based on Problem Based Learning, associating the curriculum contents of the discipline with the reality of the professional world, with a view to the formation of the future digital designer.

Theoretical themes of the discipline, such as the Ergonomic Criteria presented by Scapin and Bastien, which need to have their foundations understood through reading, are arranged in the classroom through case studies, where the student is encouraged to verify how concepts are applied to digital products on the market and, consequently, he realizes that "the real ultimate objective of problem-solving learning is to make the student get into the habit of proposing problems and solving them as a form of learning" (Echeverría and Pozo 1998).

Each ergonomic criterion presented by Scapin and Bastien was studied by the students to understand their meaning within a digital project, as the concept of the criterion was created to improve the user experience and how the criterion can be verified in the digital product, in this study aimed at an e-commerce. A first assessment of the reliability of the set of criteria was performed in a classification task (Bastien and Scapin 1992).

After presenting the definition of e-commerce elaborated by Tom Venetianer, a specialist in digital marketing, denominating it as "the set of all the commercial transactions carried out by a firm, with the objective of attending, directly or indirectly, its customers, using, for both the facilities of communication and data transfer mediated by the worldwide Internet network" (Venetianer 2000), each group of students received a set of plasticized fiches with the definitions of the ergonomic criteria of Scapin and Bastien, as presented in item 1.2 of this article.

Then, when each criterion was studied and understood, the students were instructed by the teacher to verify in the case/problem, the e-commerce selected, if the criterion in question was applicable to the studied project, how the interface used the criterion and if even met the concepts defined by Scapin and Bastien.

The objective of the debate on a given problem was to make the teacher cease to be the holder and transmitter of knowledge and be recognized by the group as a manager that promoted in the study environment the exchange of ideas, thoughts and reflections, providing the rise of new professional performances in the education of the student.

2.2   The Case Study - Americanas.Com E-Commerce

This article will exemplify the application of ergonomic criteria performed in the **Americanas.com** e-commerce conducted by a group of students in the classroom, because among the companies studied this was the site where the verification of the criteria allowed a better understanding of the importance of the study of ergonomic criteria in digital products.

Fig. 1. E-commerce interface. Source: https://www.americanas.com.br/

With the Guidance criterion, it was analyzed how the site made the "invitation", that is, how the e-commerce interface presented its products and services to the users, in an attractive way, allowing the user to have an interest in e-commerce and, in this way, increase the possibility of (see Fig. 1).

In the opening screen of e-commerce, you can check phrases such as: "have everything, you can look for:)", "enjoy", "take a look", "we will get $ 15 off the first purchase" that "invite" the user to interact with the site. The color company code, red, was used to emphasize the central range of the site, where a carousel was placed with the main offers of the company, as well as to highlight important points like "offer of the day" or "buy by department".

When analyzing the interface by Guidance criterion, it was also verified that the items of **location, format and feedback**. The **location** item used spatial structures already known to the user along the route of the site, repeating with each new page the upper structure with search information and shopping basket, company logo and others. The **format** linked real-world experience to the digital world by incorporating icons with similar characteristics to the real world and/or to images already enshrined in the digital world. The **feedback** item where each action established by the user, results in a system orientation, is present in various actions of the site. In Fig. 2, you can see that by hovering over the shopping cart, the system automatically records the **feedback** that no purchase has been made so far. Thus, in the Guidance criterion, all these items had a satisfactory response in the evaluation of the site.

With the criterion **Workload** was verified that the **Americanas.com** e-commerce worries that the user travels the smallest way to carry out an action of brief form, facilitating to the user to reach quickly to its objective. The site is organized in such a way that the similar steps are concise in their actions, creating minimal actions for the user to quickly identify their interest. In Fig. 3, in the search space, only two letters were typed, and several options have already been made available so that the user does not have to write the whole word, for example.

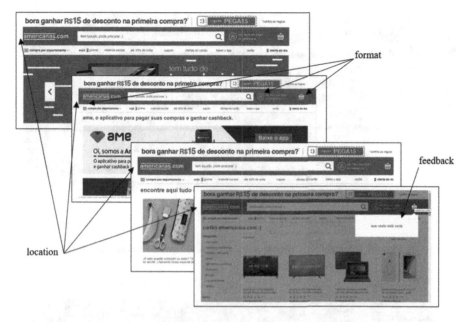

Fig. 2. Location, Format and Feedback Criteria. Source: https://www.americanas.com.br/

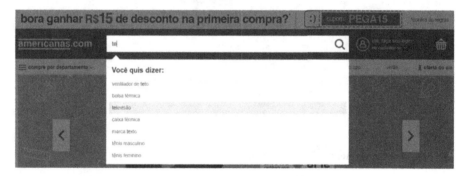

Fig. 3. Workload Criteria. Source: https://www.americanas.com.br/

It was possible to verify through the **Adaptability** criterion, that the site provides the user to perform an action in different ways, considering, mainly, their experience as a client. In this way, more experienced users can dispense with some feature, while novice users need to travel longer ways to carry out the activity with more security (see Fig. 4). On the homepage of the site, the user can access the "school material" tab in three different ways, in the hamburger menu, the carousel and the central band button.

In **Error Management**, the research identified that in several situations the Americanas.com e-commerce anticipates the needs and doubts of the user, presenting solutions before the error even occurs, signaling how the action should be carried out and/or warning the user that something needs to be changed or filled out. When filling

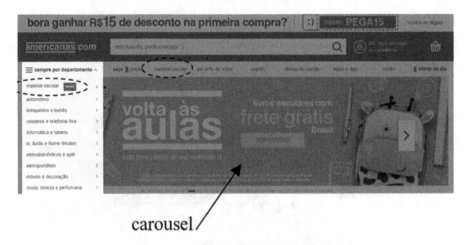

carousel

Fig. 4. Adaptability Criteria. Source: https://www.americanas.com.br/

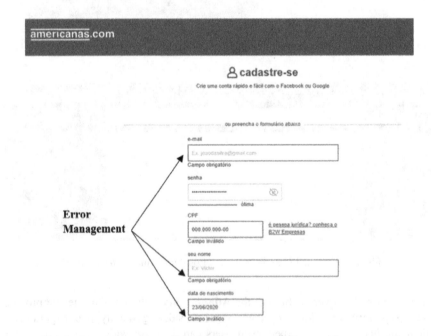

Fig. 5. Error Management Criteria. Source: https://www.americanas.com.br/

in the registration, for example, the user is oriented in each space with a template of how to fill in the blank field and, if you fill in the field in the wrong way, by pressing the "create your registration" button, automatically fields with problems are identified (see Fig. 5).

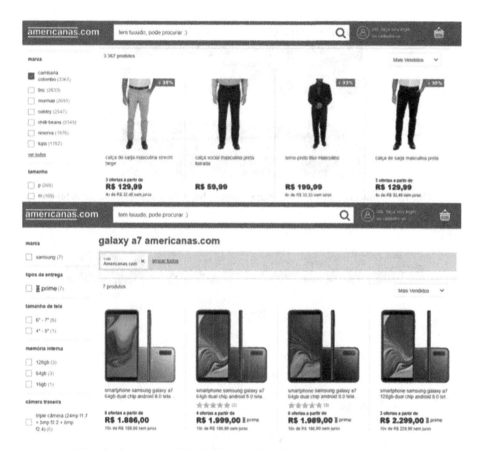

Fig. 6. Consistency Criteria. Source: https://www.americanas.com.br/

The **Consistency** criterion seeks to create homogenous areas so that the user can identify the actions to be performed even if they are on different pages. In Fig. 6 are exemplified two pages of the site, one sells masculine clothing and the other cellular. Even though it is different, the product layout is the same to facilitate the user's purchase action.

When applying the criterion **Significance of Codes**, it was observed that icons and forms were used with consecrated and universal messages so that the user could understand the meaning of the action to be performed. In Fig. 7, the icon known as the "hamburger menu" was highlighted to facilitate access to the various sales departments of e-commerce.

With the Compatibility criterion, it was verified in the **Americanas.com** e-commerce that the actions that need to be carried out in a certain way so that the processing of the data does not change, are adapted to the user. For example, in the field for filling in a numerical data, such as a user ID, there is only the possibility of entering numerals (see Fig. 8), and in this way the system induces the user to fill in the data correctly.

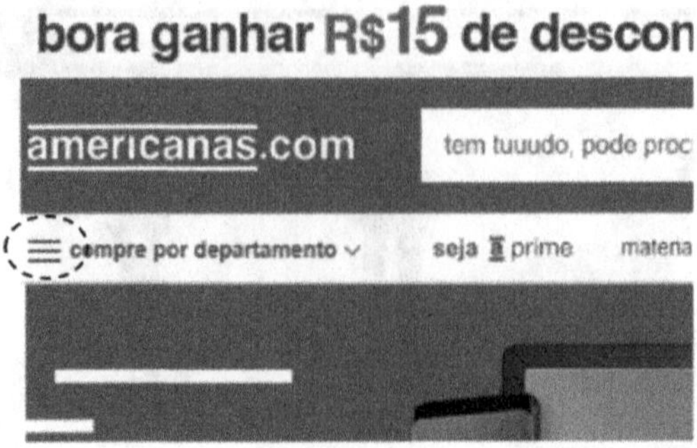

bora ganhar R$15 de descon

americanas.com   tem tuuudo, pode proc

≡ compre por departamento ∨   seja 🛒 prime   matena

Fig. 7. Significance of Codes Criteria. Source: https://www.americanas.com.br/

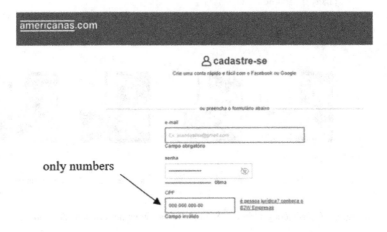

Fig. 8. Compatibility Criteria. Source: https://www.americanas.com.br/

By verifying each criterion applied to the existing e-commerce site in the market, students were able to understand that when designing a digital product, it is necessary to understand how the user will go through the interface.

Future digital designers need to understand that when a user is in front of the interface of an e-commerce, there is no one who can assist him in how to use the platform, in other words, there is no operating manual, in this way, when applying the ergonomic criteria elaborated by Bastien and Scapin, it is possible to anticipate how the user could face a certain situation.

As a result, this work promoted student's development of a training focused on reflective thinking and sensitivity to understand the world where they live, using technological process and expression related to Human Computer Interactions concepts for daily necessities identification.

3   Conclusion

Nowadays, within the higher courses, where the student has access to information in the palm of his hands, the 21st century teacher needs to create situations that establish a bridge of communication with the students, so that they become involved in the topics inherent to the several important disciplines for your academic background.

It is important that the teacher prepares your work material using the means and tools that are part of the daily life of the students, so that they feel part of their learning process and, in this way, better understand the importance of the contents of the subjects for the formation of a professional working in the market.

In this context, the discipline of Ergonomics of the Digital Design course aims to combine methodologies that make it possible to transform the space of the classroom into a welcoming environment for the practice of research and development of the study of the themes inherent to Ergonomics applied to the digital products.

During the research, the performance of the heuristic evaluation using the Ergonomic Criteria of Scapin and Bastien, different e-commerce websites were compared allowing students to diagnose errors and/or omissions in the products analyzed with respect to the user and deficiencies regarding readability and conduction of the studied interfaces.

In this article, one of the studies carried out in the classroom by the students of the Digital Design course at Anhembi Morumbi University, was presented to illustrate how the theoretical content on ergonomic criteria can be studied by students, in order to contribute to the formation of future professionals in the area of Digital Design.

In presenting a case/problem related to the real world, such as the study of an e-commerce, the teachers of the discipline of Ergonomics promote an interaction between the theoretical knowledge studied by the students and the application of content with the objective of finding new solutions to quotidian problems faced by Digital Design professionals.

The methodologies worked together were used as a learning process so that the students could verify their knowledge applied to reality. The main objective was to establish a dynamic of teaching where the student becomes the protagonist of his knowledge, starting from his previous knowledge, where the concepts of Ergonomics, could be raised, instigated and absorbed as an important contribution to their professional qualification.

As a result, this work promoted student development of a training focused on reflective thinking and sensitivity to understand the world where they live, using technological process and expression related to Human Computer Interactions concepts for daily necessities identification.

When applying Ergonomic Aspects of Scapin and Bastien, associated with the Piaget Constructivist concept, the Active Methods and using Problem-Based Learning, the work was done on the quality of the e-commerce websites, for example.

All of that enabled the students to return the sense of analysis and interpretation of data from the Human Computer Interactions, in addition to verifying that the digital device must be aimed at the needs of the user.

Based on the assumption that the legacy of the Human Computer Interaction is to improve people's life, and according to the Professor Itiro Iida, Ergonomics is "the study of the adaptation of work to the human being" (2005).

All things considered, this work enabled the students' autonomy in the elaboration of projects that involve the principles related to the Human Computer Interaction, where interconnected information mobilize students and to improve their knowledge to find new solutions to social needs.

References

Bastien, J.M.C., Scapin, D.L.: A validation of ergonomic criteria for the evaluation of human–computer interfaces. Int. J. Hum.–Comput. Interact. (1992)

Cybis, W., et al.: Ergonomia e Usabilidade: conhecimentos, métodos e aplicações. Novatec Editora, São Paulo (2010)

Iida, I.: Ergonomia: Projeto e Produção. Edgard Blucher, São Paulo (2005)

Venetianer, T.: Fundamentos do comércio eletrônico. In: Como vender seu peixe na Internet. Editora Campus, Rio de Janeiro (2000)

Echeverría, M., Pozo, J.: Aprender a resolver problemas e resolver problemas para aprender. In: Pozo, J. (ed.) A solução de problemas: aprender a resolver, resolver a aprender. Artmed, Porto Alegre (1998)

Why and Why Not Use My Face?—A Case Study of Face Recognition Solutions in the Workplace

Sinan He[1(✉)], Yi Zhang[1], Jingya Zhang[1], Xiaofan Li[1], Zhun Wu[1], Jun Niu[2], and Daisong Guan[1]

[1] Baidu AI Interaction Design Lab, Beijing, China
hesinan01@baidu.com
[2] Baidu Business Platform and Intelligent Technology, Beijing, China

Abstract. Face recognition (FR) technology is permeating and changing our lives from mobile phone to public space in China. Baidu utilizes advanced FR technology to support tens of thousands of employees in their daily access and payments. However, as a new way of human–machine interaction, a handful of researches of face interaction in the field of HCI were conducted. This study aimed to solve three issues: Users' behavior during face interaction; What are the reasons for using and not using FR? What are the advantages of user experience of FR? With the methodology of field observation and interviews, we studied the face interaction on five typical scenarios, including the gate barriers, corridors, canteen, supermarket, and vending machines. Through the analysis of these issues, we had a comprehensive and in-depth understanding of experience problems and advantages of face interaction in public space. Basing on our findings, design implications were given focusing on reducing or avoiding these problems, and strengthen the advantages of face interaction. We believe it would be beneficial for the FR which is at the early stage of HCI research.

Keywords: Face recognition · Face interaction · Face swiping · Face access · Face payment · User experience

1 Introduction

Face recognition (FR) technology is permeating our daily lives in China. From the applications on personal devices, such as unlocking the phone or logging in the app with face, to public use, for example, the face access at tourist sites, airports and train stations, etc. The word "face-swiping", has gained popularity and become part of our lives.

Baidu has done in-depth work on the technology of FR. It supports tens of thousands of face interactions every day. However, when we wanted to optimize the interaction and design of FR, we found researches of FR in the field of HCI were so few that we didn't know where to start. We didn't know how users use it, if there were any patterns of behavior, why and why not they use it, what experience advantages FR had, and what aspects could be strengthened, what aspects should be avoided, and so on.

© Springer Nature Switzerland AG 2019
A. Marcus and W. Wang (Eds.): HCII 2019, LNCS 11586, pp. 485–504, 2019.
https://doi.org/10.1007/978-3-030-23535-2_36

As a new way of interaction, current researches of FR mainly focus on the technological aspects, It is seldom discussed from the user's perspective. Only a handful of researches were conducted on human–computer interaction and user experience. For the early stage of HCI research, it is necessary to learn the real behavior of interaction and understand users' inside thoughts, and Baidu provides us with an excellent scenario for case study. This paper aims to solve the following core issues:

1. *Users' behaviour: Under what circumstances are users prone to use FR? And what behaviors do users have?*
2. *Reason mining: Why do/do not users use FR?*
3. *Advantage of user experience: What are the advantages of "swiping face" from the user's perspective compared to other methods?*

Through a hybrid method we answered these questions and based on these findings, we extended some deeper problems and discussions as the basis of design optimization.

Different from other researches, we conducted the research in real life instead of experimental environment. It mainly covers two categories of application in the company: access and payment. The access category includes the gate barriers and corridors (Fig. 1), and the payment category includes the company's canteens, supermarket, and vending machines (Fig. 2), which amount to 5 typical scenarios.

Usually, the FR devices are made up of an electronic screen with a camera connected to the access control or payment system. The face detecting process is performed by the camera. The authentication status (including the status of face detecting and recognizing) and the user's information (including the employee's name, the greeting words and the amount spent) are shown on the screen. There are also imperceptible FR devices in the company. With no screen, the detection process is performed by an independent camera. Such devices are installed in the corridors, and the light strips on the door shows the result of the recognition.

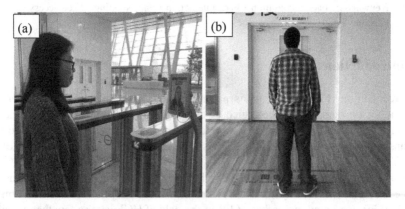

Fig. 1. Paying at the Gate Barrier (pic. a), and Corridor (pic. b). (Figures in the pic. are examples of researchers, not users)

Fig. 2. Paying at the Canteen (pic. a), Supermarket (pic. b) and Vending Machine (pic. c). (Figures in the pic. are examples of researchers, not users)

The usage process and characteristics of the five scenarios studied in this paper are illustrated as following (Table 1).

Table 1. The summary of the comparison among the 5 scenarios

Scenario	Interaction method	Screen	Feedback method	Traffic characteristics
Gate barrier	Face/card	Yes	Screen + voice	Has obvious peaks, but no lining-up
Corridor	Face/card	No	Light strip	Has no peak
Canteen	Face/card	Yes	Screen	Users line up all the time
Supermarket	Face/card/phone	Yes	Screen + voice	Users sometimes line up
Vending machine	Face/phone	Yes	Screen + voice	Users do not line up due to dispersed user traffic

2 Related Work

2.1 Face Recognition and Usability Researches

The current literature on FR still focus on exploring technology, and there are few studies based on the perspective of user experience or human–computer interaction. In terms of the application of FR technology, relevant researches in China have mainly been news commentary and lacks in-depth research. There are some international studies on biometric authentication that revolve around user experience to compare usability between various methods of authentication (including face, voiceprint, hand gesture, iris, retina etc.).

Comparisons between the various methods of usability primarily take place in lab research of mobile phone screen unlocking. The IBM Watson Center (2012) compared voice, fingerprint, hand gestures and FR as alternatives and found that face and voice recognition were more efficient than passwords or hand gestures. Users also displayed varying response, with some users finding photo-taking troublesome, while others think it is convenient [1]. Rasekhar et al. found that convenience and usability are key factors for users deciding to opt for biometric technology [2]. Alexander De Luca also pointed out that users ranked from most to least important the reasons for using face unlock as safety, curiosity, usability, novelty, emotional factors, prestige and reliability, while ranking the reasons for refusing to use face unlock (in the same order) as usability, reliability, external factors, emotional factors, security, lack of necessity, technology and misunderstanding [3].

There has been a small amount of research on face authentication in the real world. Kvarnbrink et al. performed a case study on the transition from magnetic key cards to FR in the largest gym in Europe and found that users thought FR was favorable and simple. The study revealed that users enjoyed not using swipe cards, and this also benefited the gym given that non-members can no longer borrow membership cards for access [4].

There is a similar study about the application of biometrics in the workplace (2006). It proposed two areas of focus in designing face authentication devices: the physical environment and interaction with the device. However, some of the technological aspects of facial authentication in this relatively old study are no longer applicable. For example, users have to remove their glasses for FR, and this would lead to the trouble of unable to see the screen clearly and voice prompts do little to assist them in positioning themselves accurately. This shows that such technology lacks usability [5]. Wayman et al. also mentioned that different environments can affect device performance, such as whether detection is overt or covert, whether the user is habituated or non-habituated to the device, and whether the device is supervised or unsupervised, standard or non-standard, public or private etc. The device's surrounding environment can be subject to such classifications [6].

2.2 Face Recognition and Technology Acceptance Model

There are few articles based on technology acceptance model (TAM) to study the factors affecting the willingness of using FR. Qingjie et al. [7] have studied the contribution of various factors. Although there were sources of factors, most of them based on the use of mobile phone, and none of them originated from the research of FR. When summarized the reasons for using and not using faces, we found it difficult to put all the reasons into a traditional usability or user experience framework, such as some environmental and risk factors. Through desk study of TAM, we thought it was applicable to our reason induction.

TAM is a classical model in the field of information technology, which takes willingness to use as a dependent variable and is widely validated and applied. Perceived usefulness and perceived ease of use as independent variables originate from the classical model [8], which are the most basic factors in all related studies.

Perceived Usefulness refers to the individual's perception of performance improvement after the usage of a system. Perceived Ease of Use reflects the individual's experience that a system is easy to operate [8].

Use Context originated from Heijden [9], Gan [10] who supplemented the classical TAM when they studied the mobile payment system. It referred to the specific environment in which users used the information system.

Perceived Enjoyment was derived from Serenko [11], Mun et al. [12], Lee et al. [13], Duamasbi et al. [14] supplements to TAM. It referred to the degree of personal enjoyment in the process of interaction with the system, excluding the results of performance.

Perceived Risk originated from Heijden [8], Lee [15], and Qingjie's [7] supplements to the classical TAM in their research on e-commerce and payment system. It referred to the individuals' subjective feelings resulting from their inability to judge whether adverse consequences have occurred.

In summary, previous studies mainly focused on the interaction of FR on personal mobile phones, and the conclusions may not necessarily applicable to the public space; moreover, the research based on public space lacked representativeness because of either the special scenes (gym) or the earlier time; finally, the research related to technology acceptance model also lacks the source from the real use of FR.

3   Method

We adopted a mixed-methods approach that includes field observation and interviews in this study. Field observation served two objectives: first, to learn and record the real behavior and then code some of them for the description and analysis of users' behavior patterns; second, to select users with typical behavior characteristics as the sample of interview research. Interview was mainly used for in-depth excavation of reasons.

3.1   Field Observation

We conducted four days of field observation in the Baidu Technology Park, focusing on the five scenarios of FR: gate barrier, corridor, canteen, supermarket, and vending machine. There were multiple FR (observation) points for each of the above scenarios given the park's large area. For each scenario, we selected observation points with large traffic flows, meaning more users and higher frequency of usage. We also observed these points during their idle and busy hours in order to learn about their usage in a more inclusive manner. As observation at different scenarios were conducted during overlapping times, the study was completed through the collective efforts of four researchers. The main researcher delivered standardized training for all participating researchers the day before the observation commenced to ensure the study's consistency. In the standard process, we ensure users are informed of the observations and records.

GoPro cameras in prominent locations were also deployed at each observation point before coding analysis was performed to quantify typical user behavior. These served as a supplementary form of data collection to the researcher's observation. Table 2 shows the duration and traffic recorded by GoPro cameras at each observation point. The cumulative observation time was 21.5 h, of which 13.5 h were coded and 1141 samples were coded. The corridors and vending machines saw lower traffic without no obvious peak periods, which meant a smaller number of users overall.

Table 2. Observation and coded video length, and sample size at the five scenarios

Senario	Observation length	Coded video length	Coded sample size
Gate barrier	4h	2h	339
Corridor	4.5h	4.5h	62
Canteen	6h	2h	402
Supermarket	3h	1h	329
Vending machine	4h	4h	9
Total	21.5h	13.5h	1141

Table 3. Video coding principles and coding methods

Coding indices	Coding method	Implications of each index
Use face or not	• Used • Not used	Classification of users
Hands occupation	• One hand occupied • Both hands occupied • No hands occupied	Confirms whether the user's hands were free or occupied and whether this has a bearing on using FR
Card placement	• Held in hand • Retrieved from pocket • Hung around neck • Unavailable	Reflects the employee card's accessibility to the user and whether this has a bearing on using FR
(For face users) Users' actions	• Looked at the camera in advance • Adjusted posture • No special action	Reflects users' prior planning and willingness to adjust for FR

Within a week of completing the data collection, we selected some recorded video clips based on sample size and traffic flow to encode users' behavior (Table 2). The coding principle and method are shown in Table 3.

3.2   Interview

In addition to field observations, to explore reasons for use/not use and the advantage of experience, four other researchers (who received standard training one day in advance) conducted intercept interviews at the same time. The samples in each scenario are shown in Table 4. The sample covers a variety of functional roles in the company, including product manager (PM), research and development (R&D), sales and sales etc.

Table 4. Sample size of the interviews in 5 scenarios

Scenario	Used	Not used	Total
Gate barrier	21	5	26
Corridor	16	3	19
Canteen	19	11	30
Supermarket	13	10	23
Vending machine	3	0	3
Total	72	29	101

(The number of Use/Not Use doesn't represent the usage rate, which depends on the success rate of intercept interviews)

3.3   Data Integration and Analysis

Both of the analysis of quantitative and qualitative samples provides evidences for the findings and discussion of this paper.

Quantitative Samples and Analysis. Quantitative samples based on GoPro video coding are mainly used to describe users' behavior, and further analyze if there are some patterns of the behavior. We used spss20.0 to analyze the quantitative data to explore the influence of different factors, such as the relationship between the face swiping behavior and whether the hands are occupied or the position of the card.

Qualitative Samples and Analysis. Qualitative samples which gathered from interviews are mainly used to mine the reasons why users use/do not use FR, and to explore the experience advantages of FR. Inductive method was used to summarize.

4   Findings

4.1   Users' Behavior

In this section, we describe uses' behavior from two aspects: ① Under what circumstances are users prone to use FR? We analyzed the influence of two coded factors: "hands occupation" and "card placement" through non-parametric test. ② What behaviors do users have? We analyzed the "users' actions" among the people who use FR though descriptive statistics.

Under What Circumstances Are Users Prone to Swipe Their Faces? To understand under what circumstances users would choose FR, we carried out non-parametric test and post-hoc comparison to examine users' use of FR in different hand-occupied situations. We found that in the scenario of gate barrier, canteen and supermarket, different situations of hand occupation would affect their use of FR (canteen: $\chi^2 = 28.098$, p = 0.000; supermarket: $\chi^2 = 20.394$, p = 0.000; the gate barrier: $\chi^2 = 25.041$, p = 0.000). When both hands were occupied, users were much more likely to use FR than in any other conditions. In the corridor scenario, whether users' hands are occupied has no significant influence on whether users choose FR ($\chi^2 = 0.152$, p = 0.927). The scenario of vending machine was not analyzed because of the small sample size (Table 5).

Table 5. Different kinds of hand occupation/whether they use FR in different scenarios

		Access		Payment	
		Gate barrier	Corridor	Canteen	Supermarket
One hand occupied	Used	13.6%	71.7%	22.3%	11.1%
	Not used	86.4%	28.3%	77.7%	88.9%
Both hands occupied	Used	51.9%	72.7%	85.7%	50.0%
	Not used	48.1%	27.3%	14.3%	50.0%
No hands occupied	Used	15.3%	80.0%	26.4%	20.0%
	Not used	84.7%	20.0%	73.6%	80.0%

Another factor that affects users' usage of FR is the position of the employee card. In the canteen, the supermarket, and the gate barrier scenarios, users are more likely to use FR when employee cards are invisible. With cards in sight, we further examined the relationship between the position of the card and whether users choose FR through non-parametric test and pairwise comparison, and found that the position of the card could affect whether users choose FR. (the gate barrier: $\chi^2 = 16.222$, p = 0.000; canteen: $\chi^2 = 18.159$, p = 0.000; supermarket: $\chi^2 = 8.787$, p = 0.013) When the cards were hanging around their neck rather than in their hands, user's willingness to use FR was significantly increased. The vending machine scenario was not included also. In the corridor scenario, the placement of employee cards has no significant influence on whether users choose FR ($\chi^2 = 5.784$, p = 0.055). The scenario of vending machine was not analyzed because of the small sample size (Table 6).

Table 6. The position of the card/whether users use FR in different scenarios

		Access		Payment	
		Gate barrier	Corridor	Canteen	Supermarket
Held in hand	Used	3.8%	61.5%	5.4%	6.7%
	Not used	96.2%	38.5%	94.7%	93.3%
Retrieved from pocket	Used	7.1%	28.6%	14.3%	0.0%
	Not used	92.9%	71.4%	85.7%	100.0%
Hung around neck	Used	18.3%	77.8%	21.7%	18.1%
	Not used	81.7%	22.2%	78.3%	81.9%

Except for vending machine, the corridor was completely different from other scenarios, which may be related to its property and interactive method. As an imperceptible way of interaction, it has no screen and locates directly above the user's movement. It can detect and recognise successfully as long as the user does not look down at the mobile phone or wear a hat, which is less affected by the user's subjective choice and other factors.

What behaviors do users have? The descriptive analysis of "Users' Actions" shows that: Of the 254 users who use FR, 235 (92.5%) adapted to different degrees of posture. Among them, 191(75.2%) adjusted their facial orientation in advance and actively looked at the camera. Another 44(17.3%) adjusted their standing position or changed body posture to adapt to the camera after their first standing. We think that these actions on the one hand indicates not only the usage of users, but also with the actively cooperative actions, which to some extent reflects a high level of acceptance. On the other hand, it shows that our FR equipment are not friendly enough and requires additional actions for users which can be optimized.

4.2   Reason Mining: Why Use/Not Use FR?

We interviewed 72 face users and 29 non-face users in 101 qualitative samples respectively (The number of users and non-users does not represent the usage rate, but is affected by the success rate of interception interview). The open-ended answers were summarized as Tables 7 and 8. Since the purpose of this study was to collect the complete set of reasons and the reasons of universality in the workplace as the basis of follow-up research, there was no emphasis on the differences of scenarios in the interviews and the summary.

Reasons and Frequency of Use/Non-use

Table 7. Reasons and frequency of use

Reason	Count
1. Less motion, no need to pick up the employee card or cell phone from pocket	31/72 (43.1%)
2. No longer need to bring the employee card	14/72 (19.4%)
3. Fast	13/72 (18.1%)
4. Hands occupied	11/72 (15.3%)
5. The screen is just facing the face	5/72 (6.9%)
6. Can only use face without employee card	3/72 (4.2%)
7. Feel like looking in a mirror	2/72 (2.8%)
8. Sense of Technology and Freshness	2/72 (2.8%)
9. Simple and smooth interaction	2/72 (2.8%)

(Please note that the denominator is the sample size of users, and each user may have multiple answers so that the total is not necessarily 100%)

Table 8. Reasons and frequency of non-use

Reason	Count
1. Slow	11/29 (37.9%)
2. Previous failure	10/29 (34.5%)
3. Be accustomed to employee card/phone	10/29 (34.5%)
4. Worried about mis-swipe	3/29 (10.3%)
5. Worried about the security of personal information	3/29 (10.3%)
6. The incomplete deployment makes people feel that it is still in the test period and the system is unstable	3/29 (10.3%)
7. It's considered not as reliable as employ card	2/29 (6.9%)
8. Dislike the notification of hi (office communication software within the company, integration of various office functions)	2/29 (6.9%)
9. There is a long queue behind	2/29 (6.9%)
10. The employ card is just in hand	2/29 (6.9%)
11. See others using employee cards	2/29 (6.9%)
12. The balance is insufficient, so turn to mobile payment (face and employee cards are the same payment system, while phone is another)	1/29 (3.4%)
13. The process of registration is troublesome	1/29 (3.4%)
14. Dislike taking pictures (users think face interaction is like taking pictures)	1/29 (3.4%)

(Please note that the denominator is the sample size of non-users, and each user may have multiple answers so that the total is not necessarily 100%)

Reasons Induction Based on TAM. We tried to further summarize these reasons within the same framework, but find that some of them cannot be included in the traditional framework of usability or experience evaluation of web pages or systems (such as Useful, Usable, Desirable). For example some environmental factors: the placement of equipment, the long queue behind etc., and some risk factors: mis-swipe, the security of personal information and so on. Therefore, based on the framework of usability and experience assessment, we used the technology acceptance model (TAM) [8] to summarize the above reasons (Table 9).

Table 9. Reasons and frequency of use based on TAM

Category	Reason	Count
Perceived usefulness	Less motion, no need to pick up the employee card or cell phone from pocket (31/58)	58/83(69.9%)
	No longer need to bring the employee card (14/58)	
	Fast (13/58)	
Perceived ease of use	Simple and smooth interaction (2/2)	2/83 (2.4%)
Perceived enjoyment	Sense of technology and freshness (2/4)	4/83 (4.8%)
	Feel like looking in a mirror (2/4)	
Use context	Hands occupied (11/19)	19/83 (22.9%)
	The screen is just facing the face (5/19)	
	Can only use face without employee card (3/19)	

(Please note that the denominator refers to the frequency mentioned, which is different from Tables 7 and 8.)

Through the frequency, we can see that perceived usefulness is the most important factor that mentioned by both users and non-users. In addition, users have a high degree of agreement on its convenience, which is reflected in 45/58 users mention about "less motion" and "no longer need to bring the employee card" (Table 10).

Use Context is the second important factor for the face users, which indicates that there are still some random factors in the user's choice of using face. We will explain further in the discussion section.

Perceived Risk and Perceived Ease of Use are the second most important factors for non-users, and the perceived risk has been discussed a lot in previous studies. The presentation of face and name would affect the user's risk perception, which can be optimized by design.

Previous failure accounts for the vast majority (10/11) of perceived ease of use, which means that users would abandon FR because of previous failure and change from users into non-users. From interviews, we know that users usually do not know the cause of errors when they occur, so we need to pay attention to effective guidance after errors occur.

Table 10. Reasons and frequency of non-use based on TAM

Category	Reason	Count
Perceived usefulness	Slow (11/24)	24/53 (45.3%)
	Be accustomed to employ card/phone (10/24)	
	Dislike the notification of HI (IM app within the company, integrated various office functions) (2/24)	
	Dislike taking pictures (users think face interaction is like taking pictures) (1/24)	
Perceived ease of use	Previous failure (10/11)	11/53 (20.8%)
	The process of registration is troublesome (1/11)	
Perceived risk	The incomplete deployment makes people feel that it is still in the test period and the system is unstable (3/11)	11/53 (20.8%)
	Worried about the security of personal information (3/11)	
	Worried about mis-swipe (3/11)	
	It's considered not as reliable as employ card (2/11)	
Use context	There is a long queue behind (2/7)	7/53 (13.2%)
	The employ card is just in hand (2/7)	
	See others using employee cards (2/7)	
	The balance is insufficient, so turn to mobile payment (face and employee cards are the same payment system, while phone is another) (1/7)	

(Please note that the denominator refers to the frequency mentioned, which is different from Tables 7 and 8.)

4.3   User Experience: The Advantage of FR Compared to Other Methods

Based on interviews and qualitative observation, we summarize the experience advantages of FR applications into two major aspects:

A More Natural Way of Interacting. For individual users, FR relies on their inherent features to authenticate the identity, which is more convenient and easier. They no longer need to bring an "extra item" with them, instead they are unimpeded by using FR. At the same time, FR needs a smaller range of motion. Users only need to make a short stay within the lens coverage, and occasionally make small angle adjustments, without "taking out employee card or mobile phone", "bending over to swipe card", or "holding the card or mobile phone at a certain height".

For group users, this natural way of recognition will not interrupt ongoing conversations. In a corridor, employees usually walk in groups. If swiping card is needed, one of them needs to temporarily leave the crowd to swipe the card, and the conversation will be temporarily interrupted. However, FR will open the gate for users silently without their notice, and thus it will not interrupt the conversation. This is similar to the observation of smart speaker by Cathy Pearl, the author of Designing Voice User Interfaces [16]. "(During the meal) If one queries a problem through a mobile phone, he will be separated from the group conservation. Of course, they maybe will suspend the conservation and wait for that person to continue. But if he asks a smart speaker to answer the question, everyone could hear the question and its answer, just as the speaker briefly joins the current conversation."

Emotional Interactive Experience. Compared with the original card swiping, FR is not just an instrument, but a richer feedback mode which allows the emotional communication between human and machine.

"I often have to work overtime. When I leave at night, when I pass the gate barrier using FR, it says 'You've been working very hard'. At this time, I respond to it in my heart, 'Yes indeed'." (Ms. Liu, 31–35, sales)

"Special greetings or decorations can be added to the festival", "warm greetings can be added to the rainy and snowy weather"…

The personalized expectation of employees in feedbacks to the FR gate barrier reflects their needs of emotional communication. If this could be achieved, the company's access control system would no longer be a cold security tool, but a security guard with humanistic care, who would protect and greet you; the payment system would become a smart and considerate salesperson. Such "special employees" allows employees to feel the cares from the company, strengthens the "family ties" between employees and enterprises, enhances the sense of group security, value and the feeling of presence. Also, it increases employees' sense of dependence and acceptance toward the organization. Finally, their sense of belonging will be enhanced [17].

5 Discussion

In the findings, we find some contradictions, such as the perception of security and time, which we dug further and presented in the discussion section. In addition, we add a point based on observations that users seem not to be aware of as a supplement to the reason.

5.1 Different Perceptions of Security

In the part of experience advantage, some users thought swiping their faces were safer because everyone's face is unique in terms of biometric authentication, and no one can substitute or impersonate the other to pass or pay. However, the employee card can be borrowed to others, and some users also mentioned that they "will swipe for a colleague who does not take the employee card."

Some users mentioned that security was one of the reasons why they didn't use FR. On the one hand, they worry about mis-swipes which may cause property loss. People can choose to display or hide their mobile phones and employee cards, but they cannot hide their "faces", and their facial image can be captured directly by camera without noticing them. The feeling of "passive payment" makes users uneasy. In terms of behaviour, some users keep a distance from others when they pay, or do not open the face payment function at all. On the other hand, they worry about the safety of their personal information. The exposure of users' personal information on the screen in the interactive feedback, including users' names, their real-time facial images, and the amount of consumption in the payment, will also make users feel that their privacy is violated. Researchers have pointed out that users value the way their data is used and stored, and are most reassured when the data is only stored in their devices [3]. During the interview, one user made it clear that "it is acceptable in the company because people around me are my colleagues; but if it is in public, my name and expending details are all displayed on the screen, and will be seen by others. Why would I let strangers see my personal information?" (Mr. Gao, 26–30, RD)

5.2   Different Perceptions of Time

In the process of mining the reason of why and why not using FR, we found an interesting conclusion: among the reasons for use and non-use, time is in the top three (Tables 7 and 8). Why time was the main reason for both using and not using FR? And why there were two completely different attitudes? This is a question worth discussing.

It showed that efficiency was an important consideration for users to make decisions. In addition to, we further explored the reasons:

First, the objective data indicated that it took no more than 2 s on average for access and payment. What were the user's real concerns when both of them took no more than 2 s?

When we asked the users who thought it took too long to swipe their face, "How much do you think swiping your face is slower than swiping the card?" Some users would answer "maybe swiping face wasn't that slow, just because I am used to cards", and some users will answer, "2–3 s slower." For such users, we would further ask, "Why would you care about these 2–3 s?" Then we have obtained some inner thoughts of the users, including: 1 worry about the unpredicted waiting time; 2 bad experiences before (waiting for a long time); 3 fears that more time will be wasted if FR does not work; 4 possible embarrassment caused by the pressure from people lining up behind. As a user said, "Because it is in the canteen, so many people are lining up behind and waiting for me, and on this occasion, I don't feel like wasting a single second." (Mr. Sun, 26–30, RD) Apart from embarrassment, the other three users' thoughts were related to their uncertainty about the new technology. But users who thought swiping face was quicker were less likely to hold such concerns.

Embarrassment has also been mentioned in other FR studies. Many unfamiliar bystanders around will cause embarrassment [18]. Users believe that unlocking the screen of mobile phone by using face in public places is more likely to cause embarrassment than other unlocking methods because "It looks like I'm taking selfies all day." [3]. Although the reasons for embarrassment are different, it may be due to the pressure of the queuers behind, maybe due to the pressure of the queuers behind, and maybe due to holding a cell phone at a specific angle in a public place and so on, embarrassment should be a consideration for extending FR to a wider range of public space applications.

5.3   Supplementary Reasons: Observations on the Route of Movement

Based on the 21.5 h observation, we found that whether users opted to swipe their face was related to the route of his movement approaching to the device, although users seemed not be aware of the subtle impact of this factor since it is not mentioned in the interview.

Accessibility. Take gate barrier access for instance: As the device is positioned at the rightmost gate for both entrance and exit, users who approached from the right would opt for FR whereas those coming from the left would choose to swipe their employee cards. The findings showed that users would not take a few extra steps just to use FR.

Discontinuity of Movement. In addition, a few users mentioned "sense of discontinuity" of FR when they asked to compare the experience between face and card. This made us think that the screen of FR usually had a certain angle with the user's approaching direction. Users need to turn their heads to swipe their faces, which would interrupt the progress to a certain extent.

This has been validated after we have fully measured the height and angle of the device, learned the technical parameters of the camera and the setting of the quality detection strategy of the product: Based on the current configuration of gate barrier, users have to turn their heads in order to achieve recognition (Fig. 3).

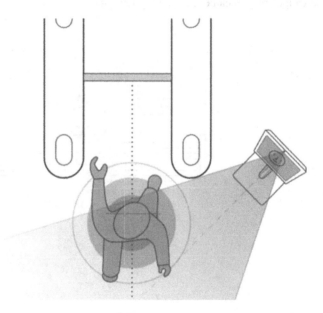

Fig. 3. Based on the current configuration (including device height, angle, technical parameters, etc.), users must turn their heads to interact with FR

There is no such "discontinuity" in the corridor, as the users approach from a distance. Their face can be captured by the camera and successfully recognized as long as they don't look down at their phones or wear hats. Passing through the gate entails a similarly smooth movement of the user walking in a straight path. As for card swiping, however, the user must digress from the original route and swipe on or off against the wall before returning to the gate. Therefore, users in the corridor preferred "FR" as their primary means of access. In comparing the corridor and gate barrier scenarios, users preferred the former. Such oblivious and uninterrupted movement made them relieved of the need to turn, pause and turn again.

6 Design Implication

Based on the findings of this paper, the experience optimization of each scenario can proceed from two major directions: reduce risk perception of non-use reasons and strengthening advantage experience.

6.1 Reducing Risk Perception Through Circulation and Interaction Design

To solve the problem of : "mis-swipe", the spatial layout can be optimized by circulation design [19], separate the crowd and distinguish the purpose of use. In the canteen, through proper planning of spatial functions, and designers can keep the devices apart from areas for picking chopsticks and napkins which have high traffic. A payment area can be set in the canteen so that users with no intention of paying will not be caught by the camera as readily (Fig. 4).

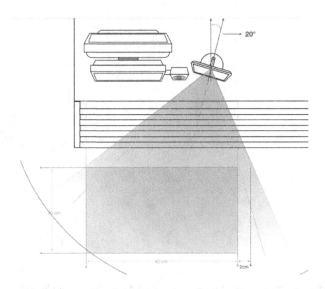

Fig. 4. A payment area can be set in the payment scenario so that users with no intention of paying will not be caught by the camera as readily.

In addition, by adding state feedback and confirmation step in the process of interaction, providing users with clearly causes of error and recovery methods, adding confirmation step with amount before payment, etc., can enhance the user's sense of control of the system and reduce perception of risk (Fig. 5).

· Confirm with motion   · Confirm with staring   · Confirm with click

Fig. 5. Add confirmation step to reduce perception of risk.

6.2   Make Interaction More Natural from the Perspective of Ergonomics

As mentioned in the findings, users have perceived some experiential advantages of using face in natural interaction. On this basis, we can add some optimization of ergonomics angle, such as placing equipment and setting technical parameters according to human comfortable interaction distance and turning angle, so as to reduce user's adaptation to equipment and make user's face interaction more labor-saving.

In addition, the angle of the screen and user's approaching direction can be reduced as much as possible, so that the sense of discontinuity caused by turning head or even the turning direction can be reduced (Fig. 6).

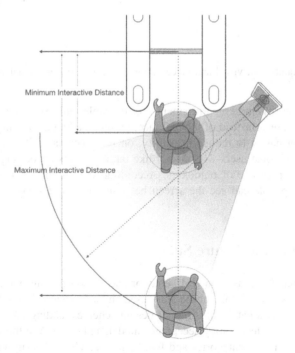

Fig. 6. Place equipment according to users' comfortable distance and angle, set technical parameters, so as to reduce users' action and discontinuity.

6.3   Enhancing Emotional Experience Through Visual and Voice Design

As mentioned in findings, compared with employ card, FR make it possible for affective interactions, and can play a role in many dimensions.

Increase the concern of enterprises. Based on festivals, weather, overtime work and so on, different visual and greetings can be designed to enhance the sense of belonging of employees.

Increase the interestingness of interaction. By changing the different feedback, adding AR expression to the user's face, the interestingness of face interaction can be enhanced, thus enhancing the perceived enjoyment (Fig. 7).

Fig. 7. Examples of visual and voice design to enhance the emotional experience

Reduce insecurity and embarrassment. For example, only showing the contour of the head on the screen instead of the real face, on the one hand, reducing the exposure of personal information to reduce insecurity, on the other hand, it also alleviates the embarrassment of some users who do not like taking photos or looking in the mirror, especially in the presence of onlookers. According to Kvarnbrink et al., users don't mind that other people can see the screen because the author's case only shows the user's sihouette.

7   Limitations and Future Study

This research mainly focuses on real behavior and reason mining, which provides us with a lot of inspiration for subsequent research and design, but still lacks some validation, such as validation of different design schemes, adding factor analysis and structural equation on technology acceptance model, and so on. And this study does not distinguish between two categories and five scenarios. The follow-up research can be the separated studies of specific scenarios.

8 Conclusion

In this study, we have conducted in-depth research on the user's behavior and inner thoughts of using FR, laying the foundation for our follow-up research on face interaction and HCI practice.

Through the research of users' behavior coding, we found that among the people who use FR, they have a high degree of acceptance, not only use, but also actively cooperate. The occupancy of hands and the location of employee cards affect people's choice of faces in some scenarios.

Based on interviews, the reasons mentioned by users are focused on "less motion", "no longer need to bring the employee cards", "fast" and "hands occupied". The reasons not used are focused on "slow", "previous failures" and "be accustomed to employ card/phone". In addition, the immediate environment (use context) can also affect users' choices even though sometimes they are not aware of it. Risk are important factors of non-use besides usefulness and ease of use. At the same time, users affirmed the advantages of face in natural and emotional interaction.

Follow-up research and practice can be conducted focusing on reducing users' perception of risk and enhancing the advantages of experience.

References

1. Trewin, S., Swart, C., Koved, L., Martino, J., Singh, K., Ben-David, S.: Biometric authentication on a mobile device: a study of user effort, error and task disruption. In: Proceedings of the 28th Annual Computer Security Applications Conference, pp. 159–168. ACM (2012)
2. Bhagavatula, R., Ur, B., Iacovino, K., Kywe, S.M., Cranor, L.F., Savvides, M.: Biometric authentication on iPhone and Android: usability, perceptions, and influences on adoption. In: USEC 2015, 8 February 2015, San Diego, CA, Proceedings, pp. 1–10 (2015)
3. De Luca, A., Hang, A., Von Zezschwitz, E., Hussmann, H.: I feel like I'm taking selfies all day!: towards understanding biometric authentication on smartphones. In: Proceedings of the 33rd Annual ACM Conference on Human Factors in Computing Systems, pp. 1411–1414. ACM (2015)
4. Kvarnbrink, P., Fahlquist, K., Mejtoft, T.: Biometric interaction: a case study of visual feedback and privacy issues in new face recognition solutions. In: CHI 2013 Extended Abstracts on Human Factors in Computing Systems, pp. 2367–2370. ACM (2013)
5. Maple, C., Norrington, P.: The usability and practicality of biometric authentication in the workplace. In: The First International Conference on Availability, Reliability and Security, ARES 2006, p. 7. IEEE (2006)
6. Wayman, J., Jain, A., Maltoni, D., Maio, D.: An introduction to biometric authentication systems. In: Wayman, J., Jain, A., Maltoni, D., Maio, D. (eds.) Biometric Systems. Springer, London (2005). https://doi.org/10.1007/1-84628-064-8_1.pdf
7. Qingjie, Z., Hanshi, G., Information, S.O.: An empirical study on users behavioral intention of face identification mobile payment. In: The Theory and Practice of Finance and Economics (2018)
8. Davis, F.D.: Perceived usefulness, perceived ease of use, and user acceptance of information technology. MIS Q. 13(3), 319–340 (1989)

9. Heijden, H.V.D., Ogertschnig, M.: Effects of context relevance and perceived risk on user acceptance of mobile information services. In: ECIS 2005 Proceedings, p. 7 (2005)
10. Gan, C.: The impact of use context on mobile payment user adoption: an empirical study in China. In: WHICEB, p. 31 (2016)
11. Serenko, A.: A model of user adoption of interface agents for email notification. Interact. Comput. **20**(4–5), 461–472 (2008)
12. Mun, Y.Y., Hwang, Y.: Predicting the use of web-based information systems: self-efficacy, enjoyment, learning goal orientation, and the technology acceptance model. Int. J. Hum. Comput. Stud. **59**(4), 431–449 (2003)
13. Lee, M.K.O., Cheung, C.M.K., Chen, Z.: Acceptance of Internet-based learning medium: the role of extrinsic and intrinsic motivation. Inf. Manag. **42**(8), 1095–1104 (2005)
14. Djamasbi, S., Strong, D.M., Dishaw, M.: Affect and acceptance: examining the effects of positive mood on the technology acceptance model. Decis. Support Syst. **48**(2), 383–394 (2010)
15. Lee, M.C.: Factors influencing the adoption of internet banking: an integration of TAM and TPB with perceived risk and perceived benefit. Electron. Commer. Res. Appl. **8**(3), 130–141 (2009)
16. Pearl, C.: Designing Voice User Interfaces: Principles of Conversational Experiences (2016)
17. Zheng, Z., Yongtai, L.: Seven influencing factors on sense of belong of staff. Reg. Econ. Rev. **8**, 48–49 (2007)
18. Stolorow, R.D.: The shame family: an outline of the phenomenology of patterns of emotional experience that have shame at their core. Int. J. Psychoanal. Self Psychol. **5**(3), 367–368 (2010)
19. Ajzen, I., Fishbein, M.: Attitude-behavior relations: a theoretical analysis and review of empirical research. Psychol. Bull. **84**(5), 888–918 (1977)

Usability of University Recruitment Web Pages from International Doctoral Students' Perspectives

Li-Min Huang$^{(\boxtimes)}$ and Dania Bilal

University of Tennessee, Knoxville, TN 37996, USA
lhuang23@vols.utk.edu, dania@utk.edu

Abstract. This study examined a group of international doctoral students' interactions with the recruitment web pages at the University of Tennessee, Knoxville (UTK). It employed eye-tracking and exit interviews. Students performed six assigned search tasks, and their task outcomes were measured based on success, dwell time, and time-based efficiency. Time to first eye fixation and fixation counts were measured using heatmaps and Area of Interests (AOIs), respectively. The findings showed that while the students were able to use the websites and find answers to most of the search tasks, they faced challenges with the usability of these websites. The findings have implications for designing recruitment web pages that are user-centered and supportive of international doctoral students' information needs and interaction behaviors.

Keywords: International doctoral students · Website usability · Eye-tracking

1 Introduction

The top principle of human-centered design from a Cognitive Load Theoretical perspective is that the design will never take users even a millisecond to think of "how to use" [1]. One of the persistent challenges in interface design is how to accommodate diversity in cultures, human abilities, background, and personalities, among other factors [2]. In fact, the current trend in globalization calls for universal design of interfaces and tools to meet the needs of all users. Additionally, globalization has become one of the strategic goals of academic institutions in the US [3].

The primary pathway for attracting international diverse students to US institutions of higher education is through the recruitment (admissions) websites [4]. Nonetheless, studies have revealed that these websites require substantial improvements for accommodating international students' information seeking and needs [5]. While previous studies have examined international graduate students' information behavior and needs (see for example, [6, 7, 8]), scarce research has addressed international doctoral students' interactions with university recruitment web pages. The present study should fill this gap.

The purposes of this study are to: (1) examine international doctoral students' interactions with university recruitment websites, and (2) explore their perceptions of the usability of the websites based on their own experiences.

© Springer Nature Switzerland AG 2019
A. Marcus and W. Wang (Eds.): HCII 2019, LNCS 11586, pp. 505–521, 2019.
https://doi.org/10.1007/978-3-030-23535-2_37

Findings from this study should provide a basis for designing user-centered university recruitment websites that seek to attract and meet the needs of international doctoral students. The fact that these students may share similar information needs and cultural background, among others, with other international students, the findings could also serve as benchmarks for providing highly usable websites that are supportive of diverse international graduate students.

2 Related Literature

2.1 University Website Evaluation Through Usability

Compared with recruiting domestic students in the US, the ways to attract international students tend to be more limited to word-of-mouth and information on university programs' websites [4]. From the marketing perspective, the usability of recruitment websites of an organization can impact the user's perception of that organization [9]. Researchers have investigated the usability of university websites using various approaches. One of these is administering a standard evaluation scale, such as the Website Analysis and MeasureMent Inventory (WAMMI). This scale consists of five main factors: Attractiveness, controllability, efficiency, helpfulness, and learnability. Mentes and Turan [10], for example, applied this scale in a study that examined 339 students' perceptions of the Namik Kemal University website in Turkey. They found that all factors, except for controllability, are positively associated with the students' perceptions of the usability of the website.

Rahman and Ahmed [11] adapted 34 items from four different usability scales (Questionnaire for User Interface Satisfaction, JISC checklist for academic websites, QUIS, and WAMMI) to evaluate the usability of the University of Dhaka's website in Bangladesh. They categorized five factors to examine usability: (1) navigation, searching and interface attractiveness, (2) interactivity and functionality, (3) accuracy, currency and authority of information, (4) accessibility, understandability, learnability, and operability, and (5) efficiency and reliability. Students were moderately satisfied with the usability of the website (average rating = 4/7).

Hasan [12] gathered students' perceptions of the usability of nine different university websites in Jordan using five usability factors: (1) navigation, (2) architecture, (3) easy of use and communication, (4) visual design, and (5) content. The top three important factors to the students were content, navigation, and ease of use. Poor visual design (e.g., colors and fonts) and inconsistency in visuals across web pages within a specific website surfaced as problems.

Tuzun, Akinci, Kurtoglu, Atal, and Pala [13] investigated ten students' information seeking of the Hacettepe University Registrar's Office web page in Turkey using eye tracking and retrospective think aloud protocol. Students performed ten assigned search tasks. Eye-tracking data analysis revealed that students frequently scrolled down and up the main page of the website and scanned looking for information on the search tasks. Students' attention was distracted by the blank area of the page. Interview data revealed that the webpage small font size, labeling of menu items, and disorganization of contents (e.g., relevant links spread across different parts of a page) were problematic.

One recent study [5] evaluated 42 US doctoral programs websites in special education from prospective students' (master's) point of view using a survey instrument with eight components (Navigation, program description, an application element, homepage links, doctoral page elements, homepage organization, faculty information, and overall experiences). The researchers collected data in 2006, 2008, 2011 and 2014. Forty-two students evaluated two websites each time. Key findings revealed that over the 8-year study period (i.e., 2006–2014), there was no significant improvement in website usability. Students rated most questions as "somewhat agree."

The reviewed studies revealed usability issues in university websites. In these studies, students were native speakers of the languages of the websites. It can be assumed that non-native speakers (e.g., international students) are likely to face more or different usability issues when they interact with websites that are not written in their native languages. For example, Huang and Bilal [14] interviewed 33 international doctoral students and explored their information needs, information seeking behaviors, feelings, and overall experiences during the process of applying for doctoral study in the US. They found that students had two primary information needs (where to apply and how to apply) and used two categories of resources to meet those needs, Experiential Resources (EXR) (e.g., peers, social networks, and social media), and Authorized Resources (AUR) (unofficial and official websites). The many issues and challenges students faced in using university recruitment websites resulted in negative feelings about the overall application process. Students made several suggestions for enhancing the usability of the websites.

In [14], Huang and Bilal employed individual interviews. Given that students were asked to recall their experiences with the application process from memory, and due to the nature of interviews that rely on subjective experiences, it is possible that the students' accounts are prone to inaccuracies. As a follow-up, we conducted a case study (reported in this paper) using empirical observations in conjunction with exit interviews and examined international doctoral students interactions with the University of Tennessee recruitment websites and associated web pages.

3   Research Questions

The following research questions guided this study:

RQ 1: How do international doctoral students interact with the University of Tennessee recruitment websites and associated web pages?

RQ2: How do international doctoral students evaluate the usability of the University of Tennessee recruitment websites and associated web pages based on their own experiences?

4 Research Method

4.1 Mixed Method

This study is exploratory in nature. We employed both quantitative and qualitative methods for data elicitation. For the quantitative method, we used eye tracking in Tobii X2-60 Eye Tracker to record the students' (hereafter, participants) eye movements, and Tobii Studio to capture their interaction behaviors with recruitment websites/pages. For the qualitative method, we utilized exit interviews to gather insights about the students' experiences with the websites/pages. Eye tracking generates quantitative data allowing for identifying Areas of Interests (AOIs) on a web page, eye movements, and eye fixations, among other factors [15, 16]. Qualitative data using interviews provide understanding of data generated from the quantitative method, while allowing for exploring the students' experiences with and assessment of the usability of websites/pages.

4.2 Population and Sample

In phase one of this study [14], we recruited 33 international doctoral students from the University of Tennessee, Knoxville (UTK), and accounting for 5% of the total enrollment of doctoral international students [17]. In the present study (phase two), we recruited five international doctoral students in the College of Communication and Information (CCI) at UTK, as of the writing of this paper. Given that around 80% of usability issues will be detected by the first five participants in a usability study [18], we believe that the sample size is somewhat adequate for reporting the preliminary findings of this study.

4.3 Instruments

Questionnaire. We developed both a brief questionnaire to gather participants' demographic and background information (e.g., age, gender, country of origin, department, and years in the doctoral program), and an interview instrument based on the WAI Site Usability Testing Questions [19] for user-centered design.

Search Tasks. We assigned the participants six search tasks (Table 1) and provided a scenario to contextualize the tasks. These tasks varied in terms of requirements. A search task may be simple and fact-finding in that it requires finding a target answer (e.g., T-1), while another task may be somewhat complex in that it requires finding relevant information for more than one facet or component (e.g., T-4).

Scenario. A friend from your home country is interested in applying to your doctoral program. Your friend asked for specific information about the program, which is reflected in the six search tasks. Find the information that your friend has requested. All search tasks were contextualized in this scenario.

Table 1. Search tasks.

Task	Description
1	Find a UTK web page you think can best provide background information about UTK for your friend. When you find the page, please highlight its URL. If you cannot find such a web page, it's fine, click on "Exit" of the browser to go to the next search task
2	Your friend's research interest is similar to yours. Find the following information and highlight the information on the web page: a. The names of two faculty members that match your friend's research interest in your program b. Look for the citations of two of the most current publications of each faculty of these two faculty members
3	Your friend wants to know about possible careers after graduating from your program. Find and highlight the career information on your program's website
4	Use the UTK website to help your friend find the following information Highlight the answers you find a. The application deadline of the UTK Graduate School b. All the application requirements of UTK admissions office c. The link to the application
5	Use your program's website to help your friend find the following information Highlight the answers you find a. The application deadline b. All application requirements of your program c. The link to your program's application
6	Your friend asks you an application question that you are not able to answer. Please find a person on your program website who can help answer the question Highlight the name and contact information of that person

4.4   Search Task Outcome Measures

Search task outcomes were measured in terms of (a) success, (b) dwell time, and (c) time-based efficiency.

(a) Success. We used a three-point success scale (1 = success, 0.5 = partial success, and 0 = no success). Success means that a participant found the correct answer or relevant information for a search task. Partial success means that a participant found the correct answer or relevant information for some parts of a search task. No success indicates that a participant did not find any information on a search task, or that the information found was incorrect. For tasks with sub-tasks (T-2, T-4, T-5), success was assigned a"1" (success = 1), which we divided equally across the subtasks. For example, T4-a (success = 0.33), T4-b (success = 0.33), and T4-c (success = 0.33).

(b) Dwell Time. We measured the viewing time of a web page in seconds, from the time a page is loaded after being clicked by a participant to the time the participant leaves the page by closing the browser.

(c) Time-Based Efficiency. We measured time-based efficiency by accounting for both success and dwell time on all six search tasks across all five participants. The measure uses the following equation [20].

$$\frac{\sum_{j=1}^{R} \sum_{i=1}^{N} \frac{t_{ij}}{n_{ij}}}{NR} \, (\text{Sec.}/\text{task})$$

Where:

N = total number of tasks (6)
R = number of participants (5)
n_{ij} = success rate on task i by participant j
t_{ij} = time spent by participant j to complete task i

4.5 Setting and Procedures

The data collection took place in the College of Communication and Information (CCI) User eXperience Laboratory. The Lab is equipped with Tobii Eye-Tracker X2-60 and Tobii Studio. We recruited five participants through personal networks (doctoral students in CCI) to participate in this study (as of the writing of this paper). Following the study approval by UTK Institutional Review Board (IRB), we invited the five participants to take part in this study. We scheduled the participants' visits to the Lab. Prior to the visits, we integrated the six assigned search tasks and respective scenario into Tobii Studio along with instructions. The search tasks appeared on the computer screen in sequence.

During each participant's visit, we introduced the purposes of the study, provided an introduction to the Lab and its equipment, and asked the participant to read and sign an informed consent form. Next, the participant was seated in front of the desktop that has the Tobii Eye-Tracker and Studio. The participant's eyes were calibrated by the Eye-Tracker. Each participant was assigned an ID under which we saved all eye tracking and interaction activities as well as the recorded exit interview.

Each participant's experimental session was recorded in the Eye Tracker and Studio, saved, and exported for analysis. Upon completing the six search tasks, the participant was interviewed to elicit data about his/her experiences in using the recruitment websites/pages. The interview was audio-recorded using a digital recorder. Recorded interviews were transcribed, coded, and analyzed using NVivo 12 software.

4.6 Data Analysis

We employed descriptive statistics (e.g., Mean value) to analyze the data gathered from the demographic questionnaire. We coded the interview data using open coding to generate themes [21]. As to the recorded interaction activities, we replayed each participant's recorded task session and examined the texts and URLs the participant highlighted as the answer or relevant information, and judged task success accordingly (see Sect. 4.4). Additionally, we calculated each participant's dwell time on each search task. As to recorded eye-tracking data, we used heatmaps and AOIs generated by Tobii Studio. Heatmaps provide visualizations that show the general distribution of a participant's gaze points and the elements on a page that receives more attention than others. AOIs are applied to investigate where the participants looked first (time to the first fixation), or elements on a page that first attract a participant' attention. We also generated fixation counts, that is, the number of times a participant looked in an AOI on a page. Typically, an area that receives higher fixation count than other areas on a page could indicate difficulty in locating information [22].

5   Results

We present the results in the context of the two research questions that guided this study: (1) How do international doctoral students interact with the University of Tennessee recruitment websites/pages?, and (2) How do international doctoral students evaluate the usability of the University of Tennessee recruitment websites/pages based on their own experiences? We present the participants' demographic and background information first, followed by the results that answered the research questions.

5.1   Participants' Demographics

Five international doctoral students participated in this study, one male and four females, aged 28 to 43 years. Three participants are from Asia and two are from Europe.

5.2   Participants' Interactions with Recruitment Websites

Participants performed six assigned search tasks. Their task outcomes were measured based on success, dwell time, and time-based efficiency. Their interactions with recruitment websites/ pages were analyzed using heatmaps and AOIs.

Success on Search Tasks. Each participant completed six search tasks, totaling 30 across the five participants. The average success rate on tasks one to six (T-1 to T-6) was 0.7, 1.0, 0.6, 1.0, 1.0, and 1.0, respectively; and the grand average of the participants' success across the six tasks is 0.88 (Table 2).

Dwell Time. Participants took the shortest time viewing pages for T-1 and the longest time viewing pages for T-5 (93.60 s versus 216.20 s respectively). The average dwell time on T-1 to T-6 across the five participants is 140.73 s (Table 2).

Time-Based Efficiency. As shown in Table 2, the average time-based efficiency per task ranged from 94.8 s (T-6) to 216.2 s (T-5). The grand average of time-based efficiency across the six search tasks the five participants performed is 159.32 s (Table 2).

Table 2. Task success, dwell time, and time-based efficiency

Task	Success	Dwell time (s)	Time-based efficiency (s)
1	0.70	93.60	133.71
2	1.00	208.20	208.20
3	0.60	122.00	203.33
4	1.00	109.60	109.60
5	1.00	216.20	216.20
6	1.00	94.80	94.80
Grand average	0.88	140.73	159.32

Eye-Tracking Data. We analyzed eye movement and fixations on three web pages that all five participants used in performing the six search tasks: (1) UTK Graduate School Admissions (https://gradschool.utk.edu/admissions/), (2) College of Communication and Information (CCI) homepage (https://www.cci.utk.edu/), and (3) CCI PhD Admissions page (https://www.cci.utk.edu/phdadmissions).

UTK Graduate School Admissions. Participants used this page to complete T-1 and T-4. Figure 1 shows the two sections (in yellow and red) that received the participants' most attention. The first section is the middle column of the page titled, *Office of Graduate Admissions.* On this page, the top paragraph in this column has a description of the goal of the *Office of Graduate Admissions* and provides links to a "wide range of graduate degree offerings, how and when to apply, and what to expect upon admission", among others. The second section is the right side menu with links to *the Office of Graduate Admissions, Applying to Graduate School, Application Status, Application Deadlines, Graduate Programs*, and *After Admission*. Participants also gazed at the left side menu, but paid more attention to information in the middle column of the page and the left right menu items.

We generated AOIs around eight areas that received eye fixation on the *UTK Graduate School Admissions* page. As seen in Fig. 2, these areas are: the search bar (A), left side menu (B), cover image (C), first paragraph of text in the middle column (D), other paragraphs on the page (E), short description referring to international students (F), right side menu (G), and contact information (H).

Figure 3 shows that the participants' mean time to first fixation on the page is longest on (F) (Mean time = 84.88 s), followed by (A) (Mean time = 70.71 s), and (E) (Mean time = 11.76 s), while it is shortest on H, D, C, B, and E, respectively. As to eye fixation count, participants fixated most on area (G) (Mean count = 41.14 times), followed by (D) (Mean count = 39 times), and (B) (Mean count = 31.57 times), while they fixated the least on areas E, C, H, A, and F, respectively (Fig. 3).

CCI Homepage. Participants viewed the CCI homepage as a starting point for T-2, T-3, T-5, and T-6. They seemed to browse the whole page to find information on these tasks (Fig. 4). Three parts received participants' highest attention (in red) on this page: (1) the middle part of left side menu, which includes the labeled links: *Graduate, Schools, People, Research*, and *Alumni & Friends*; (2) the left and right bottom part of the image (located on the left side of the middle column), and (3) the top part of the main content that includes two news headlines. We generated AOIs (Fig. 5) around eight parts of the page that received eye fixation. These are: the search bar (A), left side menu (B), blank area on the left side of the page (C), cover image at the top page (D), cover image caption (E), main content-*News* (F), *Upcoming Events* (G), and *More News* (H).

Figure 6 shows that the participants' mean time to first fixation on the page is longest on G (Mean time = 16.15 s), while it is shortest on areas D, H, B, C, A, F, and E, respectively. As to eye fixation count, participants fixated most on area (F) (Mean count = 84.4 times), followed by (G) (Mean count = 36 times), (B) (Mean count = 34 times), and D (Mean count = 26.8 times); while they fixated the least on areas C, E, H, and A, respectively.

CCI PhD Admissions Web Page. Participants used this page to find the answers for search task (T-5) (i.e., application requirements, application deadline, and application link). Figure 7 shows that participants spent the longest time from first fixation on three parts of the page (in red and yellow): *Application link, Application deadline,* and *Financial Aid.* We generated AOIs (Fig. 8) around eight areas that received eye fixations on the page: the search bar (A), left side menu (B), and five parts of the main content of the page, including the blank area on the left side of the page (C), requirements (D), application link (E), requirements in another part of the page (F), deadline (G) and financial aid and other information (H).

Figure 9 illustrates that participants mean time to first fixation on the page is longest on area (C) (Mean time = 45.44 s), followed by (B) (Mean time = 36.24 s), (G) (Mean time = 25.35 s), and (H) (Mean time = 23.96 s), while it is shortest on areas F, E, and D, respectively. As to eye fixation count, participants fixated most on area (G) (Mean count = 43.75 times), followed by (D) (Mean count = 30.25 times), (E) (Mean count = 26.26 times), (F) (Mean count = 26.25 times), and (H) (Mean count = 25.25 times). It is noteworthy that area (A) or the search bar received zero count, indicating that participants browsed and did not perform any searches in the three pages to find information on search task five (T-5).

Fig. 1. Heatmap of the UTK Graduate School Admission web page (Color figure online)

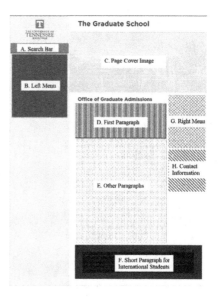

Fig. 2. AOIs on the UTK Graduate School Admission web page

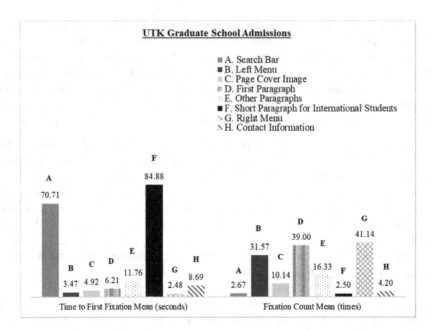

Fig. 3. AOIs (Time to First Fixation Mean and Fixation Count Mean) on the UTK Graduate School Admissions web page

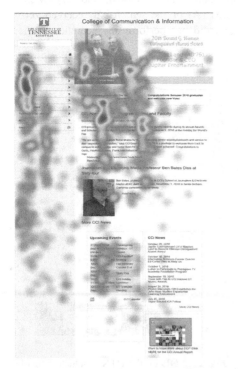

Fig. 4. Heatmap of the CCI Homepage (Color figure online)

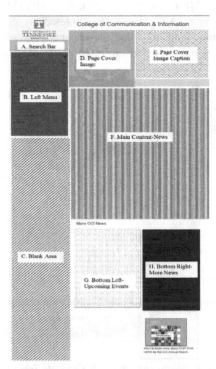

Fig. 5. AOIs on the CCI Homepage

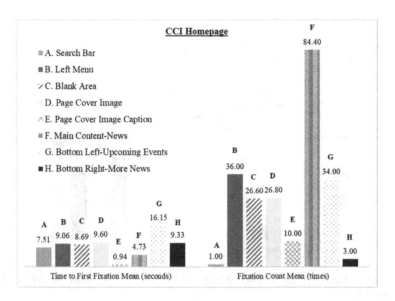

Fig. 6. AOIs (Time to First Fixation Mean and Fixation Count Mean) on the CCI Homepage

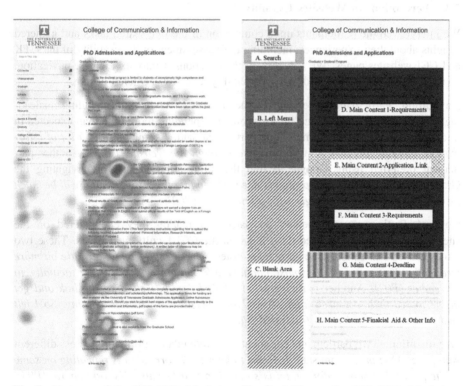

Fig. 7. Heatmap of the CCI PhD Admission web page (Color figure online)

Fig. 8. AOIs on the CCI PhD Admission web page

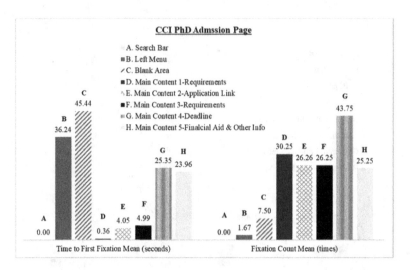

Fig. 9. AOIs (Time to First Fixation Mean and Fixation Count Mean) on the CCI PhD Admission web page

5.3 Perceptions of Websites Usability

We interviewed the participants upon completion of the five search tasks and gathered insights about their experiences, including their assessment of the usability of the UTK and CCI websites/pages. We categorized their responses into six themes: navigation, content, organization, visual design, learnability, and user-centered design.

Navigation. Participants experienced issues related to navigation, including misleading headings, difficulty locating information, and spending more time than expected in finding information. For example, one participant said: *I know there is a lot of information, but I'm not sure how to navigate through the website. (P05).* Another participant preferred using Google to find the information instead of navigating the Graduate School's website: *I probably need 30 s to find the answer, but it will be much faster by just searching Google with a few words (P02).*

Content. Participants commented on dated information they encountered on the sites/pages and two mentioned dead links on the CCI faculty web pages. These two issues caused frustration. One participant noted: *They need to update a little bit more frequently. You can see the most updated information was last year actually in November (P02).* Another participant indicated: *I couldn't click on the link and get inside to see their research interests and stuff because it was not working. So I felt really uncertain and kind of frustrated (P01).*

Organization. Two participants commented on redundant information across different web pages. One participant said: *It seems to be some information is repeating on some of the pages, but some information is so hard to find because it's too general (P03).* The other participant suggested change to the organization of websites across units (e.g., College, Schools/Departments, and the Graduate School): *There are 20 bars. It's* *just too much. I'll say narrow it down or summarize it better, like to Apply, Go [Click] here. (P05).*

Visual Design. Participants suggested improving the visual design of UTK and CCI websites/pages, including augmenting pictures and using different colors to highlight important or key information. One participant commented: *Probably they can highlight some information, use highlight in different color to make people know this is important (P02)*. Another participant suggested augmenting the CCI page with photos of students and the College and improving the quality of posted photos: *...Like some alumni who got achievement recently, we have a photo on the home page of our program. I think this is a good promotion information (P05)*.

Learnability. Two participants found the interfaces of the websites and pages hard to learn. One participant mentioned: *I wouldn't be able to figure out it all on my own where to go and where to find it starting from let's say the calendar, I needed to email someone (P03)*. The other participant noted that at the time of applying to the doctoral program, he/she *needed physical human assistance to get the information from the website...The information is out there, just I couldn't get to it (P05)*.

User-Centered Design. All participants perceived no differences between international students and native speakers in terms of how the websites/pages are designed, organized, and written. They indicated that if the university or academic programs aim to attract international applicants, their websites should provide a specific section or even a page designed for international students. For example, one participant mentioned: *Probably they want to have a separate button just for international applicants where there'll be all information just for international applicants (P03)*. Another participant commented on feeling welcomed as an international student: *I think probably you can take a photo of the international students and put it on the home page to let applicants from other countries to know that they are not alone ... and [that] you are welcome here (P02)*.

6 Discussion

6.1 Search Task Outcomes

Success. Participants completed four of the six search tasks successfully (success rate = 66%). The two tasks that participants did not complete successfully are T-1 and T-3. For T-1, participants had to find a page that best provide background information about UTK. One participant, for example, chose the CCI PhD Admission page while the other participant viewed the *UTK International Student and Scholar Services*. Although the latter is specifically designed for international students, it provides information about what to do after being admitted to UTK.

As to T-3, participants had to find possible career development information after graduating from UTK. The two participants who did not complete this task successfully indicated that such information is not available on the site. Eye-tracking data shows that these two participants browsed the CCI page and, although they fixated their eyes on the *CCI Doctoral Students & Alumni* link, they did not click on it. Instead, one participant clicked on links at bottom of the left side menu including, *Diversity & Communication in the Workplace*, and the other participant visited the *CCI Doctoral Students & Alumni* page that has a link to the *PhD Alumni Spotlights* but did not click on it. It could be that the labeling of this link was not meaningful to that participant. It is noteworthy that while the *PhD Alumni Spotlights* provides information about featured alumni and their careers, the CCI website does not have a separate category or page on careers. In a previous study [14], we found that international doctoral students were interested in finding information on future careers on the university and program websites that they visited. The study by [23] echoes these findings. Accordingly, we suggest that doctoral program recruitment websites not only include the achievements of featured alumni, but also provide a page dedicated to careers.

Dwell Time and Time-Based Efficiency. As was anticipated, participants spent the shortest time viewing pages on T-1, which is fact-based, and longest time on T-5. The latter task is somewhat complex as it has three requirements or facets (a, b, and c) combining findings target answers and relevant information. As was found in a previous study, the more complex a search task is in terms of its requirements or facets, the longer it takes to complete [18].

By combining dwell time and success, participants' time-based efficiency across the six search tasks is surprising (Mean = 159.32 s or nearly 2.5 min). This could be due to failure on two of the six search tasks. Though inconclusive, analysis of additional data from additional participants (in progress) should provide better understanding of participants' time-based efficiency.

Eye Fixation. The findings show that the dark background in both the UTK *Graduate School Admissions* page received the longest first fixation time. Long fixation time is negatively associated with search efficiency [22, 24]. To be noted, the text with the dark blue background in this page is specifically intended for international applicants and contains a link to *Admissions for International Students* page. Surprisingly, no participant clicked on that link. The location of this text toward the bottom of the page could have minimized the participants' perception of its importance. Additionally, the visual design may not have supported the participants' cognitive and physical affordances [25]. Accordingly, we suggest that website designers avoid placing key information on dark backgrounds or in locations that are not prominent on a web page.

6.2   Usability Evaluation

Participants thought that while they were able to use the UTK Graduate Admissions and CCI recruitment web pages, the faced issues pertaining to the content, organization, visual design, and learnability. Lack of user-centered design exacerbated these problems. This finding aligns with Sundeen et al. [5] whose study revealed that students need to find key information easily on websites and without resorting to others (e.g., staff) for assistance. As the usability of recruitment websites and pages influence prospective students' perceptions of a university [9], they should be designed from the students' perspectives to support their information needs and interaction behaviors.

6.3 Implications

The findings from this study are preliminary. Nevertheless, they have implications for improving the usability of the UTK Graduate School Admissions and College of Communication and Information websites/pages to support international doctoral students' information needs and interaction behaviors.

6.4 Limitations

One of the main limitations of this study resides in the small sample size. However, as was mentioned earlier, this study reports the preliminary findings based on five international doctoral students. Although the sample is small, the findings provide a strong basis for recruiting additional participants to further evaluate the usability of the UTK recruitment websites and pages.

Another limitation resides in the nature of interviews used in this study. Interviews are based on participants' self-reporting and, therefore, tend to be prone to inaccuracies.

7 Conclusion

The case study reported in this paper was conducted at the University of Tennessee, Knoxville campus. It explored international doctoral students' interactions with the recruitment websites/pages of the Graduate School Admissions and College of Communication and Information using eye tracking. It employed exit interviews and gathered data from participants about their experiences with these websites and pages. Participants performed six assigned search tasks. Their eye movements and fixations were calculated to detect AOIs on these pages. Combining eye-tracking with exit interviews provided understanding of the participants' interaction behaviors and unveiled usability issues in these websites/pages from their perspectives. Interestingly, participants seemed to prefer browsing through the websites/pages to searching, especially on the three web pages for which we calculated fixation times and counts. Although inconclusive, this could be due to the nature of the search tasks they performed. Future studies should elicit participants' reasons for browsing instead of searching. Although the findings are based on five participants, they convey the need for additional research in this area of study. The six search tasks the participants performed in this study are based on international doctoral students' information needs expressed in a previous study [14]. These tasks should be effective for use in future work.

References

1. Oviatt, S.: Human-centered design meets cognitive load theory: designing interfaces that help people think. In: Proceedings of the 14th ACM International Conference on Multimedia, pp. 871–880. ACM, New York (2006)
2. Shneiderman, B., Plaisant, C., Cohen, M., Jacobs, S.: Designing the User Interface: Strategies for Effective Human–Computer Interaction, 5th edn. Prentice Hall, Boston (2010)

3. Grapin, S.L., Lee, E.T., Jaafar, D.: A multilevel framework for recruiting and supporting graduate students from culturally diverse backgrounds in school psychology programs. School Psychol. Int. **36**(4), 339–357 (2015)
4. Westrick, S.C., Kamal, K.M., Moczygemba, L.R., Breland, M.L., Heaton, P.C.: Characteristics of social and administrative sciences graduate programs and strategies for student recruitment and future faculty development in the United States. Res. Soc. Adm. Pharm. **9** (1), 101–107 (2013)
5. Sundeen, T., Garland, K.V., Wienke, W.: Perceptions of special education doctoral websites: a multiyear investigation of website usability and navigability. J. Res. Technol. Educ. **47**(4), 273–293 (2015)
6. Chen, L.H.: East-Asian students' choice of Canadian graduate schools. Int. J. Educ. Adv. **7** (4), 271–306 (2007)
7. Chung, E., Yoon, J.: International students' information needs and seeking behaviours throughout the settlement stages. Libri **67**(2), 119–128 (2017)
8. Yoon, J., Kim, S.: Internet use by international graduate students in the USA seeking health information. Aslib J. Inf. Manag. **66**(2), 117–133 (2014)
9. Braddy, P.W., Meade, A.W., Kroustalis, C.M.: Online recruiting: the effects of organizational familiarity, website usability, and website attractiveness on viewers' impressions of organizations. Comput. Hum. Behav. **24**(6), 2992–3001 (2008)
10. Mentes, S.A., Turan, A.H.: Assessing the usability of university websites: an empirical study on Namik Kemal University. Turk. Online J. Educ. Technol. TOJET **11**(3), 61–69 (2012)
11. Rahman, M.S., Ahmed, S.Z.: Exploring the factors influencing the usability of academic websites: a case study in a university setting. Bus. Inf. Rev. **30**(1), 40–47 (2013)
12. Hasan, L.: Evaluating the usability of educational websites based on students' preferences of design characteristics. Int. Arab J. e-Technol. **3**(3), 179–193 (2014)
13. Tuzun, H., Akinci, A., Kurtoglu, M., Atal, D., Pala, F.K.: A study on the usability of a university registrar's office website through the methods of authentic tasks and eye-tracking. Turk. Online J. Educ. Technol. TOJET **12**(2), 26–38 (2013)
14. Huang, L.M., Bilal, D.: Speaking out: international doctoral students' information needs, seeking behaviors, feelings, and experience during the process of applying for graduate study in the US. Libri Int. J. Libr. Inf. Stud. (2019). (in press)
15. Lazar, J., Feng, J.H., Hochheiser, H.: Research Methods in Human–Computer Interaction. Morgan Kaufmann, Burlington (2017)
16. Bilal, D., Gwizdka, J.: Children's eye-fixations on Google search results. In: Proceedings of the 79th ASIS&T Annual Meeting: Creating Knowledge, Enhancing Lives through Information and Technology, pp. 89–94. Wiley, Hoboken (2016)
17. UTK FactBook: Headcount Enrollment by College, Level, Gender, and Race/Ethnicity Fall 2018. https://oira.utk.edu/wp-content/uploads/sites/66/2018/10/FB-2018-Headcount-Enroll ment-By-College-Level-Gender-and-Race_Ethnicity-3.pdf. Accessed 5 Dec 2018
18. Nielsen, J., Landauer, T.K.: A mathematical model of the finding of usability problems. In: Proceedings of the INTERACT'93 and CHI'93 Conference on Human Factors in Computing Systems, pp. 206–213. ACM, New York (1993)
19. Web Accessibility Initiative: WAI Site Usability Testing Questions. https://www.w3.org/WAI/EO/Drafts/UCD/questions.html. Accessed 25 Jan 2019
20. Mifsud, J.: Usability metrics—a guide to quantify the usability of any system. https://usabilitygeek.com/usability-metrics-a-guide-to-quantify-system-usability/. Accessed 25 Jan 2019
21. Corbin, J.M., Strauss, A.: Grounded theory research: procedures, canons, and evaluative criteria. Qual. Sociol. **13**(1), 3–21 (1990)

22. Holmqvist, K., Andersson, R.: Eye Tracking: A Comprehensive Guide to Methods, Paradigms and Measures. Lund Eye-Tracking Research Institute, Lund (2017)
23. Srivastava, S.K., Srivastava, A.K., Minerick, A.R., Schulz, N.N.: Recruitment and retention of international graduate students in US universities. Int. J. Eng. Educ. **26**(6), 1561–1574 (2010)
24. Orquin, J.L., Loose, S.M.: Attention and choice: a review on eye movements in decision making. Acta Physiol. **144**(1), 190–206 (2013)
25. Norman, D.: The Design of Everyday Things: Revised and expanded. Basic Books, New York (2013)

Redesigning a Main Menu ATM Interface Using a User-Centered Design Approach Aligned to Design Thinking: A Case Study

Arturo Moquillaza[1,2(✉)], Fiorella Falconi[1], and Freddy Paz[1]

[1] Pontificia Universidad Católica del Perú, Lima 32, Lima, Peru
{amoquillaza, ffalconit, fpaz}@pucp.pe
[2] Universidad San Ignacio de Loyola, Lima 12, Lima, Peru
miguel.moquillaza@usil.pe

Abstract. Currently, development teams face many challenges when designing user interfaces. There are more, and more, new methodologies, processes and techniques to make user-centered design. However, these teams often lack specific techniques or methods to accomplish these designs themselves in a real-world development process. The following is a proposal of a user-centered design approach through a case study. The approach was applied to successfully redesign the main menu of an ATM interface of a Peruvian Bank. In this iteration, the convenience of aligning the proposal with proven methodologies such as Design Thinking was observed. This proposal continues to be applied successfully in the development process of the ATM team of said bank.

Keywords: Human-computer interaction · User-centered design · Usability · Automated teller machine · Design Thinking

1 Introduction

According to the work of Granollers et al. [1], there is a growing interest in the Latin American software development industry in HCI (Human–Computer Interaction), Usability and UX (User Experience) topics. In this context, in BBVA Peru, a leading bank in that country, in its process of digital transformation and adoption of agile and user-centered technologies and processes, a collaboration was initiated between the ATM application development team and the academic community of HCI, especially with the Pontifical Catholic University of Peru. This collaboration has been reported in works presented as [2–5] and others in progress.

In this context, in the development team, we proposed an approach that consisted of a series of steps and techniques focused on the user to make the designs and redesigns that were requested. This proposal has been in use since 2017, and it was presented at Interaccion 2017 conference [3].

The need to propose an appropriate approach was due to the lack of formal proposals for methodologies for the design of ATM interfaces, as reported by Aguirre et al. in [5], and due to the tight time tables in software development processes aligned to agile methods where it is expected that the team delivers with shorter delivery periods each time.

© Springer Nature Switzerland AG 2019
A. Marcus and W. Wang (Eds.): HCII 2019, LNCS 11586, pp. 522–532, 2019.
https://doi.org/10.1007/978-3-030-23535-2_38

The Bank itself has adapted Design Thinking as a process for its specific Design areas, and for all areas in general. However, this methodology in principle involved much more time and a higher level of maturity.

According to the above, and given the maturity of the processes related to the design, the proposal was presented by the development team, in order to align it with Design Thinking and to avoid prescribing specific techniques, but to instead propose and adapt according to the project in execution. Later, this improved proposal was applied in a project entrusted to the team: Redesign the main menu of the ATM application.

Thus, all of the execution of the proposal was carried out with positive results, not only according to the feedback received in the user tests, but also by the internal users and the Bank's quality assurance personnel.

2 Background

2.1 Design Thinking

According to Lockwood, Design Thinking is "*a human-centered innovation process that emphasizes observation, collaboration, fast learning, visualization, and rough prototyping. The objective is to solve not only the stated problem at hand, but the real problems behind the obvious.*" [10].

BBVA has adapted Design Thinking based on authors as Lockwood and Tim Brown (IDEO) [11]. In this implementation, four phases are defined: Comprehension, Ideation, Prototyping and Evaluation, as illustrated in Fig. 1.

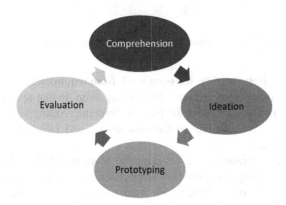

Fig. 1. Phases of design thinking. (adapted from BBVA)

2.2 Usability

Usability is defined in ISO 9241 (2010) as "*The effectiveness, efficiency and satisfaction with which specified users achieve specified goals in particular environments.*" [7].

2.3   Usability Test

According to the study performed by Holzinger [8], there are several methods, which are divided into two groups: usability inspection methods and usability testing methods. According to Paz et al. [9], the main difference between them is that in inspection methods, usability problems are detected by specialists, and in testing methods, usability problems are found through the user's observations while they are using or making comments about the interface of the system.

2.4   Initial Approach

The initial approach proposed by Moquillaza et al. in [3], consisted in seven specific steps for obtaining a ready-to-implement design. Those steps are in Fig. 2.

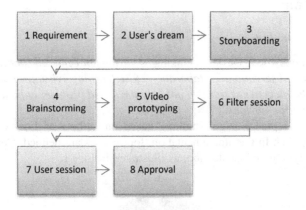

Fig. 2. Initial approach presented in Moquillaza et al. [3]

As we can see, those steps let the team work from requirements until the approval, with steps for proposing ideas and steps for filtering them. In that sense, those steps can be aligned to the phases presented for Design Thinking, adding steps for evaluation. This evaluation step is according to the conclusions and future works described in Moquillaza et al. [3].

Besides, in new iterations, the development team noted that, depending on the nature of the project, they could use additional techniques, or not use some of them. In that sense, some steps must change their names in order to suggest techniques, not prescribe them. Many other techniques can be reviewed in ISO 13407 [6].

2.5   Updated Approach

According to the previous section, the proposed approach was updated to include nine steps, aligned to Design Thinking. Design Thinking is the method used by the BBVA as toolset for any problem or project in the Bank. The updated approach is shown in Fig. 3.

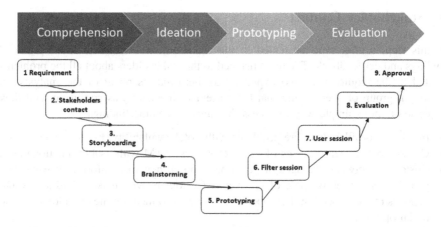

Fig. 3. Updated approach for design of user interfaces for ATM

3 Case Study

3.1 Purpose of Study

The purpose of this study was to redesign the main menu of the ATM application by applying the updated approach.

The development team was required to analyze, propose and test a proposal of redesign of the main menu and withdrawal operation in the ATM application.

The project got the participation of stakeholders and had as principal input information of real customers by verbatim quotations [12]. Verbatim quotations are spontaneous opinions of customer that they fulfill in surveys made periodically by quality-control division of the Bank and external institutions. From those verbatim quotations, it was detected that the current main menu had usability problems that negatively affected the user experience.

3.2 Methodology

This requirement was developed following the updated process described in previous sections. Furthermore, the team executed the nine steps since August, 2018, as we describe:

3.3 Requirement

The team received the requirement, and selected two persons from the team to lead the whole design process. Verbatim quotations and survey results were received and analyzed. In addition, stakeholders were identified. The techniques we used in this step were the following: tag cloud, data analysis, and stakeholder identification.

4   Stakeholder Contact

In this step, results were presented to the stakeholders in order to share principal findings and get feedback. The team listened to the stakeholders about all the problems related to the requirement, and explained to them that as result of the analysis, an important group of users found that the current main menu was confusing, and they requested a more simple way to access the functions. Some findings:

- In all user profiles there are problems with notes availability.
- Customers between the ages of 18 to 25 request ATM with usable functionalities.
- Customers between the ages of 26 to 35 express their discomfort with what they perceive as "excessive sale of products". Customers who make withdrawals and deposits request speed in their operations. They also mention the complexity of the initial options.
- Customers between the ages of 36 to 45 state that steps have been added to withdrawals and that some of these lead to error. They also mention the difference in experience among ATMs.
- Customers between the ages of 46 and over consider that there are many icons on the first screen menu and that it would be useful to place instructions. In addition, these customers mention the need to have larger texts and more lit ATMs.
- In addition, from the analysis of transactions per month, the Pareto principle is applied, and it has been found that four ATM transactions represent 93% of the transactions carried out. These four operations are Withdrawals, Check balances, Query movements, and Deposits.

In that sense, then main conclusion drawn at the meeting is to work in a new taxonomy for the menu. The techniques we used in this step were the following: face-to-face meeting and user profiles.

4.1   Storyboard

The team made some storyboards showing the principal findings of previous steps. This exercise let the rest of the team take contact of the results and state of the project. The techniques we used in this step were the following: Storyboarding and visual thinking.

4.2   Brainstorming

In order to redesign the taxonomy of the current menu, the team could take into account information of other channels of the same Bank, the Bank in other countries, and ATMs of competitor banks. With this data as reference, it was convenient to apply Card sorting with stakeholders in a brainstorming session.

The objective was to identify a taxonomy of the main menu that is simple and clear for customers, giving priority to the most used operations.

The team used 29 cards with the names of the operations that currently exist in ATMs and blank cards to be able to propose new names for existing transactions or new group names. Results of this session can be visualized in Figs. 4 and 5.

The techniques we used in this step were the following: Brainstorming, competitor analysis, card sorting.

Fig. 4. Results of Card sorting in brainstorming

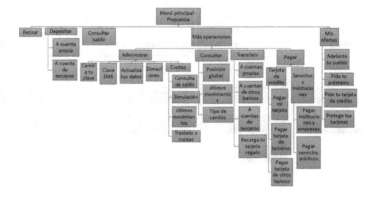

Fig. 5. Taxonomy proposed from the brainstorming

5   Prototyping

In this step, the team prepared some proposals for implementing the new taxonomy. The team based its work in these premises:

- Simplify steps for withdrawals, deposits and inquiries.
- Organize better buttons on the result of the previous activity.
- Do not affect sales flows.
- Do not affect interactive advertising.
- Focus on clients' pain points.

Four proposals were prepared. In Fig. 6, we can see initial menu. In Fig. 7, and Fig. 8, we can see some proposals. The technique we used in this step was the following: Prototyping.

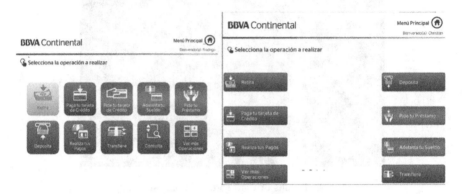

Fig. 6. Initial main menu (touch and buttons)

Fig. 7. Proposal N°1 (touch and buttons)

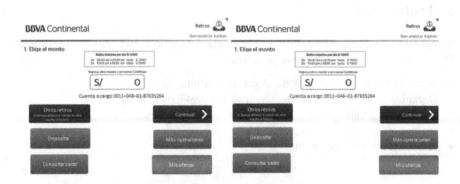

Fig. 8. Proposal N°2 (touch and buttons)

6   Filter Session

This session was made with stakeholders in order to get feedback directly. In this session two proposals were discarded and several changes were suggested. The technique we used in this step was the following: Face-to-face meeting.

7   User Session

This session was made in order to keep with the proposal ready-to-development. Proposal N°1 was selected, but users asked the team if they could evaluate proposal two in parallel. The technique we used in this step was the following: Face-to-face meeting.

8   Evaluation

For this step, the team completed in a prototyping tool, a complete navigation for two proposals. In that sense, the complete withdrawal could be evaluated.

This step was developed in two parts. In a first part, the team asked feedback to UX team in the Bank. UX team principally attends on web projects, but two assessment-meetings were held and the proposals were updated with this feedback.

In a second part, a heuristic evaluation was made over two proposals. Experts in Usability made Heuristic Evaluation. 19 items were reported, 13 were solved. Besides, user evaluations were made after changes in order to validate the proposals. The techniques we used in this step were the following: Heuristic evaluation, user evaluation and assessment meeting.

9   Approval

In this final step, ready-to-implement interfaces were presented to stakeholders, this session got positive feedback. Stakeholders asked for new requirements of redesign and asked for monitoring the present proposal once implemented and released. Figures 9, 10 and 11 show final proposal ready-to-implement. The techniques we used in this step were the following: Face-to-face meeting.

Fig. 9. Proposal ready-to-implement (part 1)

Fig. 10. Proposal ready-to-implement (part 2)

Fig. 11. Proposal ready-to-implement (part 3)

10   Conclusions and Future Work

At the end of this process, we can conclude that interfaces delivered permit the user more freedom and use of the system with better satisfaction, especially in the main menu and withdrawal operations.

Given the results obtained in all the process, especially from the usability test, we can affirm that the interfaces, which were developed, are adequate for implementing in BBVA ATMs, because of the approach followed and the users acceptance.

In that sense, we conclude that this updated approach is useful and meets its objectives in the process of designing user-centered interfaces. Additional steps permitted to deliver a product with better quality and with better Usability.

The process for ATM design should be the same as it is for any other app. However, ATM applications are different from desktop and mobile apps and it is important for a designer to consider those when applying a user-centered design approach.

Finally, we recommend BBVA that it implements a systematic process of interaction design based on the techniques described in this work.

As future work, we continue maturing this process, and evaluating and comparing with other proposals.

Acknowledgements. The authors thank to all the participants involved into the experience required to perform the presented study, especially the ATM development team. The study was highly supported by BBVA Perú, and by the Human-Computer Interaction and Design of User Experience, Accessibility and Innovation Technologies (HCI-DUXAIT) group from PUCP. We also want to thank to Dave Kinskey for his constant support during the writing process of this paper.

References

1. Granollers, T., Collazos, C., González, M.: The state of HCI in Ibero-American countries. J. Univ. Comput. Sci. **14**(16), 2599–2613 (2008)
2. Moquillaza, A., et al.: Developing an ATM interface using user-centered design techniques. In: Marcus, A., Wang, W. (eds.) Design, User Experience, and Usability: Understanding Users and Contexts, pp. 690–701. Springer, Cham (2017)
3. Moquillaza, A., Paz, F.: Applying a user-centered design methodology to develop usable interfaces for an Automated Teller Machine. In: Proceedings of the XVIII International Conference on Human Computer Interaction—Interacción 2017, pp. 1–4 (2017). https://doi.org/10.1145/3123818.3123833
4. Moquillaza, A., Paz, F., Falconi, F., López, R.: Application of the communicability evaluation method to evaluate the design of a user interface: a case study in an ATM system. Revista Colombiana de Computación **19**(2), 46–58 (2017). https://doi.org/10.29375/25392115.3442
5. Aguirre, J., Moquillaza, A., Paz, F.: Methodologies for the Design of ATM Interfaces: A Systematic Review. ISHED, p. 6 (2018)
6. Maguire, M.: Methods to support human-centred design. Int. J. Hum-Comput Stud. **55**, 587–634 (2001). https://doi.org/10.1006/ijhc.2001.0503
7. ISO: ISO 9241-210:2010 Ergonomics of Human–System Interaction—Part 210: Human-Centred Design for Interactive Systems (2010). https://www.iso.org/standard/52075.html
8. Holzinger, A.: Usability engineering methods for software developers. Commun. ACM **48** (1), 71–74 (2005)
9. Paz, F., Villanueva, D., Rusu, C., Roncagliolo, S., Pow-Sang, J.A.: Experimental evaluation of usability heuristics. In: Proceedings of the 2013 10th International Conference on Information Technology: New Generations, pp. 119–126 (2013)

10. Lockwood, T.: Design Thinking. Lockwood resource.com (2015). https://lockwoodresource.com/insight/design-thinking/
11. BBVA: Design Thinking. Serie Innovation Trends. BBVA Innovation Center (2015). https://www.bbva.com/wp-content/uploads/2017/10/ebook-cibbva-design-thinking_es_1.pdf
12. Corden, A., Sainsbury, R.: Exploring 'quality': research participants' perspectives on verbatim quotations. Int. J. Soc. Res. Methodol. **9**(2), 97–110 (2006). https://doi.org/10.1080/13645570600595264

Towards the Meaningful 3D-Printed Object: Understanding the Materiality of 3D Prints

Beth Nam[1](✉), Alex Berman[2], Brittany Garcia[1], and Sharon Chu[1]

[1] Embodied Learning and Experience Lab, University of Florida, Gainesville, USA
{bnam,b.garcia,slchu}@ufl.edu
[2] Department of Computer Science, Texas A&M University, College Station, USA
anberman@tamu.edu

Abstract. Digital fabrication (e.g. 3D printing) provides opportunities for people to act as a product designer and create or adapt objects to their needs and preferences. While research has frequently studied the applications of 3D printing, little is understood on how people engage with the 3D-printed objects after production. This paper begins to fill in this gap by investigating how people perceive 3D-printed objects at two levels: first, basic material properties, and second, meaning or interpretation. A study was conducted with 22 participants comparing 3D-printed objects made of two materials (SLA resin and PLA) with mass-manufactured plastic objects. Qualitative and quantitative results revealed that people perceive material differences in texture, shine, and quality, and that they interpret 3D-printed and mass-manufactured objects differently. The study results can inform the design of 3D printing technology and software such that resultant objects are better aligned with users' design intents and preferences.

Keywords: 3D printing · Materials · Materiality

1 Introduction

Much has been written about how 3D printing technology is set to disrupt, if not transform, economies and manufacturing [35]. It has opened up possibilities of a shift in both production methods and consumption patterns. In terms of production, artifacts can now be made using processes and materials that are starkly different from those used for mass- manufactured products. In terms of consumption, consumers can now potentially participate in the production of usable objects – "prosumers" making, creating, and innovating using affordable 3D printers [38].

The bulk of the research literature on the subject so far has focused on types of applications of 3D printing (e.g., [36,39,46]), innovations in 3D printing technologies and materials (e.g., [28,43]), and disruption of business models (e.g., [37]). Some research has addressed who the users of 3D printing are, and why and

© Springer Nature Switzerland AG 2019
A. Marcus and W. Wang (Eds.): HCII 2019, LNCS 11586, pp. 533–552, 2019.
https://doi.org/10.1007/978-3-030-23535-2_39

Fig. 1. Materials and objects used in the study (from left, PLA, SLA resin and mass-manufactured plastic)

how they engage in the practice (e.g., [20]). However, little is understood on how people engage with 3D-printed objects, or in other words, on the outcomes of 3D printing. This paper investigates people's perception of 3D-printed objects in terms of objective value and subjective meaning through a within-subjects lab-based study with 22 participants.

The success of mass-manufactured products is such that it has established certain expectations about objects for use. These expectations are evident in, for example, literature comparing consumer perceptions of mass-manufactured and handmade products (e.g., mass-manufactured products are perceived as less authentic [17]). 3D-printed objects are neither mass-manufactured, nor hand-made. Rather, they are customizable like handmade objects but made through less intimate and perhaps production-like methods as in mass-manufacturing. Thus 3D-printed objects have unique qualities that remain to be investigated. Cost and quality level are unlikely to be the only limiting factors in the adoption of 3D printing and use of 3D-printed objects in regular, everyday scenarios for meaningful purposes. Like with other technologies, attitudes and perceptions are bound to have significant influences on meaning. We propose that 3D printing technologies today have reached a level of development that warrants investigations to understand user perception of 3D-printed objects. Such investigations can provide useful (and necessary) knowledge to inform directions for further development of different facets of 3D printing technologies, especially 3D design interfaces and support software.

Following, we first review the literature on 3D printing and the importance of materiality to situate our work within the broader context of the material turn in HCI. We then describe our study design, protocol, and results. We conclude with a discussion of the significance of our study results for future research on 3D printing design software, as well as more generally for understanding materiality in HCI.

2   Background: An Overview of 3D Printing

3D printing typically refers to additive manufacturing techniques that create objects by depositing materials layer by layer [9]. Its ability to deliver one-of-a-kind objects [32] to people with relatively low expertise in design and manufacturing has ignited the public's imagination in recent years [49]. Beaman [5] argues that 3D printing has blurred the roles between designer and consumer, subverting the usual 'design for manufacturing' model to become closer to 'manufacturing for design'.

A wide variety of materials can be utilized in 3D printing, but the choice of materials is contingent on the type of production process desired [51]. The most common production method is Fused Deposition Modeling (FDM). FDM melts filament-formed material into a heated nozzle to extrude the 3D part layer by layer [19]. Polylactic Acid (PLA) is the most easily accessible and commonly used material for FDM. PLA can provide a good level of detail, but has high stiffness and a somewhat rough texture. Stereolithography (SLA) is another production method that entails a layered manufacturing process whereby the material is cured via projecting ultra violet laser beams to turn liquid resin into a solid [42]. SLA employs photopolymer resin as material, which when cured has fine features, high stiffness, and a smoother surface finish.

Initial 3D printing technologies in the early 1990s produced objects that were visibly of lower quality, and were thus used almost exclusively for rapid prototyping of single discardable items [37]. Yet, even with tremendous advances in these technologies, the use of 3D printing for prototyping is still dominant today while final production applications (ready-for-consumption products) are much scarcer [26]. This may suggest that there are barriers to the full-fledged adoption of resultant objects from 3D printing for common and casual use. The typical production process of an object involves three key stages: design, manufacturing, and distribution [38]. Research in 3D printing has coalesced around the first two stages, with HCI addressing the use of 3D design software (e.g., [18,21]), and literature from engineering addressing manufacturing systems and methods heavily [7,31]. Research on the distribution and delivery stage of 3D printing can be found mostly in the discipline of business and management, and often addresses models of supply chain (e.g., [6,8,53]). However, for 3D printing to be effective for final production applications, it is imperative for insights to be gained as well on the consumption aspect of 3D printing. These insights can inform the prior stages of the production cycle.

3   Related Work: Consumption of 3D-Printed Objects

The most common class of users of 3D printing currently are specialized industry-based users and amateur Makers, both of whom have a relatively high level of knowledge of design and manufacturing processes. We are interested in potential users who have been called 'casual makers' [20] or 'everyday designers' [27,47]. Baudisch et al. [4] argued that personal fabrication, "the ability to design and produce your own products, in your own home, with a machine that combines consumer electronics with industrial tools" [13], is not out of the question, although there are many barriers to overcome for it to become pervasive across societies.

We are not aware of any work to date that has directly investigated people's perception of 3D-printed objects. The literature on the consumption aspect of

3D printing tends to revolve around how and why casual users may decide to 3D print an object, which is still relevant for our investigation. We review this literature focusing on factors that have been identified as being significant in 3D printing design and the resultant objects. Further, we also describe some work analyzing attitudes towards handmade objects as it may help to contextualize our work on 3D-printed objects.

Shewbridge et al. [40] investigated what people may want to design if they had a 3D printer at home. Their findings showed that material type and functionality are important dimensions that people consider for objects that they would like to print (e.g., wooden parts, metal objects). The authors also highlight that these potential everyday users of 3D printers lack the needed 3D design and modelling skills.

Lee et al. [27] studied the process that people use to decide what they would want to 3D-print in terms of furniture for their homes. They found that the design requirements of users for furniture include aesthetics (namely color, style and size), ergonomics (e.g., comfortability of the material) and functionality. They suggest that users need support to understand interdependencies of design decisions within printed objects.

Based on a large-scale survey of peer production communities, Moilanen and Vadén [31] found that the top five wanted features for 3D printing relate to the physical aspect of the process, specifically 'object quality', 'speed', and 'cheaper material prices'. The most critical bottleneck that users reported seeing was 'materials and quality'.

Overall, the literature on 3D printing motivations for casual users seems to indicate that materiality, with emphasis on certain properties, is an essential aspect of 3D-printed objects. With respect to literature on handmade objects, values seem to be more positive for this class of object as compared to mass-manufactured products. After conducting four studies investigating various production modes on perceived product attractiveness for items presented as handmade vs. machine-made, Fuchs et al. [11] found a positive effect on attractiveness for handmade products. Participants perceived products described as handmade more positively. Further, participants preferred objects if they were marketed as handmade and were willing to pay more for them. Groves [17] compared people's perceptions of home-made food items with mass-manufactured food. She found that home-made food was seen as being more authentic. Higher prices for an item also led people to perceive the item to be of higher quality and more authentic, suggesting that consumers have high expectations for home-made food.

4   Theoretical Foundation: Materiality in HCI

To provide a basis for understanding 3D-printed objects, we adopt the material perspective in HCI. Research in HCI has traditionally emphasized use and functions in the study of objects. Spurred particularly by the increase in digital interfaces, researchers have called for a return to the study of form, materials and materiality. We describe below a few prominent perspectives in that paradigm.

Wiberg [50] suggested using a "material lens" to explore interaction design from the perspective of materials as the basic components of design. He operationalized this "material lens" into a methodology that consists of analyzing designs at four levels: materials, details, texture, and wholeness. At the level of materials, the properties, character, potential and limitations of materials are analyzed. At the level of details, attention is paid to aesthetics and quality of the object. At the level of texture, focus is on appearance and authenticity, with authenticity being defined as the true relationship between materials, material composition, and appearance. And finally, at the level of wholeness, all the different aspects of the object are brought into a composite so as to enable the study of object meaning to an observer.

Jung and Stolterman [24] conceptualized the study of artifacts in HCI as encompassing form and materiality. They suggest three perspectives on form: material, shape, and making (production method). Two perspectives are relevant for materiality: meaning (how objects are understood in personal and social life), and material ecology (connections among multiple artifacts in use).

Fuchsberger et al. [12] applied McLuhan's theories to the study of materiality in HCI. McLuhan's proposition that the medium is the message highlights the distinction between sensory impressions and sensory effects (seeing a comic illustration of a bang and actually feeling like you hear a bang). Thus McLuhan ascertained that the medium affects more senses than just the mode of presentation. Similarly, materials may have greater effects than what their properties suggest.

Giaccardi and Karana [14] proposed the 'materials experience' framework as a way of understanding materiality in HCI. They ascertain that materials are experienced only through a dynamic relationship among materials, people, and practices. And thus, the experiential qualities of materials are dependent on factors such as the properties of a material, the specific artifact in which it is embedded, the user's previous experiences and expectations, and social and cultural values.

They propose a framework consisting of four experiential levels: sensorial, interpretive, affective, and performative. At the sensorial level, materials impact the basic human sensory system of touch, vision, smell, sound and taste. At the interpretive level, people interpret materials and attribute situated meanings. At the affective level, the qualities of the material trigger specific emotions, even if unconsciously so. And at the performative level, all levels of experience from perceptions, meanings and affects are combined to create a certain usage and behavioral pattern towards the object.

Last but not least, the notion of affordances needs to be reviewed in a discussion on materiality. Gibson [15] defined object affordances as preconditions for activity, or possibilities in the environment that spur certain kinds of interactions. Affordances are properties of the object, present in the world irrespective of users and their presence, and independent from influences such as experiences and culture [16]. Applying Gibson's idea to HCI, Norman [33] put forth that affordances provide critical clues to a user for the operation of an object.

However, he also offered a fundamentally different perspective from Gibson in that there are two kinds of affordances: real affordances are the actual properties of objects such as physical form, material, and character. Perceived affordances are what a user perceives an object about an object in terms of what it is and how to use it. Perceived affordances are dependent on one's prior experiences and culture.

Taken together, the literature on materiality in HCI informs us of the following: (i) There are clearly two levels that need to be taken into account in the study of materiality: an object's material properties that are more or less objective, and a more holistic understanding of the object (Wiberg's wholeness, Jung and Stolterman's meaning, Fuschberger's sensory effects, Giaccarda's interpretive); and (ii) Previous and current factors affect a user's understanding of the object: the object's production process, other surrounding objects, the specific situation of use, the user's practices, and social and cultural values.

5   Study Description

5.1   Research Questions

The overarching goal of our study was to investigate how 3D-printed objects are perceived as compared to their mass-manufactured counterparts. As per the insights gained from our literature review on materiality, we examined the issue at two levels, first, at level of the basic material properties and second, at the more holistic level of object meaning or interpretation. The specific research questions were as follows:

RQ 1: a. Are there differences in how people perceive the material properties of 3D-printed objects as opposed to those of mass-manufactured objects?; b. If so, what are these differences in perception?

RQ 2: a. Do people interpret 3D-printed objects differently than mass-manufactured objects?; b. If so, what are the differences in interpretation?

5.2   Study Materials

To enable the conduct of the study, two types of objects were prepared as probes: Object A was a small white cube and object B was a white round clothing button. The objects were chosen based on the following rationale: Object A was a simple geometric object, and was thus assumed to have no obvious functionality and minimal cultural biases. Object B had a rather evident function as a fastener as per their common use in many cultures.

Each of the two objects were 3D-printed with two types of materials: (i) PLA; and (ii) SLA photopolymer resin. Mass-produced versions of each plastic object were also used in the study. In total 6 objects, shown in Fig. 1, were used as probes (2 objects X 3 materials). Mass-manufactured objects were first bought off-the-shelf, and 3D digital model of the mass-manufactured objects were subsequently created. The 3D models were then 3D printed using the SLA printing method and the FDM method using 100% infill and the highest quality printer settings. The Formlabs Form 2 printer was employed for the SLA resin objects, and the Ultimaker 3 printer with a 0.4 mm nozzle was employed to print the PLA objects. The PLA and resin objects were 3D-printed to match, as exactly as possible, the mass-produced objects in terms of color, shape, and size. The white color was chosen in order to avoid judgment based on specific colors. All of the 3D-printed objects were slightly sanded by hand after printing to remove rough edges while preserving the initial look and feel. The final study objects are shown in Fig. 1.

5.3   Study Design and Protocol

Our study had a within-subjects design with two independent variables, object and type of material. Object had 2 levels: cube, where participants engaged with the cube objects, and button, where participants engaged with the button objects. Material type had 3 levels: PLA where participants engaged with objects 3D-printed using PLA, SLA resin, where participants engaged with objects 3D-printed using the SLA method, and mass-manufactured plastic, where participants engaged with objects bought off-the-shelf.

The study involved 22 participants (13 males and 9 females with mean age = 30.2). All participants had no prior experience with 3D printing technology. Their demographics were as follows: White 45.5% (n = 10); Asian 22.7% (n = 5); Hispanic 18.2% (n = 4); Black 4.5% (n = 1); Native American 4.5% (n = 1); and Mixed Races 4.5% (n = 1). Recruitment was made through university listserv email announcements. Participants were individually contacted on a first-come, first-served basis for study sessions at mutually agreed times. Participants were asked to come to an on-campus lab for one session which lasted approximately 1 h and 30 min. A summary of the study protocol is shown in Table 1.

Table 1. Study protocol

#	Activity
1	Briefing
2	Pre-questionnaire
3	Evaluation for each project
	a. Give descriptions
	b. Write notes in hypothetical contexts
	c. Give price
	d. Questionnaires (PERVAL, PANAS-X)
4	Post-questionnaire (Repertory Grid)
5	Interview

At the beginning of the session, participants were given a consent form to sign, were briefly introduced to the study, and were asked to fill in a pre-questionnaire that asked demographic information and prior knowledge in 3D printing or 3D tools. Then, participants were handed the 6 objects (see Study Materials section), one at a time. After the participant had examined and interacted with an object, he or she was engaged in a short interview and asked to fill in a questionnaire. The contents of the interview and question are described in the "Measures" section below. The order of presentation of the objects were randomized for each participant. After a participant had reviewed all the objects, he or she was asked to fill in a final questionnaire.

6   Measures and Data Analysis

Data about user perception was collected and analyzed both quantitatively and qualitatively. For RQ1 relating to object material properties, assessment was done by asking participants to fill a repertory grid after having reviewed all the objects. The repertory grid is a technique used to elicit a participant's personal constructs without the biases of the researchers [45]. Although typically an interview-based technique, it has also been used in a questionnaire form [52].

Participants are asked to list adjectives or phrases to compare and contrast at least 3 objects. They are then asked to list the opposites of the descriptive terms. For example, if a participant used the term "smooth" to describe one object, he or she may put down the bipolar opposite of the term to be "rough", thereby creating a "smooth-rough" bipolar construct. And finally they are asked to either assign a value or ranking for each object based on each construct. In our study, participants assigned rankings to the six objects for each construct that they came up with. We note here that the repertory grid could also capture aspects of RQ2 on the object meaning since it was open-ended in nature.

For RQ2 relating to the meaning or interpretation of the objects, assessment was done in four ways: (i) Participants were asked to bid for each object on a scale of 1 to 100 cents ("how much would you pay for this object out of 100 cents?"). Such a simulated bidding process has been used successfully by others to assess object value [34]. (ii) Participants were asked to handwritten notes about each object under three given hypothetical scenarios – first, giving the object as a gift to someone close; second, receiving the object from someone close; and third, presenting the object as an artifact in a museum – so that we could capture the diversity of possible interpretations; and (iii) Participants were asked to complete the Perceived Value Scale (PERVAL) by [44] that measures the following constructs using 5-point likert scales (example items are given in brackets) – "quality/performance" (e.g., Is well made); "price/value for money" (e.g., Is reasonably priced); "social value" (e.g., Would make a good impression on other people); and "emotional value" (e.g., Is one that I would enjoy).

For the 'price/value for money' construct, the actual (purchase/production) cost of each object at the time of the study was given (cube: $1.73 mass-manufactured, $4.93 PLA-printed, $14.81 SLA-printed; button: $0.49 mass-manufactured, $2.50 PLA-printed, $2.50 SLA-printed), and the participant was asked to indicate how much he/she agreed with the price. Prices for the 3D printed objects were the price paid in a University 3D Printing Shop, where students could request a 3D design be printed on a variety of printers and materials for a cost that scales with the duration of the print and quantity of material consumed. As the buttons required less time and less material to print, they cost the minimum charge of the shop ($2.50). (iv) And finally, participants were asked to fill the PANAS-X scale [2, 48] that measures one's distinguishable affective reactions. The PANAS-X provides a list of 60 adjectives (e.g., "calm", "inspired") on which the participant rates each object using a likert scale (6-point likert scale was used in this study). The adjectives in the PANAS-X can be grouped into 2 general higher-order concepts (Negative affect and Positive affect), and 11 specific affects (Fear, Sadness, Guilt, Hostility, Shyness, Fatigue, Surprise, Joviality, Self-Assurance, Attentiveness, and Serenity).

Quantitative data from the PERVAL and PANAS-X variables, and the bidding prices given by participants for each object were collected from post-question naires. PERVAL data was aggregated by subconstruct. As per instructions on the scoring of the PANAS-X [48], responses to the adjectives making up each affect scale were summed. All quantitative data was entered into the SPSS statistical analysis software package. Repeated measures ANOVAs were conducted to test the effects of material (PLA vs SLA resin vs Mass-produced plastic) and object (Cube vs Button). Greenhouse-Geisser corrections were applied when sphericity assumptions were not met.

Qualitative data from the participants' verbal object descriptions and handwritten notes about the objects were transcribed and imported into the qualitative analysis software, MaxQDA. A total of 396 handwritten notes were collected. A qualitative analysis was performed on the verbal descriptions to identify key concepts that the participants associated with the objects. The coding process consisted of two cycles, first using the open coding approach whereby concepts were labelled using either descriptive or in-vivo codes, and then using the axial coding approach whereby relationships were found among codes and categories [10].

The bipolar constructs from all the participants' repertory grids were collated. Using a process similar to affinity diagramming, constructs that were semantically the same or that had close relationships to each other were grouped. For instance, "Glossy - Matte" was grouped with "Shiny - Dull". "Classy - Unsophisticated" was grouped with "Distinct - Generic". Each group thus indexed a dimension of meaning, and was given a unique ID. A dataset was constructed with the constructs, their associated group ID, and the ranks given on each construct for each of the objects. Friedman tests (since the data was ordinal and the study design was within-subjects) were ran on the dataset to see whether there were significant differences in ranks among the cube and then button objects.

7   Results and Findings

We present our findings by assessment or measure below. For quantitative analyses, only significant results are reported.

Table 2. Semantic groups from repertory grid

ID	Group label	Example construct	No. of instances
1	Texture	Smooth-Rough	28
2	Shine	Glossy-Matte	27
3	Distinctiveness	Fancy-Plain	22
4	Material Strength	Soft-Hard	13
5	Quality	Expensive-Cheap	11
6	Size/Weight	Large-Small	10
7	Production State	Finished-Crude	8
8	Object State	Clean-Dirty	5
9	Shape	Round-Flat	5
10	State of Use	New-Used	4
11	Function	Functional-Useless	2
12	Temperature	Hot-Cold	1
13	Transparency	Translucent-Opaque	1

7.1 Repertory Grid

We found 13 groups of semantically unique constructs from the repertory grid responses. These are listed in Table 2 with the total number of instances of all constructs represented in each group.

The Friedman test was ran for each group of constructs that had 10 or more instances (see Table 2) to compare whether there was a significant different in given rankings among materials. Tests were ran for the cube and button objects separately. Out of the 6 groups tested, only 3 had a statistically significant difference in given ranks based on material for both objects. Values are shown in Fig. 2.

		CUBE		BUTTON	
ID	Group	X^2	p	X^2	p
1	Texture	9.214	.010	23.357	.000
2	Shine	13.981	.001	20.916	.000
5	Quality	11.091	.004	14.364	.001

Fig. 2. Repertory grid results. Note: Only groups that showed an overall significant difference are shown.

Median ranks for each material in each of these 3 groups are given in Fig. 3. Post-hoc analyses (see Fig. 3) showed that with respect to texture for the cube object, there were no significant difference among the specific materials despite an overall significant difference in ranks. However, there were statistically significant rank differences among all the materials for the button object on texture.

ID	Group	CUBE Median			CUBE Post-hoc			BUTTON Median			BUTTON Post-hoc		
		PLA	SLA	Mass	PLA - SLA	PLA - Mass	SLA - Mass	PLA	SLA	Mass	PLA - SLA	PLA - Mass	SLA - Mass
1	Texture	2.29	2.18	1.54	.590	.021	.029	2.61	2.07	1.32	.007*	.000*	.002*
2	Shine	2.20	2.37	1.43	.353	.006*	.005*	2.24	2.46	1.30	.291	.002*	.000*
5	Quality	2.45	2.36	1.18	.850	.010*	.002*	2.64	2.27	1.09	.285	.004*	.002*

Fig. 3. Repertory grid post-hoc results. Note: Only groups that showed an overall significant difference on the Friedman test are shown. Median ranks are from the Friedman test. Post-hoc results are from the Wilcoxon Signed Ranked test, and show p values. Significant values are marked with an *. The lower the rank on 'texture' the smoother, on 'shine' the shinier, and on 'quality' the higher the quality.

With respect to shine as well as quality, there were significant differences between both PLA and SLA resin, as compared to mass-manufactured plastic for both objects.

7.2   Bidding Price

There were both a significant main effect of material ($F^{(2,42)} = 9.72, p = .000, partial \eta^2 = .316$) and of object ($F^{(1,21)} = 13.40, p = .001, partial \eta^2 = .389$). No interaction effect was found. Post-hoc tests showed that only PLA objects (M = \$0.36) were significantly different ($p = .000$) from mass-manufactured objects (M = \$0.52).

7.3   PERVAL Scale

On 'Quality', there were significant main effects of both object ($F^{(1,21)} = 5.75, p = .026, \eta^2 = .159$), and material ($F^{(2,42)} = 22.70, p = .000, \eta^2 = .519$). Post-hoc tests showed that both PLA ($p = .000$) and SLA resin objects ($p = .000$) were significantly different from the mass-manufactured objects.

On 'Price/Value', there was only a significant main effect of material ($F^{(2,42)} = 73.31, p = .000, \eta^2 = .778$). Post-hoc tests showed that both PLA ($p = .000$) and SLA resin objects ($p = .000$) were significantly different from the mass-manufactured objects.

On 'Social value', there was a significant main effect of material ($F^{(2,42)} = 9.46, p = .000, \eta^2 = .310$), as well as a significant interaction effect of Object X Material ($F^{(2,42)} = 3.95, p = .027, \eta^2 = .158$). Post-hoc tests showed that both PLA ($p = .004$) and SLA resin objects ($p = .001$) were significantly different from the mass-manufactured objects.

And on 'Emotional value', there were both a significant main effect of object ($F^{(1,21)} = 12.16, p = .002, \eta^2 = .367$), and a main effect of material ($F^{(2,42)} = 4.63, p = .015, \eta^2 = .181$). No interaction effect was found. Post-hoc tests showed that only SLA objects (p = .007) were significantly different from the mass-manufactured objects.

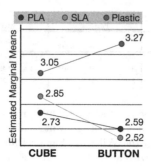

Fig. 4. Object X Material interaction effect on Social Value

CONSTRUCT	Cube	Button	PLA	SLA Resin	Mass. Plastic
BIDDING PRICE	$0.54	$.33	$0.36	$0.43	$0.53
QUALITY	3.75	3.51	3.31	3.44	4.14
PRICE/VALUE	-	-	2.11	1.84	3.77
SOCIAL VALUE	-	-	2.66	2.69	3.16
EMOTIONAL VALUE	3.45	2.85	3.09	2.91	3.44

Fig. 5. Means of each condition for main effects on PERVAL. Note: bidding price values indicate amounts given by participants. For PERVAL constructs, values are on a 1–5 agreement scale. The higher the value, the better on that construct.

Figure 5 shows the mean values for each condition for bidding price and the PERVAL constructs for the main effects reported above. The means for the Object X Material interaction effect for the social value construct is shown in Fig. 4.

7.4   PANAS-X Scale

No significant differences were found on the two high-level scales of negative and positive affect. Significant differences were found for only 4 specific affects. Main effects of material were found on "shyness" ($F^{(2,44)} = 3.30, p = .046, \eta^2 = .130$), "joviality" ($F^{(2,44)} = 6.64, p = .003, \eta^2 = .232$), and "attentiveness" ($F^{(2,44)} = 4.97, p = .011, \eta^2 = .184$). A marginal main effect of material was seen on "fatigue" ($F^{(2,44)} = 3.84, p = .056, \eta^2 = .149$) Main effects of object were found only on "shyness" ($F^{(2,44)} = 3.84, p = .039, \eta^2 = .179$), and "fatigue" ($F^{(1,22)} = 4.50, p = .045, \eta^2 = .109$). No significant interaction effects were obtained.

Mean scores of the main effects are shown in Fig. 6. Post-hoc pairwise comparisons showed that there were no significant specific differences among materials for "shyness". On "joviality", both PLA ($p = .028$) SLA ($p = .025$) were significantly different from mass-manufactured plastic. On "attentiveness", the only significant difference was between PLA and SLA ($p = .007$).

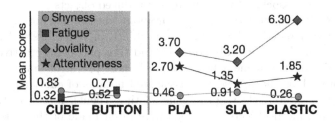

Fig. 6. Mean scores for main effects on PANAS-X scales

7.5   Handwritten Notes

From our qualitative analysis of the 396 object notes collected from participants, we uncovered five themes of interest with respect to the kinds of meanings that participants associated with the objects. Descriptions of the themes are summarized in Fig. 7, together with example notes.

	Theme	Description	Example Object Note
1	Replicability	Possibility of an object to be mass-produced or not	*"Here is a sample of the marble that we will be extracting in bulk and shipping to you next week."* [SLA Cube – P4M]
2	Flexibility	Potential of an object for customization, personalization, or artistic expression	*"Feel free to paint it, draw on it or even wrap it. Just make sure to keep it."* [PLA Cube – P12F]
3	Participation in production	Whether and how much specific individuals participated in the making of the object	*"Hey, I saw that your coat was missing a button, I made one that shouldn't stick out too much compared to the other one. Sewing kit not included. James."* [PLA Button – P5M]
4	Representation	Object is seen as symbolizing other objects, identities or histories	*"This cube was a part of the great buildings during the gladiator times.* [SLA Cube – P9F]
5	Material simulation	Ability of the object to convey a specific material feel	*"Here is an old marble cube - was found with newspaper clippings from the David vandalism that happened in the 70's."* [SLA Cube – P18F]

Fig. 7. Themes from qualitative analysis of the object notes

Theme 1: Replicability is about the possibility of an object to be mass-produced or not. While the main use of 3D-printing currently is for rapid prototyping or the production of single objects, the notes associated with the 3D-printed objects showed that people perceive 3D-printed objects to have replicability potential as well. This replicability potential was expressed in terms of, for example, the object being a part of a larger set, a sample from a batch, the first of many more to come, something that can also be sent to others. The theme of replicability is highly encouraging for the possibility of 3D-printed objects to enter mainstream markets.

Theme 2: Flexibility entails the potential of an object for customization, personalization, or artistic expression. Aspects of participants' notes that were coded as addressing the theme of flexibility included emphases on the ability of the object user to change the object's properties like color and general appearance, in scenarios such as incorporating the objects as part of art projects (e.g. making a table out of buttons or building blocks). This theme was less pronounced in notes associated with the mass-produced objects.

Theme 3: Participation in production is about whether and how much specific individuals participated in the making of the object. In-vivo codes such as "I built this object", "this is a handcrafted object", and "it is part of my creative process" were indicative of this theme, which was much more prevalent in the 3D-printed objects' notes. This theme also had associated notions of effort contributed to the creation of the objects (e.g., amount of time spent). In contrast, in notes about mass-produced objects, mentions were often made of the object having been found, bought, or given.

Theme 4: Representation relates to the fact that the object is seen as symbolizing other objects, identities or histories. This was often seen in notes for 3D-printed objects where participants perceived the objects as being about more than just the objects, for example, as being representative of historical events, a specific process, or a specific famous person.

Theme 5 Material simulation refers to the ability of the object to convey a specific material feel. Many of the notes for the 3D-printed objects specified the objects as being made of other materials such as wood, limestone, marble, plastic, resin, and synthetic material. This theme was also often based on descriptions of the object's properties that were coded as addressing size/weight, quality, shine and texture.

8   Discussion

We were interested in how people's perception of 3D-printed objects differ from that of mass-manufactured objects. We first summarize the results from the various conducted analyses, and then integrate them to answer our research questions. We wrap up by identifying implications for design and by listing the limitations of our study.

8.1   Summary of Results

The repertory grid indicated a list of 13 dimensions that participants found salient among the three objects compared. Only three dimensions of object rankings were significantly different (texture, shine and quality). In these dimensions, mass-produced objects were ranked as the smoothest, shiniest, and of the highest quality. No main effect on object dimension was found. Mass-produced objects were also assigned the greatest dollar amount during the bidding process among the three material types. Only the mean cost assigned to PLA objects (not SLA) was significantly different from that of mass-produced objects. This trend persisted for the results of the four constructs from the PERVAL scale. Scores for mass-produced objects were always the highest among the three materials, followed by PLA and then SLA, except on the 'price/value' construct where PLA objects were seen as having better price for value than SLA resin objects. Main effects of object on the PERVAL also showed that there were significant differences between the cube and the button object types on the 'Quality' and 'Emotional value' constructs, where the cube had higher scores than the button. Interestingly, there was an interaction effect on the 'Social value' construct whereby the mass-produced button had a higher mean score than the 3D-printed buttons, but the same didn't apply for the cube objects.

Ratings on the PANAS-X were significantly different on material type for only three (shyness, joviality and attentiveness) out of the 11 specific affects that the scale measures. Mean scores for mass-produced objects were significantly higher that of mass-produced objects on "joviality", and PLA objects mean was significantly higher than that of SLA-made objects on "attentiveness". Last but not least, five themes (replicability, flexibility, participation in production, representation, and material simulation) emerged from our qualitative analysis of the notes that participants wrote about the objects in different hypothetical scenarios.

8.2 Answering Our Research Questions

RQ1a asked whether there are differences in how people perceive the material properties of 3D-printed objects as opposed to those of mass-manufactured objects. Our results showed that people perceive a clear difference in the properties of the various objects, but mostly generally between 3D-printed objects and mass-produced objects. Material property differences were not evident between the two types of 3D-printed objects (PLA- and SLA-made).

RQ1b asked what the differences in perception of material properties consist of. We know from the repertory grid results that the material property differences manifested themselves perceptibly only in terms of texture and shine. Mass-produced objects were perceived to be smoother and shinier than both 3D-printed objects, regardless of object type. Codes from the notes analysis corroborated this with these two properties being the most prominent in terms of the *material simulation* theme.

RQ2a asked whether people interpret 3D-printed objects differently than mass-manufactured objects. Our results provide evidence that the interpretation of 3D-printed objects vary from mass-produced objects on certain dimension of meanings but not all.

To answer **RQ2b** about the nature of these differences in interpretation, people valued 3D-printed and mass-manufactured objects differently at monetary, social and emotional levels, and perceived them to be different quality.

At a monetary level, the bidding price and PERVAL price construct analyses tell us that mass-produced objects are seen as being more valuable. People were willing to pay more for mass-produced objects.

Interestingly, our 3D-printed objects costed more than mass-manufactured products, mostly because of the material and time spent during their production process. It is possible that increasing people's knowledge of the 3D printing process may lead them to assign a greater monetary value to 3D-printed objects. Other work (e.g., [41]) has found results with respect to craft objects that support this hypothesis.

At the social level, the PERVAL results suggest that not only are 3D-printed objects considered to be less acceptable than mass-produced objects in social settings, but this seems to be especially so for functional objects (the buttons in our study). This is highly indicative of the polarizing effect of mass-manufactured commodity objects.

At an emotional level, PERVAL results show that both object type and material type have an effect. People seem to enjoy the cube more than the button, perhaps because of its non-descriptive functionality. For material type however, mass-produced objects are seen as more enjoyable than SLA-printed objects, but not significantly more enjoyable than PLA objects. This finding is echoed in the PANAS-X results, which showed that people felt more 'jovial' towards mass-produced objects. An explanation for this may be found in the findings from the notes. SLA-made objects were assigned adjectives such as "old" "historic" and "fragile"whereas mass-produced objects had more instances of "related to high-technology"and "fun" This result is reminiscent of findings from Isbister et al.'s study [23], where they found that participants perceived smooth and round objects as "happy"or "fun"as compared to other object shapes and forms.

In terms of quality, people perceived 3D-printed objects to be worse than mass-produced objects. This finding is consistent across the Repertory Grid and PERVAL results. Despite the remarkable advancement of 3D printer technology, it appears that mass manufacturing presently remains the benchmark of quality. Beyond assessments of material properties such as durability, this quality judgment may be because of anchored societal conventions. It may be that over time, expectations will shift to allow people to perceive 3D-printed objects as more valuable without requiring them to be exactly like mass-manufactured objects.

Finally, we do see potential in 3D-printed objects to become everyday objects in the themes of replicability, representation and material simulation. Currently, the value of 3D-printed object seems to be explained largely in terms of the themes of flexibility and participation of production.

8.3   Implications for Design

From our results as a whole, we see two major implications for the HCI community:

(1) The potential for 3D-printed objects to move to everyday consumption for casual users is at least partly dependent on people's perceptions of and attitudes towards them. There is still improvement needed for 3D-printed objects to be perceived on at least a similar status as mass-produced objects. With current 3D printing technologies, the focus for 3D-printed objects is on use and functionality,

and by and large they can serve the function for which they are designed. However, our study indicates that people perceive and approach 3D-printed objects differently than mass-produced objects, especially in social settings where people find 3D-printed objects less acceptable. It is perhaps possible that attitudes towards 3D-printed objects will change as 3D printers increase in sophistication. For example, state-of-the-art printers are already able to accommodate a variety of materials such as foods [30], felts [22], and ceramics [29].

(2) Scaffolds should be designed to support materiality as a key design parameter in 3D printing customizers. It was evident from our findings that resultant 3D-printed objects are distinctively perceived. However, current 3D design software that are used for 3D printing do not scaffold any aspect directly related to materiality. Research in 3D design software and editors for 3D printing are presently heavily focused on supporting users in handling geometry. For example, Hofmann et al. [18] proposed a framework called *PARTs* that can accommodate users' design intents of a 3D model by visualizing assertions of the functional geometry to meet semantic expectations, and Kim et al. [25] developed the *FitMaker* editor to attenuate measurement errors in design. It provides a library of standardized format for CAD models to support novice users to adjust the 3D design models to fit their needs and design intent. The focus on geometry is warranted because of the emphasis on functionality for 3D-printed objects, and functions like scaling, adjustment and placement in 3D editors are typically very challenging for inexperienced users.

We argue that in order for the creativity and 3D-printed objects to be consumed by everyone, the user's design intent, in which materiality has a large influence, needs to be better supported. Possibilities should include the user. For example, being able to express through the interface that "I want a vintage photo frame to give to my grandmother for her birthday" leading the modeling software to recommend printing with an SLA printer with specific parameters.

8.4   Study Limitations and Future Work

Our study has a few limitations that need to be kept in mind: First, different 3D printers with the same production process, environment, and settings may still result in objects with slight variations in appearance, potentially affecting people's perceptions of them. Second, the probe objects in our study were relatively small in size. We note that bigger objects may allow material properties to be more evident, leading to varying participant interpretations. And third, we looked only at the immediate effects of 3D-printed objects.

Longer-term effects may be different since people tend to project additional meaning on objects over time through an appropriation process [17].

9   Conclusion

This study investigated the perception of 3D-printed objects. Participants were given objects 3D-printed in PLA and SLA resin to evaluate as compared to mass-produced versions of the objects. Results showed that people distinguish between 3D-printed and mass-produced objects on specific dimensions, both at the material properties level and at an interpretive level associated with, for instance, quality, price, social, and emotion. Only small differences were found in perception between the two types of 3D-printed materials, suggesting that 3D-printed objects overall as a class of objects are distinct from mass-manufactured objects. We propose that for the vision of everyday 3D printing [1,3] to become a reality, further research need to be done on people's perceptions of 3D-printed objects and the notion of materiality in 3D design customizers.

References

1. Anderson, C.: Makers. Nieuw Amsterdam, Amsterdam (2013)
2. Bagozzi, R.P.: An examination of the psychometric properties of measures of negative affect in the PANAS-X scales (1993)
3. Bardzell, J., Bardzell, S., Lin, C., Lindtner, S., Toombs, A., et al.: HCIs making agendas. Found. Trends® Hum.-Comput. Interact. 11(3), 126–200 (2017)
4. Baudisch, P., Mueller, S., et al.: Personal fabrication. Found. Trends® Hum.-Comput. Interact. 10(3–4), 165–293 (2017)
5. Beaman, J.: 3D printing, additive manufacturing, and solid freeform fabrication: the technologies of the past, present and future. Bull. Am. Phys. Soc. 60 (2015)
6. Berman, B.: 3-D printing: the new industrial revolution. Bus. Horiz. 55(2), 155–162 (2012)
7. Bhushan, B., Caspers, M.: An overview of additive manufacturing (3D printing) for microfabrication. Microsyst. Technol. 23(4), 1117–1124 (2017)
8. Chan, H.K., Griffin, J., Lim, J.J., Zeng, F., Chiu, A.S.: The impact of 3D printing technology on the supply chain: manufacturing and legal perspectives. Int. J. Prod. Econ. 205, 156–162 (2018)
9. Conner, B.P., et al.: Making sense of 3-D printing: creating a map of additive manufacturing products and services. Add. Manuf. 1, 64–76 (2014)
10. Corbin, J., Strauss, A., Strauss, A.L.: Basics of Qualitative Research. SAGE, Thousand Oaks (2014)
11. Fuchs, C., Schreier, M., Van Osselaer, S.M.: The handmade effect: what's love got to do with it? J. Mark. 79(2), 98–110 (2015)
12. Fuchsberger, V., Murer, M., Tscheligi, M.: Materials, materiality, and media. In: Proceedings of the SIGCHI Conference on Human Factors in Computing Systems, pp. 2853–2862. ACM (2013)
13. Gershenfeld, N.: FAB: the Coming Revolution on Your Desktop-From Personal Computers to Personal Fabrication. Basic Books, New York (2008)
14. Giaccardi, E., Karana, E.: Foundations of materials experience: an approach for HCI. In: Proceedings of the 33rd Annual ACM Conference on Human Factors in Computing Systems, pp. 2447–2456. ACM (2015)
15. Gibson, E.J.: Where is the information for affordances? Ecol. Psychol. 12(1), 53–56 (2000)
16. Greeno, J.G.: Gibson's affordances. Psychol. Rev. 101(2), 336–342 (1994)
17. Groves, A.M.: Authentic British food products: a review of consumer perceptions. Int. J. Consum. Stud. 25(3), 246–254 (2001)

18. Hofmann, M., Hann, G., Hudson, S.E., Mankoff, J.: Greater than the sum of its parts: expressing and reusing design intent in 3D models. In: Proceedings of the 2018 CHI Conference on Human Factors in Computing Systems, p. 301. ACM (2018)

19. Huang, Y.M., Lan, H.Y.: Compensation of distortion in the bottom exposure of stereolithography process. Int. J. Adv. Manuf. Technol. **27**(11–12), 1101–1112 (2006)

20. Hudson, N., Alcock, C., Chilana, P.K.: Understanding newcomers to 3D printing: motivations, workflows, and barriers of casual makers. In: Proceedings of the 2016 CHI Conference on Human Factors in Computing Systems, pp. 384–396. ACM (2016)

21. Hudson, N., Lafreniere, B., Chilana, P.K., Grossman, T.: Investigating how online help and learning resources support children's use of 3D design software. In: Proceedings of the 2018 CHI Conference on Human Factors in Computing Systems, p. 257. ACM (2018)

22. Hudson, S.E.: Printing teddy bears: a technique for 3D printing of soft interactive objects. In: Proceedings of the SIGCHI Conference on Human Factors in Computing Systems, pp. 459–468. ACM (2014)

23. Isbister, K., Höök, K., Sharp, M., Laaksolahti, J.: The sensual evaluation instrument: developing an affective evaluation tool. In: Proceedings of the SIGCHI Conference on Human Factors in Computing Systems, pp. 1163–1172. ACM (2006)

24. Jung, H., Stolterman, E.: Digital form and materiality: propositions for a new approach to interaction design research. In: Proceedings of the 7th Nordic Conference on Human-Computer Interaction: Making Sense Through Design, pp. 645–654. ACM (2012)

25. Kim, J., Guo, A., Yeh, T., Hudson, S.E., Mankoff, J.: Understanding uncertainty in measurement and accommodating its impact in 3D modeling and printing. In: Proceedings of the 2017 Conference on Designing Interactive Systems, pp. 1067–1078. ACM (2017)

26. Laser, O.: Additive manufacturing: an industry growing in relevance and applications. Appl. Des. 30–32 (2017)

27. Lee, B., Han, G., Park, J., Saakes, D.: Consumer to creator: how households buy furniture to inform design and fabrication interfaces. In: Proceedings of the 2017 CHI Conference on Human Factors in Computing Systems, pp. 484–496. ACM (2017)

28. Leigh, S.J., Bradley, R.J., Purssell, C.P., Billson, D.R., Hutchins, D.A.: A simple, low-cost conductive composite material for 3D printing of electronic sensors. PLoS ONE **7**(11), e49365 (2012)

29. Lewis, J.A., Smay, J.E., Stuecker, J., Cesarano, J.: Direct ink writing of three-dimensional ceramic structures. J. Am. Ceram. Soc. **89**(12), 3599–3609 (2006)

30. Liu, Z., Zhang, M., Bhandari, B., Wang, Y.: 3D printing: printing precision and application in food sector. Trends Food Sci. Technol. **69**, 83–94 (2017)

31. Moilanen, J., Vadén, T.: 3D printing community and emerging practices of peer production. First Monday **18**(8) (2013)

32. Mota, C.: The rise of personal fabrication. In: Proceedings of the 8th ACM Conference on Creativity and Cognition, pp. 279–288. ACM (2011)

33. Norman, D.A.: Affordance, conventions, and design. Interactions **6**(3), 38–43 (1999)

34. Norton, M.I., Mochon, D., Ariely, D.: The IKEA effect: when labor leads to love. J. Consum. Psychol. **22**(3), 453–460 (2012)

35. Petrick, I.J., Simpson, T.W.: 3D printing disrupts manufacturing: how economies of one create new rules of competition. Res.-Technol. Manag. **56**(6), 12–16 (2013)

36. Pfister, A., Landers, R., Laib, A., Hübner, U., Schmelzeisen, R., Mülhaupt, R.: Biofunctional rapid prototyping for tissue-engineering applications: 3D bioplotting versus 3D printing. J. Polym. Sci., Part A: Polym. Chem. **42**(3), 624–638 (2004)
37. Rayna, T., Striukova, L.: From rapid prototyping to home fabrication: how 3D printing is changing business model innovation. Technol. Forecast. Soc. Chang. **102**, 214–224 (2016)
38. Rayna, T., Striukova, L., Darlington, J.: Co-creation and user innovation: the role of online 3D printing platforms. J. Eng. Tech. Manag. **37**, 90–102 (2015)
39. Rengier, F., et al.: 3D printing based on imaging data: review of medical applications. Int. J. Comput. Assist. Radiol. Surg. **5**(4), 335–341 (2010)
40. Shewbridge, R., Hurst, A., Kane, S.K.: Everyday making: identifying future uses for 3D printing in the home. In: Proceedings of the 2014 conference on Designing interactive systems, pp. 815–824. ACM (2014)
41. Smith, R.K.: The creative process and the construction of value. Ph.D. thesis, Yale University (2017)
42. Sood, A.K., Ohdar, R.K., Mahapatra, S.S.: Experimental investigation and empirical modelling of FDM process for compressive strength improvement. J. Adv. Res. **3**(1), 81–90 (2012)
43. Sun, K., Wei, T.S., Ahn, B.Y., Seo, J.Y., Dillon, S.J., Lewis, J.A.: 3D printing of interdigitated Li-Ion microbattery architectures. Adv. Mater. **25**(33), 4539–4543 (2013)
44. Sweeney, J.C., Soutar, G.N.: Consumer perceived value: the development of a multiple item scale. J. Retail. **77**(2), 203–220 (2001)
45. Tan, F.B., Hunter, M.G.: The repertory grid technique: a method for the study of cognition in information systems. MIS Q. **26**, 39–57 (2002)
46. Ventola, C.L.: Medical applications for 3D printing: current and projected uses. Pharm. Ther. **39**(10), 704 (2014)
47. Wakkary, R., Maestri, L.: The resourcefulness of everyday design. In: Proceedings of the 6th ACM SIGCHI Conference on Creativity & Cognition, pp. 163–172. ACM (2007)
48. Watson, D., Clark, L.A.: The PANAS-X: manual for the positive and negative affect schedule-expanded form (1999). https://ir.uiowa.edu/cgi/viewcontent.cgi?article=1011&context=psychology_pubs
49. The White House: President Barack Obama: remarks by the president at the white house maker faire (2014). https://obamawhitehouse.archives.gov/the-press-office/2014/06/18/remarks-president-white-house-maker-faire
50. Wiberg, M.: Methodology for materiality: interaction design research through a material lens. Pers. Ubiquit. Comput. **18**(3), 625–636 (2014)
51. Yap, Y., Yeong, W.: Additive manufacture of fashion and jewellery products: a mini review. Virtual Phys. Prototyp. **9**(3), 195–201 (2014)
52. Yee, S.L.C.Y., Marsh, T.: Investigating fun and learning in educational games using the repertory grid technique (2009)
53. Yeh, T., Kim, J.: CraftML: 3D modeling is web programming. In: Proceedings of the 2018 CHI Conference on Human Factors in Computing Systems, p. 527. ACM (2018)

Optimization of User Interfaces in the Digitization of Paper-Based Processes: A Case Study of a Mobile Aviation Application

Paige L. Sanchez[(✉)] and Meredith B. Carroll

Florida Institute of Technology, Melbourne, FL 32901, USA
sanchezp2015@my.fit.edu

Abstract. Many companies across several industries have made the switch from paper to electronic documentation with the goals of improving efficiency, lowering costs, and providing employees with ways to easily access important information all at their fingertips. In the aviation industry, Electronic Flight Bags (EFBs) have transformed all required inflight, paper documentation into digital formats that are easily accessible to pilots on the flight deck. Unfortunately, in the development of first generation EFB documentation applications, and many other document-rich applications in industry, little attention has been paid to human factors design principles, resulting in applications that are inefficient and can burden user performance. This paper describes a usability analysis that was performed on a current EFB application used by a major U.S. air carrier, and provides redesign recommendations to increase usability of the EFB and streamline pilot performance. These results provide insight into potential problems to avoid in future flight deck application design, as well as for applications that serve to digitize paper-based process. Additionally, the results provide guidelines to help ensure effective and efficient user interfaces.

Keywords: Usability · Interface design · Electronic Flight Bag

1 Introduction

From user manuals, to company records, forms, and documents, "paperwork" remains a significant element of task performance across many industries. Although several industries, such as construction, insurance, and real estate still heavily rely on paper to conduct business, many industries have digitized paper-based processes with the hopes of increasing productivity, mitigating risks, lowering costs, and collecting data easily to produce company insight [7]. In the medical industry, hospitals have started to adopt tablet-based applications to store patient records, medical images, and medical journals [5]. Manufacturing companies have started to adopt the use of tablets to store all drawings, specifications, and work instructions to ensure that the most up-to-date documents are referenced and to provide easy access to important maintenance

© Springer Nature Switzerland AG 2019
A. Marcus and W. Wang (Eds.): HCII 2019, LNCS 11586, pp. 553–564, 2019.
https://doi.org/10.1007/978-3-030-23535-2_40

procedures [2]. In the aviation industry, the use of Electronic Flight Bags (EFBs) has transformed all required inflight paper documentation into electronic formats accessible to pilots on a tablet [3]. In the early 2000s, EFBs emerged on commercial airline flight decks as a means to reduce operating costs and to provide pilots with the most up-to-date information to more efficiently manage their flight tasks [6]. Further, with technological advancements, increasingly sophisticated EFB applications are becoming available for pilots to use as additional sources of information on the flight deck. EFBs are capable of providing an array of information to pilots such as company manuals, checklists, navigation charts, satellite weather information, traffic, performance data, airport moving maps, route profile optimization, and electronic technical logs [3].

However, in the development of first generation EFBs, little attention was paid to human factors design principles, resulting in EFB applications that are inefficient and can burden pilot performance. Pilots have had to deal with the aftermath of poor application design, which has added to the workload of an already demanding high-workload environment. The design of these applications is often driven by the attributes of the paper-based tools, utilizing the easiest, quickest and cheapest way to transform the paper tools into electronic tools, with little focus on effective task performance in the operational environment. In order to effectively integrate such information-heavy applications into high-workload environments, it is important for application designs to follow a human centered design approach that takes into account the task, the user, and the environment and builds the technology around these elements [1]. The objective of this paper is to describe a usability analysis that was performed on a current EFB application used by a major U.S. air carrier. This application was designed to store all required inflight and out-of-flight documents and paperwork, and we provide here redesign recommendations to increase usability of the EFB and streamline pilot performance. These results provide insight into potential problems to avoid in future flight deck application design, as well as for applications that serve to digitize paper-based process. Additionally, the results provide guidelines to help ensure effective and efficient user interfaces.

2 Usability Heuristic Principles

A heuristic evaluation is a commonly used inspection method conducted to evaluate the usability of interfaces. A heuristic evaluation is carried out by experts who often conduct task analyses of primary user tasks, and identify problems that users may experience while interacting with the interface [8]. Nielson and colleagues have developed a set of usability principles, or heuristics, used to identify problems with, and design solutions for user interfaces. These heuristics aim to ensure that interactive products are "easy to learn, effective to use, and enjoyable from the user's perspective" [8]. Ten commonly cited heuristics for interface design, defined in Table 1, focus on usability goals by evaluating system visibility, design intuitiveness, consistency, efficiency, user support, user control, and design conciseness.

Four of the ten heuristics were extremely applicable for the optimization of the EFB under evaluation and served as a framework for the EFB usability analysis described herein. These four heuristics include: (1) Match between the system and the real world (i.e., "the system should speak the user's language, with words, phrases and concepts familiar to the user"), (2) Recognition rather than recall (i.e., "minimize the user's memory load by making objects, actions, and options visible") (3) Flexibility and efficiency of use (i.e., design features of the system that "speed up the interaction for

Table 1. Usability heuristics for interface design [8]

#	Heuristic	Description
1	Visibility of system status	The system should always keep users informed about what is going on, through appropriate feedback within reasonable time.
2	**Match between system and the real world**	**The system should speak the users' language, with words, phrases and concepts familiar to the user, rather than system-oriented terms.**
3	User control and freedom	Users often choose system functions by mistake and will need a clearly marked "emergency exit" to leave the unwanted state without having to go through an extended dialogue. Support undo and redo.
4	Consistency and standards	Users should not have to wonder whether different words, situations, or actions mean the same thing. Follow platform conventions.
5	Error prevention	Either eliminate error-prone conditions or check for them and present users with a confirmation option before they commit to the action.
6	**Recognition rather than recall**	**Minimize the user's memory load by making objects, actions, and options visible. The user should not have to remember information from one part of the dialogue to another.**
7	**Flexibility and efficiency of use**	**Accelerators – unseen by the novice user – may often speed up the interaction for the expert user such that the system can cater to both inexperienced and experienced users. Allow users to tailor frequent actions.**
8	**Aesthetic and minimalist design**	**Dialogues should not contain information which is irrelevant or rarely needed. Every extra unit of information in a dialogue competes with the relevant units of information and diminishes their relative visibility.**
9	Help users recognize, diagnose, and recover from errors	Error messages should be expressed in plain language (no codes), precisely indicate the problem, and constructively suggest a solution.
10	Help and documentation	Even though it is better if the system can be used without documentation, it may be necessary to provide help and documentation. This information should be easy to search, focused on the user's task, list concrete steps to be carried out, and not be too large.

the [user]"), and (4) Aesthetic and minimalist design (i.e., "dialogues should not contain information which is irrelevant or rarely needed") [8].

3   Methods

This research utilized a five-step process to evaluate the usability of an EFB application that is used by a major U.S. air carrier to store all required inflight and out-of-flight documents and paperwork, including (1) a technology review, (2) pilot-user interviews, (3) a task analysis, (4) a heuristic evaluation, and (5) development and prototyping of redesign recommendations.

3.1   Technology Review

First, we performed a Technology Review. The primary goal of the Technology Review was to learn the functionality and composition of the EFB application. Introductory meetings were held with the airline's EFB subject matter experts (SMEs) to collect information about the current structure of the application, the functions within the application, and the features that are both frequently, and infrequently, utilized by pilots as they interact with the application.

3.2   Pilot-User Interviews

Next, we performed interviews with pilots who were users of the EFB application and this provided the richest source of information in identifying use case scenarios and usability issues. We conducted three interviews with two EFB SMEs to get alternate viewpoints regarding the primary uses of the application, the priority of information used by pilots, current design issues, to identify less frequently used functions, and to collect feedback on the newly constructed prototype.

3.3   Heuristic Evaluation

Using the results of the technology review and pilot interviews, we identified four usability heuristics on which to focus our evaluation efforts: (1) recognition rather than recall, (2) match between system and the real world, (3) flexibility and efficiency of use, and (4) aesthetic and minimalist design. To evaluate the efficiency of the application, we analyzed the number of clicks needed to access low and high priority information in the application. Based on the interviews, we defined high priority information as information that is needed for preflight preparation before every flight. Additionally, we evaluated the number of clicks needed to perform the primary task of preflight preparation to determine the efficiency of the application in a use case scenario.

3.4   Redesign Recommendations and Prototyping

Based on the results of the analysis, we developed several redesign recommendations to improve interface effectiveness and efficiency. Further, to illustrate these recommendations, we constructed a low fidelity prototype using a wire-framing tool. Two pilots performed an informal evaluation of the prototype and made additional design recommendations.

4 Results

4.1 Information Priority

The most common use of the EFB application, as identified in the pilot interviews, is preflight preparation. The interviews revealed that pilots primarily use this application right before, and during, flight to comply with company documents and to open documents required for inflight use. The documents most frequently accessed include flight and aircraft manuals, the EFB manual, airport diagrams, the Minimum Equipment List/Configuration Deviation List (MEL/CDL), comply documents, and company documents. Additionally, the results of the pilot interview revealed that the documents that are less frequently used are the training and procedures documents, which are used monthly for studying.

4.2 Menu Structure and Depth

Based on the task analysis and heuristic evaluation, we developed a representation of the navigation structure of the application to show the levels of information within each navigation tab (See Fig. 1). The application's structure consists of six main navigation folders on Level 1, with varying levels of information in each folder. The numbers represented in Levels 3–6 are the number of documents stored at each Level. All of the primary information used by pilots is stored under the first folder, "All Documents", resulting in six levels of menus that pilots must navigate through in order to access important information. Most of the information that pilots must access inflight is found in Level 4, however, it is typically recommended that critical information should not exceed a menu Level of 2 or 3 [4]. Deeper menus promote poor information retrievability, and poor recognition, as users can easily get lost in menus and are required to

Menu Depth	Navigation Menu							
Level 1	All Documents				Favorites	Company Docs	View	Unused Tab	Recently Viewed
Level 2	Tab 1	Tab 2	Tab 3	Tab 4	Tab 1	Tab 1	Tab 1		Tab 1
Level 3	1	4	6	6					
Level 4		3	9	30					
Level 5			13	28					
Level 6			4	3					

Fig. 1. Structure and menu depth of current EFB application representing Number of Documents stored in Levels 3–6

memorize where they are at in the application [9]. The remaining five navigation folders include information such as Company Documents, Favorites, View, Recently Viewed, and an unused folder that the EFB SME identified. These folders are easily accessible on the first menu level, and contain only two levels of information, despite their infrequent use.

4.3   Task Analysis

Based on information obtained from the pilot interviews we performed a task analysis of the most frequent and critical tasks performed by pilots. The task analysis resulted in a breakdown of steps pilots perform to complete the primary task on the EFB application. This included steps taken during preflight preparation to sync the application 24 hours before flight, read and comply with company documents, and find and open required documents for inflight use. A simplified version of this task analysis was later used to evaluate a use case scenario during the heuristic evaluation.

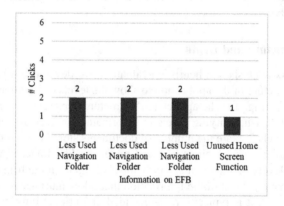

Fig. 2. Number of clicks needed to access low priority information for current design

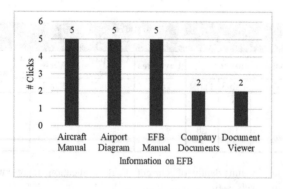

Fig. 3. Number of clicks needed to access high priority information for current design

4.4 Document Accessibility

The results of the heuristic evaluation, presented in Figs. 2 and 3, illustrate how the inefficient use of menus creates performance inefficiencies. Several high priority documents take up to five clicks to access compared to lower priority information that can be accessed in as little as two clicks. High priority information should be accessible with fewer clicks to promote ease of access [9]. These results indicate an efficiency issue that needed to be addressed in the redesign recommendations.

The number of clicks needed to complete the task of preflight preparation was evaluated. This task included five steps to set up the document viewer: (1) Add manual #1, (2) Add manual #2, (3) Add airport diagram #1 (4) Add airport diagram #2, and (5) Add the EFB manual. A total of 19 clicks were needed to access and add all documents to the document viewer, due to the extensive menu depth associated with Folder 1, "All Documents", where the flight information is stored.

4.5 Pilot Performance Problems

The pilot interviews revealed the primary issues that pilots encounter when completing their daily flight tasks on the application. The main usability problems identified by the SME pilots are information accessibility, limited visibility in the document viewer, poor presentation of the application's alerts, confusing information or icons, and a limited search feature.

Menu Navigation. According to the pilots interviewed, long lists of documents and deep menus make it difficult for pilots to find important documents needed for flight. Menu depths make navigation a tedious job, costing the pilots valuable time on the flight deck. Further, as menus are selected, the menus are layered on top of each other, often resulting in three or four layered menus and the users "getting lost" and not knowing where they are in the application or how to get to where they want to go. Additionally, when pilots need to load multiple documents into the viewer, pilots must open each document in the viewer and then close out of the viewer in order for the document to become available for later access, resulting in the pilot constantly navigating through multiple windows. These menu issues emphasize the need to address efficiency, minimalist design, and design that promotes recognition.

Document Organization. The document viewer, in which there can be many documents open at one time, does not provide any format of organization that facilitates awareness of what documents are open, nor does it provide an easy way to navigate to a desired document. As a result, users spend valuable time swiping back and forth to find a document that is open. The user can easily get lost in the viewer if there are several documents open because all of the tabs do not fit on the user's screen, and there is excessive screen switching that occurs when additional documents need to be opened. This results in poor organization, visibility, recognition, and accessibility.

Icon Usage. The EFB application also uses redundant and confusing icons, which result in misinterpretation of the icons' functions and users mistakenly selecting icons that they did not intend to select. Further evaluation of the document viewer shows that there are multiple 'x' icons with different functions. Pilots reported often confusing the two icons and mistakenly closing one window when they intended to close a different window. There are also icons in the document viewer, such as the annotation icon, that are not intuitive and can be confusing to the user.

Alerts. Pilots voiced concerns about the large banner used for alerts on the home screen. This banner does not allow pilots to acknowledge that they have read and addressed the alerts. Pilots often become complacent to the alerts banner being visible every time the application is opened. Additionally, because the banner cannot be closed once it has been read and acknowledged, the banner wastes valuable real estate in the application.

4.6   Application Redesign

Design Recommendations. Based on the results described above, we developed six redesign recommendations to address the usability issues discovered in the EFB application:

1. Reorganize information to reduce search time. This includes reducing menu depth and reorganizing the information based on its priority of use.
2. Create organization and visibility in the document viewer. This includes organizing open documents by type in a menu-type format while still allowing users to easily toggle between documents.
3. Eliminate unused functions, tabs, and folders to improve visibility of important information.
4. Ensure icons and symbols are intuitive to users. Each icon must have a unique function and cannot represent multiple functions on different pages.
5. Relocate frequently used functions to within the first two levels of menus. Ensure that functions used every time the application is open remain at a Level 1.
6. Alerts must be salient, and must allow the users to acknowledge them, resulting in reduced salience, in order to prevent complacency or alert blindness.

These redesign recommendations not only address the primary goals of airlines who have created document-based applications, but of companies seeking to digitize paper-based processes. These recommendations have the potential to improve the usability of, and operator performance with, the resulting design, including time savings, improved organization, effective alerts, and easy access to information.

Redesign Implementation. We implemented the six redesign recommendations in a wireframe prototype in order to illustrate the envisioned interface. To reduce menu depth, we eliminated unused functions from the primary navigation bar, and distributed high priority information along the navigation bar to improve accessibility. To create organization and visibility in the document viewer, we added a document menu that lists all open documents organized by document type to the document viewer. This menu can be open and hidden at any time, and allows users to easily navigate to, or close, any document that is open.

We utilized consistent and intuitive icons and added a toggle switch to all documents listed in the application. The toggle switch is labeled "Add to viewer" and allows users to add a document to the viewer in one click, without having to open the document. We moved the Sync function, which is used every time a pilot is going to use the EFB for flight, along with a "last updated" feature, to the status bar at the top of the application that is visible on every navigation tab, allowing for Level 1 access. The Sync function is used every time a pilot is going to use the EFB for flight. Therefore, we moved this function to the bar that is visible on every navigation tab so that the users can easily access it and know when they last synced. Instead of including a permanent banner for alerts on the home page, we converted the alerts feature to a banner that the user can open and close, saving valuable real estate in the application. Additionally, we included an alert notification that tells the user how many new alerts there are. While the alert banner is open, the pilot has the option to mark the alerts as read, or unread, so that they are no longer notified of alerts that they have already acknowledged. This alert banner automatically appears when there are new notifications to ensure pilots' attention is drawn to new alerts that they need to review.

Redesign Analysis. After implementing the redesign recommendations, we used the same use case analysis conducted on the original design to conduct a use case analysis on the redesigned prototype to evaluate its efficiency. The redesigned navigation structure, in Fig. 4, shows significant improvements in menu-depth and information accessibility. We eliminated unused navigation tabs replaced them with more frequently accessed folders and information, reducing menu-depth. As a result, the flattened menu-structure moved important flight information that was once at a Level 4 or 5 to a Level 2 or 3. Additionally, we reevaluated the number of clicks needed to access high priority information, shown in Fig. 5. The aircraft manual, airport diagram, and

Menu Depth	Navigation Menu																	
Level 1	Company Docs		Viewer	Flying						Not Flying					Favorites	Admin		
Level 2	Tab 1	Tab 2	Tab 1	Tab 1	Tab 2	Tab 3	Tab 4	Tab 5	Tab 6	Tab 1	Tab 2	Tab 3	Tab 4	Tab 5	Tab 1	Tab 1	Tab 2	Tab 3
Level 3				16			4	3	5	15	23	7	23	1			5	12
Level 4				5			1	3	2	1	6		2				1	

Fig. 4. Structure and menu depth of redesigned EFB application representing Number of Documents stored in Levels 3–6

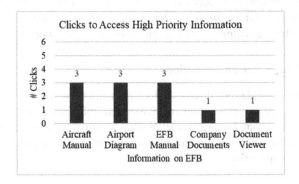

Fig. 5. Number of clicks needed to access high priority information for application redesign

EFB manual can now be accessed in three clicks versus five clicks previously. Company documents and the document viewer can now be accessed in one click, versus two clicks previously. As a result, the number of clicks needed to complete the task of preflight preparation was reduced to 10 clicks, versus 19 clicks previously. The redesigned application cuts the number of clicks, and thus the time needed to access the documents, approximately in half.

5   Discussion

Addressing the four heuristic design principles improved the overall efficiency of the EFB application by improving the user's orientation, creating visibility of open documents, and reducing the number of clicks needed to perform primary tasks.

5.1   Prototyped Design Recommendations

Task-Driven Organization. To properly address these principles in a human centered design approach, the primary tasks of the application need to be researched and well understood. As the primary tasks are documented, the priority of information used in the application also becomes known. When approaching the organization of an application that has a large number of documents, understanding the user's priority of information becomes especially important. Information-rich applications can easily result in deep menus, information overload, and tedious navigation. Therefore, information that is accessed most frequently must be accessible within a Level 1 or Level 2 menu to prevent the user from getting lost in the application and from spending extra time accessing important information.

Improved Visibility. Second, applications that store a large number of documents must promote increased visibility. In the EFB application, pilots are required to have multiple documents opened at once. Users should be able to quickly view a list of all of their open documents to improve awareness of which documents have been accessed. Additionally, visibility should be improved in the menu structure of the application. A greater number of menu options should be visible in a single menu or on a single page, instead of requiring these options to be accessed in new windows. This can be accomplished by implementing drop-down menus and slider navigation bars, which allow users to view more options without opening additional windows or layered menus.

5.2   Future Design Recommendations

Other design recommendations discussed during the pilot interviews, but not addressed in the application redesign due to implementation feasibility, include: (1) improving the usability of the search function, (2) consolidating information across the required flight manuals, and (3) reducing the amount of information that is distributed to the pilots through the EFB application.

Usable Search Functions. Both pilots during the pilot interviews discussed the inefficiencies of the search function. Because the documents in the application are uploaded as PDFs, in order for the document search to be effective, pilots must search the exact words and phrases that are used in the flight manuals and documents. As a result, pilots often cannot find what they need using the search function and find it especially difficult to use in high workload situations. In the future, documents should be uploaded in a less rigid electronic format so that a more versatile search function can be employed.

Information Consolidation. Pilots also discussed the need to consolidate the manuals used on the flight deck, as there is a great deal of redundant information across the multiple manuals that they use. As a result, pilots often do not know which piece of information is in which manual and must do without the information if it requires too much time or effort to access.

Information Prioritization. Lastly, since the introduction of the EFB on the flight deck, pilots are now flooded with more information than ever before. Air carriers now have the ability to send out any piece of information with a click of a button. This includes critical documents that must be read and complied with before flight, as well as "nice to know" information that can be read at a pilot's convenience. As a result, pilots have encountered an overload of information, making it extremely difficult to quickly and easily identify which information must be read at what point in time. This results in pilots quickly skimming through this information, or skipping over it all together. The information that is streamed through the EFB application must be prioritized before it is sent out to ensure that pilots can allocate their attention appropriately to safety critical, and high priority information.

6 Conclusions

We performed a usability analysis on an EFB application used by a major U.S. air carrier to store all required inflight and out-of-flight documents and paperwork, and identified several redesign recommendations that could optimize pilot performance both on and off the flight deck. We developed redesign recommendations and implemented the recommendations into a low fidelity prototype. The evaluation results indicted improvements to menu structure and significant decreases in time to access high priority information. These recommendations are not only applicable to the range of EFBs currently available on the flight deck, but also to many types of mobile applications that provide users with a large amount of information in safety critical environments. Such applications should be designed to take into account the user, the environment, and the tasks to be performed. Implementing human-centered design recommendations in the digitization of paper-based processes will allow this transition to serve both the company and their employees. Companies can benefit from the efficiency and cost savings through the elimination of paper, and employees can be supported in the workplace with tablet-based applications that focus on effective task performance in their operational environments.

References

1. Abras, C., Maloney-Krichmar, D., Preece, J.: User-centered design. In: Bainbridge, W. (ed.) Encyclopedia of Human-Computer Interaction, vol. 37(4), pp. 445–456. Sage Publications, Thousand Oaks (2004). https://doi.org/10.1.1.94.381
2. Chaneski, W.: Expanding the Use of Tablets in Manufacturing (2015). https://www.mmsonline.com/columns/expanding-the-use-of-tablets-in-manufacturing
3. Croft, J.: Next-Generation EFBs Integral to NextGen Cockpit. Aviation Week Network (2015). http://aviationweek.com/aftermarket-solutions/next-generation-efbs-integral-nextgen-cockpit
4. Dance, J.: Flat navigation is better than deeper navigation. Fresh Consulting (2016). https://www.freshconsulting.com/uiux-principle-23-flatter-navigation-is-better-than-deeper-navigation/
5. Eastwood, B.: 12 Ways the iPad is Changing Healthcare. CIO from IDG (2012). https://www.cio.com/article/2369341/healthcare/78144-12-Ways-the-iPad-Is-Changing-Healthcare.html#slide8
6. Johnstone, N.: The Electronic Flight Bag Friend or Foe. Air Safety Group Report Nr, 104 (2013)
7. Lee, J.: Paper in a Digital World. CIO from IDG (2012). https://www.cio.com/article/3149529/data-center/paper-in-a-digital-world-time-to-eliminate-the-inefficiency-and-waste.html
8. Preece, J., Rogers, Y., Sharp, H.: Interaction Design: Beyond Human–Computer Interaction. Wiley, New York (2002)
9. Whitenton, K.: Flat vs. Deep Website Hierarchies. Nielsen Norman Group (2013). https://www.nngroup.com/articles/flat-vs-deep-hierarchy/

From Hardware to Software: Evaluating the Swipe Gestures Navigation Feature on Mobile Phones

Lúcia Satiko Nomiso[✉], Eduardo Hideki Tanaka,
and Raquel Pignatelli Silva

Eldorado Research Institute, Campinas, SP, Brazil
{lucia.nomiso, eduardo.tanaka,
raquel.silva}@eldorado.org.br

Abstract. This paper presents the user experience evaluation of a smartphone feature to allow users to do gestures in a small, pill-shaped button that replaces the typical Android navigation bar. This proposed pill-shaped button, located at the bottom of the screen, allows swipe and tap gestures to do the same functions available on the navigation bar: go back, go to home screen and open the recent apps. However, the pill-shaped button is smaller than the whole navigation bar, which leaves more space to the apps to show their content on screen. In order to evaluate this feature, 252 participants were invited to use it during about 3 months and report any issues using some apps to describe them as well as collect logs remotely. Also, participants were also invited to answer a few user satisfaction surveys after some time using the feature. Based on the findings from this evaluation process, it was possible to fix the issues found and improve the overall usability before the feature hit the market.

Keywords: User trial · User experience · Remote evaluation

1 Introduction

It is nearly impossible to imagine the world without smartphones. Since 2007, when the first iPhone was launched and Google announced Android, smartphones and their apps have become virtual partners of people in everyday life, from the time people wake up until they go to bed, deeply embedded into people's social lives [1]. According to Google Consumer Barometer [2], in 2017, 67% of people in Brazil were smartphone users. In more developed countries, the numbers are even higher: for example, in USA, 78% of population uses a smartphone whereas, in United Kingdom, 77% of population is smartphone users.

Given its small screen size, smartphone apps have adopted some techniques and patterns to prioritize content instead of navigation. One of the most common solution are the hamburger menus [3]. Alternatively, on-screen gestures such as swipe, pinch, tap and hold and others can be adopted to replace the same functionality of buttons, menus and links in an app, although those gestures are hard to discover and learn [3].

© Springer Nature Switzerland AG 2019
A. Marcus and W. Wang (Eds.): HCII 2019, LNCS 11586, pp. 565–579, 2019.
https://doi.org/10.1007/978-3-030-23535-2_41

Based on those principles to prioritize content, Lenovo Motorola introduced the One Button Nav feature to replace the typical Android navigation bar that appears at the bottom of the screen in the Moto G family released in 2017. The first versions of One Button Nav relied on gestures on the fingerprint sensor of the smartphones to provide the same functionalities present in the Android navigation bar (go back, go home, open recent apps). However, in some of the most recent devices released by Lenovo Motorola, the fingerprint sensor moved from the front-bottom of the device to the back or even to the right edge, making it more difficult to continue use those gestures in the sensor at any time. Thus, Lenovo Motorola proposed a newer version of One Button Nav in 2018, this time creating a simple thin, pill-shaped button that appears the bottom of the screen and allows users to swipe, tap, and long press and, with these gestures, have the same functionalities of the first version of One Button Nav.

This paper continues a research published and presented on HCI International 2018 [4] by evaluating the user experience of this new version of One Button Nav before hit the consumers. Once again, the process involved a remote user experience evaluation through log collection and by providing apps to the users to describe any issues they found as well as to answer user satisfaction surveys. The next sections will describe the One Button Nav, highlighting the similarities and differences between the hardware and the software solutions, the user evaluation process, and the major findings from this evaluation.

2   One Button Nav vs Soft One Nav

The One Button Nav, introduced by Lenovo Motorola in their smartphones in 2017, completely replaces the typical Android navigation bar (back, home and recent apps), providing the same functionality on the fingerprint sensor of the smartphones, as seen in Table 1. As a result, navigation bar is not shown at the bottom of the screen and, consequently, there is an increase of the useful area of the display. Figure 1 shows a Moto G5 Plus, one of the first Lenovo Motorola devices to have a fingerprint sensor capable of recognize One Button Nav gestures.

Table 1. One Button Nav gestures.

Gesture	Function
Tap on the sensor	Go to home screen
Swipe from right to left on the sensor	Go back
Swipe from left to right on the sensor	Open recent apps
Touch and hold the sensor until a short buzz	Turn the screen off (lock the device)
Touch and hold the sensor until a long buzz	Launch Google assistant

Fig. 1. Moto G5 Plus with the fingerprint sensor highlighted.

Smartphones with large screen sizes are increasingly in the market and become the trend in different regions, as seen in the charts of Fig. 2 [5]. In North America, 44% of users have smartphones with diagonal size between 5.5 and 6", whereas in South America this number is lower, 32%. Asia has the highest number of users with large screen sizes, with 47% of users having a smartphone with screen size between 5.5 and 6". On the other hand, Europe has the lowest number, with 23% [5]. Following this trend, all smartphones released by Lenovo Motorola in 2018 had at least 5.34" of diagonal size. More specifically, Moto Z3 Play, which was the device object of this research, has 6" of screen size.

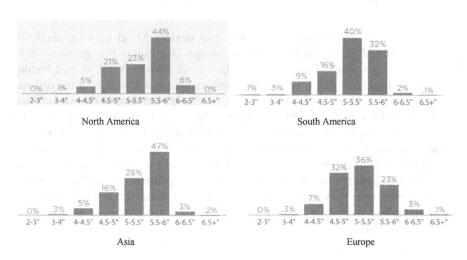

Fig. 2. Smartphone screen sizes in different regions [5].

In order to offer a larger the screen size to consumers, Moto Z3 Play and other smartphones from its generation moved the fingerprint sensor to the right edge of the device, as shown in Fig. 3, so that it became not natural to keep the One Button Nav gestures in the sensor to replace the Android navigation bar.

Fig. 3. Moto Z3 Play smartphone with fingerprint sensor to the right edge.

As many users of previous Lenovo Motorola devices would miss the ability to access the Android navigation bar functions through One Button Nav gestures, "Soft One Nav" was proposed. The "Soft One Nav" is an on-screen, pill-shaped button, placed at the bottom of the screen, which provides the same functions of the original One Button Nav. Although "Soft One Nav" is not exactly the same as the original One Button Nav, which works with the fingerprint sensor, due to marketing decisions, the same name was kept to the consumers (One Button Navigation). Figure 4 shows the onboarding screens of the two versions whereas Fig. 5 shows some screenshots of Moto Z3 Play with the "Soft One Nav" and the Android navigation bar. As seen in Fig. 5, the pill-shaped button of "Soft One Nav" is a very discreet element in the screen and a little bit smaller than the Android navigation bar. In other words, although it is on screen as Android navigation bar, "Soft One Nav" allow users to see more content on screen as it is smaller.

Fig. 4. Onboarding screens of One Nav 1.0 (based on fingerprint sensor) and "Soft One Nav".

Fig. 5. "Soft One Nav" and Android navigation bar in Moto Z3 Play.

Table 2 presents all functions available on the "Soft One Nav". Compared to the previous gestures and functions of the original One Button Nav (as shown in Table 1), the only change was with the touch and hold until a short buzz to lock the device.

Given that there were complaints about falsings (some users did this by mistake and ended up having to unlock the device again to continue using it), the decision was to remove it from "Soft One Nav".

Table 2. "Sotf One Nav" gestures.

Gesture	Function
Tap on the software button	Go to home screen
Swipe from right to left on the software button	Go back
Swipe from left to right on the software button	Open recent apps
Touch and hold the software button until a short buzz	*Turn off screen - Removed*
Touch and hold the software button until a long buzz	Launch Google assistant

Not only Lenovo Motorola adopted a solution to replace the default Android navigation bar. Even Google proposed a solution in Android 9.0 (Pie), as seen in Fig. 6. Technical media articles compared these solutions [6] and stated that Lenovo Motorola delivers a better user experience.

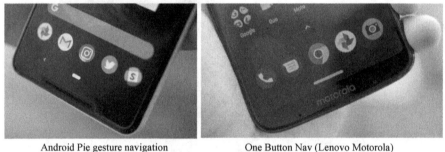

Android Pie gesture navigation   One Button Nav (Lenovo Motorola)

Fig. 6. Android Pie gesture navigation and One Button Nav.

3   Remote Evaluation of User Experience

To evaluate this new version of One Button Nav ("Soft One Nav"), 252 participants from all over the world were recruited and remotely monitored between March and June/2018. In order to test the One Button Nav, all participants received a Moto Z3 with Android O. In addition, a pre-installed tool in the smartphones allowed the participants to report issues, describing what they were doing when an issue occurred and attaching screenshots if they found it useful. By default, One Button Nav was disabled, but participants were asked to enable it and give all feedbacks by using this pre-installed tool or reporting in an online, internal forum, which allowed them to interact with other participants. Furthermore, during the evaluation period, four user satisfaction surveys were applied to rate agreement/disagreement with some user experience statements using a Likert Scale [7].

Internal forum was used most of the times for positive feedback, announcements or to confirm with other users if they are seeing same behaviors or problems in daily use, like seen in Fig. 7.

Fig. 7. Internal forum to share issues and feedback about the One Button Nav with other participants.

In total, 40 issues were manually raised by the participants. The distribution of the raised issues through the evaluation period and also how they were classified can be shown in Figs. 8 and 9. The classification of the issues and details about them can be seen in Table 3.

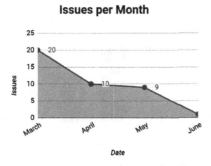

Fig. 8. Issues raised during the evaluation period distributed by months.

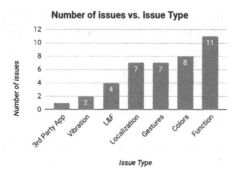

Fig. 9. Issues raised during evaluation period according to pre-defined classification.

Table 3. Classification of the issues.

Issue type	Description
3rd party app	Issue related to the usage of One Button Nav with another (3rd party) app. The responsible of the 3rd party app was notified about the issue to work on a fix
Vibration	Two issues were related to a misunderstanding of using Android vibration configuration and One Button Nav
Look and feel (L&F)	Issues related to objects not properly aligned
Localization	Most of them were related to some sentences not translated
Gestures	When some of the gestures were not working properly. Also regarding gesture to turn off screen, which users also complained about this removal
Colors	Issues related to color contrast and color combination
Function	Performance issues; although 5 of them here were related to a specific software build in which One Button Nav stopped working

Compared to the user experience evaluation done for the first version of One Button Nav, the amount of issues decreased, as shown in Fig. 10, although the number of participants were not the same: for the first version, there were 115 participants whereas, for the "Soft One Nav" evaluation, there were 252 participants.

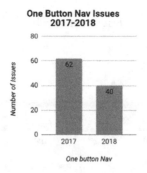

Fig. 10. Amount of issues of One Button Nav in 2017 (first version) and 2018 (new version, "Soft One Nav").

After the development team analyzed all the issues manually raised by the participants, this number decreased to 10 unique, valid issues – from all issues, 57.5% were duplicated, 22.5% were fixed, 12.5% considered as working as designed, 2.5% cancelled by the development team, 2.5% were invalid and 2.5% were not resolved. Figures 11 and 12 show some charts summarizing how the issues were handled by the development team.

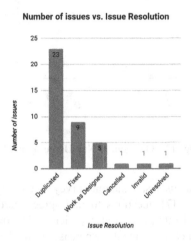

Fig. 11. One Button Nav issues resolution.

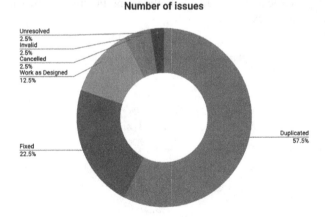

Fig. 12. One Button Nav issues resolution (distribution).

The usage of One Button Nav gestures were tracked over the time and, as seen in Fig. 13, it increased during the weeks. In the first week, 8.7% of the participants used One Button Nav whereas, in the last week, almost 32% of the participants used it. In the previous study of the first version of One Button Nav, less than 24% of the participants were effectively using the feature at the end of the evaluation period [4].

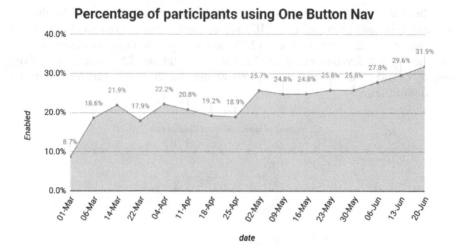

Fig. 13. One Button Nav Usage by week.

During this study, four user satisfaction surveys were applied. The surveys were composed by Likert Scale [7] questions to rate agreement/disagreement with some statements about the One Button Nav user experience. The first survey collected only 60 responses from distinct participants whereas in the last one 159 participants answered. The surveys were applied when the users changed their devices to newer ones containing hardware changes and when a new software version containing One Button Nav improvements was available to the users. Figure 14 shows the number of participants in each survey.

Fig. 14. Number of participants in each survey.

As previously mentioned, from Moto Z2 Play to Moto Z3 Play, the fingerprint sensor moved from the bottom of the screen to the right edge of the device. Also, One Button Nav was moved from the fingerprint sensor to a "software" button pill drawn at the bottom of the screen. Considering these hardware changes, a comparison between the two devices was made to evaluate overall satisfaction with the fingerprint sensor. For Moto Z2 Play survey, 73 responses were collected whereas for Moto Z3 Play 159 responses were collected. The results from the surveys showed that the fingerprint location at the right edge was not rated as positively as at the bottom of the screen, as seen in Fig. 15.

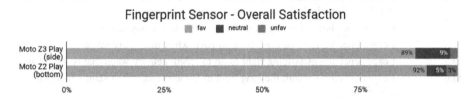

Fig. 15. Overall satisfaction with the Fingerprint sensor.

In addition, One Button Nav was also evaluated in these surveys, as shown in Table 4 and Fig. 16. Overall, there was a more positive response for the newer version of One Button Nav ("Soft One Nav") than for the previous version based on the fingerprint sensor.

Table 4. Overall satisfaction with One Button Nav.

Version	Fav	Neutral	Unfav
"Soft One Nav" (Moto Z3 Play)	88%	9%	3%
One Button Nav 1.0 (Moto Z2 Play)	80%	12%	8%

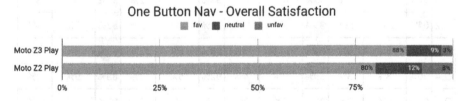

Fig. 16. Overall satisfaction with One Button Nav in Moto Z3 Play ("Soft One Nav") and in Moto Z2 Play (One Button Nav 1.0).

From the first study [4] to the new one, the questions in the surveys were updated according to the changes in One Button Nav. The updated questions are presented in Table 5.

Table 5. Survey questions for the new version of One Button Nav.

Question ID	Question
Q.0	Overall how satisfied are you with the Gesture navigation performance of your device?
Q.1	How frequently did you experience issues with Gesture navigation Performance?
Q.2	I prefer to use Gesture Navigation as opposed to using Touch Screen Buttons (TSB soft keys include back, home and recently activity)
Q.3	I experience issues tapping to go home when that is my intent
Q.4	I experience issues swiping left to go back when that is my intent
Q.5	I experience issues swiping right to go to recent activity when that is my intent
Q.6	I experience issues with the long hold to launch Google Assistant when that is my intent
Q.7	I experience issues with the haptics used for Gesture Navigation

Table 6 presents the results from the applied surveys and the charts in Figs. 17 and 18 present the specific results from the first and the last survey. The evolution of favorable responses during the surveys is also shown in Fig. 19.

Table 6. Survey questions for the new version of One Button Nav.

	Survey 01			Survey 02			Survey 03			Survey 04		
	fav	neutral	unfav	fav	neutral	unfav	fav	neutral	unfav	fav	neutral	unfav
Q.0	90%	5%	5%	88%	9%	6%	88%	9%	3%	88%	9%	3%
Q.1	92%	3%	5%	93%	4%	4%	93%	5%	2%	90%	6%	3%
Q.2	64%	23%	13%	86%	2%	13%	71%	14%	16%	82%	9%	9%
Q.3	92%	8%	0%	84%	11%	6%	90%	6%	3%	93%	6%	1%
Q.4	90%	8%	3%	89%	7%	4%	92%	5%	3%	88%	9%	3%
Q.5	92%	5%	3%	93%	6%	2%	92%	5%	3%	93%	6%	1%
Q.6	82%	12%	6%	76%	18%	7%	91%	8%	1%	92%	8%	0%
Q.7	90%	5%	5%	89%	6%	6%	96%	3%	1%	96%	5%	0%

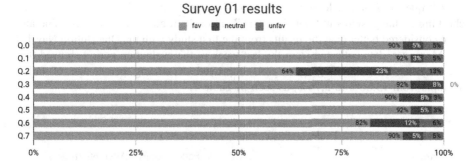

Fig. 17. Results of the first survey (01).

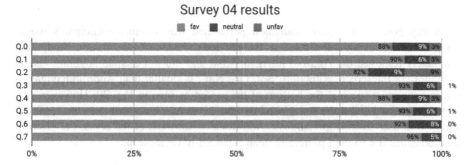

Fig. 18. Results of the last survey (04).

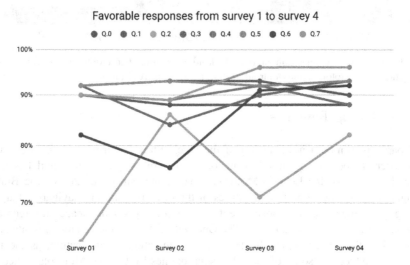

Fig. 19. Evolution of the favorable responses during the surveys.

All questions had at least 82% of favorable responses in the last Survey. Thus, checking all the gestures in "Soft One Nav", all of them got more than this value and were considered better than the results from the first study with the One Button Nav 1.0 [4]. Moreover, data collected from the last week of the evaluation period showed that accuracy to recognize fingerprint also improved decreasing percentage of failed attempts from 13.66% to 5.76%, as seen in Table 7.

Table 7. Fingerprint failed attempts (%).

Product	Failed (%)	Failed (times)	Attempts (times)
"Soft One Nav" (Moto Z3 Play)	5.76	335	5811
One Button Nav 1.0 (Moto Z2 Play)	13.66	1382	10118

A key point in the user evaluation performed was whether participants would complain about losing screen area, as the previous version of One Button Navigation completely removed the Android navigation bar and did not include anything else at the bottom of the screen. Although "Soft One Nav" is smaller than Android navigation bar, it occupies a space at the bottom of the screen as seen in Fig. 20. However, few users complained about the space used by "Soft One Nav", according to the feedback provided in user satisfaction surveys. Additionally, for most of the users, the gestures were considered easy and preferable than Android navigation bar.

Android O   Motorola   Android P

Fig. 20. Navigation comparison among Android navigation bar (Android O), One Button Navigation from Motorola and Android gesture navigation (Android P).

4   Concluding Remarks

This paper presented a new version of the One Button Navigation, a feature which allow users to perform gestures in an, on screen, pill-shaped button and has been shipped in some of the Lenovo Motorola smartphones since mid-2018. One Button Navigation offers the same functionalities of the ordinary Android navigation bar (go back, go to home screen and open recent apps), but using smaller space on screen and having a more modern look and feel. The One Button Navigation version presented and evaluated in this paper is actually the second generation of the feature, as the first version, introduced in some of the 2017 smartphones by Lenovo Motorola, relied on the fingerprint sensor.

The user evaluation performed showed very positive results, indicating high user satisfaction. Moreover, comparing to the first One Button Navigation version, the favorable responses were even higher. This kind of evaluation was incredibly valuable to assess the feature before hitting the market, making the stakeholders confident about its usability and utility to the users.

References

1. Kakihara, M.: Grasping a global view of smartphone diffusion: an analysis from a global smartphone study. In: Proceedings of the 13th International Conference on Mobile Business (2014)
2. Consumer Barometer with Google. https://www.consumerbarometer.com/en/trending. Accessed 24 Oct 2018
3. Budiu, R.: The State of Mobile User Experience. https://www.nngroup.com/articles/state-mobile-ux/. Accessed 31 Jan 2019
4. Nomiso, L.S., Tanaka, E.H., Silva, R.P.: Improving mobile user experience of new features through remote tests and evaluation. In: Kurosu, Masaaki (ed.) HCI 2018. LNCS, vol. 10902, pp. 565–575. Springer, Cham (2018). https://doi.org/10.1007/978-3-319-91244-8_44
5. Mobile Overview Report April–June 2018, pp. 2–3 (2018). (https://www.scientiamobile.com/wp-content/uploads/2018/08/MOVR-2018-Q2-final.pdf. Accessed 24 Oct 2018
6. Android Pie should just adopt Motorola's one-button navigation gestures instead. https://www.androidcentral.com/android-p-should-just-adopt-motorolas-one-button-navigation-gestures-instead. Accessed 24 Oct 2018
7. Wuensch, K.L.: What is a Likert scale? And how do you pronounce 'Likert?' East Carolina University, 27 October 2017 (2005)

The Use of the Virtual Fashion Tester: A Usability Study

Ademario S. Tavares[1(✉)], Marcelo Soares[3], Márcio Marçal[2],
Luiz W. N. Albuquerque[1], Aline Neves[1], Jaciara Silva[1],
Samantha Pimentel[1], and José C. Ramos Filho[1]

[1] Federal University of Pernambuco, Recife, Brazil
ademariojr@hotmail.com, ctiwilson@gmail.com,
linebelar@gmail.com, jaciaraclarissa@gmail.com,
samanthagcpimentel@gmail.com,
calixto.ramos@hotmail.com
[2] Federal University of the Vales do Jequitinhonha e do Mucuri,
Diamantina, Brazil
marcio@nersat.com.br
[3] Hunan University, Changsha, People's Republic of China
soaresmm@gmail.com

Abstract. Internet shopping has been around for a number of years, changing the way companies deal with their customers and technologies have followed that process through new tools and experiences. The fashion industry has followed these changes and has modernized itself to the point where consumers can get clothes without leaving their homes through the use of virtual tasters. From the simplest models that use few anthropometric measures to the most advanced ones with Augmented Reality, avatars and body movements, virtual testers have become allies for both business profits and user experiences. This paper portrays the experience of using a virtual fashion taster by a group of Fashion Design students at a university in Brazil. After evaluating this tool and answering a questionnaire about usability, some questions about ergonomic factors were discussed and proposals were generated for future designs.

Keywords: Ergonomic factors · Usability · Virtual fitting room

1 Introduction

E-commerce has taken an unprecedented proportion nowadays, being possible to buy virtually any product or service over the internet. Consumers are using e-commerce due to numerous advantages compared to going to physical stores, for example: the ease of buying 24 h a day, faster price searches, the convenience of buying at home without the need to leave and face the difficulties of daily life, such as traffic, queues, violence, tight shops, lack of architectural accessibility, etc. Meanwhile, entrepreneurs and owners of virtual stores also find several advantages in maintaining a virtual store, whether in conjunction with a physical store or not.

Shopping websites have a basic structure, with simple access and information about the products and other general data, such as company history, fashion tips, interviews,

© Springer Nature Switzerland AG 2019
A. Marcus and W. Wang (Eds.): HCII 2019, LNCS 11586, pp. 580–595, 2019.
https://doi.org/10.1007/978-3-030-23535-2_42

publications, photo gallery, payment methods, etc. However, it does not have a seller on the job, give you more information, and increase your shopping experience.

In recent years this process has changed and technology has brought new perspectives. In times of competition, it has become important to provide users with more than a visual experience. In this scenario came a resource that brought a new way of defining choice and purchase: the virtual fashion taster. That is, a digital way of choosing your outfit without users leaving their home.

However, this has become a major challenge for many professionals involved with the development of websites. Moving from a real to a virtual experience has many variables that range from usability and technology issues to emotional, social, financial, and behavioral issues. In view of the above and considering HCI as the discipline related to the evaluation of interactive computer systems for human use, this article brings the results of usability evaluation of a shopping site with virtual fitting room.

Twenty students from an undergraduate course in Fashion Design used the virtual fitting room in some Brazilian e-commerce sites and simulated the purchase of some pieces of clothing, verifying the possibilities that this tool provides. The students analyzed usability according to the hybrid model of Usability of Leventhal and Barnes [20] and made observations according to the Basic Ergonomic Factors of Gomes Filho [14]. After finding positive and negative points, the students brought a number of contributions that can be used in future versions or updates of this tool, taking into account the experience of using the tool, the information it provides, the experience and the empathy with the user.

2   Fashion Industry

Retail stores are changing the way they sell their products since the rise of Internet sales, drawing attention to the reflections and adaptations of the physical stores. Several researches address the future of traditional e-commerce versus e-commerce, drawing attention to this new way of dealing with an increasingly connected, technology-savvy public who wants new alternatives [31].

While interior designers, architects and shopwindows work tirelessly to create showcases and flashy decorations to attract as many customers as possible, another team of professionals working in the computer and information industry (digital programmers, Information Technology engineers, Web designers, etc.) seek to reduce the existing gap that differentiates the actual shopping experience from what happens on websites, in a virtual way [3].

This new process has also led to a growth in competition, modifying the sales policy of companies, putting pressure on the creative sectors, generating more discussions about the consequences and implications of online sales, requiring new directions for the production chain, logistics and supply, and the consumer a more essential element in the sales process [13]. One of the main innovations was systems that virtually test fashion products, also known as virtual fitting room.

2.1   Virtual Fitting Room

Traditional cloth tasters are physical spaces located within commercial establishments, usually in the form of booths. Consumers can experiment and evaluate clothing and accessories in front of mirrors. It is a place of great importance because it is where the consumer can make his purchase decision. In the case of the virtual fashion taster, the consumer does not necessarily have to be present in the physical store and can virtually "taste" any clothing product. It can even be done at home, in front of the computer or smartphone.

This tool appeared in some Brazilian sites some years ago in order to solve the problem that the consumers found to choose their products in more detail, especially referring to the size and comfort. Researchers point out that the installation of the Virtual FashionTaster brings benefits to shopkeepers who have shops in digital format [3, 13]. Among the benefits are increased profits, increased technology investments (generating new applications, usage alternatives, and experiences) and increased consumer curiosity about product characteristics, which in turn increases online shopping, and offline (in the physical store) as it became common for the consumer to try at home and then go to the store to make the purchase. The Fig. 1 shows an example of virtual fitting room.

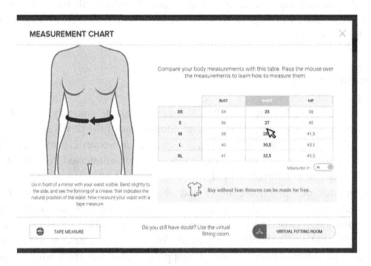

Fig. 1. A 2D female avatar and her body measurements. References: https://sizebay.com/en/ (Authorized by Sizebay).

There are several models with various configurations and possibilities of use. From 2D models accessed with just a few mouse clicks (or on the display), with scrollbars, buttons, and fields for numeric data to models that use the computer or smartphone camera, where the user captures his or her own photo and through the overlap of images it is possible to "mount" the clothing in your own body. There are still the most advanced models, installed in physical stores, that capture the real image of the body through complex algorithms present in sensors installed in mirrors. This body reading performs a scanning and capturing of the body sizing, generating an avatar with the precise measurements of the body, simulating the "virtual assembly" of the clothes in the user with great detail, using a pre-existing database [26, 27].

It can observed the use of Virtual Reality (VR) and Augmented Reality (RA) technology in more advanced models, especially those that use avatars. In fact the term "3D avatar" corresponds to a graphic, digital, complete and personalized representation of a person. There are several models and the main attributes that the deference is the realism, the level of detail and the movements [4]. Some examples of virtual fitting room and/or technologies that use RA for fashion use are: "1Measure", "Viubox", "FaceCake", "Swivel", "Fitiquette", "Zugara", "triMirror", "bodyvisualizer", "Fitnect", "Bodi.me".

2.2   Fashion in the Virtual World

The use of RV and RA is one of the great advances in the user experience. The global market for virtual environments (especially those using VR and RA as technology) undergoes exponential growth, from \$6.1 billion in 2016 to a projection of \$209.2 billion in 2022. The figures indicate that there are huge investments, opportunities and expectations [28].

According to Flavián [12] state-of-the-art technologies that utilize RV in favor of customers can be a great alternative against competition when used commercially. The authors cite as an example the early visualization of the new decoration of a room before the project is even finalized or virtually experience the clothes before they go to the store. This interaction can be a great competitive advantage, including influencing the purchase intention.

Empirical tests with new techniques, types of virtual fashion tasters using real consumers and comparative tests help companies to understand the function of this technology, facilitating the selection of the best model to meet their needs and their objectives related to production, logistics, sales, marketing and the relationship they maintain with their customers [2, 9, 15, 24, 32]. The comparative results bring new insights into the interaction with environments and virtual elements, whether physical (through body tracing) to cognitive, emotional and sentimental aspects, and are configured as hybrid experiences [5, 6].

3   Usability

The term usability is a concept of fundamental importance to the design and its applications. If the purpose of a product or system is to meet the needs of the user, usability is the element that will provide the execution of the activity and the satisfaction of the user. The usability process "begins by looking at who uses the product, understanding its objectives and needs" [10], and then defining the most appropriate technique to meet the needs and provide a correct interaction between the user, the product and the task.

ISO 9241-11 [18] defines usability as the "reach by which a product can be used by certain users to achieve specific goals with effectiveness, efficiency and satisfaction in a certain context of use." This definition highlights both the complexity and the usability scope. Without usability, the product or system tends to fail, causing several problems, such as user dissatisfaction, loss of time and expenses, extra costs, generating low productivity, among others [21].

The methods of usability evaluation evolved from the first initiatives in the 1980s, becoming constants, enabling increasingly successful interactive experiences [11, 17, 21]. More than the technique and technology used in application development, user experience and satisfaction during and after its use have become valuable elements for websites [1].

However, the virtual world is still a great novelty for many people. Some difficulties that the online clothing trade encounters are distrust and uncertainty of the user, lack of experience in the use of new technologies, doubt in the veracity of the description of the product information, the quality of the product, exchange problems or to the question of the future performance of the product and its durability [7]. Behavior change includes acceptance and trust in the internet, the perception and frequency of use of this technology, clarity and understanding, social influence and opinion of the people [16].

According to Nielsen [22] the usability tests bring countless benefits to both the users and the professionals who develop the systems. In addition to identifying usage problems that may make it difficult or impossible to perform the task, the tests can generate improvements suggested by the users themselves through feedbacks. Tests may occur in a natural environment (field test) or in a controlled environment (laboratory test), however it is important to consider the use context that, in addition to the environment, includes users, the tasks that will be [10, 18].

3.1 Leventhal and Barnes Usability Model

The various types of existing usability tests use different metrics, factors, and parameters, depending on the product or system to be analyzed for use. The model of Leventhal and Barnes [20] has the characteristic of being hybrid because it brings together the main factors of three usability models: Eason [8], Shackel [25] and Neilsen [23].

The authors believe that gathering a set of variables related to a use situation (including the task, user and interface) may result in a more adequate diagnosis of good or bad usability. The model developed by Leventhal and Barnes is divided into two types of variables: situational and user interface, according to Table 1. The definitions of each variable are reported below [10, 20, 21, 29, 30]:

Table 1. Model of usability of Leventhal and Barnes [20], adapted from Falcão and Soares [10].

Situational	Variables	User interface variable
Task variable	User variable	–
Frequence		Easy of learning
Rigidity		Ease of use
Limitations of the situation		Ease of relearning
		Flexibility
		Satisfaction
		Task matching

- Frequency - interferes with usability because the sequence of steps to accomplish a task becomes easier if it is performed regularly thanks to the human memory factor.
- Rigidity - the amount of options that allow the accomplishment of a de-terminated task can influence usability. If the number of paths is large, the stiffness will be low. But with few steps it is possible that the ta-refa is simple, setting itself as high stiffness.
- Limitations of the situation - attribute related to possible barriers that may hamper the accomplishment of the task, causing failures and failures. For example, instruction in a language other than native language may make it difficult to understand and accomplish the task.
- User variables - User characteristics can influence usability, such as motivation and experience, including ability to solve problems.
- Ease of learning - Can novice users learn to use the interface? Is it easy to understand and memorize the steps?
- Ease of use - Is the process of using the interface easy or not? Usability will occur if there is facility.
- Ease of relearning - After using the first time, will the user be easy to use the second time or will he/she encounter difficulties?
- Flexibility - in the event of an unforeseen event, does the interface facilitate the solution and the resumption of the task? For example, if you have the "Undo" button, it will override some inappropriate command, returning to the immediately preceding stage.
- Satisfaction - If the interface is easy to use and learn it is likely to be satisfying. Understand the difference between expectations and the performance of a product or system after its use.
- Task Matching - Proper correlation between the interface and the task helps both the novice and the seasoned user schematize their understanding, after all, a good combination of tasks facilitates understanding.

3.2 Basic Ergonomic Factors

Ergonomics is a scientific discipline whose use of its principles is present in the most diverse situations and contexts of daily life. This condition is possible due to the presence of several factors that are part of the project development process and are also part of ergonomic research. It is likely that a product that provides safety and comfort during its use can be considered a good product. Therefore, the "safety" and "comfort" factors should be considered by the industry in general, used as requirements in the development of their products and, where possible, informed to consumers.

Professor and ergonomist Gomes Filho [14] developed a technical ergonomic reading system that relates factors that can be used in projects in the areas of product design, graphic design, architecture and interfaces. This system considers some factors to be basic and very important for design because of its breadth of reach and benefits. Although each project has characteristics, configuration, function, context and specific uses, these factors have a strong influence on the various stages of project development.

The ergonomic factors cited by Gomes Filho [14] are divided into three blocks of variables according to Table 2, and will be explained briefly below.

Table 2. Basic ergonomic factors, adapted from Gomes Filho [14].

Project requirements	Handling actions	Perception actions
Task	Operational handling	Visual
Safety	Cleaning	Auditive
Comfort	Maintenance	Tactile
Reach Wrap	Spatial arrangement	Kinesthetic
Posture		Vibration
Application of force		
Popular stereotype		
Materials		

Project Requirements

- Task - Knowing how, why and why the public will wear a garment is crucial for the fashion designer, preventing him from designing something out of context, especially if they are clothing for specific use.
- Safety - Protection of the human body is the main function of dressing, but in some situations safety is paramount. For example, to protect against accidents, mainly uniforms and sportswear.
- Comfort - The perception of comfort is somewhat subjective. However, comfort must provide physical and sensory well-being, suitability during use without causing temporary or intense discomfort and that do not interfere with the performance of domestic, work or leisure tasks.
- Reach Wrap - Understands the area or spatial volume where the people perform their activities without adopting inappropriate postures that can cause muscular fatigue. Some clothing may hinder or prevent full reach of the arms to the closing systems.
- Posture - Posture depends heavily on the wearer's attitudes rather than on clothing. But improperly sized clothing or asymmetric structure may disrupt posture.
- Application of force - Are the physical movements and efforts made by the user in relation to the handling and control of certain products. Some clothes, like the corselet, require the user's physical strength to dress.
- Popular stereotype - Corresponds to common usage practices, known by the population of a given location. It has to do with culture, customs, beliefs and corresponds to the way systems and products are used.
- Materials - The choice of materials is of fundamental importance because their characteristics can influence in different conditions: use, laundry function, economy, aesthetics, comfort, cleanliness, safety (inflammability, toxicity, etc.). Even the materials can be decisive for the success of the other ergonomic factors.

Handling Actions

- Operational handling - Act or physical action that relates to the handling or operation of any product. The use of most of the products occurs through physical contact through the handles and knowing them is important.
- Cleaning - Fundamental to task functionality and efficiency, this variant is a desirable feature in any product.
- Maintenance - represents the preservation of the configuration and function of the product. Knowing the correct maintenance procedures for a garment facilitates interchangeability and can influence the performance of the task and the useful life.
- Spatial arrangement - Can be understood as the best possible organization of the elements of a garment, allowing the proper distribution of the items as required.

Perception Actions

- Visual - Being the main element of perception of the human being, the vision exerts a great influence in the decision making of purchase in the industry of the model. The product is "pleasing to the eye" even before use.
- Auditory - This perception can complement, reinforce, or replace the assimilation of certain information captured by vision. Or, if used improperly, it can cause noise that hinders silence.
- Tactile - It has intense relation with the materials. The contact and pressure of the clothing on the body can assume diverse perceptions and sensations depending on the type of material and accessories. Is the fabric light or heavy? Smooth or rough?
- Kinesthetic - It has to do with the multisensory perception and with the muscular movements, position and weight of the body. It is a relatively complex perception action.
- Vibration - Understands the vibrations that occur with the use of the object and can be felt. For example, tasks that require a lot of movement from the user, if your uniform has accessories that can cause vibration, balance or trepidation, the task may be poorly executed.

4 Case Study

The case study was carried out with students of the course of Fashion Design of two colleges in the state of Pernambuco, Brazil. Of the 48 students involved, only 20 were selected (14 women and 6 men) for meeting the following criteria: to be at least 18 years of age; have completed more than half the course; being enrolled in the discipline Ergodesign and; never have used a virtual fitting room.

Purchasing should be done on personal computers, as ease of use of the hardware would allow exploring all elements of the virtual fitting room.

4.1 Methodology and Initial Procedures

The approach of this study was objectivist, since there was a preliminary investigation to obtain the knowledge and later practical application. The character of the study is descriptive, since it was observed the phenomenon, the record of the events and the analysis of the data collected.

After studying the methodologies of Leventhal and Barnes and Gomes Filho, the students simulated for 20 min the purchase of clothes using the virtual suppliers in Brazilian sites of clothes retail sales. After the use experience, they answered a questionnaire using the five-level Likert scale. Although it is possible to adopt other levels according to the precision of the answers, the context of the respondents' understanding or specific details [19], the original model was chosen.

No guiding or supplementary questions were elaborated, only the statement of each variable and factor composed the questionnaires. Students assigned a score of 1 to 5 to identify the positive and negative points of virtual tasters. In the end, the students presented their opinions and generated recommendations.

The caption adopted was as follows:

- Strongly agree = worth 5 points;
- Somewhat agree = worth 4 points;
- Neither agree nor disagree = worth 3 points;
- Somewhat disagree = worth 2 points;
- Strongly disagree = worth 1 point.

4.2   The Choice of Website

The 20 students accessed a number of Brazilian websites, but found few virtual fashion tasters. Most sites provided only measurement tables and some had 2D avatars, signaling some parts of the body. However, one kind of virtual fashion taster platform was replicated on most of the sites found and all students chose to evaluate its usability.

It is the Sizebay platform (https://sizebay.com/en/), a company that was born in 2014 in Brazil and offers the virtual taster system for more than 100 virtual stores, in various fashion segments, such as sportswear and uniforms. The Fig. 2 shows one of the steps of the sizebay virtual fitting room.

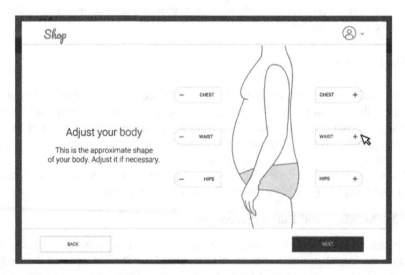

Fig. 2. One of the screens of the virtual fitting room of Sizebay, 2019. References: https://sizebay.com/en/ (Authorized by Sizebay).

4.3   Usability Evaluation

The Leventhal and Barnes usability test is divided into variables and students should analyze each of them during the use of the virtual provider. The standard question to be answered was this: "Is this variable present in the virtual taster?".

The twenty students were represented by codes, distributed at random, from S1 to S20. The order of numbers had no meaning or interference in the answers. Table 3 presents the final result, where S1 stands for "Student n.1" and V1 is the "variable n. 01 "and the values were explained in Sect. 4.1.

Table 3. Result of the usability evaluation according to Leventhal and Barnes [20]

Participant	V1	V2 *	V3 **	V4 ***	V5	V6	V7	V8	V9	V10
ST1	5	5	5	5	5	5	5	5	5	5
ST2	5	4	5	4	4	5	5	5	5	5
ST3	4	4	4	4	5	5	5	5	5	5
ST4	4	5	5	3	4	5	4	5	5	5
ST5	3	2	5	2	4	3	3	5	4	4
ST6	5	4	5	4	4	4	4	5	5	5
ST7	5	5	5	5	5	5	5	5	5	5
ST8	5	5	5	5	5	5	5	5	5	5
ST9	4	4	5	4	4	4	3	4	5	4
ST10	5	4	5	5	5	5	5	5	5	5
ST11	5	4	5	4	5	5	5	5	5	5
ST12	5	5	5	5	5	5	5	5	5	5
ST13	5	5	5	4	4	5	5	5	5	5
ST14	4	4	5	4	4	4	3	5	5	5
ST15	4	5	4	5	5	5	5	5	5	5
ST16	4	5	5	5	5	5	5	5	5	5
ST17	5	5	5	4	5	5	5	5	5	5
ST18	5	4	5	4	4	4	4	4	5	4
ST19	5	4	4	3	4	4	3	4	5	5
SP20	5	5	5	4	5	5	4	5	5	5
Total	92	88	97	83	91	93	88	97	99	97

Attention: Although there is a standard question, some variables require a complement, and the items below, with asterisks, tell you about the complements.

*The rigidity to perform the task is high.

**There are no limitations of the situation in the virtual taster.

***The variables of a beginning user do not influence the use of the taster.

4.4   Basic Ergonomic Factors

Each student researched a website and evaluated the data available on it, the step-by-step usage, seeking information related to basic ergonomic factors. In all there were 9 sites with virtual tasters and some of them were analyzed by more than one student. The amount of data generated was enormous and would not fit into this work for reasons of space limitations.

However, Tables 4, 5 and 6 provide an overview of students' perceptions.

No site or type of clothing has been contemplated and the results below do not specify any of them. The tables only demonstrate in a global way the students' perception and critical sense of the ergonomic issues.

Table 4. Assessment of basic ergonomic factors - project requirements.

Project requirements	Situation found in the virtual fitting room	Recommendations
Task	- The clothes available on the websites are conventional, for day-to-day use, and it is not necessary to specify the suitability of the clothes for their respective specific tasks	- Use this feature on websites that sell clothing for corporate, industrial, sports or medical use. Risk and safety are important in these contexts
Safety	- Some websites sold uniforms, which require more information because they are special clothing	- Clothing of specific use, work or intense effort, such as industrial uniforms, sports clothes (especially radicals), and their accessories should mention safety
Comfort	- In this sense, facing various categories of comfort, only visual comfort is possible, because physical comfort requires direct contact with clothing	- It would be interesting to contain additional information, such as thermal comfort, whether the drying is fast, whether it has a size adjustment system, whether the clothing has UV protection, etc.
Popular stereotype	- The websites visited only sell national clothes. Therefore, local customs have been respected and it is likely that all clothing will be easy to use	- Clothing that has closure systems that are more difficult to trigger, or that come from other cultures and countries, should have additional information
Reach Wrap	- Most of the clothes tested have front or side closure systems, with easy reach and actuation	- The website should inform if there is cloth with closure systems in an area that is difficult for the user to reach, making their autonomy difficult
Posture	- The clothes sold on the sites are conventional and did not influence the user's posture. It is important to remember that this is a user behavioral issue	- It is not possible to control the posture of the users and often he is responsible for maintaining his correct posture. In the case of clothes used in specific situations, where tasks require inappropriate postures, this information can be included in the Task item. Remembering that there are special clothes with postural brokers

(continued)

Table 4. (*continued*)

Project requirements	Situation found in the virtual fitting room	Recommendations
Application of Force	- The clothes simulated by the students have a closure system with simple shapes and easy-to-execute actuations	- Clothing that has complex closure systems that require application of force or help from third parties for the act of undressing or dressing should contain additional information. If possible, contain illustrations
Materials	- It was possible to observe in some sites that the materials were cited, but with little information	- Knowing the characteristics and comportamento of the materials helps in the choice of clothes, such as resistance, temperature provided, texture, elasticity, compression, reflex, etc.

Table 5. Assessment of basic ergonomic factors - handling actions.

Handling actions	Situation found in the virtual fitting room	Recommendations
Operational handling	- The clothes on the websites have simple functional systems and the handling for wearing or undressing is relatively simple	- Clothing with closure systems with different formats must contain usage information and enlarged images of the systems
Cleaning	- No information was found to facilitate the cleaning process	- It is recommended that the website has information on the cleaning materials to be used in the clothes, especially in the case of clothes that need special cleaning
Maintenance	- There was no information on maintenance of the clothes or accessories	- Usually the maintenance information comes on the label, but it could come on the website, including information about the accessories
Spatial arrangement	- The human models using the clothes give a correct dimension of the configuration of the clothes and their configuration, especially through the frontal view	- Allowing the visualization of the clothes in various views and angles facilitates the understanding of the clothing in the body, and can facilitate the choice

Table 6. Evaluation of basic ergonomic factors – perception actions.

Perception actions	Situation found in the virtual fitting room	Recommendations
Visual	- The images and their enlargements show the structure of the clothing, its details, acuity, legibility and the whole as a whole	- The images are enough to demonstrate the configuration of the clothes. If possible, insert videos with moving models
Auditory	- No information was found on auditory perception	- It is important to give details about clothes with accessories or elements that can emit sounds (such as touching metal parts)
Tactile	- Some websites contain information about materials, but there is a lack of data on tactile perception	- The sensation of the touch should be mentioned in the clothes, for it has to do with physical comfort
Kinesthetic	- There are no references to kinesthetic or synesthesia	- It is important to make clothes visible in different angles or a landscape behind the clothes to simulate an environment
Vibration	- No vibration data found on clothing	- Accessories that can swing or shake should be reported

4.5   Positive and Negative Points Found in the Study

At the end of the assessments, students should report positives and negatives (success or failure) of the experience of using virtual fashion tasters. The positive points were the following:

- The experience was satisfactory and interesting.
- I found it easy to use, even easy to learn.
- It is easy to buy, because the virtual taster takes some doubts regarding the body and its proportions.
- It is possible to have a mean base of body measurements and physical type.
- Having the notion that the clothing meets my expectations makes all the difference.
- There is a table with standard measures in case of doubts.
- I found the procedures quick, better than leaving the house to buy

  The negatives points were the following:

- None of the websites reported on the homepage that has the virtual fashion taster option, it is necessary that the consumer first click on some clothing to see the option. It should be more perceptive.
- The websites found have few pieces to use the virtual fashion taster, not all can be simulated, which left a feeling of frustration.
- The difficulty in finding stores with virtual fashion tasters was high, showing that this technology still needs to be spread.

- Some websites have misleading advertising, as they claim to have the virtual fashion taster and when we visit we only find a table of measurements, without the adjustment and simulation capabilities of the human body.
- Some websites claim to have the virtual fashion taster option but the link is inactive or indicates an error.
- Most sites with virtual fashion tasters use the same Sizebay software, evidencing the little investment of this technology in national clothing sites.
- The virtual fashion taster does not allow 360-degree rotation, and a multi-angle view is not possible.
- It was not possible to observe the trim of the clothing on the body.
- There was a lack of organization of clothing sizes on the site I researched.

The positives and negatives refer to the experience with the websites and the virtual fitting room. The opinions are general, not specific.

5 Final Considerations

The usability assessment of the virtual taster was an enriching experience for Fashion Design students. It allowed them to evaluate the functionality through the application of knowledge on Ergonomics and the usability test. The presented suggestions were pertinent and the present observations in this work are only a summary of the final content of the discipline Ergodesign. The main objective was achieved and the final result indicated a high level of satisfaction in the use of the virtual test, even though it is a new resource for students.

Applying the basic ergonomic factors in fashion was a major challenge, requiring insight, sensitivity, critical sense and detail on the part of the students, bringing new ways of seeing the products, focusing on the user experience.

It was agreed among students that the convenience provided by online shopping helps increase the presence of this type of business transaction worldwide. The speed in evaluations and comparisons of the products that are coming is one of the great benefits, especially if the consumer does not need to leave the house. This technology is a strong ally to meet this need and to consider ergonomics in this process is of fundamental importance.

References

1. Arslan, H., Yuksek, A.G., Elyakan, M.L., Canay, O.: Usability and quality tests in software products to oriented of user experience. J. Qual. High. Educ. 4(3), 81 (2018)
2. Ayalp, N., Yildirim, K., Bozdayi, M., Cagatay, K.: Consumers' evaluations of fitting rooms in retail clothing stores. Int. J. Retail Distrib. Manag. 44(5), 524–539 (2016). https://doi.org/10.1108/IJRDM-06-2015-0085
3. Beck, M., Crié, D.: I virtually try it… I want it ! Virtual fitting room: a tool to increase online and off-line exploratory behavior, patronage and purchase intentions. J. Retail. Consum. Serv. 40, 279–286 (2016). https://doi.org/10.1016/j.jretconser.2016.08.006

4. Berdic, N., Dragan, D., Mihic, S., Anisic, Z.: Creation and usage of 3D full body avatars. Ann. Fac. Eng. Hunedoara **15**(1), 29–34 (2017)
5. Cheng, L.-K., Chieng, M.-H., Chieng, W.-H.: Measuring virtual experience in a three-dimensional virtual reality interactive simulator environment: a structural equation modeling approach. Vir. Real. **18**(3), 173–188 (2014). https://doi.org/10.1007/s10055-014-0244-2
6. Datcu, D., Lukosch, S., Brazier, F.: On the usability and effectiveness of different interaction types in augmented reality. Int. J. Hum.-Comput. Interact. **31**(3), 193–209 (2015). https://doi.org/10.1080/10447318.2014.994193
7. Dimoka, A., Hong, Y., Pavlou, P.A.: On product uncertainty in online markets: theory and evidence. MIS Q. **36**(2), 395–426 (2012)
8. Eason, K.D.: Towards the experimental study of usability. Behav. Inf. Technol. **3**(2), 133–143 (1984)
9. Erra, U., Scanniello, G., Colonnese, V.: Exploring the effectiveness of an augmented reality dressing room. Multimedia Tools Appl. **77**(19), 25077–25107 (2018). https://doi.org/10.1007/s11042-018-5758-2
10. Falcão, C.S., Soares, M.: Usability of consumer products: an analyzes of concepts, methods and applications. Estudos em Design **21**(2), 01–26 (2013)
11. Fernandez, A., Insfran, E., Abrahão, S.: Usability evaluation methods for the web: a systematic mapping study. Inf. Softw. Technol. **53**(8), 789–817 (2011). https://doi.org/10.1016/j.infsof.2011.02.007
12. Flavián, C., Ibáñez-Sánchez, S., Orús, C.: The impact of virtual, augmented and mixed reality technologies on the customer experience. J. Bus. Res. (2018). (in Press). https://doi.org/10.1016/j.jbusres.2018.10.050
13. Gallino, S., Moreno, A.: The value of fit information in online retail: evidence from a randomized field experiment. Manuf. Serv. Oper. Manag. **20**(4), 767–787 (2018). https://doi.org/10.1287/msom.2017.0686
14. Gomes Filho, J.: Ergonomia do Objeto, 2nd edn. Editora Escrituras, São Paulo (2010)
15. Gultepe, U., Gudukbay, U.: Real-time virtual fitting with body measurement and motion smoothing. Comput. Graph. **43**, 31–43 (2014). https://doi.org/10.1016/j.cag.2014.06.001
16. Guzzo, T., Ferri, F., Grifoni, P.: A model of e-commerce adoption (MOCA): consumer's perceptions and behaviours. Behav. Inf. Technol. **35**(3), 196–209 (2016). https://doi.org/10.1080/0144929X.2015.1132770
17. Hussain, A., Mkpojiogu, E.O.C., Kamal, F.M.: A systematic review on usability evaluation methods for M-commerce apps. J. Telecommun. Electron. Comput. Eng. **8**(10), 29–34 (2016)
18. ISO 9241-11: Ergonomic requirements for office work with visual display terminals (VDTs). Part 11: Guidance on usability. International Organization for Standardization, Geneva, Switzerland (1998)
19. Joshi, A., Kale, S., Chandel, S., Pal, D.K.: Likert scale: explored and explained. Br. J. Appl. Sci. Technol. **7**(4), 396–403 (2015)
20. Leventhal, L., Barnes, J.: Usability Engineering: Process, Products and Examples. Pearson Education, Inc., Hoboken (2008)
21. Madan, A., Dubey, S.K.: Usability evaluation methods: a literature review. Int. J. Eng. Sci. Technol. **4**(2) (2012)
22. Nielsen, J.: Designing Web Usability: The Practice of Simplicity. New Riders Publishing, San Francisco (1999)
23. Nielsen, J.: Usability Engineering. Academic Press, Boston (1993)
24. Noordin, S., Ashaari, N.S., Wook, T.S.M.T.: Virtual fitting room: the needs for usability and profound emotional elements. In: 6th International Conference on Electrical Engineering and Informatics (ICEEI), pp. 1–6 (2017). https://doi.org/10.1109/iceei.2017.8312427

25. Shackel, B.: Ergonomics in design for usability. In: People and Computers. Cambridge University Press (1986)
26. Song, C.: System development and realization of computer-aided clothing remote design. RISTI [Revista Iberica de Sistemas e Tecnologias de Informacao], (E9), pp. 1–13 (2016). http://risti.xyz/issues/ristie9.pdf. Accessed 31 Jan 2019
27. Song, D., Tong, R., Du, J., Zhang, Y., Jin, A.Y.: Data-driven 3-D human body customization with a mobile device. IEEE Access **6**, 27939–27948 (2018). https://doi.org/10.1109/ACCESS.2018.2837147
28. Statista: Forecast augmented (AR) and virtual reality (VR) market size worldwide from 2016 to 2022 (in billion U.S. dollars). https://www.statista.com/statistics/591181/global-augmented-virtual-reality-market-size/. Accessed 31 Jan 2019
29. Sukinah, A.N., Adzhar, K., Azliza, Y., Suhana, S.N.: Assessing website usability attributes. Aust. J. Basic Appl. Sci. **8**(4), 192–198 (2014)
30. Tavares, A., Souza, C., Araújo, J.: Análise da usabilidade de controles remotos de aparelhos condicionadores de ar. Tecnologus (12), 5 (2017)
31. Wilson, M.: Reimaging stores: as digital commerce forces brick-and-mortar stores to innovate, industry experts share their views on the future of physical retail. Chain Store Age **93**(3), 18–23 (2017)
32. Zuraj, M., Sparl, P., Znidarsic, A.: Analysis of individual aspects influencing non-purchasing in an online environment and consumer willingness to purchase custom-made apparel. Organizacija **50**(4), 352–363 (2017). https://doi.org/10.1515/orga-2017-0026

Exploring the Relationship Between Web Presence and Web Usability in Peruvian Universities

Luis Torres Melgarejo, Claudia Zapata Del Río[✉],
and Eder Quispe Vilchez

Pontificia Universidad Católica del Perú, Lima, Peru
{luis.torres,zapata.cmp,eder.quispe}@pucp.edu.pe

Abstract. Currently the use of the internet is an essential requirement for any business that aspires to reach many customers, sharing the information of their products, their achievements, their day to day, etc. This leads to the generation of a quantity of information year after year by these companies, which allows them to gain presence in the network. This reality also applies to the education sector, so this work will focus on Peruvian universities. Universities generate a large amount of content, and therefore it is necessary to be easy to find and read. In this way they will not be at a disadvantage compared to other universities that compete to attract more applicants. Our motivation is based on a study conducted in Turkey whose results show that the universities with the greatest web presence in that country have better usability. With this motivation, it was decided to do this work that, repeating the Turkish experience, verifies if there is a relationship in the Peruvian universities with greater presence, according to a ranking of universities called Webometrics. This evaluation takes as reference other usability studies, among them those that use tests with users and questionnaires, to obtain a ranking of web usability and to be able to contrast it with the web presence ranking.

Keywords: Web presence · Usability · University

1 Introduction

In today's competitive world there is a wide variety of solution options from many organizations to different needs. These organizations seek to be constantly in the sights of their potential stakeholders in order to have more possibilities to offer their services. For this reason, they are interested in having an Internet presence, since it is one of the main mass media.

This is not different in the education sector, where universities constantly seek to be an option for potential students. Using a web page, these educational centers show the information to the possible applicant and their parents as: university programs, the benefits of their campuses, extracurricular activities, quality of teaching, libraries, among many others.

© Springer Nature Switzerland AG 2019
A. Marcus and W. Wang (Eds.): HCII 2019, LNCS 11586, pp. 596–615, 2019.
https://doi.org/10.1007/978-3-030-23535-2_43

The information they offer is abundant and quite diverse. However, people have an idea of the information they are looking for when accessing a university website, so it is necessary to make it easy to find for them. This requirement, as in any business, must be focused on the target audience, which consists mostly of young people who are in their last year of high school and their parents.

There are currently recommendations to help websites to better achieve the objectives for which they were created, a high level of usability. The term "usability" refers to "the extent to which a product can be used by specific users to achieve specific goals with effectiveness, efficiency and satisfaction in a context of specific use" [13]. The universities that apply these recommendations in the most appropriate way will have a competitive advantage.

In other countries, such as Turkey, studies have been conducted that show that universities with a greater web presence have better usability [15]. This seen in another way may mean that a university with less presence worries less about its usability. Studies have been sought, like that of Turkey, conducted here in Peru but to date they do not exist.

For this reason, it has been decided to carry out this work that includes the evaluation of web pages of Peruvian universities and a comparison of their position in the Webometrics ranking. The result of this research allowed us to see if in Peru there is also that relationship usability-presence web, as well as to obtain recommendations on the usability of the websites that were tested.

1.1 Usability

According to ISO 25010 [8], Usability is understood as the ability of the software product to be understood, learned, used and attractive to the user, when used under certain conditions. A usable system complies with the following sub-characteristics:

- Allows the user to understand if the software is suitable for their needs.
- Allows the user to learn their application.
- Allows the user to operate and control it easily.
- It can protect users from making mistakes.
- It has a nice user interface and satisfies the interaction with the user.
- Allows it to be used by users with certain characteristics and disabilities.

It is an essential feature that every website must have for the dissemination of information to the public [22]. This also includes university websites that communicate information about their academic programs, teaching facilities, research, etc. [15].

1.2 Webometrics

Ranking Web Webometrics is the largest academic ranking of Higher Education Institutions. Cybermetrics Lab (CSIC) provides multidimensional and updated information about the performance of universities around the world based on their presence and impact on the web every 6 months.

Its main objective is to promote the academic web presence, supporting the initiatives of Free Access to increase the transmission of knowledge. To achieve this goal, the publication of rankings is one of the most powerful and successful tools to initiate and consolidate the processes of change in academia, increasing the commitment of academics.

The information published is only the positioning of these institutions. It does not show the values obtained that result from the counts or formulas that apply. The positioning methodology is based on these 4 indicators [23] (Table 1):

Table 1. Webometrics indicators

Indicators	Description	Source	Weight
Presence	Size (number of web pages) of the main web site of the institution	Google	5%
Visibility	Number of external networks that originate links to the web pages of the institution	Ahref Majestic	50%
Transparency	Number of citations of the main authors according to the source	Google Scholar	10%
Excellence	Number of jobs among the top 10% most cited in 26 disciplines	Scimago	35%

1.3 Web Presence

According to Webometrics [23], Web Presence is understood as the size or number of web pages of the main web domain of the institution. It includes all subdomains that share the same web domain and all file types, including rich ones like PDF documents. Webometrics obtains this information from the Google search engine, as indicated on its website.

It is expected that this indicator reflects the activities of an organization because it is related to its volume of content.

1.4 Usability Testing with Users

It is a technique to evaluate the system performing tests with users and whose objective is to obtain direct information about how the real user uses the system [9].

When performing these tests, the following benefits will be sought [21]:

- Know if participants can complete the specified tasks successfully
- Identify how long it takes to complete specified tasks
- Know how satisfied the participants are with the website.
- Identify opportunities for improvement in performance and user satisfaction
- Analyze the performance of the website in relation to its usability objectives.

In order to perform a user test, the following steps are followed [17]:

1. Development of research questions or test objectives.
2. Use of a representative sample of end users.
3. Representation of the real work environment.
4. Observation of end users who use the product.
5. Interviews and surveys of the participants by the moderator of the test.
6. Collection of quantitative and qualitative performance and measures of preference.
7. Recommendation of improvements to the product design.

A user test does not guarantee the success of the product evaluated at 100%, even if it is carried out with complete rigor. The reasons are the following [17]:

- Tests are artificial situations due to elements that can affect the results.
- The results do not show that a product works even if the tests have significant statistical results.
- Participants do not usually fully represent the population
- The tests are not necessarily the best techniques to use and it depends on the time, cost, precision and the time to apply them.

1.5 Questionnaires

Questionnaires are widely used to measure users' perception and satisfaction when using a system [7]. They are composed of several questions, each one of them seeks to cover a quality construct [12].

Their main advantage is that they are relatively inexpensive and can generate many responses, rather than observation-based tests that require a laboratory, observation personnel, recruitment participants and other logistics issues [12].

2 Background

An important part of all research is to be able to review what has been studied previously on the corresponding topic. For this reason, a systematic review of all studies and research related to usability studies was carried out taking into account the level of web presence of several universities, regardless of the country. This allowed us to know what methodology and tools they have used and what conclusions they have reached based on their results in order to use them for the study in Peru.

The process of searching, filtering and selecting articles was carried out on April 22, 2018. Initially, 276 articles were found and 13 were selected.

The results of the search for related studies are based on a selection of primary and secondary studies, which are grouped according to the research question to which they respond, as shown in the Table 2. In addition, the percentage of studies that offer classified answers according to research topic is shown.

Table 2. Systematic review results

Research questions	Answers	Papers	Percentage
What studies show relationships between usability and web presence in universities?	Find a correlation between usability and web presence	2	15.4%
	Use web presence only as a selection criterion	1	7.7%
	Does not use web presence	10	76.9%
What methodology or criteria have been used to evaluate and compare them?	User tests	3	23.1%
	Expert analysis	4	30.8%
	Automatic tools	5	38.5%
	Questionnaires	4	30.8%
	Statistical correlation with web presence	2	15.4%

2.1 Usability Studies on University Websites

The study by Peker, Kucukozer-Cavdar and Cagilta [15] establishes a correlation between web usability and web presence for universities in Turkey. To do this, it evaluates the usability of the 5 websites of universities with the greatest web presence, according to the Webometrics ranking. The evaluation consists of user tests, which measured the time and achievement of previously defined tasks, and satisfaction questionnaires. The universities were classified according to their web usability and web presence, and subsequently a correlation between both values was calculated.

In the study by Torres, Méndez and Orduna-Malea [20] an evaluation is made of applications or webs of libraries of 50 universities selected from the Webometrics ranking. In this evaluation, 14 criteria are considered based on content that a web or library application must contain, and a total score is applied. Finally, based on that score, they are given a position and compared to their position in the Webometrics ranking and a correlation is sought.

A study like the previous one is carried out by Aziz et al. [2], which seeks to raise awareness about the importance of usability and accessibility for universities and other educational centers in Malaysia. In his work, he carries out a usability analysis and includes metrics such as number of broken links, page size and speed according to whether it is a public or private university, polytechnics and community colleges.

The study by Panigrahi et al. [14] shows a relationship between the gross enrollment rate and the level of web usability for distance education. In this paper an analysis of 15 universities in the United States, Australia and India is carried out, checking the presence of 23 attributes that they should fulfill for distance learning. An expert analysis was done for the websites and questionnaires and interviews were conducted to find the real reasons for the low recruitment. Finally, with this data, a linear regression is performed to verify the relationship between enrollment and usability criteria.

The study by Huang and Huang [5] focuses on evaluating university websites from subjective and objective points of view. For this, the behavior of the users during the tasks (user tests) is evaluated, obtaining objective information and grouped in diffuse clusters (where an element can belong to more than one cluster). In addition, a questionnaire is made to users where they can place values between 0 and 1 as a response and obtain subjective information. Finally, both data are combined giving them weights and a relation is found.

2.2 Methods Used in the Web Evaluation

In the studies found, only in [15, 20] we seek to establish a statistical relationship between web presence and web usability. In addition, in [10] the web presence was used as a selection criterion for the sample, but it was not encouraged to establish a correlation with web usability. Also, the other works showed web usability analysis but did not use web presence.

On the evaluation methodology, only in [3, 5, 15] were user tests, which will be used in this work. In the case of expert analysis, in [4, 10, 14, 20] an analysis was performed reviewing usability attributes in each web by themselves to obtain results. Finally, in [1, 2, 6, 11, 16] automated tools were used to help perform performance tests, content evaluation and structure. However, they do not make an in-depth usability analysis because they cannot show the accomplishment of needs of the user.

In addition, [3, 5, 15, 18] web usability questionnaires were used to obtain additional information. Of these studies, the questions were shown only in [5] and the questionnaire used was Palmer. Instead, in [18] questions were asked based on Nielsen's heuristics. In both cases, only multiple-choice questions were used.

In [3, 15], the questionnaire contained demographic information questions, multiple choice questions (satisfaction) and open questions (feedback). In [3] it is indicated that the CSUQ questionnaire is used, unlike [15] where they do not give more information.

Finally, only in [15, 20] it is sought to find a correlation between usability level and web presence by analyzing the collected data. In [14] a statistical correlation between web usability and recruitment problems is sought.

3 Methodology

The present research work focuses on conducting a web usability evaluation of Peruvian universities that are within the Webometrics ranking. The data collection consisted of a user test and a questionnaire. Subsequently, an analysis of the information was carried out to obtain a correlation between its positioning according to usability and web presence.

3.1 Selection of Websites

The universities considered for the evaluation were the first 10 in web presence in the Webometrics ranking. This ranking currently considers 182 universities or colleges. This work was carried out in the second semester of 2018. It has been decided to hide the identity of these universities and they are named as follows (Table 3):

Table 3. Selected universities

Position	1	2	3	4	5	6	7	8	9	10
University	A	B	C	D	E	F	G	H	I	J
Category	Private	State	State	Private	State	Private	Private	State	Private	Private

3.2   Participant Profile

The selection of participants focused on those who are potential users of universities.

- Age: ages between 18 and 34 will be considered because they represent the highest number of visitors to a university website.
- Experience: At least one basic level in the use of web pages will be considered.
- Previous use: Participants will not be able to participate in the evaluation of websites they have visited previously.

3.3   User Testing

The evaluation of the selected websites consisted in the observation of the participants and how they interact with it. In order to carry out this evaluation in a correct way and that does not negatively influence the execution of the same, this procedure has been designed considering the following points.

Participants

The number of participants was 20 people. Each participant evaluated 4 websites, having a total of 80 evaluations. That means that there were 8 evaluations per web, which is enough to find their deficiencies.

Tasks

The tasks defined for this test can be performed for any of the 10 websites chosen. They consist of very basic instructions for the participants to seek information and answer the questions. The tasks consist in looking for information about:

- University Programs: (4 questions)
- Admission process (5 questions)
- Research Projects (3 questions)

It will be verified if the user manages to complete the objective and the time it takes to execute the task will be measured.

The score was calculated as follows for each task:

- Percentage of compliance (Pc) for each task that is equal to the number of correct answers among the total of questions.
- Task score (Pt) equal to the compliance percentage will be divided by the task execution time in seconds. If the task was not fulfilled, the result will be zero.
- Maximum score (Pm) that will be equal to the highest task score (Pt) of all the universities in that task.
- Score per university (Pu) averaging the corresponding homework scores (Pt).
- Final score per university (PFu) is equal to the score per university (Pu) between the maximum score (Pm)

The final position of each university will be determined by the median of the positions in each task. Finally, the universities will be ordered according to their median. If a university has the lowest median, the first position corresponds to it and if it has the highest median it corresponds to the tenth position.

Questionnaires

The questionnaire to be used for the evaluation of the websites is WAMMI [24] and has been chosen for the following reasons:

- Specializes in websites, unlike other questionnaires that are software oriented in general.
- It is not complex or extensive for the participant.

Calculation of the Score of the WAMMI Questionnaire

If a question seeks to confirm any strength or positive point on the website, the following score will be assigned:

1. Strongly disagree (1 point)
2. Disagree (2 points)
3. Neither agree nor disagree (3 points)
4. Agree (4 points)
5. Strongly agree (5 points)

Otherwise, if you want to confirm a problem or negative point, the following score will be assigned:

1. Strongly disagree (5 points)
2. Disagree (4 points)
3. Neither agree nor disagree (3 points)
4. Agree (2 points)
5. Strongly agree (1 point)

The total score of the questionnaire consists of the sum of the individual scores of each question, being able to reach from 20 to 100 points. According to this score will be given a positioning to universities.

3.4 Statistical Analysis

Once obtained the positions for web presence, user tests and questionnaire; are compared:

- User test positions with web presence positions.
- The questionnaire positions with web presence positions.

However, it is necessary to define the most appropriate correlation coefficient for these positions. The most popular coefficients to compare rankings are Kendall's Tau and Spearman's Rho. For this experiment it has been decided to use Kendall's Tau-b for the following reasons:

– Kendall's Tau is best in small data set [25]
– Spearman's Rho is more sensitive to differences between any pair and is more
  appropriate to use when a significant difference in a single pair is critical.

4   Results

The evaluation of the university websites was agreed with different users and they were programmed within a range of 10 weeks. Next, a summary of all the data obtained in the user tests and in the questionnaires will be displayed.

20 people were contacted, and the corresponding user tests were carried out. The shortest duration of the test was approximately 40 min and the longest time was approximately 1 h and 30 min. There were users of different ages in a range between 19 and 31 years old, and 40% of them were between 25 and 28 years old. In addition, 25% of the users were women.

About the Internet experience, in Fig. 1 a large majority (85%) prefer the Google Chrome browser, 10% prefer Mozilla FireFox and 5% prefer Safari. In addition, 40% dedicate more than 8 h a day to surf the Internet and 25% dedicate between 4 and 7 h a day. The rest of the users invest between 1 and 3 h a day.

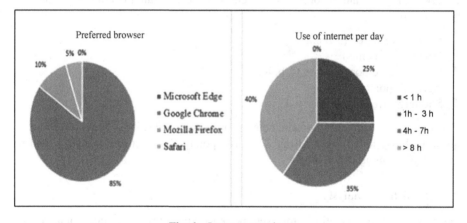

Fig. 1. Internet experience

4.1   Task 1: University Programs

The first task was for users to search for information about any university program they want. They were asked to write the name of the program they chose, the number of semesters in length, the number of courses in the fifth level and whether they found the number of credits per course.

As noted in Fig. 2, University E has the first place in the university careers section. In second place is the University A that has a close score, next to the University F and the University J.

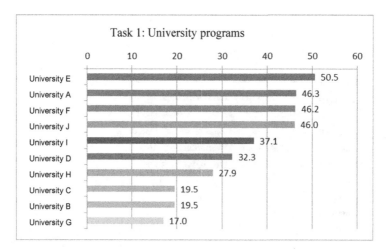

Fig. 2. Task 1

The University E, the direct access to a university program is easier in the main menu but the information about its courses should be looked for in an embedded PDF that is not friendly. University A has a large list of all the programs, and it makes you invest more time searching. However, the information within each program is well distributed and easy to find. This is reflected in the measurements made because both have almost the same effectiveness, but University E has better times in the achievement of the task.

4.2   Task 2: Admission Process

The second task was for users to seek information about the admission process. They were asked to indicate if they found the following information: date and cost of the exam; contents that will be evaluated; detailed steps of the process; and scholarships.

As noted in Fig. 3, University J has the first place in the Admission section. The difference in score with respect to the University G and the University H is not very big.

The University J has elements in its design that confuse the user at the beginning but is sufficiently ordered to find it quickly. In contrast, the University G does not have an ordered content to help the user; and University H has a more modern design with respect to the other universities, but the information is a little less orderly.

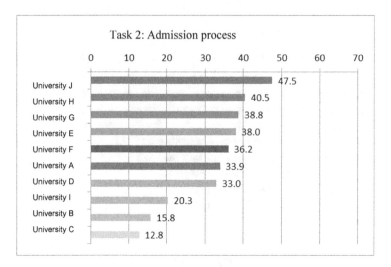

Fig. 3. Task 2

4.3   Task 3: Research Projects

The last task consisted in the search of information about research projects of the university. Users were asked to name a project, the leader or principal responsible and the budget assigned to that research.

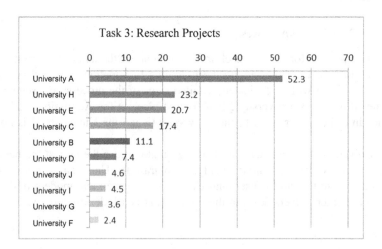

Fig. 4. Task 3

As observed in the Fig. 4, University A is the university that has better usability in the Research section, with a great difference compared to other universities. The information is concise and well structured, allowing a shorter time to find it.

The other universities have a more complicated navigation. Users often cannot find the information they were asked for, and users who found it have delayed doing so.

4.4 Questionnaire

After using each website, users answered a questionnaire with questions about positive aspects, negative aspects and suggestions they would make to the portal.

The questionnaire used was WAMMI and consists of 20 multiple-choice questions.

As observed in Fig. 5, University A has the first place in user satisfaction due to the orderly structure of its website and easy access to information. University D has the second highest score according to the opinion of the participants even though some of its pages could not be seen at times.

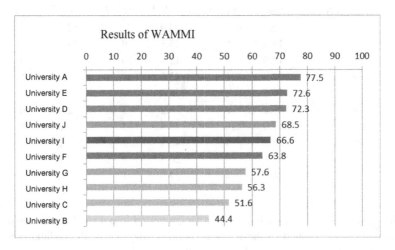

Fig. 5. Results of WAMMI

5 Data Analysis

As described in the previous section, two methods of usability measurement have been carried out: user tests and satisfaction questionnaires; and the data have been obtained to be able to assign positions to each of the 10 universities. These positions have been defined for each of the 3 tasks and for the questionnaire.

The hypothesis for this research was:

- H0: There is no correlation between usability and web presence positions
- H1: There is a correlation between usability and web presence positions

where H0 is the null hypothesis that will be rejected.

When defining the correlation coefficient to be used for the analysis, this null hypothesis will be considered based on the chosen correlation coefficient.

- H0: $\tau = 0$
- H1: $\tau <> 0$

where τ is Kendall's Tau-b correlation coefficient between web presence and the usability of Peruvian universities, with a significance level of 0.05 in a bilateral contrast. That is, the p-value must be less than 0.025. This value is the most used for experiments whose cost per error is low.

5.1   User Testing of All Universities

First, the comparison will be made with the positioning obtained in the user tests, so a summary of the information obtained in Table 4 is shown.

Table 4. Web presence and test user positions

University	Position web presence	Score task 1	Position task 1	Score task 2	Position task 2	Score task 3	Position task 3
A	1	46.3	2	33.9	6	52.3	1
B	2	19.5	9	15.8	9	11.1	5
C	3	19.5	8	12.8	10	17.4	4
D	4	32.3	6	33.0	7	7.4	6
E	5	50.5	1	38.0	4	20.7	3
F	6	46.2	3	36.2	5	2.4	10
G	7	17.0	10	38.8	3	3.6	9
H	8	27.9	7	40.5	2	23.2	2
I	9	37.1	5	20.3	8	4.5	8
J	10	46.0	4	47.5	1	4.6	7

The partial positions of each task must be converted into a single final position, so the median will be applied to these values because they are of the ordinal type. The mean is not used on an ordinal scale because the successive intervals on the scale are of unequal size [19]. It is not possible to apply mode in these cases because several universities have different positions in each task there is no value that is the most frequent.

From the median, the final position is calculated by university. That final position, shown in Table 5, will be compared with the web presence position. To do this, both sets of positions are processed and the bivariate correlation coefficient "Kendall's Tau-b" is calculated. Once the analysis is executed, the result shown in Fig. 6 is obtained.

The correlation coefficient is almost zero (-0.092) and the level of significance (0.717) is much higher than the p value defined above. Therefore, a correlation with the obtained data cannot be established.

Due to this, it has been decided to look for it in subsets of universities. In this work the universities were grouped into state and private universities, and a correlation was sought between the universities within these groups.

Table 5. Final positions

University	Position task 1	Position task 2	Position task 3	Median	Final position
A	2	6	1	2	1
B	9	9	5	9	9
C	8	10	4	8	7
D	6	7	6	6	6
E	1	4	3	3	3
F	3	5	10	5	5
G	10	3	9	9	9
H	7	2	2	2	1
I	5	8	8	8	7
J	4	1	7	4	4

			Web presence	User test
Tau_b de Kendall	Web presence	Correlation coefficient	1,000	-,092
		Sig. (bilateral)	.	,717
		N	10	10
	User test	Correlation coefficient	-,092	1,000
		Sig. (bilateral)	,717	.
		N	10	10

Fig. 6. Correlations: web presence – user test (All Universities)

5.2   User Testing with Private Universities

Once again, we carried out a positioning of the universities according to their scores in the user tests, but this time only the private universities are chosen (Table 6).

Table 6. Private universities positions

University	Position web presence	Position task 1	Position task 2	Position task 3	Median	Final position
A	1	1	4	1	1	1
D	2	5	5	2	5	5
F	3	2	3	6	3	2
G	4	6	2	5	5	5
I	5	4	6	4	4	4
J	6	3	1	3	3	2

			Web presence	User test
Tau_b de Kendall	Web presence	Correlation coefficient	1,000	,072
		Sig. (bilateral)	.	,845
		N	6	6
	User test	Correlation coefficient	,072	1,000
		Sig. (bilateral)	,845	.
		N	6	6

Fig. 7. Correlations: web presence – user test (Private Universities)

Figure 7 shows the results obtained. Again, the correlation coefficient is almost zero (0.072) and the level of significance (0.845) is much greater than the p value. Therefore, a correlation with the data obtained with this group cannot be established.

5.3   User Testing with State Universities

A final positioning of the universities was made according to their scores in the user tests, but this time the state universities will be included.

Figure 8 shows the results obtained. Both positions have a perfect negative correlation. That is, the greater the web presence (content) of a public university, the lower its usability level. The level of significance obtained is 0, so it is a valid correlation (Table 7).

Table 7. Private universities positions

University	Position web presence	Position task 1	Position task 2	Position task 3	Median	Final position
B	1	4	3	4	4	4
C	2	3	4	3	3	3
E	3	1	2	2	2	2
H	4	2	1	1	1	1

			Web presence	User test
Tau_b de Kendall	Web presence	Correlation coefficient	1,000	-1,000*
		Sig. (bilateral)	.	.
		N	4	4
	User test	Correlation coefficient	-1,000**	1,000
		Sig. (bilateral)	.	.
		N	4	4

Fig. 8. Correlations: web presence – user test (Public Universities)

5.4   Satisfaction Questionnaires for All Universities

A correlation with the results obtained from the satisfaction questionnaire will also be sought. To do this, first a summary of the scores obtained and their position according to these scores is shown. In addition, the positions according to the web presence according to Webometrics are also displayed in Table 8.

Figure 9 shows the results obtained. The coefficient is practically zero and the level of significance is very high, greater than the p-value, and this result cannot be considered. Therefore, no correlation can be established with this data and the next steps would be to look for the correlation for state and private universities separately.

Table 8. Scores and positions – WAMMI (All Universities)

University		A	B	C	D	E	F	G	H	I	J
Position web presence		1	2	3	4	5	6	7	8	9	10
Questionnaire	Score	77.5	44.4	51.6	72.3	72.6	63.8	57.6	56.3	66.6	68.5
	Position	1	10	9	3	2	6	7	8	5	4

			Web presence	User test
Tau_b de Kendall	Web presence	Correlation coefficient	1,000	-,022
		Sig. (bilateral)	.	,929
		N	10	10
	User test	Correlation coefficient	-,022	1,000
		Sig. (bilateral)	,929	.
		N	10	10

Fig. 9. Correlations: web presence – WAMMI (All Universities)

5.5   Satisfaction Questionnaires for Private Universities

We again take the subset of private universities and assign the web presence orders and questionnaire scores for these. The new order can be seen in the Table 9.

Table 9. Scores and positions – WAMMI (Private Universities)

University		A	D	F	G	I	J
Position web presence		1	2	3	4	5	6
Questionnaire	Score	77.5	72.3	63.8	57.6	66.6	68.5
	Position	1	2	5	6	4	3

Figure 10 shows the results obtained. We see a weak correlation between both orders and with a level of significance greater than the p value. Therefore, it can not be concluded that there is a correlation.

			Web presence	User test
Tau_b de Kendall	Web presence	Correlation coefficient	1,000	,333
		Sig. (bilateral)	.	,348
		N	6	6
	User test	Correlation coefficient	,333	1,000
		Sig. (bilateral)	,348	.
		N	6	6

Fig. 10. Correlations: web presence – WAMMI (Private Universities)

5.6   Satisfaction Questionnaires for Public Universities

Once again, we take the subset of public universities and assign them the new web presence orders and questionnaire scores. The new positions can be seen in the Table 10.

Table 10. Scores and positions – WAMMI (Public Universities)

University		B	C	E	H
Position web presence		1	2	3	4
Questionnaire	Score	44.4	51.6	72.6	56.3
	Position	4	3	1	2

			Web presence	User test
Tau_b de Kendall	Web presence	Correlation coefficient	1,000	-,667
		Sig. (bilateral)	.	,174
		N	4	4
	User test	Correlation coefficient	-,667	1,000
		Sig. (bilateral)	,174	.
		N	4	4

Fig. 11. Correlations: web presence – WAMMI (Public Universities)

Figure 11 shows the results obtained. A strong correlation is seen between both orders but with a level of significance greater than the defined p-value. Therefore, it cannot be concluded that there is a correlation.

6   Conclusions

According to the results, a zero relation was obtained for the user tests and a weak relation in the case of the questionnaire. However, p-value was lower than the level of significance and the null hypothesis could not be rejected. Therefore, it was decided to look for a correlation considering separately the private universities and the state universities.

In the case of private universities, a strong relationship was obtained for the user tests and a weak relation was obtained for the questionnaire. However, p-value was lower than the level of significance and again the null hypothesis could not be rejected. It can be interpreted that private universities update their website according to priorities different from the amount of content they publish, and that usability is affected for that reason. These universities are self-sustaining, so starting from their priorities is to make a profit.

In the case of state universities, a perfect inverse relationship was obtained in user tests, so the hypothesis can be rejected in the case of these universities. According to this, it can be interpreted that a web with a greater amount of content is more difficult to find something specific if there is not a design that really helps to do it. The estates universities always have several applicants much greater than the number of vacancies, so they do not need the web to be a tool to attract applicants. For that reason, they could be neglecting its usability. In the case of the questionnaires, a strong inverse relationship was found but again the p value was lower than the level of significance and the null hypothesis could not be rejected.

However, only an inverse relationship between usability and the web presence of Peruvian public universities has been found, but only in user tests. This result is quite different from that obtained in the Peker study, where a strong direct relationship was found in user tests and questionnaires for the 5 universities. Being different countries, it is possible that the way in which usability is prioritized is different.

It is considered necessary to carry out an additional study to confirm this relationship between usability and web presence in Peruvian state universities. This new study should have a methodology designed especially for these universities. The reasons are as follows:

- The difference between two public universities was almost nil, so it would be better to corroborate this in a new study. If the universities had different positions, the correlation obtained would not have statistical significance.
- The user tests had to include workable tasks in the 10 private and state universities that were not homogeneous with each other. The new study should include tasks designed especially for Peruvian state universities.
- The state universities considered in this study were only 4, so the sample is small to conclude a sufficiently convincing correlation.

Finally, the users mentioned more frequently negative aspects related to the location of the content they seek and the information that is published. This result was obtained from the open questions of the questionnaire. This would show that in many of these websites the information that the university considers necessary is published, but without considering an adequate maintenance of the same.

References

1. Adepoju, S.A., Shehu, I.S.: Usability evaluation of academic websites using automated tools. In: 2014 3rd International Conference on User Science and Engineering (i-USEr), pp. 186–191 (2014)
2. Aziz, M.A., et al.: Assessing the accessibility and usability of Malaysia higher education website. In: 2010 International Conference on User Science and Engineering (i-USEr), pp. 203–208 (2010)
3. Benaida, M., Namoun, A.: An exploratory study of the factors affecting the perceived usability of Algerian educational websites. Turk. Online J. Educ. Technol. **17**(2), 1–12 (2018)
4. Chamba-Eras, L., et al.: Usabilidad Web: situación actual de los portales Web de las Universidades de Ecuador. In: Gestión de las TICs para la Investigación y la Colaboración (2016)
5. Huang, T.-K., Huang, C.-H.: An integrated decision model for evaluating educational web sites from the fuzzy subjective and objective perspectives. Comput. Educ. **55**(2), 616–629 (2010)
6. Doulani, A., et al.: Analysis of Iranian and British university websites by world wide web consortium. J. Scientometr. Res. **2**(1), 74 (2013)
7. Gediga, G., Hamborg, K.-C., Düntsch, I.: The IsoMetrics usability inventory: an operationalization of ISO 9241-10 supporting summative and formative evaluation of software systems. Behav. Inf. Technol. **18**(3), 151–164 (1999)
8. ISO/IEC: ISO/IEC 25000. Software product quality requirements and evaluation (SQuaRE). The International Organization for Standardization, vol. 41 (2005)
9. Nielsen, J.: Usability 101: Introduction to Usability. Nielsen Norman Group, Fremont (2012)
10. Kargar, M.J.: University website ranking from usability criteria perspective; a case study in IRAN. Int. J. Adv. Comput. Technol. **3**(11), 246–251 (2011)
11. Kaur, S., et al.: Analysis of website usability evaluation methods. In: 2016 3rd International Conference on Computing for Sustainable Global Development (INDIACom), pp. 1043–1046 (2016)
12. Lew, P., et al.: Using web quality models and questionnaires for web applications understanding and evaluation. In: 2012 Eighth International Conference on the Quality of Information and Communications Technology, pp. 20–29 (2012)
13. Mentes, S.A., Turan, A.H.: Assessing the usability of university websites: an empirical study on Namik Kemal University. Turk. Online J. Educ. Technol. **11**(3), 61–69 (2012)
14. Panigrahi, G., et al.: A study to increase effectiveness of distance learning websites in India with special reference to the state West Bengal to increase the present GER of higher education through incorporation of Elearning facility in a better way. Proc. Soc. Behav. Sci. **15**, 1535–1539 (2011)
15. Peker, S., et al.: Exploring the relationship between web presence and web usability for universities: a case study from Turkey. Program **50**(2), 157–174 (2016)
16. Rekik, R., Kallel, I.: Fuzzy reduced method for evaluating the quality of institutional web sites. In: 2011 7th International Conference on Next Generation Web Services Practices, pp. 296–301 (2011)
17. Rubin, J., Chisnell, D.: Handbook of Usability Testing: How to Plan, Design, and Conduct Effective Tests. Wiley, New York (2008)
18. Saeed, S., Amjad, A.: Understanding usability issues of Pakistani university websites. Life Sci. J. **10**(6s), 479–482 (2013)
19. Stevens, S.S.: On the theory of scales of measurement. Science **103**(2684), 677–680 (1946)

20. Torres-Pérez, P., et al.: Mobile web adoption in top ranked university libraries: a preliminary study. J. Acad. Librariansh. **42**(4), 329–339 (2016)
21. U.S. Department of Health & Human Services: Usability Testing. https://www.usability.gov/how-to-and-tools/methods/usability-testing.html
22. Antona, M., Stephanidis, C. (eds.): Universal Access in Human–Computer Interaction. Design and Development Approaches and Methods, pp. 277–287. Springer, Berlin (2017). https://doi.org/10.1007/978-3-319-58706-6
23. Methodology | Ranking Web of Universities: More than 28000 Institutions Ranked. http://www.webometrics.info/en/Methodology
24. WAMMI - Home. http://www.wammi.com/
25. Field, A.: Discovering Statistics Using SPSS. SAGE Publications Ltd, Los Angeles (2009)

Research on Factors Affecting Behavior of Taking Selfies in China Based on Logistic Regression Analysis

Si-qi Wu[1,2(✉)], Wen-jun Hou[1,2], and Meng-yun Yue[1,2]

[1] School of Digital Media and Design Arts,
Beijing University of Posts and Telecommunications, Beijing 100876, China
1519390005@qq.com
[2] Beijing Key Laboratory of Network Systems and Network Culture,
Beijing University of Posts and Telecommunications, Beijing 100876, China

Abstract. With the popularity of smartphones and photo-based social networking sites, taking selfies have become a trend among young people. A number of camera apps developed by third-party with face-beauty feature have become popular in China and original camera apps (developed by phone manufacturer) such as HUAWEI have also added face-beauty feature. However, smartphones such as iPhone without face-beauty feature are criticized by the majority of Chinese users. At present, there is little research on the design of original camera apps. In this paper, behavior of taking selfies of Chinese users were focused. An online questionnaire was used to investigate Chinese behavior of taking selfies and the design of face-beauty feature in original camera apps. The analysis of variance and Ordinal Logistic Regression analysis were used as the primary method of data analysis. This study concluded the factors affecting the user's frequency of taking selfies, high-frequency scenes of taking selfies, the relationship between face-beauty feature and recognition of taking selfies, the function usage of original camera apps and third-party camera apps, as well as the influence of face-beauty feature on taking selfies. It can help to design the functions of original cameras of foreign smartphone brands entering the Chinese market to a certain extent.

Keywords: Behavior of taking selfies · Logistic regression ·
Face-beauty feature

1 Introduction

Selfie is a self-portrait photograph taken for oneself. The history of selfie can be traced back to 1839. The history of self-portrait can be traced back to 1839. Robert Cornelius, the pioneer of American photography, used Daguerre photography to take the first portrait of a human figure outside his own store, which was also the first self-portrait photograph in human history [1]. However, due to the limitation of devices, taking selfies did not get popular until Steve Jobs launched the "smartphone" iPhone 4 in 2010, and the era of taking selfies really came.

© Springer Nature Switzerland AG 2019
A. Marcus and W. Wang (Eds.): HCII 2019, LNCS 11586, pp. 616–629, 2019.
https://doi.org/10.1007/978-3-030-23535-2_44

According to Zenith's mobile advertising forecast in 2017, 66% of people 52 of key countries would have smart phones in 2018, and China, as the country with the largest number of smartphone users, will have 1.3 billion users [2]. This widespread popularity of smartphones has created a boom in taking selfies in China. After the emergence of a third-party camera app called "Metuxiuxiu" in 2012, many third-party camera apps such as "camera 360", "Chaozipai" and "tiantianPtu" emerged in endlessly in China. The third-party camera apps also promote the development of original camera apps (developed by phone manufacturer). Huawei, OPPO and other Chinese mobile phone brands have vigorously promoted their face-beauty features during brand promotion. There is even a "Meitu" mobile phone in the Chinese market which is mainly aimed at taking photos, especially selfies. However, there are few face-beauty features added to the iphone, which has a high market share in China, so whether the face-beauty features will become a factor affecting the Chinese users' behavior of taking selfies has become a trigger point of this study.

This study aimed to explore the use of original camera apps in taking selfies by Chinese users, and how face-beauty features affect the behavior of taking selfies. Based on the previous research, the development of behavior of taking selfies and the development of China's original camera apps and third-party camera apps were summarized. The research involved the purpose of taking selfies in China, frequency of taking selfies, whether the original camera apps have face-beauty features, the satisfaction of the original camera apps, and the function selection of third-party camera apps, etc. Factors affecting Chinese users' satisfaction with original camera apps are still being explored. The variables affected were presented in the form of scales. Therefore, multiple ordered logistic regression is considered for subsequent data processing and analysis.

Logistic Regression, also known as generalized linear model, belongs to a statistical model. The goal of Logistic Regression is to find the most appropriate model to describe the relationship between explanatory and interpreted variables, which can help predict the discrete results of a group of variables, which may be continuous, discrete, dichotomous, or a mixture of these variables [3]. Logistic Regression model of binary data includes Simple Logistic Regression model and Multivariate Logistic Regression model. The first type involves the modeling of the relationship between an explanatory variable and binary explained variables. The second type can be used to model K explanatory variables, each explanatory variable has m levels. The application of Logistic Regression also extends to the case where the dependent variables appear in the form of ordered categorical response, also known as Ordinal Logistic Regression model [4]. Ordinal Logistic model can be applied to epidemiological investigation, which can be divided into first, second, third and fourth levels of illness. It can also be applied to many sociological studies that classify people's well-being or satisfaction [5].

According to the presentation of the dependent variables in this study, Ordinal Logistic Regression is used as the primary method for data analysis.

2 Method

2.1 Procedures

This research mainly adopted the methods of literatures, interviews and questionnaires. The research was divided into two stages. The first stage mainly carried on methods of literatures and interviews. Some users whose frequency of taking selfies were in low, medium and high three categories were consulted about reasons for taking or not taking selfies and the usage of face-beauty features and third-party camera apps, etc. The above work helps to improve the presupposed answers in the questionnaire and design the overall logic of the questionnaire. In the second stage, the questionnaire release, data recovery and analysis were mainly carried out. During the research phase, we ensured that all the participating users clearly understood the purpose of our research.

2.2 Materials

The questionnaire in this study is divided into six parts.

Part 1: Demographic Information
Questions including gender, educational background, age and region were designed to ensure the validity of sampling.

Part 2: User Classification
The users were divided into four types including: non-self-timer users (never took selfies), low-frequency users (sometimes take selfies except taking lots of selfies in certain circumstances), medium-frequency users (often take selfies per week), high-frequency users (always take selfies every day).

Part 3: Reasons for Taking or Not Taking Selfies
This part mainly inquired about the reasons and frequencies related to taking selfies. The relationship of the purposes and frequency were analyzed by Logistic Regression. Then, purposes of taking selfies which had positive and negative correlation effects on frequency of taking selfies can be obtained. It can help determine high-frequency scenarios and low-frequency scenarios of taking selfies in order to determine the functions that the camera may need according to the situation.

Part 4: Investigation of the Original Camera Apps (Developed by Phone Manufacturer)
This part included questions like "Is there any face-beauty features in your **original camera apps**?", "How much do you approve of your **original camera** apps?", "What are the common face-beauty features you always use when taking selfies", etc. Then, we focused on whether the original camera apps had face-beauty features or not would affect the recognition of the original camera apps, and whether the recognition will affect the use frequency of the original camera apps and the third-party camera apps.

Part 5: Investigation of the Third-Party Camera Apps

This part included the reasons for using third-party camera apps and the commonly used functions of third-party camera apps. Logistic Regression was used to analyze which functions led users to use third-party camera apps and which functions led users to take selfies with original camera apps.

Part 6: Relationship Between Face-Beauty Features and Taking Selfies

According to different types of users, whether face-beauty will affect the frequency of behavior of taking selfies was focus in this part.

2.3 Participant

A total of 430 respondents completed the questionnaires and 413 questionnaires were valid. Questionnaires were sent out through links in Chinese social networking app called WeChat. The user's age range was from 8 to 60 years old. Within this age group, users had a clear understanding of selfie behavior. Among them, 28% respondents were under 18 years old, 48% respondents were between 18 and 30 years old, and 24% respondents were between 30 and 60 years old. 84% of them have undergraduate education or above. 34% respondents were male users and 66% respondents were female users.

2.4 Data Analysis Methods

The main purpose of the data analysis is to find out the correlative factors that significantly affect behavior of taking selfies. The main methods used are Ordinal Logistic Regression analysis and chi-square test. We focused on (1) the correlation between purposes and frequency of taking selfies, (2) the relationship between face-beauty features and recognition of taking selfies, (3) whether recognition of taking selfies affected the usage of third-party camera apps, (4) which factors would lead users to use third-party camera apps or original camera apps, and (5) whether face-beauty features will affect frequency of taking selfies.

3 Results and Discussion

3.1 User Classification

In this questionnaire, all users were asked to choose their own frequency of taking selfies. There were five situations: "never took selfies", "almost take no selfies", "only take selfies in certain circumstances (such as travel, gathering, etc.)", "often take selfies per week" and "always take selfies every day". Users who didn't take selfies or almost took no selfies were both classified as users who never took selfies. The proportion of four types of participants is shown in Fig. 1. The proportion of different types of male and female participants in their respective gender is shown in Fig. 2.

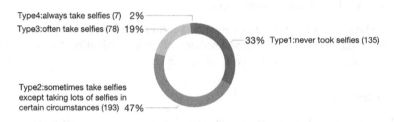

Fig. 1. Participants classification

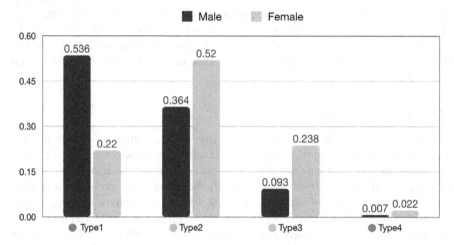

Fig. 2. The proportion of different types of male and female participants in their respective gender

According to the cross-analysis in this study, most of Chinese users had no regular behavior of taking selfies, in which the proportion of female users in irregularly taking selfies has exceeded half of female users, and the data of male users of taking no selfies had exceeded half of male users. High-frequency users who took selfies every day still accounted for a small value. Female users who took selfies every week were more than one-fifth of the female users who never took selfies.

The frequency of female users' behavior of taking selfies was significantly higher than that of male users. Most users focused on irregular selfie behavior, that is, frequency of taking selfies is not high, but once taking a selfie, there would be a large number of continuous behavior. We suspect that the frequency of taking selfies will be affected for most user-specific scenarios and purposes.

3.2 Effect of Selfie Purpose on Selfie Frequency

The purpose of taking selfies was taken as the explanatory variable, and the frequency of taking selfies was taken as the explained variable to carry out an Ordinal Logistic Regression analysis. Table 1 shows the test results of parallel lines. According to the parallel line test, if significance level alpha is 0.97, the null hypothesis cannot be rejected because the probability p-value is greater than significance level alpha, indicating that there is no significant difference in the slope of each model, so it is appropriate to choose the Logit connection function.

Table 1. The test results of parallel lines[a] for effect of selfie purpose on selfie frequency

Model	-2Log-Likelihood	Chi-Square	Df	Sig.
Null Hypothesis	280.388			
General	278.070	2.317	8	.970

The null hypothesis states that the location parameters(slope coefficients) are the same across response categories.
a. Link function: logit

Table 2 shows the statistics of goodness of fit described by the model. The value of Nagelkerke is 0.393, which is not close to 1 which indicates that more of the variation is explained by the model, while the value of McFadden is 0.250, which is not in the range of 0.3–0.5. The goodness of fit is not good enough.

Table 2. Pseudo R^2 values for effect of selfie purpose on selfie frequency

Cox and Snell	0.218
Nagelkerke	.248
McFadden	0.117

Link function: logit

Table 3 shows the significance test results of zero model and current model regression equation. It can be seen that the log-likelihood value of −2 times of zero mode is 378.657, the current model is 1059.715, the likelihood ratio is 98.270, and the probability P-value is 0.000. If the significance habit-level is 0.05, the null hypothesis is rejected, indicating that the significant linear relationship between all explanatory variables and the connection function is selected correctly.

Table 3. Model-fitting information for effect of selfie purpose on selfie frequency

Model	-2Log-Likelihood	Chi-Square	Df	Sig.
Intercept Only	378.657			
General	280.388	98.270	8	.000

Link function: logit

Table 4 shows the results of parameter estimation of the output model. Reason4 "self appreciation", reason7 "pass the boring time" and reason8 "show yourself on social platforms" have significant relevant with frequency of taking selfies based on the 0.05 significance level. According to the positive or negative of the estimates value of the logit coefficients, people who chose these three reasons were more likely to take selfies with high frequency.

Table 4. Parameter estimates of the relationship between reasons and frequency of taking selfies

		Estimate	Std.Error	Wald	df	Sig.	95% Confidence Interval	
							Lower Bound	Upper Bound
Threshold	[frequency=3]	5.227	.790	43.726	1	.000	3.678	6.776
	[frequency=4]	8.873	.010	77.209	1	.000	6.894	10.852
Location	reason1	-.088	.190	.217	1	.641	-.460	0.238
	reason2	.148	.201	.543	1	.461	-.246	0.543
	reason3	-.342	.189	3.284	1	.070	-.713	0.028
	reason4	.427	.195	4.801	1	.028	.045	0.809
	reason5	.237	.205	1.335	1	.248	-.165	0.640
	reason6	.130	.188	.483	1	.487	-.237	0.498
	reason7	.569	.211	7.281	1	.007	.156	0.983
	reason8	.526	.178	8.718	1	.003	.177	0.876

Link function: logarithm

Reasons for taking selfies were divided into two categories: category 1 = external reason {commemorating special events, recording daily life, displaying social activities} and category 2 = internal reason {self-appreciation, interesting, showing yourself to good friends or relatives, passing boring time, showing yourself on social platforms}. We sum them up by the frequency at which we always, often, and sometimes take selfies and ranked them from highest to lowest as shown in Fig. 3. In the sample data, "commemorating special events", "recording daily life", "displaying social activities" were three kinds of reasons to motivate users to take selfies. However, according to the data shown in Table 4, these three reasons did not increase the users' frequency of taking selfies. Therefore, external reasons are the factors that drive most users to take selfies, but the self-timer frequency can only be improved by internal reasons. In design, external drivers are mostly generated by specific situations, so combining situational awareness may be a way to improve self-timer user experience.

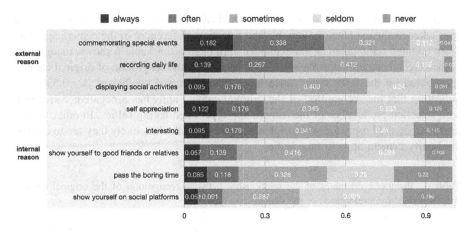

Fig. 3. Reasons for taking selfies

3.3 The Effect of Face-Beauty Features on Recognition of Original Camera Apps and the Effect of Original Camera Recognition on Camera Selection During Taking Selfies

Taking face-beauty features as the explanatory variable and recognition of original camera apps as the explained variable, Ordinal Logistic Regression was conducted. The result was shown in Table 5. Face-beauty1 "the original camera apps come with facebeauty features" has significant relevant with recognition of original camera apps based on the 0.05 significance level. According to the positive or negative of the estimates value of the logit coefficients, when the original camera apps have face-beauty features, the recognition of the original camera apps will be higher. To some extent, it can be explained that the face-beauty features of smartphones can improve the user experience when taking selfies with original camera apps. Due to the space limitation and to avoid repetition, the evaluations of the Logistic Regression Model like Tables 1, 2 and 3 would not be described in the following text of this paper.

Table 5. Parameter estimates of the relationship between face-beauty features and recognition of original camera apps

		Estimate	Std.Error	Wald	df	Sig.	95% Confidence Interval	
							Lower Bound	Upper Bound
Threshold	[recognition1=1]	-2.694	.302	79.559	1	.000	-3.286	-2.102
	[recognition1=2]	-1.234	.192	41.248	1	.000	-1.610	-.857
	[recognition1=3]	-.112	.171	.432	1	.511	-.448	.223
	[recognition1=4]	1.294	.189	46.981	1	0.000	.924	1.664
Location	face-beauty1	.670	.220	9.294	1	.002	.239	1.101
	face-beauty0	0[a]	.	.	0	.	.	.

Link function: logit

a. This parameter is redundant, so set to 0

Ordinal Logistic Regression was conducted with recognition of the original camera apps taken as the explanatory variable and selection preferences of the camera app type when taking a selfie taken as the explained variable. As the Table 6 shows, recognition of the original camera apps has significant relevant with recognition of original camera apps based on the 0.05 significance level. The estimated coefficient is $-0.536 < 0$, indicating that the recognition of the original camera apps has a negative correlation with selection preferences of the camera app type when taking selfies. In other words, the more satisfied users are with original camera apps, the less likely they are to use the third-party camera apps to take selfies.

Table 6. Parameter estimates of the relationship between recognition of the original camera apps and selection preferences of the camera app type

		Estimate	Std.Error	Wald	df	Sig.	95% Confidence Interval	
							Lower Bound	Upper Bound
Threshold	[choice=1]	-3.112	.412	57.090	1	.000	-3.919	-2.305
	[choice=2]	-2.069	.390	28.101	1	.000	-2.834	-1.304
	[choice=3]	-1.517	.381	15.851	1	.000	-2.264	-.770
	[choice=4]	.692	.393	3.104	1	.078	-.078	1.461
Location	recognition	-.536	.099	29.244	1	.000	.730	-.342

Link function: logit

In summary, face-beauty features can make the user experience better and gain more recognition when taking selfies with original camera apps, while the user will choose to use original camera apps more when the recognition of original camera apps is higher. In other words, users will use third-party camera apps less often when the face-beauty features are available on original camera apps. In essence, both the original camera apps and the third-party camera apps aim to provide users with satisfactory selfie results. The above conclusions also verify the existence value of the current third-party camera apps online, that is, to provide effects that the native camera is not enough to achieve, such as beauty effect, stickers and so on. There's still plenty of room for original camera apps to be optimized for selfies.

3.4 The Effect of the Reasons for Using Original Camera Apps and Third-Party Camera Apps on Selection Preferences of the Camera App Type

Table 7 shows that reason(2)3 "I am used to taking photos with an original camera app and then using a third-party camera app for photo processing." is more likely to lead users to use original camera apps. Similarly, Table 8 shows that reason(3)3 "Face-beauty feature of third-party cameras are powerful and need not edit later" and reason (3)4 "All processes can be implemented in one application" are more like to cause people to use third-party cameras, while reason(3)6 "I used to take photos with the original camera and use the third-party camera for post-processing" are more likely to cause people use original cameras as result shown in Table 7.

Table 7. Parameter estimates of the relationship between the reasons for using original camera apps and selection preferences of the camera app type

		Estimate	Std.Error	Wald	df	Sig.	95% Confidence Interval	
							Lower Bound	Upper Bound
Threshold	[preference=1]	-.239	.289	.684	1	.408	-.805	.327
	[preference=2]	1.592	.319	24.886	1	.000	.967	2.218
	reason(2)1	-.294	.309	.909	1	.340	-.899	.311
	reason(2)2	-.120	.317	.144	1	.704	-.742	.501
	reason(2)3	1.007	.348	8.369	1	.004	.325	1.690
	reason(2)4	0.522	.470	1.234	1	.276	-.399	1.444
Location	reason(2)5	-.012	.427	.001	1	.977	-.849	.824
	reason(2)6	-.430	.425	1.026	1	.311	-1.263	.402
	reason(2)7	.665	.509	1.704	1	.192	-.333	1.662
	reason(2)8	.289	.986	.086	1	.770	-1.644	2.221
	reason(2)9	-.046	.541	.007	1	.932	-1.106	1.014
	reason(2)10	-.383	.347	1.216	1	.270	-1.063	.298

Link function: logit

Table 8. Parameter estimates of the relationship between the reasons for using third-party camera apps and selection preferences of the camera app type

		Estimate	Std.Error	Wald	df	Sig.	95% Confidence Interval	
							Lower Bound	Upper Bound
Threshold	[frequency(3)=3]	.449	.434	1.071	1	.301	-.402	1.300
	[frequency(3)=4]	4.004	.577	48.172	1	.000	2.873	5.134
	reason(3)1	.209	.448	.217	1	.641	-.669	1.087
	reason(3)2	.175	.409	.184	1	.668	-.627	.977
	reason(3)3	1.655	.434	14.520	1	.000	.804	2.507
	reason(3)4	1.356	.435	9.731	1	.002	.504	2.208
Location	reason(3)5	.082	.737	0.012	1	.911	-1.363	1.527
	reason(3)6	-1.469	.659	4.964	1	.026	-2.760	-.177
	reason(3)7	-.187	.883	.045	1	.832	-1.918	1.543
	reason(3)8	.608	.825	.543	1	.461	-1.008	2.224
	reason(3)9	.731	.878	.693	1	.405	-.990	2.453
	reason(3)10	.422	.507	.693	1	.405	-.571	1.415

Link function: logit

Figure 4 shows reasons why users use native camera apps and third-party camera apps in order of frequency. According to the ranking of the frequency of the reasons, it can be concluded that the main reason for users to use the third party is the post-processing and rich face-beauty effects. On this basis, users do not want to leave the current app for post-processing, and users prefer to solve the problem of photo optimization in the same app. And the effects of many original camera apps are not mirror images, which also lead users to choose third-party camera apps. The advantages of the original camera apps are the realism and simple operation. Compared with the complicated retouching, the users hope to get a high-quality selfie quickly and easily. Therefore, when face-beauty features are added to the original camera apps, try to add a one-click beauty effect which is not exaggerated to ensure the formality and quality of the photos.

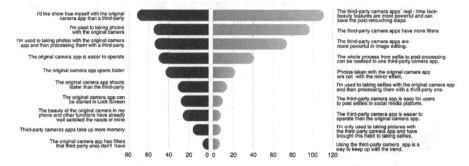

Fig. 4. Reasons why users use native camera apps and third-party camera apps

Figure 5 shows the features selected by the participants in the study taking selfies with original and third-party camera apps. Both cameras have the highest usage rate when users choose one button of beauty, which indicates that most users need a simple operation. The difference is that third-party filters are more abundant, so most users choose filters when using third-party camera apps. On the contrary, the filter function of the original camera apps ranks fourth, which is lower than whitening and adjusting the beauty level, indicating that the original filter is single. Among them, whitening, smooth and enlarging eyes are the most frequently used functions, which show the aesthetic convergence of Chinese users. In other words, Chinese users generally think that white skin, small face and big eyes are kind of beauty.

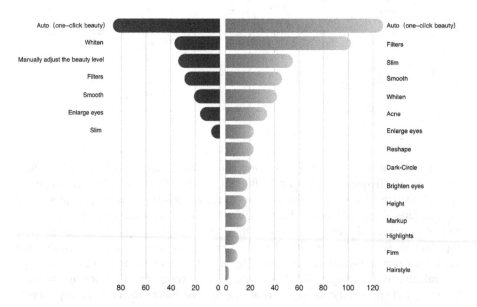

Fig. 5. Features of native camera apps and third-party camera apps

3.5   The Effect of Face-Beauty Features on the Frequency of Taking Selfies

A question "If one day, all the face-beauty feature of camera apps in the world suddenly disappear, will your frequency of taking selfies be affected?" was asked in the questionnaire. Figure 6 obtained by cross analysis shows that people of Type1 won't be affected by missing face-beauty feature. Some high-frequency users of Type4 and Type5 will reduce taking selfies. However, a number of users of Type4 and Type5 get almost no impact. In conclusion, taking selfies is an objective requirement for users. Although face-beauty features can affect the frequency of taking selfies to a certain extent, users still choose self-portraits in the absence of face-beauty feature and most people will not greatly reduce their frequency of taking selfies.

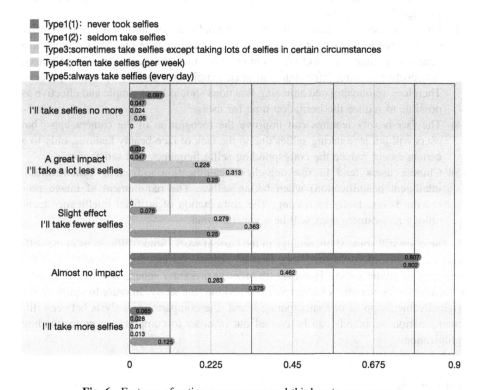

Fig. 6. Features of native camera apps and third-party camera apps

4   Conclusions

This study reflected the current situation of self-timer behavior of Chinese users, including purposes of taking selfies, frequency of taking selfies and usage of camera apps. According to Ordinal Logistic Regression analysis and cross-analysis, the design suggestions of original camera apps were obtained. The specific conclusions are as follows:

(1) The majority of Chinese users taking selfies are still female, and most of them do not take selfies regularly, which is largely related to the scene of the user at that time. When optimizing the self-timer mode of the camera, the combination of situational awareness should be considered to improve the user's self-timer experience.

(2) The user's behavior of taking selfies is dominated by the environment, but the frequency of selfie is largely influenced by the internal purpose. High-frequency selfie-takers often take a large number of selfies because they are bored to kill time, consider taking selfies as an interesting thing and eager to show themselves on social platforms. The function design of camera selfie mode should not only meet the basic selfie needs, but also provide more interesting and social functions for high-frequency users.

(3) Most Chinese users take selfies with original camera apps and use third-party camera apps to apply photo retouching, but users are more inclined to complete a series of operations of photo retouching within the same app. Users not only need rich post-processing effect but also need simple and flexible operation process. Therefore, retouching and adjusting functions should be as simple and effective as possible to reduce the hesitation time for users.

(4) The face-beauty features can improve the recognition of the camera apps, but users will not stop taking selfies due to the lack of face-beauty features, only to a certain extent reduce the corresponding selfie frequency and satisfaction.

(5) Chinese users tend to use one-click beautification (advanced beautification, intelligent beautification) when taking selfies. The requirement of image processing is constantly increasing. The combination of artificial intelligence technology and camera apps will be a general trend.

There are still some shortcomings in the current work. Some differences in the self-timer effects of different smartphone brands' original camera apps will also affect the frequency of taking selfies. However, in order to present a general rule, this study did not introduce the variable of smartphone brand into the study. In order to optimize the original camera app of one smartphone brand, the comparative analysis between different smartphone brands can be carried out in order to complete the corresponding optimization.

References

1. Pu, Y.Q.: Study of the self-expression in taking selfies. Master's thesis, Central Academy of Fine Arts (2017)
2. Hou, W., Chen, X.: Application of logistic regression analysis of smartphone speech interaction usage in China: a questionnaire-based study of 622 adults. In: Kurosu, M. (ed.) HCI 2018. LNCS, vol. 10903, pp. 133–151. Springer, Cham (2018). https://doi.org/10.1007/978-3-319-91250-9_11

3. Hosmer, D.W., Lemeshow, S.: Applied Logistic Regression, 2nd edn. Wiley, New York (2004)
4. Lokosang, L.: Statistical analysis of determinants of household food insecurity in post conflict Southern Sudan. Master's thesis, University of KwaZulu-Natal (2009)
5. Xue, W.: Data Analysis Based on SPSS, 4th edn. China Renmin University Press, Beijing (2017)
6. Chen, H.B., Zhu, H.L.: Study of the factors affecting the satisfaction of residents' cultural consumption. Stat. Decis. **14**, 104–107 (2014)
7. Wang, Z.W., Xiang, Y.T., Gao, L., Lyu, X.B.: Study of the factors impacting the taxi-hailing apps market based on the logistic regression model. Sci. Technol. Innov. Herald **13**(8), 80–83 (2016)
8. Manovich, L., Huang, J.H.: The aesthetics of automation: artificial intelligence and image culture. J. Beijing Film Acad. **6**, 75–79 (2014)
9. Zhang, Z.H.: Study of the internal drive psychological in beauty camera. Pop. Lit. **1**, 171 (2017)
10. Yang, J., Zhang, Y., Zha, S.Y.: The social function and the psychology analysis of taking online selfie. J. Chang. Educ. Inst. **34**(02), 48–52 (2018)

A Study of Usability Design of Baren Products

Ke Zhang[(✉)] and Xiaoli Dong

School of Design, South China University of Technology, Guangzhou 510006,
People's Republic of China
kezh@scut.edu.cn

Abstract. In recent years, with the rapid development of the domestic cultural economy, the development of the printmaking market is also at a good opportunity. As an important rubbing tool in the production of prints, baren plays an important role in the effect of printmaking. The development of printmaking determined that baren has a significant commercial development value and design research significance. However, the user may experience hand soreness, chassis edge puncture paper, chassis wear during the process of using the baren to rubbing prints. This paper creatively introduces the usability analysis into the design research of baren from the perspective of user experience.

Keywords: Print rubbing tools · Baren · Product design · User experience · Ease of use

1 Introduction

Printmaking is a comprehensive art that combines painting, engraving and printing with a knife as a substitute for a pen. There are two ways of engraving rubbings, one is to use the engraving machine for rubbings and the other is to use baren for manual rubbings. Compared with other paintings, the charm of printmaking lies in its "craftsmanship" and "operability". In the process of printmaking creation, as shown in Fig. 1, rubbings are used to express their thoughts and the world in their eyes. Hand-printed prints can improve the coordination and use ability of hands, eyes and brain, enhance the control ability of hands, and make the image more in-depth and detailed [1].

2 Manual Baren

There are very few articles on the design and research of baren products in domestic and foreign literatures, and most of them are about the content of print art. Only during the research of printmaking, they mentioned some information about the appearance, materials, production process, etc. of baren products. In general, there is no systematic research literature on baren products, whether foreign or domestic. Therefore, the baren product design research based on man–machine force analysis not only has the innovation of product design practice, but also a theoretical academic innovation attempt.

A. Marcus and W. Wang (Eds.): HCII 2019, LNCS 11586, pp. 630–644, 2019.
https://doi.org/10.1007/978-3-030-23535-2_45

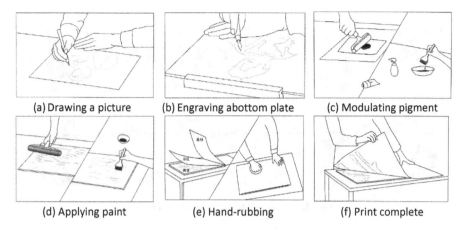

(a) Drawing a picture   (b) Engraving abottom plate   (c) Modulating pigment

(d) Applying paint   (e) Hand-rubbing   (f) Print complete

Fig. 1. Manual printing flow chart of printmaking.

On the one hand, the baren products provided by this research topic are visited by the painters in the form of field visits, obtained in the printmaking village and the Chinese New Year paintings base, and on the other hand through online shopping. Then through the desktop research method, collect the data related to the baren products on the network, organize the baren product introduction and user review data on the e-commerce platform, and compare and analyze the material and user evaluation, and provide the baren products. The information is summarized as following and illustrated in Fig. 2:

According to the market research results, baren is called differently in different places, but its functions are similar. Up to now, baren can be roughly divided into two categories: traditional baren and modern baren [2].

China is the first country in the world to invent engraving and printing, and the birthplace of printmaking. Tangzi is a tool for embossing paper in the printing of ancient Chinese New Year paintings. Tangzi is made of old palm tree bark. Of course, some exquisite Tangzi also use horsetail, which has few impurities and is durable [3].

The traditional Japanese printmaking method uses a tool called "Tuobao", which is a baren. It is a printing tool developed by Japanese prints based on the techniques of studying ancient Chinese prints. It is also loved by Western printmakers. The traditional Japanese baren is made of bamboo skin (required bamboo skin are large enough and complete), wood boards and hemp ropes. Compared with the traditional Chinese Tangzi, the traditional baren of Japan has the characteristics of strong force and control flexibility, which is very suitable for the use of a small number of watermark prints [4].

Nowadays, many artists use a mushroom-like baren. This tool is preferably made of hard wood. Both ends of the head and the handle can be used. The head is used to grind a large area, and the handle can be used to grind a part of the work. The general specification is that the handle is 10 cm long, the chassis diameter is 4.5 cm, and the weight is 30 g. South Korea has improved its styling on the basis of traditional wood mushrooms. On the basis of South Korea, Germany added a 5 mm thick felt base to the baren friction surface, which can be used for imprinting or other purposes.

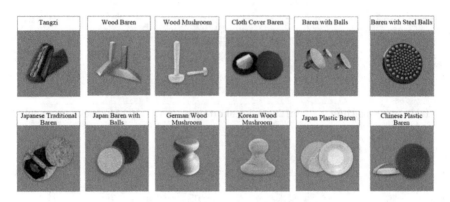

Fig. 2. Baren products across the world.

Steel ball baren is also a newly invented printing tool in recent years. It is divided into two types, one is that the beads can be rolled, and the other is a steel ball that cannot be moved. The surface is smooth, wear-resistant, and has a certain pressure, so it is relatively easy to use. But these two have one thing in common. The product form is more clumsy and expensive. The market price is around 1000 yuan, which is not very popular. Compared with the thicker metal baren made in China, the Japanese baren is lighter and made of wear-resistant resin and stainless steel beads. When printing, you need to exert relatively large strength, but you can print beautiful effects. If you print a large work, or a large number of repetitive prints, your hands will feel tired and painful.

The invention of plastic baren originated from Akira Korosaki, a famous Japanese print artist, who designed plastic baren on the basis of traditional baren. The innovation of baren is that the friction surface of the chassis can be removed and replaced with a new one after long-time wear and tear. When the plastic baren evolved into the Chinese market, it became simple but difficult to use without replaceable friction surfaces.

During the investigation, a wooden baren was obtained from Taiwan. It has a smooth wooden surface, which gives a very comfortable feel, and the side surface of the chassis has a concave and convex surface, which makes it easier for people to hold. The handle looks a bit awkward compared to the chassis. McMade's painting company sells a baren with wood-bonded fabric. This fabric has a smooth texture and is suitable for grinding, but the wooden structure is too simple, the handle is uncomfortable to use, and the user's reflection is easy to loose.

To sum up, due to the uncertainty of pressure in the process of baren's use, it is difficult to analyze the force of man-machine interface by establishing a more objective virtual model. Therefore, this project intends to study the usability test by means of satisfaction test and fatigue index test of physical prototype. The fatigue test was evaluated by the reduction of the right arm grip strength before and after the experiment.

3 User Requirements for Usability of Baren Product

3.1 Objectives and Methods

What kind of baren can solve the above problems? Based on this question, this chapter carries out an experiment combining observation and interview to explore users' perception of baren product usability standards.

Identify and Segment Target Users. In the early stage of baren's design and research, users should be stratified and target users should be established. Only by combining the needs of target users can products satisfying target users be designed [5]. Baren's users are widely distributed, including primary school students, middle school students, high school students, undergraduates, graduate students, professional printmakers, amateur printmakers and so on.

The users involved in the survey recruited 20 master's and undergraduate students (including 14 females, average age: 23 years old) with experience in making woodcut prints from the school of design of the author's university. Participants were required to: (1) be able to critically analyze the form and function of all products; (2) be able to discuss usage scenarios without experiencing future conceptual design; and (3) be able to speak out their needs in conversation.

Baren Product Design User Survey. From the perspective of psychology and behavior, what people say or think is often different from what they do [6]. Therefore, semi-structured interview method and observation method are combined to design survey method. First, we conducted a semi-structured interview to understand the target users' feelings and opinions on existing baren products in the market, and sorted out the problems that users encountered in the process of using baren products. Then, in order to facilitate discussion and obtain users' use of the product under the most real conditions, baren products will be provided for users' operation experience during the interview, so as to observe users' use more comprehensively. The combination of these two survey methods can better analyze the real needs of users in the process of experience and the potential needs hidden under the surface behavior.

3.2 Baren Product Usability Attribute Induction

All contents of semi-structured interviews and observations were recorded, and then iterative analysis was carried out using grounded theory research [4] to obtain the usability attributes of baren products. The records collected about 70 items, only 35 of which met our research questions and were considered valid.

Through open coding, these contents are grouped into similar patterns without any presets, and are arranged into 10 patterns according to the similarity of the contents. For example, from the phrase "plastic baren will wear out the chassis soon", it can be deduced as "the wear resistance of the product materials" that is one of the powerful usability attributes. Then, it also can be analyzed what product elements are associated with each usability attribute, and group them by the mode of the axial coding in terms of how the user behavior is derived. In this way, the two levels can be identified that included four product usability attributes, as shown in Fig. 3.

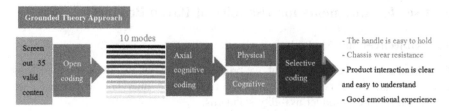

Fig. 3. Analytical research method for obtaining user's demand for usability of baren.

From the results of interviews and observations, it can be found that the usability of baren products can be attributed to the usability at the physical level and the usability at the cognitive level. The usability of the physical level is summarized as the handle is easy to hold and the chassis is resistant to wear. The usability of the cognitive level focuses on the ease of use perceived by the user, and users' expectations for cognitive usability mainly include product interaction of a clear and easy to understand and a better emotional experience.

Usability Attributes of Physical Level. *The Handle is Easy to Hold*. Users reflected that when using baren products, the handle design was unreasonable, which caused an uncomfortable experience for users. For example, there will be a situation of grinding the hand, and the dimensional distance with chafing chassis is too narrow, so that the finger is completely gripped, and a feeling of pressure will appear; the palm is in a state of no support during the process of moving the rubbing in the grip state. The angle between the arm and the palm is too large, causing the wrist to withstand greater pressure and causing soreness. This kind of easy use that affects people's physiological acceptability should also be analyzed from the perspective of ergonomics, so as to design a baren handle form that is more easy to use. Therefore, this phenomenon and demand can be summarized as the physical "handle is easy to grasp".

Chassis Wear Resistance. Especially the domestic plastic baren used for a long time, the chassis will appear partial wear, and the Japanese plastic baren, in order to maintain the durability of the product, the design for the replacement of the chassis. Most college students use plastic baren, so it is generally reflected that they hope baren can be more wear-resistant and minimize local wear.

Usability Attributes of Cognitive Level. *Clear and Easy to Understand Product Interaction*. In the process of operating baren, good communication between products and users is essential. The quality of product interaction affects the user's usability experience. The clarity and understanding of product interaction is reflected in the form of the product. Specifically, the structure of the product makes it easy for the user to understand how to operate and guide the user to use it correctly, so as to avoid the user's unfamiliar user experience in understanding the way the baren product is held.

It has been observed that the operator's holding method for the same product is different, as shown in Fig. 4. For example, users use plastic baren mainly in two ways, and due to the size of the palm is not the same in both men and women, it leads to the male adopting the holding mode. The female adopts the holding mode, which shows that the original plastic baren product form is lacking in guiding the user to use correctly. Just based on their own understanding and exploratory grip, the user experience is different from the different grip styles. Therefore, in the design of the new baren product, it is urgent to design a simple and clear product interaction interface to guide the user.

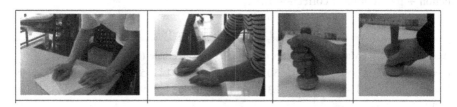

Fig. 4. Example of different ways of baren operation.

Better Emotional Experience. The design of the product not only has to have practical functions, but if it can convey the product semantics which are more in line with the user's psychological needs through the point, line and surface of the product, it can bring a better emotional experience to the user [7]. When users use baren, especially the ugly baren or the cheaper baren, they will feel that they are not confident in their use, and couldn't reflect the own taste. Even if they are preliminary learners, they may not be used frequently. They also have high expectations for the design of the new baren. For example, if the design of the baren product can be conveyed in the popular animation culture, traditional culture, etc. through the shape, color, material, etc., or it may look more personalized and fashionable. A strong look is more attractive to them to buy and use.

4   Analysis of Factors Influencing Usability of Baren Product

The usability of baren products is affected by many factors, including physiological state and behavior, psychological characteristics, using environment and basic functions of the products. These factors are analyzed in detail in order to obtain the preliminary design guidelines related to the new baren product design.

4.1   Physiological Status Analysis of Users

Human Hand Size. The rubbing of baren products requires direct contact with the products by hand. Therefore, the design of the holding part directly affects the usability of baren products, and the design of the holding part is closely related to the size of the hands. In the design of new baren products, if the size of the hand is not taken into account, the size of the holding part of the product is not designed properly, which will inevitably affect the user's usability experience of baren products.

By referring to the measurement standard of Chinese human hand data, as shown in Table 1 it indicates the length and width of Chinese male and female hands as well as their percentiles. The peak at the 50th percentile is the average value, as shown in

Fig. 5. From Table 1, it can be found that the adult male with the 50th percentile has a hand length of about 183 mm and a hand width of about 82 mm. Adult female hands are about 171 mm long and 76 mm wide. The size calculation in baren product design can be based on the following set principles of product functional size:

Product optimal functional size = human body size percentile + functional correction + psychological correction [27].

Table 1. Human hand size [8].

Age group	Male (16–60 years old)							Female (18–55 years old)						
Percentile	1	5	10	50	90	95	99	1	5	10	50	90	95	99
Hand length (mm)	164	170	173	183	193	196	202	154	159	161	171	180	183	189
Hand width (mm)	73	76	77	82	87	89	91	67	70	71	76	80	82	84

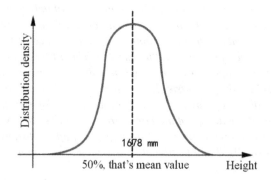

Fig. 5. Normal distribution of human body size [9].

The length of the holding part of the baren product studied in this paper is mainly affected by the palm width of the hand, as shown in Table 1 so the palm width of the hand can be substituted into the formula to calculate the length of the holding part of the product. Data are obtained as shown in Table 2.

Table 2. Baren product recommended holding area length range.

Result of holding area length range for baren product	
Maximum (male)	Product size: 82 + 0.4 (glove correction) + 0.6 (anti-slip texture parameter) = 83 (mm)
	83 + 10 (reserved movable size on the left side of palm) + 10 (reserved movable size on the right side of palm) = 103 (mm)
Maximum (female)	Corresponding product size: 76 + 0.4 (glove correction) + 0.6 (anti-slip texture parameter) = 77 (mm)
	77 + 10 (reserved movable size on the left side of palm) + 10 (reserved movable size on the right side of palm) = 97 (mm)

In the process of using baren, if the whole palm is controlled on the chassis, the chassis should be as wide as or slightly wider than the width of the palm, so as to more easily control the product's range of motion to achieve the desired effect. Therefore, using the width of the palm as the basic reference, the approximate width range of the baren chassis is calculated. The palm width dimension used here refers to the total width including the palm width and thumb width. Its total width can be taken as the human body size value input by the formula by using the width of thumb in the hands of Chinese adult male and female at the 50th centile, as shown in Table 3. The total width size data are 104 mm and 91 mm, respectively. Under the guidance of ergonomic hand size design principles, the chassis size of baren products studied in this paper was estimated, and the chassis width was about 92 mm–105 mm, as shown in Table 4.

Table 3. Total human hand width (with thumb).

Percentage	5%	50%	95%
Adult male (mm)	94	104	112
Adult female (mm)	81	91	102

Table 4. Recommended chassis width range for baren product.

Result of baren product recommended chassis width range	
Maximum (male)	Product size: 104 + 0.4 (glove correction) + 0.6 (anti-skid texture parameter) = 105 (mm)
Maximum (female)	Product size: 91 + 0.4 (glove correction) + 0.6 (anti-skid texture parameter) = 92 (mm)

In the process of using baren, most of the time the fingers need to be bent and grasped. In the extreme grasping state, only one palm area is left between the hand and the baren chassis from a vertical view, so the length of the baren chassis should be greater than the length of the palm. From the above analysis, it can be concluded that the length range of baren chassis is greater than the length of palm and less than the length of hand. The size of palm length can be obtained by regression equation of male and female hand control parts [10]. The regression equation of male palm length was: palm length (male) = 7.89 + 0.53 hand length (male), while the regression equation of female palm length was: palm length (female) = 3.20 + 0.55 hand length (female). Combining the size of male and female palm length and hand length, according to the range value principle of "take the maximum and the minimum" in mathematical calculation, the analysis shows that the chassis length range of baren product is between 105 mm and 174 mm.

Based on the above data of human hand size calculation, it can be determined that the shape of baren chassis is roughly oval. Baren products recommend holding area length greater than 97 mm less than 103 mm; The recommended width range of the massage chassis of baren products should be greater than 92 mm and less than 105 mm; Baren chassis length shall be greater than 105 mm and less than 174 mm.

It should be noted that in this paper, the parameters when wearing gloves are taken into account as a possibility correction, corresponding to the functional correction in the design principle formula, and the anti-skid texture parameters of the product are set as the psychological correction.

Range of Motion of the Hand Joints. The rubbing of baren products requires direct contact with the products by hand. Therefore, the design of the holding part directly affects the usability of baren products, and the design of the holding part is closely related to the size of the hands. In the design of new baren products, if the size of the hand is not taken into account, the size of the holding part of the product is not designed properly, which will inevitably affect the user's usability experience of baren products.

Wrist joint activity is one of the main types of hand joint activity. The range of wrist joint activity can be divided into transverse range of motion and longitudinal range of motion. The longitudinal range of motion of the wrist is palmar flexion toward the palm and dorsal flexion toward the hand, as shown in Fig. 6. The lateral range of motion of the wrist is radial deviation toward the thumb and ulnar deviation toward the little finger, as shown in Fig. 7. Figures 6 and 7 marked by many experiments in determination of activity of several limit [11], it is important to note the wrist joint can activities to the limit, but in close to the limit state of work is very tired, and keep wrist extreme bending force operating state for a long time, on each muscle in the arms of operation will also affect. Therefore, it should be avoided to keep the wrist in the limit state of joint degree for a long time [11].

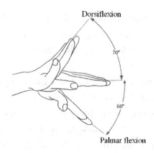

Fig. 6. Longitudinal range of motion of the wrist joint.

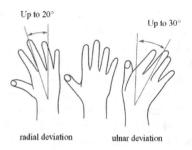

Fig. 7. Lateral range of motion of the wrist joint.

So for the wrist structure, what is the Angle at which the wrist is bent, and what is the most comfortable hand? In response to this question, the authority has proved through many experiments that the most comfortable state is when the Angle between the palm and the stressed plane is between 15 degrees and 30 degrees under the stress state of the wrist joint of the hand. If it goes beyond this range, the forearm muscles will be in an uncomfortable stretching state, and if you press hard again, the blood vessel flow may be reduced [12], resulting in numbness of the muscles around the wrist. These data conclusions are the results of long-term practice, so they can be used as a reference in the design of new baren products.

Hand area pressure perception. When holding a baren product to print a print, it is necessary to exert a large amount of strength, and the hand is deformed by the force, which causes a feeling of discomfort such as soreness, which is related to the muscles and nerves of the hand part, and due to the muscles of different parts of the hand. Differences with the distribution of nerves can also cause different pressure deformations and perceptions in different regions. Therefore, according to these factors, the relationship between the bearing capacity of different parts of the hand and the distribution of muscles and nerves should be analyzed, so as to better guide the layout of the main bearing area of the product interface of baren product and avoid the discomfort such as soreness during use.

Tao guoqiang, a master student of zhejiang university of technology, has divided his hands in detail in the research on the establishment of virtual model of handgrip [13]. He divided the hand into 19 regions, as shown in Fig. 8, in which 14 fingers were

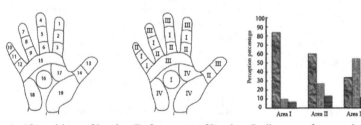

A: 19 partitions of hand   B: four areas of hand   C: diagram of comprehensive physiological perception

Fig. 8. Pressure distribution in different areas of hands [13, 14].

divided into 14 regions, and the palm was divided into four areas according to the distribution of muscles and other soft tissues of the hand.

Because the tissues and structures of different parts of the hand are different, the magnitude of the force that can be sensed and withstood by different areas of the hand is also different. In areas where the muscles are more developed and the nerve tissue is less, the force that can be tolerated is greater. On the contrary, there are fewer hand muscles, but the areas with dense nerve distribution can withstand less force. The pressure that different areas of the hand can bear is shown in Fig. 8.

It can be seen from the Fig. 8 that the pressure bearing values of partitions 18 and 19 are the highest, followed by zones 1, 4, 7 and 13. Because the function of baren determines that a considerable amount of force should be exerted by hands in the operation process, the main force point layout of baren should be placed in the 18 and 19 regions with more muscles as far as possible. The application point of guiding direction control can be placed on the fingertip fingertip segments in regions 1, 4, 7 and 13, where the fingertip muscles are relatively abundant, and the first web where the nerve tissue is less. Among them, when using the finger for power control, the thumb has the strongest power control ability, so the thumb can be considered to control the direction movement.

Xia rulong, a master student of zhejiang university of technology, divided the center of the palm into four zones when studying the comfort of holding tools. Each zone has different perception of pain, pressure and pain [14], as shown in Fig. 8. The palmar and interphalangeal muscles are particularly sensitive to tingling sensation. If the design of the handle is not reasonable, the muscle between the palm and the interphalangeal will bear a lot of local pressure during the manipulation, which may cause numbness and tingling sensation for a long time [15]. Therefore, the force point of the baren product handle and the force position of the guiding direction should not correspond to the interphalangeal muscle of the palm as far as possible, as shown in Fig. 9.

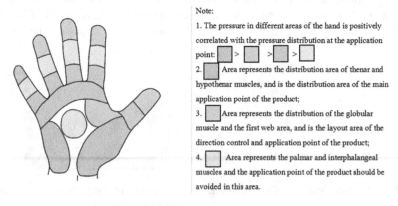

Note:

1. The pressure in different areas of the hand is positively correlated with the pressure distribution at the application point: ☐ > ☐ > ☐ > ☐

2. ☐ Area represents the distribution area of thenar and hypothenar muscles, and is the distribution area of the main application point of the product;

3. ☐ Area represents the distribution of the globular muscle and the first web area, and is the layout area of the direction control and application point of the product;

4. ☐ Area represents the palmar and interphalangeal muscles and the application point of the product should be avoided in this area.

Fig. 9. Baren product force point layout.

4.2   User Behavior Analysis

Operator Posture Analysis. Based on the particularity of the rubbing print process, most of them use stand-up work. The operation diagram is shown in Fig. 10. From the analysis in the Fig. 10, the operator can take care of the larger work when using the "upright" work posture. The area can also make greater force on the hand. When standing and operating, 1. can try to control the large space; 2. The hand can make more force; 3. Effectively use the visual space to operate other parts.

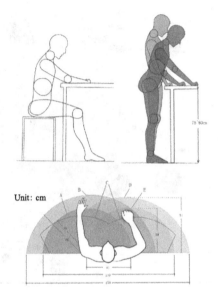

Left sitting position is generally adopted for the the process of painting, engraving and other operations

The right side position is generally adopted for the process of rubbing.

A: Left hand normal work area

B: left hand maximum working area

C: hands combined with the usual work area

D: right hand maximum working area

E: Right hand normal work area

Fig. 10. Analysis of operation posture.

Different Holding Methods and Strength Analysis. Table 5 summarizes some basic ways of holding different baren products.

As can be seen from Table 5, wooden mushrooms belong to the most common incomplete holding posture. Although they are small and elegant in shape, they need fingers to manipulate, press and move, which will result in large local strength of fingers, which is not conducive to power transmission. Other baren products are held in a relatively reasonable way, and the last complete holding method in the Table 5 is the best. According to the research, the holding force of baren products changes with the distance between the top of thumb and the top of other four fingers. The holding force is greater when the finger-spacing is between 2.5 cm and 7.5 cm. The finger range is closest to that of a half-clenched fist in its natural form. For the palm, it is to try to meet the user's comfort in this form when using the product.

Table 5. Classification of different baren holding methods.

Classification of operation mode	Operating characteristics	Operational diagram	Representative product
Non-complete hold	The grip of the thumb and two fingers is close to the middle.If the palm contact grip, will cause palm discomfort.		
Complete hold	The fingers are close to the palm of the hand, and most of the fingers and the inner surface of the palm are in contact with the object.		
Complete hold	The inner surface of the entire palm grips the handle completely. Such a type of grip is often referred to as "power grip."		

4.3   Analysis of Users' Psychological Characteristics

The design of products should not only meet the practical functions of the products, but also meet the growing psychological and emotional needs of people. The inner meaning expressed by the products and the emotional needs caused by them are increasingly valued by people in the design [16]. Psychological factors affect the emotional experience of the whole product. The main judge of baren's usability is the user. Users of different ages have different needs for ease of use. Therefore, it is necessary to fully understand the psychological factors of users in order to make the product design positioning more accurate.

Professional printmakers and teachers of printmaking have high expectations for baren due to their profound artistic and cultural deposits. Primary and secondary school users prefer those products with interesting shapes, rich imagination, gorgeous colors, rich fairy tale colors and safe features. University student users attach importance to the psychological and emotional satisfaction brought by the product, such as differentiated, personalized and diversified experience. Therefore, when targeting the target audience as a group of students in college printmaking, they should consider them as artistic students. Compared with ordinary college students, they may have more requirements for the beauty of baren products. Therefore, when designing baren products for college students, we should pay more attention to the beauty of the products.

4.4   Product Use Environment Analysis

The creation environment of the engraving is relatively dirty and messy, which makes the following factors need to be considered in the usability design of baren products:

Easy Cleaning. Oily inks and gouache pigments are used in the process of making prints. Under such an operating environment, baren's surface and chassis are likely to turn black. This determines that the outer surface of baren should be as smooth as possible and the material should be washable.

Easy to Receive. Print creation to use more tools, print baren size should be within a reasonable range, not too large or too small, and other products should be combined with the common storage space.

Versatility. Refers to the versatility of some operation modes. The tools needed for engraving creation are messy and each tool has different function. We hope to consider functional composition in the design of the new baren, so as to reduce the number of tools and make the desktop more concise.

4.5   Analysis of Product Functional Constraints

Tactile Comfort. Users report wrist pain and other phenomena when using baren. The tactile comfort of baren products is closely related to the materials, so in the later shaping of product forms, materials that can bring more comfortable tactile sensation should be considered in the selection of materials.

Durability. After using plastic baren for a long time, the chassis will produce wear phenomenon, reducing the service life of the product. The baren, handmade with bamboo skin and cloth covers, will soon wear out. This decided to consider the use of high friction resistance coefficient, the use of good performance of the material.

Less Mistakes. In print art, a knife is used to carve uneven patterns on basswood to express the work. This makes it easy for the plastic baren to break the paper on the board during the rubbing process. Therefore, users hope to reduce the chance of breakage through the shape design of the product. And when the rubbing engraving left hand to press on the edge of the board, because the plastic baren chassis thin, it will appear sharp, easy to rub in the rubbing to the left hand near the finger, causing pain.

5   Conclusion

In this paper, the research and design of baren products innovatively introduces usability analysis into the design research of baren by focusing on the usability of plastic baren. This topic introduces the concept of usability for the design and research of new baren products, and has the following results:

(1) Through market research, pre-interview and observation method, the problems of baren products at home and abroad are summarized. After analysis, the user's usability for baren products is summarized.
(2) Multi-dimensional analysis of the factors affecting the usability of baren products, combined with the basic design elements of the product.
(3) Through the induction of the usability requirements, the factors affecting the usability are analyzed.

The result of the study will be used for further design a brand new baren product that satisfies targeted users.

Acknowledgements. This research is supported by Guangdong Province "Twelfth Five-Year Plan" project funding GD14HYS01.

References

1. Song, Y.: The Research of Engraving into the Regular Classroom Teaching of Fine Arts in Primary Schools. Zhejiang Normal University, Jinhua (2015)
2. Dong, X.: Research on the Usability of New Baren Product Design. South China University of Technology, Guangzhou (2018)
3. Chen, J.: China's print market, which is in urgent need of development. J. Zhuzhou Norm. Coll. **1**, 104–106 (2007)
4. Su, X.: Engraving Techniques (Part 1). Peking University Press, Beijing (2008)
5. Lin, Q.: User-Centered Home Health Care Product Development. South China University of Technology, Guangzhou (2016)
6. Wang, Y.: Research on Urban Public Toilet Design Based on Usability Theory. Hebei University of Technology, Tianjin (2007)
7. Muller, M.J., Kogan, S.: Grounded Theory Method in HCI and CSCW. IBM Center for Social Software, Cambridge (2010)
8. Li, C.: Humanized industrial design. Beauty and Age, vol. 3 (2004)
9. GB/T16252-1996: People's Republic of China National Standard: Adult Hand Size. China Standard Press, Beijing (1996)
10. GB/T12985-1991: Apply the Percentile Rule of Body Size to Product Design. China Standard Press, Beijing (2008)
11. Ruan, B., Shao, X.: Industrial Design Ergonomics, pp. 127–128. Machinery Industry Press, Beijing (2018)
12. Yan, S., Xu, H.: Ergonomics and Product Design. Harbin Engineering University Press, Harbin (2003)
13. Tao, G.: Virtual Hand Model for Grip and Finite Element Analysis of Grip. Zhejiang University of Technology, Hangzhou (2012)
14. Yang, D.: A Finite Element Model for Grip Analysis of a Hand-Held Tool Handle. Zhejiang University of Technology, Hangzhou (2012)
15. Xia, R., Li, J., Jiang, X., Zhu, Q.: Research on the zone pressure measurement method for hand grip comfort application. Mech. Des. Manuf. Eng. **8**, 14–17 (2013)
16. Zhang, F.: Research on man-machine relationship design of hand held tools. Guangxi Light Ind. **11**, 60–61 (2010)

Correction to: A Systematic Literature Review of Usability Evaluation Guidelines on Mobile Educational Games for Primary School Students

Xiao Wen Lin Gao, Braulio Murillo, and Freddy Paz

Correction to:
Chapter "A Systematic Literature Review of Usability Evaluation Guidelines on Mobile Educational Games for Primary School Students" in: A. Marcus and W. Wang (Eds.): *Design, User Experience, and Usability*, LNCS 11586, https://doi.org/10.1007/978-3-030-23535-2_13

The book was inadvertently published with an incorrect version of an author's name in Chapter 13. It has been corrected as "Braulio Murillo" in the corresponding chapter.

The updated version of this chapter can be found at
https://doi.org/10.1007/978-3-030-23535-2_13

Author Index